Contents

⊲ **W9-CCT-183**

These are, the Michelin Maps to use with this guide:

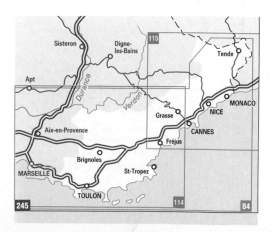

Principal sights

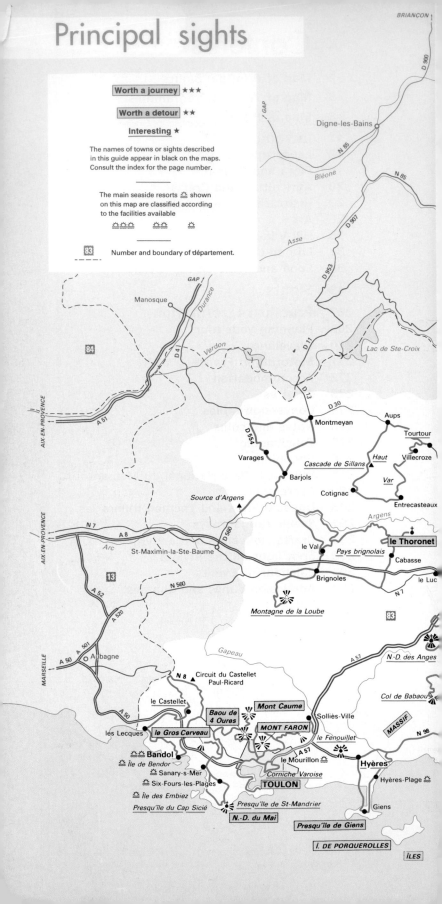

Worth a journey ★★★

Worth a detour ★★

Interesting ★

The names of towns or sights described in this guide appear in black on the maps. Consult the index for the page number.

The main seaside resorts ⚓ shown on this map are classified according to the facilities available

⚓⚓⚓   ⚓⚓   ⚓

83   Number and boundary of département.

Touring programmes

Route des Grandes Alpes : 100 km-62 miles (1 day)

Massif des Maures and Haut-Var :
550 km-342 miles (5 days)

Massif de l'Esterel and Préalpes de Grasse :
250 km-155 miles (4 days)

Riviera and Nice hinterland :
500 km-311 miles (6 days including 1 day in Nice)

Overnight stop

Vallée du Loup ★★   Name under which a route is described

★★★ = 🏛🏛🏛
★★ = 🏛🏛
★ = 🏛

0 _____ 20 km

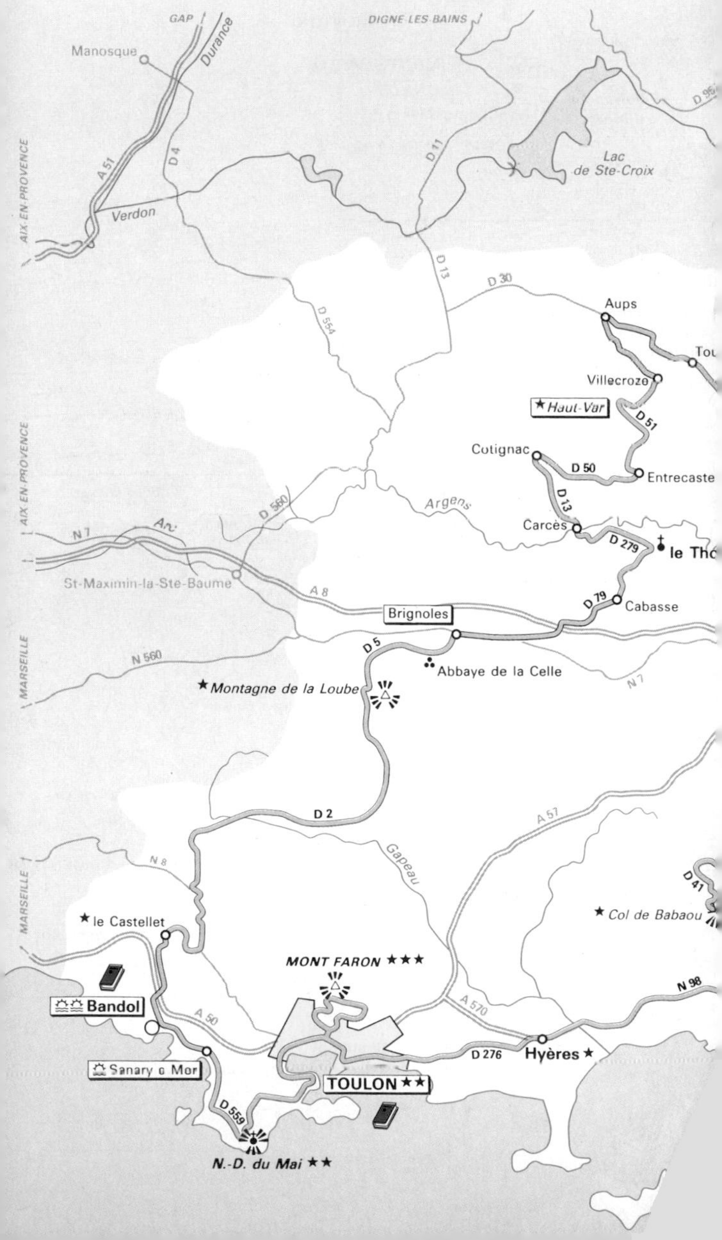

GAP

Manosque

Durance

DIGNE LES BAINS

DIGNE-LES-BAINS

D 96

AIX EN PROVENCE

A 51

D 4

Verdon

D 11

Lac de Ste-Croix

D 554

D 13

D 30

Aups

Tou

Villecroze

★ Haut-Var

D 51

AIX EN PROVENCE

Cotignac

D 50

Entrecaste

D 560

Argens

D 13

Carcès

D 279

le Tho

N 7

Ar

N 7

St-Maximin-la-Ste-Baume

A 8

Brignoles

D 79

Cabasse

MARSEILLE

N 560

D 5

Abbaye de la Celle

N 7

★ Montagne de la Loube

D 2

A 57

Gapeau

D 41

★ Col de Babaou

MARSEILLE

N 8

le Castellet

MONT FARON ★★★

N 98

🏛🏛 Bandol

A 50

A 570

🏛 Sanary ₀ Mer

D 276

Hyères ★

TOULON ★★

D 559

N.-D. du Mai ★★

TORINO

Col de Tende
Colle di Tenda

TOUR

Valdeblore
le Boréon
Cascade de l'Estrech
St-Martin-Vésubie
Venanson
Colmiane
Roquebillière
Vallée des
Merveilles
Vallon de la Gordolasque
l'Authion
H^te Vallée
Roya
Tende
la Brique
N.-D. des Fontaines
Gorges de Bergue
Saorge
Gorges de Saorge

ARRIÈRE-
Forêt de Turini
Cime de Peira-Cava
Breil-s-Roya

Vallée de la Vésubie
PAYS
Lucéram
Sospel

ITALIA
GENOVA

l'Escarène

S 20
A 10
SAN REMO

Var
NIÇOIS
N 202
Peillon
Ventimiglia
N 7
MENTON

A 8
Èze
MONTE-CARLO
MONACO
Villefranche-s-Mer
Beaulieu-s.-Mer
NICE
CORNICHES DE LA RIVIERA
Cap Ferrat
Cagnes-s-Mer

Antibes

JUAN-LES-PINS ♨♨♨
Cap d'Antibes ♨
Golfe-Juan ♨♨

Lérins

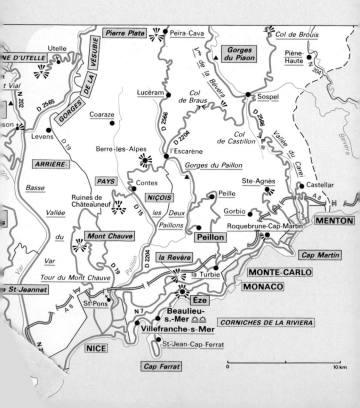

Pierre Plate
Peïra-Cava
Col de Brouis
Utelle
GORGES DE LA VÉSUBIE
V^ée de la Bévéra
Gorges du Piaon
Piène-Haute

NE D'UTELLE
t Vial
N 202
D 2565
GORGES
Lucéram
Col de Braus
Sospel
D 204

Coaraze
Col de Castillon
Vallée du Carei

D 2566
D 2566
Bévéra

Levens
D 19
Berre-les-Alpes
l'Escarène
D 2204

son
D 2566

ARRIÈRE-
PAYS
Contes
Gorges du Paillon
Ste-Agnès
Castellar
A 8

Basse
NIÇOIS
Peille
MENTON
Ruines de Châteauneuf
les Deux Paillons
Gorbio
Roquebrune-Cap-Martin
Vallée
D 15
Peillon
du
Mont Chauve
Cap Martin

Var
Tour du Mont Chauve
la Revère
la Turbie
MONTE-CARLO
MONACO

St-Jeannet
D 19
Paillon
D 2204
St-Pons
N 7
Èze
Beaulieu-s.-Mer ♨♨
Villefranche-s-Mer
CORNICHES DE LA RIVIERA
A 8

NICE
St-Jean-Cap-Ferrat

Cap Ferrat
0   10 km

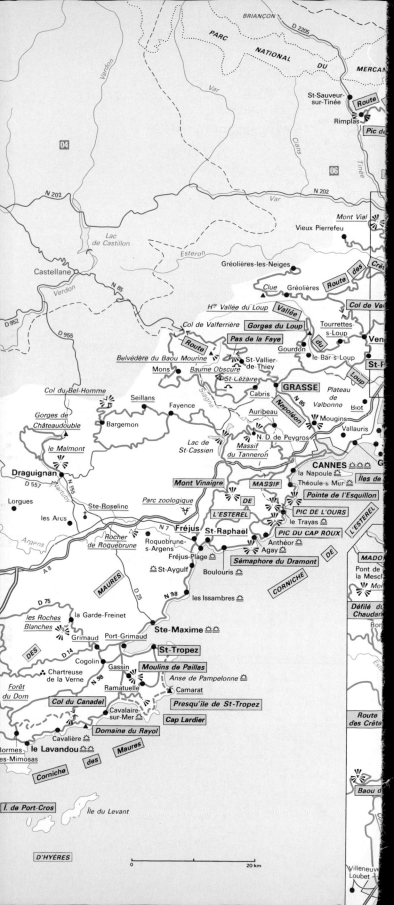

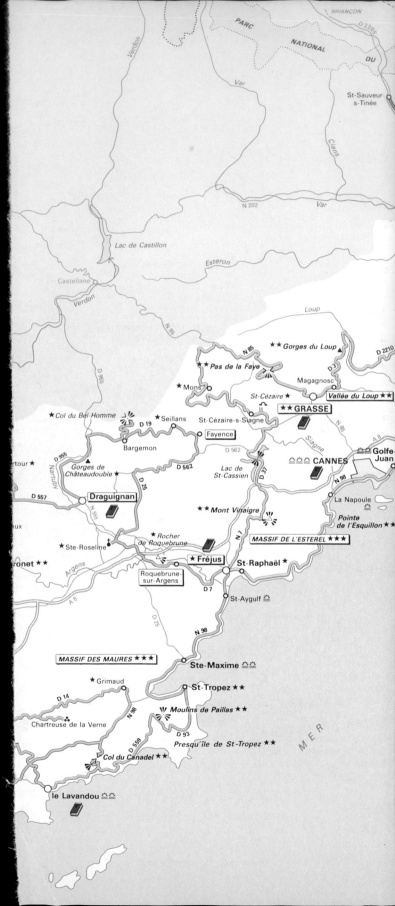

Interested in gardens?

Cap d'Antibes: Jardin Thuret

Cap Ferrat: Gardens of the Fondation Ephrussi-de-Rothschild

Èze: Jardin exotique

Grasse: Jardin de la Princesse Pauline and Parc communal de la Corniche

Hyères: Jardins Olbius-Riquier and Parc St-Bernard

Menton: Jardin du Val Rameh and Jardin des Colombières

Monaco: Jardin exotique, Jardins St-Martin and Jardin japonais

Nice: Cimiez Gardens, Jardin Albert-Ier and Parc Phoenix

PLACES TO STAY MAP

The map below indicates towns selected both for the accommodation and leisure facilities which they offer and for their attractive settings.

Overnight stops are large towns or cities with good accommodation facilities and a number of sights to see.

Monte-Carlo, Nice and Cannes merit **a short stay** such as a weekend, by virtue of their rich collections of monuments and museums and the important events which they host. The map also shows the many and varied **seaside resorts**, several winter sports resorts and **a spa**, as well as certain **mountain resorts**, which are good starting points for walks and rambles.

Other places to stay have been chosen for their welcome and the charm of their setting. Coastal resorts with **marinas** are indicated by a special symbol.

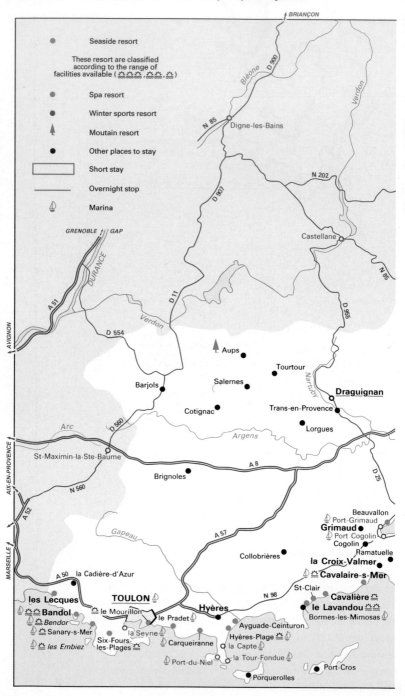

The **Michelin Red Guide FRANCE** and the **Michelin Guide Camping Caravaning France** are annual publications which list a selection of hotels and restaurants and camp sites, classified according to the standard of comfort of their amenities and selected following on-the-spot visits and enquiries.

Local tourist offices also provide information about different types of accommodation; their addresses and telephone numbers are listed at the end of this guide *(see Admission times and charges; see also Practical information: Accommodation).*

It is advisable to book well in advance for the holiday season.

Michelin maps nos 114 and **115** provide a range of information about the places marked – type of road, location of isolated sights, beaches, swimming places in rivers, swimming pools, golf courses, racecourses, airfields and gliding fields...

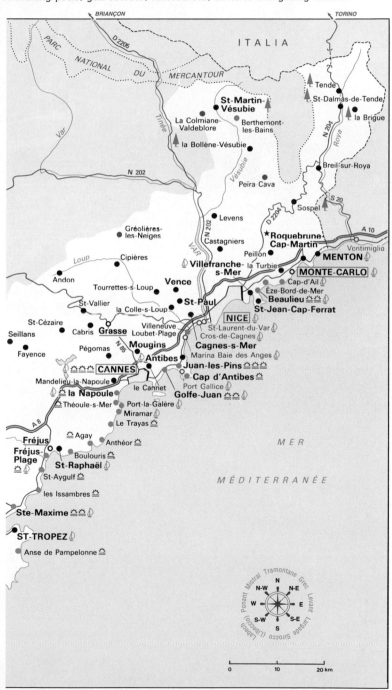

Le Trayas on the Esterel coast

Introduction

Landscape

This guide describes the Riviera from Les Lecques to Menton and the mountainous hinterland which comprises the Provençal Tableland, the Pre-Alps of Grasse and the high country north of Nice. The adjacent regions are described in the Michelin Green Guides *Provence* – available in English – and *Alpes du Sud* (Southern Alps) – available in French.

CONTRASTS

This is a country of contrasts:

...**in coastline** – The Riviera extends from Les Lecques to Menton and is extremely varied *(see The Coast below)*. The little sheltered inlets between the porphyry promontories of the Esterel differ markedly from the great sweeping bays with flat shores which gently punctuate the coastline; while elsewhere on the coast, mountains plunge steeply into the sea, sheer as a wall, as at Cap Sicié.

...**in relief** – A countryside just as varied lies inland. The fertile plains and foothills of Provence are typically Mediterranean in their vegetation but among them are barren, rugged heights like those to the north of Toulon.
Then follow the mountain masses of the Maures and the Esterel which rise to no more than 800m – 2 600ft: the first is crisscrossed by many valleys and ravines and covered with fine forests of cork oak and chestnut; the second massif is dominated by the outline of Mont Vinaigre and the peaks of Pic de l'Ours and Pic du Cap Roux. The country behind Cannes and Nice is one of undulating hills stretching to the Pre-Alps of Grasse, where gorges have been cut into the plateaux and the mountain chains are split by rifts *(clues)*, particularly in Haute-Provence. Lastly, behind the Riviera the peaks of the Pre-Alps of Nice rise to more than 2 000m – 6 560ft, while further to the north and northeast the true Alpine heights tower on the Italian border.

...**in climate** – There is a winter warmth on the Nice coast (the average temperatures for January in Nice are max 13°C – 55°F; min 4°C – 39°F) and, less than two hours away by car, the icy air of the ski slopes; the summer heat of the coast and the exhilarating coolness of the mountain resorts; the cold *mistral* wind and the burning *sirocco*; long days of drought, dried-up rivers and, suddenly, tremendous downpours and overflowing torrents.

...**in vegetation** – The forest of Turini, with its centuries-old beeches and firs, is like that of a northern land; the woods of the Maures and the Esterel are typically southern with their cork oaks and pines, periodically ravaged by forest fires. The wild scrub and underbrush of the *maquis* is far from the orderly rows of the orange and lemon groves; the lavender and thyme growing wild from the vast cultivated fields of flowers; the palm trees, agaves and cacti of the coast from the firs and larches of the highlands.

...**in activity** – The coast attracts all the activity of the area: the busiest roads, the most important towns and the varied and the best equipped resorts are concentrated there. Inland, however, there is peace and quiet, even complete solitude; sleepy little towns and old villages, perched like eagles' nests high up on the hillsides but now almost deserted *(see HILL VILLAGES)*.

...**in economy** – Nice is the coast's tourist capital; Monte-Carlo, a great gambling city. The busy flower trade and the production of perfume exist side by side with the new research centres dealing with oceanography and data processing.

Land of the Sun – Such a multiplicity of impressions has one common factor – the Mediterranean climate. In the Land of the Sun the sun shines continually (2 725 hours annually in Nice compared with 1 465 hours in London).
Except in high summer, outlines are sharpened and natural features acquire an architectural aspect in the clear air. The shining blue of the sea and sky blends with the green of the forest, the silver-grey of the olive trees, the red porphyry rock and the white limestone.

TERRAIN

Provence was formed from two mountain systems: one very old – the Maures and the Esterel – the other much younger – the Provençal ranges of Pyrenean and the Pre-Alps of Alpine origin.

The Maures – This crystalline mountain mass spreads from the River Gapeau in the west to the Argens valley in the east, from the sea in the south to a long depression in the north, beyond which are the limestone Pre-Alps. Long low parallel ranges, covered with fine forests which have not escaped the forest fires, make up the Maures massif; the highest point is La Sauvette (779m – 2 556ft).

The Esterel – The Esterel, separated from the Maures by the lower Argens valley, has also been eroded by time and is, therefore, also of low altitude, its highest peak being Mont Vinaigre at 618m – 2 027ft. The deep ravines cut into its sides and its jagged crests dispel any impression of mere hills.

The Esterel, like the Maures, was once entirely covered with forests of pine and cork oak but these have been ravaged periodically by forest fires.

Quantities of shrubs and bushes grow beneath the trees: tree heathers, arbutus, lentisks and lavender, while scrub *(maquis)* covers the open ground. In spring the red and white flowers of the cistus, yellow mimosa and broom and white heather and myrtle form a brilliant floral patchwork.

Provençal Ranges – These short limestone chains, arid and rugged, rise to heights of 400 to 1 150m – 1 200 to 3 500ft. Of Pyrenean origin with a highly complex structure, they do not have the continuity of those of Alpine origin such as the Southern Pre-Alps. The most southerly peaks, just north of Toulon are the Gros Cerveau (429m – 1 407ft), which is bisected by the Ollioules gorges, Mont Faron (542m – 1 778ft), which dominates the town, and Le Coudon; Montagne de la Loube rises 28km – 17 miles to the north. Between the ranges are fertile valleys where the traditional crops of cereals, vines and olives are cultivated.

Maritime Alps and Mercantour – Away to the northeast the horizon is dominated by a vast mountainous mass (altitude: 1 500 to 2 900m – 4 922 to 9 515ft), which is dissected by the upper valleys of the Var, Tinée, Vésubie and Roya. On the Italian border these mountains meet the great crystalline massif, Le Mercantour, the peaks of which exceed 3 000m – 9 843ft.

Pre-Alps – This region contains a large part of the Southern Pre-Alps. Between the rivers Verdon and Var the **Pre-Alps of Grasse** are formed by a series of parallel east-west chains, with altitudes varying between 1 100 and 1 600m (3 609 and 5 249ft) which are frequently indented by wild and narrow rifts *(clues)*.

The **Nice Pre-Alps** rise from the coast in tiers to a height of 1 000m – 3 281ft, affording a wide variety of scenery inland from Nice and Menton. These ranges, which are Alpine in origin, run north-south before changing direction abruptly to finish up parallel with the coast.

Provençal Tableland – From Canjuers plateau to the Vence pass, the Pre-Alps are rimmed with a tableland of undulating limestone plateaux, similar to the *causses*, into which water infiltrates, penetrating through rifts to feed resurgent streams like the Siagne. The River Loup has carved out a very picturesque gorge.

Below lies a **depression** or "lowland" where the towns of Vence, Grasse and Draguignan are situated. Beyond the River Argens, the depression extends east down the river to Fréjus and west towards Brignoles; the main axis, however, is southwest to Toulon to the northern slopes of the Maures and Le Luc basin.

13

RIVERS

Mediterranean rivers are really torrents and their volume, which varies considerably from a mere trickle to a gushing flood, is governed by melting snow, rainfall and evaporation, depending on the season.

The lack of rain and the intense evaporation of the summer months reduce the rivers to little dribbles of water along their stony beds.

In spring and autumn the rains fall suddenly and violently and even the smallest streams are immediately filled with rushing water; little brooks, trickling through the undergrowth, soon turn into torrents and their raging waters advance at the frightening speed of a galloping horse.

The flow of the Argens varies from 3m³ to 600m³ – 660 to 132 000 gallons a second and that of the Var from 17m³ to 5 000m³ – 3 790 to over a million gallons. At the height of its spate the Var is more than half a mile wide and the stain of its muddy waters can be seen in the sea as far away as Villefranche on the far side of Nice.

The water level in rivers in limestone regions is always very uneven. The rains seep into the ground through numerous fissures to reappear often a considerable distance away as large springs gushing out from the sides of valleys. Some of the springs rise in riverbeds, such as the gushers *(foux)*, which cause the River Argens to flood. Most of the rivers with torrential rates of flow transport material but the River Argens is the only one to have built up an alluvial plain comparable to those of the Languedoc coast. All the torrential rivers have created beautiful valleys, deep gorges (the Loup and the Siagne gorges) or rifts (*clues* – the Clue de Gréolières), which are among the attractions of inland Provence.

CAVES AND CHASMS

In contrast to the deeply dissected green valleys, such as the gorges of the Loup and the Siagne, the Caussols plateau *(see ST-VALLIER-de-THIEY)* rolls away to the far horizon, stony and deserted, a typical karst relief. The dryness of the soil is due to the calcareous nature of the rock which absorbs rain like a sponge.

Water infiltration – Rainwater, charged with carbonic acid, dissolves the carbonate of lime to be found in the limestone. Depressions, which are usually circular in shape and small in size and are known as **cloups** or **sotchs**, are then formed. The dissolution of the limestone rocks, containing especially salt or gypsum, produces a rich soil particularly suitable for growing crops; when the *cloups* increase in size they form large, closed depressions know as **dolines**. Where rainwater infiltrates deeply through the countless fissures in the plateau, the hollowing out and dissolution of the calcareous layer produces wells or natural chasms which are called **avens**. Little by little the chasms grow, lengthen and branch off, communicating with each other and enlarging into caves.

Development of a resurgent spring

Underground rivers – The infiltrating waters finally produce underground galleries and collect to form a more or less swiftly-flowing river. The river widens its course and often changes level, to fall in cascades. Where the rivers run slowly they form lakes, above natural dams, known as **gours**, which are raised layer by layer by deposits of carbonate of lime. The dissolution of the limestone also continues above the water-level in these subterranean galleries: blocks of stone fall from the roof and domes form, the upper parts pointing towards the surface of the earth. When the roof of the dome wears thin it may cave in, disclosing the cavity from above and opening the chasm.

THE COAST

The mainly rocky coastline reflects the different types of mountain and plateau to be found inland emerging as cliffs and rocks where they meet the sea.

The Toulon Coast – This highly indented section of the coast provides well-sheltered harbours; Bandol and Sanary bays and the outstanding Toulon anchorage. The stretches of almost vertical cliffs are interrupted by some fine beaches.

The Maures Coast – Between Hyères and St-Raphaël, the Maures massif meets the sea and the coastal scenery offers charming sites and enchanting views.

The Giens peninsula, formerly an island, is now joined to the mainland by two sandy isthmuses. Nearby are the Hyères islands, densely covered with vegetation, and the Fréjus plain, once a wide bay but now filled by alluvial deposits brought down by the Argens. Characteristic also of this particular section of the coast are great promontories such as Cap Bénat and the St-Tropez peninsula, narrow tongues of land such as Cap Nègre and Cap des Sardinaux and wide bays like the Bormes anchorage and the gulf of St-Tropez.

The Esterel Coast – The porphyry rocks of the Esterel massif, steep and rugged, make a striking contrast with the blue of the sea. Along this stretch of coast the mountains thrust great promontories into the sea, between inlets *(calanques)* and small bays. Offshore, the surface of the sea is scattered with thousands of rocks and small, green moss-covered islets, while submerged reefs can be seen beneath the clear water. The Corniche d'Or *(see Massif de l'ESTEREL)* is reputed internationally for its breathtaking scenery, superb viewpoints and various resorts.

The Antibes Coast – The vista changes once again between Cannes and Nice. The shore is no longer eaten away by the sea; it is flat and opens into wide bays. It is a smooth, unbroken coast on which the Cap d'Antibes peninsula is the sole promontory.

The Riviera Proper – From Nice to Menton the Alps plunge abruptly into the sea. Here the coastline forms a natural terrace, facing the Mediterranean but isolated from its hinterland. Cap Ferrat and Cap Martin are the two main promontories along this stretch of coast. The term Riviera, which has already passed into the language of geography, is applied to this type of coast line. A triple roadway has been cut over the steep slopes, lined with villas and terraced gardens.

Roquebrune – Cap Martin

THE MEDITERRANEAN SEA

The Mediterranean is Europe's bluest sea. The shade – cobalt blue to artists – comes from the clarity of the water. Visitors soon realise that the colour often changes depending on the nature of the sky, the light, the seabed and the depth of water so that at times the "blue Mediterranean" is opal or a warm grey.

The water – The temperature of the water, governed on the surface by the sun's heat, is constant (13°C – 55.4°F) from 200m to 4 000m – 650ft to 13 000ft downwards, whereas in the Atlantic it drops from 14°C to 2°C (57.2°F to 35°F). This is an important factor in the climate, for the sea cools the air in summer and warms it in winter. Rapid evaporation makes the water noticeably more salty than that of the Atlantic. The waves are small, short and choppy; storms come and go quickly.

The tides – Tides are almost non-existent (about 10in – 25cm). Sometimes when the wind is very strong the tide may reach as much as three feet – 1m. These figures are markedly different from the tides of the Atlantic or from the tides of 13 to 15m – 40 to 50ft round Mont-St-Michel off the Normandy coast. This relative tidal stability has resulted in the Mediterranean being chosen as the base level for all French altitudes.

The Provençal coastline drops sharply into water that becomes relatively deep a short distance from the shore. Between Nice and Cap Ferrat soundings indicate a depth of 1 000m – 3 280ft about half a mile out.

THE SEASONS

A superb climate – Crowds come flocking in summer and the tourist season lasts almost the whole year.

The Côte d'Azur is one of the most inviting names in the world! Properly speaking, the name Riviera applies to the French coast between Nice and Menton and to the Italian coast between Ventimiglia and Genoa. English visitors, at first for the sake of health but later more and more in search of pleasure, were attracted to the Riviera (especially Nice) in the 18C. The Côte d'Azur (Les Lecques to Menton) has become widely known as the French Riviera.

Winter – The proverbial mildness of the French Riviera is due to a number of factors: a low latitude, the presence of the sea which moderates temperature variations, a wholly southern aspect, and the screen of hills and mountains which protects it from cold winds. The average temperature for January in Nice is 8°C – 46°F. The unfavourable winds blow from the east and from the southeast bringing rain. Fog and sea-mists are rare except on the coast in the height of summer, harsh winters with ice and snow are practically unknown.

The thermometer may rise to 22°C (72°F) but at sunset and during the night the temperature drops suddenly and considerably. There is little rainfall: it is the dew that keeps the vegetation fresh. The hinterland is cold and often snow-covered but the air is limpid and the sun brilliant – an ideal climate for winter sports.

Spring – Short but violent showers are characteristic of springtime on the Riviera. This is when the flowers are at their best and a joy to look at. The only drawback is the *mistral*, which blows most frequently at this season, especially west of Toulon. The mountain, however, act as a buffer and the wind is never as intense as it can be in western Provence and the Rhône Valley.

The Romans made a dreaded god of this fearsome wind. It comes from the northwest in cold gusts; after several days – three, six or nine – this powerful blast of clean air has purified everything and the wind-swept sky is bluer than ever.

Summer – The coast offers an unchanging blue and an average temperature of 22°C (72°F) throughout July and August. The heat, however, is bearable because it is tempered by the fresh breeze that blows during the daytime. This is not the season for flowers: overwhelmed by drought the vegetation seems to sleep. When the hot breath of the *sirocco* comes out of the south everyone grumbles.

The hinterland offers a wide variety of places to stay at varying altitudes up to 1 800m (5 905ft); the higher one climbs the more vital the air.

Autumn – Autumn is the season for violent storms after which the sun reappears, brilliant and warm. In the whole year, there is an average of only 86 days of rain in Nice (150 in London), but the quantity of water which falls is higher (34in – 863mm in Nice against under 24in – 609mm in London). There are plenty of perfect days during the Mediterranean autumn.

Flora and Fauna

Plants and trees do not grow in the same way on the Riviera as they do further north. New shoots appear, as they do elsewhere, in the spring but a second growth begins in the autumn and continues throughout most of the winter. The dormant period is during the summer when the heat and dryness of the climate favour only those plants which are especially adapted to resist drought. These have long tap roots, glossy leaves which reduce transpiration, bulbs which act as reservoirs of moisture and perfumes which they release to form a kind of protective vapour.

TREES

Olive Trees – 2 500 years ago, the Greeks brought olive trees to Provence where they grow equally well in limestone or sandy soils. The olive has been called the immortal tree for, grafted or wild, it will always grow from the same stock. Those grown from cuttings die relatively young, at about three hundred years old. Along the coast, the trees reach gigantic dimensions, attaining 20m – 65ft in height, their domes of silver foliage 20m – 65ft in circumfer-

Olive tree

ence and trunks 4m – 13ft round the base. The olive tree, which has more than sixty varieties, is found up to an altitude of 600m – 2 000ft and marks the limit of the Mediterranean climate. It grows mainly on valley floors and on the hillsides. The trees begin to bear fruit between their sixth and twelfth year and are in full yield at 20 or 25. The olives are harvested every two years. Olive groves are numerous in the areas around Draguignan, Sospel and at Breil, in the Roya valley.

Oak Trees – The oaks native to the Mediterranean region are evergreen. The **durmast oak** grows in the scrub *(garrigue)*. The **holm oak** grows in chalky soil at altitudes below 800m – 2 500ft. As scrub-oak, it is a characteristic feature of the *garrigue* (rocky, limestone moors). In its fully developed state it is a tree with a short thick-set trunk covered in grey-black bark and with a dense, rounded crown. The **cork oak** is distinguished by its large dark-coloured acorns and its rough bark. Every eight to 12 years the thick cork bark is stripped off exposing a reddish brown trunk.

Umbrella pine   Aleppo pine

Pine Trees – The three types of pine to be found in the Mediterranean region have unmistakable silhouettes.

The **maritime pine**, which grows only in limestone soil, has dark, blue-tinged green needles and deep red bark.

The **umbrella pine** is typically Mediterranean and owes its name to its easily recognisable outline. It is often found growing alone.

The **Aleppo pine** is a Mediterranean species which grows well in chalky soil along the coast; it has a twisted, grey trunk and lighter, less dense, foliage.

Other Provençal Trees – The smooth-trunked **plane tree** and the **lotus tree** shade the courtyards, streets and squares and also line the roads.

The dark silhouette of the coniferous, evergreen **cypress** is a common feature of the countryside; planted in rows, the pyramidal cypress forms an effective windbreak.

The common **almond tree**, a member of the Rosaceae, is widespread in Provence and blossoms early. The robust **chestnut** flourishes in the Maures massif. Certain mountain species of **fir** and **larch** are to be found in the Alps; the forest of Turini is a fine fir-growing region.

Almond tree

Exotic Trees – In parks and gardens and along the roads stand magnificent **eucalyptus trees**. This hardy specimen is well adapted to the climate. In winter another Australian import, **mimosa**, covers the slopes of the Tanneron massif with a yellow mantle.

The greatest concentration of **palm trees**, is to be found in the Hyères district. The two types most common to the Riviera are the date palm with its smooth, tall trunk sweeping upwards and the Canary palm which is much shorter and has a rough scaly trunk.

Orange and **lemon** groves flourish on the coastal stretches between Cannes and Antibes and Monaco and Menton.

Use the Map of Principal Sights to plan a special itinerary

BUSHES AND SHRUBS

The **kermes oak** is a bushy evergreen shrub, which rarely grows more than three feet – one metre in height. Its name comes from the kermes, an insect halfway between a cochineal fly and a flea, which lives throughout its existence attached to the stems of the oak.

The **lentisk** is an evergreen shrub with paired leaves on either side of the main stem and no terminal leaf. The fruit is a small globular berry, which turns from red to black when it is mature.

The **pistachio** is a deciduous shrub which can grow to a height of 13-16ft – 4-5m. The leaves grow in groups of five to eleven, one of which is terminal. The fruit is a very small berry, red at first, ripening to brown.

The Mediterranean **thistle** is a perennial, which attains a height of 1m – 3ft. The irregular pointed leaves are bright green on top and covered with white down on the underside.

The Garrigue – Some of the limestone areas are so stony (Vence pass road and the D 955 from Draguignan to Montferrat) that even thorns (kermes oak, gorse and thistle) and aromatic plants (thyme, lavender and rosemary) can survive only here and there in between the bare rocks; this is the *garrigue*.

The Maquis – The scrub *(maquis)* thrives on sandy soil and forms a thick carpet of greenery, which is often impenetrable. In May and June when the cistus is in flower it is a marvellous spectacle, especially in the coverts of the Esterel.

Mediterranean thistle

SUCCULENTS

Some varieties of succulents are African in character: Barbary figs, agaves, cacti and aloes grow in open ground. Ficoids with large pink and white flowers cling to old walls.

The **aloe** has thick and fleshy leaves, from which a bitter juice is extracted for medicinal use.

The **Barbary fig** is an unusual plant from Central America, which grows in arid soil in hot climates; its broad, thick, fleshy leaves bristle with spines. The Moroccans call it the Christian fig; it is also known as the "prickly pear".

Barbary fig

Aloe

For a wider knowledge of exotic flora, take a stroll in

> *Jardin exotique in Monaco*
> *Jardin de la Villa Thuret in Cap d'Antibes (see ANTIBES)*
> *Several botanic gardens in Menton*
> *Domaine du Rayol (including Val Rameh) (see CAVALAIRE)*
> *Jardin Olbius Riquier in Hyères*

FOREST FIRES

From time immemorial the scourge of the Provençal woodland, especially in the Maures and the Esterel, has been the forest fire, which causes more damage than deforestation by man, now carefully monitored, and destruction by goats which live on the tender young shoots. During the summer the dried-up plants of the underbrush, pine needles, resins exuded by leaves and twigs are highly combustible and sometimes catch fire spontaneously. Once started, a fire may spread to the pines with disastrous results in a strong wind. Great walls of flame, sometimes 10km – 6 miles in length and 30m – 100ft high, spread at speeds of

5-6km – 2-3 miles per hour. When the fire has passed, nothing remains standing except the blackened skeletons of the trees while a thick layer of white ash covers the ground.

The Riviera Corniches between Nice and Menton, the slopes of Mont Férion in the Nice Hinterland and the region from Grasse to Mandelieu still bear the scars of the particularly severe forest fires which raged during the summer of 1986, and it will be many years before regeneration of their natural habitat is complete.

Preventive measures include the removal of undergrowth near residential areas, creation of fire-breaks and the appointment of fire-watchers and patrols. Active intervention is provided by the regular fire brigade and the airborne water carriers based in Marignane. In the event of a major fire risk, the ALARME plan enables access roads to private homes to be cleared for firefighters and limits the movements of walkers. For information on the closures in the forests, there is a recorded message service (☎ 04 94 47 35 45) for the use of ramblers.

MEDITERRANEAN MARINE LIFE

Life in the Mediterranean Sea resembles a house full of animal tenants with astonishing characteristics living one above the other. During an underwater dive, the following species may be observed.

Brown grouper – Depending on its age and size, the grouper is first female, then male. It changes sex at about 9 years old when it weighs 10 kilos – 22 lb. Since the fish can live for about 50 years, it spends most of its life as a male. The young female grouper lives on rocky seabeds in shallow water (less than 10m – 33ft deep) which makes it an easy prey for underwater hunters and other predators. As it reaches adulthood it makes its home in holes in the rocks at a depth of at least 50m – 164ft where it lives as a formidable carnivore at the extremity of the marine food chain. It may eventually reach a length of 1.20m – 4ft and weigh 30 or 40 kilos – 66 lb or 88 lb. This fish, which had become very rare in the Mediterranean, has benefited from a 5-year moratorium prohibiting the catching of groupers.

A project currently under way, led by the Parc naturel de Port-Cros, is designed to protect the grouper within an area around the island.

Jellyfish – Jellyfish, which appear seasonally in coastal waters, sometimes cause problems for holidaymakers. The most common species, pelagia, can sting with its mouth, tentacles and umbrella. The poison, which is intended to immobilise prey, is powerful enough to cause redness and burning of the skin. The population of **pelagia** follows a 12-year cycle, depending on climatic conditions, and their arrival is usually pre-

S. de Wilde/JACANA

Brown grouper

ceded by a very dry spring. Another species of jellyfish, the Portugese Man-of-War has long tentacles (up to 10m – 33ft), which are invisible to swimmers and have a very powerful sting. They are fortunately rare in the Mediterranean.

Posidonia – This flowering plant, which has bunches of long dark-green leaves, plays an essential role in the Mediterranean environment. Its rhizomes grow slowly, thus allowing it to fix the sediments from the coast and create a habitat rich in oxygen and favourable to many animal species. When the posidonia dies, these animal species either die out or migrate.

A dive into the colourful world of the posidonia provides the possibility of seeing many amazing species. The **sea cucumber**, also known as holothurian, is the dustbin of the sandy seabed and lives only in the posidonia. The **sea-slug**, found all over the Mediterranean, is a white mollusc with brown spots which contrasts with the red sponges. The **striped weever fish** lives on the seabed near the posidonia, buried in the sand with just its head visible. It has a very poisonous dorsal fin the sting of which can be serious. The **sea-horse** likes to hide near its relative, the **pipefish**, whose amazing threadlike form, with trumpet-shaped mouth, mimics the leaves of the posidonia among which it lives. In the last few decades harbour works and construction along the coast have caused much sedimentation and the resultant pollution is endangering the fragile habitat. Since 1989 one of the six varieties of tropical algae already identified in the Mediterranean, the non-toxic **taxifolia**, has spread rapidly along the French Riviera. It is feared that the spread of this alga may be harmful to the posidonia, although it seems to thrive in areas which are very acid and where the posidonia does not grow.

Agriculture and Crafts

FLOWERS AND EARLY VEGETABLES

Cut Flowers – Alphonse Karr *(See ST-RAPHAËL)*, a political refugee living in Nice before the annexation, is generally credited with having founded the flower trade. With the help of an associate, Karr began large-scale cultivation and had the idea of sending bunches of fresh violets and small packets of mixed seeds to Paris. From this modest start the trade in cut flowers and mimosa has developed considerably owing to irrigation and hothouses.

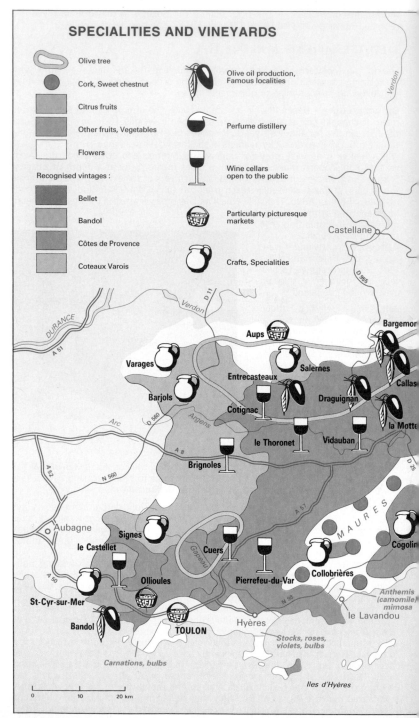

SPECIALITIES AND VINEYARDS

Olive tree

Cork, Sweet chestnut

Citrus fruits

Other fruits, Vegetables

Flowers

Olive oil production, Famous localities

Perfume distillery

Wine cellars open to the public

Particularty picturesque markets

Crafts, Specialities

Recognised vintages :

Bellet

Bandol

Côtes de Provence

Coteaux Varois

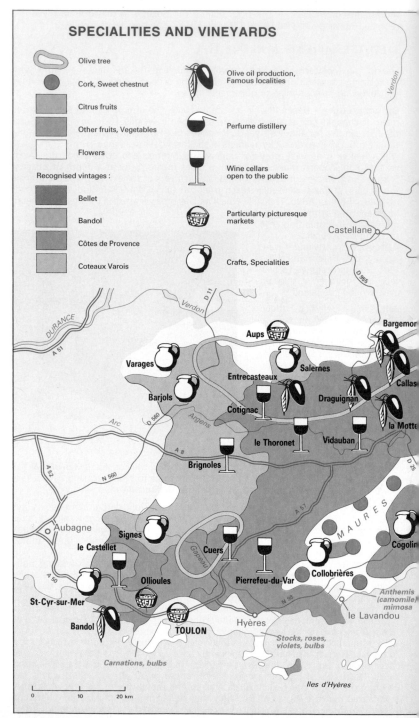

Flowers and Scented Plants of the Grasse Region – The two main flower crops of this area are roses and jasmine. The May tea-rose is the same as that grown in the east but the Mediterranean variety has a fine scent. Jasmine is of the large flowered variety which has been grafted on to jasmine officinalis. It is a particularly costly and delicate plant which flowers from the end of July to the first winter frosts.

The orange blossom used for perfume is obtained from the bitter fruit tree, known as the Seville orange *(bigaradier)*. Orange-flower water is made from direct distillation. The cherry laurel, eucalyptus and cypress are distilled both for essence and for toilet water. Mimosa is used for the production of essence by extraction. Sweet basil, clary (sage), tarragon, melissa or balm mint, verbena, mignonette,

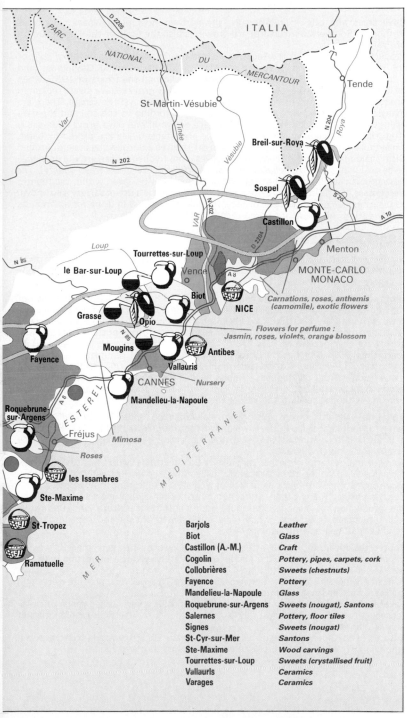

Barjols	Leather
Biot	Glass
Castillon (A.-M.)	Craft
Cogolin	Pottery, pipes, carpets, cork
Collobrières	Sweets (chestnuts)
Fayence	Pottery
Mandelieu-la-Napoule	Glass
Roquebrune-sur-Argens	Sweets (nougat), Santons
Salernes	Pottery, floor tiles
Signes	Sweets (nougat)
St-Cyr-sur-Mer	Santons
Ste-Maxime	Wood carvings
Tourrettes-sur-Loup	Sweets (crystallised fruit)
Vallaurls	Ceramics
Varages	Ceramics

peppermint and geranium all yield products used in perfumery, confectionery and pharmacy. Scented plants include wild lavender, aspic, thyme, rosemary, sage, etc. Le Bar-sur-Loup, Golfe-Juan, Le Cannet and Vallauris as well as Seillans (Var *département*), are major centres for the production of natural aromatic raw materials, although it is Grasse which is number one in this domain.

This luxury industry, which caters mostly for the export market, is supplemented by the synthetic perfume industry. The French perfume industry's exports exceed 1 000 million francs ($ 184 500 000), the most important customers being the United States, Japan, Germany and the United Kingdom.

Early vegetables – After North Africa, Spain and Italy, the region of Toulon and Hyères provides the earliest vegetables and fruit. The Var is noted for the cherries of Solliès-Pont and the peaches of the Fréjus area.

Olive trees and oils – Traditionally, the northernmost place where olive trees (symbol of Southern agriculture) are grown, is also the limit of the Midi or South of France.

Production of olive oil in the region accounts for more than two-thirds of that of the whole country, and is spread throughout the Var, around Draguignan and Brignoles, and in the Bévéra and Roya valleys. Following the frosts of 1956, when nearly a quarter of the olive trees died, the olive groves have been replanted progressively with two more hardy species: the **aglandau** and the **verdale**. There are many other varieties, with flavours which vary according to the soil and the date of harvest. Traditionally several varieties are grown in one olive grove. Harvest is from the end of August, depending on the area; table olives are picked by hand, while those destined for miling are shaken off the tree and collected in nets. Around Nice, shaking *(gaulage)* is always used. Olives from Nyons *(tanches)* are the only ones to be designated AOC *Appellation d'origine contrôlée – of guaranteed quality).* The **belgentiéroise** olive, harvested at the end of August, can be eaten within the month; the **grossane**, is a fleshy black, salted olive, the **salonenque** is a green variety also known as *olive des Baux*. The **cailletier**, or little Nice olive, is stored in brine for six months before eating. All these are both eaten at table and made into oil.

CRAFT WORKSHOPS

Numbers of craftsmen have moved into the old inland villages, which they have often restored with care, and are producing traditional objects made by the old methods or highly original creations.

Biot – The production of large earthenware jars in Biot goes back to the days of the Phoenicians. In the Middle Ages Biot was an important centre for ceramics and it was not until the 19C that it was eclipsed by Vallauris. There are several modern workshops specialising in traditional earthenware jars, pottery, ornamental stoneware and metalwork.

Since the 1960s Biot has owed its growing international reputation to its glass craftsmen. By visiting a glass workshop one can see how the various pieces are made using the old techniques. Exhibits include carafes, bottles, glasses, little oil lamps and the traditional Provençal jugs with long spouts *(calères, ponons)* for drinking without touching the vessel with the lips.

Vallauris – Ceramics from Vallauris have a worldwide reputation. In 1947 Picasso came to work in a studio in the town and attracted a crowd of followers. Nowadays it is difficult to distinguish between the mass-produced pot and the hand-made article in the shop windows.

Many of the potters – whether they use the old methods (wood firing) or the new techniques – produce attractive work: glazed kitchenware (tureens, bowls, jugs), handsome stoneware, various glazed or unglazed articles and clay pipes.

Besides pottery many other interesting activities have been introduced including the production of hand-crafted puppets, handsome furniture and decorative sculpture made from olive wood, colourful painted chests and cupboards, fine hand-woven linen and furnishings.

Tourrettes-sur-Loup – Tourrettes has been revived by its craftsmen. It was an important weaving town in the Middle Ages and renewed its connection with this craft after the Second World War.

It has become a centre for hand-woven fabrics. The weavers produce very high quality goods in small quantities.

Several of the workshops in the winding streets offer a very varied range of cloth: reproductions of old Provençal fabrics, shot material for the high fashion market or furnishings, hand-woven ties.

Tourrettes also houses potters (making earthenware sheep using a Mexican process, engraving in vivid enamels), painters and sculptors in olive wood.

Historical Table and Notes

Events in italics indicate milestones in history.

BC	
1000	The Ligurians occupy the Mediterranean seaboard.
600	Foundation of Massalia (Marseille) by the Phocaeans. They bring olive, fig, nut, cherry trees, the cultivated vine; they substitute money for barter.
5-4C	The Greek colonists in Marseille set up trading posts: Hyères, St-Tropez, Antibes, Nice and Monaco. The Celts invade Provence mingling with the Ligurians.

Gallo-Roman Provence

122	The Celts are defeated by the Romans.
102	Marius defeats the Teutons from Germania, near Aix.
58-51	*Conquest of Gaul by Julius Caesar.*
49	Julius Caesar founds Fréjus.
6	Building of the Alpine Trophy at La Turbie.
AD	
1, 2 and 3C	Roman civilization in evidence in some coastal towns (Fréjus, Cimiez, Antibes); the Via Aurelia (Ventimiglia-Brignoles-Aix) is the country's main highway.
313	*Constantine grants Christians freedom of worship by the Edict of Milan.*
4, 5C	Christianity takes root in the coastal towns, then inland.
5, 6C	Vandals, Visigoths, Burgundians, Ostrogoths and Franks invade Provence in turn.
496	*Clovis, King of the Franks, defeats the Alemanni from Germania at Tolbiac.*
8C	The Saracens sack the seaboard in the first half of the century.
800	*Charlemagne is crowned Emperor of the West.*

Provence up to the "Reunion"

843	*Treaty of Verdun* regulates the division of Charlemagne's Empire between the three sons of Louis the Debonair. Provence is restored to Lothair (one of Charlemagne's grandsons) at the same time as Burgundy and Lorraine.
855	Provence is made a kingdom by Lothair for his son, Charles.
884	The Saracens capture the Maures and for a century terrorise the land.
962	*Restoration of the Western Empire as the Holy Roman Empire under Otto I.*
10, 11C	Provence, after passing from hand to hand, is finally made part of the Holy Roman Empire. Despite this, the Counts of Provence enjoy effective independence. The towns are freed and proclaim their autonomy.
12C	The County of Provence passes to the Counts of Toulouse, then to the Counts of Barcelona. The Counts maintain an elaborate court at Aix.
1226	*Accession of Saint Louis.*
1246	Charles of Anjou, brother of Saint Louis, marries the daughter of the Count of Barcelona and becomes Count of Provence.
1254	Landing of Saint Louis at Hyères on return from the 7th Crusade.
1308	Overlordship of Monaco is bought from the Genoese by a member of the Grimaldi family.
1343-82	Queen Jeanne becomes Countess of Provence. Plague decimates the population.
1388	Nice hands itself over to the Count of Savoy.
1419	Nice is officially ceded to the Duke of Savoy.
1434	René of Anjou "Good King René" becomes Count of Provence.
1481	Charles of Maine, nephew of René of Anjou, bequeaths Provence (except Nice, which belongs to Savoy) to Louis XI.
1486	Reunion of Provence with France ratified by the "Estates" of Provence (assembly of representatives of the three orders); Provence attached to the Kingdom "as one principal to another".

Provence after the "Reunion"

1501	Establishment of Parliament at Aix (Parliament of Provence), sovereign court of justice, which later claims certain political prerogatives.
1515	*Accession of François I.*
1524	Provence is invaded by the Imperialists, commanded by the High Constable of Bourbon.
1536	Invasion of Provence by the Emperor Charles V.
1539	Edict of Villers-Cotterêts decrees French as the language for all administrative laws in Provence.
1543	Nice besieged by French and Turkish troops. Catherine Ségurane instrumental in causing the Turks to withdraw.
1562-98	*Wars of Religion.* Promulgation of the Edict of Nantes.
1622	Louis XIII visits Provence.
1643-1715	*Reign of Louis XIV.*
1691	Nice taken by the French.
1696	France returns Nice to Savoy.
1707	Invasion of Provence by Prince Eugene of Savoy.
1718	County of Nice becomes part of the newly created Kingdom of Sardinia.
1720	The great plague decimates the population of Provence.
1746	Austro-Sardinian offensive is broken at Antibes. Austrian War of Succession.
1787	Reunion of the "Estates" of Provence.
1789	*The French Revolution.*

Revolution-Empire

1790	Provence divided into 3 *départements:* Bouches-du-Rhône, Var, Basses-Alpes.
1793	Siege of Toulon, in which Bonaparte distinguishes himself. Nice is reunited with France.
1799	On 9 October, Bonaparte lands at St-Raphaël on his return from Egypt.
1804	*Coronation of Napoleon.*
1814	*Abdication of Napoleon, at Fontainebleau, 6 April.* Embarkation of Napoleon at St-Raphaël, 28 April, for the Island of Elba. The County of Nice is restored to the King of Sardinia.
1815	Landing of Napoleon at Golfe-Juan, 1 March. *Battle of Waterloo, 18 June.*

19th Century

1830	*Accession of Louis-Philippe.*
1832	The Duchess of Berry lands at Marseille, hoping to raise Provence in favour of a legitimist restoration.
1852-1870	*Reign of Napoleon III.*
1860	County of Nice restored to France.
1878	Opening of the Monte-Carlo Casino. Development of the winter tourist season of the Riviera.
late 19C	St-Tropez School of Painting.

20th Century

1914-18	Many village populations depleted by First World War.
1940	The Italians occupy Menton.
1942	The Germans invade the Free Zone. The scuttling of the French Fleet in Toulon harbour.
1944	Liberation of Provence.
1946	First International Film Festival in Cannes.
Since 1946	Development of summer tourist trade on the Riviera. Harnessing of the rivers Durance and Verdon.
1947	Upper valley of the Roya incorporated into France.
1970	International technopole opened at Sophia Antipolis near Valbonne reflects increasing emphasis on development of the region into a hi-tech industrial belt.
1980	The Provençal Motorway (A8), links the Rhône and Italian networks.
1989	Law passed to strengthen measures against forest fires which pose an increasing threat to the region.
1989	The TGV (*train à grande vitesse* – high speed train) arrives on the Riviera.
August 1994	Celebration of the 50th anniversary of the Liberation of Provence.
1996	A high speed boat service (NGV) between Nice and Corsica.

ALLIED LANDING IN PROVENCE (1944)

Operation "Dragon" – This was the aftermath of operation "Overlord" which had liberated Normandy three months earlier. At a critical moment in the battle of Normandy the Allies landed on the coast of Provence (fortified by the Germans under the name "Südwall" with the American 7th Army under **General Patch**, of which the French Ist Army (composed mostly of African soldiers) formed the principal part.

"Nancy a le torticolis" – (Nancy has a stiff neck) This laconic message, broadcast on the BBC in the evening of 14 August announcing the landings in Provence, raised the hopes of the Resistance groups which had been on alert since the projected landings reported on 6 June 1944. Between June and August, the dropping of arms by parachute was stepped up, notably in the *pouvadous* (dry and stony moors); these arms were destined for the Maquis (Resistance) in the Maures, the Alps, Besillon and Ste-Baume. In the early hours of 15 August, airborne Anglo-American troops were dropped around Le Muy to take control of the strategic communications route, RN 7. The village of **La Motte** became the first Provençal village to be liberated. At the same time, French commandos from Africa landed on the left wing at Cap Nègre, and on the right wing at Esquillon Point, while American Special Forces attacked the Iles d'Hyères. Thus protected, the main army, assembled on the 2 000 ships, including 250 battleships, landed at 0800 on the beaches of Cavalaire, St-Tropez, Le Dramont and the Esterel. Despite a rapid advance, the two sectors were still separated at the end of the day by pockets of German resistance at St-Raphaël and Fréjus which fell only the following day. On 16 August the B Army under General De Lattre landed at Cavalaire Bay and in the gulf of St-Tropez and, having relieved the Americans, attacked the defences of Toulon. General Montsabert outflanked the town to the north to fall on Marseille. After the fall of Hyères and Solliès, Toulon was reached on 23 August but fighting continued until 28 August with the surrender of the St-Mandrier peninsula. On the same day, after 5 days of fighting, Marseilles was liberated.

To the east, the Americans of the First Special Force advanced to the Alpes-Maritimes to back up the Resistance forces and drive the Germans back into the Italian Alps: Nice fell on 30 August and Menton on 6 September. In the hinterland, the Massif de l'Authion, transformed into an entrenched camp by the Germans, was the site of hard fighting for 8 months. L'Authion was overcome on 13 April 1945, Saorge on 18 April but Tende was liberated only on 5 May, 3 days before the general Armistice!

Provence had been liberated in less than 15 days. The Allies pursued the Germans, who retreated up the Rhône valley; the 1st French Army under De Lattre de Tassigny effected a link-up with the 2nd amoured division under Leclerc in Côte d'Or south of Châtillon-sur-Seine.

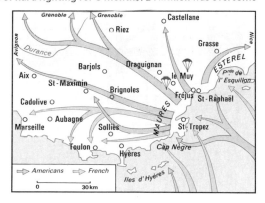

Art

ABC OF ARCHITECTURE

To assist readers unfamiliar with the terminology employed in architecture, we describe below the most commonly used terms, which we hope will make their visits to ecclesiastical, military and civil buildings more interesting.

Ecclesiastical architecture

illustration I ▶

Ground plan: The more usual Catholic form is based on the outline of a cross with the two arms of the cross forming the transept: ① Porch – ② Narthex – ③ Side aisles (sometimes double) – ④ Bay (transverse section of the nave between 2 pillars) – ⑤ Side chapel (often predates the church) – ⑥ Transept cros-

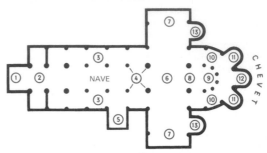

sing – ⑦ Arms of the transept, sometimes with a side doorway – ⑧ Chancel, nearly always facing east towards Jerusalem; the chancel often vast in size was reserved for the monks in abbatial churches – ⑨ High altar – ⑩ Ambulatory: in pilgrimage churches the aisles were extended round the chancel, forming the ambulatory, to allow the faithful to file past the relics – ⑪ Radiating or apsidal chapel – ⑫ Axial chapel. In churches which are not dedicated to the Virgin this chapel, in the main axis of the building, is often consecrated to the Virgin (Lady Chapel) – ⑬ Transept chapel.

Romanesque — Gothic

◀ illustration II

Cross-section: ① Nave – ② Aisle – ③ Tribune or gallery – ④ Triforium – ⑤ Barrel vault – ⑥ Half-barrel vault – ⑦ Pointed vault – ⑧ Buttress – ⑨ Flying buttress – ⑩ Pier of a flying buttress – ⑪ Pinnacle – ⑫ Clerestory window.

◀ illustration III

Gothic cathedral: ① Porch – ② Gallery – ③ Rose window – ④ Belfry (sometimes with a spire) – ⑤ Gargoyle acting as a waterspout for the roof gutter – ⑥ Buttress – ⑦ Pier of a flying buttress (abutment) – ⑧ Flight or span of flying buttress – ⑨ Double-course flying buttress – ⑩ Pinnacle – ⑪ Side chapel – ⑫ Radiating or apsidal chapel – ⑬ Clerestory windows – ⑭ Side doorway – ⑮ Gable – ⑯ Pinnacle – ⑰ Spire over the transept crossing.

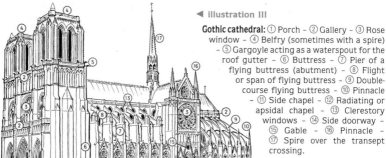

◀ illustration IV
Groined vaulting:
① Main arch –
② Groin –
③ Transverse arch.

illustration V ▶
Oven vault:
termination of a barrel vaulted nave.

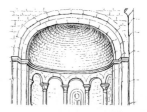

illustration VI

Lierne and tierceron vaulting: ① Diagonal – ② Lierne – ③ Tierceron – ④ Pendant – ⑤ Corbel.

illustration VII

Quadripartite vaulting: ① Diagonal – ② Transverse – ③ Stringer – ④ Flying buttress – ⑤ Keystone.

▼ **illustration VIII**

Doorway: ① Archivolt. Depending on the architectural style of the building this can be rounded, pointed, basket-handled, ogee or even adorned by a gable – ② Arching, coving (with string courses, mouldings, carvings or adorned with statues). Recessed arches or orders form the archivolt – ③ Tympanum – ④ Lintel – ⑤ Archshafts – ⑥ Embrasures. Arch shafts, splaying sometimes adorned with statues or columns – ⑦ Pier (often adorned by a statue) – ⑧ Hinges and other ironwork.

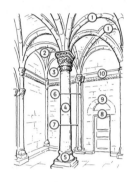

illustration IX ▶

Arches and pillars: ① Ribs or ribbed vaulting – ② Abacus – ③ Capital – ④ Shaft – ⑤ Base – ⑥ Engaged column – ⑦ Pier – ⑧ Lintel – ⑨ Discharging or relieving arch – ⑩ Frieze.

Military architecture

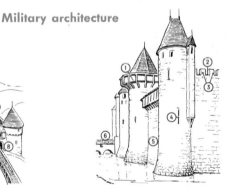

illustration X

Fortified enclosure: ① Hoarding (projecting timber gallery) – ② Machicolations (corbelled crenellations) – ③ Barbican – ④ Keep or donjon – ⑤ Covered watchpath – ⑥ Curtain wall – ⑦ Outer curtain wall – ⑧ Postern.

illustration XI

Towers and curtain walls: ① Hoarding – ② Crenellations – ③ Merlon – ④ Loophole or arrow slit – ⑤ Curtain wall – ⑥ Bridge or drawbridge.

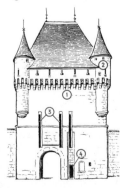

◀ **illustration XII**

Fortified gatehouse:
① Machicolations – ② Watch turrets or bartizan – ③ Slots for the arms of the drawbridge – ④ Postern.

illustration XIII ▶

Star fortress: ① Entrance – ② Drawbridge – ③ Glacis – ④ Ravelin or half-moon – ⑤ Moat – ⑥ Bastion – ⑦ Watch turret – ⑧ Town – ⑨ Assembly area.

Aisle: illustration I

Altarpiece or retable: illustration XIV

Ambulatory: illustration I

Amphora: (Greek) vase used for storing and transport of oil or wine; antique vase with two handles. The base was sometimes replaced by a point for standing in the sand.

Antiphonary: a book of antiphons or anthems.

Apse: generally rounded east end of a church. In French churches the exterior is known as the chevet (*see chevet*).

Apsidal or radiating chapel: illustration I

Aqueduct: elevated or underground artificial channel for carrying water.

Illustration XIV

Altar with retable or altarpiece:
① Retable or altarpiece – ② Predella –
③ Crowning piece – ④ Altar table –
⑤ Altar front.

Arabesque: Arab ornamentation combining letters, flowing lines and intertwining foliage.

Arcade: succession of small arches; when attached to a wall they are known as blind arcades.

Architrave: lowest part of the entablature.

Arrow slit: illustration XI

Atlante: male figure used as a support.

Atrium: in a Roman house a large rectangular court; under the central section, open to the sky, is the impluvium or basin to catch the rainwater.

Axial or Lady Chapel: illustration I

Baldachin or baldaquin: canopy supported by columns, usually over the high altar.

Balusters or banister: uprights supporting the handrail of a staircase.

Balustrade: row of balusters or short pillars or posts surmounted by a railing or a coping.

Baptismal font: basin with a base, usually placed in a chapel near the entrance to the church.

Baptistery: building, often separate from the church or cathedral, used for baptisms.

Barrel vaulting: illustration II

Bartizan: illustration XII

Basin or bowl: of a fountain and usually shallow.

Basket-handled arch: depressed arch common to late medieval and Renaissance architecture.

Bastion: illustration XIII

Bay: illustration I

Biscuit: unglazed white porcelain with an imitation marble grain.

Bond: an arrangement of stones or bricks.

Broken barrel vaulting: see below the cross section of a Provençal Romanesque church.

Buttress: illustrations II and III

Capital: illustration IX

Caryatid: support in the form of a carved female figure.

Chancel: illustration I

Chapter house: place of assembly for the members of any monastic order or canons of a collegiate church or cathedral.

Chevet: French term for the east end of a church; illustration I

Chimera: grotesque monster with a lion's head, goat's body and dragon's tail.

Ciborium: canopy over the high altar or a receptacle for the Eucharist.

Cippus: small pillar used to mark a burial place or serve as sepulchral monument.

Clerestory: upper stage of an elevation consisting of a range of tall windows.

Coffered ceiling: vault or ceiling decorated with sunken panels.

Console: moulding to carry a cornice or balcony.

Corbel: illustration VI

Corinthian order: Greek architectural order characterised by scroll capital almost entirely covered in curled acanthus leaves.

Cornice: projecting moulding to carry a balcony.

Crenellations: illustration XI

Crypt: underground chamber or chapel.

Cuneiform: wedge-shaped; applies to characters of the ancient Middle Eastern (Persian, Assyrian) civilizations.

Denticular: having dentils.

Dentil: small rectangular block, used as a decorative pattern in the entablature of Classical orders.

Dolmen or cromlech: megalithic monument consisting of a large flat stone resting horizontally on several upright ones.

Doric order: Greek architectural order with plain capitals.

Emblasoned: adorned with a coat of arms or other heraldic devices.

Entablature: in Classical architecture the element of a temple above the columns, supporting the wooden roof.

Etching: process of print making using nitric acid etched plates.

Ex-voto: offering or inscription made in pursuance of a vow.

Festoon: ornamentation in the form of a garland of foliage, fruit and flowers.

Flamboyant: last phase (15C) of French Gothic architecture; name taken from the undulating (flame-like) lines of the window tracery.

Fluted: vertical grooves in column shafts.

Foliated scrolls: sculptural or painted ornamentation depicting foliage, often in the form of a frieze.

Forum: large square, surrounded by a portico, which was the centre of public and commercial life in Roman towns.

Fresco: mural painting executed on wet plaster.

Frieze: illustration IX

Gable: triangular part of an end wall carrying a sloping roof; the term is also applied to the steeply pitched ornamental pediments of Gothic architecture; illustration III

Gallery: illustration II

Gargoyle: illustration III

Groined vaulting: illustration IV

Guilloche: in gold and silver work criss-cross hatching of engraved lines.

High altar: church's main altar usually placed in the chancel.

High relief: haut-relief; sculpted relief figures which are proud of their background by more than half their thickness.

Historiated: decorated with figures of people or animals.

Hypocaust: in Antiquity an underground furnace designed to heat the water or the rooms of a house.

Illumination or miniature: painted decoration of a letter or writing with colours. Typical of medieval manuscripts.

Impost: a member in wall formed of a bracket-like moulding supporting an arch.

Incunabula: work printed prior to 1500.

Ionic order: Greek architectural order with double scroll capitals.

Keep or donjon: illustration X

Lantern: small turret crowning a roof or dome.

Lectern: reading or singing desk, often pivoting, in a church.

Lintel: illustrations VIII and IX.

Loggia: covered gallery, often arcaded, on the outside of a building.

Lombard arcades: decorative blind arcading composed of small arches and intervening pilaster strips: typical of Romanesque art in Lombardy.

Loophole or arrow slit: illustration XI

Low relief: bas-relief; carved or sculpted figures which are slightly proud of their background.

Machicolations; illustration X

Maroufle: French word for a very strong glue used to apply a painting on canvas to another surface.

Merlon: illustration XI

Miniature: has superseded the word illumination since the 16C; see illumination.

Misericord: illustration XVII

Monolith: single block of stone.

Monstrance: receptacle for displaying the Host; usually made of silver or gold and embellished with precious stones and often surrounded with a sunburst.

Mosaic: pictures or decorative patterns composed of small pieces of stones or marble set in cement.

Mullion: a vertical post dividing a window.

Narthex: illustration I

Nave: illustration I

Niche: wall recess often adorned with a statue or vase.

Oculus: round window.

Ogee arch: arch consisting of two double (S-shaped) curves, concave below and convex above, meeting in a point at the top.

Organ: illustration XV

Oven vaulting: illustration V

Overhang or jetty: overhanging upper storey.

Palestra: in Antiquity a public place for practising wrestling and athletics.

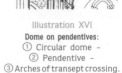

Illustration XV
Organ:
① Great organ case –
② Little organ case –
③ Caryatids – ④ Loft.

Illustration XVI
Dome on pendentives:
① Circular dome –
② Pendentive –
③ Arches of transept crossing.

Panel: compartment or shutter of a wainscot, door or window, often sunken or raised.

Patio: Spanish word to designate an inner court, open to the sky.

Pediment: low-pitched gable above the main entrance of a building; a broken pediment is one open at the apex.

Pendentives: usually dome on pendentives; illustration XVI

Pepperpot roof: conical roof

Pergola: covered walk in a garden created by trelliswork covered with climbing foliage.

Peristyle: a range of columns surrounding or on the façade of a building.

Pier: illustration VIII

Pietà: Italian term designating the Virgin Mary with the dead Christ on her knees.

Pilaster: engaged rectangular column.

Pilaster strip: decorative feature characteristic of Romanesque architecture in Lombardy consisting of shallow projecting pilasters and blind arcading.

Pointed arch: diagonal arch supporting a vault; illustrations VI and VII

Pointed or ogive arch: arch consisting of two curves meeting in a point at the top; it is called an equilateral arch when the radii equal the span.

Polychrome: multicoloured.

Polyptych: several painted or carved panels hinged together.

Porch: covered approach to the entrance to a building.

Postern: illustrations X and XII

Predella: illustration XIV

Pulpit: an elevated structure in the nave of a church for the preacher or reader; often elaborately carved and provided with a sounding board.

Punic: pertaining to Phoenician colonies in North Africa and especially to Carthage.

Quadratura: 16C term derived from Italian designating pictural representation in *trompe l'œil* of architectural or decorative motifs.

Quadripartite vaulting: illustration VII

Rampant vault: see below the vertical section of a Provençal Romanesque church.

Recessed tomb: funerary niche.

Relics: part of a saint's body or one of his personal belongings.

Reliquary: casket to hold a relic or relics of a saint; it sometimes takes the form of the relic eg arm reliquary.

Retable: see altarpiece.

Reticular: in the form of a network.

Rocaille: decorative patterns derived from shell forms.

Rococo: decorative style popular during the reign of Louis XV. It is characterised by curving lines.

Rood-beam or tref: illustration XVII

Roman milestone: milestones placed at 1.5km (1 Roman mile) intervals along Roman roads.

Rose or wheel window: illustration III

Rustication: large blocks of masonry often separated by deep joints and given bold textures (rock-faced, diamond-pointed or vermiculated). Commonly employed during the Renaissance.

Saddleback roof: usually of a tower where two gable ends are connected by a ridge roof.

Sanguine: red chalk drawing.

Santon: fired and gaily painted clay figurines; traditionally used in the Christmas cribs in Provence.

Sarcophagus: Stone or marble coffin.

Segment: part of a ribbed vault, compartment between the ribs.

Semicircular arch: round-headed arch.

Sexpartite vaulting: six compartments formed by three intersecting diagonals.

Spire: illustration I

Stalls: illustration XVII

Stele: upright slab bearing inscriptions or low reliefs commemorating a victory or a person.

Stucco: mixture of powdered marble, plaster and a strong glue; used for decoration.

Transept: illustration I

Transverse or diaphragm arch: arch separating one bay from the next in certain Romanesque churches.

Triforium: illustration II

Triptych: three panels hinged together, chiefly used as an altarpiece.

Trompe-l'œil: illusionist painting.

Twinned or paired: columns or pilasters grouped in twos.

Tympanum: illustration VIII

Wainscot or panelling: timber lining to walls.

Wall belfry: wall, usually rising above the west front, pierced by openings in which hang the bells.

Watchpath or wall walk: illustration X

Illustration XVII

Stalls: ① High back –
② Elbow rest –
③ Cheek-piece –
④ Misericord.

THE ARTS

Compared with Provence, which is rich in monuments of all sorts, the Riviera has less to offer. Here, however, the sightseer will discover art in its earliest forms side by side with its most modern expressions. Right up until the 19C the art of the region remained highly conservative. When the Romanesque and Gothic styles were flourishing elsewhere in France, the Riviera remained untouched.

Architecture

Gallo-Roman Antiquities – Provence and particularly the Riviera have been thriving areas since Roman times. As later generations took the materials used by the Romans for the construction of their own new buildings, only a few fragments of the ancient civilization have survived. In the districts of Fayence, Fréjus and St-Raphaël, Roman works are still being used to carry water.

The Roman ruins at Cimiez *(see NICE)* are extensive. At Fréjus *(see FRÉJUS)*, as well as the arena, there are traces of the harbour installations. The Alpine Trophy at La Turbie *(see LA TURBIE)* is of especial interest; it is one of the few such Roman trophies still in existence. Buildings from the Merovingian and Carolingian periods include the bapistery at Fréjus; and the chapels of Notre-Dame-de-Pépiole and La Trinité at St-Honorat de Lérins.

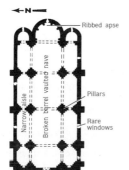

Plan of a Provençal
Romanesque Church

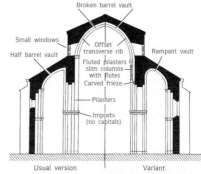

Vertical section of a
Provençal Romanesque Church

Amphorae

From ancient times, the Provençal coasts have been visited by numerous merchants ships often of imposing size (more than 30m – 98ft long) and heavily laden (up to 8 000 amphorae). The problems of manœuvring these heavy boats with oar and sail and lack of knowledge of the reefs led to innumerable shipwrecks. The wrecks salvaged with their cargoes of amphorae bear witness to the busy commercial exchanges between areas of production and the consumers in urban centres. Navigation took place between April and September when the weather conditions were most favourable. Food products transported were wine, oil and fish. The cargo on these boats was arranged at right angles to the keel; the pointed ends of the amphorae were wedged in place by the branches of trees, and the empty spaces between their necks were filled with the next row, thus assuring that the whole was stable. Some holds contained up to four levels of amphorae.

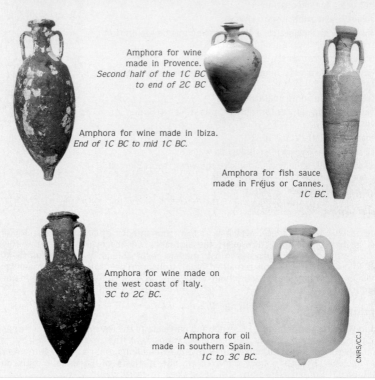

Amphora for wine made in Provence.
Second half of the 1C BC to end of 2C BC

Amphora for wine made in Ibiza.
End of 1C BC to mid 1C BC.

Amphora for fish sauce made in Fréjus or Cannes.
1C BC.

Amphora for wine made on the west coast of Italy.
3C to 2C BC.

Amphora for oil made in southern Spain.
1C to 3C BC.

CNRS/CCJ

Regulations concerning underwater archeological finds.
All cultural goods from the sea (amphorae etc) found on public property belong to the State. Therefore anyone diving who finds any archeological remains must leave them in place and not touch them.
In the event of objects being brought up by chance (in nets, for example), it is forbidden to dispose of them and the find should be reported to the nearest Affaires Maritimes within 48 hours. Offenders are dealt with in the High Courts.
Lastly, a small consolation, divers who have declared a find of a wreck or archeological remains could benefit from a reward fixed by the government.

Romanesque Period – In the 12C an architectural renaissance in Provence blossomed in the building of numerous churches. The Romanesque style here is more eclectic than innovative, resulting not in large buildings, such as those in Burgundy, but rather in unpretentious churches, remarkable for the bonding of their evenly cut stones with fine mortar work.
The churches are plain outside, their façades being often poor in style; the only break in the flatness of the sides comes from powerful buttresses. The square belfry and the east end are sometimes decorated with applied blind arcades, known as **Lombard bands**, evidence of northern Italian influence.
On entering, the visitor is struck by the simplicity and austerity of the interior which often consists of a single nave and a shallow transept. If aisles form part of the plan, the apse ends in a semicircle flanked by two apsidal chapels.

Eclectic architecture

Villa Mauresque, Hyères

Ste Jeanne d'Arc (1934), Nice

Château Smith, Nice

Baroque house (1890), Nice

Jardin Japonais, Monte-Carlo

Hôtel de l'Ermitage, Monte-Carlo

Russian Orthodox Cathedral, Nice

The interesting abbey of Le Thoronet *(See LE THORONET)* contains a church of the Cistercian Order with the wide transept and bare appearance characteristic of the churches built by the Benedictines. In contrast, however, the roof of broken barrel vaulting and the semicircular apse show the influence of the local craftsmen.

Gothic to Baroque – There are few Gothic buildings in the region. Provençal Gothic is a transitional style which depends heavily on Romanesque traditions. The style is represented in the powerful groined vaulting at Fréjus and Grasse. The cloisters at Fréjus are remarkable.

In the 15C Good King René brought numerous Italian craftsmen to Provence, but, though Provençal painting was influenced by the Renaissance, architecture remained untouched.

C. Moirenc/DIAF

Menton Cathedral

Classical buildings, however, abound (17C and 18C). Design lost its original style and became more severe and majestic. In the towns the wealthier citizens built town houses. The development of the Baroque style is to be seen in ecclesiastical buildings in the County of Nice at Sospel, Menton, Monaco, La Turbie and Nice. Façades are adorned with pediments, niches and statues; inside, the architectural lines are often hidden by altarpieces, panelling and baldaquins of great richness.

Modern Period – The 19C showed little originality and Baroque continued to be favoured for new constructions and restorations. The Romanesque-Byzantine style was employed in the church of Notre-Dame-de-la-Victoire-de-Lépante, St-Raphaël, the neo-Gothic on the west front of the church at Cimiez and neo-Romanesque for Monaco's cathedral. Slightly later, the Casino in Monte-Carlo and the Hôtel Negresco in Nice were designed in an ostentatious style borrowed from the Belle Epoque (*c*1900).

Examples of 20C works include the Church of Ste-Jeanne-d'Arc in Nice, the country church of St-Martin-de-Peille and the Chapelle Matisse at Vence. The Fondation Maeght in St-Paul, the Musée Marc-Chagall in Nice, and the striking property development at the Baie des Anges Marina at Villeneuve-Loubet or Port-Grimaud are other fine examples of modern architecture.

Pierre Puget (1620-94)

This native of Marseille, was one of the greatest French sculptors of the 17C. He began by carving the prows of ships and later developed huge carved poops. During a journey in Italy he developed his talents by working as a pupil of Pietro da Cortona.

After the fall of Fouquet, his patron, he established himself away from Versailles and was appointed director of the port of Toulon by Colbert who thought well of him. Jealousies and intrigues soon brought him into disgrace, so he threw himself into the embellishment of Toulon. His best known works are the atlantes supporting the balcony of Toulon Town Hall and the *Milo of Croton*, which is exhibited in the Louvre in Paris. His Baroque style could express power, movement and pathos.

Painting

Primitives – From the middle of the 15C to the middle of the 16C a school of painting, at first purely Gothic then influenced by the Italian Renaissance, flourished in the County of Nice. It is best known through the works of **Bréa** and **Durandi**. It is said of Louis Bréa that he was a "Provençal Fra Angelico" praise justified by the sincerity and sobriety of his brush and his gift for stressing the humanity of his subjects. However, his simplicity is a far cry from the mysticism of Fra Angelico, and his colours and dull tones lack the quality of the great Italian genius. These Provençal artists worked mainly for the penitent brotherhoods, which explains why their paintings are scattered in many churches and pilgrim chapels. They can be seen in Nice (where Brea's brother Antoine and nephew François are represented), Gréolières, Antibes, Fréjus, Grasse and Monaco.

St Martin by
Louis Bréa

P. et G. Leclerc, Nice

During the same period, the humblest churches of the County of Nice were decorated with the most striking mural paintings. These are to be seen at Coaraze, Venanson, Lucéram, Saorge and Notre-Dame-des-Fontaines where Renaissance Primitive **Giovanni Canavesio**, working beside **Jean Baleison**, created Gothic-inspired works of exceptional quality.

The Classical Period – The 17C and 18C were marked by the fine pictures of the Parrocles, the Van Loos, Joseph Vernet and Hubert Robert. It is **Fragonard**, however, who is the pride of Provence. Rakish scenes were his favourites; he painted them with great enthusiasm and exquisite style. He often used as background to his jubilant party scenes, the landscapes flooded with light and the gardens full of flowers seen round his native town of Grasse.

Modern Painting – At the end of the 19C numerous artists, representing the main trends in modern painting, were fascinated by the clear light of the Mediterranean South of France.

Impressionism – The Impressionists sought to portray the subtle effects of light on Mediterranean landscapes. Berthe Morisot lived in Nice, Monet in Antibes and **Renoir** in Cagnes where he spent his last years, painting flowers and fruits, landscapes and people of the South.

Impressionism gave birth to a new school, **Pointillism**, a method of painting created by Seurat, which consisted of dividing shades into tiny dots of pure colour distributed so as to intensify the effect of light.

Signac, Seurat's disciple, established himself in 1892 in St-Tropez, to which he attracted some of his friends, among whom were Manguin, Bonnard and Matisse.

Fauvism – Matisse and Dufy, who were established in Nice, reacted against Impressionism and, through the use of pure and brilliant colours, juxtaposed in simplified forms and perspectives, tried to express not just the fleeting sensation evoked by the spectacle of nature but the very thoughts and emotions of the artist.

Contemporary Movements – **Picasso**, founder with Braque of Cubism – an art concerned above all with form – was in his turn seduced by the Riviera, and lived in Vallauris in 1946, then in Cannes and finally in Mougins.

Braque spent his last years painting in Le Cannet while **Fernand Léger**, another Cubist painter, lived in Biot.

Dunoyer de Segonzac was untiring in his portrayal of St-Tropez.

Chagall found the light and flowers of Vence a marvellous stimulus to his multicoloured dreams.

Other artists, such as **Kandinsky** in La Napoule, **Cocteau** in Menton, **Van Dongen**

L'Estaque by Georges Braque

Musée de l'Annonciade, St Tropez

in Cannes, **Magnelli** in Grasse and **Nicolas de Staël** in Antibes, although not spending much time in the region, nevertheless marked their stay in an unforgettable manner.

At the same time in Nice in the 1960s a group of artists including **Arman**, **César**, Dufrêne, Hains, **Klein**, Raysse, Rotella, Spoerri, Tinguely and Villeglé formed the **Nouveau Réalisme** joined later by Niki de Saint-Phalle, Deschamps and Christo. They were reacting against abstraction, which was preponderant in artistic circles after the war, and experimented with new approaches to reality making use of objects found in the modern industrial and consumer world. Alongside these innovators were the members of the **Nice School**, who each sought his own vision (**Ben**, Bernar Venet, Sacha Sosno); and **Bernard Pagès** and **Claude Viallat**, who, closely linked to the theories of Conceptual Art, led to the creation of the Support-Surface in the 70s *(for more on contemporary movements see NICE Musée d'Art moderne et d'Art contemporain).*

The chapter on art and architecture in this guide gives
an outline of artistic achievement in the country
providing the context of the buildings and works of art
described in the Sights section
This chapter may also provide ideas for touring
It is advisable to read it at leisure

Hill Villages

Many old villages may be seen perched like an eagle's nest on a hilltop or set on the flank of a hill; some are practically deserted, while others have been restored. For centuries the peasants built their villages in this way, at a distance from their lands and water supplies, and surrounded them with ramparts.

This was a wise precaution in the days of the great Germanic invasions, the Moslem pirates, and the attacks by the mercenaries of the Middle Ages and the Renaissance. The coming of security, better communications and the development in agricultural techniques in the 19C ended this isolation. Villages began to develop in the plains, sometimes doubling in size, and country dwellers were able to live on the land they cultivated and build their house there. Gourdon, Èze, Utelle, Peille and many other villages *(see map below)* still bear witness to the ancient Provençal way of life.

These isolated villages are picturesque to visit. Built with stones from the hillsides, they seem to blend with the countryside. The winding streets and alleyways **(calades)**, which are steeply sloped and only to be traversed on foot, are paved with flagstones or cobbles, intersected by tortuous stairways and crossed overhead by vaults and arches. Sometimes arcades follow one another at ground level, affording the passerby shelter from the sun and rain.

Lucéram

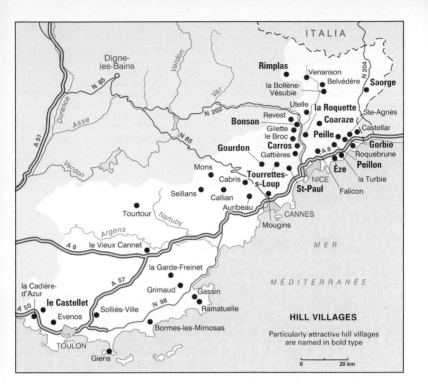

HILL VILLAGES

Particularly attractive hill villages
are named in bold type

0   20 km

The houses, roofed with curved tiles, have high narrow fronts, worn by the
centuries. They buttress each other and surround the church or château, which
dominates the village. Old nail-studded doors, wrought-iron hinges and bronze
knockers, still adorn the more substantial dwellings.
Sometimes the little townships, which have attracted many craftsmen, are still
enclosed by ramparts and one enters by a fortified gate.

Life on the Riviera

ON THE COAST

The Riviera has attracted man since earliest times and strongholds have been built
on isolated hills; the curious village of Èze is the best example.
Since the great expansion of the tourist trade, life on the Riviera is dominated by
a beach and holiday atmosphere nearly all year round. Local life is gradually
disappearing from view under the great influx of visitors.

Holiday resorts – The visitor who is seeking fashionable and elegant surroundings
can choose between the animation of Cannes and Monte-Carlo or the quieter and
more discreet life of Hyères, Beaulieu, Menton, Cap Ferrat or Cap Martin. Those
who are looking for the liveliness of a large town with all its amusements will
undoubtedly turn to Nice. Lively St-Tropez will attract a large number of summer
visitors; the seeker of solitude will find isolated inlets and localities; and a full range
of hotels in the large resorts caters for every budget.
There are also charming country houses, built in Provençal rustic style, with pink
or ochre-coloured walls, overhanging red-tiled roofs and arbours covered with
wistaria and climbing plants. There are, too, beautiful gardens in which great
earthenware jars, which once held olive oil or wine, are now purely decorative.
Magnificent parks offer fine views from their terraces, and everyone can enjoy the
light and colour in an atmosphere of charm and relaxation.
Numerous constructions are invading the coast and one can see here and there
towns built over water, such as the lake town of Port-Grimaud, the Cogolin Marina
and the marine city of Port-la-Galère.
Ambitious building projects, some of which are out of all proportion, have sprung
up on all sides; a great number of private properties are situated even along the
coast itself, but in fact the public has right of access all along the coast.

Ports and fishing – The naval port of Toulon is in a league of its own on the popular recreational coast. Cannes, Monaco and Menton are long-established pleasure boat ports: beautiful yachts with shining steelwork lie at anchor in the bay or are moored to the quays. Fishing on the Riviera is confined to the coast and, as the catch is insufficient for the area, it has to be supplemented by shipments from the Atlantic.

There are no large fishing ports but numerous little harbours along the coast – Bandol, St-Tropez, St-Raphaël, Villefranche-sur-Mer, for example, are adapting to the demands of tourists and equipping themselves with moorings for pleasure boats. For some years past the Nice region has made efforts to modernise the fishing industry and increase the number of boats in use. This has been achieved through the use of very large running nets known as *lamparos* and *seinches* and the construction of fish canneries.

The markets – Most of the coastal towns have their own flower and fish markets where, to the colourful banks of flowers and stalls of gleaming fish, are added the noisy bustle and the warmth of the local accents of buyers and sellers, creating a truly meridional scene.

INLAND

The interior reveals the last vestiges of what was once a rough and precarious way of life. Valley sides and hill slopes were terraced with stone walls retaining small strips of soil growing cereals or two or three rows of vines and a few olive and almond trees. The *garrigue* where small flocks of sheep and goats were put to graze formed a sharp contrast with the fertile valleys and irrigated plains of the lowlands and the coast, where cereals, early vegetables and flowers were harvested and vines and fruit trees flourished. The lonely villages clinging to solitary ridges *(details above)* and small farms lying abandoned among their terraced walls bore no resemblance to the market towns of the plains, spread along the main roads, or to the farms *(mas)* scattered in the midst of large cultivated areas.

The centre of the village is the little square *(cours)* shaded by plane trees round a small fountain. This is where the cafés are to be found, always full in this region where people love social life, conversation and politics and where much of the day is spent away from the houses, which are left with the shutters closed to keep out the heat and insects.

THE GAME OF BOULES

This, the most popular game of the region, is played with ironclad balls. Matches are between teams of three players *(triplettes)* or four *(quadrettes)*. The *pointeurs* (attackers) must throw their balls as close as possible to a small ball *(cochonnet)*, acting as a jack, which is set at the limit of the pitch. The *tireurs* (defenders) must knock away the balls of their opponents by striking them with their own and the best players can do this so that their ball takes the exact place of the one knocked away. Over short distances, in which it is forbidden to move the feet, the play is *à la pétanque*. Over long distances (10m – 30ft or more), where the players throw their balls after making three hopping steps, the play is *à la longue*. The intense concentration of the players, often mirrored in their facial expressions, and the passionate disputes which break out when judging the distance between balls make this a fascinating game to watch.

Pétanque in St-Tropez

Food and wine on the Riviera

The main features of Provençal cooking are garlic and frying in oil (preferably olive). Garlic has inspired many poets who have written of the "Provençal truffle", the "divine condiment", "man's friend". Olive oil is used wherever butter would be used farther north. "A fish lives in water and dies in oil" acording to a local proverb.

Bouillabaisse – Here we salute the most celebrated of Provençal dishes. The classic bouillabaisse must consist of the "three fishes": scorpion fish *(rascasse)*, red gurnet and conger eel. Several other kinds of fish and shellfish are usually added – it is essential that the fish used is fresh and cooked in a good quality of olive oil. The seasoning is just as important as the fish: salt, pepper, onion, tomato, saffron, garlic, thyme, bay leaves, sage, fennel and orange peel. Sometimes a glass of white wine or brandy gives the final flavour to the broth, which is poured onto thick slices of bread.

Aïoli – *Aïoli* is another Provençal speciality and is a mayonnaise made with olive oil, strongly flavoured with crushed garlic. Comparing the northern variety of mayonnaise with *aïoli*, Mistral dismissed it as insipid "jam". *Aïoli* is served with *hors-d'œuvres*, or with *bourride* (a soup of angler fish, bass and whiting, etc), or many other dishes.

Fish – One of the Mediterranean's tastiest fish is the red mullet *(rouget)*, which the famous chef, Brillat-Savarin, called the "woodcock of the sea" probably because gourmets cook it without first scaling or cleaning it. The *loup* (local name for bass) grilled with fennel or vine shoots, is also a delicious dish. *Brandade de morue* is a purée of pounded cod mixed with olive oil, some garlic cloves and truffle slices.

Aromatic herbs – Considered with garlic and olive oil to be one of the basics of Southern cooking, aromatic herbs, cultivated or growing naturally on sunny hillsides, perfume gardens and markets and enrich dishes. Known as *"herbes de Provence"*, the mixture includes savory *(sarriette)*, used to flavour goats' and ewes'milk cheeses; **thyme** *(thym)* cooked with most vegetables and also grilled meat; **basil** *(basilic)*, **sage** *(sauge)*, **wild thyme** *(serpolet)*, **rosemary** *(romarin)* wich is good for the digestion, **tarragon** *(estragon)*, **juniper** *(genièvre)* used to flavour game, **marjoram** *(marjolaine)* and **fennel** *(fenouil)*. It is used in many dishes and can, according to taste, be a main constituent or just a trace.

Thirteen desserts – Provençal tradition presents diners at Christmas with 13 desserts (representing Christ and the 12 apostles): raisins, dried figs, walnuts, hazelnuts, almonds, raisins on the vine, apples, pears, black nougat (made with honey), *fougasse* (sort of brioche), prunes stuffed with almond paste, melons stored in straw and dry cakes flavoured with orange blossom.
At Epiphany, a **galette des rois** is served in the form of a brioche crown covered in sugar and candied fruits and containing a china figure.

Wines – Vines have been cultivated in Provence since Antiquity.
The **rosé wines**, their glowing colour achieved by a special process from black grapes, are gaining increasingly widespread popularity; pleasant and fruity to the palate, they go well with any dish.
The **white wines** are generally dry in character but have a good bouquet and are an excellent accompaniment to shellfish and Mediterranean fish.
There is a wide variety of full-flavoured **red wines**: full-bodied or subtle and delicate depending on whether they come from Bandol or the southern slopes of the Maures or, on the other hand, from the Argens valley or St-Tropez.
The most popular wines are from the region of Bandol, Ollioules, Pierrefeu, Cuers, Taradeau and la Croix-Valmer, from the Niçois area and particularly the wines of Bellet, La Gaude, St-Jeannet and Menton *(see Wine Tasting in the Pratical Information at the end of the Guide)*.

SPECIALITIES FROM NICE

Niçois cuisine, a lively expression of the character of Nice, is inspired by the cooking of Provence and of Liguria in Italy as it is the meeting point of the two traditions. The narrow streets of Old Nice, clustered at the foot of the castle hill, overflow with opportunities to try the best known specialities as well as seasonal variations. Two well-known examples of the cooking of Nice are an **onion tart** *(pissaladière)*, garnished with a thick anchovy sauce *(pissala)* and black Nice olives, and **salade niçoise**, a tasty combination of local tomatoes, cut into four, beans, radishes, peppers, onions, hard-boiled eggs and Nice olives, garnished with anchovy fillets and basil leaves and moistened with olive oil.
For a snack to be eaten in the street there is a large chick-pea flour pancake *(socca)*, divided into portions and accompanied by a small glass of local wine *(pointu)*: it is sold in and around Place St-François.
At lunchtime recharge the batteries for more sightseeing with a round sandwich (**pan bagnat** meaning soaked bread) containing tomatoes, onions, anchovies and olives, moistened with olive oil and flavoured with garlic.

Teatime hunger *(merenda)* can be appeased with fried slices of a thick chick-pea pancake *(panisses)*.

Salad or soup or omelette may accompany a marinade of young fish **(poutina)** which are caught with the permission of the local authorities between Antibes and Menton in Febuary. During the rest of the year gourmets may console themselves with a **fish soup** *(soupe aux poissons de roche)* made with little crabs *(favouilles)*.

The evening menu may be enlivened by a slice of **sucking pig** *(porchetta)* stuffed with herbs and its own offal, served with a mixed salad *(salade de mesclun* in the local dialect) composed of 14 types of young salad plants picked in the area.

The dishes on offer in the tiny restaurants in the villages inland include – stuffed courgette flowers *(fleurs de courgette farcies)*; a vegetable stew *(ratatouille)* made of tomatoes, aubergines, peppers and courgettes gently cooked in oil; shell-shaped pasta *(gnocchi)* made of wheat and potato flour and served with a thick sauce *(daube)*; deep-fried pastry parcels *(barbajouan* meaning Uncle John) filed with rice, squash, garlic, onion and cheese; a stockfish dish known as **estocaficada** *(see below)*. The convivial family dish, known as **pistou**, is a vegetable soup to which is added an unctuous concoction of basil, garlic, tomatoes and unstinted olive oil.

For dessert there is a sweet tart **(tourte de blea)** garnished with chopped chard leaves, pine kernels and currants.

Halfway through Lent the pastry cooks' windows display small sweet pastry cushions known as **ganses**. A cake flavoured with orange flower water *(fougasse)* is sold all year round; in Monace it is decorated with aniseed in the national colours of red and white.

One may resist the torpor of midday by sitting in the shade with a glass of crushed ice flavoured with mint *(gratta queca)*.

Estocaficada – This is the local version of the stockfish of Marseille, known for short by old hands as "estocafic". As it takes a whole day to prepare, it has become a dish for special occasions. To fillets of stockfish (dried cod), flaked with a fork and lightly browned, are added peeled and de-seeded tomatoes, the tripes of the stockfish cut into strips, chopped olives and bouquets of herbs including fennel, marjoram, parsely, thyme, bay and savory. The dish is braised for three to four hours, generously laced with brandy *(la brande)*. When the liquor has reduced to a level which only the vigilance of the cook can determine, a good measure of stock is added to the pot.

At a family gathering this imposing dish is accompanied by a full-bodied wine from Le Bellet.

Pan Bagnat – Cut a round loaf of wholemeal bread in half horizontally. Moisten the interior with a generous measure of olive oil and rub vigorously with a clove of garlic.

On the lower half lay slices of tomato, rings of white onion, black Niçois olives and cover with de-salted anchovy fillets. Garnish with salt and chopped basil leaves.

Cover with the upper half, wrap in a cloth and leave for a good hour for the flavours to mingle – a good dish for a picnic.

The French Riviera, one of the most famous holiday destinations in the world, has a reputation largely founded on the growth in popularity of winter "Grand Tourism". Nowadays, the crowds of royalty, the flashy, stucco-laden palaces and the enormous luxury yachts are no longer the main attraction; the compelling charm of the region lies in the wide variety of its attributes: hot sun and warm sea; red cliffs and golden beaches; peaceful villages and throbbing night-clubs; world-famous festivals and rich museums; traditional celebrations, markets and locally grown produce; architectural treasures set against a magnificent backdrop of mountains.

A few reasons for visiting the French Riviera

- **Tour of the modern art museums**. This can be undertaken at any time during the year, but some museums are shut in November and December.
- **Monte-Carlo Motor Rally.** *End of January*.
This is undoubtedly the supreme championship in the world line-up of rallies.
- **Nice Carnival.** *Fortnight around Shrove Tuesday*.
One of the longest-lived traditions of the Nice region, dating from the 13C. There are light shows, parades of decorated floats, balls, carnivals and a battle of flowers.
- **Cannes International Film Festival.** *May*.
Essential date in the diaries of all the big names in the world of cinema since 1946. New films, famous actors, "rising stars" and fans.
- **Monaco Formula I Motor Grand Prix.** *Weekend after Ascension*.
Breathtaking spectacle of racing cars hurtling round a wildly twisting track laid out through the town centre.

Curiosities of the Riviera

- **Exotic places**
Villa grecque Kérylos in Beaulieu-sur-mer
Mosquée soudanaise and Pagode boudhique in Fréjus
Conservatoire botanique du Rayol in Rayol-Canadel
Églises russes in Nice, Cannes and Menton
Jardin japonais in Monte-Carlo
- **Experiencing nature**
Sentier sous-marin in Port-Cros
Jardin sous-marin in Rayol
Killer whales at Marineland in Antibes
Vallée des Merveilles and rock carvings
Village des tortues in Gonfaron
- **Museums and special collections**
Musée des Amoureux de Peynet in Antibes
Prison du Masque de fer on l'Ile Ste-Marguerite
Changing of the guard in Monaco
Noël des Bergers in Lucéram

Villefranche-sur-Mer

Sights

ANTIBES★★

Population 70 006
Michelin map 84 fold 9 or 115 folds 35 and 40 or 245 fold 37

The much frequented resort town of Antibes, built between the bays of La Salis and St-Roch, lies on the west of the Baie des Anges facing Nice. It has its own harbour, **Port Vauban**, and the Cap d'Antibes *(see CAP d'ANTIBES below)*, nearby, is a pleasant place to explore.

The Antibes region is one of Europe's great centres for the commercial production of flowers. About 800 firms keep some 300ha – 750 acres under glass frames or greenhouses. Roses take first place, followed by carnations, anemones and tulips. Evergreens and spring vegetables are also grown.

HISTORICAL NOTES

Greek Antipolis – From the 4C BC the Greeks of Massalia set up a chain of trading posts with the Ligurian tribes along the coast. A new city sprang up opposite Nice; Antipolis, the Greek name for Antibes, may mean the town opposite but the derivation is disputed. Antipolis was contained between the present Cours Masséna and the sea, the Greeks holding only the area commanded by their ships, their warehouses and their ramparts. Mistrust reigned; the Ligurians never entered the town, which had only one gate opposite the present town hall; all transactions took place outside the town walls.

The Greeks were succeeded by the Romans, and they in turn by the Barbarians whose invasions ruined the city's prosperity.

Antibes, frontier outpost – The kings of France realised the important military role that Antibes could play, above all from the end of the 14C when the town stood at the Franco-Savoyard frontier. It was the property of the Grimaldis from 1386 and was purchased by Henri IV (1589-1610).

Each reign brought improvement or enlargement to its fortifications until the work was completed by Vauban in the 17C. Only the Fort Carré and the seafront remain.

Bonaparte at Antibes – In 1794 Bonaparte, charged with defending the coast, settled his family in Antibes. He was a general but his pay seldom arrived on the appointed day. Times were hard. Mme Lætitia, his mother, did the household laundry herself in a nearby stream. His sisters made furtive expeditions to the artichoke and fig plantations and were chased away by the landowner but the future princesses were fleet of foot and escaped. After the fall of Robespierre, Bonaparte was imprisoned for some time in the Fort Carré.

Notable inhabitants – **General Championnet**, born in Valence, died in Antibes in 1800, from the cholera which was ravaging his army; this unselfish leader, who had distinguished himself in the German and Italian campaigns, was only 38. He asked to be buried in the moat of the Fort Carré. His bust stands in Cours Masséna.

ANTIBES

Albert 1er (Bd)
Nationale (Pl.) 4
République (R. de la)

Andreossy (R.)	3
Arène (Av. P.)	5
Bas-Castellet (R. du) ...	6
Bateau (R. du)	7
Clemenceau (R. G.)	15
Close (R. J.)	16
Horlog (R. de l')	29
Maizière (Av. Général) ..	32
Masséna (Cours)	36
Orme (R. de l')	43
Revely (R. du)	49
Revennes (R. des)	50
Saleurs (Montée des) ..	57
Touraque (R. de la)	63

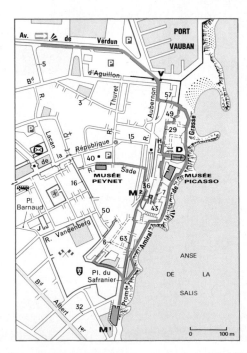

D Église de
l'Immaculée-
Conception
M1 Musée archéologique
M2 Musée de la Tour
des arts et
traditions
populaires
V Porte marine

Old town, Antibes

M. Trigalou/PIX

Maréchal Reille (1775-1860) was born in Antibes. Aide-de-camp to Masséna, Reille distinguished himself in all Napoleon's campaigns. Later, rallying to the monarchy, he was made a marshal by Louis-Philippe and died a senator during the Second Empire. **Nicolas de Staël** (1914-55) painted his last canvases in Antibes, before killing himself. A young glamorous American couple, Sara and Gerald **Murphy**, fell in love with Antibes in the mid-1920s, and their villa became a favoured holiday haunt for their many American friends, including the **Fitzgeralds** and **Hemingway**.

★ OLD TOWN *1 hour 45min*

Avenue de Verdun – From this road, skirting St-Roch Bay, there is a good **view** of the marina and of the 16C Fort Carré isolated on its rock with Cagnes and the heights of Nice in the background to the right.
Enter by the old sea gate (V) and follow Montée des Saleurs as far as avenue Amiral-de-Grasse.

Promenade Amiral-de-Grasse – This road, once the seafront promenade, runs along the only remaining part of 17C ramparts facing the sea and below the old cathedral and castle (Musée Picasso). It gives a fine **view★** of the coastline towards Nice with the Alps rising in the background, snow-covered for most of the year.

Musée archéologique (**M'**) ⊘ – The Bastion St-André, part of Vauban's fortifications, houses a **collection of archeological items** illustrating 4 000 years of history. At the back of a large vaulted room built on a reservoir notice a bread oven and, to the right, the reconstruction of a Roman ship used for transporting amphorae.
Some of the particularly interesting exhibits include a copy of the Mask of Silenus in bronze (the handle of a vase; the original is in the Musée archéologique in Nice) and an ornamented lead sarcophagus. Local excavations are continually adding to the exhibits of pottery (Massaliote, Greek and Roman amphorae) as well as objects salvaged from shipwrecks from the Middle Ages to the 18C. The Greek writer Nikos Kazantzakis, author of *Zorba the Greek* (written in Antibes), lived at 8 rue du Bas-Castellet, where there is a plaque inscribed with a phrase encapsulating his philosophy.
Turn back and take rue de la Touraque straight ahead.

Old streets – To left and right are picturesque side streets, bright with flowers in season and barely a stone's throw from the sea. Cours Masséna serves as the market place.
To reach Place Nationale turn left into rue Sade.

★ **Musée Peynet** ⊘ – Located in an old 19C school are severas hundred works (lithographs, theatre decors, ink drawings, watercolours, sculpture, greeting cards, dolls...) of Raymond Peynet (born 1908). The famous cartoonist is known for his two young lovers, Les Amoureux (appeared in various publications – *Paris Match, Marie-Claire, Elle*...). The subjects illustrated include the seasons, town life, music, etc.
Return to Cours Masséna.

Musée de la Tour des arts et traditions populaires (M²) ⊙ – *In Cours Masséna*. This **museum of folk arts and tradition** is located in the Tour de l'Orme and contains a good selection of local costumes, everyday objects and traditional furniture dating mostly from the 18C and 19C. Note also the water skis belonging to Léo Roman who initiated this sport in Juan-les-Pins in 1921.

Take the rue de l'Orme and then the rue du Bateau to get to the Château Grimaldi.

Château Grimaldi (Musée Picasso) ⊙ – The original castle was built in the 12C on a terrace overlooking the sea on the foundations of a Roman camp situated on the Antipolis acropolis. It was reconstructed in the 16C but the square Roman tower, the battlement walk and pairs of windows remain from the original structure. The castle, which was the bishops' residence in the Middle Ages, was lived in by the Grimaldi family until the 17C.

Inner courtyard – In the courtyard there is a composition by the sculptor Arman depicting guitars, reminiscent of a painting by Picasso, *A ma Jolie*. In the chapel hangs the **Deposition from the Cross★** (1539) by Antoine Aundi, which contains the earliest known view of Antibes.

Terrace – In the terrace garden, fragrant with aromatic plants, are displayed seven statues by Germaine Richier and works by Miró, Pagès, Amado Spoerri and Poirier.

Archeological Collection – The Musée Picasso contains Roman pottery, friezes, funerary urns and stelae; one bears the touching inscription: to the spirit of Septentrion, 12 years, who danced at the Antibes theatre for two days and was a success.

★ **Donation Picasso** – *This is on the first floor of the museum.* Soon after his arrival on the Riviera in the autumn of 1946, Pablo Picasso (1881-1973), who had part of the castle at his disposal, started work on some large scale paintings. His output was amazing; the majority of the paintings, lithographs and drawings on view in the castle were the result of one season's work. The original supports used by the artist, of fibro-cement and plywood, symbolise the shortages of the post war period.

La Joie de Vivre, a huge work in fibro-cement, is a smiling pastoral composition of a plant-woman dancing among exuberant goats and satyrs. Preliminary sketches and drawings are also on view.

La Joie de Vivre or *Antipolis* (1948)
by Pablo Picasso *(detail)*

Musée Picasso, Antibes – © SPADEM 1996

His other **paintings** are in the main joyful works full of imagination, inspired by the marine and mythological life of the Mediterranean (fish, sea urchins, fishermen, centaurs...): *Ulysses and the Sirens, The Oak Tree* and a huge triptych – *Satyr, Faun* and *Centaur with Trident*. Two still-lifes of exceptional quality – *Fish* and *Watermelon* – illustrate strict geometrical design.

The showcases hold an impressive collection of Picasso's **ceramics**. His great powers of imagination and ingenuity are revealed in the variety of decoration and the beauty and originality of form, often quite humorous. With some pieces, decoration and form combine to suggest a silhouette: woman, owl, bull, goat... These were created at Vallauris between 1948 and 1949.

The prints and drawings of the Vollard collection, which are grouped around monumental statues, date from the 1930s.

On the second floor, works by Nicolas de Staël are on display in Picasso's old studio. Note in particular, *Still Life with Chandelier, Fort Carré* and the gigantic canvas entitled *Grand Concert*. The pieces by Nicolas de Staël are the result of a winter which he spent in Antibes.

The stairwell contains a display of some of the collection of modern art: works by Arp, Magnelli, Ernst.

On leaving, turn right down the steps towards the church.

Immaculée-Conception (D) – Of the original Romanesque church, which served as a cathedral in the Middle Ages, only the east end remains. The belfry is a converted 12C watch tower. The west front (carved **door panels** – 1710) is in the 17C Classical style. Among the art treasures are: a wooden Crucifix (1447) in the choir, a former pagan stone altar in the south apsidal chapel; an **altarpiece** (1515) by Louis Bréa in the south transept – the centre panel has been touched up but the 13 surrounding panels and the predella are treated like miniatures; a 16C **Recumbent Christ** carved in lime wood.

Take rue de l'Horloge *(right)*, rue du Revely *(left)* and rue Aubernon *(right)* for a picturesque route to return to the port.

Port Vauban – As well as being a marina – one of the largest in the Mediterranean – this port is also used by luxury cruise ships. Perhaps owing to a premonition, Maupassant *Bel Ami* his boat moored here in the 19C century.

⌂ CAP D'ANTIBES
Round tour of 10km - 6 miles - about 2 hours

Strictly speaking the name Cap d'Antibes refers only to the most southerly tip of land but it has come to mean the whole peninsula, which is an enchanting garden dotted with sumptuous hotels and villas catering for summer and winter visitors.

Pointe Bacon (Z) – This point gives a **view**★ of Antibes and the Fort Carré, extending across the Baie des Anges in front of Nice and the surrounding countryside to Cap Ferrat and even Cap Martin near the Italian frontier.

Plateau de la Garoupe (Z) – On the summit of the plateau are a chapel, a lighthouse and a viewing table *(table d'orientation)*.
Viewing table – Fine **panorama**★★ stretching from the Esterel to the Alps.
Sanctuaire de la Garoupe (Z E) ⊘ – Outside this church are two 17C wrought-iron grilles. Inside, two adjoining chapels, communicating by wide arches, form two aisles.
The widest aisle is ornamented with a fresco by J Clergues. It also contains an interesting **collection of votive offerings**; the oldest dates back to 1779.
On either side of the altarpiece over the high altar are: on the left the **Sebastopol icon**, a magnificent Russo-Byzantine work, believed to be from the 14C, and on the right the *plachzanitza* of the Woronzoffs, a splendid painted silk, also brought back at the time of the siege of Sebastopol.

In the second aisle, decorated with frescoes by Edouard Colin, are some 60 naval votive offerings and maritime souvenirs as well as a gilded wood statue of **Notre-Dame-de-Bon-Port** (Our Lady of Safe Homecoming), patron saint of sailors. Every year on the first or second Sunday in July the statue of Our Lady, taken on the previous Thursday to the old Cathedral in Antibes, is brought back in procession to La Garoupe by the seamen. Beside the sanctuary stands the curious Oratoire de Ste-Hélène, first patron of Antibes, who has been worshipped here since the 5C AD in what was originally a pagan shrine.
Phare ⊘ – The **lighthouse**, one of the most powerful on the Mediterranean coast, with a luminous intensity of 2 300 000 candelas, has a beam which nominally carries 52km – 32 miles out to sea and 100km – 33 000ft up to aircraft. The radio beam has a range of 185km – 100 nautical miles.
★ **Jardin Thuret (Z F)** ⊘ – These **botanical gardens** covering 4ha – 2.5 acres bear the name of the scientist Gustave Thuret, who created them in 1857. He sought to acclimatise plants and trees from hot countries, successfully spreading the

CAP D'ANTIBES

E Sanctuaire de la Garoupe
F Jardin Thuret
M Musée naval et napoléonien

different species throughout the region: the first eucalyptuses, from Australia, were planted here. Bequeathed to the state, the gardens are administered by the National Institute of Agronomic Research.

They contain a magnificent collection of rare plants and trees: among the 3 000 species are palm trees, mimosas, eucalyptuses, cypresses...

Villa Thuret, the gardens' botanical centre, contains offices and research laboratories.

Musée naval et napoléonien (Z M)Ⓥ – The former Le Grillon battery has been transformed into a naval and Napoleonic museum. At the entrance stand two replicas of a magnificent Louis XIV bronze cannon. Inside, the construction of ocean-going sailing ships is explained using models in showcases. Also on display are **Napoleon's bust** sculpted by Canova in 1810, model soldiers and officers of the Great Army, Napoleon's autograph and imperial proclamations.

From the roof, there is a fine **view**★ over the wooded headland to the Iles de Lérins and to the distant Alps.

Port de l'Olivette (Z) – From this harbour, there is a **view** over the Golfe Juan, the heights of Super-Cannes, Pointe de la Croisette and the Iles de Lérins. The coast road, avenue du Maréchal-Juin, follows the seashore to Juan-les-Pins and overlooks **Port Crouton** and **Port Gallice**.

EXCURSIONS

EDEN-ROC, an Edwardian paradise

This majestic palace surrounded by an estate (8 ha – 20 acres) is set on a promontory of Cap d'Antibes. Famous for its beach huts *(cabanes)* and its private beach, it has become an essential port of call for film stars visiting the Riviera. For a century it was also the favoured hotel of royalty from all over the world. A wonderful party given by Russian princes in Spring 1870 launched the Grand Hôtel du Cap. After a quiet period, during which Stephen Liégeard compared the hotel to Sleeping Beauty's castle, the Grand Hôtel was relaunched under the patronage of the American Gordon Bennett. In 1914 an annexe, the Eden Roc together with its private beach, was built, foreshadowing the popularity of the Riviera as a summer resort. Since then, it has known unfailing success, with a varied and cosmopolitain clientele such as General Eisenhower, who used it for winter quarters, the painters Picasso and Chagall, who worked here and various rich eccentrics such as the oil magnate Gulbenkian *(Mister 5%)*.

The swimming pool is open to non-residents (admission charge payable).

★ **Marineland**Ⓥ – *4km – 2.5 miles north towards Nice*.

This, the first marine zoo in Europe, consists of many large pools containing **killer whales** (large voracious cetaceans which even attack other whales), dolphins, elephant seals, seals and maned and Californian sea-lions. The dolphins and the killer whales give regular acrobatic displays. In a penguin enclosure *(manchotière)* about 20 king penguins have been reared. An animation, **"Sharks"**, includes a tunnel passage 30m – 98ft long with a view of a dozen grey sharks and tiger sharks swimming in a vast tank. The zoo has been successful in breeding from many species which rarely reproduce in captivity; killer whales, maned sea-lions and king penguins. Amongst other activities intended to protect the marine environment, specialists from Marineland offer a veterinary service to marine mammals in the Mediterranean.

Marineland also houses a little museum containing a fine collection of models, marine instruments and other items.

Parc Aqua-SplashⓋ – *Entrance via Marineland*. This water leisure park offers a range of water games: a swimming pool with waves, water chutes, giant pool.

La jungle des papillonsⓋ – *Entrance via the Marineland car park*.

To get the best out of this **butterfly centre**, *visitors are advised to wear brightly coloured clothing, which encourages the butterflies to fly up to them, and to choose a bright sunny day for their visit.*

This pleasantly arranged glasshouse houses 15 species of diurnal butterfly from all over the world and a large number of chrysalises, since the average life span of a butterfly is three weeks. Besides this, there are regular exhibitions on themes from the animal kingdom.

★ **Biot** – *8km – 5 miles north. See BIOT*.

Les ARCS

Population 4 744
Michelin map 84 fold 7, 114 fold 23 or 245 fold 35

The town, in the heart of vineyards which produce excellent wines, vies with Brignoles *(See BRIGNOLES)* for the title of capital of the Côtes de Provence wines. It is dominated by the ruins of Villeneuve castle, where St Roseline was born, and which is the starting point for the Provence wine circuit.

Church⊙ – It attracts many visitors to its **mechanical crib** *(left on entering);* the backdrop is the old village of Les Arcs. The side chapels are painted with frescoes: *(left)* the miracle of St Roseline's roses by Baboulaine; *(right)* a **polyptych**★ in 16 sections by Louis Bréa (1501) of the Virgin and Child surrounded by Provençal saints.

Le Parage – *From Place de l'Église take rue de la Paix leading up to the keep.* Around the ruins of the medieval castle are the stepped streets and alleys of the old town winding between and beneath the houses. In the Middle Ages, from the keep, a watch was kept against Saracen invasions.

EXCURSION

Ste-Roseline *4km – 2.5 miles east of Les Arcs by D91.*

In the quiet countryside and vineyards around Les Arcs stands the chapel of Ste-Roseline, part of the old abbey of La Celle-Roubaud, founded in the 11C. In the 13C it became a charterhouse and flourished during the priorate of **Roseline de Villeneuve** from 1300 to 1328. The 12C cloisters and the Provençal style Romanesque chapel are all that remain.

★ **Interior**⊙ – On the right of the nave is the shrine of St Roseline, whose corpse is amazingly well-preserved. Pilgrimages take place five times a year, the most popular being on Trinity Sunday and the first Sunday in August. A Renaissance chancel grille surmounted by a polychrome statue of St Catherine of Alexandria divides the nave; on the high altar stands a superb early 16C Baroque altarpiece depicting the Descent from the Cross; the delicately carved choir stalls date from the 17C. The altar at the far end of the nave bears a Renaissance altarpiece showing the Nativity; on the left of the chancel hangs a precious 15C predella. Contemporary works of art include a great mosaic by Chagall (south aisle) inspired by the legend of St Roseline; a bronze low relief illustrating St Roseline and the miracle of the roses and a lectern in the shape of a bush by Alberto Giacometti's brother, a stained-glass window in iridescent colours (rose petals) by Bazaine and others by Ubac.

AUPS

Population 1 796
Michelin map 84 fold 6, 114 fold 21 or 245 fold 34

From the foot of the Espiguières hills, Aups overlooks the Uchane plain, a fertile area of gently rounded hillocks, which is bordered to the northwest by the steep highlands of Haute-Provence. To the south, the Massif des Maures dominates the horizon. Aups is renowned for its honey.
Ramparts and a ruined castle evoke the past. The huge main square planted with magnificent plane trees, the many fountains and the picturesque old streets add to the charm of this delightful old town; there is a fine wrought-iron belfry in rue de l'Horloge.

Collégiale St-Pancrace ⊙ – The collegiate church of St Pancras is 15C Provençal Gothic with a Renaissance doorway; the simple nave ends in a square apse. The church treasury houses some interesting 15C-18C gold- and silver-plate.

Musée Simon-Ségal⊙ – *Rue du Maréchal-Joffre.*
This museum of modern art contains 280 pictures, of which 175 are by the Paris School, on display in the former Ursuline Convent's chapel.

Black gold of the Haut-Var

The truffle (called *rabasse* in Provence) is a fungus which grows on the secretions which seep out of diseased oak trees. There are two categories of truffle: the white, which are not particularly good to eat, and the black which ripen in the autumn and are recognisable by their distinctive smell. They are harvested from November to February by dogs or by sows which take two years to train. The largest truffle market in the Var takes place in Aups every Thursday during the gathering season. The uninitiated may be surprised by the unusual air of excitement which pervades transactions. In addition, there is a large truffle fair in Aups on the fourth Sunday in January. In this truffle-producing region many restaurants offer dishes cooked with truffles – spinach or salad or eggs for example.

EXCURSION

* **Haut-Var** – *Round tour of 53km – 33 miles – about 5 hours. From Aups take D 77 east.*

The road winds along the steep slopes of the Espiguières hills. Soon after Château de la Beaume bear left into D 51 towards Tourtour.

* **Tourtour** – *See TOUR-TOUR.*

Villecroze – *See VILLE-CROZE.*

Salernes – *5km – 3 miles southwest of Villecroze.* Facilities. An agricultural and industrial centre, Salernes is known for the manufacture of floor tiles and pottery. The church, set among 17C houses, boasts a belfry at either end. Fountains abound and trees shade the main square.

The D 31 follows the Bresque valley south.

Entrecasteaux – *See EN-TRECASTEAUX.*

From Entrecasteaux take D 31 south; turn right into D 50.

Cotignac – *See COTIGNAC.*

Take D 22 north. There is a good view back over the site of Cotignac. Further on to the right the Cascade de Sillans can be spied through the trees.

* **Cascade de Sillans** – *30min on foot return. Before entering the village turn right into a path (sign; car park).* In a sylvan setting the Bresque cascades over a 42m – 138ft drop; in summer the volume of water is diminished.

Sillans-la-Cascade – An attractive, once fortified village on the Bresque, with a few picturesque streets near the post office, which boasts a pinnacle turret.

Continue on D 22 to return to Aups.

Old town, Aups

J. L. Gallo/MICHELIN

BANDOL ♨♨

Population 7 431
Michelin map 84 fold 14, 114 fold 44 or 245 folds 45 and 46

Bandol is a pleasant small resort lying beside a pretty bay and sheltered from the north wind by high wooded slopes. It has three sandy beaches: the Lido facing east, the well-sheltered Renecros facing west and the Casino facing due south.

Beyond the villas scattered in groves of pine and mimosa behind the seafront are fields of flowers and vineyards which produce the best known of the Côtes-de-Provence wines.

Allée Jean-Moulin ★ and Allée Alfred-Vivien which line the harbour are bordered with pines, palms and flowers.

From the **chemin de la corniche** round the perimeter of the little peninsula with Bendor island lying off shore, there is a good view along the coast from Cap de l'Aigle to Cap Sicié.

EXCURSIONS

Jardin exotique et zoo de Sanary-Bandol ⊘ – *3km – 2 miles north; 500m – 550yds after passing over the motorway (A50), turn right (sign "Zoo-jardin exotique").*

In these shady gardens cacti and tropical plants grow to remarkable sizes. Among hundreds of rare plants animals from all over the world can be seen – monkeys (marmosets, Capuchin monkeys, gibbons and their offspring) and also coatis, lemurs, fennecs, kinkajous, peccaries, deer, ponies, miniature goats and llamas as well as the noisy, colourful worlds of parrots and of pink flamingoes and cranes.

⚓ Ile de Bendor ⓥ

The **boat trip** to the island makes a pleasant summer excursion. The island is an attractive tourist centre offering fine beaches, a harbour, a Provençal village with craft shops and a conference centre with lectures. The Espace Culturel Paul-Ricard, open to young painters and sculptors, offers art lessons.

Exposition universelle des vins et spiritueux ⓥ – In a large hall decorated with frescoes, this curious exhibition covers the production of wine, aperitifs and liqueurs in 51 different countries; 8 000 bottles are on display as well as a collection of glasses and decanters.

★ Hill Villages of Pays de Bandol

Round trip of 55km – 29 miles – about 3 hours. From Bandol take D 559 northeast; turn left into D 559ᴮ towards Le Beausset and pass under the railway bridge.

In Le Beausset turn right into N 8 towards Toulon. After 1km – half a mile turn right.

The narrow winding road climbs through olive groves, orchards and vineyards dotted with broom and cypress trees.

Notre-Dame du Beausset-Vieux ⓥ – *Leave the car below the chapel.*
The **chapel** has been restored by voluntary workers. It is a bare Provençal Romanesque structure with barrel vaulting in the nave and oven vaulting in the apse. The Virgin and Child in the choir comes from Pierre Puget's studio. In the left niche a group of 400-year-old **santons** illustrates the Flight into Egypt. Some of the votive offerings (side aisle) date back to the 18C.
From the terrace above the chapel a circular **view**★ takes in Le Castellet, Ste-Baume, the Gros Cerveau and the coast from Bandol westwards to La Ciotat.

Return to the N 8; and continue north towards Aubagne.

Circuit du Castellet Paul-Ricard ⓥ – *8km – 5 miles north of Beausset by N8.* This track, built in 1970 on 1 000 ha – 2 471 acres of desolate scrubland, has become an essential feature in the professional life of Formula 1 and Formula 3 racing drivers. The track (5.8km – 3.5 miles long) was officially opened on the occasion of the first Grand Prix de France, won by Jacky Stewart. Since then, many international drivers, such as Alain Prost in 1976, have attended the driving school at the circuit. Developments to comply with new competition regulations, as well as the airfield at Castellet, have allowed a greater variety of track events as well as air shows. Among meetings which appeal to the layman are the Grand Prix historique de Provence and the Deux Tours d'Horloge (shows and races for vintage vehicles). In May every year at a colourful truck show, the **Grand Prix International de Camions**, there are stunts, vintage vehicles and a concours d'élégance – a competition to find the most creatively decorated juggernaut.

The Mecca of motorcycling – The introduction of the Motorcycle Grand Prix de France *(July)* and, since 1973, the famous endurance test, le **Bol d'Or** *(September)*, have made the "two-wheeler" one of the most popular stars at Castellet.

Musée du modelisme ⓥ – Situated at the entrance to the track, this modelling museum contains some interesting reconstructions and dioramas, including a very realistic reproduction of the Paul-Ricard circuit. Upstairs, several fine animated scenes represent the world of the railway.

On leaving the circuit, turn left into RN 8 towards Aubagne. At the Camp-du-Castellet crossroads, turn left and left again into D 26 towards le Beausset. 3km – 2 miles before the hill to le Beausset, turn right into D 226 towards le Castellet.

★ **Le Castellet** – Perched on a wooded hill above the vineyards, this remarkable stronghold, formerly owned by the Lords of Les Baux and then by King René, has well preserved ramparts, a carefully restored 12C church, a castle dating back in part to the 11C. From beyond the gate in Place de la Mairie there is an attractive **view** inland towards Ste-Baume. Many houses date from the 17C and 18C. There are art and craft workshops – painting, pottery, hollow-ware, weaving and leatherwork.

Leave Le Castellet going downhill towards D 66.

La Cadière-d'Azur – This very old hill town, which had 4 000 citizens at the Revolution, produces Bandol wine. Some of its former defences remain. The 13C Peï Gate, in front of the town hall leads to a maze of picturesque old streets. From the eastern end of the village there is a fine **view**★ inland over Le Castellet to Ste-Baume.

Follow D 66 to Les Lecques.

Les Lecques – *See Les LECQUES.*

From Les Lecques the road south via La Madrague affords fine **views** of the coast and hinterland before joining D 559 which returns to Bandol.

BARGEMON

Population 1 069
Michelin map 84 fold 7, 114 fold 23 or 245 fold 35

An old stronghold at the foot of the Provençal Tableland, Bargemon still recalls its past in its old streets, its broken ramparts, ruined castle and 12C fortified gateways (in particular the so-called "Roman" gate, Place de la Mairie). Large shady squares and many fountains add to its charm while the presence of mimosa and orange trees indicate a mild climate.

Church – The 15C building near the town gateway was incorporated in the defences. Its square belltower is 17C. It has a fine flamboyant **doorway**. Pierre Puget is the putative artist of the angel heads on the high altar.

Notre-Dame de Montaigu – The village is dominated by the spire of the **chapel** which contains three fine altarpieces supported by wreathed columns. It has been a place of pilgrimage since the 17C when a miraculous statue of the Virgin was brought there from Belgium by a monk who was a native of the village (the statuette, carved in olive wood, is shown only on Easter Monday).

BARJOLS

Population 2 166
Michelin map 84 fold 5, 114 fold 19 or 245 fold 33

The small town lies in a natural amphitheatre in lush green country fed by many springs and streams. Barjols contributes to traditional Provençal life by making tambourines and flutes *(galoubets)* and holding an unusual festival.

Festival of St Marcel – *(See Calendar of events).* From time immemorial the people of Barjols have killed an ox each year to celebrate their survival during a siege. In 1350 a group of pious citizens, rescuing the relics of St Marcel (a 5C bishop) from the abandoned abbey near Montmeyan, fell in with the other celebrants and the religious and secular festivities were combined.

St Marcel was adopted as the patron saint of Barjols and each year in January his bust is carried in procession through the town. Sometimes an ox is decorated and blessed by the priest in front of St Marcel's statue. While it is led round the town on its way to the abattoir, the people sing compline and light a bonfire. The following day after High Mass the statue, escorted by the clergy and the band, joins the float bearing the ox on a spit and proceeds to the main square where the ox is roasted whole, the people celebrate in true Provençal style with flutes, tambourines, music and dancing. On the third day the roast ox is distributed to the crowd.

"The Mushroom", Barjols

E. Baret

OLD TOWN

The old town contains 12 wash-houses and 30 **fountains**. The most remarkable fountain, near the town hall, is a limestone-encrusted mushroom-shaped one, known locally as the "Champignon". A magnificent plane tree (circumference 12m – 39ft), said to be the largest in Provence, dominates the town hall square. In the lower town, the Pontevès House, named after an old Provençal family from a nearby village, is enhanced by a Renaissance doorway.

Clinging to the hillside, north of the church, is **Réal**★, the town's oldest quarter. Inhabited since the 12C, it has been occupied for the most part by tanners (as water is an essential tool of their trade); 3 levels of partially troglodyte (16C-17C) soaking and rinsing basins were excavated in the 1980s. Nearby, under a vault, is the entire text of the Déclaration des Droits de l'homme et du citoyen, carved on glazed stelae.

Church – The original Romanesque structure was rebuilt in the 16C with a fine Gothic nave. The organ loft, choir panelling and carved misericords are 17C. To the right of the entrance, behind a beautiful 12C font, is the original carved tympanum depicting Christ the King with angels and the symbols of the Evangelists.

Provençal belltowers in the Var	
Les Arcs	Tour de l'Horloge (18C)
Aups	Tours de l'Horloge (Clock tower)
Carces	Belltower on top of a fortified gateway (17C)
Carmoules	Belfry (17C)
Cotignac	Belltower (16C)
Flassans	Belltower (18C)
Salernes	Steeple (18C)
Tavernes	Finely carved belltower (18C)

EXCURSIONS

Source d'Argens – *15km – 10 miles to the southwest. From Barjols take D 560.*

Vallon de Font-Taillade – The road plunges into a green valley of fields and meadows and follows a winding stream. On the slopes vineyards alternate with pines and holm oaks.

500m – 547yds after Brue-Auriac a narrow path to the left leads to a chapel.

Notre-Dame – Next to a graveyard stands an abandoned Romanesque chapel built from the local red stone. Its pleasant façade, pierced by an oculus and a bay and topped by a wall-belfry with twin windows, is obscured by undergrowth.

Return to the D 560 and turn left. Park the car after 3km – 2 miles, in front of the bridge.

Source d'Argens – On the right of the road a path leads through the bushes straight to the spring which is one of the sources of the River Argens.

Plateaux du Haut-Var

Round tour of 52km – 32 miles – half a day.

Varages – This pleasant village shaded by plane trees was once a rival to Moustiers in the production of faïence. Decoration here is often similar to that found in Moustiers – the craftsmen responsible sometimes worked in several ceramicist centres – and the production of faïence continues today in two factories in Varages, which export much of their production. A fair dedicated to faïence, *Terre et Feu* (earth and fire), takes place each summer with an exhibition of works.

Church ⊘ – Built in the 17C in the Provençal Gothic style, the church has a fine belltower cover in glazed multicoloured tiles. Inside, the altar of St Claude, patron saint of faïence-makers, is decorated with medallions and crosses made locally.

Musée des faïences ⊘ *(place de la Libération)* – This museum, housed in the maison Gassendi, contains a complete retrospective of the history of faïence in Varages from the end of the 17C, displayed on two levels. In the many glass cases the different techniques used by the local dynasties such as the Armand, Clerissy and Niel families, are explained: hand decoration, decoration with stamps and enamelling techniques. On the first floor, there is a remarkable 19C **faïence fountain** by Mazières.

The factory, **"Manufacture des Lauriers"** continues the tradition and produces many Provençal items.

A workshop nearby, **"atelier de faïence"**, exhibits its products and it is possible to watch the decorators at work.

To the north of Varages, D 554 runs between hills planted with vines and olive groves interspersed with holm oaks and pines.

La Verdière – This village, on the slopes of a hill, is dominated by its church and castle. The fortress, built in the 10C by the Castellane family, was acquired in the 17C through a marriage by the rich Forbin d'Oppède family. The castle today, in a dilapidated condition, shows the results of Louis-Roch de Forbin to make the building more comfortable in the 18C.

East of La Verdière take D 30 towards Montmeyan.

The road crosses a barren limestone plateau covered with sparse vegetation typical of such an area. There are junipers, holm oaks and hawthorn bushes as well as Scots pine which indicate that this is at the northern edge of the region. This forest of stunted trees is scattered with piles of stones, the remains of attempts to clear and acclimatise the land during the rural expansion of the 19C.

Montmeyan– This medieval village, perched on a hill, looks over the entrance to the Verdon gorge. There is a fine **view**★ from the southern entrance to the village over the rocky ridge of the Castellane Pre-Alps to the east. After passing the Tour Charlemagne, part of the remains of the 14C castle, there is a panoramic viewpoint overlooking the whole plateau.

Take D 13 south from Montmeyan to Tavernes.

Tavernes– This is pleasant village, set in the midst of olive groves and vineyards, in an attractive dip surrounded by hills: there is a square belfry with an 18C wrought-iron campanile on top, and the remains of medieval walls. At the top of the village sits N-D de Bellevue, a chapel dedicated to Our Lady of Bellevue.

Le BAR-SUR-LOUP

Population 2 465
Michelin map 84 fold 9 or 115 fold 24 or 245 fold 37

Between the River Loup and its tributaries, Le Bar is attractively **sited**★ on a hillside surrounded by terraces of orange trees and beds of jasmine and violets. There is a perfume factory on the edge of the village.

Admiral de Grasse – Le Bar was part of the estate of the Counts of Grasse and Admiral François de Grasse (1722-88) lived in the castle as a youth. He had a distinguished career and fought valiantly in the American War of Independence. He was rewarded by a grateful Congress with four artillery pieces taken from the English forces. The brave admiral was taken prisoner on his ship (1782) after a hard battle lasting some ten hours.

THE TOWN

The narrow streets of the old town wind round the massive 16C castle with its four corner towers and ruined keep.

St-Jacques – Embedded in the stonework at the foot of the **church**'s belltower is a Roman tombstone. The magnificently carved **panels** of the Gothic door are attributed to the sculptor Jacques Bellot, who was responsible for the choir stalls in Vence.

A fine **altarpiece** by Louis Bréa consists of 14 scenes in three tiers painted on a gold background (high altar) depicting the apostle James the Greater (St Jacques le Majeur) and the Virgin and Child surrounded by 12 saints; the pediment above is adorned with the Trinity and the symbols of the Evangelists.

Under the gallery is the **Dance of Death★**, a curious 15C painting on wood, naïve in technique; it includes a poem in Provençal. The composition illustrates a legend: the Count of Bar gave a ball during Lent and his guests were struck dead in the middle of the revels. The Dance of Death was painted to record the divine punishment. Death, in the guise of an archer, strikes down the dancers with his arrows and their souls, escaping from their bodies through the mouths as little naked figures, are weighed in the balance by St Michael, at the feet of Christ, and are flung headlong into the gaping maw of a monster representing the entrance to Hell.

★ **Viewpoint** – From the church square (Place de l'Église) there is an oblique view up the Gorges du Loup and eastwards over the hills to Vence.

BEAULIEU-SUR-MER ⚌⚌

Population 4 013
Michelin map 84 folds 10 and 19 or 115 fold 27 or 245 fold 38
Local map see Corniches de la RIVIERA

This fashionable resort lies close under a ring of hills which protect it against north winds and make it one of the warmest spots on the Riviera – an asset especially in winter. The town is also an oasis of peace and quiet. For the tourist, the charm of Beaulieu is centred chiefly round the **Baie des Fourmis★** and boulevard Alsace-Lorraine, lined with attractive gardens.

★ **Villa grecque "Kérylos"** ⊘ – This faithful reconstruction of a sumptuous Greek villa of ancient times was conceived by the archeologist **Théodore Reinach**, and built in 1902 by the architect Pontremoli. It was bequeathed to the French Institute in 1928. On a **site★** reminiscent of the Aegean, the villa stands in a pleasant garden above the sea looking out over the Baie des Fourmis, Cap Ferrat, Èze and Cap d'Ail. Precious materials such as Carrara marble, alabaster and rare and exotic woods were used on the interior. The frescoes are reproductions or variations of originals. The furniture, made of wood inlaid with ivory, bronze and leather, is modelled on examples seen on vases and in mosaics. Some of the pieces are originals: mosaics, amphorae, vases, lamps, statuettes. Although the villa is well-equipped with modern conveniences these are all well concealed.

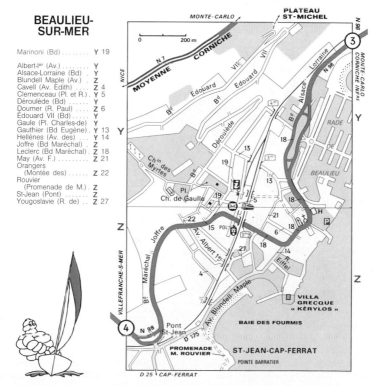

BEAULIEU-SUR-MER

Marinoni (Bd) .... Y 19

Albert-Ier (Av.) .... Y
Alsace-Lorraine (Bd) . Y
Blundell Maple (Av.) . Z
Cavell (Av. Edith) .... Z 4
Clemenceau (Pl. et R.) . Y 5
Déroulède (Bd) ...... Y
Doumer (R. Paul) .... Z 6
Édouard VII (Bd) .... Y
Gaule (Pl. Charles-de) . Y
Gauthier (Bd Eugène) . Y 13
Hellènes (Av. des) ... Y 14
Joffre (Bd Maréchal) . Z
Leclerc (Bd Maréchal) . Z 18
May (Av. F.) .... Z 21
Orangers
   (Montée des) ..... Z 22
Rouvier
   (Promenade de M.) . Z
St-Jean (Pont) .... Z
Yougoslavie (R. de) .. Z 27

WALKS

★★ **Sentier du plateau St-Michel** – *1 hour 45min on foot return – stiff climb.*
Starting north of boulevard Edouard-VII. The path leads up the Riviera
escarpment to the plateau (viewing-table), affording wonderful views from Cap
d'Ail to the Esterel.

★ **Promenade Maurice-Rouvier** – *1 hour on foot return.*
This remarkable promenade runs parallel to the shore from Beaulieu to
St-Jean-Cap-Ferrat. On one side are fine white villas in beautiful gardens and on
the other the sea with distant views of the Riviera and peninsular point of
St-Hospice.

BIOT★

Population 5 575
Michelin map 84 fold 9 or 115 fold 25 or 245 fold 37

Biot (the final "t" is voiced) is a picturesque village on rising ground some 4km
– 2.5 miles inland. Cut flowers – roses, carnations, mimosa and anemones – are
grown here for market. Since 1960 its name has been inseparably linked with that
of Fernand Léger.

2 500 years of history – There is evidence of settlement by the Celto-Ligurians,
Greeks and Romans from finds made in the area and in La Brague plain. In 1209
the Templars took over from the local lords and unified the village. In 1312 the
deeds passed to the Hospitallers of St John of Jerusalem and order reigned. In the
14C Biot suffered from the Black Death and warring factions; the decline was
reversed only following an edict promulgated in 1470 by Good King René allowing
40 families from Oneglia and Porto Maurizio (now Imperia on the Ligurian coast)
to settle in the village.

Crafts – Biot has long been known for its pottery, as the area is rich in clay, sand,
manganese and volcanic tufa (stone used for ovens). Amphorae from Biot were very
popular until the mid-18C and were exported through the ports of Antibes and
Marseille.
It has now diversified and has developed into an important craft centre *(see Crafts)*.

SIGHTS

★★ **Musée National Fernand-Léger** ⊙ – *Southeast of the village, just off D 4
(signed).*
Built in 1960 by A Svetchine, the architect from Nice, the museum, which

J. Mer/EDIMEDIA – © SPADEM

Birds on a Yellow Background
Musée Fernand Léger, Biot

contains 348 works by Léger
(1881-1955), and the gardens
were given to the French nation
by Mme Nadia Léger and
Georges Bauquier.
The façade is decorated by a
vast **mosaic** (500m²-5 382sq ft)
celebrating sports, designed for
the Hanover Stadium. On the
left is a monumental ceramic:
Children's Playground and two
large bronzes *Women with Parrot* and *Walking Flower*.
Displayed in the entrance hall,
lit by a stained-glass window, is
a large tapestry in beige and
grey: *The Bathers*.
The ground floor gallery presents original ceramics produced between 1950 and 1955
in the Brice workshop in Biot
and **paintings** showing the artist's evolution from 1905 to his
death.
Portrait of the Uncle (1905)
and *My Mother's Garden* are
impressionist in style while Cézanne's influence is evident in
Study of a Woman in Blue
(1912) and *14 July*. Between
the two World Wars the artist

experimented with contrasting primary colours (unusual *Gioconda with Keys* – 1930) and geometrical compositions (*The Great Tug* – 1923). In the *Study of Adam and Eve* (c1934), the artist shows a total disregard for facial features – which was to become the rule – and the characters become secondary to the general composition.

At a later stage (1942) Léger gave equal importance to colour and line *(Divers)* used at random within a strict composition.

After 1945 the artist painted large canvases celebrating work and industrial civilization – *Builders*, 1950, marks a significant achievement in style and inspiration – relaxation and joie de vivre *(Campers)*. *The Great Parade* (1954) is evocative of the fabulous world of the circus.

A staircase lit through a stained-glass window leads to the graphic arts room on the ground floor, in which drawings and gouaches reflecting the artist's various phases of development are on display.

Outside, this wing features huge mosaic works (including one of 300m² – 3 230sq ft) executed in 1990 following original designs by the artist. On the west front is a design planned for the Triennale de Milan; another version of *Les oiseaux sur fond jaune* adorns the east façade.

Bonsaï arboretum ⊘ – *Chemin du Val de Pôme, 100m – 109yds south of the Musée Fernand Léger.*
This sloping garden (53 000m² – 32 300sq ft), displays a large collection of bonsai trees against the backdrop of a reconstructed Japanese garden, as well as other tropical plants in nearby greenhouses.

Verrerie de Biot ⊘ – *At the foot of the village, on the D 4 going southeast, near the museum.*
The glassworks were opened in 1956 and produce a great variety of articles which are in great demand. Visitors can watch the different stages of glass blowing – in this case the Biot bubble glass.

Old village – The evening is the best time to appreciate the authentic charm of the picturesque streets, starting from the tourist information centre (syndicat d'initiative) and following the arrows, through the town gates, Porte des Migraniers (grenadiers) and Porte des Tines (both 16C), and emerging into the beautiful **Place des Arcades** with its rounded and pointed arches.

Musée de Biot ⊘ – *Entrance from the tourist information centre.* This museum of local history and ceramics is situated in the ruined Chapelle des Pénitents Blancs, topped by a three-sided pinnacle, and traces the main events in Biot's

---

For those interested in modern art

Antibes: Musée Picasso

Biot: Musée Fernand-Léger

Cagnes-sur-Mer: Musée Renoir and Musée d'Art moderne méditerranéen

Menton: Musée du palais Canolès, the salle des mariages in the Hôtel de Ville and the Musée Jean-Cocteau

Nice: Musée Marc-Chagall, Musée des Beaux-Arts, Musée Matisse and the Musée d'Art moderne et contemporain

St-Paul: Fondation Maeght

St-Tropez: Musée de l'Annonciade

Vallauris: Musée national "La Guerre et la Paix" and the donation Magnelli

Vence: Chapelle du Rosaire (chapelle Matisse)

Villefranche: Chapelle St-Pierre (chapelle Jean-Cocteau)

Where to see the works of the great masters:

Chagall:	Musée national du message biblique in Nice
Cocteau:	Chapelle St-Pierre in Villefranche-sur-mer, Musée Jean-Cocteau and the salle des mariages in the Menton town hall, chapelle N-D-de-Jérusalem in Fréjus
Dufy:	Collection Raoul Dufy in the Galerie-musée Raoul-Dufy in Nice
Léger:	Musée national Fernand-Léger in Biot
Matisse:	Musée Matisse in Nice and the Chapelle du Rosaire in Vence
Picasso:	Musée Picasso in Antibes and Musée national "La Guerre et la Paix" in Vallauris
Renoir:	Musée Renoir in Cagnes-sur-mer

history. A collection of 19C domestic water cisterns in yellow enamel streaked with green and brown, jars bearing the marks of former craftsmen and a reconstructed local kitchen are of great interest.

Church – It overlooks Place des Arcades and its multicoloured pavement. Rebuilt in 15C it was decorated with murals which the bishop of Grasse considered undecorous and had painted over.

On the west wall is the **altarpiece★** of the Virgin of the Rosary in red and gold attributed to Louis Bréa: on the central panel a Virgin of Pity covers the Child Jesus, clerics and laymen with her cloak and stands against a blue-green sky, holding a rosary in her hands. A graceful Mary Magdalene is depicted twisting a strand of golden hair between her fingers.

On the right at the far end of the church there is another altarpiece attributed to Canavesio who married a local girl: an **Ecce Homo** with two cherubs and the instruments of the Passion; above the Flagellation, Christ Reviled and the Resurrection.

BORMES-LES-MIMOSAS★

Population 5 083
Michelin map 84 fold 16, 114 fold 48 or 245 fold 48
Local map see Massif des MAURES

Bormes-les-Mimosas stands in an agreeable **setting★**, near the sea and on a steep slope at the entrance to the Forêt du Dom. It is an attractive place to stay with its colourful profusion of mimosa, oleander, camomile and eucalyptus. The road from Le Lavandou affords the best view of the town.

Bormes has 17km – 10.5 miles of beach, and 850 pleasure boats can berth at the marina.

Two inhabitants of Bormes played an important part in the wars of independence in Latin America in the 19C. **Hippolyte Mourdeille** (1758-1807) lost his life chasing the Spaniards out of Montevideo and **Hippolyte Bouchard** (1780-1837) organised the Argentinian navy. Bormes honours their achievements by celebrating Argentina's national day on 9 July.

SIGHTS

Place St-François – A statue commemorating Francesco di Paola, who is said to have saved Bormes from the plague in 1481, stands in front of the solid 16C Chapelle St-François surrounded by dark cypress trees. Among the exotic plants in the neighbouring graveyard with its 18C tombs is a monument to the painter Jean-Charles Cazin, who was particularly attached to the place.

Terrace – It is in front of the chapel and affords a good **view** of Bormes anchorage and Cap Bénat. The round tower to be seen in the distance is the base of an old mill.

Musée "Arts et Histoire" ⊙ – *65 rue Carnot.*
This museum presents the history of Bormes, of Fort Brégançon and of the Chartreuse de la Verne; also the lives of Bouchard and Mourdeille *(see above)*. A century of regional painting, particularly the works of Cazin (1841-1901), landscape painter and decorator, is also on show.

St-Trophyme – The robust three-aisled church near the town hall was built in the 18C in the Romanesque style. The façade bears a sundial with the Latin inscription: *Ab hora diei ad horam Dei* (from daily time to divine time). The interior is decorated with 14 oil paintings by Alain Nonn (1980) depicting the Way of the Cross. Six reliquary-busts crowning the pillars date from the 18C.

★ **Old streets** – Below the church the streets of old Bormes are typical of a Provençal village. Several covered passageways run between the lanes, providing shade for passers-by. Many steep alleyways tumble down from the castle: the steepest of these, known as "neck-breaker" *(Rompi-Cou)*, is laid with smooth paving stones separated by a central drain.

Château – The signs *"parcours fleuri"* near the church lead to a flower-lined walk round the castle, which has been partially restored to provide a dwelling. Beyond the castle the terrace provides a fine **view★** over Bormes, the anchorage, Cap Bénat and the islands of Port Cros and Le Levant.

EXCURSIONS

Cap de Brégançon – At the eastern edge of Hyères harbour a fortress sits on a rocky promontory. The **fort de Brégançon**, which has been the President's summer residence since 1968 *(not open to the public)*, is built on a little island linked to the shore of Cap Bénat by a footbridge. It was neglected from the beginning of the 18C but the young General Bonaparte began its restoration, which was completed between the two World Wars. The oldest parts of the building date from the 16C. The drawbridge and the two crenellated towers can be seen from the beach beside the walls.

The three musketeers of the "silent world"

In August 1937, before the fort became the presidential summer retreat, two young divers with makeshift equipment based on recycled inner tubes, attempted to beat a harpooning record. In the absence of any substantial booty, J-Y Cousteau and P Taillez found that their dive in the midst of (at that time still trusting) shoals of grouper and bass revealed the potential of underwater exploration. A third leading harpoonist, J Dumas, soon joined them and the hunt for pictures superseded the hunt for sea-bass. In the autumn of 1943, Dumas, experimenting with an aqualung, dived to a depth of at least 62m – 203ft and was affected by nitrogen narcosis (rapture of the deep). After the Second World War the underwater explorers' odyssey was immortalised on film and their craft, *Calypso*, was seen all round the world.

★★ Route des Cols

Round tour of 109km – 68 miles. See Massif des MAURES

BREIL-SUR-ROYA

Population 2 058
Michelin map 84 fold 20 or 115 fold 18 or 245 fold 26
Local map see NICE HINTERLAND

Breil lies astride the River Roya – its waters are contained by a small dam – near the Italian border below the summit of l'Arpette (1 610m – 5 282ft) on the main road from Ventimiglia to Turin via the Col de Tende (pass).
Several small industries – leather, olives, dairy farming – sustain the town, which is known for fishing and water sports (canoeing competitions).

M. Braun

Breil-sur-Roya

"A Stacada" – This unusual and highly-coloured event takes place every four years *(last in 1994)* to commemorate the abolition of the *droit du seigneur* brought about by the rebellion of the inhabitants of Breil who had been subjugated by a local tyrant. Some of the villagers, adorned with rich medieval costumes, process through the town, stopping along the way to perform scenes from this historical event. The unexpected arrival of the lord allows the inhabitants to demand reparation. After many races between the lord's Turkish guard and the nobles, the latter are at last captured and put in chains *(a stacada)*.

OLD VILLAGE

Situated on the east bank it consists of picturesque streets where traces of the ramparts and gateways can be seen among the old buildings. The Renaissance Chapelle Ste-Catherine with its doorway flanked by two Corinthian pillars stands south of the parish church.

Sancta-Maria-in-Albis – The vast 18C church with its carved doors (1719) and Baroque interior on a Greek cross plan, is adorned with an ornate 17C **organ loft** of carved and gilded wood (gallery) and an early **altarpiece** (1500) to the left of the chancel: St Peter as Pope with the triple crown between St Paul and St Jerome and above St Catherine and St Bartholomew on either side of The Transfiguration.

Écomusée du haut-pays ⊙ – This museum is located in an old engine shed where the border station of Breil once stood. It presents an interesting summary of the evolution of public transport in the Nice hinterland since the beginning of the century. The display includes a tram dating from 1900, identical with those which ran between Menton and Sospel, and a 141 R steam train. Another part of the exhibition takes the theme of agricultural activity in the region.

BRIGNOLES

Population 11 239
Michelin map 84 fold 15, 114 folds 20, 32, 33 and 34 or 245 fold 47
Local map see Excursions below

The narrow twisting streets of old Brignoles terrace the northern side of a low hill crowned by the venerable crenellated castle of the Counts of Provence. The new town is developing in the plain. All around, green rolling countryside stretches over the broad Carami valley.

This rich market town produces peaches, honey, olives and oil, and the exhibition-fair which is held annually in the first fortnight in April has made the town the wine capital of the Var and of Provence. The marble quarries situated at Candelon *(southeast of the town)* were once renowned.

Brignoles plums – Brignoles plums were famous throughout the kingdom until the 16C. As sugar-plums, they were a delicious addition to the sweetmeat dishes of the time: the Duke of Guise was nibbling one a few minutes before he was assassinated at Blois. All the plum trees used to belong to a local lord but during the League in the 16C, the people of Brignoles ransacked his lands and destroyed 180 000 trees. Since then "Brignoles plums" have actually come from Digne.

OLD BRIGNOLES

South of Place Carami, picturesque old streets lead to the church of St-Sauveur and to the castle of the Counts of Provence. Walk along the covered rue du Grand-Escalier (**8**), rue du St-Esprit (**18**) and rue des Lanciers (**9**), in which there is a **Romanesque house** (**E**) with twin windows.

St-Sauveur – This church has a lovely exterior Romanesque doorway (12C) framed by Ionic columns. The simple interior consists of a nave in Provençal Gothic style. The 15C low reliefs in gilded wood, depicting the sacrifice of Abraham and the distribution of manna, frame the high altar. The south

Brignoles Church *(detail)*

BRIGNOLES

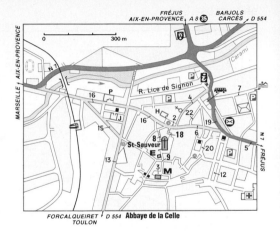

E Maison romane
M Musée du Pays brignolais

chapel contains a **Descent from the Cross** by Barthélemy Parrocel, who died at Brignoles in 1660 and whose descendants were also painters. The door to the sacristy is 16C.

Musée du Pays brignolais (M) ⊙ – This regional museum is in a building which dates in part from the 12C, formerly the castle of the Counts of Provence. The chief exhibit is the **La Gayole tombstone★** (late 2C – early 3C) illustrating the transition from pagan to Christian iconography (bust of Apollo, the Sun God on the left).
Also on the ground floor are a reproduction of an 18C Provençal kitchen and an exhibition on the local mining of bauxite, with a reconstruction of a mine gallery. On display is a cement boat by Joseph Lambot who invented reinforced concrete. There is some fine 17C woodwork in the castle chapel, as well as a beautiful 11C **black Virgin and Child** in carved wood.
Barthélemy and Joseph Parrocel and Montenard (1849-1926) are represented in the gallery of religious and pagan art upstairs. An exhibition on local customs includes a **crib**, created in 1952 in the Provençal tradition.

Abbaye de la Celle ⊙ – In the 13C the Benedictine convent attracted the daughters of the Provençal nobility, but by the 16C standards had fallen so low that the nuns were distinguished from other women only by their dress and their lovers.
Efforts at reform failed and the convent was closed in 1660 on the orders of Mazarin.
The 17C Prioress' house has been converted into a country hotel. The cloisters, chapter-house and refectory can be visited. The austere Romanesque abbey church is now the parish church, containing a striking 15C Crucifixion.

Continue on D 405 and then turn left into D 5 going south.

EXCURSIONS

★ ① **Brignoles Country** *Round tour 56km – 35 miles – about 3 hours – local map below*

The dark green of the pines in this undulating countryside contrasts with the varied colours of mixed farming, dominated by vineyards, and with earth stained red by bauxite; until the 1970s the mining of bauxite was the main local industry.

Le Val – The village lies beside the Roman Via Aurelia and was once enclosed by ramparts. Its narrow houses cluster around an elaborate 18C wrought-iron campanile. Skilled development of the site has preserved its Provençal character. On the way into the village is the **Hôtel des vins** which has on its façade a fresco painted by a pupil of Dali. The Romanesque church still has some beautiful 18C frescoes as well as some 16C polychrome statues.
The old communal oven (12C) houses the **Musée du Santon** ⊙. Displayed in glass cases in the long vaulted bakehouse is a varied collection of Provençal *santons* as well as cribs from Venice, Israel, Latin America and Africa. The oven contains a large crib of Neapolitan origin.
In the penitents' chapel (16C) is the **Musée d'Art Sacré** ⊙ which contains a sizeable collection of commemorative plaques dating from the 17C onwards, statues and richly embroidered pastoral robes.
At the eastern edge of the village there is a picturesque old wash-house framed by lovely columns. A little further on is the **Musée de la Figurine historique** ⊙. On the ground floor of this museum are antique toys, some dating from 1850, while

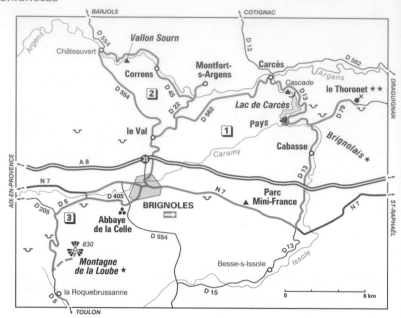

old figurines and some antique military uniforms are displayed on the first floor. Remarkable dioramas of the Napoleonic period can be seen together with old sheets of paper soldiers.

A former olive oil mill houses the **"maison de l'olivier"** ⊘. This museum has an exhibition of illustrations showing the history of the olive tree.

Go to Carcès, 17km – 10.5 miles northeast.

Vineyards alternate with lavender fields and pine plantations.

Carcès – Tall narrow houses beneath flat roofs cover the hillside below the Gros Bessillon. The town produces oil and honey and has extensive wine cellars.

2km – 1 mile south of Carcès *(towards Cabasse)*, the tree-lined D 13 comes to a **waterfall** where the river drops 7m – 22ft in several stages.

Lac de Carcès – The pine-clad shores are a favourite haunt of fishermen. The reservoir, retained by the beaten earth dam, supplies Toulon and other coastal towns. There is a fine **view** from the southern end of the lake.

Continue on D 13.

Red bauxite mines become more frequent. Turn left into D 79 for the Abbaye du Thoronet.

★★ **Abbaye du Thoronet** – *Cistercian abbey. See Abbaye du THORONET.*

Return to D 13 and turn left towards Cabasse along the Issole valley.

Cabasse – *See Cabasse.*

Parc Mini-France – *11km – 7 miles southwest of Cabasse, off N 7.* This floral park has reproduced, in miniature, a selection of France's monuments and characteristic regional sites (Cathédrale de Reims, Château de Chenonceau, a Breton village, etc).

Return to Brignoles on the D 79 past more red bauxite deposits.

Turn right into N 7 to return to Brignoles.

② **Vallon Sourn**

Round tour 39km – 25 miles – about 1 hour – local map above

From Brignoles take D 554 north. In Le Val turn right into D 562 and then left into D 22.

Montfort-sur-Argens – The ramparts and ruins of a forbidding feudal castle mark this former Templar commandery, which now produces excellent grapes and peaches. Two square towers remain, with mullioned windows, as well as a fine 15C spiral staircase.

Return to the crossroads and turn right into D 45.

The road follows the Argens upstream.

Correns – This riverside village with its fountains beneath the towering Gros Bessillon is known for its white wine. The castle keep has interesting gargoyles.

Vallon Sourn – In Provençal *sourn* means sombre, used here to describe the upper valley of the River Argens, which is enclosed between steep cliffs riddled with caves where people sought refuge during the Wars of Religion.

In Châteauvert turn left into D 554 to return to Brignoles.

★ ③ Montagne de la Loube

14km - 10 miles southwest - about 3 hours - local map opposite

From Brignoles take D 554 south. Turn right into D 405; turn left into D 5.

The countryside is pitted with red bauxite mines.

1km - half a mile before La Roquebrussanne, turn left into a narrow road closed to traffic where there is room to park.

★ **Montagne de la Loube** – *2 hours on foot return.* The narrow road up this mountain *(closed to vehicles)* bordered by flowers in springtime, passes strangely shaped rocks resembling animals and human beings.

The last stage of the ascent is a rock climb (not dangerous) near the telecommunication mast.

From the summit (830m – 2 723ft), there is an interesting **panorama★**. In the valleys the farmland is hemmed in by barren ridges and on the hillsides the bauxite mines show like red gashes in the green covering of pine and holm oak. Beyond the Carami valley to the north are the hills of Haute Provence; to the east are the Alps; to the south the mountains round Toulon, and to the west the long ridge of Ste-Baume.

Return to Brignoles by D 5 and N 7.

La BRIGUE

Population 618
Michelin map 84 folds 10 and 20 or 115 fold 9 or 245 fold 26
Local map see NICE HINTERLAND

Among the vineyards in the beautiful Levense valley, tributary of the Roya, near a Romanesque bridge, stands the charming village of La Brigue. Its old green schist houses below the ruins of the castle and tower of the Lascaris, local rulers from the 14C to 18C, give some idea of its age.

Old village – Some of the houses are built over arcades; on some of the others the lintels are carved, often with a heraldic device. From the square there is a fine **view** of Mont Bégo.

To the right of the parish church stand two penitents' chapels: the 18C **Chapelle de l'Assomption** ⊙, Baroque façade with a graceful Genoese belltower; and to the left the **Chapelle de l'Annonciation** ⊙, also Baroque on a hexagonal plan. The latter houses the church treasure and a collection of ecclesiastical ornaments.

★ **Collégiale St-Martin** – This parish church has a fine late 15C square Romanesque belltower; Lombard bands decorate the gable end and the side aisles. The doorway, framed in the Antique style (1576) with an older (1501) green schist lintel, opens onto a sumptuously decorated gilded nave in the Italian style. The 17C organ in the gallery was repaired in the 19C by the same Italians who worked at Saorge. The white marble font is covered by a painted and gilded conical baldaquin.

The church contains a remarkable collection of **primitive paintings from the Nice School★**. Chapels along the south aisle contain a Crucifixion with Saints and donors comparable with Louis Bréa's in Cimiez; an altarpiece of St Martha recounting on the predella the local legend of her arrival at Marseille on a boat, here pictured as a sailing ship; the Sufferings of St Elmo, revealing a cruel realism unusual in the gentle Bréa; also by Bréa the fine altarpiece of the **Adoration of the Child**; and, finally, by the same school, the central panel of a triptych representing the Assumption.

On the north side, the first chapel contains a triptych of the Italian Fuzeri of **Our Lady of the Snows** (1507) with its 18C Baroque frame.

CABASSE

Population 1 182
Michelin map 84 folds 6 and 16, 114 fold 21 or 245 folds 34 and 47
Local map see BRIGNOLES: Excursions

The village on the Côtes de Provence wine road has a shady square around a mossy fountain. The green valley site has seen many generations of human habitation as the nearby dolmens, standing stones and Gallo-Roman ruins prove.

St-Pons ⊙ – The 16C church has two aisles and a 16C doorway although the tympanum was carved in 1900. In the fifth bay an altarpiece of the Rosary is made up of several small paintings. Most noteworthy is the **high altar**★ of carved and gilded wood in Spanish Renaissance style (1543). The altarpiece depicting the Virgin and Child with St Michael and St Pontius is crowned by an elegant canopy. In the side aisle the ribbed vaulting is supported on pendants representing faces with grotesque or gentle expressions. There are also Gallo-Roman remains: cippi, ruined sarcophagi, capitals. Milestones stand near a 2C funerary inscription set in the outside wall.

CABRIS★

Population 1 307
Michelin map 84 fold 8 or 115 southwest of fold 24 or 245 fold 36

This charming village occupies a magnificent **site**★ on the edge of the Provençal plateau, looking out over the Grasse countryside to the sea (20km – 12 miles). Its name recalls the Marquise de Cabris, Mirabeau's sister, a restless character. The village and its neighbourhood have long been a favourite haunt of writers and artists.

Church – The 17C church contains a painted wooden pulpit and a fine rustic altarpiece under the gallery. Behind the altar hangs a copy of a Murillo painting.

Castle ruins – From the defensive wall and terrace, there is a superb **view**★★: southeast to Mougins and the hills running down to le Cannet, out to sea over La Napoule bay to the Iles de Lérins, south beyond Peymeinade and over the brow of the Tanneron to the Esterel, swinging westwards to the Lac de St-Cassien with the Massif des Maures in the distance.

Grotte des Audides ⊙ – *On leaving Cabris, take D 4 towards St-Vallier-de-Thiey for 4km – 2.5 miles. The entrance to the cave is located below the level of the road to the left coming from Cabris. It is advisable to wear waterproof shoes.* This cave, discovered in 1988 and explored to a depth of 186m – 610ft, is a chasm in which concretion is still taking place, which has given rise to a small underground river. Visitors take a narrow staircase *(275 steps)* down to a depth of 60m – 197ft, where a permanent flow of air keeps the air fresh. All the way down there are beautiful concretions to be admired: "giant medusas" and stalagmites in the process of being formed.

The site encompasses six caves, of the chasm type, which were for the most part inhabited during prehistoric times.

Outside in a park are reconstructed scenes of life in prehistoric times, as well as exhibits dug up during excavation and exploration of the caves: carved tools, fossils and various bone fragments. Other geological exhibits include strange limestone shapes, some containing giant grooves eroded by water.

CAGNES-SUR-MER★

Population 40 902
Michelin map 84 folds 9 and 18 or 115 folds 25 and 26 or 245 fold 37

Cagnes-sur-Mer is set in a landscape of hills covered with olive and orange trees and cultivated flowers (carnations, roses, mimosa). The town comprises: Haut-de-Cagnes, dominated by a medieval castle, Cagnes-Ville, the modern residential and commercial quarter and Cros-de-Cagnes, an unusual fishing village and beach.

The picturesque upper town has become the home of many painters who come each year in great numbers, attracted by the beautiful setting and the incomparable light. A large racecourse, serving the whole of the Riviera, has a varied programme throughout the season from December to March and in August and September each year.

The Grimaldis of Cagnes – The history of Cagnes is that of its castle. This was originally a fortress built by Rainier Grimaldi, Lord of Monaco and Admiral of France, after he became Lord of Cagnes in 1309. A branche of the Grimaldi family *(see MONACO)* remained in possession of Cagnes up to the Revolution.

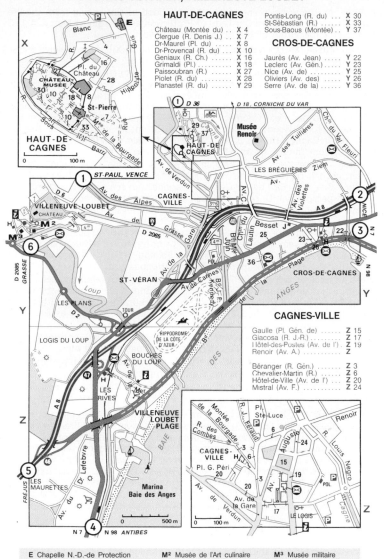

HAUT-DE-CAGNES

Château (Montée du) ..	**X** 4
Clergue (R. Denis J.) ..	**X** 7
Dr-Maurel (Pl. du)	**X** 8
Dr-Provencal (R. du) ...	**X** 10
Geniaux (R. Ch.)	**X** 16
Grimaldi (Pl.)	**X** 18
Paissoubran (R.)	**X** 27
Piolet (R. du)	**X** 28
Planastel (R. du)	**Y** 29

Pontis-Long (R. du) ...	**X** 30
St-Sébastian (R.)	**X** 33
Sous-Baous (Montée)..	**Y** 37

CROS-DE-CAGNES

Jaurès (Av. Jean)	**Y** 22
Leclerc (Av. Gén.)	**Y** 23
Nice (Av. de)	**Y** 25
Oliviers (Av. des)	**Y** 26
Serre (Av. de la)	**Y** 36

CAGNES-VILLE

Gaulle (Pl. Gén. de)	**Z** 15
Giacosa (R. J.-R.)	**Z** 17
Hôtel-des-Postes (Av. de l') .	**Z** 19
Renoir (Av. A.)	**Z**
Béranger (R. Gén.)	**Z** 3
Chevalier-Martin (R.)	**Z** 6
Hôtel-de-Ville (Av. de l') ...	**Z** 20
Mistral (Av. F.)	**Z** 24

E Chapelle N.-D.-de Protection   **M²** Musée de l'Art culinaire   **M³** Musée militaire

Rainier's castle was converted in 1620 by Henri Grimaldi into a finely decorated château. Entirely loyal to the King of France, he persuaded his cousin, Honoré II of Monaco, to renounce Spanish protection and to place himself, by the *Treaty of Péronne* (1641), under French protection. Heaped with honours and riches by Louis XIII and Richelieu, Henri led a life of luxury at Cagnes. This was the zenith of the family's power. When the Revolution broke out, the reigning Grimaldi was driven out by the inhabitants and took refuge in Nice.

★HAUT-DE-CAGNES

It is advisable to walk up to Haut-de-Cagnes along Montée de la Bourgade.

The **Porte de Nice** near the church tower is 13C.

St-Pierre (X) ⊙ – The door of the church opens into the gallery. The early Gothic nave contains the Grimaldi tombs. The larger nave added in 18C houses an altarpiece of the 18C Spanish School portraying St Peter receiving the keys to Paradise and an 18C statue of the Virgin and Child *(south side of chancel)*.

★ **Old town** – The picturesque town with its steep streets and vaulted passageways has many 15C and 17C houses (Renaissance houses with arcades near the castle).

Notre-Dame-de-Protection (X E) ⊙ – *Access on foot up Montée du Château.* The Italianate porch and belltower of this chapel inspired Renoir. The apse is decorated with rather stilted 16C **frescoes**: on the dome the Evangelists, Isaiah, the Sibyl; on the walls, scenes from the childhood of Christ and from the life of the Virgin; in the centre Our Lady of Protection as a Virgin of Mercy. A 17C altarpiece of the Virgin of the Rosary is in the north chapel.

★ **Château-Musée** (**X**) ⊙ – A double staircase and a Louis XIII doorway give access to this imposing castle crowned with machicolations.

Ground floor – The Renaissance **patio★★** has an agreeable freshness and elegance in sharp contrast to the feudal castle's austere façades. Two storeys of marble columned galleries decorated with arabesques surround the courtyard where thick foliage adds a note of greenery. Eight low vaulted medieval rooms open onto the patio galleries: Rooms 1 and 2 (fine Renaissance fireplace) present medieval history; Room 6 contains Roman sculpture dating from the 2C discovered in Cagnes. Rooms 3, 4 and 5 form a **Museum of the Olive Tree**: its history and cultivation, the use of its wood, pressing and olive oil.

First floor – Receptions were held in these 17C rooms. The ceiling of the banqueting hall represents the **Fall of Phaeton★**; this *trompe-l'œil* was painted between 1621 and 1624 by the Genoese, Carlone, and conveys an extraordinary illusion of perspective. Once he had finished, the artist could not bring himself to leave it: "My beautiful Fall," he sighed, "I shall never see you again." As it happened, he died only six weeks after he left Cagnes.

In the former boudoir of the Marquise of Grimaldi, there are 40 portraits, the **Suzy Solidor Bequest★**, given by the famous singer: paintings of herself done by famous contemporary artists. The ceiling of the adjoining oratory is decorated with Louis XIII style plasterwork *(gypseries)*. An antiphonary dates from 1757.

Musée d'Art moderne méditerranéen – This museum of modern Mediterranean art is housed in the banqueting hall on the first floor and in the apartments on the second floor. The rich collection of works by 20C painters who were either born on the shores of the Mediterranean or came to live there, such as Dufy and Vasarely, is shown in rotation or in temporary exhibitions.

Tower – From the top of the tower there is a fine **view★** over the roofs of Old Cagnes to the sea, from Cap Ferrat to Cap d'Antibes and the Alps.

International Art Festival – Every year since 1969, during the three summer months, the castle has held a large exhibition of contemporary art.

ADDITIONAL SIGHTS

Musée Renoir (**Y**) ⊙ – This memorial museum is located at Les Collettes, where Pierre-Auguste Renoir (1841-1919) spent the last 12 years of his life. The artist's house and two studios *(first floor)* have been preserved just as they were.

Ten of his **canvases** are exhibited on the ground floor; they belong to his last, especially sensual period; a shimmering palette expressing the beauty of nature with lovely rounded female forms (second version of his *Bathers*, 1901-02). It is also at Cagnes that he attempted sculpture and a few masterpieces (*The Shepherd Paris*, 1915), are on display. Right in front of the house stands **Venus Victrix★**; the large bronze statue overlooks the lovely garden, landscaped with olive, orange and lemon trees.

Renoir at Les Collettes

Pierre-Auguste Renoir, the painter, was born in Limoges but, as a young man, he went to Paris where his talents soon developed under the influence of the Impressionists and the world of art. From 1882 he made several visits to Provence, particularly in the company of Cézanne, and learned to appreciate the Mediterranean light and landscape. In 1900, as he was suffering from rhumatism, his doctor advised him to try a change of climate and he spent some time near Grasse with his wife and younger son Jean, who later became a film producer. Once his reputation was universally established he settled permanently in the South of France and in 1907 he bought the property of Les Collettes in Cagnes-sur-Mer, attracted by the view of the sea and the old village. Four of his paintings were inspired by the surrounding countryside. In 1913, at the suggestion of his friend Vollard, he took up sculpture with a pupil of Maillol called Guino and built a studio in the garden of Les Collettes where he worked. Under his directions, Guino created a little Venus and then the famous *Venus victrix*, which is displayed in the garden of the Museum. Renoir's last years were saddened by the death of his wife, his sons being wounded in the First World War and the inexorable progress of his illness, which confined him to a wheelchair; he managed to paint despite the arthritis which paralysed his right hand. As his physical capacity diminished, he stated that "he was beginning to know how to paint". In August 1919, in addition to having received many honours and having his work hung in the major museums of the world, he was officially accepted by the Louvre where several of his works are displayed. On 2 December 1919, just before his death, he began to paint a bouquet of anemones.

Baou de St Jeannet

EXCURSIONS

Villeneuve-Loubet, Marina Baie des Anges – *9km – 5.5 miles south. Take avenue de Grasse to Villeneuve-Loubet. See VILLENEUVE-LOUBET.*

★ Les Baous and the Corniche du Var

Round tour of 32km – 20 miles – about 1 hour 15min (excluding the ascent of Baou de St-Jeannet).

From Cagnes take avenue Auguste-Renoir and D 18 north to La Gaude.

The road runs past elegant residential properties, olive groves, market gardens and flower fields, with **views** of Vence, the hills and La Gaude.

La Gaude – From the ridge above the River Cagne La Gaude, which earned its living from vineyards and flower cultivation, now houses research centres in the fields of data processing, agronomy and horticulture. The 14C castle in the St-Jeannet district is thought to have been built by the Templars. At the crossroads in Peyron continue north on D 18 through orchards and vineyards.

St-Jeannet – The charming village occupies a remarkable **position★** on a scree terrace at the foot of Baou St-Jeannet, among orange groves, flower fields and vineyards producing good quality wine. Behind the church on the left a sign "Panorama" points to a terrace offering a **view★** of the peaks *(baous)*, the coast and the Var valley.

★★ **Baou de St-Jeannet** – *2 hours on foot return. The signposted path starts from Place Ste-Barbe by Auberge St-Jeannet.*
A sheer cliff 400m – 1 312ft high dominates the village. From the top *(viewing table)* a huge **panorama★★** extends from the Esterel to the French and Italian Alps.
Return to D 18 towards La Gaude. Turn left into D 118.

Centre d'Études et de Recherches IBM – The huge buildings on the left of this IBM Research and Study Centre, consisting of two opposing Y-shapes raised on concrete pillars to accommodate the uneven ground, were designed by Breuer and are a good example of architecture harmonising with its natural surroundings.

★ **Corniche du Var** – This scenic road follows the ridge or clings to the hillside on the west bank of the Var with a clear view of the river valley and the Nice hinterland. The steep slopes of the valley are covered with the flower fields and olive groves.

St-Laurent-du-Var – Until the County of Nice passed to France in 1860, the Var formed the frontier with the Kingdom of Sardinia. Passengers usually forded the river, often on another man's back. The first permanent bridge was built downstream in 1864.
Near the mouth of the river Var, a vast lake, protected by a dyke, has been developed into a yachting harbour (over 1 000 moorings).
Return to Cagnes by N 7.

CANNES ✿✿✿

Population 68 676
Michelin map 84 fold 9 or 115 folds 38 and 39 or 245 fold 37
Local map Massif de l'ESTEREL

Cannes stands on the shores of La Napoule bay, a superb anchorage dominated by the Esterel heights. The town owes its popularity to the beauty of its **setting**★★, its mild climate and magnificent festivals. From its early fame as the winter salon of the world's aristocracy, it has developed into an important resort and conference centre.

HISTORICAL NOTES

Cannes, the coastal watchtower – By the 10C, following the earlier Ligurian oppidum of Ægitna and the Roman settlements (42BC), a small cluster of dwellings, constructed by Genoese families, stood at the foot of the rock known today as Mont Chevalier or Le Suquet. The place was called Canoïs, cane harbour, after the reeds *(cannes)* that grew in abundance in the surrounding marshes.

In 1131, the Count of Provence, Raymond Bérenger II, gave the settlement to the abbots of Lérins. They built a tower and fortifications to protect the fishermen against possible attack from the Saracens. As soon as the first enemy ships

appeared on the horizon, the Lérins watchers gave the alarm. The defences were directed by the religious orders – first the Templars, then the Knights of Malta. The Fathers of Mercy dealt with the ransoming of prisoners.

Lord Brougham and the origin of the resort (1834) – Cannes' riches and renown are due to the misfortune of a Lord Chancellor of England (1830-34). Lord Brougham (politician, famous orator; he designed the four-wheeled one-horse carriage, which bears his name, the brougham), who was on his way to Nice in 1834. Cholera in Provence prevented the wealthy traveller crossing the *cordon sanitaire* to Nice; he returned to Cannes. The place, then a small fishing village, pleased him so much that he built himself a house there. For the next 34 years, right up to the time of his death (*d* 1868), Lord Brougham exchanged the winter fogs of London for the Mediterranean sunshine. His example was soon followed by the English aristocracy of the time and the town's population of 4 000 grew rapidly.

Two famous French writers dearly loved Cannes: Prosper Mérimée died there in 1870; Guy de Maupassant anchored his yacht in the bay between 1884 and 1888 and wrote his enthusiastic impressions of the town in his story *Sur l'Eau* (On the Water). Frédéric Mistral, the Provençal poet, celebrated Cannes and there is scarcely a famous person in art or literature who has not visited Cannes.

Cannes Festivals – The Cannes Festivals are world famous. Among the most popular are the international regattas, the International Record and Music Market (MIDEM) which takes place in January and the International Market for Television Programmes in April and May. The International Film Festival is the most glittering artistic gathering on the Riviera; each year in May Cannes becomes the film capital of the world.

★★ SEA FRONT *by car: 30min*

★★ **Boulevard de la Croisette (BCDZ)** – Local residents stroll here in winter. This elegant promenade, bordered by palm trees and gardens, overlooks a fine sandy beach.

Luxury hotels and elegant shops line the front and the side streets as far as rue d'Antibes. Here among the galleries and antique shops, the cinemas and night clubs, the smart set are to be found. At the top end of La Croisette, east of the port, is the new **Festival and Conference Centre** (Palais des Festivals et des Congrès), which includes the municipal casino, designed by P Braslawsky, F Druet and Sir Hubert Bennet. Its ultra-modern facilities comprise a 2 400-seat auditorium, Debussy Theatre (1 000 seats), broadcasting studios, meeting rooms overlooking terraces, press offices...

Dominating the bay is an open-air theatre (Théâtre de la Mer) seating 1 200. To the east of the conference centre lies the verdant Esplanade Président-Georges-Pompidou, affording lovely views of La Napoule bay.

La Croisette, Cannes

Between the conference centre and the gardens lies Allée des Stars, where the handprints of the great movie stars who have passed through have been set in the concrete.

Further east on the opposite side of the road, beyond the sumptuous Majestic Hotel, is a private 19C mansion, **la Malmaison** ⊙, once part of the Grand Hotel; it now houses the municipal cultural service and art exhibitions. Nearby stands the Hôtel Noga-Hilton, incorporating the façade of the old Palais des festivals, which was demolished in 1988 after 40 years as the venue for the Cannes Film Festival. Further on beyond the rose gardens is Port-Canto, a sports and cultural centre and marina (capacity up to 650 boats). From the promenade there are fine views of La Napoule bay and the Esterel heights.

★ **Pointe de la Croisette** (X) – Proceed east along boulevard de la Croisette to the Pointe de la Croisette. The spit of land owes its name to a small cross which used to stand there. It offers splendid views of Cannes, La Napoule bay and the Esterel, particularly at sunset. In addition to the beautiful gardens, modern tourist developments have provided artificial beaches and the Palm Beach and Mouré Rouge marinas.

Beyond Palm Beach (summer casino) round the point, a **view**★ of Golfe-Juan and Cap d'Antibes opens up. Boulevard Gazagnaire follows the seafront and avenue Maréchal Juin goes back into town.

CANNES

André (R. du Cdt) ..... CZ
Antibes (R. d') .... BCY
Belges (R. des) .... BZ 12
Chabaud (R.) .... CY 22
Croisette (Bd de la) . BDZ
Félix-Faure (R.) ...... ABZ
Foch (R. du Mar.) .... BY 44
Joffre (R. du Mar.) ... BY 60
Riouffe (R. Jean de) .. BY 98

Albert-Edouard (Jetée) . BZ
Alexandre-III (Bd) ..... X 2
Alsace (Bd) .... BDY
Anc. Combattants
d'Afrique du Nord (Av.) AYZ 4
Bachaga Said Boualam . AY 5
Beauséjour (Av.) ..... DYZ
Beau-Soleil (Bd) ...... X 10
Blanc (R. Louis) ...... AYZ
Brousailles (Av. des) .. V 16
Buttura (R.) .... BZ 17
Canada (R. du) .... DZ
Carnot (Bd) X
Carnot (Square) ...... V 20
Castre (Pl. de la) ..... AZ 21
Clemenceau (R. G.) ... AZ
Coteaux (Av. des) V
Croix-des-Gardes (Bd) . VX 29
Delaup (Bd) .... AY 30
Dr-Pierre Gazagnaire (R.) AZ 32
Dr-R. Picaud X
Dollfus (R. Jean) ..... AZ 33
Etats-Unis (R. des) ... CZ 35
Faure (R. Félix) ...... ABZ
Favorite (Av. de la) ... X 38
Ferrage (Bd de la) .... ABY 40
Fiesole (Av.) .... X 43
Gallieni (R. du Mar.) .. BY 48
Gaulle (Pl. Gén.-de) ... BZ 51
Gazagnaire (Bd Eugène) . X
Grasse (Av. de ...... VX 53
Guynemer (Bd) .... AY
Hespérides (Av. des) .. X 55
Hibert (Bd Jean) ...... AZ
Hibert (R.) .... AZ

Isola-Bella (Av. d') X
Jaurès (R. Jean) ... BCY
Juin (Av. Mar.) ...... DZ
Koenig (Av. Gén.) .... DY
Lacour (Bd Alexandre) . X 62
Latour-Maubourg (R.) . DZ
Lattre-de-T. (Av. de) .. AY 63
Laubeuf (Quai Max) ... AZ
Leader (Bd) .... VX 64
Lérins (Av. de) ...... X 65
Lorraine (Bd de) ..... CDY
Macé (R.) .... CZ 65
Madrid (Av. de) ...... DZ
Meynadier (R.) .... ABY
Midi (Bd du) X
Mimont (R. de) ...... BY
Mont-Chevalier (R. du) AZ 72
Montfleury (Bd) ...... CDY 74
Monti (R. Marius) .... AY 75
Noailles (Av. J.-de) ... X
Observatoire (Bd de l') . X 84
Oxford (Bd d') .... X 87
Pantiéro (la) .... ABZ
Paradis-Terrestre
  (Corniches du) .... V 88
Pasteur (R.) .... DZ
Pastour (R. Louis) .... AY 90
Perier (Bd de) .... V 92
Perrissol (R. Louis) ... AZ 93
Petit-Juas (Av. du) ... VX
Pins (Bd des) .... X 95
Pompidou (Espl. G.) . BZ
Prince-de-Galles
  (Av. du) .... X 96
République (Bd de la) . X
Riou (Bd du) VX
Roi-Albert (Av.) X
Rouguière (R.) .... BY 100
St-Antoine (R.) ...... AZ 102
St-Nicolas (Av.) ..... BY 105
St-Pierre (Quai) ..... AY
Sardou (R. Léandre) .. X 108
Serbes (R. des) ...... BZ 110
Source (Bd de la) .... X 112
Stanislas (Pl.) .... AY
Strasbourg (Bd de) ... CDY
Teisseire (R.) .... CY 114

Tuby (Bd Victor) ... AYZ 115
Vallauris (Av. de) .... VX 116
Vallombrosa (Bd) .... AY 118
Vautrin (Bd Gén.) .... DZ
Vidal (R. du Cdt) .... CY 120
Wemyss
  (Av. Amiral Wester) . X 122

LE CANNET

Aubaréde (Ch. de l') .. V 8
Bellevue (Pl.) .... V 13
Bréguières (Ch. de) ... VX 14
Cannes (R. des) ..... V 19
Carnot (R. de) V
Cheval (Av. Maurice) .. V 23
Collines (Ch. des) V
Doumer (Bd Paul) V
Écoles (Av. des) ..... V 34
Four-à-Chaux (Bd du) . V 45
Gambetta (Bd) ...... V 50
Gaulle (Av. Gén.-de) .. V
Jeanpierre (Av. M.) ... V 58
Mermoz (Av. Jean) ... V 68
Monod (Bd Jacques) .. V 68
Mont-Joli (Av. du) .... V 73
N.-D.-des-Anges (Av.) . V 79
Olivet (Ch. de l') .... V 85
Olivetum (Bd) .... V 86
Paris (R. de) .... V 89
Pinède (Av. de) ...... V 94
Pompidou (Av. G.) V
République (Bd de la) . V
Roosevelt
  (Av. Franklin) ...... V 99
St-Sauveur (R.) ...... V 106
Victor-Hugo (R.) ..... V 119
Victoria (Av.) V

VALLAURIS

Cannes (Av. de la) .... V 18
Clemenceau (Av. G.) .. V 25
Fournas (Av. de) ..... V 46
Golfe (Av. du) .... V 52
Isnard (Pl. Paul) ..... V 56
Rouvier (Bd Maurice) .. V 102
Tapis-Vert (Av. du) ... V 113

A   B

CANNES

0   200 m

↙ ÎLES DE LÉRINS   B

A

D   Château (Musée National
« La Guerre et la Paix »)
M   Musée de la Poterie

OLD CANNES AND THE HARBOUR

1 hour 30min

Allées de la Liberté (ABZ) – Beneath the plane trees, a morning flower market
is held, overlooking the harbour where pleasure craft and fishing boats are moored.

Take rue Félix-Faure and rue Rouguière to rue Meynadier.

Rue Meynadier (ABY) – Formerly the main street linking the new town with
Le Suquet, it is lined with a variety of shops and some fine 18C doorways.

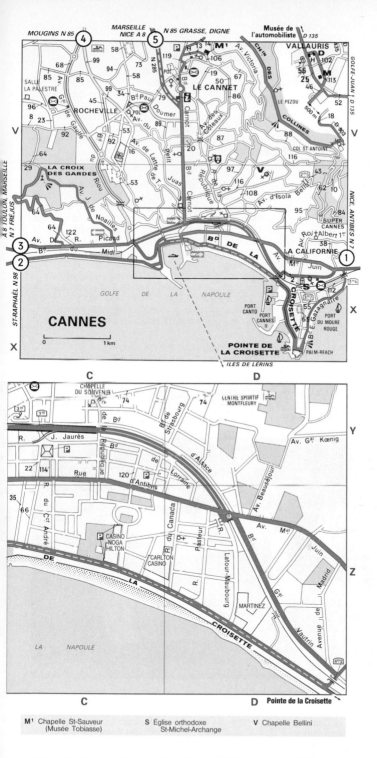

M¹ Chapelle St-Sauveur   **S** Église orthodoxe   **V** Chapelle Bellini
(Musée Tobiasse)   St-Michel-Archange

Go to Le Suquet via rues Louis-Blanc, Félix-Faure and Mont-Chevalier.

Le Suquet (AZ) – The old town, built on the site of the former Canoïs castrum on the slopes of Mont Chevalier, is known locally as Le Suquet. Rue Perissol leads to Place de la Castre surrounded by a defensive wall and dominated by the church of Notre-Dame-d'Esperance, which was built in the 16C and 17C in the Provençal Gothic style.

The old belltower leads to a long tree-lined terrace offering a fine **view** of the town and harbour and Ile Ste-Marguerite.

Cannes Film Festival

In 1939, Jean Zay, Popular Front minister of Beaux-Arts, created the International Film Festival at Cannes, chosen for its sunny climate. The inauguration, planned for 1 September, was cancelled when the declaration of war intervened two days later.

The real launch of the international career of the Festival took place on 20 September 1946 in the former Casino Municipal near the Old Port... a location returned to 40 years later at the time of the inauguration of the Nouveau Palais des Festivals in 1983.

In 1949 the festival moved to the Palais de la Croisette (demolished in 1990).

In spite of its suspension in 1948 and 1950 for financial reasons and an interruption in May 1968, the fame of the festival has grown over the years, with a prestigious jury presided over by such celebrities as J Romains, M Pagnol, J Cocteau, J Giono and R Clair. As it became a forum for international cinema, the Festival brought together an impressive number of participants and works. In 1994, 2 000 professionals (buyers and sellers) were present at the projection.

During the 10 days of the event, several competitions take place: the Selection Officielle (competing for the Palme d'Or), the Hors-Compétitions, the category "Un certain Regard" and parallel sections (Semaine de la Critique and Quinzaine des Réalisateurs). The great media interest in the various ceremonies of the Festival offer a unique springboard to all films, whether prizewinning or not, and confirms its role in uncovering talent in the 7th art.

Which films are shown? To be selected, films have to have been made during the preceding 12 months and must not have been shown at another such event.

They must not be distributed outside their country of origin before their selection. All the showings are reserved for professionals and admission is by invitation only. Only films entered in the category "Un certain Regard" are open to the public.

Carole Bouquet and Michel Blanc at the Cannes Film Festival

★ **Musée de la Castre (AZ)** ⊙ – The old Cannes castle, built in the 11C and 12C by the Lérins monks to watch over the harbour, houses important collections of archeology and ethnography brought from the five continents and bequeathed by two learned travellers in the 19C.

The small Cistercian Chapelle Ste-Anne, at the entrance, holds temporary exhibits. The rooms that follow are concerned with religion and mythology (works from the Fontainebleau School) as well as paintings of Provence and Cannes by 19C and 20C artists.

Room 4 looks out on the inner courtyard; here stands the 12C square watchtower (22m – 72ft), **Tour du Suquet**, where temporary photographic exhibits are held. From the top there is an extensive **view★** of La Croisette, La Napoule bay, the Iles de Lérins, the Esterel heights and the hills to the north of Cannes (raised relief model).

The extensive archeological collection displays objects from the Mediterranean Basin and the Middle East (Iran, Lebanon, Syria, Cyprus, Egypt, Etruria, Rome...) as well as primitive art from Africa, Oceania, the Americas (North and South), and Asia. Contemporary works of art are also exhibited.

Follow rue J-Hibert and rue J-Dollfus to reach Square F Mistral where a statue of the "immortal bard of Provence" was erected in 1930 to commemorate the centenary of his birth.

The harbour – Boulevard J-Hibert runs parallel with Midi beach round the point to the harbour with its ranks of fishing boats and luxury yachts. Larger cruise liners and merchant shipping anchor further out. The west side of the harbour is lined with shops and restaurants. In the northeast corner is the **shipping terminal** (large frieze runs along it, at the top) and embarkation quay for trips to the Iles de Lérins.

QUARTIER DE LA CALIFORNIE

This district to the east of the old town consists of luxurious villas set in magnificent gardens. Mostly built during the last century, there are stunning examples of exotic architecture with exotic and strange neighbours (pagodas and Moorish minarets, façades surmounted by turrets and colonial villas, bow-windows and moucharaby etc). All are private residences and the view of the exterior is often obscured by thick foliage.

Certain unique houses *(private property; not open to the public)* have contributed to the history of Cannes.

Avenue Roi Albert Ier: **Villa Kazbeck**, known for the parties given by the Grand Duc de Russie and **Villa Champfleuri**, famous for its exotic gardens which can be seen in the film *Macao, enfer du Jeu* by J Delannoy.

Avenue Jean-de-Noailles: **Villa Marie-Thérèse** and **Villa Béatrice** (1881), formerly Rothschild properties, built in the Classical style, which now house the Médiathèque de Cannes.

Avenue Maréchal Juin (eastern edge of town): **château Scott**, an amazing mixture of styles, dominated by Flamboyant Gothic; *Le Mystere de la Chambre Jaune* by M l'Herbier was filmed here in 1930.

Avenue Victoria (in Cannet): **Villa Yakimour** (see LE CANNET).

Chapelle Bellini (X V) ⊘ – *From the Cannes-Nice motorway, take the first exit to the left towards Vallauris, turn right into avenue de Vallauris. At no 67, turn right into avenue Poralto, then left into Allée de la Villa Fiorentina.*

This chapel was included in the grounds of the sumptuous Tuscan palace "Villa Fiorentina" built at the end of the last century for the Balkan nobility.

This religious building, in elaborate Baroque style, has the coat of arms of Count Vitali on its west face. The interior retains several works by the last owner, the Cannes painter Bellini (1904-89) who had his studio here.

Église orthodoxe St-Michel-Archange (X S) ⊘ – 30 bd Alexandre III. Since the Empress Maria Alexandrovna, wife of Tsar Alexandre III, regularly spent the winter in Cannes, it was necessary to build a church large enough to accommodate her court. The construction of the church was supervised by the Cannes architect Nouveau and its inauguration took place in November 1894. The richly orna-mented interior contains some remarkable icons (one of which represents **St Michael the great captain**) and banners received from the Russian imperial family. The spire with its onion-shaped dome is of a later date than the main building.

The church's choral group is particularly renowned for its interpretations of the liturgy. The crypt *(closed to the public)* contains the bodies of members of the imperial family who died in exile and of the white Russian general Youdenitch who took part in the siege of Petrograd in 1919.

Opposite the church, and slightly to its right, in Alexandra Square, is the **chapelle Tripet-Skryptine**, a neo-Byzantine building which was the first Russian Orthodox church in Cannes.

LE CANNET

See plan of Cannes. Leave Cannes by boulevard Carnot (X)

There is no break between Cannes and Le Cannet which is reached by boulevard Carnot.

Admirably protected from the wind by a circle of wooded hills, Le Cannet, at an altitude of 110m – 361ft, complements the climate of Cannes. This very busy resort has been popular with many artists: the actress Rachel, the painter Renoir and the playwright Victorien Sardou. The artist Pierre Bonnard (1867-1947) stayed here and spent the last years of his life painting views of Le Cannet from Villa Le Bosquet (avenue Victoria).

Le Vieux Cannet – The old town is reached by rue St-Sauveur *(mostly pedestrianised)* which has 18C houses with interesting façades as well as pleasant small squares shaded by plane trees and linked by alleyways. At no 19, where a side road goes up to the left, a blank façade has been covered with a mural by Peynet representing *Les Amoureux* (the lovers). Further on the left is the little 15C **chapel of St-Sauveur (VM¹)** sheltering behind a large lime tree, with a pediment decorated with polychrome mosaics. The **Musée Tobiasse** ⊘, inside the chapel, is a museum exhibiting mosaics, wooden panels adorned with figures (to be read from right to left) and objects made by the artist. The whole is lit through five stained-glass windows of vivid design by Tobiasse.

Place Bellevue (**V 13**) overlooks the square tower of Ste-Philomène church and offers a superb view of Cannes and the Iles de Lérins. The old Calvys tower (12C) still stands nearby, as well as the taller Danys tower (14C). Both towers have fine façades topped with machicolations. There is an amusing fresco dedicated to the founding families of Le Cannet on one wall. The jardins de Tivoli can be reached from the Hôtel de Ville via the pedestrian rue Cavasse, passing some luxurious 1900 villas.

★ **Chemin des Collines** – This is a particularly attractive road along the flanks of the hills above Cannes. There are many fine views over the built-up area, the gulf of La Napoule and the Iles de Lérins to reconcile the driver to the winding road. Continue to the east, to the Col de St-Antoine.

It is possible to return to Cannes by avenue Victoria.

On the left in the avenue Victoria, at the top of a magnificent avenue of populars, sits the **Villa Yakimour** *(private property, no visiting)*. This oriental residence was given by the Aga Khan to his wife Yvette Labrousse (Yakimour is derived from their initials and *amour*).

To continue to Vallauris, over the Col de St-Antoine, turn left into D 803.

Vallauris (**V**) – *See VALLAURIS*

⌂⌂ **Golfe-Juan** – *2km – 1.2 miles southeast of Vallauris by D 135. See GOLFE-JUAN* On returning towards Cannes on N 7, the road skirts round the hills of Super-Cannes while on the horizon can be seen the Iles de Lérins and the red barrier of the massif de l'Esterel; the **view**★ is at its best at sunset.

Return to Cannes along the seafront.

EXCURSIONS

★★ **Iles de Lérins** – *Boat trip half a day. See Iles de LÉRINS.*

★ Croix des Gardes (X)

Round tour of 8km – 5 miles (steep climb) plus 15min on foot return. Leave Cannes on avenue Dr-Picaud. At the traffic lights near the Sol-hôtel turn right into boulevard Leader. 100m – 110yds beyond the entrance to the Pavillon de la Croix des Gardes, turn right into avenue J-de-Noailles and leave the car 100m – 110yds further on in the car park provided.

Take a footpath on the right which leads to the top of the hill (alt 164m – 538ft), where there is a large cross 12m – 39ft high. This strategically placed feature, which has given its name to the hill, has been a permanent lookout post since the 16C. From the foot of the cross there is a marvellous **panorama**★ over Cannes and its setting, the Iles de Lérins, the Esterel and, in clear weather, the St-Tropez peninsula.

Continue along avenue J-de-Noailles to return to Cannes.

★★★ **Tour of the Massif de l'Esterel** – *96km – 60 miles – half a day.*
We recommend that the round tour be made in the direction in which it is described, from Cannes to St-Raphaël by the inland route and from St-Raphaël to Cannes by the coast road *(see Massif de l'ESTEREL ④ and ① respectively)*. Tours of the interior of the massif can be made using the local map on *(see Massif de l'ESTEREL)*.

★ **Massif du Tanneron** – *Round tour of 56km – 35 miles – 1 hour 30min. See Massif du TANNERON.*

The attraction of the French Riviera for the Russian aristocracy gave rise to a large number of Russian Orthodox churches

In Cannes – *St-Michel-Archange (1894)*
In Menton – *the Russian sanatorium chapel (1908)*
In Nice – *the church in the rue Longchamp (1858), which is the oldest, and St-Nicholas (1912), the most recent and most magnificent.*

CAP FERRAT★★

Michelin map 84 folds 10 and 19 or 115 fold 27 or 245 fold 38
Local map see Corniches de la RIVIERA

Cap Ferrat, originally the southernmost tip, has now given its name to the whole peninsula, which protects the Villefranche-sur-Mer anchorage and Baie des Fourmis towards Beaulieu. Elegant houses shelter discreetly in the dense vegetation, which tends to obscure a view of the shore except from the streets of St-Jean, the lighthouse or St-Hospice point.

Starting from Pont St-Jean (bridge) follow the route shown on the plan.

★★ Fondation Ephrussi-de-Rothschild

The foundation which was bequeathed to the Institut de France on behalf of the Academy of Fine Arts in 1934 by the Baroness Ephrussi de Rothschild, has an incomparable **setting★★★** in magnificent gardens on the narrow neck of the peninsula and enjoys fine view of the Villefranche and Beaulieu anchorages. Inside is a museum exhibiting more than 5 000 works of art.

★★ **Musée Ile-de-France (M)** ⊘ – The villa which houses this museum was built in the Italian style soon after 1900 to hold the furniture and works of art that the Baroness collected throughout her life. Her favourite period was the 18C. Pink marble columns from a palace in Verona surround a covered patio in which pieces of medieval and Renaissance furniture stand on an 18C Savonnerie carpet and a mosaic floor; the walls are hung with 16C and 17C Flemish tapestries. It is decorated with a collection of medieval and Renaissance works of art: a late 15C altarpiece depicting St Bridget of Ireland; a Carpaccio painting depicting a Venetian condottiere.

The surrounding rooms and galleries display works of art from various periods: 18C furniture (some items belonged to Marie-Antoinette), Savonnerie carpets, Beauvais, Aubusson and Gobelins tapestries, canvases by Boucher, Coypel, Fragonard, Lancret, Hubert Robert, terracottas by Clodion and candelabra by Thomire. The private apartments of Madame Ephrussi which can be seen include her bedroom, bathroom, her boudoir and the Sèvres diningroom.

On the first floor, the exceptional collection of porcelain from Vincennes, Sèvres and Dresden adds to the dazzling effect of the whole collection. The curious monkey room ("Salon des Singes") evokes the theme of animals which was so dear to Baroness Ephrussi; note in particular the unusual monkey orchestra in Meissen porcelain. Two Chinese lacquer panels open into the gallery of Far Eastern art, arranged in a Gothic décor and including lacquerwork from Coromandel, Chinese vases and carpets and a series of Mandarin costumes in an adjoining room. the Impressionists' Gallery contains landscapes by Monet, Renoir and Sisley.

ST-JEAN CAP-FERRAT

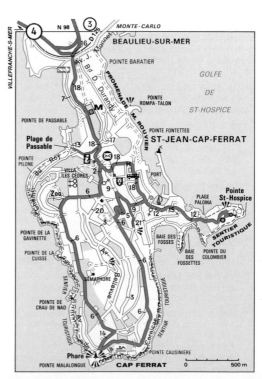

Villa Ile-de-Frances, Cap Ferrat

★ **Gardens** – Magnificent gardens (7ha – 17 acres) surround the villa. The French garden abounds in Mediterranean plants and terminates in a stepped cascade spilling into a rockery by a Temple of Love copied from Versailles. Broad steps lead down among the arums, papyrus, pomegranates and daturas of the Spanish garden, which is followed by the Florentine garden with its graceful marble statue. Fountains, columns, gargoyles and sculptures, both medieval and Renaissance, ornament the Stone Garden. A delightful Japanese garden contrasts with the unusual plants in the tropical garden. The Baroness Ephrussi was very partial to roses, a great variety of which can be seen in the rose garden.

★★ TOUR OF THE CAP *Round tour of 10km – 6 miles – about 3 hours*

Plage de Passable – This gently sloping shingle beach faces Villefranche anchorage.

Zoo ⊘ – A dried-out lake in grounds which once belonged to Leopold II of Belgium has been converted into a **tropical garden** in which a zoo covering some 3ha – 7 acres has been established. It contains 350 species of animals and exotic birds. Several times a day a performance is given by a troop of chimpanzees.

Phare ⊘ – The beam of this **lighthouse** is visible at 46km – 30 miles. From the top (164 steps), there is a **panorama**★★ from Bordighera point in Italy to the Esterel heights including the Alps and Pre-Alps. The Sun Beach swimming pool has been hollowed out of the rocks nearby.

★ **St-Jean-Cap-Ferrat** – Once a fishing village, St-Jean is now a quiet resort, its old houses looking down on the harbour of pleasure craft.
The stepped street to the south of boulevard de la Libération leads to a **viewpoint**★ from which Èze, the Tête de Chien, Mont Agel and the Alps on the Italian border can be seen.

Pointe St-Hospice – A pleasant stroll up between the private houses, past an 18C prison tower, leads to a 19C chapel, which replaces an old oratory dedicated to St Hospice, a hermit from Nice. From the chapel there is a good **view**★ of the coast and inland from Beaulieu to Cap Martin.

WALKS

From St-Jean, visitors can take pleasant walks, mostly in the shade.

★ **Promenade Maurice-Rouvier** – *1 hour on foot return.*
Starting at the northern end of Plage de St-Jean, the walk follows the coast towards Beaulieu with views of Èze and the Tête de Chien.

★ **Sentier touristique de la pointe St-Hospice** – *1 hour on foot return.*
Take avenue J. Mermoz to the Paloma-Beach restaurant and then go down the steps on the left. The path winds along the shore past Paloma Beach with a view of Èze, Monaco and Cap Martin. Once round the Pointe St-Hospice, it skirts the Pointe du Colombier and leads along the shoreline of the Baie des Fossettes before rejoining avenue J. Mermoz.

CAVALAIRE-SUR-MER ⚓

Population 4 188
Michelin Map 114 folds 49 and 50, or 84 fold 17 or 245 folds 48 and 49

Framed by Cap Cavalaire and to the east by Cap Lardier, and backed by the range of Pradels mountains, this family resort has a superb beach of fine sand (4km – 2,5 miles long). The yachting harbour (over 1 000 berths) makes Cavalaire an ideal base for summer boating.
On 15 August 1944 part of the American army landed in Cavalaire bay.

EXCURSIONS

★★★ Iles d'Hyères ⊙ - *See Iles d'HYÈRES.*

★★ CAP LARDIER

PRACTICAL INFORMATION

It is not advisable to attempt the whole route. Wear good walking shoes to cross the steep rocky points where the path has collapsed and remember to take plenty do drink. Avoid the hottest hours of the day when visibility is reduced by a heat haze. The sandy beaches are small at Gigaro, Briande and l'Escalet; however the path winds along beside many creeks which are an invitation to wander in unspoilt contryside.

Sentier du littoral de Gigaro au cap Taillat – *This path starts from the beach at Gigaro. There is a car park on the sea front or on the left just before the pinewood. In season there is an information post near the sign at the edge of the Gigaro pinewoods. The section of the route beyond Cap Taillat is described from the St-Tropez peninsula towards Cap Camarat.*
Most of the route falls within the protected side of cap Lardier managed by the Coastal Conservatory (Conservatoire du Littoral). The coast path runs along an uninterrupted succession of steep cliffs from which there is a view of the Briande bay ending in the east in the characteristic silhouette of Cap Taillat.
The area has a good collection of forest species. Beyond the forest the countryside is covered with vineyards. **Cap Taillat** is in fact a growing sand bar connecting the rocky reef to the coast, turning it into a peninsula. At the very end is a semaphore signal.
The path cuts across the base of the headland and disappears into scrub vegetation dominated by ilex until l'Escalet beach. *(It is possible to join the route from the customs shed at the entrance to the car park at l'Escalet.)*
For a description of the rest of the route, see ST-TROPEZ Peninsula.
It is possible to return to Gigaro from Briande beach by the inland path (route DFCI) through dense pinewoods which ends at the information post at Gigaro.

History of the Cap Lardier estate

In Edwardian times a remarkable vineyard occupied the site of the present development and Mas de Gigaro; these date from the 1950s when the estale was sold and turned into a camp site. At the beginning of the 1970s, a banking institution purchased the estate, as well as some additional land up to Brouis beach, with a view to building a marina. The residents rallied against this plan, and when the Coastal Conservatory (Conservatoire de l'Espace Littoral) bought the estate in 1976, the conservation of this unspoilt part of the coastline was assured.

★★ Domaine du Rayol ⊙ *7km – 4,5 miles west by D 559.*

The turning for Domaine du Rayol is on the left at the beginning of Rayol village; quick tour (30min) or more extensive tour (1 hour 30min to 2 hours).
The domaine du Rayol, evidence of a period of luxury, was created at the beginning of the century when European industrial and banking families built holiday resorts on previously undeveloped sites overlooking the sea, surrounded by lush vegetation. Rayol itself is on an exceptional **site★**, rising in a semicircle on wooded slopes among cork-oaks, mimosa and pines, in one of the most beautiful positions on the Var coast. In 1910 a Parisian banker, Courmes, after travelling extensively, had a house built here surrounded by exotic gardens. The stock market crash in 1929 put an abrupt end to the development of the estate. The aeronautics engineer Potez, who was forced to take refuge on the coast in 1940, renovated the property and the garden. The belvedere by Patek, with

its circular pergola, is linked to the coast by a magnificent flight of steps, and the garden is now glorious. In 1989 the Conservatoire du Littoral bought the whole estate (20 ha – 49,5 acres) after several decades of neglect, in order to preserve some of the last wild shores of the corniche des Maures. The landscape gardener Clément created a patchwork of gardens here planted with vegetation found growing in Mediterranean climates all over the world. There are dragon trees in the jardin des Canaries, agaves from central America, extremely rare honey palms and Andean araucarias from Chile, eucalyptus, bottle brush and blue gum trees from Australia, strelitzia from South Africa and bamboos from China. Between each continent the winding paths offer glimpses of the turquoise sea and a headland covered with pines. During the

Cactus in bloom, Jardin du Rayol

summer season, there are evening concerts of classical music here, with the opportunity to walk in the floodlit gardens during the interval.

★ **Jardin marin** ⊘ – A trip from the little beach at Rayol offers an unusual view of underwater life in the Mediterranean. This tour, accompanied by wardens from the Conservatoire, is preceded by an introduction to the principal species likely to be seen, their description and the best place to look for them among the posidonia. Among the discoveries to be made are the amazing life of the sea cucumber, the tireless activity of the gobies, real caretakers of the seas with their constant curiosity and the strange sexuality of the rainbow wrasse. Other finds might include sea slugs (a local species), the distracting ballet of a shoal of bream, the sparkling colours of a solitary wrasse or a conger eel lying in wait in a crevice in the rocks which are scattered around the bay.

COARAZE★

Population 540
Michelin map 84 fold 19 or 115 folds 16 and 17 or 245 south of fold 25
Local map see NICE HINTERLAND

Coaraze is situated at an altitude of 640m – 2 100ft on the **Col St-Roch** road (altitude of pass: 990m – 3 248ft), also called the Route du Soleil ("Sunshine Road"), which links the upper basins of the two Paillon Rivers. The name of the village is derived from "coa" and "raza" (*queue rasée* – bobbed tail) and has been given different interpretations.

Craftsmen have taken up residence in this nicely restored medieval village with its picturesque **old streets★**, long vaulted passageways and pretty little squares adorned with fountains.

From the terraced gardens, flanked by cypress trees, there is a lovely view down into the valley and north to the upper slopes of Rocca Seira.

The square is decorated with sundials designed by Cocteau, Goetz and Ponce de Léon.

Church – The old cemetery, where cement boxes take the place of vaults because it is impossible to carve into the rock, leads to the church. The interior is Baroque. At the far end hangs an early painting of St Sebastian pierced by arrows.

Take the D 15 north and turn left almost immediately into a narrow road.

Notre-Dame-de-la-Pitié ⊘ – The "blue chapel" was decorated in 1962 with blue monochrome scenes from the life of Christ. Behind the altar a glass panel enhances a metal *Pietà*. The terrace gives a lovely view of the village.

COGOLIN

Population 7 976
Michelin map 84 fold 17, 114 fold 36 or 245 fold 48
Local map see Massif des MAURES

This typical Provençal village with trading and industrial interests lies along the foot of a slope overlooked by an ancient tower and a ruined mill.

Many of the villagers are employed in the manufacture of carpets, pipes and bottle corks, and in the collection of reeds and canes from the marshes suitable for use in clarinets, fishing rods, furniture, etc. It is also a wine growing centre.

OLD VILLAGE

At the top of the village, behind the *Hôtel de Ville,* the many alleyways joined by vaulted passages preserve their medieval character. There is an original fountain in the place Dolet, and, in **rue Nationale,** fine Renaissance doorways in green serpentine stone, some of which date from the 12C; the bourgeois building at no 46 is know as château Sellier. At the top of the hill is the **clock tower** (14C), all that remains of the fortified castle *(access at the end of rue Nationale, via montée de Horloge).* Coming back down to the left, the **chapelle Ste-Croix** in place Bellevue is decorated with contemporary works.

Église St-Sauveur – Parts of the church date from the 11C and a fine Renaissance serpentine gateway remains. Inside, a side chapel houses a fine altarpiece by Hurlupin (1540) depicting Saint Antony accompanied by Saint Eligius and Saint Pons, as well as a beautiful 17C Baroque bust.

Espace Raimu ⊙ – *Avenue Georges-Clemenceau.* Located on the ground floor of the local cinema, this centre pays homage (posters, photographs, memorabilia) to the French actor Jules Auguste César Muraire (1883-1946), better known as Raimu. Raimu is best known to the English-speaking public for his interpretation of César in the trilogy *Marius, Fanny, César* by Marcel Pagnol and for his role in *La Femme du Boulanger,* also by Pagnol.

CENTRE FOR ARTS AND CRAFTS

Cogolin pipes Briar roots from the nearby Maures forest provide the raw material for the manufacture of pipes. In the avenue Clemenceau many workshops, including the Maison Courrieu, more than 200 years old, are open to visitors and show manufacturing techniques as well as beautiful collections of the finished product.

"Manufacture de tapis de Cogolin" ⊙ – *10 boulevard Louis-Blanc (off avenue Georges-Clemenceau).* At the beginning of the 1920s, some Armenian refugee weavers settled in Cogolin, and the **carpet factory** was established in 1928, with the transfer of some high warp looms from Aubusson. Two production methods are now used: hand weaving on request (using low warp looms – **la basse lisse**), and hand tufting, the technology of which permits very intricate decoration. The tour also includes the workshops where furnishing fabrics and carpets are made, including knotted deep pile wool carpets in the Aubusson style.

MARINES DE COGOLIN

5km – 3 miles northeast by N 98 and D 98A

Near Cogolin is a fine sandy beach, and a marina (22ha – 54 acres) with more than 1 500 moorings. The 4 basins are surrounded by a residential complex built in a unique architectural style. There are regular boat shuttle services to the other ports nearby.

CONTES

Population 5 867
Michelin map 84 fold 19 or 115 south of fold 17 or 245 fold 38
Local map see NICE HINTERLAND

Originally a Roman settlement, the village is built on a rocky eminence which rears above the River Paillon de Contes like a ship's prow; modern constructions extend into the valley. A tale tells of a plague of caterpillars in the 16C. The intruders were solemnly tried and sentenced to exile. The villagers organised a procession, and the caterpillars obediently left the village forever.

Church ⊙ – The south chapel contains a remarkable altarpiece of the Nice School (1525). The central panel representing St Madeleine has disappeared but the **predella** ★ illustrates her life in five scenes. The woodwork is 17C; doorway, gallery, pulpit. An elegant Renaissance fountain plays in front of the church. From the terrace there is a fine view of the valley.

EXCURSION

Châteauneuf-de-Contes

6km – 4 miles by D 715 to La Grave; cross the Paillon and take D 815.

The road (D 815) winds uphill beneath the shade of pines and olives above the Paillon, until one can look down on Contes, on its rocky spit and on Berre-des-Alpes.

The village nestles against the hillside among olive groves on the site of a Ligurian settlement, later a Roman camp, overlooking the Paillon de Contes valley. The 11C Romanesque **church, "Madone de Villevieille"** ⊙, is decorated with festoons and Lombard bands. A Roman inscription is incorporated into the façade. The east end with its massive buttresses has been cleared.

The interior was restored in the 17C and frescoes painted on the ceiling; behind the high altar, a fine plaster altarpiece frames a 15C wooden statue of the Virgin and Child.

2km – 1.25 miles further on turn left to the ruins.

Old Châteauneuf – *30min on foot return.* The deserted ruins of walls and towers make a strange spectacle against the rocky landscape. The people of Châteauneuf-de-Contes retreated up here in the Middle Ages to be safe from attack. From the top of the bluff there is a huge **panorama**★ taking in Mont Chauve and Mont Férion (west) and the Alps (northeast).

COTIGNAC

Population 1 792
Michelin map 84 folds 5 and 6, 114 fold 21 or 245 fold 34

★ **The site** – This village seems to flow down from a cliff (80m – 262ft high) of varying colours, shaped by the course of the Cassole and riddled with caves.
Some of the chasms are more than 50m – 164ft deep. On top of the cliff are two 14C towers, the remains of Castellane castle. There is a good view of the site from the D22 on the way from Sillans.

Village

Several fountains and elm and plane trees add to the charm of the old streets with their 16C and 17C doorways.
From Place de la Mairie, the belltower leads to the 16C Romanesque church, the front of which was rebuilt in the 18C.
A path goes up from the church to a two-storey cave which gives a good **view** of the village and its surroundings. At the foot of the rock is an open-air theatre where performances are given in summer *(see Calendar of Events).*
The village is well known for its honey, oil and wine.

Notre-Dame-des-Grâces – *1km – half a mile south on D 13 and a side road to the right.*
The chapel, surmounting Mont Verdaille, is connected with an appearance of the Virgin in the 16C, which is depicted in a painting above the altar. In 1660 young Louis XIV came here on pilgrimage with his mother Anne of Austria, an event commemorated by a black marble tablet on a pillar.
From the esplanade around the church, there is a pleasant **view** especially of Carcès, the Argens valley and the Brignoles region to the south.

DRAGUIGNAN

Population 30 183
Michelin map 84 fold 7, 114 fold 23 or 245 fold 35

Draguignan, situated between the Haut-Var and the Haute-Provence plateau, developed from a Roman fort built on an isolated knoll where the clock tower now stands.
On market day, the otherwise peaceful streets fill with people from the surrounding wine growing district.

From the Middle Ages to the present – In the 13C the town grew at the foot of the hill, and a defensive wall with three gates, two of which remain (the Portaiguières and Romaine), and a keep (on the bluff) were built. Louis XIV ordered the keep to be razed in retribution for the conflict between local factions in 1649. In 1797 the town became the administrative centre (Préfecture) of the Var by order of Napoleon; in 1974 Toulon took over. In the 19C Barons Azémar and Haussmann, both prefects of the Var, laid out tree-lined walks and straight boulevards to the west and south of the town.

An American Cemetery, to the east of the town, and a monument to the Liberation (**Z**) on the corner of avenue Lazare-Carnot and avenue Patrick-Rosso, recall the severe fighting that took place in the region in August 1944, notably around Le Muy, where 9 000 British and American soldiers were parachuted or landed from gliders on the morning of 15 August. The town has been the home of an artillery school since 1976.

St Hermentaire and the dragon – The name Draguignan is derived from Draconio, from the Latin *draco* meaning dragon.

Legend has it that, in the 5C, pilgrims on their way from Ampus to the renowned Lérins abbey via Lentier encountered a dragon roaming the marshes, now meadows watered by the Nartuby. The terrified pilgrims appealed for the help of a hermit, Hermentaire, who lived in the area. He overcame the dragon and built a chapel dedicated to St Michael the Archangel.

The existing church of **St-Michel** (**Y**) ⊘, north of place du Marché, contains an 18C statue of St Hermentaire in gilded wood.

OLD TOWN (Y)

To the east of boulevard de la Liberté, between two of the original gateways – the **Portaiguières**, pierced in a 15C square tower, and the Romaine (14C) – a network of picturesque streets lined with ornate doorways and houses at odd angles constitutes the old town (pedestrian precinct). The marketplace is set with fountains and shaded by plane trees. The vast façade (**B**) of an old 13C synagogue in rue de la Juiverie and the old mansion at no 42 (**D**) are of interest.

Clock Tower, Draguignan

S. Viron/DIAF

Tour de l'Horloge (**Y**) ⊘ – The **clock tower** replaces the keep, which was demolished in 1660. It has four flanking turrets and an ornate wrought-iron campanile. The **view** from the top takes in the town and the Nartuby valley; on the horizon are the Maures mountains.

SIGHTS

Musée (**Z M¹**) ⊘ – The museum, an old Ursuline convent built in the 17C and remodelled in the 18C by the Bishop of Fréjus for use as his summer residence, displays some interesting and rare items, as well as old furniture, sculpture, ceramics from France (Vallauris, Moustiers, Sèvres) and the Far East, most of which come from the old Château de Valbelle at Tourves.

Galleries 1 and 2 contain three paintings by Ziem (1821-1911), including two of Venice, *The Deliverance of St Peter* by J-B Van Loo, a suit of parade armour made between 1570 and 1575 for François de Montmorency, and a graceful composition sculpted by Camille Claudel (1903). The next room, devoted to French and Dutch 17C painting, displays a Rembrandt *(Child Blowing Bubbles)*, a small Frans Hals *(Kitchen Interior)* and a *Head of Christ* by P de Champaigne.

In the adjoining gallery – archeology – there is a collection of Etruscan vases and a handsome Roman lamp found at Vidauban.

DRAGUIGNAN		Gay (Pl. C.)	Y 6	Marché (Pl. du)	Y 16
		Grasse (Av. de)	Y 8	Martyrs-de-la-R. (Bd des)	Z 17
Cisson (R.)	YZ 3	Joffre (Bd Mar.)	Z 9	Marx-Dormoy (Bd)	Z 18
Clemenceau	Z 3	Juiverie (R. de la)	Y 12	Mireur (R. F.)	Y 19
		Kennedy (Bd John)	Z 13	Observance (R. de l')	Y 20
Clément (R. P.)	Z 5	Leclerc (Bd Gén.)	Z 14	République (R. de la)	Z 23
		Marchands (R. des)	Y 15	Rosso (Av. P.)	Z 24

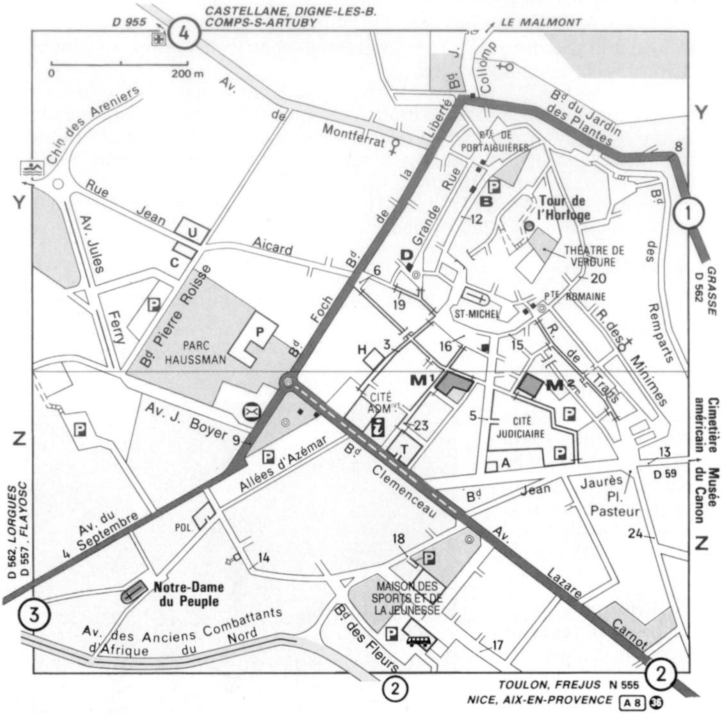

B Façade d'une ancienne
   synagogue
D Vieil hôtel

M¹ Musée
M² Musée des Arts et Traditions
    de moyenne Provence

In Gallery 5 are exhibited a bust of the Count of Valbelle, Marquis of Tourves, by Houdon and 17C-18C paintings: pastels by the Boucher school, two canvases by Teniers the Younger, a charming *Portrait of a Young Girl* by Greuze and *St Peter's Basilica* by Panini.

The final room is devoted to archeology and displays items discovered during the excavation of Gallo-Roman sites of St-Hermentaire and medieval ones of the town.

★ **Musée des Arts et Traditions populaires de moyenne Provence** (Z M²) ⊙ – The traditional activities of the region encompassing the Provençal tableland, the Haut Pays Varois, the Maures and the Esterel are exhibited in this museum. It was essentially an agricultural region where cereals (primary crop), vineyards (in Provence since Antiquity), olive trees and cork (cork-maker's workshop) were cultivated. Other activities included bee-keeping, sheep-raising, hunting, arts and crafts (floor tiles from Salernes, glassworks from the area around Fayence to Fréjus) and the raising of silkworms. Everyday life is evoked with displays of religious objects, domestic furnishings, costumes...

At the junction of allées d'Azémar, shaded by six lines of hundred-year-old plane trees, and boulevard Clemenceau is a bronze bust of Clemenceau by Rodin.

Notre-Dame-du-Peuple (Z) – A chapel was built in the 16C in Flamboyant Gothic style and enlarged later (west front in 19C). It is dedicated to the Virgin who saved the town from the plague *(pilgrimage, 8 September)* and contains many votive offerings. On the north wall is the central panel of a 16C altarpiece of the Nice School representing the Virgin saying her rosary.

Cimetière américain et mémorial du Rhône ⊙ – *Leave Draguignan by boulevard J-Kennedy.*

In the landscaped cemetery (5ha – 12 acres) are the graves of 861 American soldiers of General Patch's 7th Army who fell in Provence during the campaign launched on 15 August 1944 in support of the Normandy landings. At the foot of the memorial a bronze relief map traces the troop movements. The names of the fallen are inscribed on the supporting wall. The chapel is decorated inside with mosaics by the American Austin Purves.

Musée du canon et des artilleurs ⓥ – *3km – 2 miles east of Draguignan by boulevard J-Kennedy and D 59; at the artillery school's main entrance, in a military zone.*

The artillery school (f 1791) was transferred to Draguignan in 1976; it merged in 1983 with the anti-aircraft school from Nîmes.

The museum, which the school uses for military instruction, presents the evolution of weapons systems and tactics from ancient times until 1945.

The ground floor contains displays of heavy arms. Old-fashioned small arms are represented by various types of gun – coastal guns, naval guns, drill guns, siege guns, field guns – and rockets. The display of modern artillery comprises field weapons, trench equipment, fortifications, mountain weapons, anti-tank weapons and anti-aircraft defence equipment. A life-size diorama illustrates the use of the French 75mm guns during the First World War and the crucial role played by the artillery in the Battle of Garigliano during the 1944 Italian campaign. On the mezzanine, seven tents, representing a military camp at the time of the Second Empire, house a display on the evolution of small arms since the invention of the gun.

EXCURSIONS

Pays Dracénois

★ **Malmont Viewpont** (Table d'orientation du Malmont) – *6km – 4 miles – about 45min. From Draguignan take boulevard Joseph-Collomp north. After 6km – 4 miles, the road reaches a pass. Turn left into a narrow road which leads to a viewing table 300m – 330yds away.*

An extensive **view**★ covers Mont Vinaigre in the Esterel range, Agay anchorage, the Argens valley, the Maures heights and Toulon.

Trans-en-Provence – *5km – 3 miles from Draguignan. Leave Draguignan by ② on the plan and then take N555.*

This lively village was renowned until the last world war for its silk spinning, the power for which came from about 20 mills on the Nartuby river.

The town hall, built in 1779, with its lovely Louis XV **façade**★ decorated in *trompe-l'œil,* is a rare example of 18C civic architecture.

There is a fine reredos in St-Victor (14C church).

Gorges and waterfalls of the Nartuby – A path leads from the place de la Mairie in front of the town hall to the bridges. This outstanding **site**★ can be viewed from between the Pont Vieux and the Pont Bertrand.

Puit aérien – *Chemin du Cassivet.* This "aerial well" was an original design by the Belgian engineer, Knapper, who built it in 1930. The well, which has never been used, works by recovering moisture during the night to water crops.

Flayosc – *7km – 4.5 miles – about 45min. From Draguignan take D 557, ③ on the plan, going west.*

This typical local village, looking down on a smiling countryside of vineyards, fields and orchards, has retained its 14C fortified gates. The typically Provençal **place de la Reinesse** has plane trees, a mossy fountain and a small wash-house; the Romanesque **church** has a massive square belltower. From the terrace a long **view** of the countryside and the Massif des Maures.

★ Gorges de Châteaudouble

41km – 26 miles – about 1 hour. From Draguignan take D 955, ④ on the plan.

Pierre de la Fée – The "fairy's stone" is a fine dolmen of which the table, 6m – 19.5ft long, 4.50m – 14.5ft wide and weighing 40 metric tons, rests on three raised stones more than 2m – 6ft high.

★ **Gorges de Châteaudouble** – The deep, green, serpentine gorge was created by the Nartuby, a tributary of the Argens.

Before reaching Montferrat, return to Le Plan and turn right into D 51.

The road goes through the old village of Châteaudouble.

Châteaudouble – This village occupies an exceptional site on the top of a cliff overhanging the gorges of the Nartuby by 100m – 330ft. Its medieval charm can be seen by following the many passages interspersed with little squares adorned with fountains. Notre-Dame de l'Assomption, 16C church, flanked by a Romanesque belltower, has a fine studded portal. The Saracen tower offers a superb **view**★ over the whole village and the rough outlines of the gorges. From the gorges, several quite steep paths lead to the prehistoric caves of Mouret, Chèvres and Chauves-Souris.

From Châteaudouble drive north towards Ampus.

The D 51 crosses a plateau through the Bois des Prannes.

Ampus – The village church is a well restored Romanesque building. At the back of the church, a path marked by modern Stations of the Cross (1968) leads to a rocky outcrop.

Return to Draguignan on the D 49 which gives a good **view** of the town.

★ **Ste-Roseline** – *10km – 6 miles south of Draguignan by N 555, ② on the plan; turn right into D 91. See Les ARCS.*

Les Arcs – *10km – 6 miles south of Draguignan by N 555, ② on plan; turn right into D 555. See Les ARCS.*

Îles des EMBIEZ ⚓

Michelin map 84 fold 14, 114 fold 44 or 245 fold 46
Local map see SANARY-SUR-MER: Excursions

The Embiez archipelago lies off Port du Brusc on rich fishing banks, which are the delight of the amateur angler. It consists of three islands, the largest of which, officially named **Ile de la Tour Fondue**, is commonly known as Les Embiez. The second largest, **Grand Gaou**, with its public park, is linked to the mainland by a footbridge. The **Ile du Grand Rouveau** has an automatic lighthouse. **Petit Rouveau** is a bird reserve dedicated to the reproduction of gulls among others. The smallest, **Petit Gaou**, serves as a car park on the road from Le Brusc.

Ile des Embiez

L'ILE PRINCIPALE ⊘

Ile des Embiez (95ha – 235 acres) has an astonishing variety of natural features: fine gravel beaches, wild coastline with many coves, salt marshes, umbrella pine woods and vineyards which produce a popular rosé wine.

There is a busy modern marina overlooked by the ruins of the medieval château de Sabran, with houses built in the Provençal style. Those interested in diving will find waters full of an exceptional variety of fauna; beginners and those interested in Mediterranean wildlife will find information from the **Centre de plongée des Embiez** ⊘. For the less adventurous there is the small train which tours the island as well as a chance to view the underwater world from on board l'Aquascope ⊘.

★ **Institut océanographique Paul Ricard** ⊘ – The old naval gun site on St-Pierre promontory houses an oceanographic institute which contains research laboratories dealing with marine biology, fish farming and pollution of the sea.

A **museum** on the ground floor displays the principal Mediterranean environments and the species which live in them, including an extensive collection of molluscs, stuffed fish and fossils.

About 20 large seawater **aquariums** *(first floor)* provide a natural environment for some hundred species of Mediterranean aquatic animals, some in gorgeous colours: gorgonias, hermit crabs, grouper, blue lobsters, spider crabs, octopi, sting rays, scorpion fish, little eels.

ENTRECASTEAUX

Population 709
Michelin Map 245 fold 34 or 114 fold 21

Built halfway up a hill on the banks of the Bresque river, this village prides itself on its public gardens attributed to Le Nôtre. It is a pleasure to wander through the old Provençal streets under an old fortified church with a buttress spanning a road. The main avenue, shaded by hundred-year-old plane trees, is a very lively thoroughfare. Decorative carpets are produced here, as well as olive oil.

Château  – This austere 17C building overlooks the valley of the Bresque, a tributary of the Argens. Its high façade is topped by a double row of tiles and wrought-iron balustrades. The château was the stronghold of the Castellane, followed by the Grignan (who received the Countess de Sévigné) before passing to the Bruni family. This family included **Admiral Bruni d'Entrecasteaux** who died at sea in 1793 during an expedition to find the explorer La Pérouse who had disappeared five years earlier.

After a long period of neglect, the château was restored by the British painter Ian McGarvie-Munn who turned part of it into a museum before his death in 1981. The tour now includes the former castle kitchen and outbuildings in the basement, the guardrooms and the salons on the ground floor.

EXCURSIONS

St-Antonin-du-Var

8km – 5 miles east by D50; turn right at the cemetery into D250.

This undulating region, irrigated by tributaries of the Argens, is distinguished by a very diverse habitat and by about ten castles buried in the lovely forest: the most impressive castle, Château du Clos *(private property)* displays a fine classical façade at the end of a park with ornamental lakes. The parish church in the main village is of Romanesque style, its fine south front endowed with semicircular openings.

Massif de l'ESTEREL★★★

Michelin map 84 fold 8 or 115 folds 33 and 34 or 245 folds 36 and 37

The Esterel between St-Raphaël and La Napoule is an area of breathtaking natural beauty. One of the loveliest parts of Provence, it was opened to large scale tourism by the Touring Club's creation in 1903 of the scenic tourist road known as the "Corniche d'Or" (Golden scenic route).

The contrast between the busy life along the coast and the loneliness of the inland roads is extraordinary – the latter will appeal to tourists who prefer to leave the well beaten track for the pleasure of exploring on their own.

GEOGRAPHICAL NOTES

The massif – The Esterel, which is as old as its neighbour the Maures from which it is separated by the Argens valley, has been worn down by erosion so that its highest point, Mont Vinaigre, is a mere 618m – 2 027ft. However, in this mountain mass, the deep ravines and broken skyline dispel any impression of this being mere hills. The Esterel is made up of volcanic rocks (porphyry), which were forced up during the Hercynian foldings, thus differentiating it from the Maures. These hard porphyry rocks, which give the range its characteristic profile, its harsh relief and vivid colouring, appear in full beauty in the red tints of the Cap Roux range. Agay is where the blue porphyry is found from which the Romans made the column shafts for their monuments in Provence; elsewhere the colours are green, yellow, purple or grey. The jagged relief extends even to the waterline: the mountains thrust promontories into the sea; the sea cuts deep into the mountains. On the mainland rugged points alternate with minute bays, narrow strands and small shady beaches or creeks between vertical walls; offshore are thousands of rocks and islets coloured green with lichen, while underwater there are reefs which can be clearly seen.

The fiery red of the rocks makes a striking contrast with the deep blue of the sea.

Fragile flora – The Esterel, like the Maures, was until the first World War entirely covered with thick pine and cork-oak forests. Following the widespread forest fires which ravaged practically all the Esterel in 1943, 1964, 1985 and 1986, the forest exists today in only a few places *(see Forest Fires)*. Reafforestation involves an immense amount of work. Over the past century, scrub *(maquis)*, which was unknown in 1903, has taken over more than 60% of the Esterel area. The maritime pine, which is at present affected by a disease preventing it from reaching maturity, accounts for more than half of the coniferous trees. L'Office National des Forêts has undertaken much replanting, introducing new species (coniferous and broad-leaved) and cutting back shoots of cork-oak. By 1993 the forest was made up of more than half maquis, 18 % cork-oak and 13 % maritime pine. Other species present in smaller numbers are the Aleppo pine, umbrella pine and holm oak. The Massif de l'Esterel also boasts fine shrubby vegetation which holds down the soil and slows erosion: heathers, arbutus, lentisk, cistus, gorse and lavender. In spring and at the beginning of autumn their flowers provide a glorious multicoloured and fragrant display.

Diverse fauna – In the heart of the massif are many herds of wild boar, as well as partridge, pheasant and hares. Roedeer have been succesfully reintroduced into the area.

HISTORICAL NOTES

Via Aurelia – The Esterel was bounded on the north by the Via Aurelia (Aurelian Way) constructed during the reign of Aurelius. It ran from Rome to Arles, via Genoa, Cimiez, Antibes, Fréjus and Aix, and was one of the most important roads in the Empire. The roadway, paved and cambered and more than 2.5m – 8ft wide, was laid upon a cement base, as is the N 7, which follows much the same route. In the local dialect it

---

PRACTICAL INFORMATION ABOUT VISITING THE MASSIF

- Roads belonging to the DFCI (Défense forestière contre l'incendie – forest fire-fighters) are closed to public traffic. They count as private roads; an open barrier does not indicate that access is permitted. Parking in front of these barriers is prohibited and cars should be parked well to the side of narrow roads to allow the passage of emergency vehicles. Pedestrian access is always possible.
- During periods of high fire risk, the ALARME plan is put into action and certain public roads (classed as major fire risks) may be closed to vehicles. Offenders are liable for heavy fines. Walkers are strongly advised to avoid such areas for reasons of safety.
- Camping is prohibited in the massif and within 200m – 656ft of any of the forests.
- While walking in the massif, respect plants and wild animals and do not touch them, stay on the paths and keep dogs under control.
- For up-to-date information on the conditions in the massif, ☎ 04 94 47 35 45.

is still called *lou camin aurélian*. Taking the shortest route, it made use of many bridges and other civil engineering works. At the end of each Roman mile (1 478m – 1 617yds) distances would be indicated by a tall milestone – one of these can be seen in the museum at St-Raphaël (Musée archéologique). As the road approached the towns, it had raised pavements for pedestrians, which also served as mounting blocks. Stage posts, equipped with hostelries, horses and workshops, minimised delays to the imperial post.

Esterel Gap – The road round the north side of the Esterel, which was for many years the only land route to Italy, was rife with highwaymen; "to survive the Esterel Gap" became a local saying. The most dangerous spot was to the west of Mont Vinaigre; in those days the coach road left the N 7 at the Carrefour du Logis-de-Paris and ran nearer the foothills past the forester's lodge (M F du Malpey) at Le Malpey (Evil Mountain). The exploits of **Gaspard de Besse** in the 18C have remained legendary. After attacking and plundering the coaches and horsemen passing within reach, Gaspard and his band took refuge in a cave on the side of Mont Vinaigre. The brigand chief loved elegance: he wore a splendid red costume adorned with precious stones and fine silver buttons and buckles. For many years the mounted constabulary were at his heels. He also frequented the inn at Les Adrets (Auberge des Adrets), on the N 7. Arrested in another inn near Toulon, he was broken on the wheel in 1781 at the age of 25. His head was nailed to a tree on the road which had been the scene of his many escapades.

Even in 1787 the naturalist Saussure showed real courage in exploring the region on foot. Until the end of the 19C the massif remained the refuge of convicts escaping from Toulon.

Le Dramont and Ile d'Or, Esterel Coast

★★★ CORNICHE DE L'ESTEREL

① St-Raphaël to Cannes
40km – 25 miles – about 5 hours – local map below

★ **St-Raphaël** – *See ST-RAPHAËL.*
From St-Raphaël take N 98, ① on the plan.
The road skirts the marina. On the seafront is a memorial to the campaigns of the French Army in Africa.

⌂ **Boulouris** – This small resort, where villas are scattered among pines in beautiful gardens, has several little beaches and a pleasure boat harbour.

Plage du Dramont – A stele, to the right of the road, commemorates the landing of the US Army, 36th Division on 15 August 1944. The beach is bordered by the Dramont forest which covers the headland.
Immediately after the Dramont camping site, turn right. 100m – 110yds further on, leave the car and take a lefthand path leading up to the signal station.

★★ **Sémaphore du Dramont** – *1 hour on foot return; the path is paved and signposted.* From below the signal station there is a **panorama★★**: to the southwest of the Maures, of the two porphyry rocks guarding the entrance to the gulf of Fréjus (the Sea Lion – *Lion de Mer* – and the Land Lion – *Lion de Terre*), Ile d'Or with its tower. On the horizon to the north is Mont Vinaigre; behind the Rastel d'Agay peak in the foreground, can be seen the rocks of the Cap Roux range and lower down, on the right, the Agay anchorage. To descend, take the signposted path which leads to the little port; attractive glimpses of clear water inlets much favoured by nature lovers.
The road passes the beautiful Camp-Long beach before reaching Agay.

⌂ **Agay** – The resort borders a deep anchorage, the best in the Esterel and used in earlier centuries by the Ligurians, the Greeks and the Romans. Roman *amphorae*, which came, no doubt, from a ship which must have sunk some 2 000 years ago, have been found in these waters.
The bay is overlooked by the **Rastel d'Agay**, its slopes resplendent in red porphyry, and is lined by a large and sunny beach, which extends eastwards as far as the small jetty, and beyond by a more popular shady beach.

⌂ **Anthéor** – The resort of Anthéor is dominated by the three peaks of the Cap Roux range.
Just before the Pointe de l'Observatoire, there is a **view** inland of the red rocks of St-Barthélemy and Cap Roux.
The road to the summit (pic) of Cap Roux is described under ② below.

★ **Pointe de l'Observatoire** – The ruins of a blockhouse look out over a beautiful **view★** with the blood-red porphyry rocks against the cobalt blue of the sea. From the point can be seen Anthéor, Cap Roux and Esquillon points and La Napoule bay further north along the coast.
At this point the magnificent red rocks of the Esterel drop sheer into the sea.

⌂ **Le Trayas** – The resort is divided into two parts: one terraced on wooded slopes, the other by the seashore. The creeks and inlets which mark the coast include many small beaches, the largest of which lies at the end of Figueirette Bay. This bay was a centre for tunny fishing in the 17C, when nets were cast offshore and left for four months. To watch the nets a tower was built on the shore.

Miramar – This elegant resort, with its private harbour, lies in Figueirette Bay.
On a bend near the Hôtel Tour de L'Esquillon, pull off the road into the car park. A path (sign) leads up to the Pointe de l'Esquillon.

Massif de l'Esterel

The Kingdom of Auguste 1

Off Dramont beach is a small island of red porphyry, l'**Ile d'Or**, marked by a strange tower which appears to grow out of the rock. This rock, less than 1 hectare – 2.5 acres in area, has an unusual history which has contributed to the myths which form part of the Riviera. When it was put up for auction by the Domaines in 1897, a Parisian doctor bid for it. Doctor Auguste Lutaud transformed the island into the realm of the operetta and built a four-storey tower in medieval style out of the red stone of the Esterel. Thus the building merged both with its foundations and with the backdrop of the Esterel. The eccentric proprietor proclaimed himself King Auguste 1er of the Ile d'Or. He became the darling of fashionable society on the coast and organised lavish receptions. Many celebrities of the Belle Époque attended these parties, among them general Galliéni and the academician Jean Aicard. The monarch died in 1925 and is buried in his kingdom. Since then the island, still private property, has changed hands several times.

The cartoonist Hergé, who created Tintin, used the island as inspiration for his book *L'Ile Noire*.

★★ **Pointe de l'Esquillon** – *15min on foot return.* A beautiful **panorama**★★ *(viewing table)* of the Esterel heights, the coast, Cap Roux, the Iles de Lérins and Cap d'Antibes.

La Galère – The resort is built on wooded terraces on the slopes of the Esterel where it forms the western limit of La Napoule bay. Below the road, the seaside development of **Port-la-Galère** *(private port)*, an astonishing design by the architect Jacques Couelle, seems to merge into its rocky environment. The fronts of the houses are strangely hollowed to give the effect of a honeycomb.

The road rounds Pointe de l'Aiguille, opening up a **view**★ of La Napoule bay, Cannes, the Iles de Lérins and Cap d'Antibes.

G. Simeone/DIAF

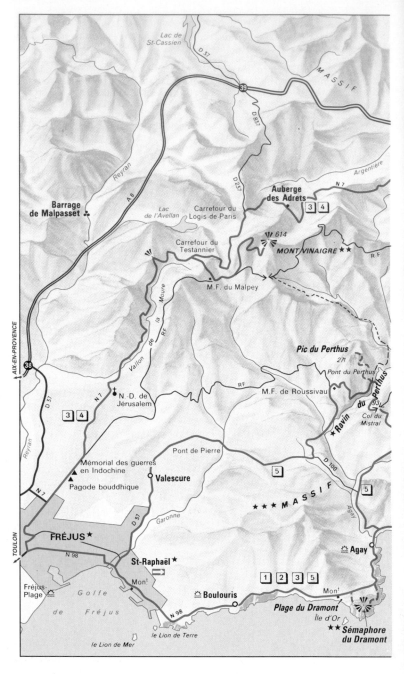

⌂ **Théoule-sur-Mer** – This resort, which is protected by the Théoule promontory, has three small beaches. The crenellated building on the shore, now a château, was a soap factory in the 18C.

⌂ **La Napoule** – *See La NAPOULE.*

After crossing the River Siagne, the N 98 skirts La Napoule bay.

⌂⌂⌂ **Cannes** – *See CANNES.*

★★ PIC DU CAP ROUX

② **From St-Raphaël**

38km – 24 miles – about 2 hours (excluding walks) – local map above

★ **St-Raphaël** – *See ST-RAPHAËL.*

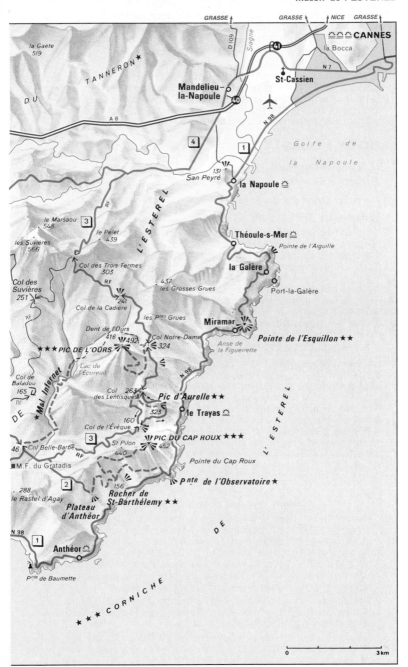

From St-Raphaël take N 98, ① on the town plan: the cliff road, the Corniche de l'Esterel, as far as Agay is described in ⑪ above.
From Agay take the Valescure road; at the fork bear right towards Pic de l'Ours. Beyond the Gratadis forester's lodge (M F du Gratadis) bear right. After fording the River Agay, bear right again around the north side of the Rastel d'Agay towards the Rocher de St-Barthélemy. Leave the car in the Plateau d'Anthéor car park.

Plateau d'Anthéor – *Picnic area.* There is an overall view of the sea to the right and of neighbouring peaks to the left.

The road continues to climb: **view**★ of steep slopes plunging into the sea *(right)*, of the red rock of St-Pilon and Cap Roux *(left)*; in the background is the Pic de l'Ours.

91

★★ **Rocher de St-Barthélemy** – *30min on foot return from the car park.*
A staircase, carved into the stone, leads to the top of the rock for a magnificent
view★★ of the Agay anchorage and Fréjus bay on one side, and the *calanques*
du Trayas and La Napoule bay on the other.

★★★ **Pic du Cap Roux** – *2 hours on foot return from the car park.* The path leading
to the Cap Roux peak is indicated by arrows and orange marks. From the summit
(452m – 1 483ft), there is a marvellous **circular view**★★★ *(viewing-table).*
From the Rocher de St-Barthélemy it is possible to take a footpath to rejoin the
coast road, the RN 98. This excursion can be done in reverse, leaving the car
at the place where the footpath branches off the RN 98.

★★ PIC DE L'OURS

③ From St-Raphaël

53km – 33 miles – about 2 hours 30min (excluding walks) – local map above

The roads taken are steep, narrow and not always surfaced.

★ **St-Raphaël** – *See ST-RAPHAËL.*

*From St-Raphaël take N 98, ① on the plan; the cliff road, the Corniche de
l'Esterel, as far as Agay is described in ① above. From Agay take the Valescure
road and bear right towards Pic de l'Ours. After Gratadis forester's lodge (M F du
Gratadis), bear right and, having forded the River Agay, leave the Plateau
d'Anthéor on the right and bear left to the Pic de l'Ours (Moutrefrey crossroads).*
The road climbs to the summit past evergreen oaks, barren land and red rocks,
with the Mal Infernet ravine in the distance. Winding round the north side of
St-Pilon and Cap Roux, the road reaches the passes, Col de l'Évêque and then
Col des Lentisques *(one-way traffic between the two passes: take the road to
the east of the peak on the outward journey, and the interior road on the return),*
with frequent **glimpses** of the sea to the right.

★★ **Pic d'Aurelle** – *1 hour on foot return by a marked path starting from the Col
des Lentisques.* The Aurelle is one of the major peaks in the coastal chain of the
Esterel. From the top (323m – 1 060ft) a fine **panorama**★★ takes in the area
between the Cap d'Antibes and Pointe de l'Observatoire.
From the Col des Lentisques to the Col Notre-Dame is one of the most beautiful
drives in the Esterel. Immediately overlooking the coast, the road offers
breathtaking **bird's-eye views**★ of the Corniche de l'Esterel cliff road and splendid
perspectives of the shore looking towards Cap d'Antibes. From the Col
Notre-Dame (323m – 1 060ft), a remarkable **panorama** extends over Cannes, the
Iles de Lérins and La Napoule bay.

Different types of pine growing on the Riviera

Maritime Pine – This is the original species of the Mediterranean coast,
growing thickly in the past. In spite of its very combustible nature, it had
the advantage of being able to regenerate itself speedily after fires. It has
been attacked by another enemy in the last 25 years – a parasitical insect,
the Matsucocus Feytaudi, has brought about its downfall by preventing it
attaining maturity. This explains its often bare appearance. It still
represents 60% of the species in the coastal forests.

Umbrella Pine – As well as having an attractive appearance, which suits the
Mediterranean setting, this tree is preferred for replanting the maquis. It
casts a welcome ring of shade.

Aleppo Pine – More common inland, this tree will grow on dry soils up to an
altitude of 500m – 1640ft. This tree, which is usually seen growing on land
left fallow or on isolated south-facing slopes, can be recognised by its
red-brown bark and the curve of its trunk.

Scots Pine – this tree flourishes in the climate of the plateaux of the Haut
Var and the north of the Alpes-Maritimes. Together with the fir it forms
magnificent forests.

★★★ **Pic de l'Ours** – *1 hour 30min on foot return. Car park at Col Notre-Dame.* The
series of hairpin bends by which the road *(private vehicles prohibited)* reaches
the summit affords constantly changing views of the wooded ranges of the
Esterel and the deeply indented coastline. The remarkable **panorama**★★★ from
the summit (496m – 1 627ft) where there is a television transmitting station,
includes the coast – from the Maures to the Alps – the Esterel range, dominated
by Mont Vinaigre and the Var countryside.
From Col Notre-Dame, drive to Col des Trois Termes.

From the Col Notre-Dame, the road *(surfaced for 5km – 3 miles)* clings to the peaks of the Petites Grues and the Grosses Grues before reaching the Col de la Cadière where the **view**★ opens to the north towards La Napoule and the Massif du Tanneron. At the Col des Trois Termes, take the track on the right (almost hairpin back on yourself) to join the N 7.

Return to St-Raphaël on N 7 or by returning along the route described above.

★ VIA AURELIA

④ Cannes to St-Raphaël

46km – 29 miles – about 6 hours – local map above

⌂⌂⌂ **Cannes** – *See CANNES.*

From Cannes take N 7, ③ on the town plan.

For most of the way this route runs through the Esterel forest. After passing through the industrial zone of La Bocca, the road crosses the alluvial plain of the River Siagne.

Turn left into the road leading to Cannes-Mandelieu airport, then right.

Ermitage de St-Cassien – The 14C chapel set on a low rise in an oak plantation with a few cypress trees standing guard makes a charming picture. Tradition says it was once the site of a Roman temple; it is now a place of pilgrimage.

Return to N 7.

Mandelieu-la-Napoule – Population 16 493. Mimosa capital along the Siagne. The N 7 runs along the valley between the Esterel and Tanneron massifs.

Auberge des Adrets – This inn was the favourite haunt of the highwayman Gaspard de Besse.

At the crossroads, Carrefour du Logis-de-Paris, the road skirts the foot of Mont Vinaigre, the highest peak in the Esterel (618m – 2 027ft).

At the Carrefour du Testannier, turn left into a road marked "Forêt domaniale de l'Esterel". At the Le Malpey forester's lodge, follow the sign to Mont Vinaigre.

★★ **Mont Vinaigre** – *30min on foot return.* A path leads to the top which offers a splendid **panorama**★★★ on all sides: on the coast Cap d'Antibes, Pointe de la Croisette, Cannes and La Napoule bay, Pic de l'Ours with its tower and TV mast, Pic du Cap Roux and Fréjus bay, inland the Massif des Maures and the Argens valley, and the limestone hills of Provence. On a fine day one can see as far as the Alps and Ste-Baume.

Return to N 7.

At the bend, there is a **view** on the right towards Fayence; then the road follows the valley of the Moure. The original Via Aurelia, however, followed the line of the forest road on the opposite bank.

★ **Fréjus** – *See FRÉJUS.*

Return to St-Raphaël by boulevard S-Decuers.

★ **St-Raphaël** – *See ST-RAPHAËL.*

★ ROUTE DU PERTHUS

★ ⑤ Perthus

20km – 12 miles – allow 3 hours – local map above

★ **St-Raphaël** – *See ST-RAPHAËL.*

Leave St-Raphaël at ① on the map; at the Gratadis forester's lodge, turn left towards the Col de Belle-Barbe. Car park on the Col. The track beyond is prohibited to traffic.

★ **Ravin du Mal Infernet** – *2 hours on foot return.*

Follow the footpath which leads into the wooded ravine of Mal Infernet, a majestic setting overlooked by many jagged rocks. The path goes as far as the Lac de l'Écureuil. This lake contains a fine variety of fish: roach, tench, carp, perch and trout. It is possible to continue on foot as far as the Col Notre-Dame by going round the Pic and the Dent de l'Ours to the north.

Return to the Col de Belle-Barbe.

Take the road heading northwest towards the Roussivau forester's lodge (Maison Forestière) going round the Perthus peaks to the south.

Leave the car in one of the car parks on the Roussivau plain.

★ **Ravin du Perthus and Pic du Perthus occidental** – *1 hour 30min on foot.* Near the first car park a footpath leads off into the pretty Perthus ravine. It offers a nice setting for some easy rambles before heading off towards the foothills of Mont Vinaigre. Near Pont de Perthus, a marked out footpath leads to the western Perthus peak (271m – 889ft), with its scarlet porphyry rocks towering above the southern limit of the Esterel forest.

Return to the car park on the Roussivau plain and head towards Valescure on the Roussivau forest road.

This road makes a sudden transition from the rocky, wooded isolation of the Esterel massif to the more cultivated countryside of sloping plots studded with umbrella pines and eucalyptus.

Valescure – The villas of this resort, the aristocratic extension of St-Raphaël, are scattered over the wooded hillsides in a landscaped park. The resort owes its reputation to the English, who used to come for the golf, the mild climate and the tranquillity.

Return to St-Raphaël by D 37.

ÈZE★★

Population 2 446
Michelin map 84 folds 10 and 19 or 115 fold 27 or 245 fold 38
Local map see Corniches de la RIVIERA

Èze, a strange isolated village, is a prime example of a hill village *(see Hill Villages)*: it clings, like an eagle's nest, to a rock spike towering 427m – 1 410ft above the sea. Each year numerous painters and tourists in search of the picturesque crowd its **site★★**.

Legend claims that it was founded by the Saracens but in origin it was a Celto-Ligurian settlement, which subsequently came under the rule of the Phœnicians, Romans and Saracens and then of various families, even rising to the status of a county in the 16C.

In 1986 the area was extensively damaged by fire.

★OLD VILLAGE

A 14C double gateway with crenellations and a sentry walk leads into the steep narrow streets, sometimes stepped and sometimes running beneath the carefully restored houses which are now smart boutiques and artists' studios. At every corner there are flowers, shrubs, fountains and breathtaking views of the sea and mountains.

Chapelle des Pénitents Blancs (B) ⊙ – The simple 14C chapel is decorated with enamelled panels illustrating the life and death of Christ and his mother.

To the left on entering is a Crucifixion, an early example of the Nice School; on the high altar an unusual Catalan crucifix, dating from 1258, in which Christ is smiling; on the right a 16C hexagonal ciborium in mahogany; on the left a 14C statue, the Madonna of the Forest, so called because the child she is holding has a pine cone in his hand. A 16C wooden crucifix hangs on a pilaster in the gallery.

Jardin exotique ⊙ – Many varieties of succulents and cacti flourish in the gardens crowned by the remains of a château built in the 14C and dismantled on the orders of Louis XIV in 1706. There is a splendid **panorama★★★**, from the terrace, of the Riviera (on a fine morning Corsica is visible).

ÈZE

Brec (R. du)	2
Centenaire (Pl. du)	3
Château (R. du)	4
Colette (Pl. de la)	5
Église (Pl. de l')	6
Paix (R. de la)	7
Pise (R. de la)	8
Planet (Pl. du)	9

B Chapelle des Pénitents Blancs

Eze

Church – The church was rebuilt in the 18C with a classical façade and a two-storey tower. The Baroque interior contains a fine statue of the Assumption (18C) attributed to Muerto and an emblazoned 15C font.

Parfumerie Fragonard ⊙ – This annexe of the Grasse perfumery displays the various stages in the manufacturing process of essential oils and cosmetics.

★ **Sentier Frédéric-Nietzsche** – *About 2 hours on foot return*. Nietzsche thought out the third part of his masterpiece *Thus Spoke Zarathustra* on the picturesque mule path which winds down towards the Corniche Inférieure. It leads through pinewoods and olive groves to the seaside resort of Èze-Bord-de-Mer.

FAYENCE

Population 3 502
Michelin map 84 folds 7 and 8, 114 folds 11, 24 or 245 fold 36

Fayence lies on the edge of the Provençal tableland (view of the Signal de Lachens beacon – alt 1 715m – 6 626ft), opposite its twin village, Tourrettes, on the road from Draguignan to Grasse, overlooking an important gliding field. It has an enviable position, between the mountains and the sea, ringed by picturesque villages and only 10km – 6 miles from the Lac de St-Cassien. Potters, stone and wood carvers, weavers, painters and coppersmiths work there.

Church – This church was built in the mid-18C, replacing the smaller, older church unable to hold a growing congregation. The interior is very Classical with tall pillars supporting a gallery round the nave. The high altar, Baroque in style, is the work of the Provençal marble mason, Dominique Fossatti (1757). In the nave's south aisle, a 16C gilded altarpiece represents scenes of the Passion and the Glorification of Christ; Christ in Agony is in the centre with a giant St Christopher carrying the Infant Jesus below.
From the terrace, to the right of the church, the **view**★ extends beyond the gliding field, in the foreground, to the Maures and Esterel heights.

Panorama de l'ancien château – *Follow the signs from the church*. The view is to the north to the Provençal tableland, the Pre-Alps of Castellane and Grasse.

Old town – Below the church, steep streets, lined by handsome doorways of houses and a 17C gateway, lead to the town gates. The Porte Sarrasine is still crowned by machicolations.

EXCURSIONS

Col du Bel-Homme *Round tour of 64km – 40 miles – about 4 hours*

From Fayence take D 563 south.

Almost immediately on the right, then the left, is the turning *(signpost)* to Notre-Dame-des-Cyprès.

Notre-Dame-des-Cyprès ⊙ - In a setting of tall cypress trees, the Romanesque chapel (12C) looks out over Fayence and Tourrettes. The oven-vaulted apse contains a 16C altarpiece set in a Baroque frame: scenes from the life of the Virgin painted on wood in a naïve style flank a painted wooden statue.

Return to D 563 which skirts Fayence airport and turn right into D 562 which crosses several streams as it winds among the trees.

To the north the villages of Fayence, Tourrettes and Montauroux are strung out along the ridge.

At Les 4 Chemins turn right into D 25 (towards Callas).

Callas - Grouped round the castle ruins against a hillside of olive, oak and pine trees, Callas is still a typical village of the Haut-Var. A fire alarm unfortunately disfigures the campanile. The Romanesque **church** ⊙, heavily restored in the 19C, displays a 17C altarpiece above nine hooded penitents on their knees.

From the terrace the **view** south takes in the Maures and Esterel heights.

Continue along D 25 which goes over the Col de Boussague and winds up a pleasant valley to Bargemon.

Bargemon - *See BARGEMON.*

From Bargemon take D 25 west.

The road climbs steeply offering fine views of Bargemon and its surroundings.

★ **Col du Bel-Homme** - Alt 951m - 3 210ft. A path on the left leads to the top. From the viewing table a **panorama**★ extends south to the coast, northeast to Grasse, north to the Canjuers plateau and the mountains round Castellane.

Return to Bargemon and take D 19 towards Fayence.

The road climbs above the town before turning eastwards through pine trees, evergreen holm oaks and broom. On the southern horizon rise the Maures and Esterel heights.

★ **Seillans** - *See SEILLANS.*

N-D-de-l'Ormeau - *See SEILLANS.*

Return to Fayence on D 19 with open views of the countryside.

Lac de St-Cassien - *Round tour of 29km - 18 miles - about 2 hours.*

From Fayence take the road to Tourrettes.

Tourrettes - The unusual castle, modelled on the St Petersburg Cadet School, was built in about 1830 for a general under the Empire.

Turn left into D 19, D 562 and D 56 to reach Callian.

Callian - Streets lined with old houses wind round the castle on a delightful **site**. A fountain plays under the trees of the main square, from where **views** look southwest over the local flower fields to the Lac de St-Cassien beneath the Tanneron heights. The Esterel and Maures heights dominate the horizon to the south.

North of the village take D 37 to Montauroux.

The road offers pleasant views of Callian and Montauroux.

Montauroux - Many craftsmen have settled in the village. There are 17C and 18C houses in rue de la Rouguière, and the **view**, from the square, takes in the Lac de St-Cassien, the Tanneron heights, with a glimpse of the Maures and the Esterel. Set apart is the **Chapelle St-Barthélemy**, the former parish church (12C); the chapel is Romanesque.

Continue on D 37 crossing D 562.

Lac de St-Cassien - From the Pré-Claou bridge, there is a **view** of the whole lake which supplies water for irrigation. Its wooded slopes attract game hunters and fishermen. Water sports are allowed on the lake (no motor boats) and there are swimming places.

Return to Fayence by D 37; turn left into D 562 and right into D 19.

FRÉJUS★

Population of conurbation 73 967
Michelin map 84 fold 8, 114 fold 25, 115 fold 33 or 245 fold 36
Local maps see Massif de l'ESTEREL and Massif des MAURES

Fréjus lies between the Maures and the Esterel, in the alluvial plain of the Lower Argens, where vineyards and fruit orchards flourish. The town itself is built on a rock plateau whose slopes descend gently towards the sea about a mile away. Fréjus attracts lovers of the past; its Roman ruins, although unspectacular, are among the most varied in France and its cathedral close is of architectural interest. The construction on the coast of Port-Fréjus has encouraged a local tourist industry.

HISTORICAL NOTES

Birth and heyday (1C BC) – Fréjus takes its name from **Forum Julii**, a village founded by Julius Caesar in 49BC, as a trading and staging post on the great coastal road which was to become known as the Via Aurelia.

Octavian, the future Emperor Augustus, turned the market town into an important naval base (39BC), where he built and trained the fast, manoeuvrable light galleys which were later to win the battle of Actium (31BC) against the heavy ships of Cleopatra and Antony.

Augustus established, in the town then called Colonia Octavanorum, a large colony of his veterans (soldiers who had finished their military duties and to whom a sum of money and some land were given, along with the full rights of a Roman citizen). The city developed (construction of the Platform or military headquarters and the Butte St-Antoine) until it numbered 40 000 inhabitants. It was exceedingly prosperous.

Fréjus 2 000 years ago – *See plan under Roman City below.*

Ramparts surrounded it, pierced by four gateways corresponding to the two broad streets, quartering the town, in the tradition of Roman settlements. Soldiers, sailors and citizens enjoyed the arenas, theatre and baths free of charge.

An aqueduct 40km – 25 miles long brought fresh water from the Siagnole near Mons *(See MONS)* as far as the water tower from which it was piped to the fountains and public buildings.

Among the naval bases of the Roman world only Fréjus and Ostia, in Italy, offer sufficient remains to be reconstructed: from the eastern end of the Esplanade Paul-Vernet (Roman forum), one can look down on the plain where the port lay 2 000 years ago and, with the aid of the vestiges still standing, one can evoke fairly easily its shape, size and facilities.

The port, which was created in the first place by dredging and deepening a lagoon, was reconstructed during the reign of Augustus.

The harbour of some 22ha – 54 acres, a considerable area for those times, included well over 2km – 1 mile of quays of which traces still remain.

It was linked with the sea by means of a canal, protected from the *mistral* by a wall, and approximately 30m – 98ft wide and 500m – 1 640ft long – the shore line has receded since Roman times. The entrance was guarded by two large symmetrical towers, of which one, bearing Augustus' Lantern, still rises high above the plain at the end of the south quay. An iron chain, which lay on the bottom all day, was stretched between the towers at night.

A strong outward current, obtained by a secondary canal from the Argens, prevented the harbour from silting up.

A large tower, boatyards, baths and buildings – the harbour-master's office, a health control office and laundry – completed the installations, together with the *palaestra* (sports ground) and hospital, of which traces are to be found at the Villeneuve farm, southwest of the town.

Decline – During the long years of Roman peace, the military aspect of the port declined and in the late 2C AD the fleet was moved away but the port remained a lively commercial centre until the 4C. Under Constantine an archbishopric was established. The harbour and canal, however, were neglected and began to silt up. At the beginning of the 10C the town was destroyed by the Saracens. In 990 under Bishop Riculphe, the city rose again on a much smaller scale; the medieval town walls *(plan overleaf)* followed the line of rue Jean-Jaurès and rue Grisolle. Henri II turned Fréjus into a large naval base.

Finally, under the Revolution, the whole port was sold as a national estate and was filled in by its new owner.

★★ CATHEDRAL CLOSE ⊙ *time: 45min*

This fortified unit comprised: the cathedral, the cloisters and annexes, the baptistery and the bishop's palace.

From place Formigé go down a few steps beneath the cathedral porch until you come to the stairway into the cloisters.

Portal – Under an ogee arch are two **panels★** (1) carved in the 16C to illustrate scenes in the life of the Virgin, St Peter and St Paul, portraits and military motifs.

★★ **Baptistery** – This baptistery, one of the most ancient buildings in France, is thought to date back to the 5C. Separated from the cathedral by the porch, it has a square external appearance with sides about 11m – 36ft long. The inside is in the form of an octagon with alternate curved and rectangular niches separated by black granite columns. These are topped by capitals of marble taken from Fréjus' ancient forum. Excavations have uncovered the original white marble pavement and the piscina.

A wrought-iron grille (2), given by Cardinal de Fleury, tutor and minister to Louis XV, who was at one time Bishop of Fréjus, leads to the baptistery. Formerly the two doors on either side of the grille were used: by the lower door (3) the candidates for baptism entered and, after being baptised by the bishop, left by the upper, triumphal door (4) as new Christians. Dressed in a white tunic, they then went to the cathedral, attended full mass for the first time and received their first communion. Baptism was often administered to

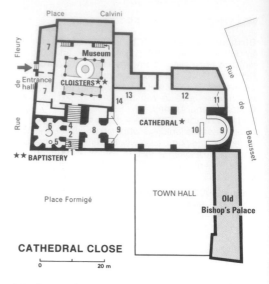

adults. It is believed that originally the bishop washed the feet of candidates in an earthenware basin *(dolium)* (5) found in the ground. Then immersion took place in the octagonal font (6) situated in the centre of the baptistery. A curtain, fixed to columns, surrounded the font. Unction was then administered on the head with holy oil.

Fréjus Cathedral cloisters

★★ **Cloisters** – The 12C-13C cloisters were intended for the chapter canons and comprised two storeys; only one upper gallery remains. The ground level clerestory is formed by a series of twin columns of white marble with varied capitals. The groined vaults which once covered the galleries were replaced by a pine-wood ceiling with exposed beams, decorated in the 15C with curious little **painted panels**★ of animals, chimerae, grotesques and characters from the Apocalypse. On the first floor the columns are finer and the arches round; on the ground floor the arches are pointed – such variations are often found in the architecture of Provence. In the garth there is a well. The west gallery is flanked by a once fortified building (7), where the monks lodged.

Archeological Museum – *First floor.* This museum contains a good collection of Gallo-Roman antiquities recovered from the Fréjus excavations. Particularly outstanding are a rare Roman mosaic with floral motifs and geometrical designs found undamaged, a two-headed Hermes in marble (uncovered in 1970), a head of Jupiter (1C BC) and several statues in marble and bronze.

Cathedral ⊘ – The cathedral is dedicated to Our Lady (south aisle) and to St Stephen (north aisle) and is an early example of Gothic art in Provence. Some parts of the building may date back to an earlier basilica.

The porch (**8**) supporting the 16C belfry was erected 200 years later. Over the apse rises the battlemented tower which once defended the episcopal palace. In the 12C the north aisle was largely rebuilt and covered by a semicircular vault while in the 13C the nave was roofed with pointed vaulting supported on heavy square pillars.

The lovely **choir stalls** (**9**) date from the 15C and the high altar (**10**) of white marble from the 18C. There are also two 14C tombs (**11**); the **altarpiece of St Margaret** (**12**) above the sacristy door is by the Nice artist, Jacques Durandi, and at the end of the aisle, near the tombs (**14**) of the bishops of Camelin (17C), is a remarkable Renaissance Crucifix (**13**) in wood.

Old Bishop's Palace – The façade on the square is modern; the other overlooking rue du Beausset formed part of the palace dating from the 14C which was built in pink Esterel sandstone. It is now the town hall.

Chapter-house – The rusticated façade of the chapter-house, which is known locally as "Le Capitou" or the Provost's House (Maison du Prévôt), looks down on rue de Fleury (**7**). The doorway pierces a fortified tower at ground level; on the first floor are twin windows beneath round arches.

★ ROMAN CITY *1 hour*

Gauls' Gate – The old gateway through the Roman ramparts is half-moon shaped. Of the two towers which once flanked it only one remains. The Roman city covered about 40ha – 99 acres.

★ **Amphitheatre** ⊘ – Built outside the city in the 2C, the amphitheatre is 114m long by 82m wide – 124yds by 93yds (Nîmes 143yds by 109yds; Arles 149yds by 117yds), and could accommodate approximately 10 000 spectators. Half the amphitheatre lies against the flank of the hill crowned by ramparts.

Destined primarily for the pleasure of soldiers and veterans, it was clearly built with an eye to austerity and economy. It differs in this respect from the amphitheatres which were erected at Arles and Nîmes. These were destined for a much more sophisticated public. Bull-fights and other spectacles are held here in summer. On the esplanade is a sculpture, *Le gisant*, which commemorates the Malpasset disaster in 1959. Two columns discovered on a Roman wreck in the gulf of St-Tropez and erected at the junction of the N 7 and D 37 can be seen to the southwest from the lawn surrounding the arena.

In summer a little train *(train de soleil)* ⊘ provides a tour of the site starting from the Esplanade.

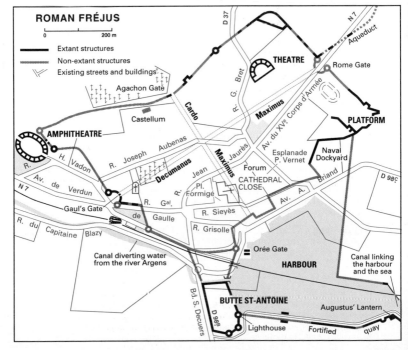

Theatre – This theatre, contemporary with the amphitheatre, consists now of only the radial walls on which once rested the arches supporting the tiers of seats. It measures 84m by 60m – 92yds by 66yds.

Inside, the orchestra pit is clearly visible, together with the stage foundations and the slot into which the curtain was lowered.

Aqueduct – Only pillars and ruined arcades now remain of the aqueduct which reached the city at the height of the ramparts. The water was then carried round beneath the northern parapet walk as far as the water-tower *(castellum)* from which the distribution conduits started. Some interesting remains can be seen in avenue du XVᵉ-Corps-d'Armée.

Platform – Still known as the eastern citadel, this area shows traces of a Roman platform which served as the military headquarters *(praetorium)*: offices, storerooms, lodgings and baths. To the south lay the naval dockyard.

Orée Gate – The gate consists of a fine arch most likely the remains of a chamber which formed part of the harbour baths.

Butte St-Antoine – This mound formed a western citadel as a counterpart to the platform. Boulevard S-Decuers skirts the western wall; the eastern wall would have overlooked the harbour; some towers remain on the southern front, one of which may have been a lighthouse.

Nearby stood the military laundry where the soldiers' uniforms were cleaned by a process using fuller's earth and sulphur vapour.

Augustus' Lantern – *Follow the signed path skirting the south face of the Butte St-Antoine.*

Beside the base of a tower the path turns right on to the southern quay; part of the defence wall still exists.

At the far end of the quay a tower marked the entrance to the harbour and the beginning of the canal leading out to sea. Although the tower was a ruin by the Middle Ages a construction known as Augustus' Lantern was erected on it to act as a landmark to sailors entering the harbour. The wall marking the line of the sea canal stretches away to the southeast.

OLD TOWN *45min on foot*

Starting in place Formigé, walk north towards rue Jean-Jaurès.

Rue de Fleury crosses the cathedral close; at the end *(no 92 right)* there is a handsome doorway in green serpentine from the Maures.

In rue Jean-Jaurès *(left)* the old 18C town hall *(no 112)* has an interesting façade decorated with a curved balcony and a loggia supported on columns. The street follows the line of the medieval ramparts.

The doorway *(no 53 rue Sieyès)* framed by two 17C stone atlantes is all that remains of the former mansion of Abbé Sieyès.

Rue Grisolle follows the line of the medieval enclosure; there is a handsome round tower *(no 71)* and a medieval façade *(no 84 right)*.

The picturesque **passage du Portalet** *(at the end of the street)* connects a string of little old squares.

From place Paul Vernet return to place Formigé.

PORT FRÉJUS

In 1989, after 10 years' work, Fréjus renewed contact with its ancient maritime past in opening a yachting harbour. The complex, the architecture of which, inspired by the work of the Italian architect Palladio, seems to link the town with its Roman origins, offers a complete range of services and accommodation. The different areas are joined by gangways which are the scene in summer of much colourful and lively activity. In the shelter of a breakwater (220m – 240 yards long) there are berths for more than 750 boats. Work presently underway, together with access to a future canal, will provide an additional 1 000 places.

≈ **Fréjus-Plage** – The magnificent beach of fine sand which extends this new area stretches for several kilometres to the west of St-Raphaël. Beside the sea is a memorial recalling the sacrifice of Senegalese infantrymen (l'Armée Noire).

This guide, which is revised regularly,
incorporates tourist information provided at the time of going to press
Changes are however inevitable owing to improved facilities and
fluctuations in the cost of living

SOUVENIRS OF THE NAVY

In 1910 Fréjus resumed an active military rôle with the creation of the first air and sea base in France, where Rolland Garros became famous. At the beginning of the First World War this became a centre for colonial troups from Africa and Asia who established a rest and recreation base here. Fréjus thus became the principal naval base in France. The different cultures represented in the armies at that time have left a legacy of exotic buildings.

On 23 September 1913 the pilot Roland Garros took off from the naval air base at Fréjus in a Morane-Saulnier seaplane to make the first air crossing of the Mediterranean between Fréjus and Bizerte in just over 8 hours.

Take avenue du XV Corps and then N 7 (avenue Général Callies) towards Nice. Leave the car in the car park midway between the two monuments.

Pagode Bouddhique Hong Hien ⊘ – This Buddhist pagoda stands in the centre of an Asian garden. The pagoda was built in 1917 by Vietnamese soldiers who had come to fight in France, then restored and extended during the 1970s. Traditional Vietnamese architecture was the inspiration for the building and the statues in the garden are arranged according to Buddhist tradition. The garden around the Pagoda is planted with exotic flora, including some superb lotus, and contains impressive representations of sacred animals and guardian spirits (dragons, white elephants...).

Leave the car in the car park and continue on foot.

Mémorial des guerres en Indochine ⊘ – At the foot of a hill this imposing circular necropolis symbolically faces the sea.

Since 1987, the remains of 24 000 soldiers and civilians who died on active service in former Indochina have been repatriated and collected here. The bodies of soldiers are housed in a vast colombarium while unidentified bodies are in an ossuary in the crypt. In the historical room in front of the necropolis the events and battles in the history of Indochina are displayed. Illuminated maps and models are used to describe the geographical locations of these events.

From Fréjus take avenue Verdun west and then D 4 for 3km – 2 miles towards Fayence.

Missiri Mosque, Fréjus

G. Biollay/DIAF

Mosquée de Missiri – In a pinewood *(left)* stands a large ochre Sudanese mosque, built in the 1920s by Senegalese soldiers from the naval camp. It is a concrete replica of the celebrated Missiri de Djenné mosque in Mali and consists of a central courtyard with a first-floor gallery around which one can walk, despite the rather dilapidated appearance of the building. Two false termite mounds have been raised nearby to create an impression of Africa.

1km – 0.5 miles after D 4 joins the motorway the Musée des Troupes de marine is on the right.

Musée des troupes de marine ⊘ – This museum is attactively housed in a modern building and contains fine collections of objects and documents which are arranged in chronological order to trace the history of the Marine Corps who, since 1622, have played a decisive rôle both overseas and in world wars. The expeditions during the great colonial period from the Second Empire (1852-70) to 1914 (Africa, Indochina, Madagascar) are recreated using a collection of pieces of equipment, arms, pennants and local crafts, as well as many illustrations (watercolours, drawings, photographs). There are many belongings of General Galliéni, including his study in Indochina and the car which he used in Madagascar from 1900 to 1905. On the first floor there is a table in rare wood inlaid with mother-of-pearl featuring a map of Hanoi in 1906 as well as the famous "zinc palm" from Djibouti.

In the crypt are buried unknown marines from the Infantry Division who fell when fighting the Bavarians at Bazeilles (Ardennes) in 1870.

EXCURSIONS

★ **Parc zoologique** ⊙ - *5km - 3 miles. From Fréjus take avenue de Verdun (N 7) west. Turn right into D 4. After 3km - 2 miles bear right into a narrow road which crosses the motorway.*

The Zoological Park covers about 20ha - 49 acres in the foothills of the Esterel massif. Visitors may walk or drive beneath the umbrella pines, cork oaks and olive trees to see a great variety of birds (pink flamingoes, vultures and parrots) and many wild animals (African elephants, zebras, primates such as lemurs etc) Animal training shows.

Notre-Dame-de-Jérusalem ⊙ - This tiny chapel, situated in the Tour de Mare district near the RN 7, was the last building to be designed by Jean Cocteau. He had finalised the layout and the interior décor as early as 1961 but the chapel remained unfinished until after the poet's death in 1963. It was completed in 1965, thanks to Édouard Dermit.

Remains of Malpasset Dam - *From Fréjus follow the signs to "Nice par l'autoroute A 8". At the last roundabout before the motorway sliproad, take D 37 signposted "Barrage de Malpasset" for 5km - 3 miles. Park the car under the motorway viaduct; 1 hour on foot return.*

The footpath leading off from the barrier goes up the Reyran valley through sparse *garrigue* vegetation and huge scattered blocks of concrete, which were torn off the dam.

The dam is an arch dam, built in 1954 with a capacity of 49 million m³ - 1 730 million ft³. It was intended to relieve the lack of water in the Var coastal region during the summer months. On the evening of 2 December 1959 the torrential rainfall of previous weeks reached the danger limit of the dam and caused the abutments of the arch to collapse. Within 20 minutes, a 55m - 180ft high wave had surged through Fréjus, claiming 400 victims.

The footpath carries on down to the bottom of the valley, leading to the foot of the dam. From here, the size of the breach in the dam's arch makes a striking impression. The turbine is still in the middle of it.

Another viewpoint can be found by going up a footpath which forks to the left of the first one; a little lookout point overlooks the remains of the dam and the west side of the valley.

Étangs de Villepey - *5km - 3 miles. From Fréjus take N 98 west towards St-Tropez.*

These pools are fed both by sea water and by freshwater streams. The Coastal Conservators - Conservatoire du Littoral - are in the process of developing the area as a reserve. A great variety of vegetation is visible: reed-beds in the centre, umbrella pine groves in the south and brackish stretches along N98. In this protected environment more than 200 species of birds, mostly migrants, are thriving. Spring is the best time to see pink flamingoes, grey herons and egrets. Among the nesting birds are several pairs of bee-eaters.

★ **Rocher de Roquebrune** - *Round tour of 29km - 18 miles - about 1 hour 30min. From Fréjus take avenue de Verdun (N 7) west. After about 10km - 6 miles - turn left into D 7 to Roquebrune-sur-Argens. For a description of the tour see ROQUEBRUNE-SUR-ARGENS.*

La GARDE-FREINET

Population 1 466
Michelin map 84 fold 17, 114 fold 36 or 245 fold 48
Local map see Massif des MAURES

In the heart of the Maures massif, between the Argens valley and St-Tropez bay, lies La Garde-Freinet (once called Le Fraxinet). It is a flourishing craft centre. Local wares are displayed in the disused **Chapelle St-Éloi** ⊙ at the entrance to the village. In season the tourist office maintains an information post here.

From the surrounding forests of cork-oaks and chestnut trees comes the raw material for the manufacture of bottle corks and the production of sweet chestnuts sold under the name *Marrons de Luc*. In the autumn, **chestnut festivals** are organised to celebrate the harvest.

SARACEN STRONGHOLD

Owing to its strategic position La Garde-Freinet suffered over a century of occupation by Saracens. In local tradition the name Saracen is applied collectively to the Moors, Arabs, Turks and Berbers who harassed the country from the 8C to the 18C.
After being defeated at Poitiers in 732 by Charles Martel, the Arabs drifted down into Provence. Although driven back several times, they managed to hold on to the region around La Garde-Freinet. On the height which dominates the present village they built a fortress from which they used to descend to pillage inland Provence. It was only in 973 that Count William, the Liberator, managed to expel them.
In contrast to the damage they caused, the Saracens taught the Provençal people about medicine, how to use the bark of the cork-oak and how to extract resin from pine trees. They also introduced the flat house tile and the tambourine.

Ruins of Fort Freinet – *1km – half a mile – plus 45min on foot return. Take GR 9 on the south side of the village. Leave the car in the parking area levelled out at a bend in the road.* There is a good view of the Le Luc Plain and the first Alpine foothills. *A path leads first to a mission cross (the Croix des Maures) and then climbs quite steeply to the fortress ruins.*
The ruins of the feudal castle attributed to the Saracens blended in for many years with the rocky site. Excavation work carried out has resulted in the discovery and uncovering of the foundations of a 15C fortified village. From the summit, the **panorama**★ extends out to sea and a long way inland.
After returning to the car park follow the forest track for 5km – 3 miles to the sign for Roches Blanches.

★ **Panorama des Roches Blanches** – At this spot, known as White Rocks *(for access, walk round the barrier)*, there is a view in all directions: *(left)* the Garde-Freinet forest and the valley of the Argens river, *(right)*, over the slopes of the north Maures and *(east)* the bay of St-Tropez.

GOLFE-JUAN ♨♨

Michelin map 84 fold 9 or 115 fold 35 or 245 fold 37

This popular resort at the foot of the Vallauris hills, clad with orange trees and mimosa, with a 1km – 1 094yd beach of fine sand extending in a shallow curve, overlooks a good anchorage protected by Cap d'Antibes and the Iles de Lérins.
Napoleon landed here in March 1815 *(see ROUTE NAPOLEON)* after escaping from Elba with 1 100 men in the brigantine *Inconstant* and other ships. A mosaic on the quay commemorates the event. When land was sighted, Napoleon summoned the lookout and rewarded him with all the money he had in his pockets.
General Cambronne was the first to land and, in spite of the opposition of the local authorities, tricolour cockades were distributed and soon sported by all. Napoleon's proclamation including his famous remark "Victory will sweep the land; the eagle with the Tricolour will fly from steeple to steeple until he reaches the towers of Notre-Dame" was first posted here. The Emperor rested at a nearby inn while attempts were made to win over the Antibes garrison. As the move proved unsuccessful, he gave orders to march on Cannes.

★★ LA ROUTE NAPOLÉON

57km – 35 miles – about half a day. For a description of the road from Golfe-Juan to the Col de Valferrière see ROUTE NAPOLÉON. For an alternative return route to Golfe-Juan via Grasse see GRASSE: Southern foothills of the Grasse Pre-Alps (in reverse order).

For other excursions from Golfe-Juan see CANNES: Excursions.

GOURDON★

Population 294
Michelin map 84 fold 8 or 115 fold 24 or 245 fold 37

Gourdon "the Saracen" was built on a remarkable **site**★★ on a rock spur *(see Hill Villages)* more than 500m – 1 640ft above the River Loup.
The old houses have been restored and converted into boutiques and workshops.

★★ **Panorama** – There is a magnificent panorama from the little square by the church with a 50km – 30-mile radius covering the coast from the mouth of the Var to Cap Roux and from the Esterel massif inland to the Pic de Courmettes beneath which the River Loup emerges from the upper gorge and winds its way to the coast.

Château ⊘ – The old fortress of Gourdon, built in the 13C on the foundations of an old Saracen fortress and restored in the 17C, contains architectural features of the Saracens (vaulted rooms), of the Tuscans of the 14C and of the Renaissance (doorway at the far end on the main courtyard).

Musée historique – The historical museum occupies the castle's ground floor. The entrance hall contains a fine collection of arms and armour. The monumental chimney in the dining room is 14C and the furniture 17C.

In the drawing room the furniture is 16C; there is an Aubusson tapestry, a secrétaire which belonged to Marie-Antoinette, a *Self-Portrait* by Rembrandt and a fine painting (1500) of the Cologne School: **St Ursula**.

King of Marocco and his army
by Anselme Boix-Vives

The chapel contains a 16C triptych, a *Descent from the Cross* from Rubens' studio, a *Golgotha* of the Flemish School and a polychrome wood sculpture of St Sebastian by El Greco.

The Guard Room contains a collection of 16C and 17C oriental arms.

In Henry IV's Tower, the documents displayed bear the Royal Seal; an opening in the floor reveals the former dungeon.

★ **Musée de Peinture naïve** – Seven rooms on the second floor are hung with an exceptional collection of naïve painting covering the period 1925-70 and including a Douanier-Rousseau (portrait). Other artists represented are the French Séraphine, Bauchant, Vivin, Lefranc, Caillaud, Fous, Rimbert, Bombois and Lagru, the Croats Rabuzin, Kovacic and Vecenaj (all from the Hlebine School, Croatia); O'Brady an American; Greff a Belgian and Vivancos a Spaniard.

Gardens – The terraced gardens were designed by Le Nôtre on three levels and have now been transformed into a botanical centre, preserving typical flora of the Pre-Alps. From the upper terrace the **view**★★ is similar to that described from the church square.

GRASSE★★

Population 41 388
Michelin map 84 fold 8 or 115 fold 14 or 245 fold 37

Grasse has a seductive charm and much to please the visitor, as it stretches out over the foothills of the high limestone plateaux overlocking the perfumed plains which have brought it fame and riches. There are broad views from the modern town with its terraced houses with split-level gardens, while below in the old Provençal town narrow alleys are linked by steep ramps or steps which wind between houses four – or even five – storeys tall.

HISTORICAL NOTES

A small republic (12C) – In the Middle Ages, Grasse was a tiny republic, administered by a council whose members called themselves "consuls by the Grace of God". It based itself on the Italian republics and had diplomatic relations with Pisa and Genoa. By way of Cannes, it exported soap, oil and tanned skins to them; in exchange it received raw hides and arms. Raymond Bérenger, Count of Provence, put an end to this independent existence in 1227.

A great Provençal poet – Bellaud de la Bellaudière (1532-88), a soldier-poet, was born and died in Grasse although he lived mainly in Aix, Marseille and Avignon. His work, inspired by Rabelais and Petrarch, is both tender and vigorous and briefly revived the Provençal language in literature between the troubadours (12C) and Mistral (19C).

Fragonard, child of Grasse (1732-1806) – Fragonard's father, a tanner and glove-maker, tried to make his son, Jean-Honoré, become a lawyer's clerk rather than an artisan, but the young man was possessed by the urge to draw and left for Paris. He painted with Chardin and then Boucher. Winner of the Prix de Rome at the age of 20, he achieved great renown but the Revolution deprived him of his fashionable clientele and dictated a more severe style of painting.

Despite the protection of the artist David, Fragonard preferred to leave Paris and seek refuge in Grasse with his friend, Maubert. Fragonard had brought with him five of his finest canvases, painted for Mme du Barry, who on a capricious whim had refused them. He sold them to his host for a minute sum.

In time the painter became bored in Grasse and returned to Paris, where he lived frugally without, however, losing his carefree air.

One hot afternoon in August 1806 this now elderly artist entered a café to eat an ice-cream and died suddenly of a stroke.

How Grasse became a winter resort – During the winter of 1807-08 the gay and impetuous Princess Pauline Bonaparte, separated from her husband, Prince Borghese, and on bad terms with her brother, the Emperor, came to Grasse to seek relief from family worries and regain her strength in a warm climate. Every day she was carried in a sedan chair to a grove of holm oaks, which she particularly liked and which is now known as her garden "Jardin de la Princesse Pauline". Later, Queen Victoria spent several winters in Grasse at the Grand Hotel and at the Rothschild property.

Napoleon's Passage (2 March 1815) – After the cold welcome he received in Cannes, the Emperor decided to take the Alpine road (Route des Alpes) via Grenoble and advanced on Grasse, but perhaps because of fear of a hostile demonstration from the populace, the Emperor went round the town on what is now boulevard du Jeu-de-Ballon. He camped on what is now known as "Plateau Napoléon", but stayed scarcely an hour.

Perfume industry – Grasse had long specialised in leather work and glove making when in the 16C perfumed gloves came into fashion. This was the beginning of the perfume industry. The great perfume houses were born in the 18 and 19C and still enjoy an international reputation.

There are three manufacturing processes: distillation, *enfleurage* and extraction. **Distillation** is the oldest process. Flowers and water are brought to boiling point in a still. The water and essence are condensed in a "florentine" flask where they separate owing to the difference in density and to their insolubility.

In the 18C **enfleurage** was invented. It uses the property that animal fats have of absorbing the scent of flowers. Fresh flowers are repeatedly laid on different layers of animal fat; washing with alcohol separates the perfume from the fats; a pomade is obtained. Few firms use the process nowadays, as it is labour-intensive.

The latest process is **extraction** by which the flowers yield their perfume in its most concentrated form. The flowers are brought into contact with a solvent which is then evaporated. A concretion *(concrète)* is thus obtained which consists of perfume and wax. One tonne of Grasse jasmine blossoms yields 3kg of concretion – which cost 150 000–175 000F per kg in 1992. The wax is removed using alcohol and the 40% which remains is called absolute *(absolue de concrète)*.

The essences produced in Grasse, which are the base material of the perfume industry, are used locally or sent to Paris where the great perfume houses blend them according to secret formulas to produce the fascinating creations for which France is famous throughout the world.

The Grasse perfume industry has now diversified and has started production of food flavourings.

★ OLD TOWN (VIEILLE VILLE) *2 hours*

★ **Place du Cours (Z)** – This fine terraced promenade offers a charming **view**★ over the cultivated and wooded countryside, which rolls gently to the sea; the huge **fountain (Z V)** dates from the Revolution; a monument to Fragonard stands in the small square where the promenade and boulevard du Jeu-de-Ballon meet.

Go down the steps and turn left into rue Mirabeau below boulevard Fragonard.

★ **Musée d'Art et d'Histoire de Provence (Z M¹)** ⊙ – The museum is in an 18C mansion erected by Louise de Mirabeau, sister of the tribune Mirabeau, when she married the Marquis de Cabris. The mansion, called "Petit Trianon", was planned and decorated by the Marquise with a view to entertaining on a grand scale, but all she ever experienced there were days troubled by court actions and family scenes.

This museum provides a remarkable compendium of the art and history of eastern Provence.

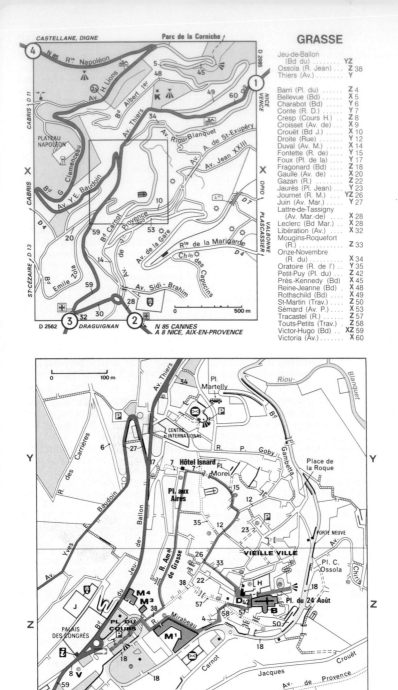

GRASSE

B	Cathédrale	M¹	Musée d'Art	M³	Musée international
D	Tour de Guet		et d'Histoire		de la Parfumerie
K	Jardin de la Princesse		de Provence	M⁴	Musée de la Marine
	Pauline	M²	Villa-musée Fragonard	V	Fontaine

Ground floor – Pottery (18C-19C) from Apt and Le Castellet is displayed in the entrance hall. Some rooms are decorated in the style of Louis XIV and Louis XV. There are two rooms devoted to paintings: one to 19C Provençal artists (Chabaud, Camoin) and the other to reconstructed scenes of life in Grasse in the 18C and 19C.

Basement – On view are the reconstructed kitchen of the Cabris mansion, fine pieces of Moustiers faience and ceramics from Biot and Vallauris. One room contains Provençal cribs and *santons*, and cherubs which once adorned altarpieces. Another features the Gallo-Roman period: pediment from a 4C funeral monument, lamps, flasks, jars. The archeological section evokes the everyday life of local people from prehistoric times to the late Middle Ages; the display includes objects used during funeral rites and in peasant life from day to day. The exhibits were unearthed in local excavations.

Continue along rue Mirabeau and turn left up the slope to place du Barri; take the Touts-Petits short cut and steps on the right to place du Petit-Puy.

Cathedral (Z B) – The cathedral dates back to the late 10C-11C but was restored and remodelled in the 17C; the double staircase at the entrance, with its wide stone handrail, and the two crypts were added in the 18C. Note the panels of the main door (1721) in the façade, adorned with horizontal bands and arcading. The high narrow nave, with heavy pointed rib-vaulting, marks the beginning of the Gothic style in Provence; together with the robust round pillars it gives a grandiose air to the whole building. The organ (1855) is by Junk of Toulouse. In the south aisle there are three **paintings**★ by Rubens *(The Crown of Thorns,* the *Crucifixion* and *St Helen in Exaltation of the Holy Cross)* executed in Rome in 1601 and offered to the town in the 19C by a citizen; a fine **triptych** attributed to Louis Bréa representing St Honoratus between St Clement and St Lambert; the *Mystic Marriage of St Catherine* by Sébastien Bourdon (17C); finally, **The Washing of the Feet**, one of the rare religious canvases by Fragonard.

Place du 24-Août (Z) – From the far side of the square, the east end and belltower of the cathedral can be seen to good effect. There is also a fine **view** eastwards over the Grasse countryside. Close at hand is the so-called Clock Tower (Tour de l'Horloge).

Return to place du Petit-Puy.

Tour de Guet (Z D) – The town hall, formerly the Bishop's Palace, boasts a massive square watchtower in red tufa stone, dating from the 12C and bearing an inscription in memory of the poet Bellaud de la Bellaudière.

Place aux Aires (Y) – At the centre stands an elegant three-tiered **fountain**. The old houses which border the square are built over uneven arcades. **Hôtel Isnard** on the north side, a town house built in 1781, has a fine door and attractive wrought-iron balcony at first floor level. Every morning there is a noisy **flower and vegetable market** in progress beneath the aged lotus trees.

Rue Amiral-de-Grasse (Z) – Fontmichel House (no 18) was built in the 17C.

ADDITIONAL SIGHTS

Villa-musée Fragonard (Z M²) ⊙ – In this elegant country house Fragonard took refuge during the Revolution, when it belonged to Maubert, a local glove-maker and perfumer. It now belongs to the municipality and serves as a cultural centre and museum devoted to a whole family of artists. A fine park surrounds it. One of the ground floor rooms contains copies (originals in the Frick Collection in New York City) of the panels painted by Fragonard between 1771 and 1772 for the Countess du Barry. The stairwell is decorated with republican and Masonic allegories executed in *trompe-l'œil* and monochrome by Fragonard's son, Alexandre-Évariste (1780-1850) at the age of 14. Upstairs the **Fragonard Room**★ displays a variety of the artist's work: original drawings and etchings, sketches, paintings – two self-portraits, *Landscape with Washerwomen*, *The White Bull* and *The Three Graces*. In a room on the left works by Alexandre-Évariste are displayed, including *Reading the Bible* after Greuze. Another room is devoted to a grandson, Théophile Fragonard (1806-76): *Embarkation for Cythera* and *Visiting the Sick*. There are also canvases by Marguerite Gérard (1761-1837), Fragonard's pupil and sister-in-law *(Portrait of a Girl)*.

★ **Musée international de la parfumerie (Z M³)** ⊙ – This museum is dedicated to one of the most famous activities in Grasse. It occupies three buildings of different periods: a mansion with neo-Classical façade from the time of Napoleon III and two late 19C buildings. The exhibits cover more than 3 000 years of the history of perfume-making in the world.

C.J. Muzzin/Musée international de la parfumerie. Grasse

Perfume bottle

The ground floor, set up like a perfume factory, presents the different techniques used to make perfume from the extraction of the sweet-smelling raw materials to the end product, with machines and explanatory panels. On the mezzanine is the research laboratory. Exhibited on the first floor are different kinds of perfume vessels (flasks, scent bottles...), boxes, chests, and posters which indicate man's involvement with perfume, and other fragrance-related products (toiletries, cosmetics...) through the ages; famous names are evoked: Guerlain, Patou, Lanvin, Chanel... Notice too the travel accessories belonging to Marie-Antoinette.

A greenhouse, on the terrace, contains many different local and tropical plants used in the manufacture of perfume.

Musée de la marine (**Z M⁴**) ⊙ – Housed in five vaulted rooms in the Hôtel Pontevès-Morel, the marine museum traces the distinguished career of Admiral de Grasse, who was born at Bar-sur-Loup *(See Le BAR-SUR-LOUP)*, and his involvement in the American War of Independence. Among the 29 models of ships are 18C sailing ships, a Maltese galley, the flagship *La Ville de Paris* (Washington and Lafayette came on board on 17 September 1781), and the cruiser *De Grasse*, decommissioned in 1974.

Perfumeries ⊙ – Fragonard *(20 boulevard Fragonard)*, Galimard *(route de Cannes)* and Molinard *(60 boulevard Victor-Hugo)* are open to the public and give a general idea of the manufacturing process.

Jardin de la Princesse Pauline (**X K**) – *Access via avenue Thiers, boulevard Alice-de-Rothschild and boulevard de la Reine-Jeanne.*
There is a good **panorama**★ of Grasse, the Massif du Tanneron, the Esterel and the coast from the viewing-table in Princess Pauline's garden.

Parc communal de la Corniche (**X**) – *Access as above; then turn a sharp left into boulevard Bellevue and then right into boulevard du Président-Kennedy; 30min on foot return.*
At the bend, a path to the right *(sign)* leads to the edge of the steep Pre-Alps of Grasse.
From the lookout point, the **view**★★ extends from Baou de St-Jeannet and from the Tanneron mountains to the peaks of the Esterel; on the horizon can also be seen the bays of La Napoule and Juan and the Iles de Lérins.

EXCURSIONS

★★ **Préalpes de Grasse** *Round tour of 104km – 65 miles – about 5 hours*

From Grasse take boulevard G-Clemenceau and turn left into D 11.

After crossing the "Plateau Napoléon", the road rises towards Cabris offering fine **views** of the Grasse countryside.

★ **Cabris** – *See CABRIS.*

Bypass Spéracèdes by turning right into D 513 at the beginning of the village.
From Tignet, there is a beautiful **view** of Cabris and Grasse. The D 13 runs through magnificent sloping olive groves, passing the La Graou prehistoric tumulus.

St-Cézaire-sur-Siagne – From its **site**★ dominating the steep valley of the Siagne, the walls and towers of this interesting village testify to its feudal past. Standing in its own churchyard is a pleasant Romanesque chapel which shelters the Gallo-Roman tomb of Julia Sempronia. From the church a marked path leads to a **viewpoint**★ *(viewing table).*
Return to the village and turn left.

Puits de la Vierge – The road makes a detour past a group of nine wells, probably Roman in origin.

From St-Cézaire take D 5, turn right into D 613 which leads to the St-Cézaire caves.

★ **Grottes de St-Cézaire** ⊙ – The caves, hollowed out of the limestone, keep a constant temperature of 14°C – 57°F. Both the stalactites, which have great musical resonance, and the stalagmites are remarkable for the variety of their shapes – toadstools, flowers, animals – and their red colour, which is due to the presence of iron oxide in the rock. There are also beautiful rock crystallisations.
The caves, which comprise several chambers with evocative names such as the "Hall of Draperies", the "Organ Chamber", the "Fairies' Alcove", the "Great Hall", are connected by narrow passages one of which arrives suddenly at the edge of an abyss, 40m – 130ft below ground level.
Return to the crossroads on D 5.

Col de la Lèque – *5km – 3 miles – about 15min.* To the right of the road leading up to the pass, near Puades, there is a group of tumuli. From the pass and on the return journey there are successive **views**★ of the Gorges de la Siagne and the village of St-Cézaire piled up in its mountainous amphitheatre on the bluff.

Continue towards St-Cézaire-sur-Siagne and turn right into D 105.

Gorges de la Siagne – The road runs up through the rich vegetation in the deep gorge which the waters of the Siagne have worn in the limestone.
After crossing the Siagne (from the bridge, **view** up and down the gorge), turn right into D 656, a very steep and narrow road.
After serpentining steeply above the gorge, the road broadens out into a colourful rock circus before entering a wooded valley which brings it to the plateau. Turn left into D 56 following the hillside. Fig and olive trees grow on the terraces which are retained by low drystone walls.

Cross the Siagnole.

Sources de la Siagnole – *30min on foot return.* On the right beyond the bridge a path leads to a very pleasant spot where several Vauclusian springs rise to form the River Siagnole.

Roche Taillée – There is a sign to indicate the remains of a Roman aqueduct *(on the left of the road)* which carried water from around Mons to Fréjus on the coast and is still in use. **View**★ eastwards towards Grasse.

Turn right into D 37 and then right again into D 563 to reach Mons.

The road is cut into the hillside high above the Siagnole gorge. Once over the Col d'Avaye, the road offers a magnificent **view**★★ reaching as far as the Esterel.

★ **Mons** – *See MONS.*
The mountainous and wooded environs of Mons give way to an arid landscape with outcrops of white rock. At the Col de Valferrière (alt 1 169m – 3 835ft) turn right into N 85, the Route Napoléon.

★★ **Route Napoléon** – *The road as far as Grasse offers spectacular views of the Riviera coast and is described in the opposite direction under ROUTE NAPOLÉON.*

★★ Gorges du Loup *Round tour of 38km – 24 miles*

From Grasse take D 2085, ① on the town plan, going northeast.

The northeastern suburb of Grasse comprises attractive villas scattered among olive, cypress and orange trees.

Magagnosc – *900m – 984yds – after the town signpost and immediately past the restaurant "La petite auberge" turn right at the sign: Église St-Laurent.* There are two churches. **St-Laurent** ⊘, in Tuscan style, is adorned with some fine stained glass and a copy of a Byzantine fresco by the contemporary painter, Robert Savary, who also decorated the walls and ceiling of **St-Michel**, the Romanesque chapel of the White Penitents.
From the churchyard there is a **view**★ of the sea near Cannes and of the Esterel massif.

Return to D 2085 and at Pré-du-Lac take the first road, D 203, to Châteauneuf-Grasse.

Châteauneuf-Grasse – This elegant hill village perched on a promontory exudes plenty of Provençal atmosphere with its lovely old houses grouped together on the overhang. The narrow stepped streets and the vaulted passageways are overlooked by the wrought-iron campanile of the church. Inside the church there is a lovely 18C altarpiece.

From the town head east towards Opio – a good view of the plain. At the crossroads turn left into D 3 and continue as far as Pré-du-Lac, turn right into D 2210.

The picturesque **site**★ of Le Bar-sur-Loup comes into view.

Le Bar-sur-Loup – *See Le BAR-SUR-LOUP.*

Continue to Pont-du-Loup. For a description of the Gorges du Loup see Vallée du LOUP. At Pré-du-Lac take D 2085 to return to Grasse.

To plan a special itinerary:
  – *consult the* **Map of Touring Programmes** *which indicates the tourist regions, the recommended routes, the principal towns and main sights*
  – *read the descriptions in the* **Sights** *section which include Excursions from the main tourist centres*
Michelin Maps nos 114 and 115 indicate scenic routes, places of interest, viewpoints, rivers, forests...

GRIMAUD*

Population 3 322
Michelin map 245, fold 48, 84 fold 17 or 114 fold 50

This large hill village owes its name to the Grimaldi family who once owned it. In the 10C Gibelin de Grimaldi received the fief from the Comte de Provence in recognition of his help in expelling the Saracens from Provence.

Isolated from the summer bustle of the coast, the village has retained its Provençal character with its little shady squares and fountains and its winding alleyways enlivened by the many craftsmen.

In summer, leave the car in the car park near the graveyard.

OLD VILLAGE

Walk towards the centre of the village from the car park and take one of the lanes which lead into place Neuve with its remarkable monumental fountain. The rue des Templiers has fine basalt arcades and serpentine doorways, for example on the maison des Templiers; this leads to St-Michel, a church built in the form of a cross in Romanesque style, dating from the 11C.

CHATEAU

The castle, built at the beginning of the 11C, originally consisted of three enclosures surrounded by four three-storeyed towers. The imposing ruins of this great building were left after the demolition ordered by Mazarin in 1655.

From the upper covered way there are fine **views**★ of the Maures and the Golfe de St-Tropez.

On summer evenings there are shows at the castle.

On the hill in the graveyard beyond there is a charming windmill, and from here a fine **view**★ of the Golfe.

EXCURSIONS

Chapelle N-D-de-la-Queste – *3km towards Port-Grimaud*. This chapel, built by the monks of the abbey of St-Victor in Marseille, houses a remarkable Baroque altarpiece in gilded wood illustrated with scenes from the life of the Virgin. There is a pilgrimage here on 15 August.

★ **Port-Grimaud** – *See PORT-GRIMAUD.*

HYÈRES*

Population 48 043
Michelin map 84 fold 16, 114 folds 46, 47 or 245 fold 47
Local map see Massif des MAURES

Hyères, lying in a well-sheltered setting, is the most southerly and the oldest of the Riviera climatic resorts. The old quarters cling to the southern slope of the Castéou hillside (204m – 670ft) and overlook the modern town and the anchorage enclosed by Cap Bénat and the Giens peninsula. The new harbour is used by pleasure boats and the ferries which ply between the mainland and the Iles d'Hyères. The modern town's most outstanding feature is its wide streets lined with magnificent palm trees.

Early history – Excavations on the coast at L'Almanarre reveal that Greeks from Marseille set up a trading station called **Olbia**, which was succeeded by a Roman town – Pomponiana – and a nunnery, called St-Pierre-d'Almanarre in the Middle Ages.

In the early Middle Ages the inhabitants moved up the hill to where the Lords of Fos had built a castle. Agriculture and particularly the salt marshes brought Hyères success and the port of L'Aygade (subsequently silted up) was a base for the Crusaders; **St Louis** disembarked there in 1254 on returning from the Seventh Crusade. Soon afterwards the town passed to the Counts of Provence. In 1620 the castle was demolished by Louis XIII and Hyères declined in favour of Toulon.

Modern revival – The town became well known in the 18C and 19C, particularly to the English, as an inland resort; 20C tourism has led to the development of the beaches.

Hyères is a lively town throughout the year and not solely dependent on tourism. The surrounding plain is extensively cultivated to produce early fruit (strawberries, peaches) and vegetables; great vineyards thrive in excellent growing conditions. The town also exports potted palms and ornamental plants.

★ OLD TOWN (VIEILLE VILLE) *1hour 15min*

Porte Massillon (Y R) – The gate leads into rue Massillon, a bustling shopping street, once the main street of the old town; many Renaissance doorways.

Place Massillon (Y 29) – In the square, where the daily market is held, stands the 12C tower, **Tour St-Blaise**, last remnant of a Knights Templar commandery. To the left is the rue Rabaton where the great preacher, Massillon (1663-1742) was born (no 7; **Y B**).

Place St-Paul (Y 49) – From this terrace square, once the site of the cloisters of the Collégiale St-Paul, there is a good **panorama★**(viewing table).

Ancienne collégiale St-Paul (Y) ⊘ – The oldest parts of the former collegiate church go back to the 12C; the belltower is pure Romanesque. A fine Renaissance door and monumental stairway give access.

The narthex, which is probably the nave of the original structure, to which a ceiling has been added, is covered with votive offerings (some dating from the 17C). To the left of the entrance is a large **crib** of Provençal *santons* with the medieval town as a backdrop. The Gothic nave, set at right angles to the original church, has Flamboyant Gothic side chapels. Altarpieces adorned with wreathed columns, reliquaries and gilded wooden statues date from 17C.

Old town, Hyères

Old streets – Porte St-Paul (gateway) near the collegiate church is incorporated in a handsome **Renaissance house (Y E)** with a turret at one corner. Pass beneath and follow rue St-Paul to rue Ste-Claire where the Porte des Princes stands framing the chevet and belltower of the collégiale St-Paul.

Retrace your steps to rue de Paradis where there is a fine **Romanesque house (Y F)** (no 6) which has been restored (twin windows with slim columns).

Return through the Porte St-Paul and take picturesque rue Barbacane to rue St-Esprit which runs into rue Bourgneuf. Continue to place de la République with its shady plane trees.

St-Louis (Y) ⊘ – This former church of the Franciscan convent has three elegant doors beneath round arches, a rose window and a corniche. It brings to mind the Italian Romanesque style. The nave, with its thick-ribbed pointed vaulting, ends in a square apse as do the side aisles. The whole is an example of the transition from Romanesque to Provençal Gothic.

Town of palm trees

Hyères is famous for palm trees as its nickname suggests. The cultivation of palms began to expand in 1867 and reached its height in the 1930s. There are now no less than ten varieties named Hyères palms. The renown of these trees has brought about their export as far as Saudi Arabia. In Hyères itself, a stroller can enjoy the exotic charm of the palms in the avenue Godillot, one of the most attractive roads in France, and in three public gardens: the Casino gardens, Roy gardens and Denis gardens. In the fine Olbius-Risquier gardens there is a complete range of existing species.

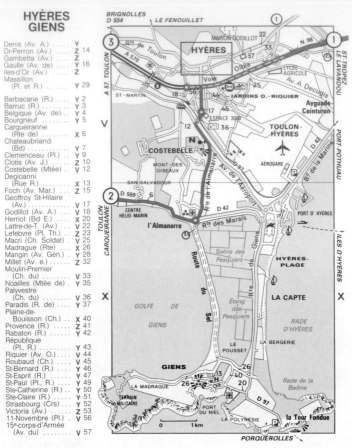

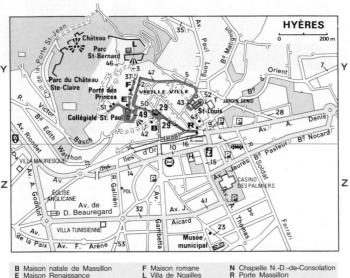

B Maison natale de Massillon
E Maison Renaissance
F Maison romane
L Villa de Noailles
N Chapelle N.-D.-de-Consolation
R Porte Massillon

ADDITIONAL SIGHTS

★ **Jardins Olbius-Riquier** (ᴠ) ⊘ – The gardens are very extensive (6.5ha – 16 acres) and grow a rich variety of tropical plants, particularly varieties of palms and cacti, in the open.
In the **greenhouse** the more delicate varieties of tropical and equatorial plants can be seen together with a few rare animals.
The gardens include a small zoo in a special enclosure, and a lake supports several species of water birds.

★ **Notre-Dame-de-Consolation (v N)** ⊘ – There has been a sanctuary on the top of Costebelle hill since the 11C. The present chapel was built in 1955. There is a huge coloured sculpture of Our Lady against the cross which forms the belltower's vertical axis. A series of sculpted groups depicting the main events in the Virgin's life are picked out in cement and stone on the principal front between the windows. The clean lines of the interior are complemented by the Apostle sculptures in the apse and the play of colours from the huge **stained-glass windows**★ designed by Gabriel Loire to illustrate the cult of Mary and the history of the sanctuary.

The neighbouring promenade *(viewing table)* gives a **view**★ of the Hyères *(left)* and Toulon *(right)* anchorages.

Parc St-Bernard (Jardin de Noailles) (Y) – *From Cours de Strasbourg drive north, take avenue Paul-Long following the signs: montée de Noailles on the left.* The park encloses the castle ruins and boasts a huge variety of Mediterranean flowers.

From the terraces there is a picturesque **view**★: from the old town and the Collégiale St-Paul, over the Pic des Oiseaux and Costebelle hill to the peninsula and the islands; to the east is the outline of the Massif des Maures.

Villa de Noailles (Y L) ⊘ – In 1923 the Noailles, a rich couple of patrons, commissioned a modern winter villa from the Belgian architect Mallet-Stevens, which was to be as open to the sunlight as possible. The villa (1 600 m² – 1914 sq yds), which includes a covered swimming pool and about 60 rooms, was one of the first modern homes on the Riviera. All the famous artists of the 1920s (Picasso, Dali...) attended the extravagant parties at the villa. The American photographer Man Ray shot some sequences of a surrealist film here and Buñuel set L'*Âge d'or* in the villa.

After a long period of neglect, the first stage of restoration in 1986 has meant that exhibitions can be organised on the first floor. After the restoration is complete, a project for a cultural centre is under consideration.

Château Ruins (Y) – *Same route as for Parc St-Bernard but go round the righthand side of the park to the car park. Take the well-trodden path up the hill (45min on foot return).*

The Château d'Hyères passed from the Lords of Fos to the Counts of Provence, who rebuilt it in the 13C. The ruins are quite extensive, particularly the towers and crenellated keep which dominate the town.

From the top *(viewing table)* a vast **panorama**★ of the coast and the interior can be seen.

Musée municipal (Z) ⊘ – The Greek and Roman archeological specimens displayed in this museum come from the excavations at Olbia.

Collections of minerals, fossils, shells, fish, birds. Gallery of local artists. Louis XV and Louis XVI furniture.

Parc du château Ste-Claire (Y) ⊘ – A fine villa built in 1850 by Colonel Voutier the man who discovered the Venus de Milo, sits in the middle of this park filled with exotic plants. The château now houses the administrative offices of the Parc national de Port-Cros.

Seaside architecture

The development of winter tourism in Hyères dates from the middle of the 19C, with the mass visits of the English, including many celebrities: Queen Victoria, the novelist R L Stevenson, and some great French figures: Victor Hugo, Michelet and Maupassant. The resort is therefore endowed with the luxurious hotels necessary for its exacting visitors: Hôtel des Palmiers, Grand Hôtel des Iles d'Or and the extension of the venerable Park Hôtel where the young Bonaparte stayed.

Alexis Godillot, supplier to the armies of the Second Empire and owner of a quarter of the town, decided to launch "his" resort by rechristening it "Hyères-les-Palmiers", and by entrusting the architect Chapoulard with the building of various follies in composite style which can still be seen, for example in avenue Riondet.

There are other buildings, in the most electic styles, throughout the residential districts; for example the "Villa Tunisienne" (XX), avenue Beauregard, built by Chapoulard around 1870, the Villa Thosolan, avenue du XVᵉ corps, the Villa Roux, rue de Verdun, the Villa Mauresque (XX) and the Collège Anglo-Français.

EXCURSIONS

★ **Le Fenouillet Summit** *4km – 2.5 miles – plus 30min on foot return*

From Hyères take avenue de Toulon then turn right into a signed road to Le Fenouillet.

From the neo-Gothic **chapel** there is a marked path to Le Fenouillet, the highest point of the Maurettes (291m – 955ft) with a very good **panorama**★ particularly of the Hyères and Toulon anchorages and the surrounding mountains.

Parc des oiseaux exotiques ⊘

East by N 98 through La Londe-les-Maures towards St-Raphaël

A signposted trail through the park of mainly eucalyptus and pine trees leads past large aviaries containing, one after another, most species of parrot, toucans, hornbills, large birds such as the hooded cassowary and emus all the way from Australia. Various types of wader complete this interesting visit.

★★ **Gien Peninsula**

Double Tombolo – The Gien peninsula is a rare natural phenomenon: the former island of Giens is linked to the mainland by two coastal bars (each 4km – 2.5 miles long). In similar cases, such as Quiberon, a single tombolo (sandbar) has formed which joins the island to the coast. At Giens, the combination of particular conditions – the mouths of two rivers, the Gapeau and the Roubaud, one on each side of Giens, coupled with strong currents at sea have allowed the formation of a double tombolo on the rocky seabed.

The parallel bars enclose a lagoon which provides an ideal habitat for birds. Pink flamingoes and avocets are common here. The best time to see flamingoes is in mid-September when up to 1 500 birds come here. An original, if not unique, vegetation has been recorded here: glasswort, sea rocket, white mignonette and thorny rushes.

A project aimed at replanting posidonia is underway in the gulf of Giens; this will halt the erosion of the sea-bed and encourage the revival of species which live in it. In fact the underwater life concentrated in this area is dependent on this plant. With its disappearance, caused by man, the sand is no longer protected and the beaches are washed away by the sea.

For three decades the west tombolo has been eroded by wind and by equinoctial storms which breach the seawalls, sweep away the beach and cover parts of the road with sand. A project by the Conservatoire du Littoral is now in progress to preserve this site.

> The western tombolo at Giens, under the protection of the Conservatoire du Littoral, is governed by strict regulations:
> - Vehicular traffic is permitted from Easter to All Saints' Day on the tombolo road, with no parking en route; the road is closed the rest of the year.
> - Parking is allowed only in the two car parks at each end of the western tombolo.
> - To reach the beaches, use only the marked paths, without walking on the dunes or vegetation, and avoiding the marked protected zones.
> - Drying sails or any canvas on the vegetation is not allowed.

L'Almanarre – Long sandy beach near the site of the Greek town of Olbia *(see above)*.

Take the salt road (Route du sel; accessible only in summer) down the western side of the peninsula.

This picturesque route passes a vast saltmarsh (400ha – 988 acres) and then L'Étang des Pesquiers, home of many waterbirds.

Marais salants – In the Hyères region are two working salt-marshes: the salins des **Pesquiers** on the Giens tombolo and the **Vieux Salins**. The combined production of the two salt-works varies between 23 000 and 30 000 tonnes a year. In the **salt tables**, vast rectangles of 2 to 4 ha – 5 to 10 acres, the sea water deposits its salt. The constant dry wind speeds evaporation while concentration is aided by mechanical gyrating movements. The "harvest" or collection of the salt takes place in the last week of August (according to tradition between harvest and grape-picking).

The operation involves first lifting the salt crust which has formed on the salt tables – this is the job of the *détoureur*. This crust, or **sel gris** (grey salt), is kept apart for use for example on snow-covered roads. The white salt, washed and fit for consumption, is collected and piled into immense white mountains **(camelles)**, which advertise far and wide the presence of salt-marshes.

Les Pesquiers salt-works, Gien Peninsula

Giens The village, in the middle of a former island, is a small seaside resort. The castle ruins form a mound from which there is a magnificient **panorama**★★ (viewing table). The poet St-John Perse stayed here and lies at rest in the cemetery. To the south is the little port of Niel, surrounded by a lovely pinewood.
Drive east from the village to the Tour Fondue.

Tour Fondue – Boats sail from here to the Ile de Porquerolles. The name comes from the fort built under Richelieu to control the narrows of la Petite Passe, which was also protected by forts on the small islands of Grand and Petit Ribaud *(private property)*. There is a beautiful view of the islands and the Giens peninsula.

Tour of the peninsula on foot – *(about 5 hours for 18km – 11 miles)*. The route, which is partly signed, links the port of la Madrague to Badine beach. Take D97 along the eastern side of the peninsula – fine views of the Hyères plain and the Maures. Continue to Hyères-Plage via la Bergerie and la Capte set in pinewoods.

Hyères-Plage – A small forest of umbrella pines shelters this village. Boats leave from the port for the Iles d'Hyères.

Ayguade-Ceinturon – This is the old port of Hyères, where St Louis disembarked on his return from the Seventh Crusade. It is now a pleasant seaside resort. Continue via **Berriau-Plage** to **Port-Pothuau**, a picturesque little fishing port.

Almanarre "funboarding" festival

Almanarre beach stretches (6km – 3.7 miles) along the salt-marshes of L'Étang des Pesquiers, facing the Golfe de Giens. On windless days it is popular with families on holiday but, when the *mistral* starts to blow, it is transformed into a mecca for "funboarding". The beach offers ideal conditions because it is protected by the slight tombolo to the east, the low-lying land to the west and by cap de Carqueiranne from the heavy swell out at sea.

Almanarre has thus become the top windsurfing location on the Riviera. in 1966 it was chosen as the venue for the European championships for production boards and funboarding.

The beach also attracts many spectators who come to marvel at the spectacular acrobatics, particularly "jibes" – amazing somersaults in the air which have become the symbol of funboarding.

There are schools all along the beach offering windsurfing lessons for beginners and for more advanced practitioners.

Iles d'HYÈRES★★★

Michelin map 84 folds 16 and 17, 114 folds 47, 48, 49 or 245 folds 47 and 48
Local map see Massif des MAURES

These well-known islands, which became detached from the Massif des Maures in a relatively recent geological age, lie close the south entrance to Hyères harbour. They are also known as the Golden Isles – Iles d'Or – a name given to them during the Renaissance, no doubt due to the fact that in certain lights their mica shale rocks have golden reflections.
The short sea crossing and the variety of walks on the islands – on the coast or inland – provide unforgettable memories.

FROM PIRATES TO LIBERATORS

Land of asylum – In the 5C the monks of Lérins arrived, succeeding the Ligurians, the Greeks and the Romans as the islands' overlords. In the following centuries they were constantly attacked by pirates until François I raised the islands of Port-Cros and Levant to the status of the marquisate of the Iles d'Or on condition that the marquis keep them under cultivation and protect them from pirates. Despite exemption from taxes, the islands lacked manpower until a right of asylum was established under which criminals were granted immunity provided they remained on the islands. This idea had unfortunate consequences; jailbirds swarmed to the islands, where they turned to piracy, even being so bold as to attempt the capture of one of the king's ships from Toulon. Only in the reign of Louis XIV did the last of these dubious characters leave.

A British coup – In 1793, after the capture of Toulon by the Revolutionaries *(see TOULON)*, British and Spanish squadrons anchored off the Iles d'Hyères. The commander of Fort Ste-Agathe at Porquerolles, forgotten on his island by the French authorities, had only the vaguest idea of what was happening on the mainland. The British admiral invited him on board his flagship and the commander went unsuspectingly. While the whisky was circulating, British sailors landed, surprised the garrison and tried to blow up the fort. The ships then raised anchor taking with them, as prisoner, the crestfallen commander.

Allied Landing (August 1944) – During the night of 14 to 15 August, American troops landed on the islands of Port-Cros and Levant and silenced German batteries which could have had Allied shipping lying at anchor within their range.

★★★ ILE DE PORQUEROLLES

Porquerolles, the largest and most westerly of the Hyères Islands, measures 7km long by 3 wide – 4 by 2 miles – and was called Protè (First) by the Greek colonists who came to live along its shores. The north coast is well supplied with sandy beaches bordered by pine trees, heather, arbutus and scented myrtle; the south coast is steep and rugged with one or two inlets which are easily accessible. There are few inhabitants inland, only vineyards, pine and eucalyptus woods and thick Mediterranean vegetation.
The major part of the island has been acquired by the State to protect the natural heritage. To this end, a **conservation area** consisting mainly of forests was set up in 1972 and a **botanical conservatory** in 1979.

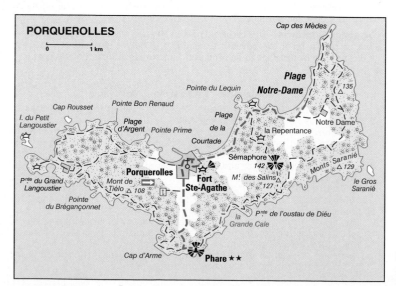

116

PRACTICAL INFORMATION ABOUT LES ILES D'OR

Access - From
- La Tour Fondue (Giens Peninsular) and Hyères port ☎ 04 94 57 44 07 (TLV, Transports Littoral Varois); in season there is a tour of the three islands *(Trois Iles)*, starting from La Tour Fondue, which includes a visit of 1 to 2 hours to each island;
- Toulon, on board the catamaran *Ville de Toulon* which offers trips with underwater views in season;
- Le Lavandou, Cavalaire (☎ 04 94 71 01 02 Vedettes des Iles d'Or), direct to Porquerolles or Port-Cros; L'Ile du Levant is accessible only on a round tour including Port-Cros.

Before leaving
During periods of major fire risk, the ALARME plan is in force (announced before embarkation); it means that access is limited to the beaches, the coast path and the villages. Bicycles are not allowed on Port-Cros.

Ile de Porquerolles
The best way to tour the island is by bicycle. Bikes can be hired near the port and in the vicinity of the town hall. There are many places for refreshment – in the road leading from the town hall, which is lined with restaurants, and in several more peaceful spots, such as at the foot of Ste-Agathe fort.
As watering-places are rare, especially in high season, it is advisable to obtain supplies at the fountain in place d'Armes before setting off round the island.

Ile de Port-Cros (National Park)

The whole of the island of Port-Cros, both land and sea, is a nature reserve to which strict regulations apply:
- vehicular traffic is prohibited on the island;
- smoking is not allowed outside the village and no plants of any kind should be removed;
- animals are permitted but must be on a lead;
- harpooning is forbidden throughout the area of the Parc National de Port-Cros; line fishing is forbidden within a radius of 50m - 164ft from the island's coast;
- drinking water should be carried since supplies are very rare on Port-Cros and there is no public watering-place; there are, however, several shops selling drinks in the village. In season there is an information centre in the first building to the left of the landing stages (☎ 04 94 05 90 17). Trips in a glass-bottomed boat are available on board *Marabel Seascope*.

Port-Cros, Iles d'Hyeres

E. Baret

Ile du Levant
The accessible areas of the island are in the west and north; in the north a channel is reserved for water sports and an area is allocated to windsurfing. Apart from the cafés on the landing stage, the only restaurants are at Héliopolis, above the port. The principal beaches, reached by the coast path on each side of the landing stages, are for the exclusive use of nudists.

Diving
The great depths and the lack of strong currents around the islands and in the Baie de Carqueiranne provide ideal conditions for diving as well as for underwater photography of the many wrecks. There are several diving clubs in Hyères and La Londe; *Sun Plongée* in Port-Cros and *Porquerolles Plongée* in Porquerolles.

La Palud cove, Port-Cros Island

An unusual destiny – For 60 years this island was the private property of one single family. In 1911, a Belgian engineer, F-Joseph Fournier, having made his fortune in Mexico, decided to give Porquerolles as a wedding gift to his young bride. Once settled on the island with his family and an army of gardeners, he attempted to recreate the atmosphere of a south American hacienda by importing exotic plants. He began with the cultivation of several exotic fruits then unknown in France: pineapple, kumquats. Along the walks are South American plants such as the bellombra with its enormous roots. Also witness to this replanting, the 180 ha – 445 acres of vines originally planted have been reduced to half the quantity but continue to produce a reputable rosé. This was the first vineyard to gain the appellation A.O.C. Côtes de Provence *(see PRACTICAL INFORMATION: Food and Drink)*.

The village – The small village of Porquerolles, which lies at the end of a minute anchorage now used as a harbour for pleasure boats, has given its name to the whole island. The village was built by the military in the middle of the 19C and consists of a main square, a modest church, containing an unusual Stations of the Cross carved by a soldier with his penknife, and a few fishermen's cottages. To this nucleus, which resembles a North African colonial settlement rather than a Provençal village, hotels and private houses have been added.

Fort Ste-Agathe ⊘ – This fort is the first building to be seen before landing on the island. The fort, topping a mound which overlooks the port, occupies an extremely strategic position. Its walls in the shape of a trapezium are surmounted by a massive corner tower, all that remains of the original structure built by François I in 1532. The English ruined and then burnt the fort in 1793 and the reconstruction was begun in 1810 with buildings adapted to new military requirements. The round tower is constructed on a massive scale: walls 4m – 13ft thick, 20m – 66ft in diameter and 15m – 49ft high. The Parc de Port-Cros has organised exhibitions in the tower's various rooms on underwater archeology, objects excavated, and on the history of the islands and Hyères harbour. The great circular room has a ceiling (6m – 20ft high) and fine wooden beams. From the terrace on top of the tower, with its five embrasures for large-bore cannon, there is a magnificent **view**★ over most of the island: la Courtade beach, Notre-Dame beach, the Sémaphore peak (summit 142m – 466ft) to the east and to the west wooded hills obscuring the beaches.

Walks

★★ **Lighthouse Walk** – *1hour 30min on foot return.*
This walk to the lighthouse *(phare)* is a "must" even for tourists with only a few hours to spend on the island. The **lighthouse** ⊘, which stands on the most southerly point of the island some 96m – 307ft up, has a beam which carries 54km – 34 miles.
There is a **panorama**★★ extending over most of the island: the Langoustier hills, Fort Ste-Agathe, the signal station and the cliffs on the south coast, the Hyères anchorage and the Maures massif.

★★ Beach Walk – *2 hours on foot return.*
This pleasant walk along sandy paths continually in the shade of the pine trees, starts from Fort Ste-

Tour of Porquerolles under sail – A race takes place every Sunday in the summer, from Whitsun, starting from the port with the object of sailing around the island in the fastest possible time.

Agathe *(bear left)* and skirts the Plage de la Courtade.
After Pointe du Lequin the path dips towards the sea, revealing the **Plage Notre-Dame**, a beautiful sandy beach bordered by pine trees.

Other Walks – The **signal station** (sémaphore), Plage d'Argent, **Pointe du Grand Langoustier** and Cap des Mèdes all make good walks.

A boat with under-water viewing facilities makes cruises off shore ⓥ

★★ ILE DE PORT-CROS

Port-Cros, which was the Mèse – Middle island – to the Greeks, owes its present name to the hollowed out *(creux)* shape of its small harbour. A few fishermen's cottages, a few shops and a small church, adorn the area around the bay which is commanded by the Fort du Moulin (also known as the "Château").

Port-Cros island is hillier and more rugged and rises higher above the sea than its neighbours; its covering greenery is unrivalled – it is a true Garden of Eden and a peaceful place in which to stay. The island is 4km – 2.5 miles long by 2.5km – 1.5 miles wide and its highest point, Mont Vinaigre, reaches 194m – 679ft. Port-Cros, together with Ile de Bagaud and the neighbouring islets, Rascas and La Gabinière and an area extending 600m – 656yds around the coastline, has been designated a **Parc national** ⓥ. The park covers 700ha – 2.69sq miles on land and 1 800ha – 7sq miles at sea and forms a unique protected site for Mediterranean flora and fauna.

The principal walks are signed at the quayside; possible variations are shown by a broken line in red on the plan.

★ Plage de la Palud – *1hour 15min on foot return; marked path.*
Climb up to the castle for a view of the neighbouring island of Bagaud. A **botanical path** planted with Mediterranean specimens winds round **Fort de l'Estissac** ⓥ, built under Richelieu and which houses exhibitions on the marine environment and the relation between man and the sea, and follows the curve of the bay before reaching the beach.

★ Underwater path ⓥ – *A preliminary visit to the Parc office in the port is strongly recommended and, in the case of a solitary dive (diver providing his own equipment, breathing apparatus only), an aquaguide which attaches to the wrist should be obtained.*

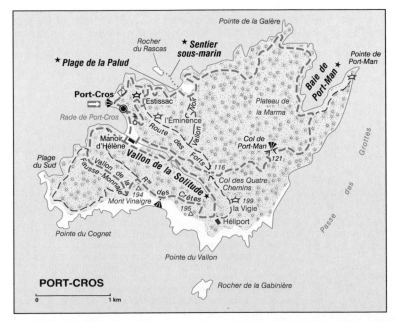

PORT-CROS

Guided tours are arranged in season with equipment provided.

In the section between the little island of Rascas and La Palud beach in an area signposted by yellow buoys, an underwater observation point, no deeper than 10m – 33ft, has been set up.

Here anyone who can swim – diving is not necessary – can see a great variety of representative Mediterranean species which live at this depth. Numbered buoys mark the best viewpoints: the highest numbered signposts indicate the best positions. Among other flora and fauna, the principal stages in the development of posidonia, and the types of animal which live in it, can be observed.

Return to the village passing between the forts of L'Éminence and l'Estissac.

* **Vallon de la solitude** – *2hours on foot return; marked paths.*

This is the classic walk for all visitors spending half a day on the island. At the beginning of the valley stands the Manoir d'Hélène – a manor house now a hotel – so called after the heroine in Melchior de Vogüé's novel *Jean d'Agrève* which is set on Port-Cros. The path is in deep shade for almost all its length.

Once in sight of Fort de la Vigie start back along the cliff walk (Route des Crêtes), which affords **views** of the sea. At Mont Vinaigre bear right into Vallon de la Fausse Monnaie (valley of false currency).

* **Port-Man** – *Round tour of 10km – 6 miles – 4 hours on foot return; marked paths.* This pleasant excursion is made along a shaded and nearly level path from which, at the end of the Col de Port-Man, there is a pretty **view** of the Ile du Levant, the coast and the Maures. It ends in **Baie de Port-Man**, a wonderful green amphitheatre or bay, which is well sheltered from the north winds. Return via Pointe de la Galère, Plateau de la Marma and Plage de la Palud.

Other Walks – These include Plage de la Palud by way of the Route des Forts and the Vallon Noir; the beach and the awesome cliffs along the south shore; Pointe de Port-Man.

There are other opportunities to discover the underwater world: a boat with underwater window sails around Porquerolles in the high season ⊘.

ILE DU LEVANT ⊘ *Local map see Massif des MAURES.*

The island consists of a rock spine 8km – 5 miles long but only 1 200m – 1 300yds wide rimmed by prodigious vertical cliffs inaccessible except at two points: the Avis and Estable *calanques.* The disembarkation point on the island is the Aiguade landing-stage from which a path leads up to Héliopolis.

When the Lérins monks inhabited the islands, the Ile du Levant was the abbey's garden and granary. The majority of the island (80%) is occupied by the Marine Nationale. Access is forbidden.

Héliopolis – In the western part of the island, the village of Héliopolis and the Grottes area attract a considerable number of nudists each summer. This part of the island *(private property)* was one of the first places where, in 1931, the nudist principles of the doctors Durville were put into practice.

In season local clubs organise diving activities which are open to the general public *(see Practical Information at the end of the Guide).*

Posidonia, lungs of the Mediterranean.

This flowering plant, which looks like bunches of long green leaves, is an essential element of marine life in the Mediterranean. It grows on sandy seabeds on the narrow coastal fringes.

Posidonia plays the same role as forests: it is a habitat for animal and plant species, a source of oxygen and stabilises the seabed. It is threatened with damage and extinction by man's intervention: unpurified sewage discharge, uprooting by boats mooring, building on the coast and by the invasion of another species *(Caulerpa taxifolia).*

JUAN-LES-PINS ☆☆☆

Michelin map 84 fold 9 or 115 folds 39 and 40 or 245 fold 37
Town plan in the current Michelin Red Guide France

This elegant winter and summer resort lies at the end of a magnificent bay, well protected by luxurious Cap d'Antibes and Pointe de la Croisette. A pinewood grows right down to a gently sloping beach of fine sand, some 2km – 1 mile long, which is well protected from the wind. **Port-Gallice** is for pleasure boats.

In the evening, activity centres on the numerous restaurants, open-air cafés and night clubs round the casino.

Juan-les-Pins beach

The "swing" era – The thriving musical nightlife of Juan-les-Pins began during the 1920s, with the arrival of the first American tourists. They revolutionised the atmosphere of the resort with their exuberance: they sunbathed on the beaches, they water-skied and they listened to strange music called jazz. A magnate named Frank Gould founded the first summer casino and the young jet set passed sleepless nights dancing to the turbulent music of Cole Porter, in the company of Douglas Fairbanks, Mary Pickford and Mistinguette.

At the end of the Second World War, immediately after the Liberation, the music started again thanks to a clientele from the US Navy based on the Riviera. In 1951 Sydney Bechet was married here in an atmosphere which owed much to New Orleans carnivals. From then on each summer Juan-les-Pins was transformed into the European jazz capital by Sydney Bechet and Claude Luter. After Bechet's death in 1959 the first jazz festival was born; its success was assured by the presence of Louis Armstrong, Count Basie, Duke Ellington, Dizzy Gillespie and Miles Davies.

Jazz is now inseparable from the name of Juan-les-Pins.

The summer season is marked by many events including the famous **World Jazz Festival** which takes place in the Palais des Congrès or under the pine trees.

The tours described under CANNES can also be taken from Juan-les-Pins.

Use the Index to find more information about a subject mentioned in the guide
– people, towns, places of interest, isolated sites,
historical events or natural features...

Le LAVANDOU ☆☆

Population 5 212
Michelin map 84 folds 16 and 17, 114 fold 48 or 245 fold 48
Local map see Massif des MAURES

This charming resort in the shelter of Cap Bénat has so far preserved its Provençal character; its name recalls the lavender fields on the banks of the Batailler. It is still active as a fishing **port** as well as offering moorings for pleasure-craft. It is also a departure point for the Iles d'Hyères.

Place Ernest-Reyer – The square, laid out as a garden, offers a **view** of the Iles du Levant and Port-Cros; a broad beach curves south towards the port of Bormes-les-Mimosas with the wooded slopes of Cap Bénat in the background.

Boulevard de-Lattre-de-Tassigny – Pleasant promenade beside the beach; **view** of the port and the coast eastwards to Cap Lardier.

BOAT TRIPS ⊘

★★★ **Iles d'Hyères** – *One day. Maps and description see Iles d'HYÈRES.*

The song of summer

The identity of the south is indelibly marked by the song of the cicada, which forms an unbreakable trio with the game of bowls (pétanque) and a siesta under the pine trees. The song of the cicada is stimulated by a combination of particular conditions – the temperature must be at least 25°C in the shade and there should not be too much noise. A tiny change – such as a cloud passing in front of the sun or the noise of the wind in the trees – is enough to interrupt the insect. Only the male cicada sings, since the noise is a mating call to females. The dawn serenade is produced when the insect contracts two rigid plates on its abdomen, cymbals, which vibrate at 500 times a second. The sound is amplified by a ventral cavity full of air which acts as a resonance chamber. When the female has located the sound using ears on her abdomen, she joins her suitor in the tree. There are nearly 15 different varieties of cicada in France, of which the most common is the *cacau gris (cicada orni),* an emblem of Provence.

J. Ch. Gérard/DIAF

Les LECQUES

Michelin map 84 fold 14, 114
fold 43 or 245 fold 45

This seaside resort (part of St-Cyr-sur-Mer *commune*) to which families come in both winter and summer, has a sheltered harbour at the far end of a tranquil bay. There is a lovely beach of fine sand bordering the fertile plain planted with vines and olives and linking Les Lecques with La Madrague, which is built at the foot of wooded hills where the coast abruptly changes to rocks and escarpments.

Drive along the coast towards La Madrague.

Musée de Tauroentum ⊘ – The museum is built on the foundations of a Roman villa; on display are some wreathed columns with Corinthian capitals from the villa's peristyle and a granite column from a pergola, 80m – 262ft long, which adorned the sea front. The museum also contains three 1C mosaics, fragments of frescoes and amphoras. In the showcases are many Greek and Roman objects: coins, pottery, glass, jewellery and figurines. In the grounds stands a double-decker tomb found in La Madrague: the burial chamber is lined with pink marble and the libation chamber above is covered with a 4C saddleback roof. Behind the museum a path leads to a pottery tile kiln and remains of houses (walls bearing traces of frescoes). **View** over Les Lecques bay.

Iles de LÉRINS★★

Michelin map 84 fold 9 or 115 fold 39 or 245 fold 37

The interest and attraction of an excursion to the Iles de Lérins lie in the enjoyment of the outing both at sea and on the islands themselves, in the fine panorama of the coast from Cap Roux to Cap d'Antibes and in the visits to the fortress on Ste-Marguerite and the keep of the old fortified monastery on St-Honorat.
In season there are **son et lumière** performances ⊙.

PRACTICAL INFORMATION

Boats sail to the Ile de Lérins ⊙ all year from Cannes and in season from St-Tropez, St-Raphaël and Nice.
L'Ile Ste-Marguerite has a few shops for its residents and several restaurants and bars.
On the island the visitor will find several watering places, but in high season it is a good idea to bring enough food and drink for the day.
L'Ile St-Honorat, entirely occupied by a Dominican monastery, has only one restaurant and no bars. Watering points are rare and water may be rationed in summer. It is essential to bring provisions for a picnic.

★★ILE SAINTE-MARGUERITE

The higher and the larger of the two islands, Ste-Marguerite, is separated from the mainland by a shallow channel 1 100m – just over half a mile wide. The island, which lies east-west and is 3km – 2 miles long and 900m – 1 000yds wide, belongs to the State except for the Domaine du Grand Jardin in the south. Pleasant walks have been laid out in the pine and eucalyptus woods.

The island in Antiquity – The Iles de Lérins were mentioned by the ancient historians. The larger was called Lero, a name, according to Strabo, which commemorates a Ligurian hero to whom a temple was dedicated. Pliny, on the other hand, talks of a Roman port and town.
Recent excavations near Fort Royal have uncovered a number of houses, wall paintings, mosaics and ceramics dating from between the 3C BC and 1C AD. Various wrecks and port substructures found to the west of the island prove that Roman ships called in at Lero.

The riddle of the "Iron Mask" – In 1687 the fortress of Ste-Marguerite, a state prison, received the famous "Man in the Iron Mask", a character who, according to Voltaire, wore a mask with a chinpiece which had steel springs. His identity has never been established with certainty. He is said to have been: an illegitimate brother of Louis XIV, a secretary of the Duke of Mantua who had tricked the "Sun King", a black sheep of the nobility, an accomplice of Madame La Brinvilliers the poisoner, etc.
According to another version: Anne of Austria's doctor, having performed an autopsy on Louis XII, expressed misgivings about the king's ability to father a child. His son-in-law, who inherited the papers, is said to have let out this state secret and he, therefore, may have been the prisoner on Ste-Marguerite.
An even more interesting theory maintains that a woman companion to the Man in the Iron Mask gave birth to a son who was immediately taken away to Corsica. Entrusted (*remis de bonne part* in French – *di buona parte* in Italian) to reliable foster parents, this nameless child is said to have been called "Buonaparte" and to have been the great-grandfather of Napoleon.
The most recent among many other conjectures is that the man was a black page given to Queen Maria Theresa by the Duke of Beaufort in 1661. The queen supposedly had an affair with her page and gave birth to a daughter, Marie-Anne, who, as Sister Louis-Marie-Thérèse, became a nun in 1695, better known as the "Moresse de Moret".
M. de Saint-Mars, charged with guarding the Man in the Iron Mask and bored to tears on Ste-Marguerite, managed to obtain the post of Governor of the Bastille in 1698. His prisoner went with him and died there in 1703.

SIGHTS *2 hours*

Forest ⊙ – For the most part the island is covered with trees: tall eucalyptus and various species of pine protect a dense undergrowth of tree-heathers, arbutus, mastic trees, cistus, thyme and rosemary.
Many rides and broad paths cut through the forest to provide charming **walks**. Starting from the landward side of the Fort, the Eucalyptus Walk – the trees are huge – leads to the Domaine du Grand Jardin; the Allée Ste-Marguerite returns to the landing place. The cliffs are mostly fairly steep making it difficult to reach the shore. There is a path right round the edge of the island (*about 2 hours walk*).

Fort Royal ⊙ – The fortress was built by Richelieu and reinforced by Vauban in 1712. Its main entrance on the west side is monumental. A small **aquarium** *(left)* contains Mediterranean specimens.

In the building beyond, Maréchal Bazaine was imprisoned from 1873 until August 1874 – when he escaped to Spain (official reports do not reveal how). From the terrace there is an extensive **view**★ of the nearby coast.

Pass behind Bazaine's quarters to reach the prisons and old castle; the latter currently houses a marine museum (Musée de la Mer).

Prisons – The entrance hall gives access to the museum *(right)* and the prisons *(left)*. Until the 19C the corridor leading to the cells used to open directly into the courtyard.

On the right is the cell of the Man in the Iron Mask. The cells opposite were occupied by six Protestant pastors imprisoned after the Revocation of the Edict of Nantes (1685); they are now a Huguenot memorial with documents on the Protestants, the Wars of Religion, the Edict of Nantes and the Revocation of the same.

Musée de la mer – The castle's ground floor was built onto the original Roman vaulted rooms. The marine museum exhibits archeological finds excavated in the fort and offshore (1C BC Roman galley, 10C Saracen ship). There is an attractive display of part of the cargo of wrecked ships: a fine collection of Roman amphorae, glass and ceramics and Arab ceramics with sophisticated decoration. Pleasure boating and regattas are the themes evoked in the other rooms.

★★ ILE SAINT-HONORAT

St-Honorat (1 500m – 1 mile long by 400m – 437yds wide) has a less hospitable coastline than Ste-Marguerite, from which it is separated by a narrow strait known as the Plateau du Milieu. The island is the private property of the monastery but walking and bathing are permitted.

Some of the land is cultivated by the monks, who make a liqueur called Lerina, but the rest is covered by a fine forest of umbrella and sea pines, of eucalyptus and a few cypress trees.

At the end of the 4C, **St Honoratus** settled on Lerina, the smaller of the two islands; his retreat soon became known and his disciples hastened to join him. Resigned to not living as a solitary, the saint founded a monastery which was to become one of the most famous and powerful in all Christendom. Pilgrims came in crowds to walk round the island barefoot – a pope on a visit followed this ancient tradition in all humility. Many of the faithful from France and Italy were buried in the monastery which governed 60 dependent priories. In 660 St Aigulf established the Benedictine Order in the monastery.

Raids by Saracens and Genoese pirates, government by commendation, attacks by the Spaniards and the arrival of military garrisons were not favourable to monastic life so that by 1788 only four monks remained and the monastery was closed. During the Revolution it was confiscated and sold.

In 1859 the monastery once more became a place of worship and in 1869 it was taken over by Cistercians from Sénanque Abbey.

SIGHTS *2 hours*

★★ **Island tour** – Starting from the landing place, an attractive shady path makes a circuit of the island. Now close to the shore, now further inland, it offers many different views of the island, its crops, its trees and wooded walks; Ile Ste-Marguerite and the coast on the mainland are also visible.

★ **Ancien monastère fortifié** ⊙ – The remarkable high "keep" or "castle" of this old fortified monastery is set on a spit of land projecting into the sea from the southern coastline. It was built in 1073 by Aldebert, Abbot of Lérins, on Roman foundations, to protect the monks from Saracen pirates.

The gate is over 4m – 13ft above ground level and access to it was by a ladder which has now been replaced by a stone stairway. Facing the entrance, a staircase leads to a barrel-vaulted storeroom. On the left, a few steps go up to the first floor.

The **cloisters** with pointed arches and 14C and 17C vaulting (one of the columns is a Roman milestone) enclose a square courtyard covering a rainwater tank paved with marble. The upper gallery, with small columns of white marble, goes to the chapel of the Ste-Croix (Holy Cross), a high room with Gothic arches still called the Holy of Holies owing to the many relics it contained.

From the platform with its 15C battlements and crenellations at the top of the old keep, the **view**★★ extends over the Iles de Lérins and the coast from the Esterel to Cap d'Antibes, with the often snow-capped peaks of the Alps in the background.

Monastery, Ile St Honorat

Monastère moderne ⊙ – *Only the museum and church are open.*
The old buildings occupied by the monks, parts of which date from the 11C and 12C, have been incorporated into the 19C "new" monastery.

Museum – Situated on the left of the cloisters, it groups Roman and Christian lapidary fragments found on the island, together with documents on the monastery's history and influence. There is also a panel from an altarpiece (St Benedict, St Peter, St John the Baptist) said to be by Louis Bréa.

Church – The abbey church was built in the 19C in the neo-Romanesque style. In the north transept is an 11C Chapel of the Dead.

Chapels – Seven chapels scattered about the island completed the monastery; they were intended for anchorites. Two have retained their former character.

La Trinité – Situated at the eastern end of the island, it pre-dates the 11C. It is built on a trefoil plan with an oval cupola on pendentives. The Byzantine influence leads some experts to date it from the 5C.

St-Sauveur – The chapel which is in the northwest corner of the island is as old as La Trinité but built to an octagonal plan. It was restored in the 17C and again more recently.

The balls of fibre which roll on the beaches and catch on the vegetation of the dunes are in fact the dry remains of posidonia. This marine plant forms "meadows" on the sea-bed and is an essential producer of oxygen.

LEVENS

Population 2 686
Michelin map 84 fold 19 or 115 fold 16 or 245 fold 25
Local map see NICE HINTERLAND

The medieval village (alt 600m – 1 968ft) has given refuge to the coastal population over the centuries. With its modern facilities it is a pleasant place for a holiday.

VILLAGE

Place de la Mairie opens into an attractive public garden, its shady terraces overlooking the valley; nearby stands the curved façade of the Baroque Chapelle des Pénitents Blancs.
In rue Masséna is the house, dated 1722, of the Masséna family; some amusing **frescoes** on the life of Marshal Masséna, executed by the artist Dussour in 1958 in the style of strip cartoons, are to be found at the town hall *(mairie)* ⊙.

Climb up towards the swimming pool.

★ **View** – From near the 1914-18 War Memorial and further as the outer boulevard loops back to the village, the view extends over the junction of the Var and the Vésubie in its setting of high mountains from the Cheiron to Le Mercantour.

EXCURSION

Duranus *8.5km – about 5 miles – 30min*
From Levens take D 19 north.

The road overlooks the deep Gorges de la Vésubie *(See Vallée de la VÉSUBIE)* from a great height, and affords a glimpse of the chapel of Madone d'Utelle *(left)* high up in the mountains.
Duranus, a pretty village, set in the midst of orchards and vineyards, was founded in 17C by the people of Rocca-Sparviero, a ruined village at Col St-Michel.
Although Queen Jeanne was in fact childless, the legend persists that she cursed the village because she was tricked by the villagers into eating her children at a banquet.
At the northern end of Duranus is the **Saut des Français**★★ (Frenchmen's Leap), marked by a viewpoint. It commemorates Republican soldiers who were hurled over the edge in 1793 by bands of guerillas from the Vésubie valley. The view is almost lost in the dizzy vertical drop to the bottom of the gorges, with Utelle and its chapel dominating the scene.

LORGUES

Population 6 340
Michelin map 84 fold 6, 114 fold 22 or 245 fold 35

Lorgues spreads up a slope towards wooded hilltops. The ground is well suited to the cultivation of vines and olives. Oil, both from olives and grape seeds, is produced in large quantities.
It is a pleasant small town where the main square with its magnificent plane trees is one of the most beautiful in the whole region.

Old town – The fortified gateways are 14C. The streets of the town radiate from a central square. A stroll along any of them reveals many interesting old houses with their attractive façades, lintels, wrought-iron work, stairways and fountains.

Collégiale St-Martin ⊘ – The 18C church was built by Bishop Fleury of Fréjus who later became a cardinal and a minister to Louis XV. It is unusually large with a dressed stone façade. The high altar in multicoloured marble is decorated with angels' heads. The Virgin and Child is attributed to Pierre Puget. The church has a fine organ and a carved pulpit.

St-Ferréol – *1km – half a mile. Follow the signs to the northeast of the town.* The chapel stands on a low wooded hill; traces of a Roman settlement.

EXCURSIONS

★★ **Abbaye du Thoronet** – *13km – 8 miles southwest. From Lorgues take D 562 towards Carcès. Bear left into D 17 and turn right into D 79. See Abbaye du THORONET.*

Notre-Dame-de-Benva ⊘ – *3km – 2 miles northwest (D 50) on the Entre-casteaux road.*
The chapel of Our Lady of Benva (corruption of Provençal Ben Vai: good journey) stands on a hillside. Its porch is built astride the old Entrecasteaux road so that passers-by should notice it. Both the porch and the interior are decorated with 15C frescoes.

Taradeau – *9km – 6 miles – southeast on D 10.*
A "Saracen" tower and a ruined Romanesque chapel crown the bluff dominating the village, which is a wine-producing centre.
Take D 73 north uphill.

Turn right into a stony path marked "Table d'Orientation 800m" *(viewing table)* and park the car. From the top there is a vast **panorama**★ over Lorgues, Les Arcs, the Provençal tableland and the Grasse Pre-Alps, the Esterel and the Maures.

This guide, which is revised regularly,
incorporates tourist information provided at the time of going to press
Changes are however inevitable owing to improved facilities and
fluctuations in the cost of living

Vallée du LOUP★★

Michelin map 84 folds 8 and 9 or 115 folds 24 and 25 or 245 fold 37

The Loup rises at an altitude of 1 300m – 4 250ft in the Pre-Alps of Grass (north face of L'Audibergue mountain). For almost all of its short journey to the Mediterranean, the river has cut a valley gorge through the mountains – and this ranks among the most beautiful natural sights of Haute-Provence. The approach roads to the gorges pass through a picturesque region where there are many hill villages. The region described below is the lower basin of the Loup valley.

★★ GORGES DU LOUP *From Vence 56km – 35 miles – about 1 day*

★ **Vence** – *See VENCE.*
From Vence take D 2210 northwest; after 2km – 1 mile bear right into a road signed "Château-restaurant des arômes".

Château Notre-Dame-des-Fleurs – *See VENCE: Excursions.*
The road is bordered by pleasant houses among the olive trees. There is a view back over the hills round Vence.

★ **Tourrettes-sur-Loup** – *See TOURRETTES-SUR-LOUP.*
The road loops round the picturesque village of Tourrettes-sur-Loup before passing the limestone fissures of the Loup valley. The hill village of Le Bar-sur-Loup appears and then Gourdon on its promontory.

Pont-du-Loup – The Draguignan-Nice railway line, which crossed the entrance to the Gorges du Loup was destroyed by the Germans in 1944; the viaduct ruins are visible.

The area has a good reputation for the fruit jellies *(pâte de fruits)* it produces.

Outside the village turn right into D 6.

The road runs through the splendid **Gorges du Loup★★**, cut vertically through the Grasse mountains, with enormous cauldron-like holes, smooth and round, hollowed out of their sides. Just before the second tunnel, in a semicircular hollow, the **Cascade de Courmes★** spills down onto a mossy bed (40m – 130ft). *Only when the site is open in season leave the car beyond the third tunnel.* Further on, amid lush vegetation, a huge megalith marks the entrance to the **Saut du Loup** ⊙, an enormous cauldron hollowed out by marine and glacial erosion in the Tertiary and Quaternary Eras, in which the waters of the Loup swirl furiously in spring. The waterfall known as **Cascades des Demoiselles** gushes down through a strange setting of mosses and vegetation petrified by the spray which has a high lime carbonate content.

Courmes waterfall

J.-P. Hervy/EXPLORER

Just before the bridge, Pont de Bramafan, turn sharp left into D 3. As the road rises to Caussols plateau, the vegetation grows sparser but as far as Gourdon there are continual **views★** down into the depths of the gorges with a particularly breathtaking **view★★** where an overhang has been built out from a sharp righthand turn *(signpost)*. Beyond the end of the gorges the view widens out southwards towards the coast.

★ **Gourdon** – *See GOURDON.*
Interesting drive downhill from Caussols plateau along D 3. In Le-Pré-du-Lac turn into D 2085.

St-Pons – The village lies on a slope where olives, vines and jasmine grow. After Le Collet bear left into D 7 and drive down a wooded valley which becomes more and more enclosed until it joins the lower Loup valley, where there is a good **view** of the river and of the precipitous Pre-Alps of Grasse in the background. After a *corniche* section (cut into the rock face with good views), the road descends to the valley floor to cross the river.

La Colle-sur-Loup – A picturesque village in the plain where fruit and flowers are cultivated. The church has a Renaissance door and a square belltower.

★★ **St-Paul** – *See ST-PAUL.*
Beyond St-Paul the **view** extends to the foothills of the Pre-Alps of Grasse.
Return to Vence by D 2 and D 236.

Le LUC

Population 6 929
Michelin map 84 fold 16, 114 fold 54 or 245 fold 47 – Local map see Massif des MAURES

This important agricultural centre, situated on the old Via Aurelia is a collection point for the harvests of the vine and olive growers of the Var plain and acts as the crossroads of the central Var region.
The village lies in the shadow of a 16C hexagonal tower (27m – 89ft high). This tower, built in the style of Italian campaniles, is used as a belltower. An identification table on the main buildings gives a detailed description of the village. The marine engineer **Jean-Baptiste Lebas** (1797-1873), born in Le Luc, was responsible for the transport of the obelisk from Luxor to the place de la Concorde in Paris (the main events of his life are chronicled in the Musée du centre-Var).

Musée historique du centre-Var ⊙ – This museum of local history is located in the 17C Chapelle Ste-Anne and displays collections of historical exhibits discovered in local excavations: fossils (dinosaur eggs); a carved Roman sarcophagus; medieval sculptures; minerals from the Maures massif; ancient weapons. There is also a historical display on Le Luc.

Musée régional du timbre ⊙ – This regional museum dedicated to the history of **postage stamps and philately** is housed in the Château de Vintimille, a striking 18C building. The clear and spacious display follows the different stages in the traditional (that is using copper-plate engraving) manufacture of postage stamps. A reconstruction of the studio of Albert Decaris, the designer and engraver of many stamps, both French and other, provides a fitting backdrop for these processes. Numerous examples of philatelic counterfeiting and non-French stamps complete the exhibition. A selection of literature *(documentation)* on philately is available for visitors to consult.

View from the oppidum de Fouirette – *(45min on foot). Walk towards the Vergeiras district, then follow the signed path which leads to the top of the hill (300m – 984ft high).* There is a wonderful **view**★ over the Maures plain, from Gonfaron to the Rocher de Roquebrune.

Campaniles in the Var	
Les Arcs	Tour de l'Horloge (18C)
Aups	Tour de l'Horloge
Carcès	Campanile atop a fortified gate (18C)
Carnoules	Belfry (17C)
Cotignac	Campanile (16C)
Draguignan	Tower (17C)
Flassans	Atop the belfry (18C)
Le Luc	Tower (16C)
St-Tropez	Campanile (19C)
Salernes	Belfry (18C)
Tavernes	Campanile (18C)
Toulon	Arsenal tower (18C)

J.-L. Gallo/MICHELIN

Campanile atop clock tower,
Toulon Arsenal

LUCÉRAM ★

Population 1 026
Michelin map 84 fold 19 or 115 fold 17 or 245 fold 25
Local map see NICE HINTERLAND

The village stands on a steep rock between two ravines in a wooded region beneath the mountain peak, Cime du Gros Braus; it was also defended by ramparts including the 13C tower which dominates the town. Lucéram not only boasts a remarkable **setting**★★ but is exceptionally rich in works of art.

★ **Noël des bergers** – Each year shepherds from the neighbouring mountains make their offering of lambs and fruit to the church to the sound of fifes and tambourines.

★OLD VILLAGE

Place de la Mairie, follow the arrows pointing to the church (église).

A maze of stepped streets and vaulted alleyways make up the medieval town. Note the Ionic columns framing a 14C doorway to the right and the many Gothic houses all along the route. From the church terrace one can look down over Lucéram, its tower and crenellated walls, and beyond the hills behind Nice to the sea.

Church ⊙ – The interior of the simple 15C church was remodelled in the 18C with elaborate plasterwork.

★★ **Altarpieces** – These form the most complete group of the Nice School and are among the best presented in the County of Nice. In the south transept is the remarkable **altarpiece of St Antony** framed in Flamboyant Gothic panelling with decorative motifs, sometimes against a gilded chequered backdrop.
Behind the high altar, the outstanding **altarpiece of St Margaret**, which is divided into 10 panels, is by Louis Bréa: around the central figure are Mary Magdalene (bottom left) and St Michael (top left).
Three fine altarpieces by the Bréa School are placed in the nave.

★ **Treasury** – It comprises some remarkable pieces: a chased silver statuette of St Margaret (1500), a finely engraved 14C reliquary, a statue-reliquary of St Rosalie from Sicily, two candlesticks and an alabaster Virgin (16C).

Other works – On the left of the entrance stands an unusual Baroque *Pietà* of painted wood and to the left of the chancel another dating from the 13C in plaster on cloth. Old processional lanterns in wrought iron are displayed.

CHAPELS

St-Grat ⊙ – *1km – half a mile to the south on D 2566.*
This chapel is decorated with frescoes attributed to Jean Baleison. Parts of the vaults show the four Evangelists writing; beneath a triple Gothic canopy are the Virgin and Child who is holding a dove, St Grat bearing the head of John the Baptist and St Sebastian in elegant attire, an arrow in his hand.

Notre-Dame-de-Bon-Cœur ⊙ – *2km – 1.3 miles northwest on D 2566, then 15min on foot return. Park the car on the open space and take the path on the left past a ruined house to the chapel.*
The frescoes, attributed to Baleison, are interesting despite some unfortunate repainting. In the porch: Good and Bad Prayer and St Sebastian; in the chapel: the Adoration of the Shepherds, the Adoration of the Magi and scenes from the life of the Virgin.

To plan a special itinerary:
- consult the **Map of Touring Programmes** *which indicates the tourist regions,*
the recommended routes, the principal towns and main sights
- read the descriptions in the Sights *section*
which include Excursions from the main tourist centres

Michelin Maps nos 8 4 and 9 8 9 indicate scenic routes, places of interest, viewpoints, rivers, forests...

Massif des MAURES★★★

Michelin map 84 folds 7, 16, 17 and 18, 114 folds 34 to 37 or 245 folds 47 to 49

The wooded Massif des Maures extends eastwards from Hyères to St-Raphaël, between the sea to the Gapeau and Argens river valleys. The coast is continuously indented, providing delightful viewpoints and beauty spots which can be seen from the magnificent tourist road, particularly the section from Le Lavandou to La Croix-Valmer known as the "Corniche des Maures". The interior is broken up by shady valleys and wild ravines.

GEOGRAPHICAL NOTES

The Maures, composed for the most part of crystalline schists (gneiss and mica-schists), are, with the Esterel range, the oldest geological area in Provence. The Hercynian folding pushed up a vast continent, Tyrrhenia, which included Corsica and Sardinia.

Successive thrusts originating from the Pyrenees and the Alps broke up this mass, forming the western basin of the Mediterranean and reshaping the Maures into four parallel lines of relief.

The Iles d'Hyères mark the southern chain which is partially submerged; the second chain along the coast reaches its highest point at Les Pradels (528m – 1 725ft); the two inland chains, La Verne and La Sauvette, are separated by the Rivers Grimaud and Collobrières. La Sauvette, the most northerly chain, includes the highest peaks, Notre-Dame-des-Anges (780m – 2 559ft) and La Sauvette (779m – 2 556ft), and ends in Roquebrune mountain overlooking the lower Argens valley.

The coastline juts out in the blunt promontories of Cap Bénat and St-Tropez peninsula, the pointed headlands of Cap Nègre and Cap des Sardinaux and retreats into the Bormes anchorage, and the bays of Cavalaire and St-Tropez.

The pines along the coast, and the cork-oaks, holm-oaks, arbutus, cistus and chestnuts inland, which form the main vegetation of the Maures, are sometimes devastated by raging forest fires. The massif's principal industry, the manufacture of bottle corks, derives from the cork-oaks which are carefully cultivated.

Massif des Maures coast

PRACTICAL INFORMATION
ABOUT VISITING THE MASSIFS

- Roads belonging to the DFCI (Défense forestière contre l'incendie - forest fire-fighters) are closed to public traffic. They count as private roads; an open barrier does not indicate that access is permitted. Parking in front of these barriers is prohibited and cars should be parked well to the side of narrow roads to allow the passage of emergency vehicles. Pedestrian access is always possible.
- During periods of high fire risk, the ALARME plan is put into action and certain public roads (classed as major fire risks) may be closed to vehicles. Offenders are liable for heavy fines. Walkers are strongly advised to avoid such areas for reasons of safety.
- Camping is prohibited in the massif and within 200m - 656ft of any of the forests.
- While walking in the massif, respect plants and wild animals and do not touch them, stay on the paths and keep dogs under control.
- For up-to-date information on the conditions in the massif, ☎ 04 94 47 35 45.

HISTORICAL NOTES

"Maouro", a Provençal word which applies to dark forests, has become "Maures" in French and is used to describe this densely wooded mountain range.

On the other hand, tradition sees in the name an allusion to the Moorish pirates from Spain, who ravaged the coast in the 8C and established themselves in the following century on the slopes around the Grimaud plain; but these pirates were really Saracens. Driven out in 973, they continued to raid the coast up to the 18C and set up a reign of terror. To defend themselves, the inhabitants withdrew from the shore, going up into the hills from where they could watch the horizon *(see HILL VILLAGES)*.

J. Guillard/SCOPE

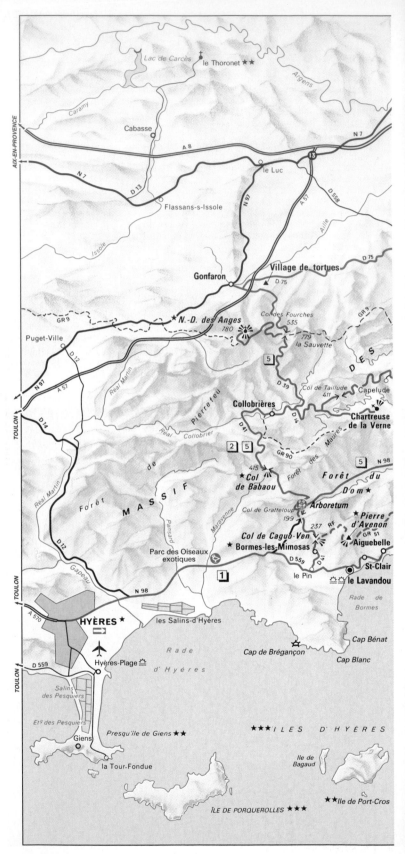

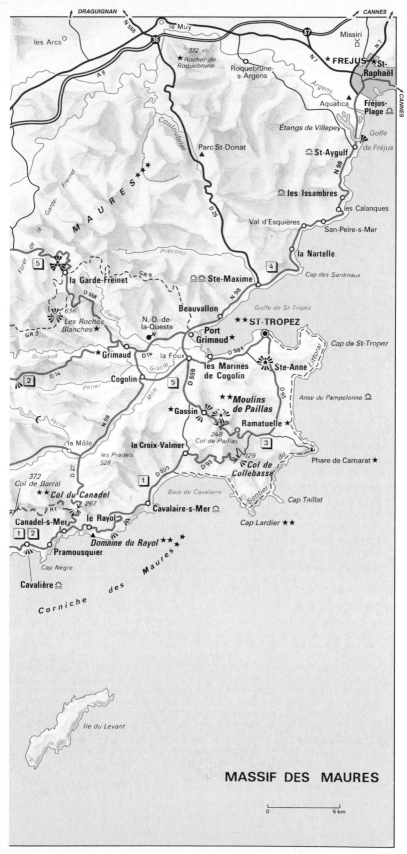

MASSIF DES MAURES

It was the 20C vogue for sea-bathing, limited at first to an aristocratic clientele, which brought this magnificent coast back to life and ended the economic isolation of the region. On 15 August 1944 the Allied and French Armies landed on the Maures beaches to liberate the south of France.

Hermann's tortoise

This tortoise, the only one native to France, appeared in Mediterranean Europe about one million years ago. It lives in the scrub *(maquis)* which provides all its food – oak leaves, fruit and molluscs. After hibernating in a tree stump until about June, the female lays her eggs in a nest which she immediately abandons. If they survive the first two months of life and predatory badgers, the baby tortoises can look forward to a life of 60 to 100 years.

Hermann's tortoise has already disappeared from mainland Spain, the Balearic Islands and part of the Balkans, because of natural predators as well as fire (which is the greater threat); it is now falling victim to alterations in its habitat caused by man and to unregulated collecting. The tortoises now survive only in Corsica and in the massif des Maures, where a tortoise village has been established to safeguard the species.

★★ CORNICHE DES MAURES

1 Hyères to La Croix-Valmer

48km – 30 miles – about 3 hours – local map above

★ **Hyères** – *See HYÈRES.*

From Hyères take N 98, ① on the town plan.

The *corniche* road along the foot of the Pradels coastal chain passes many enchanting beauty spots although the magnificence of the forest has been damaged by fire in some places.

After crossing the Gapeau, the road runs past the salt-marshes across the Hyères plain with **views** of Cap Bénat and the Ile du Port-Cros.

Le Lavandou – *See Le LAVANDOU.*

From Le Lavandou the road runs along the wooded coastline, which is bright and colourful with flowers in season.

St-Clair – The small resort of St-Clair, a short distance from the main road, has a large and beautiful beach.

Aiguebelle – Pleasant, peaceful seaside resort.

Cavalière – Cavalière has a fine beach, sheltered from the *mistral*. The view extends over Cap Nègre and the Bormes anchorage as far as the Island of Levant and Port-Cros.

Pramousquier – A modest resort with a sheltered beach of fine sand.

The road leaves the shore and winds among pine trees and gardens.

Le Rayol-Canadel-sur-Mer – Canadel, lying at the base of the last foothills of the Pradels range and flanked by superb pinewoods, possesses one of the most sheltered beaches on the Maures coast.

Cavalaire-sur-Mer – *See CAVALAIRE.*

La Croix-Valmer – Population 2 634. The village is a climatic resort and rest centre. The local wine is well considered among Côtes de Provence.

The site of La Croix village is said to be where Constantine had his vision while on his way to Rome to claim the Empire. According to tradition he saw a cross in the sky with the words "*In hoc signo vinces*: in this sign you will conquer", a prediction of his forthcoming victory which was shared by Christianity; after the battle Constantine converted to Christianity. A stone cross erected on the pass commemorates the legend and gives the village its name. An alternative tradition relates that Constantine's vision of his victory over Maxentius occurred at the Milvian Bridge outside Rome.

Col de Collebasse – Alt 129m – 43ft. *8km – 5 miles from La Croix-Valmer along the very winding D 93.* There is a superb **view★** of the Pampelonne bight, Cavalaire bay and the Iles d'Hyères.

★★ MAURES INTERIOR

2 Round tour from Le Lavandou

109km – 67 miles – one day – local map above

This beautiful circular tour, along very hilly but unfrequented roads, goes over at least seven passes *(cols)* and penetrates deep into the heart of the massif.

⚐⚐ **Le Lavandou** – *See Le LAVANDOU.*
From Le Lavandou take D 559 west and turn right into D 41.
The roads winds uphill among cypresses, eucalyptus, mimosa and white, pink and red oleanders. Fine **view** ahead of Bormes and its castle.

★ **Bormes-les-Mimosas** – *See BORMES-LES-MIMOSAS.*
Continue on D 41 to Col de Caguo-Ven; the forest road (right) is accessible only on foot. Continue downhill to Col de Gratteloup (alt 199m – 656ft). Make a detour of 2km – 1.5 miles northeast on N 98 to Maison Forestière de Gratteloup.

Arboretum de Gratteloup – *See below.*
Return to Col de Gratteloup. Turn right into D 41.
The road passes over wooded slopes of cork-oak and chestnut – deep valleys *(east)* and glimpses of the sea and the mountains round Toulon *(west)*.

★ **Col de Babaou** – Alt 415m – 1 362ft. There is an attractive **panorama**★ from the pass of the Hyères anchorage, the Giens peninsula and the Iles d'Hyères. Beyond the pass rise the tallest of the Maures summits, their slopes wooded by magnificent chestnuts and cork-oaks. The road descends to the Réal Collobrier valley which widens to form the Collobrières basin.
Turn right into D 14.

Collobrières – The picturesque houses of the well-shaded town look down on the river flowing swiftly beneath an old hump-backed bridge. The local forests provide the raw material for bottle corks and the vineyards the grapes for rosé wine. The local speciality is *marrons glacés* and other sweet chestnut products.
Continue east on D 14. After 6km – 4 miles turn right.
A narrow road leads to the ruins of the former Carthusian Monastery of La Verne, in its majestic forest setting.

Chartreuse de la Verne – *See Chartreuse de la VERNE.*
Return to D 14 and continue east.
After the Col de Taillude the road looks across the valley of la Verne to the ruins of the charterhouse crowning the opposite slope and then, after passing high above the hamlet of Capelude, makes its way into the upper valley of the Le Périer stream. From the centre of the valley there is a **vista** of the Grimaud plain and the bay of St-Tropez.
Abruptly the road turns into the valley of the Giscle (or of the Grimaud rivulet) from where Grimaud can be seen in the distance overlooked by its beautiful castle ruins.

★ **Grimaud** – *See* 5 *below.*
From Grimaud take D 558 south.

Cork-oak

The cork oak is an evergreen which requires heat and humidity. It grows near the sea up to a height of 500m – 1 640ft and has proved to be particularly resistant to fire. It is easily recognised by its large blackish acorns and heavily scored bark.

Gathering the bark *(démasclage)* takes place for the first time when the tree is 25 years old; this is known as the male bark. Subsequent harvests, which take place in July and August when the sap is rising, occur every 9 or 10 years, which is the time it takes for a new layer of cork to form; this is known as the female bark, which is highly prized by industry (manufacture of chipboard at le Muy) and by craftsmen (boards, ornamental objects and materials for ceramicists). The greater part of the production is exported, particularly to Sardinia.

In the middle of the 1960s the Maures produced 5 000 tonnes of cork per annum supplying about a hundred local firms. In 1994 the foresters of the Var region produced 500 tonnes of cork but the local firms had disappeared. The traditions of this industry are preserved in the cork museum in Gonfaron.

J.-Ch. Gérard/DIAF

Gathering cork

Cogolin – *See COGOLIN.*

Take N 98 southwest up the Môle valley. After 8km – 5 miles turn left into D 27 which winds up the north face of the coastal chain of hills.

★★**Col du Canadel** – Alt 267m – 876ft. Suddenly the sea comes into view; there is a superb **panorama**★★ of Canadel, Pramousquier beach, Cap Nègre, the Bormes anchorage, Cap Bénat and beyond, on the horizon, the island of Porquerolles.

Leave the car in the car park on the col. Take the forest track on the right to the Col de Caguo-Ven, cars prohibited.

This is a picturesque route with magnificent **views**★ of the Maures massif and, to the south, of the coast and the Iles d'Hyères.

The forest track along a ridge, bordered with chestnuts and mimosas, is shared with the GR 51 to the Col de Barral. Vieux-Sauvaire is reached after one hour's walk *(restaurant open here in season)* after which the path goes back down to the Col de Barral (372m – 1 220ft). There are fine views from the ridge which the path follows for 5km – 3 miles to the Pierre d'Avenon.

At a farm (mas) take the path to the right which climbs for 100m – 110yds (the last few yards are an easy climb).

★ **Pierre d'Avenon** – Alt 442m – 1 450ft. From the top of this huge mound of giant boulders the **view**★ extends on either hand over the whole Maures coastline from Cap Lardier to Hyères with the harbour installations of Le Lavandou and Bormes in the foreground.

From here it is a 45min walk to the Col de Caguo-Ven.

Col de Caguo-Ven – Alt 237m – 778ft. From the pass, there is a **view** of the Hyères and Bormes anchorages and the island of Porquerolles.

Return to Le Lavandou via Bormes-les-Mimosas and Le Pin.

★ ST-TROPEZ PENINSULA

③ **From Croix-Valmer to St-Tropez** – *See ST-TROPEZ PENINSULA.*

Cork-oak trees

★★ COAST ROAD

④ **St-Tropez to St-Raphaël**
39km – 24 miles – half a day excluding tours of St-Tropez and St-Raphaël – local map above

★★ **St-Tropez** – *See ST-TROPEZ 2 hours 30min.*

From St-Tropez take D 98ᴬ, ① on the town plan.

The road skirts the southern shore of the bay looking across to the opposite coast.

After 4km – 2.5 miles turn right.

Cogolin Marina – *See COGOLIN.*

Return to D 98ᴬ; turn right into N 98 and right again to Port-Grimaud.

★ **Port-Grimaud** – *See PORT-GRIMAUD.*
Return to N 98 which skirts the north shore of the bay, overlooking St-Tropez.

Beauvallon – Beauvallon is a well-situated resort on the north shore of St-Tropez bay shaded by pine and cork-oak woods.
At this spot the Maures massif slopes very gently down to the sea where the shore, with scarcely any shade, forms a series of beaches from the end of the bay right round to Ste-Maxime.

≗≗ **Ste-Maxime** – *See STE-MAXIME.*
The road, which skirts the coast closely as far as St-Aygulf, circles Cap Sardinaux.

La Nartelle – The beach of what is now the resort of La Nartelle was one of the landing points for the Allied forces in August 1944.
The coastline between La Nartelle and St-Aygulf is broken up into several inlets *(calanques)* with small beaches and rocks emerging from the sea.

≗ **Les Issambres** – This pretty resort combines with Val d'Esquières, San Peïre and Les Calanques to form a rapidly evolving tourist development. Houses of various sizes, some built in the Provençal style, have been discreetly sited in the hills. Les Issambres probably takes its name from "Sinus Sambracitanus", the Roman name for the bay of St-Tropez.

≗ **St-Aygulf** – The resort of St-Aygulf is shaded by pines, cork and holm oaks; from the beach of fine sand, ringed with rocks, there is an attractive view of Fréjus Bay and Les Issambres.
Beyond St-Aygulf there is a beautiful **panorama** of the plain of the Lower Argens which separates the Maures and the Esterel. The magnificent rocks of Roquebrune mountain stand out from the Maures massif while in the Esterel chain, behind the Dramont semaphore, one can pick out the summit of Cap Roux. To the left the road runs alongside the **Aquatica** ⊘ water sports park, before leading into Fréjus.

★ **Fréjus** – *See FRÉJUS.*
From Fréjus take boulevard S-Decuers south.

≗ **Fréjus-Plage** – *See FRÉJUS: Port Fréjus.*
Take N 98 by the sea to reach St-Raphaël.

★ **St-Raphaël** – *See ST-RAPHAËL.*

★ CREST ROAD

⑤ Round tour starting from St-Tropez

120km – 74.5 miles – half a day excluding tour of St-Tropez – local map above

This excursion passes through wooded countryside and affords some fine views. Quiet roads lead to the lower slopes of the twin peaks of N-D-des-Anges and La Sauvette.

★★ **St-Tropez** – *See ST-TROPEZ. 2 hours 30min.*
From St-Tropez take D 98ᴬ, ① on the plan.
The road skirts the southern shore of the bay of St-Tropez.
At La Foux turn left into N 98.

Cogolin – *See COGOLIN.*
Continue west on N 98 up the Môle valley.

Shortly before the village of La Môle stands a château (right) flanked by two round towers with pepperpot roofs. It was here that **Saint-Exupéry** (1900-44), aviator and writer, spent some of his childhood years. Vineyards give way to forest-covered slopes.

★ **Forêt domaniale du Dom** – This State Forest, composed mainly of pines, cork-oaks and chestnuts, spreads over the Les Pradels and La Verne ranges, which are separated by the steep-sided Môle valley. Jean Aicard (1848-1921), poet and novelist, set his work *Maurin des Maures* in this area.

1km – 0.5 mile before the pass, stop by the Maison Forestière de Gratteloup.

Arboretum de Gratteloup ⊘ – *Leave the car in the car park beside N 98.*
This arboretum, created in 1935, consists of various areas extending to nearly 3 ha – 7 acres. The first, and oldest, part contains mostly Mediterranean species (cypress, pines, juniper, yoke elms and hop hornbeams); more varied species grow in other areas: red cedar, eucalyptus, maples, alder and birch. Lastly, an area is devoted specifically to the development of the chestnut tree.

At the Col de Gratteloup turn right into D 41 continuing until Collobrières (for a description of this section see ② above). 3km – 2 miles east of Collobrières turn left into D 39.

The road winds through wooded countryside overlooking a steep-sided stream and affords the occasional glimpse of the summit of La Sauvette to the right. Shortly before Col des Fourches the road to the left leads to the Notre-Dame-des-Anges hermitage, pinpointed by the television relay mast.

★ **Notre-Dame-des-Anges** ⊘ – The **priory** near the summit (780m – 2 559ft) stands in an attractive **setting**★, amidst schist rocks where only trees such as the chestnut thrive. The Merovingian foundation may well have superseded an earlier pagan place of worship. Remodelled in the 19C, the buildings included accommodation for pilgrims and a chapel, the walls of which are covered with votive offerings.

Beyond the screen of trees surrounding the chapel there is a remarkable **view**★ *(north)* of the Argens depression backed by the Alps; *(west)* Ste-Baume; *(south)* over the Maures heights to the sea, the Hyères islands, the Giens peninsula and Toulon; and even Corsica on a clear day.

Return to the Col des Fourches and turn left towards Gonfaron.

The road passes by La Sauvette, which at an altitude of 779m – 2 556ft is the highest point in the Maures massif, before descending to Le Luc plain.

Gonfaron – This village, set against the backdrop of the Massif des Maures, is still an active centre of cork manufacture. At the north edge of the village rises an isolated hill, crowned by a chapel dedicated to St Quinis.

The Legend of the Flying Donkeys

In the 17C, during a procession in honour of St Quinis, a householder in Gonfaron refused to sweep the area in front of his house and suggested that the statue of the saint should fly over the rubish. Some time later the same man and his donkey had reached the top of a hill when the animal slipped and they both tumbled into the ravine below.

The locals saw the saint's hand in this misfortune and the legend is told in respect of this hill which rises in the Luc plain.

Écomusée de liège ⊘ – The traditions of the cork industry in the Maures region are preserved through reconstructions and display of tools.

Village de tortues de Gonfaron ⊘ – *In Gonfaron turn right into D 75. The best times to visit are during the morning (11am) and in the early evening (6pm).*

The village is a breeding centre for the almost extinct Hermann tortoise *(Testudo Hermanni Hermanni)*, one-million-year-old herbivore.

The centre also shelters France's freshwater turtle and the common or European tortoise *(Testudo Graeca)*.

The visit includes the nesting house *(écloserie)*, the nursery for the under 5 years, the terrarium for the hibernation of the young, the various enclosed areas set up according to age or species and the infirmary. Courtship occurs in April, May and September, egg-laying from mid-May to mid-June, and hatching in early September.

Continue on D 75; at the crossroads turn right into D 558 towards La Garde-Freinet.

The road climbs to La Garde-Freinet, which is dominated by the castle ruins.

La Garde-Freinet – *See La GARDE-FREINET.*

Take D 558 south.

Still descending, the road passes cork-oak and chestnut-covered slopes and affords glimpses of the bay and peninsula of St-Tropez.

★ **Grimaud** – See GRIMAUD

Return to St-Tropez by D 14 and D 98ᴬ.

Michelin Maps (scale 1: 200 000), which are revised regularly, indicate:
- *golf courses, sports stadiums, racecourses, swimming-pools, beaches, airfields*
- *scenic routes, public and long-distance footpaths, viewpoints*
- *forest parks, interesting sights...*

The perfect complement to the Michelin Green Guides for planning holidays and leisure time
Keep current Michelin Maps in the car at all times

Population 29 141
Michelin map 84 folds 10 and 20 115 fold 28 or 245 fold 39
Local maps see Excursions below, NICE HINTERLAND and Corniches de la RIVIERA
Plan of conurbation in the current Michelin Red Guide France

Menton claims to be the warmest resort on the Riviera and is a pleasant place to spend a winter holiday. Winter, however, is hardly mentioned here where the sun reigns supreme, and long sandy beaches, two marinas and festivities and cultural activities welcome the summer visitor. The town is backed by terraced slopes planted with citrus fruits and olives. The climate is particularly favourable for flowers and tropical plants; lemon trees, which die if the temperature falls below - 3° C (26°F), flourish throughout the year, providing the famous Menton lemons much sought after by connoisseurs. The picturesque old town standing out against a mountainous backdrop occupies a magnificent **site★★**.

Early history – Evidence of human settlement in the Paleolithic era from excavations near the Italian frontier is displayed in the Musée d'Anthropologie préhistorique in Monaco and in the Musée de préhistoire in Menton but little is known

Old town, Menton

J. Guillarc/SCOPE

about the town's origins. The name Menton first appears in 1261. In 1346 the town was bought by the Grimaldis of Monaco although it remained under the Bishop of Ventimiglia. Together with Monaco it oscillated between the protection of France and Sardinia until it was permanently attached to France in 1860.

Modern town – In the late 19C and early 20C Menton shared in the popularity of the Riviera with the European aristocracy. Rich and well-known foreigners came to live there as well as several writers – the New Zealander Katherine Mansfield (1888-1929), the Spaniard Blasco Ibáñez (1867-1928) and Ferdinand Bac (1859-1952), a French essayist and painter. 20C tourism brought new blood and light industry grew up in the Carei Valley, while the residential district spread west to Roquebrune-Cap-Martin and east to the Italian frontier. The old town and vast green spaces have been preserved.

"Artium civitas" – This inscription on the front of the town hall declared Menton's ambition to be a city of the arts. The aim is to offer a variety of cultural activities. Art exhibitions are held throughout the year at the Palais de l'Europe (**Z**).

The **Chamber Music Festival** has an international reputation and its guest artists are world-famous.

A prize for the best short story is awarded each year by the Katherine Mansfield Foundation.

Shrove Tuesday brings the annual Lemon Festival and there are flower carnivals throughout the summer. Festivals are also held by night in the Pian Gardens (*access from promenade de la Mer* – **Y**).

Fête du Citron (*illustration p. 266*) – The mild climate and the fertile citrus fruit orchards around Menton have given birth to a local lemon festival, which since 1934 has taken place in the Biovès Gardens. The event calls for more than 100 tonnes of citrus fruit – oranges, grapefruit and and kumquats as well as lemons – which are used to cover decorative metal frames erected in the gardens to illustrate a different theme each year. The festival closes with a procession of floats decorated with citrus fruit.

★★ SEAFRONT AND OLD TOWN *3 hours*

Start from the Municipal Casino going east.

★★ **Promenade du Soleil** (**Z**) – The promenade with its broad terraces, follows the shore beneath the old town with the Alps in the background.

Quai Napoléon-III (**Z**) – The jetty, which protects the harbour and ends in a lighthouse, is a good vantage point from which to look at the old town. There are facilities for **boat trips** ⊘.

Musée Jean-Cocteau (**Z**) ⊘ – This museum is housed in a 17C bastion built by Honoré II of Monaco. Cocteau, the "prince of the poets", worked there from 1957 onwards. It was his initiative that led to the bastion being transformed into a museum and it was he who oversaw the restoration. The remaining parts of the original building include a large vaulted salon and two small annexe rooms, one of which still contains an oven. The guardrooms and the munitions store now contain the museum.

Outside, the artist has designed pebble mosaics in traditional Menton style on several themes – Orpheus, the Faun of youth, a lass of Menton and the fisherman. The floor of the entrance is decorated with the Mediterranean emblem, the lizard, made of small grey and white pebbles. On the wall hangs an Aubusson tapestry, **Judith and Holophernes**, which Matisse described as the "only truly contemporary tapestry". The wrought-iron display cases were designed by Cocteau especially for his museum; they contain zoomorphic ceramic vases. The tapestry hanging above the stairs, *l'Age du Verseau*, was woven in the Gobelins workshops. The first floor gallery houses a series of pastels entitled *Les Innamorati* (1961), and a large portrait of the poet by Marc Avoy depicting Cocteau leaving the body of a faun.

Jetée Impératrice-Eugénie (**Y**) – From Volti's sculpture of Saint Michael (**Y V**), there is a fine **view**★ of the old town above the arcades with the mountains in the background and of the coast from Cap Martin to Bordighera in Italy; Ventimiglia is hidden by Cap Mortola.

Quai Bonaparte (**Y**) – It skirts Les Sablettes beach and the old town. A huge flight of steps leads up to the church of St-Michel between tall narrow houses.

★★ **Parvis St-Michel** (**Y**) – At the top of the steps is a charming square in the Italian style, overlooking the sea and the coast, where the concerts of the Chamber Music Festival are held during August. The square is paved with a handsome mosaic of the Grimaldi arms in grey and white and framed by typical old houses and the façades of two churches.

St-Michel (**Y F**) ⊘ – This is the largest and finest Baroque church in the region. Its two-tier **façade** in yellow and green exhibits a variety of architectural decoration. The tower (15C) on the left, which belonged to an earlier building,

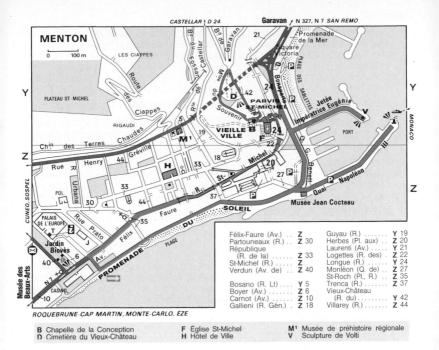

Félix-Faure (Av.) . .	**Z**		Guyau (R.)	**Y** 19
Partouneaux (R.) . .	**Z** 30		Herbes (Pl. aux) . .	**Z** 20
République			Laurenti (Av.)	**Y** 21
(R. de la)	**Z** 33		Logettes (R. des) .	**Z** 22
St-Michel (R.)	**Z**		Longue (R.)	**Y** 24
Verdun (Av. de) . .	**Z** 40		Monléon (Q. de) . .	**Z** 27
			St-Roch (Pl., R.) . .	**Z** 35
Bosano (R. Lt)	**Y** 5		Trenca (R.)	**Z** 37
Boyer (Av.)	**Z** 6		Vieux-Château	
Carnot (Av.)	**Z** 10		(R. du)	**Y** 42
Gallieni (R. Gén.) .	**Z** 18		Villarey (R.)	**Z** 44

ROQUEBRUNE-CAP MARTIN, MONTE-CARLO, ÈZE

B Chapelle de la Conception	**F** Église St-Michel	**M¹** Musée de préhistoire régionale
D Cimetière du Vieux-Château	**H** Hôtel de Ville	**V** Sculpture de Volti

was crowned with an octagonal campanile with a glazed tile roof in the 17C, and the great Genoese style campanile (53m – 174ft) on the right was added in the 18C. Above each of the three doors is a niche; the central one contains a statue of St Michael, with St Maurice on the left and St Roch on the right. The ornate interior was inspired by the Church of the Annunziata in Genoa, giving rise to the basilica plan with false transept and shallow chevet and barrel vaulting; it also resembles St-Véran at Utelle. Local artists such as Puppo and Vento contributed to the decoration of the side chapels which commemorate various local worthies.

In the first north side chapel is the fine Baroque **altarpiece** by Puppo, *Le Pape Urbain VIII intercédant auprès de l'Enfant Jésus pour les âmes du Purgatoire* (Pope Urban VIII interceding with the infant Jesus for the souls in Purgatory) framed by gilt columns wreathed with vine leaves; in front stands a marble altar under a crown-shaped canopy. Next door is a Crucifixion by Ferrari and an unusual 17C Virgin and Child. The third chapel contains an Assumption by Puppo embellished with angels, drapes and scrolls.

The choir contains the huge 17C **organ casing**; above the handsome 18C choir stalls is the **altarpiece of St Michael** (1569) by Manchello: the saint is flanked by Peter bearing papal insignia and John the Baptist; the upper sections show a fine *Pietà*. The exuberant Baroque high altar is crowned by St Michael slaying the Devil. The next side chapel is devoted to the Princes of Monaco: a late 17C painting shows St Devota, patron of the Principality, in front of the rock of Monaco. Another Ferrari, the *Adoration of the Shepherds*, hangs in the first south side chapel and in the last chapel is an altarpiece by J A Vento: *the Rest during the Flight into Egypt*. The baptistery (1806) is adorned with a dome in *trompe-l'œil*. Damask hangings from Genoa, the colour of amaranth (purple), decorate the choir and the central nave. They were presented by Prince Honoré III of Monaco on the occasion of his wedding in this church in 1757.

★ **Façade of the Chapelle de la Conception (Y B)** – On leaving the church climb a few steps on the left to admire this chapel of the White Penitents (1685, restored in 19C), with its garlands of flowers and basket-handled pediment surmounted by statues of the three theological virtues.

Climb the steps into rue du Vieux-Château, very picturesque, which leads to the cemetery.

Cimetière du Vieux-Château (Y D) – This international cemetery, laid out in the last century on the site of the old medieval castle, consists of terraces one above the other which can be seen clearly from the port. Each level contains tombs of a different religion or nationality. The cemetery is the most striking souvenir of the time when Menton was full of rich summer visitors from all over the world. Among the celebrities from this era whose fame still endures are several great Russian princes (Troubetzkoy, Volkonsky and Ouroussof), the uncle and aunt

141

(Delano) of the American president Roosevelt, Webb Ellis who is credited with inventing the game of Rugby football and the Danish architect Georg Tersling, who designed many palaces and houses on the Riviera at the beginning of the century.

From the southern corner of the English graveyard there is a beautiful view★ of the old town, the sea and the coast from Mortola point in Italy to Cap Martin.

Return to parvis St-Michel by montée du Souvenir, bordered by oleanders.

Rue Longue (Y 24) – The steps up to St-Michel are intersected by rue Longue, once the main street of the town and former Via Julia Augusta, which becomes rue des Logettes and joins rue St-Michel.

Rue St-Michel (Z) – This pedestrian lane, lined by orange trees, links the old and new towns and is full of boutiques. Below on the left, **place aux Herbes** (Z 20) with its coloured paving stones, colonnade and fountain is a pleasant corner in view of the sea; nearby the covered market offers an animated daily spectacle.

Avenue Félix-Faure, itself a lively street, leads to the Biovès gardens.

Jardin Biovès (Z) – These beautiful gardens in the town centre are bordered by palms and lemon trees, planted with flowers and ornamented by fountains and statues (*Goddess of the Golden Fruit* by Volti). The gardens follow the line of the Careï River and open up a view of the mountains behind the town. The **Palais de l'Europe**, formerly the Assembly Rooms *(right)*, in the style of the Belle Époque (*c*1900), is now a conference and cultural centre. From 1951 to 1980, it housed the Biennial International Art Exhibition which attracted painters such as Picasso, Dalì, Chagall and Matisse.

ADDITIONAL SIGHTS

★ **Musée des Beaux-Arts (Palais Carnolès)** ⊘ – *Avenue Carnot* (Z 10). This former summer residence of the Princes of Monaco was built in the 17C in the spirit of the Grand Trianon, according to plans by Robert de Cotte and Gabriel. After great modifications in the 19C, its visitors included Elisabeth-Louise, the last queen of Prussia, and Prince Metternich. It then passed into the ownership of the American Allis, a celebrated ichthyologist, on whose intructions the building was restored by the Danish architect Georg Tersling and decorated with frescoes on antique themes by Matthiessen, a German artist. The original plasterwork and gilding have survived in the Grand Salon de Musique Antoine 1er and the Salon Bleu.

Upstairs – The first floor is dedicated to the collection of early art. The beautiful 13C *Virgin and Child* is a Tuscan work by the Master of the Maddalena. The following galleries illustrate religious themes from different countries – *Virgin and Child with St Francis* by Louis Bréa, *Virgin and Child* by Leonardo da Vinci and *Holy Family* by Bernardino Luini. In another gallery hangs a *Portrait of Urban of Bologna* by Bernardino Orsi. The works of various European schools of the 16C, the 17C and the 18C include *St Benedict with the young St Maurus and St Placidus* by Philippe de Champaigne as well as works by Magnasco, Weenix, Bruyn the Elder and Verbugh.

Ground floor – A collection of contemporary and modern work is housed on the ground floor. The museum displays in rotation works from the Wakefield Mori collection (Picabia, Forain, Dufy etc), contributions from the Biennales de Peinture (up to 1980) and gifts from artists (Gleizes, Desnoyers, Delvaux, Sutherland).

Jardin d'agrumes – A vast **garden of citrus fruit trees** (grapefruit, mandarin, kumquat, orange and lemon) and avocado trees contains a number of sculptures. Space in the central alleyway, around the Palais Carnolès, is devoted to Magda Frank; in the first lateral alleyway note busts of Prince Rainier II of Monaco, Princess Grace, Katherine Mansfield and other famous people of our times. The other alleyways are decorated with works by Lazareff, Sigaldi and Gleb.

Hôtel de ville (Z H) ⊘ – The town hall is a beautiful building inspired by the 17C Italian style. The **hall**★ where marriages are performed was decorated by Jean Cocteau. On the wall at the back, the angler, who has a fish as an eye, is wearing the traditional Menton fisherman's hat; the girl opposite him is wearing a traditional hat from Nice. The walls depict Orpheus and Eurydice on one side and a fictitious marriage on the other. On the ceiling, Poetry is depicted astride Pegasus, Science is juggling with the planets, and Love is no longer blind.

In the entrance there are two Mariannes (the French Republic, represented by a woman wearing the liberty cap), drawn by Cocteau, engraved onto two large mirrors. The furniture was chosen by Cocteau himself: candelabra in the form of palm trees; Spanish style chairs; and a panther skin leading to the marriage table.

Musée de préhistoire régionale (Y M¹) ⊘ – This museum was opened at the beginning of the century in a building specially designed by the architect Adrien Rey. It houses collections from local prehistoric sites, the oldest of which come from excavations carried out by Bonfils (a 19C naturalist from Menton) in the Grimaldi caves.

Ground floor – Reconstructions of scenes of daily life illustrate the evolution of prehistoric man in the Alpes-Maritimes and Liguria from 1 000 000 BC to 1 500 BC: the taming of fire, the development of artistic expression (30 000 years ago), the beginnings of agriculture (5 000 BC) and metallurgy on Mont Bégo (1 800 BC). A film room and an interactive question-and-answer terminal enable visitors to test their knowledge.

The basement contains displays on the history of Menton and popular art and traditions. There are the reconstructions of the insides of Menton houses during the last century; a kitchen and a bedroom. Two more rooms display traditional local objects connected with the cultivation and harvesting of lemons and olives. A gallery of posters commemorates the golden age of Menton's popularity as a winter resort from 1870 to 1914.

Église orthodoxe russe ⊘ – *Rue Morillot; access via avenue Carnot* (**Z 10**). The **Russian Orthodox Church** (1892) was designed by Georg Tersling, a Danish architect. Although its small size is more appropriate to a chapel, the interior is richly decorated with murals by Prince Gagarin and many icons. The present congregation is composed of elderly people of Russian origin but in the 19C a sizeable Russian colony spent the winter on the Riviera. In 1880 they decided to found a convalescent home, La Maison Russe, so that patients with tuberculosis could benefit from the mild climate of Menton. The home, which stands near the church, was particularly helpful to the soldiers who caught tuberculosis in Manchuria during the Russo-Japanese war (1905).

★ GARAVAN AND GARDENS

From promenade de la Mer (**Y**).
Once a handful of elegant private houses set apart from Menton, Garavan has now become – especially since the building of the marina – a luxurious residential suburb of Menton, between promenade de la Mer and boulevard de Garavan, in a splendid setting.

Chapelle St-Jacques – This pretty 17C Baroque chapel houses a municipal gallery of contemporary art exhibitions.

★ **Jardin du Val Rameh** ⊘ – *From promenade de la Mer* (**Y**) *take chemin de St-Jacques.* Arranged around the Villa Val Rameh by the English during the 1930s and then the Musée d'histoire naturelle of Paris, the terraced garden includes over 700 species of Mediterranean, tropical and sub-tropical flora. All these plants are acclimatised to the Menton climate and flourish abundantly. Exotic species are dotted amidst the citrus trees: passiflora, guava, avocado etc. From the terraces there is a magnificent view of the old town and the sea.

Jardin des Colombières ⊘ – *From promenade de la Mer* (**Y**) *take avenue Blasco-Ibañez. Partial redevelopment in progress.* This garden, designed by Ferdinand Bac (1859-1952), humorous writer, architect and landscape gardener, is a homogenous architectural ensemble.

Jardin des Romanciers (Villa Fontana Rosa) ⊘ – This unusual residence can be recognised by its

Jardin des Romanciers, Garavan

J.L. Galle/MICHELIN

porch decorated with ceramics in memory of the great names of Spanish literature. It was built in 1924 by the Spanish novelist Blasco Ibañez. Only the garden is open to visitors. It consists of a harmonious sequence of pergolas and structures, interspersed with ponds and embellished with ceramics of Spanish design.

Oliveraie du Pian – *Boulevard de Garavan.* This olive grove includes more than 500 hundred-year-old olive trees.

Serre de la Madone et Clos du Peyronnet – Serre de la Madone has some plants unique to this garden and Clos du Peyronnet specialises in plants from South Africa. Although they are private properties and usually closed to the public, it is occasionally possible to visit them during events organised by the **Maison du Patrimoine** ⊙ which can provide information on the relevant dates.

Jardin de Maria Serena ⊙ – *Promenade Reine-Astrid.* This garden could be said to have the most temperate climate in France, since the temperature never falls below 5°C. It is known for its large collection of palm trees.

Katherine Mansfield (1888-1923)

This writer from New Zealand, spent a year in Menton from spring 1920. Her delicate health caused her to choose Garavan and she moved into the Villa Isola-Bella *(now in avenue Katherine-Mansfield)*. In this peaceful haven she wrote five of her best works including *The Stranger, The Chambermaid, The Girl.* Writing in her diary, she said: "The house faces the sea; on the right is the old town with its little port and pepper plants growing on a tiny quay... This old town... is the loveliest place I have ever seen."

EXCURSIONS

★ Roquebrune-Cap-Martin

Menton and Roquebrune-Cap-Martin form a ribbon of urban development. *See ROQUEBRUNE-CAP-MARTIN.*

★ L'Annonciade

Round tour of 12km – 7 miles – about 45min.

From Menton take avenue de Verdun (Z 40) running into avenue de Sospel, D 2566 going north.

Ignore a left-hand turning to L'Annonciade and continue on under the Provençal motorway. After two hairpin bends D 2566 bears right to Sospel; bear left and go under the motorway again and continue to the Auberge des Santons where the path to the monastery begins.

The **chapel** ⊙ has been a centre for pilgrimages to the Virgin since the 11C. The present building dates from the early 17C. From the terrace (225m – 738ft) there is a **panorama**★ of the coast from Bordighera point to Cap Martin and of the mountains ringing Menton.

Return by a winding road which rejoins avenue de Sospel in Menton.

Castellar

Round tour of 13km – 8 miles – about 45min. From Menton take route de Castellar (Y), north on the plan.

Castellar is an attractive hilltop village and a good centre for walking. Its parallel streets are linked by covered alleys. From the terrace in place Clemenceau, there is a good **view** of the sea and the surrounding heights. On the return drive, follow the same route for 2.5km – 1.5 miles, then turn right into the winding "Chemin du Mont-Gros". Admire the fine views.

After the cemetery there is a winding road which can be followed to rejoin the D 2566.

★ Ste-Agnès

13km – 8 miles – about 45min – local map opposite. From Menton take avenue Carnot (Z 10) north, turn right into cours René-Coty, avenue des Alliés and rue des Castagnins, D 22.

The road is uphill all the way with views of the Gorbio valley. Bear right at **Col St-Sébastien** (alt 754m – 2 474ft) which gives a particularly picturesque **view**★ of Ste-Agnès. The **site**★ is exceptional. Only 3km – 2 miles from the sea, yet at an altitude of 780m – 2 559ft, the village (the highest on the coast) is perched like an eagle's nest at the foot of a grey limestone cliff which lights up in superb shades of pink at sunset.

The picturesque cobblestone streets of the village, lined with craft shops, include rue Longue and the vaulted rue des Comtes-Léotardi.
A rocky track leads from behind the graveyard to a viewing table in the ruins of the castle. There is a marvellous **panorama**★★.

Fort Maginot de Ste-Agnès ⊘ – *At the entrance to the village, turn towards the parking Sud, and park the car on the left near the entrance to the fort.* This imposing building, camouflaged by the overhanging rocks surrounding it, was built between 1931 and 1938 as part of the reinforcement of the Alpine Maginot Line.
Its firing slots, equipped with 81mm mortars and 75/135mm guns faced southeast over Menton Bay to protect its approaches. The barracks, deep in the cliff, still house a working electric generator, a neutralisation room and the kitchens. The tour of the fort gives an insight into life in such strongholds during the Second World War.
Outside, set slightly downhill, a platform overlooking the intricacies of the Provençal motorway gives a marvellous **view**★★ of the coast from Bordighera in Italy to Cap Martin and Mont Agel to the southwest.

Col de Castillon Road *21km – 13 miles – about 1 hour 30min*

*Leave Menton by avenue de Verdun (**Z 40**) running into avenue de Sospel.*

The road over the Col de Castillon – also called the Col de la Garde – makes its way through a break in the ridge of hills running parallel to the coast and dividing the Menton district from the Sospel basin. From the pass the River Careï flows south to the Mediterranean, and the River Merlanson north to join the River Bévera.

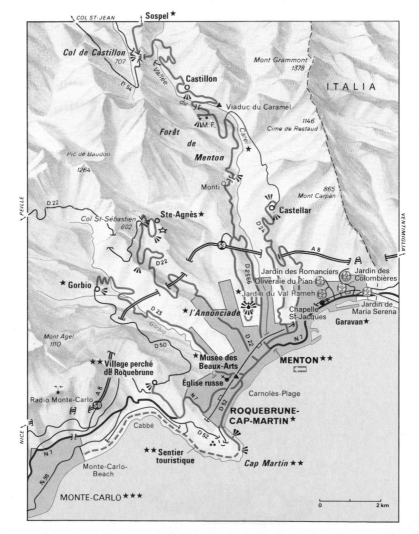

145

After passing under the motorway, D 2566 climbs, twisting and turning as it goes, up the beautiful **Careï valley**★ beneath the bare ridges of the Franco-Italian border to the east. The lemon groves give way to olive and pine trees.

Once past the hamlet of Monti, the road skirts Menton forest, offering fine views.

The tortuous little road which leads directly to the village of Castellar *(see above)* leads off from the start of a bend at the bottom of a dip.

Forêt de Menton – A variety of trees contributes to the beauty of the forest. To the left of the forest refuge *(M.F. on the local map)* a path *(1 hour on foot return)* leads to a **view**★ *(viewing table)* of the coast. The road soon passes the Caramel **viaduct**.

Castillon – On the right lies the new village of Castillon, a model of rural planning, built halfway up the hillside in the Provençal style. The village was reconstructed twice: after the earthquake of 1887 and after the bombardments of 1944. Its main district *(car park nearby)*, overlooking the village, is occupied for the most part by craftsmen.

From the summit, the **view** opens out onto the Careï valley and the Mediterranean.

After the village, the road to the Sospel valley leads off to the left, plunging in and out of tunnels following the tracks of the old tramway which ran between Menton and Sospel. The road leading off to the right soon brings you to the pass.

Col de Castillon – Alt 707m – 2 320ft. The **view** to the north takes in the Bévera valley with the Peïra-Cava and Aution peaks in the distance. To the left D 54 takes a picturesque route to the Col St-Jean.

From here the road drops gradually down into Merlanson valley. Little by little the forest is replaced by olive groves and terraced vineyards. First the stronghold on Mont Barbonnet comes into view, followed by the town of Sospel and the surrounding heights.

★ **Sospel** – *See SOSPEL.*

Vallée des MERVEILLES**

Michelin map 84 folds 9, 10, 19 and 20
or 115 folds 7 and 8 or 245 folds 25 and 26

To the west of Tende, around **Mont Bégo** (alt 2 872m – 9 423ft), lies a region of glacial lakes and valleys, rock cirques and moraines, formed during the Quaternary era, cut off by the lack of roads and the severe mountain climate. The Minière, Casterino and Fontanalbe valleys are clothed with larch woods but the Vallée des Merveilles, which lies between the Grand Capelet and Mont Bégo, has only a thin carpet of vegetation which is covered in flowers in summer. The peaks, valleys and lakes make a magnificent spectacle.

The region, which is part of the **Parc National du Mercantour** is famous for the thousands of rock engravings which have been discovered there, most of which are carved on huge slabs of schist or polished sandstone, known as *chiappes*. It is reached along a tributary valley of the Roya.

The whole of the site known as the Vallée des Merveilles consists of five distinct regions around Mont Bégo.

- the Vallée des Merveilles itself, which is the largest and contains more than half the carvings;
- the Vallée de Fontanalbe, which is narrower and contains about 40% of the carvings;
- the Valmasque, Valaurette and Sabion areas which contain only a few scattered carvings.

PRACTICAL INFORMATION

It is important to bear in mind that these sites are at high altitude (between 1 600m-2 500m/5 429ft-8 202ft) and that certain preparations are advisable – good physical stamina, mountain boots or shoes and warm clothing providing protection from cold and rain. As storms are frequent and sometimes very violent, it is wise to obtain reliable meteorological information. To study the route in advance see Map 1/25 000 Vallée de la Roya – published by the Conseil Général des Alpes Maritimes.

- Guided tours organised by the guides of the Vallée des Merveilles, are the best way of seeing those engravings which are rarely visible or difficult of access. In the high season, apply to the office in Casterino; otherwise apply to the guides office in Tendre (☎ 04 93 04 77 73).

- The Fontanalbe area may be visited without a guide from the Baisse de Valmasque up to the Fontanalbe mountain refuge using the authorised path *(about 3 hours)*. The Arpette area cannot be visited without a guide.

- The regulations appropriate to open-air sites apply within the boundaries of the Vallée des Merveilles – no domestic animals, no fire, no camping or bivouacing within an hour of the park boundaries and no disposing of waste within the boundaries.

- Visitors must not stray from the waymarked paths unless accompanied by an official guide.

- Refreshments are available; it is however wise to book in advance in the season by contacting the place directly – ☎ 04 93 04 64 64 (Refuge des Merveilles) and ☎ 04 93 04 89 19 (Refuge de Fontanalbe).
The local map shows the routes available within the approved boundaries.

OPEN-AIR MUSEUM

The name Bégo is derived from an Indo-European root which means the sacred mountain (Be) inhabited by the bull-god (Go). The region of Mont Bégo is an open-air museum comprising over 30 000 engravings. Although they were discovered and identified at the end of the 17C, it was not until 1897 that they were studied systematically by the British scholar, Clarence Bicknell. In 1947, when the region became part of France, more intensive research was carried out by a team working under Henry de Lumley, which spent 30 years recording every engraving within a wide area (12ha – 30 acres). The engravings are cut into the rock face worn smooth by glacial erosion 15 000 years ago. The linear engravings date from the Gallo-Roman period through the Middle Ages to the present. The engravings which are of most interest to the archeologists are even earlier – the majority date from the early Bronze Age (c 1800 BC to 1500 BC). A stippling technique was used: the contours and surfaces were obtained by the juxtaposition of tiny dots (between 1 and 5 mm – up to 0.2in across) punched in the rock face with flint or quartz tools.

Magic mountain – Although they lack obvious artistic merit, the engravings reveal the preoccupations of the Ligurian people who lived in the lower valleys and made pilgrimages to Mont Bégo, to which they ascribed divine power – both protective, owing to the many streams which rise there, and awesome, owing to the sudden violent storms which rage there.

The engravings exhibit five themes – horns, arms or tools, anthropomorphs, geometric figures and other unidentified images. Here as elswhere, the mountain cult was linked to that of the bull; drawings of horns and bovine creatures feature in half the engravings. Ploughs and harrows harnessed to animals suggest that agriculture was practised; some crisscross patterns may represent parcels of land. There are many representations of weapons which correspond quite well with those excavated on contemporary archeological sites. Human figures are, however, not very numerous; the best known have been given names – the Wizard, Christ, the Chieftain, the Dancer; others, which are more enigmatic, permit of a wide range of interpretation such the Tree of Life at Fontanalbe *(guided tour only).*

ACCESS ROUTES

- either by N 204 up the Roya Valley to St-Dalmas-de-Tende, by D 91 to Casterino village and by one of two footpaths:
- from Lac des Mesches to the Arpette area and the Refuge des Merveilles (3 hours walk)
- from the refuge de Casterino to the refuge de Fontanalbe and the Fontanalbe district (2 hours 30min-walk)
- or from Belvédère up the Gordalasque Valley to St-Grat *(see Vallée de la VÉSUBIE)* and the footpath to Pas de l'Arpette.

The two most popular excursions from St-Dalmas-de-Tende are described below.

WALKING TOURS ⊘

Vallée des Merveilles – *10km – 6 miles north of St-Dalmas-de-Tende by D 91; leave the car at Lac des Mesches.*
Take the signed footpath *(3 hours on foot)* to the Refuge des Merveilles and then to the Lac Long, the starting point for a guided tour of the Arpette area. It is possible to spend the night at the refuge (reservation necessary).

The following morning, walk up the Vallée des Merveilles as far as the Baisse de Valmasque *(about 2 hours 30min)* and then return by the same route to reach the car park in the late afternoon.

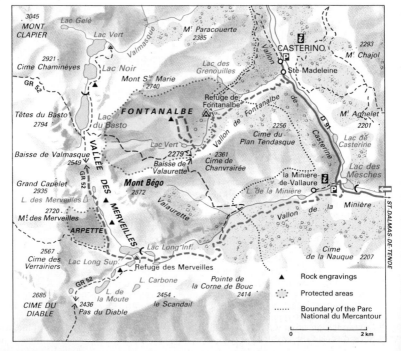

The Wizard and Mont des Merveilles

Fontanalbe – *12km – 8 miles north of St-Dalmas-de-Tende by D 91; park the car in Casterino. Allow one whole day.*
South of Casterino by the information panel *(sign: Fontanalbe)* take the wooded track west and continue to the refuge *(about 1 hour)*. Bear left of the refuge building and continue to Lac Vert *(about 45min)*. For a guided tour of the engravings continue along the side of the lake to the guides' hut at **Lacs Jumeaux**.
By staying overnight at the Fontanalbe refuge *(reservation necessary)* it is possible to climb the foothills of Mont Bégo as far as the Baisse de Fontanalbe (alt 2 568m – 8 423ft) – fine views of the three lakes in the Valmasque Valley. It is possible to continue towards the Valmasque Refuge or to return to Casterino by the outward route.

Regulations at the sites in the Vallée des Merveilles

Although the Bronze Age rock engravings are protected for most of the year by a covering of snow *(from mid-October to late June)*, in recent years they have suffered considerable damage, inflicted intentionally or unintentionally by human visitors. To prevent such defacement the trustees and the officers of the Parc National du Mercantour have limited public access to the Arpette and Fontanalbe sectors only.
Visitors may enter these two areas only if they are accompanied by approved guides *(apply to the Guides Office in Tende)* who are on duty at these two sites daily throughout the summer (2 or 3 tours, each lasting 3 hours).
The main regulations are sympolised by the signs shown below. Violations of these regulations, detected by the official park guides, are punishable by heavy fines.

Do not leave the waymarked path without an official guide

Do not touch the engravings

Do not tread on the engravings

Do not damage the engravings

MONACO***

Population 29 876
Michelin map 84 folds 19 and 20 or 115 folds 27 and 28 or 245 fold 38
Local map see Corniches de la RIVIERA
Plan of conurbation in the current Michelin Red Guide France

The Principality of Monaco, a sovereign state of only 197ha – just under 1sq mile, consists of: Monaco, the old town; Monte-Carlo, the new town; La Condamine which links them and Fontvieille the industrial section. Several million tourists flood into the Principality each year. The glamour of Monaco is embodied not least by its royal family: Prince Rainier, who lost his wife Princess Grace, the former Hollywood actress, in a tragic car accident in 1982 after 26 years of marriage, and their three children Prince Albert and Princesses Caroline and Stephanie.

Native Monégasque citizens (4 500 in 1990) are exempt from taxes and military service.

The Grimaldi family – Monaco, which was inhabited in prehistoric times and later became a Greek settlement and a Roman port, first takes its real place in history with the Grimaldi dynasty. There are numerous branches of the family in France, at Cagnes and Beuil, and in Italy, at Genoa and Naples. During the conflict between the Guelphs and the Ghibellines, François Grimaldi was expelled from Genoa and, disguised as a monk together with his men, captured Monaco in 1297; hence the two armed monks on the Grimaldi coat of arms.

A Grimaldi bought the domain of Monaco from the Genoese in 1308 and, since then, the name and the Grimaldi coat of arms have always been carried by the heirs to the title, whether these come from the House of Goyon-Matignon (1731-1949) or, as the present Prince of Monaco, Rainier III, from the House of Polignac.

A turbulent history – The history of Monaco has been fraught with: family dramas – in the 16C Jean II was killed by his brother Lucien, who in turn was assassinated by his nephew; political conflicts – in 1604 Honoré I was thrown into the sea by his subjects; foreign occupations – by the Spaniards from 1524 to 1641 (it was from the King of Spain that the Grimaldis received the title of Prince), by the French from 1641 to 1814; by the kingdom of Sardinia from 1815 to 1861, and by the French again, when Menton and Roquebrune, which belonged to the Principality, were bought in 1861 by Napoleon III, at the time of the annexation of Nice.

Birth of Monte-Carlo – The first casino was a mean establishment in Monaco itself, set up in 1856 by the Prince, who was short of funds. Only in 1862 did the casino move to its own building in Monte-Carlo where it remained in humble isolation for several years. The arrival of **François Blanc**, director of the casino in Bad Homburg, brought success. Within a few years the casino became fashionable and the surrounding land was covered with luxurious houses, most of them the property of the casino company, La Société des Bains de Mer (SBM). The gaming tables in Monte-Carlo became the most famous and most popular in Europe.

Thriving economy – To accommodate the influx of visitors attracted by the gambling tables and tax concessions, Monaco began to put up buildings at a furious pace until all the available space was occupied and the shoreline has been extended into the sea, thus gaining 22% more land.

Tourism remains the main activity. Without neglecting the traditional visitor, Monaco has sought to capture the business traveller and the conference trade. The hotel complex at Les Spélugues, built on piles below the Casino, comprises a conference centre fitted with the latest equipment and capable of holding 1 100 people. Monaco now has facilities rivalling those of Cannes and Nice. At Fontvieille light industry is being encouraged: clothing, printing, pharmaceutical products, plastics, precision engineering, perfumery, food processing. Around 40 international banking institutions count Monaco as a front-runner in the banking world. The world of the media is represented by Radio et Télé Monte-Carlo, SBM, owner of the Casino and the Hôtel de Paris, is the largest private employer in Monaco.

Original and revolutionary town-planning – The first large town-planning projects which accompanied the economic explosion of the mid-1960s were hampered by the cramped nature of the territory of Monaco.

During the first period, until the end of the 1970s, the solution favoured was to build upwards. A dozen high-rise buildings, more than 30 storeys high, were constructed and established an "American" landscape, expressing through architecture the style of the Monégasque economic expansion.

Since the 1980s a new urban plan has been developed to satisfy the growing residential and service requirements: the future of property in Monaco would seem to lie underground.

All the new access roads are now linked to the French network by deep tunnels. Connections between districts are facilitated by groups of automatic lifts *(see Practical Information)* or escalators. Behind the façade of some of Monaco's luxurious hotels are access ramps to large public car parks hollowed out of the rock.

PRACTICAL INFORMATION
Parking and public transport

Access to the Rock (Rocher) is permitted only to vehicles registered in Monaco and the Alpes-Maritimes. Public car parks in Monaco with more than 500 spaces are:

Sous-sol du Stade Louis II (1 200) **Chemin des Pêcheurs** (600)
Centre commercial de Fontvieille (680) **Les Boulingrins** (600)

There are large lifts providing swift vertical travel in certain districts. The main lifts are:

Place Ste-Dévote to Boulevard de Belgique (longest)
Plages du Larvotto (and Musée National) to Place des Moulins
Avenue Hector-Otto towards Boulevard de Belgique
Avenue de la Costa (Park Palace Building) towards Boulevard Princesse-Charlotte
Centre des Congrès (Boulevard Louis II) towards Terrasses du Casino
Parking des Pêcheurs towards Musée Océanographique
Avenue de Grande-Bretagne towards Avenue des Citronniers
Centre Commercial de Fontveille towards place d'Armes
Port de Monaco towards Avenue de la Costa

Arriving by air – Regular daily service (7min) every 20min between Monaco and the Aéroport de Nice-Côte d'Azur provided by **Héli Air Monaco** at the Héliport de Monaco-Fontvieille. ☎ (00) 377 92 05 00 50.

Money, stamps and telephones – Visitors are required to use local postage stamps and the local coins.
As well as French currency, local coins which are legal tender only in Monaco and the Alpes-Maritimes, are in circulation.
To telephone a number in Monaco, dial 00 377, followed by the number required; to telephone to France dial 00 33, followed by the number required.

Refreshment
Avenue Princesse-Grâce and Avenue des Spélungues offer plenty of opportunities to take refreshment while listening to music:

Piano bars   Harry's (avenue des Spélungues)
Discotheques   Sass Café (avenue Princesse-Grâce)
   l'X Club, Jimmy'z

All the great hotels have an American bar and several luxurious restaurants. The Café de Paris, very luxurious, has an all-night brasserie and a restaurant serving fish specialities.

Shopping
All the famous trademarks have shops in Monte-Carlo and some trade in the larger hotels (Métropole, Park Palace).
Shops specialising in traditional goods are to be found in the narrow streets of the Rock (Rocher) opposite the Palace.
The Boutique du Rocher in avenue de la Madone is the official outlet for local crafts.

Not to be missed

Changing the guard in Place du Palais daily at 11.55am precisely.

Picturesque procession on the Rocher and other cultural spectacles on the national day, 18 November.

Sciaratù Carnival during the week of Shrove Tuesday when local specialities are on offer – *barbagiuàn* and *fougasse* in red and white, the colours of Monaco. Watching the Grand Prix de Monaco from a boat moored in the middle of the port; reservations and information from the tourist office.

Before laying a bet

No-one under 21 is allowed in the gaming rooms. Free admission to the fruit machine rooms in the Café de Paris (from 10am) or in the Casino de Monte-Carlo (from 2pm); the gaming rooms and American games open in the Casino at 3pm (5pm for certain games). The Sun-Casino also has some gaming rooms.

During the summer season *(July to mid-September)* gambling takes place in the Salles des Palmiers of the Sporting-Club de Monte-Carlo (from 10pm). A tax of 100FF is payable in most of the private rooms.

In the Fontvieille district, a bus station has been built 10m – 33 ft below sea-level and a peninsula (22ha – 54 acres in area) has been reclaimed from the sea in 10 years.

Around the town at the bottom of chasms between ancient buildings minuscule excavators can be seen at work: every new building must be provided with a multi-level underground car park.

There are several projects underway and due for completion at the end of this century: an underground railway station and railway lines, the construction of a great conference and exhibition centre which will be embedded in the Larvotto shoreline. Other more long-term projects will bring into play even more daring and innovative techniques, such as the creation of artificial lagoons with a view to building districts over the shallows of Monaco's coast.

★★★ MONACO

Monaco, capital of the Principality, is picturesquely sited on a rock which juts some 800m – 875yds out to sea and drops sheer to the waves below on almost all sides. The upper part, which stands 60m – 200ft above the mainland shore, forms a terrace which is occupied by the old administrative offices of the town, the palace, the cathedral, the gardens and the oceanographic museum. Westwards, beyond the gully through which the road and railway run, are the steep cliffs and caves of the tropical gardens.

In front of the tropical gardens, the Fontvieille district, which is largely industrial, is undergoing large-scale development with the creation of new residential and recreational areas on land reclaimed from the sea *(work in progress)*.

Jardin exotique neighbourhood *1 hour 30min*

★★ **Jardin exotique (AY)** ⊘ – The tropical gardens cascade down a steep rock face which has its own microclimate favourable to cacti and other succulents, particularly arborescents: huge candelabra-like euphorbia, giant aloes, "mother-in-law cushions", Barbary figs. There are 6 000 varieties of semi-desert flora; many of the unusual shapes and vivid colours are native to Mexico and southern Africa. The garden offers many magnificent **views★** of the rock of Monaco, the harbour, Monte-Carlo, Cap Martin and the Italian Riviera *(viewing table)*.

★ **Grotte de l'Observatoire (AYB)** ⊘ – *558 steps*. The grottoes, which open off the tropical gardens, have been well arranged. The tour passes through a number of chambers at different levels, adorned with stalactites, stalagmites and other delicate and varied concretions. The rock is dolomitic limestone.

Excavations at the cave mouth have revealed signs of human habitation some 200 000 years ago; tools and prehistoric animal bones are on display in the museum.

★ **Musée d'Anthropologie préhistorique (AYM')** ⊘ – *Access via the Jardin Exotique.*

The presentation and rich diversity of the exhibits make this museum of interest even to the non-specialist. The Rainier III Room contains regional collections (animal bones and Stone Age tools). Owing to changes in climate not only reindeer, mammoths and cave bears but also elephants and hippopotamuses roamed the Riviera. The skeletons of *Homo sapiens* are impressive: Grimaldi negroids, Cro-Magnon man, collective burials etc.

J. Lebar/PIX

Monte-Carlo

The Albert-I Room contains a retrospective exhibition on the principal milestones of the evolution of mankind. One showcase is devoted to prehistoric figurines (mammoth, horse); the other showcase to the Bronze Age.

St-Martin (AY) ⓥ – The church, built on the site of a former Carmelite chapel and part of a complex in avenue Crovetto-Frères, was designed by the local architect, P Ravirino, and inaugurated in 1876.

Make for the terrace.

From the terrace there is fine **view**★ over Monte-Carlo and Cap Martin, the Rock and Fontvieille.

Enter the church at the upper level.

The sloping nave leads to the choir; a hollow cylinder of concrete suspended from the ceiling directs a shaft of light onto the altar. The colourful stained-glass windows are by Frédérique Duran: on the south wall St Martin, St Joseph, St Rita and St Antony. At the bottom of the nave hangs a striking *Crucifixion and Resurrection* by Marcel de Paredes (1974). In the Saint-Esprit chapel on the lower level the dove-shaped tabernacle hangs from the ceiling.

Fontvieille

Leave the car in the car park under the Louis-II stadium

The new sporting complex, Stade Louis-II, built on daring lines, was designed by the architect H Pottier to withstand earth tremors.

Parc paysager (BZ) – In this park plant species from all over the world are grouped around a charming lake. Adjoining this is the "Princesse Grâce" rose garden with more than 3 500 varieties of rose, some of which were created by celebrated gardeners. The statue of Princess Grâce was created in 1983, the year of her death, by Kees Verkade. On the seafront is the heliport. From here there is a panoramic view inland of the foothills of the principality: the long line of high buildings of the Espace Fontvieille and behind them the sharp outline of the Tête de Chien, dominated by Mont Agel. To the left is the marina of Port-Cap-d'Ail.

The way back towards the shopping centre passes an attractive residential area rising from which can be seen a campanile with a dome covered in glazed tiles. There are three museums on the first level of the **Terrases de Fontvieille**, over the shopping centre.

★ **Collection des voitures anciennes (AY M²)** ⓥ – About a hundred old vehicles and carriages from the royal collection are on display on the five levels of this exhibition hall. On the first level are the barouches used by Prince Charles III. Next is the De Dion Bouton (1903), the first car owned by Prince Albert I, and other famous models: a Lincoln Torpedo convertible (1928), a Packard cabriolet (1935) and the Buick Skylar (1966). The Rolls Royce Silver Cloud given by Monégasque tradesmen to Prince Rainier on his marriage in 1956, and a 1952 Austin London taxi converted for Princess Grace bring a personal touch to this collection. The milestones of the contemporary history of the motor car are represented by a tracked vehicle, Citroën de la Croisière Jaune, a fine selection of front-wheel drives, American military equipment, a Trabant and a 1986 Lamborghini built on futuristic lines.
The 1929 Bugatti (winner of the 1st Grand Prix) and a 1989 Ferrari F1 (600hp) have pride of place in the hall dedicated to Formula 1. On the left, on a pedestal surrounded by flowers, is a helmet worn by the driver Ayrton Senna (killed in 1994), a permanent reminder of the dangers of this sport.

Musée naval (AY M⁴) ⓥ – The hundred exhibits in this museum are the cream of the royal collection of model ships covering a period from ancient times to the present day. The oldest models were built by Prince Albert I in 1874. Among the most remarkable are the **Gondole impériale** made in 15 days for the inspection of Napoleon 1st at Anvers, and the *Missouri*, depicted in the state she was in on 2nd September 1945 when the armistice was signed with Japan.

Musée des timbres et des monnaies (AY M⁵) ⓥ – Housed in a very modern setting, this museum contains all the stamps produced in the Principality together with a fine retrospective of the Princes' collections. The first stamp produced with the head of a Monégasque sovereign was issued in 1885 during the reign of Charles III. Before that date, after the introduction of postmarks, Sardinian stamps were used for franking, and from 1860, overprinted "Monaco".
In the large gallery there is a line-engraving rotary press which was used for half a century to print Monaco's stamps. The rare stamps gallery contains several unique exhibits: letters sent from Fort Hercule (as Monaco was called under the Revolution), and the first stamps from Sardinia and Monaco in colour.
A set of current Monégasque stamps can be bought at reception as well as boxes of coins, both those currently in use and collectors' items.

Outstanding views – There is a view over Fontvieille from place du Palais Princier, near promenade Ste-Barbe, and from the statue of Albert I to the east over the whole of Monte-Carlo and la Condamine. On a fine evening there is a wonderful view of the lights of Monaco from the Grande Corniche or the belvedere at La Turbie.

Sea dragon

★★ **The Rock** *about 3 hours*

Park in Parking des Pêcheurs (**CY**) *and take the lift* ⓥ

★★★ **Musée océanographique** (**CY**) ⓥ – This museum, which is also an institute of scientific research, was founded in 1910 by Prince Albert I.
The founder, who was an oceanography enthusiast, devoted the museum to marine science and housed in it the scientific collections he made during his campaigns after 1885. The large imposing freestone building occupies an exceptional site on the south face of the Rock, overlooking the Mediterranean from an impressive cliff (80m – 262ft).

Basement – The **Aquarium**★★ is one of the finest in Europe. More than 4 500 fish representing 400 different species swim in 90 pools which recreate their natural habitat. The tropical species exhibit the most astounding colours. Among the most strange, magnificent or rare specimens are the flying scorpion fish, the orange clownfish, the surgeon fish and the sunfish. In a great pool (25 000l – 5 500 gallons of water) a nurse shark lives happily with large green turtles and hawksbill turtles. The live coral reef from the Red Sea is a unique exhibit.

Ground floor – On the left, the **salle d'océanographie zoologique**★ (named the Salle de la baleine) contains the skeletons of large marine mammals: a whale (20m – 66ft), washed up on the Italian coast, a killer whale, a sperm whale, a sea-cow, a narwhal as well as stuffed specimens: giant Japanese crabs (2m – 6ft wide), a giant turtle (200kg – 441lb) and casts of coelacanths. An exhibition *(art de la nacre)* of mother-of-pearl contains some splendid carved shells from Prince Albert I's collection as well as recent acquisitions.
In the atrium, opposite the entrance, are life-size models of two diving bells identical to those used on board the *Calypso*.
On the right of the atrium the former conference room has been turned into a cinema showing films made by Jacques Cousteau's team. This hall is also used for important international scientific congresses.

First floor – The central oceanographic hall features the scientific journeys of Prince Albert: models of his four research vessels, notably *Princesse Alice II*. It was on board this ship that, in 1901, the Prince collected fish from a record depth of 6 000m – 19 681ft and on an expedition to Spitzberg reached a latitude of 80°N. Nearby is the reconstruction of the laboratory installed on his last vessel, *Hirondelle II*, as well as his whaling boat from which he was able to recover animals living at great depths from the stomachs of the whales he hunted. Next is the exhibition *Découverte de l'océan* which explains the main marine phenomena: waves, salinity of the water, the effect of the ocean on the atmosphere and more complex questions such as the rise of deep water along certain coasts (upwelling). Among the remarkable animations are a reconstruction of the sinking of the *Titanic*, a gigantic model of the Marianne trench, the deepest in the world, and one of the first submarines, *Bushnell's Turtle*.

Terrace – From the second floor terrace *(lift)*, overhanging the sea, there is a magnificent **view**★★ of the coast from the Esterel to the Italian Riviera and of the Tête de Chien and Mont Agel inland.

Musée de la chapelle de la Visitation (**CY**) ⓥ – This 17C Baroque chapel houses the rich Barbara Piasecka-Johnson collection of sacred works of art. Of particular interest are works by Zurbarán, Rubens and the Italian Baroque masters.

From the museum entrance continue (right) to the Jardins St-Martin.

★ **Jardins St-Martin** (**BCZ**) – Shady walks offer glimpses of the sea through the tropical vegetation. Statue of *Prince Albert I* by François Cogné (1951). The fragments of pillars and capitals come from the church of St-Nicolas *(see below)*.
In season, a little train "Azur Express" ⓥ *makes two circuits from the avenue St-Martin.*

On the car park terraces, near the Musée Océanographique, is the **Monte-Carlo Story** ⓥ. In a large hall an audio visual production on a large screen traces the history of the Grimaldi dynasty and the development of the Principality.

Cathedral (**BY**) – The neo-Romanesque cathedral was built on the ruins of the church of St-Nicolas between 1875 and 1903 of white stone from La Turbie. The high altar, the organ loft and the Bishop's chair, its canopy supported by granite columns, are of white marble encrusted with mosaic and copper motifs. In the south transept chapel is a fine Spanish Renaissance style altar in red and gold. The Princes' tombs are in the ambulatory.
The cathedral has a collection of **early paintings of the Nice School**★★. At the entrance to the ambulatory (left) is the **altarpiece of St Nicolas** by Louis Bréa: 18 sections in glowing colours surrounded by Renaissance carving of leaves and dolphins. In the centre St Nicolas is seated on a green throne; on most panels the names of the characters appear against a gold background: St Devota, patron of Monaco, in a small painting (bottom left); a remarkable Mary Magdalene (right); St Anne curiously cradling both the Virgin as a child and the Infant Jesus in her

arms (top right). Three panels – St Roch, St Anthony and the Rosary – decorate the ambulatory. The *Pietà* of the White Penitents behind the high altar has a charming predella. In the south transept above the sacristy door is an altarpiece by Louis Bréa: a **Pietà** against a Monaco landscape.

Old town – Between the cathedral and the Palais de Justice (law courts), built in 1930 in imitation Italian Gothic, are the shady squares and narrow lanes of the old town. Rue Comte-Félix-Gastaldi (**BY 10**) (Renaissance doorways) leads to rue Princesse-Marie-de-Lorraine (**BCY 54**).

Chapelle de la Miséricorde (**BY D**) – This chapel's classic pink and white façade was built in 1646 by the Black Penitents. In a niche on the south side is a **recumbent Christ★** by the Monégasque sculptor Bosio; on Good Friday this statue is carried through the streets of the old town. *On leaving turn right into picturesque rue Basse* (**BY 3**).

Historial des Princes de Monaco (**BY M³**) ⊘ – In a suite of handsome vaulted rooms the history of the Grimaldi family is set out in 24 scenes with 40 life-size wax figures.

★ **Place du palais** (**BY 35**) – The square, ornamented with cannon given to the Prince of Monaco by Louis XIV, is bordered to the northeast by a crenellated parapet from which there is a **view** of the harbour, Monte-Carlo and the coast as far as the Bordighera headland. To the southwest is the **promenade Ste-Barbe** (**BY 60**) with a view of Cap d'Ail.
The changing of the guard takes place just before midday.

★ **Palais du Prince** (**BY**) ⊘ – The oldest parts of the palace are 13C; the buildings on the south side, in Italian Renaissance style, 15C and 16C. The formidable perimeter is built into the vertical rock. Some battlemented towers remain standing. A monumental doorway with the Grimaldi arms adorns this robust-looking ensemble.
The tour leads first of all to the Hercules gallery which overlooks the lovely **main courtyard** featuring a double staircase in white marble. The whole gallery is decorated with 16C and 17C frescoes – particularly by Ferrari. The Throne Room and the state apartments where official receptions are held are decorated with carpets and precious furniture and hung with portraits signed by Rigaud, Philippe de Champaigne and Van Loo.

★ **Musée napoléonien et des archives du palais** ⊘ – The ground floor of a wing of the palace is devoted to a museum on Napoleon, of whom the Prince of Monaco is a descendant. There are numerous souvenirs and documents: lorgnette, watch, tobacco pouch, tricolour, hat belonging to the "little corporal", King of Rome's clothes; also coins, medals, arms, uniforms, military insignia, flags belonging to the grenadiers on Elba; busts of Napoleon by Canova and Houdon, bust of Josephine by Bosio; on the wall is the family tree of the Bonapartes, originally from Florence, and that of the Prince of Monaco.
Apart from a portrait of Napoleon by Gérard, the upper floor is devoted to the history of Monaco: charter granted by Louis XII recognising the Principality's independence, collection of stamps, coins and medals.

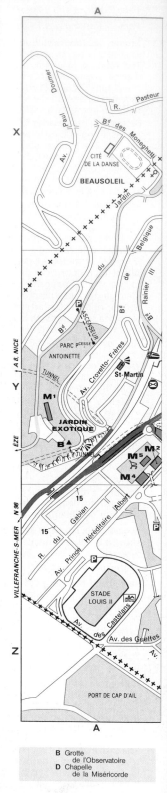

B Grotte
  de l'Observatoire
D Chapelle
  de la Miséricorde

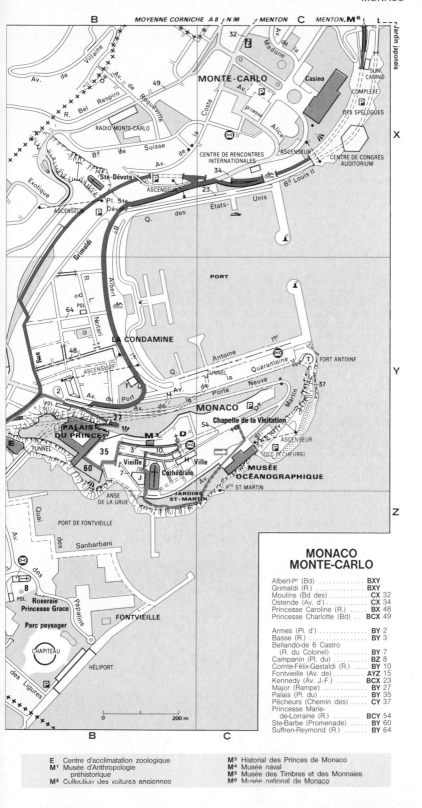

MONACO
MONTE-CARLO

E   Centre d'acclimatation zoologique
M¹ Musée d'Anthropologie
    préhistorique
M² Collection des voitures anciennes

M³ Historial des Princes de Monaco
M⁴ Musée naval
M⁵ Musée des Timbres et des Monnaies
M⁶ Musée national de Monaco

A piece of rock brought back from the moon by the American cosmonauts is also on display.

Pass under the vault to the right of the palace.

Rampe Major (BY 27) – The ramp leads down to place d'Armes, passing through 16C, 17C and 18C gates as it descends the north face of the rock overlooking the harbour and La Condamine.

Centre d'acclimatation zoologique (ABY E) ⊘ – The zoo terraces, on the southwest face of the Rock, present a large and varied collection of mammals, reptiles and birds and numerous monkeys. Fine view of the sea and Cap d'Ail.

LA CONDAMINE *30min*

In the Middle Ages this term applied to cultivable land at the foot of a village or a castle. Nowadays La Condamine is the commercial district, between the Rock and Monte-Carlo.

Port (BCXY) – Prince Albert I was responsible for the harbour which is skirted by a broad terraced promenade and crowded with luxury yachts. The Olympic swimming pool was added by Prince Rainier. In season **boat trips** ⊘ in a glass-bottomed catamaran leave from quai des États-Unis.
From the northwest corner of the harbour a valley separating La Condamine from Monte-Carlo runs up under a viaduct to the church of Ste-Dévote.

Ste-Dévote (BX) ⊘ – Built in 1870 on the ruins of an old church, it contains a fine 18C marble altar.
St Devota was martyred in Corsica in the 3C when, according to tradition, the skiff carrying her body to Africa was caught in a terrific storm and was guided by a dove towards the French coast, finally landing at Monaco.
In the Middle Ages relics of the saint were stolen and taken away by ship. But the thieves were caught and their ship burned – a legend which has given rise to the ceremony which takes place every 26 January when a ship is burned on the square in front of the church; the next day there is a procession.

Rue Grimaldi (BXY) – The busy shopping street, lined with orange trees, leads off place Ste-Dévote.

★★★ MONTE-CARLO *1 hour 15min*

Monte-Carlo is a name famous throughout the world. It brings to mind gambling and also the majestic setting of its palaces, casinos, rich villas, luxurious shops and its flowered terraces, trees and rare plants. Monte-Carlo offers visitors attractions of all kinds.
To the east of the Principality are the man-made beaches, swimming pools and ultra-modern bathing facilities of Larvotto, a luxury development partly built on land reclaimed from the sea which complements the other facilities of Monte-Carlo Beach and is linked to the Spélugues complex by avenue Princesse-Grâce.
Stroking the knee of the equestrian statue of Louis XIV in the entrance of the Hôtel de Paris is said to bring the gambler good luck.

Monte-Carlo Opera House

Casino (CX) ⊘ - The casino is surrounded by beautiful gardens and stands on a fine **terrace**★★ from which the view stretches from Monaco the the Bordighera headland. The terrace is extended by the roof-top promenades of the Spélugues complex which is adorned by a *composition in enamelled* pumice stone *by Vasarely* entitled *Hexa Grace.*

The building comprises several sections: the oldest (to the west), built in 1878 by **Charles Garnier**, architect of the Paris Opera House, faces the sea; the most recent dates from 1910. As one enters the huge central hall, the theatre is in front and the sumptuously decorated gambling rooms on the left. First are the public rooms: the Renaissance Room, the European Grand Salon, the America Room and the Room of the Graces. A small gallery separates the America Room from the rooms of the Cercle Privé (club): the two Touzet Rooms and the vast and ornate François Médecin Room. A grand staircase goes down to the Ganne Room, where there is a nightclub. There is also the auditorium, designed by Charles Garnier.

Pierrot and Dogs by Vichy (1865),
Musée national de Monaco

★ **Jardin japonais (CX)** ⊘ - *Access from boulevard Louis II.* In the extremely urban surroundings of the Larvotto district this garden provides a calm green oasis beside the sea. The garden (7ha - 17 acres), which is designed according to Shintoist principles by a great Japanese landscape gardener, is a very structured miniaturisation of the world of nature. The three fundamental elements of a Japanese garden are illustrated: the line (path), the point (pool) and the surface (waterfall). The mineral constituents come from the Auvergne (granite), from Corsica (porphyry) and from the valley of the Tinée (shingle in the pool). All the garden furniture and the planting are symbolic.

The **Pont Cintré "Taïko"** - This scarlet bridge (the colour of happiness) illustrates the difficult journey towards the gods, represented by the central islands: the one with two pine trees is in the form of a turtle, symbol of longevity; the small island, planted with a single pine, represents a nesting crane.

Near the tea room the **Jardin Zen** (Karésansuï) invites contemplation of the dry countryside outlined by the seven stones of Cap Corse. The ellipses traced on the gravel symbolise the perpetual movement of the universe.

The tea rooms with their restrained design add another oriental note to this unusual display.

★ **Musée national de Monaco** (**CX M⁶**) ⊘ - The national museum of dolls and automata, in a charming villa built by Charles Garnier and preceded by a rose garden ornamented with sculpture - note the *Young Faun* by Carpeaux - contains a collection of 19C automata and some 400 dolls dating from the 18C to the present. The very intricate internal workings are open to view; they are set in motion several times a day. There is an 18C Neapolitan crib including 250 figures.

Everyone has heard of the Monte-Carlo Rally which has taken place each year since 1911 (end January), and of the Monaco Grand Prix Automobile (May) which takes place in the streets of the Principality on a winding circuit (3.145km-2 miles).
There is also the Feast of St Dévote (27 January); the International Television Festival (February); the Spring Arts Festival and the International Tennis Championship (April); the Flower Show (May); the Monte-Carlo Golf Open on the slopes of Mont Agel (June); the concerts in the Palace courtyard and the Fireworks Festival (July-August); the National Day of Monaco (19 November); the International Circus Festival (December)...
There is no need to advertise the reputation of the Monte-Carlo Philharmonic Orchestra or of the Opera – where the work of the most famous choreographers is presented.

WALKS

★★ **Coastal Path to Cap Martin** – *3 hours on foot return (preferably in the afternoon) – local maps see MENTON: Excursions and Corniches de la RIVIERA. For a shorter walk, take the car to Roquebrune-Cap-Martin station and join the path below the station.*
On the left of the Monte-Carlo Beach Hotel, take the steps down between two houses.
For a description of the walk in the opposite direction see Corniches de la RIVIERA ③

★ **Coastal Path to Cap d'Ail** – *1 hour on foot return – local map see Corniches de la RIVIERA.*
Park the car near Plage Marquet, the beach to the west of Fontvieille.
From the beach there is a path along the shore. Monaco Rock soon disappears from sight as the path rounds the headland where the sea throws up a fine spray as it crashes on the rocks. Slowly Cap Ferrat and Beaulieu come into view. On the left of *La Pinède* restaurant, steps lead up to the road and Cap-d'Ail station. The path can be followed as far as Mala beach, then a flight of steps leads to the road back into the conurbation.

★ **Beausoleil; Mont des Mules** – *3km – 2 miles then 15min on foot return – local map and description see Corniches de la RIVIERA.*

*Admission times and charges for the sights described
are listed at the end of the guide
Every sight for which there are times and charges is identified by
the clockface symbol* ⊘ *in the Sights section of the guide*

MONS★

Michelin map 84 fold 8 or 115 fold 22 or 245 fold 36

This old village (traces of a Celto-Ligurian oppidum) is set on an isolated rock spur in the Pre-Alps of Grasse on a wild and sunny **site★** where every type of sub-Alpine Provençal plant flourishes. After several plague epidemics the village was repopulated in the Middle Ages by families from the Genoa region who were probably responsible for the skilful rebuilding of the village and also for bringing the land back into cultivation with olives, wheat and pastureland. The picturesque narrow streets and the little squares with their old fountains make a pleasant walk.

Place St-Sébastien – The square is set off by an 18C fountain; the terrace looks out over the Siagne and Siagnole valleys and provides an exceptional **view★★** which on a clear day ranges from Le Coudon (north of Toulon) via the Lérins Islands and Corsica to the Alps on the Italian frontier *(viewing table).*

Church ⊘ – The building, which was started in the Upper Provençal Romanesque style, was greatly altered in the 15C and 17C. It is fitted with unusually uniform furnishings: five Baroque altarpieces including a huge triptych dating from 1680 on the high altar dedicated to the Assumption of the Virgin and St Peter and St Paul. To the right of the high altar stands a beautiful 15C silver processional cross. The bell in the square belltower dates from 1438.

MOUGINS

Population 13 014
Michelin map 84 fold 9 or 115 south of fold 24 or 245 fold 37

On an extraordinary hilltop **site★**, clothed in flowers and bushes, the old village with its narrow lanes and restored houses is contained within the line of the earlier ramparts; the 12C fortified gateway is known as the "Saracen" gate.
There is a festive atmosphere in place de la Mairie where the solitary old elm and fountain are surrounded by bustle and restaurants. The town hall used to be a chapel for the White Penitents.
From the village there is a wide **view** of the Grasse countryside to the sea. The terrace of the church **belltower** ⊘ gives a superb **panorama★** over the surrounding countryside and the coast.
As early as 1935 Pablo Picasso discovered Mougins in the company of Dora Marr and the photographer Man Ray. He actually settled here in 1961 with his wife Jacqueline, and remained until his death in 1973. They lived in the Notre-Dame-de-Vie district in the *mas* called "L'antre du Minotaure" (The Minotaur's Lair), which became a centre for creative artists.

Musée municipal ⊙ – This museum is located on the first floor of the *mairie*, or town hall, which was built on the foundations of an old chapel dedicated to St-Bernardin. It contains an interesting retrospective of the history of Mougins using period literature. The display includes Roman funerary stelae, a 16C reliquary and numerous exhibits of local handcrafts and agricultural implements no longer in use. Part of the display is given over to **Commandant Lamy**, born in Mougins in 1858, who explored Africa and founded the capital of Chad (once called Fort-Lamy).

Musée de la photographie ⊙ – The photography museum is to be found behind the church belltower, beside the "Saracen" gate, once part of the town's ramparts. The display occupies three floors and includes a lovely collection of old cameras, such as the **cidoscope** an ancestor of animated cartoons, and numerous photographs of Picasso going about his business and of his family, by his friend André Villers. There are also works by great photographers such as Clergue, Doisneau, Duncan, Lartigue, Roth, Otero, Denise Colomb and the press photographer Ralph Gatti.
Some rooms are given over to temporary exhibitions of the works of contemporary photographers.

EXCURSIONS

Notre-Dame-de-Vie ⊙ – *6km – 3.5 miles – about 45min – east of Mougins by D 235 going northwest and D 35 east; after 2km – 1 mile turn right.*
The **site**★ is strikingly beautiful; the **hermitage** of Notre-Dame-de-Vie stands at the top of a long meadow bordered by two rows of giant cypresses (on the right beneath the trees stands a 15C stone cross). The **view**★ towards Mougins is reminiscent of a Tuscan landscape. Here Picasso chose to spend his last years; his house, well screened by trees and bushes, is just opposite.
The **chapel** ⊙ is 17C; the belltower is roofed in coloured tiles. There are three Gallo-Roman funeral inscriptions. On the high altar is a fine altarpiece of the Assumption in blue and gold; on the left-hand wall a collection of votive offerings.
N-D-de-Vie (Our Lady of Life) was a "sanctuary of grace"; stillborn babies were brought there, sometimes from great distances; during the mass the child was thought to revive for a few moments, long enough for it to be baptised.

A track suitable for motor vehicles joins D 3.

★ **Musée de l'automobiliste** ⊙ – *5km – 3 miles southeast. 772 chemin de Font-de-Currault. The* **car museum** *is situated next to the Aire Nord des Bréguières (service area on the north side) of the motorway (A 8); it can also be reached via the footbridge from the service area on the south side.*
The museum can also be approached from Vallauris (see VALLAURIS).
From Mougins take D 234 northwest; turn right into D 3 towards Cannes. Just before the motorway turn left into chemin du Belvédère which becomes chemin des Collines. At the second junction turn left into chemin de Ferrandou, then left again to cross over the motorway. Turn right into chemin de Font-de-Currault, which leads to the museum car park.

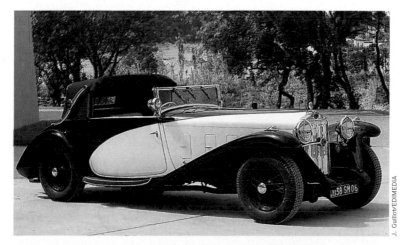

Delage D 8 SS, (1930). Musée de l'Automobiliste Mougins

The façade of the futuristic building beside the motorway is composed of concrete and glass to resemble a radiator. Two motoring enthusiasts, Adrien Maeght and Antoine Raffaelli, assisted by ESCOTA, the company which manages the French Riviera's motorways, have gathered a collection of vintage cars and more recent models, which are displayed in rotation (about 90 at a time). Each vehicle in the gleaming display is in working order; all the famous makes are represented: Benz (first serial model 1894), Bugatti (57, 1938), Ferrari, Hispano-Suiza, Delage, Rolls Royce, etc. The section devoted to racing cars, some of which have won Grands Prix, contains a series of Matras from the years 1967 to 1974. Every year two thematic exhibitions are held stressing some particular aspect of motoring. The museum cinema shows films on the history of the car and the part played in it by each make.

Various activities and competitions are held throughout the year in the entrance court: exchange mart, public auction, best turned-out vehicle etc.

La NAPOULE ⚓

Michelin map 84 fold 8, 114 fold 26, 115 folds 34 and 37 or 245 fold 37
Local map see Massif de l'ESTEREL

Part of the Mandelieu-la-Napoule *commune*, La Napoule, a seaside resort, lies on the shore at the foot of the cliff known as San Peyré or St-Pierre; it has a large marina and three sandy beaches stretching round the bay; the view is very beautiful.

Château-musée ⊙ – Two massive towers, once part of a 14C castle, were restored and converted by the American sculptor, **Henry Clews** (1876-1937), with the help of his architect wife.

The castle, which is a curious mixture of styles – Romanesque, Gothic and Oriental – occupies a magnificent **site★**. The tour includes the gardens, the main rooms, the cloisters and the sculptor's studio.

Henry Clews' **sculptures** belong to no identifiable school. He liked to model people or fabulous animals; he could portray grace and spirituality but some of his work is shockingly realistic. His work is imbued with romantic fantasy.

Art exhibitions and concerts are held at the castle in summer.

★ **San Peyré Viewpoint** – *Access from the post office by rue des Hautes-Roches plus 45min on foot return along the marked path.*

From the top of the cliff there is a view from the Tanneron massif east across La Napoule bay and Cannes to Cap d'Antibes.

NICE★★★

Population of conurbation 475 507
Michelin map 84 folds 9, 10 and 19 or 115 fold 26 or 245 fold 38
Local maps see NICE HINTERLAND and Corniches de la RIVIERA
Plan of conurbation in the current Michelin Red Guide France

Capital of the Côte d'Azur and Queen of the Riviera, no title is too great for this magnificent winter and summer resort, which is also a famous tourist centre. Standing at the head of the Baie des Anges, Nice is sheltered by an amphitheatre of hills. Its popularity comes from the charm of its **setting★★**, its artistic treasures, the wonderful climate and innumerable attractions, including the proximity of the ski slopes.

The Paillon torrent, partly covered by esplanades and above which are the theatre, the Palais Acropolis and the Palais des Expositions, cuts the city in two: to the west, the modern city; to the east, the old town and port, beneath the castle hill.

Nice Carnival in place Masséna

Festivals in Nice – The **Nice Carnival★★★** is famous. The two Saturdays and Sundays that fall within the Carnival dates are marked by processions, confetti battles, fireworks and masked balls *("veglioni")* etc. The **floral processions**, or *batailles de fleurs*, offer a picturesque spectacle and attract huge and excited crowds, drawn by the colourful fruit and flowers.

The summer season now prolongs the winter festivities with popular and fashionable festivals, horse-racing (which takes place on the course at Cagnes), floral processions, open-air theatrical performances and aquatic sports drawing huge crowds of visitors. The Jazz Festival, which attracts famous musicians to the Cimiez arena, and the International Festival of Folk Traditions are held in July (For dates *see Calendar of Events*).

King of the Carnival – The carnival tradition dates backs a long way in Nice; it was referred to as long ago as in 1294, on the occasion of the visit of the Count of Provence, Charles II. The Nice Carnival has always been a wholesome diversion from social tensions and the problems born of the conflicts which were constantly breaking out as a result of Nice's geographical location. Until the end of the 18C, the carnival took place after the Lenten fast in the form of local festivities in the old part of the city.

After a break of several years, caused by the wars of the Revolution and the Empire, the first parade of carnival floats took place in 1830 in honour of the royal visit of King Charles Félix to Nice and the return to Sardinian sovereignty. The form of the modern carnival dates back to 1873, to the impetus given by the painter Alexis Mossa and the formal systemisation of the various stages of the festivities and the setting of a different official theme every year. The Nice carnival-going families belong to long lines of tradition – verging on outright dynasties! – and each "stable" of carnival floats has its own distinguishing characteristics. On average, about a tonne of papier-mâché is used in the making of each float.

Famous painters of Nice have played their part in enriching the carnival decorations. The modern festivities begin with the triumphal entry of "Sa Majesté Carnaval" about three weeks before Shrove Tuesday, or Mardi Gras, when an effigy of the King of the Carnival is then ceremonially burned to mark the end of the carnival period. During the intervening period festivities are in full swing, with parades of carnival floats on Saturdays and Sundays and during some evenings, accompanied by groups of people on foot, in fancy-dress and wearing enormous comic heads made of papier-mâché.

FROM NIKAIA TO NISSA LA BELLA

From the Greeks to the House of Savoy – Excavations at Terra Amata *(see NICE: Additional Sights)* reveal evidence of human settlement in Nice 400 000 years ago. It was a Ligurian stronghold in early history and a trading-post founded about the 4C BC by the Greeks of Marseille under the name Nikaia. The Romans concentrated their colonisation efforts on Cimiez (Cemenelum), whose splendour obliterated the little market town on the east bank of the Paillon with a port at the eastern end of what is now quai des États-Unis.

Barbarian and Saracen invasions, however, reduced Cimiez to nothing, and it was Nice that began to develop under the Counts of Provence in the 10C.

In the 14C, the history of Nice was marked by an important event: Louis of Anjou and his cousin, Charles of Durazzo, Prince of Naples, both advanced their claims on Provence on the death of **Queen Jeanne**, Queen of Sicily and Countess of Provence, who had adopted them. Beautiful and beloved by the people of Provence, this princess was smothered to death on the orders of Durazzo (1382). **Amadeus VII**, Count of Savoy, seizing an opportune moment when troubles divided the country, moved to Provence. In 1388, working secretly with the Count of Savoy, who had been assured of the treachery of Jean Grimaldi, Governor of the town, Nice and its hinterland seceded from Provence and joined Savoy. Amadeus VII entered the city amidst great rejoicing. Along the route of his procession houses were decorated with colourful tapestries, and flowers covered the ground; people danced and sang round bonfires; merchants set up stalls in the streets; and everyone drank to the new sovereign. As Amadeus passed on horseback, cherubs on strings were hoisted into the air waving palm leaves. Except for a few short interruptions, Nice belonged to the House of Savoy until its restoration to France in 1860.

Catherine Ségurane – In the 16C Nice began to feel the effects of the rivalry between the Houses of France and Austria: François I and his Turkish allies launched military operations against the County of Nice, which belonged to the House of Savoy, allied to Charles V. In 1543 French and Turkish troops, under the redoubtable leader Barbarossa, besieged Nice.

It was then that, according to a local tradition, Catherine Ségurane, a woman of the people, earned her fame. As she was bringing food to a soldier on the ramparts, the order for the assault was given, and some Turks appeared at the top of the wall. Catherine flung herself forward, knife in hand, hurled several attackers into the moat below, seized a standard and put fresh courage into the men of Nice. The attack was repulsed. From the ramparts, as a gesture of contempt, Catherine turned her back on the Turks and lifted up her skirts. Other attacks met with greater success and the town fell after more than 20 days of siege; the defenders took refuge in the castle and their resistance was such as to force the besiegers to withdraw. A statue was erected to Catherine by her fellow citizens.

Bonaparte in Nice – The County of Nice, which under the Convention became the Département of Alpes-Maritimes, had been occupied by French troops in 1792 and re-attached to France the following year. In 1794 Bonaparte, then General of Artillery in the army fighting against the Sardinians and the Austrians in the County of Nice, lived at no 6 in the street which now bears his name, and proposed to the daughter of his landlord. It was in this house that he was arrested after the fall of Robespierre. Bonaparte had been on good terms with the Convention member whose brother was the people's representative with the army in Toulon. His detention was short as he put forward a skilful defence.

PRACTICAL INFORMATION
Tourist Information and public transport

There are several tourist information centres:
Gare SNCF, ☎ 04 93 87 07 07.
2 rue Massenet, ☎ 04 93 87 60 60.
Nice Ferber, promenade des Anglais ☎ 04 93 83 32 64. Details of events are also available on the Web: www.mice-coteazur.org.
Public transport (TNL) serves a large area around the town. The *Nice by Bus ticket (carte touristique)* is valid for 1 or 5 or 7 days. There is no public transport on 1 May.

Old town, Nice

Markets
Daily except Mondays

Fish market – the most **picturesque** – place St-François – 7am to midday
Flower market – the most **typical** – cours Saleya – 6am to 4pm; according to the season, bargains are available in the afternoon
Fruit and vegetables – cours Saleya and also the Liberation market which occupies avenue Malausséna and place Charles-de-Gaulle
Flea market – quai Papacino – daily
Antique market – cours Saleya – every Monday

On the town

A good place to pass the hottest hours of the day is in the ice-cream parlours in place Rossetti or cours Saleya. There is music in the piano bars *Mississippi (5 promenade des Anglais)* and *Tam-Tam* (rhum a speciality) *(place Masséna)*. At night the locals frequent two pubs renowned for rock music – *Master Home and Chez Wayne* – in rue de la Préfecture. The *Grand Café de Turin (place Garibaldi)* specialises in seafood. Local specialities are served in restaurants in rue St-François-de-Paule and rue Pairolière.
Casino Ruhl (promenade des Anglais) is worth a gamble.

Shopping

Most shops in Vieux Nice are closed on Mondays; in Nice as a whole many shops are also closed on Shrove Tuesday afternoon.
For local specialities –
Local olive oil from Chez Alziari, 14 rue St-François-de-Paul
Eau de Nice (mimosa scented toilet water) and many other perfumes from Au parfum de Grasse (maison Poilpot), rue St-Gaétan
Le Bellet wine (particularly Château de Bellet) from wine merchants in the old town (rue de la Préfecture) or the producer in St-Romain-de-Bellet
Glacé fruit from Auer, 7 rue St-François-de-Paul
Provençal specialities from the streets around Ste-Réparate Cathedral
– cloth *(rue Paradis and rue du Marché)*
– crafts *(rue du Pont-Vieux and rue de la Boucherie)*
– *santons (rue St-François-de-Paul)*.

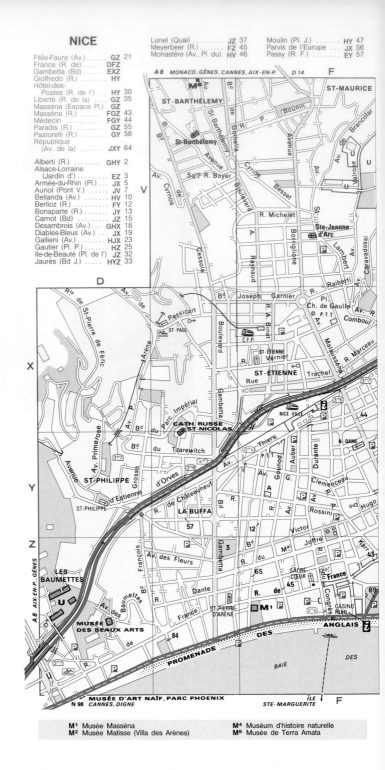

In 1796 he was in Nice again on his way to take over the post of commander-in-chief of the army in Italy. The house where he lived is in rue St-François-de-Paule, in front of the opera. He had married Josephine only a few days earlier and it was from Nice that he wrote the well-known letter: "My darling, anguish at our parting runs through my veins as swiftly as the waters flow down the Rhône... my emotion thunders in my ears like a volcano... I would like to tear out my heart with my teeth..."

At the fall of the Empire in 1814, Nice and its hinterland was handed back to the House of Savoy under the Treaty of Paris.

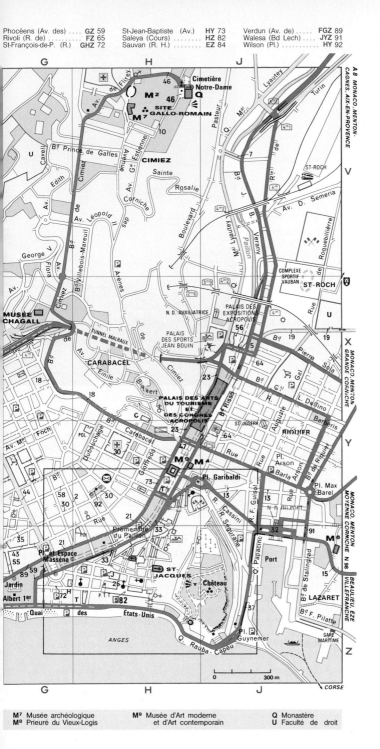

M⁷ Musée archéologique   M⁹ Musée d'Art moderne   Q Monastère
M⁸ Prieuré du Vieux-Logis   et d'Art contemporain   U Faculté de droit

Two men of Nice: Masséna and Garibaldi – **Masséna** (1758-1817), son of a wine merchant, went to sea until he was 17 and then entered French service in the Royal Italian Regiment. As he had to wait 14 years for the gold braid of a 2nd lieutenant, he left the army disappointed. At the Revolution he re-entered the service at Antibes where he was then living; by 1793 he was a divisional general. Napoleon made him a Maréchal de France, Duke of Rivoli and Prince of Essling. His military genius was accompanied by a ruthless ambition which sometimes caused scandal. During his career he is said to have shouted successively: "Long live the Nation! Long live the Emperor! Long live the King! " After Napoleon, he was the general most esteemed by Wellington.

167

Giuseppe **Garibaldi** (1807-82), one of the principal authors of the Italian Revolution of 1860, had an extraordinarily turbulent political and military life in Europe and South America. A great friend of France, he served in the ranks of the French Army in 1870 with his two sons, and commanded a brigade in the Vosges. In the First World War other members of the Garibaldi family fought in the Argonne at the head of Italian volunteers.

Plebiscite – As a result of the alliance of 1859 between France and Sardinia (House of Savoy), Napoleon III undertook to help the Sardinians drive the Austrians out of the provinces of northern Italy for which he would receive Nice and Savoy in return. But the *Peace of Villafranca*, signed prematurely by the Emperor, left Venice to the Austrians, thus not fully realising the aim of the alliance. The cession of Nice and Savoy was all the more compromised as it met with hostility from Britain. In 1860 the *Treaty of Turin* between Napoleon III and the King of Sardinia, Victor Emmanuel II, stipulated the return of Nice to France "without any constraint on the will of the people". The plebiscite was a French victory: 25 743 in favour, 260 against. The entry of French troops and the ceremony of annexation took place on 14 June 1860. On 12 September the Emperor and the Empress Eugénie received the silver-gilt keys to the city from the mayor of Nice in what is today place Garibaldi. These keys are kept in the Masséna museum.

Baie des Anges, Nice

The regions of Tende and La Brigue were to remain Italian territory for 87 years until the treaty of 10 February 1947 allowed France, once more, to extend its natural frontiers to the Alpine chain.

"L'École de Nice" – At the beginning of the 1960s Nice became one of the most lively artistic centres in Western Europe; futuristic exhibitions and other surprising events began to take place. In contrast to the painters who, during the first half of the century, worked in isolation, the new wave mixed life and art. At the instigation of **Yves Klein** who repositioned painting in a purifying movement (vacuum, monochrome paintings symbolising the sky, fire etc) and of **Arman** who elevated everyday accessories to the level of art, the "New Realists" gave a distinctive impulse to modern art in Nice. Other artists then joined the Nice School: Martial Raysse, Sosno, Verdet, Chacallis, Venet and Ben. Some of these artists' works are exhibited in the **Musée d'Art moderne et d'Art contemporain** in Nice, and modern works can also be seen in various public places around Nice.

The present – Since 1860 the development of Nice, which then had 40 000 inhabitants, has been prodigious; it is now the second largest town of Mediterranean France after Marseille and the fifth largest in France itself. Industry plays an important role in the local economy.

Nice is an administrative centre as well as a university town, and its Centre Universitaire Méditerranéen, École Nationale des Arts Décoratifs, Conservatoire de Musique, Centre National d'Art Contemporain and important museums all add to the city's cultural life.

With its Palais des Expositions (an exhibition centre with 20 000 places), its new Palais Acropolis (conference and arts centre) and its many top-rank hotels, Nice remains the foremost tourist centre in France and thereby gains its living.

★★ SEAFRONT *45min*

★★ **Promenade des Anglais (EFZ)** – This magnificent, wide promenade, facing due south and bordering on the sea for its entire length, provides wonderful views of the Baie des Anges which extends from the Nice cape to the Fort Carré at Antibes. Until 1820 access to the shore was difficult but the English

colony, numerous since the 18C, undertook the construction of a coastal path, which was the origin of the present promenade and gave it its name. The famous Promenade has retained a sort of splendour despite being taken over by motor vehicles. The white stone and glass façades of the north side, overlooking the sea, still attract the visitor: Ruhl Casino and Hotel Méridien (1973), Palais de la Méditerranée – fine example of 1930s architecture – the Negresco, a Baroque structure dating from the Belle Époque (*c*1900) and the Musée Masséna. Visible on the façade of the Élysée Palace, overlooking rue Honoré-Sauvan (**EZ 84**), is the monumental bronze *Venus* (1989) by the sculptor Sacha Sosno.

Place and Espace Masséna (KQR) – Started in 1815 in the Italian style, the buildings form an architectural unit in red ochre with arcades at street level. A fountain stands in the southern section: four bronze horses rising from a basin. The north side of the square opens into avenue Jean-Médecin (once avenue de la Victoire) which is the main shopping street, crowded with people and traffic. To the west extends what the 18C English called Newborough. Rue Masséna and rue de France, its continuation, form the axis of a pedestrian precinct; here are smart shops, cinemas, cafés and restaurants between the tubs of flowers; it is a pleasant place to stroll at any hour of the day.

Avenue de Verdun skirts the **Jardin Albert I (GZ)**, a welcome oasis of greenery surrounding a fountain, the *Three Graces*, sculpted by Volti. It is the starting point for tours by two small **tourist trains** ⊙.

★ **Musée Masséna (FZ M¹)** ⊙ – This museum, surrounded by gardens, was built in 1898, modelled on Italian residences of the First Empire, to the design of Georg Tersling and the Niçois A Messian for Victor Masséna, great-grandson of the Marshal. In 1919 his son André gave it to the town.

Ground floor – The group of **salons** in Empire style, directly inspired by the Piedmontese château at Govone, has bay windows looking out on to the promenade des Anglais. The gallery contains statues and paintings (a marble bust of Marshal Masséna by Canova, a full-length portrait of Empress Joséphine by Baron Gros, a full-length marble statue of Napoleon as Roman Emperor by Chaudet) and Thomire vases. On the staircase, two remounted canvases by François Flameng are dedicated to the Masséna family.

First floor – Exhibited in the right wing is a collection of Nice primitives *(see Introduction)*: a reredos of St John the Baptist by Jacques Durandi is remarkable for the intense expression of John the Baptist and the meticulous painted detail on the predella: and the predella of an altarpiece of St Marguerite by Louis Bréa. All these pictures come from the church at Lucéram *(see Lucéram)*. In the centre of the room is a magnificent reliquary, in silver plate and enamel, known as

"Baiser de Paix", from the Italian Renaissance. There is also a Virgin in multi-coloured stone, a 14C Burgundian piece and a 13C reliquary of Saint Commode from Limoges. Primitive Italian, Flemish and Spanish works hang on the walls, as well as a fine 16C French Crucifixion.

There are two rooms devoted to liturgical ornaments (15C to 17C) and to church silver plate as well as Germanic sculpture (16C).

Amongst a fine collection of arms and armour (14C to 18C) are a head guard belonging to Charles V, a bourguignotte (helmet) belonging to Philip II of Spain and a knight protected by German armour said to be "maximilienne cannelée" (16C).

Second floor – Jewels from all over the world are displayed here as well as watercolours by Niçois painters (Trachel, Costa, A Mossa). The exhibition of weights and measures contains a curious clock with 15 faces. The era of great Niçois (Masséna and Garibaldi) is evoked by documents from the period and sculptures and paintings (by Garacci and Detaille). The Revolution and the Empire are represented by a precious sketch of Bonaparte by David, coronation robes of Joséphine and Napoleon's first death mask. The history of Nice is illustrated by watercolours, a fine model of the town in 1890 and models of three superb ships as well as an interesting collection of aristocratic and bourgeois costumes (19C).

Quai des États-Unis (KLR) – The eastern extension of promenade des Anglais passes by two **Galeries-Musées★** devoted to three artists whose works influenced contemporary and more specifically Mediterranean art between 1860 and 1960. The first, the **Galerie-musée Raoul Dufy (KR Y)** ⊘, is devoted to the artist **Raoul Dufy** (1877-1953). Dufy's works (landscapes, still-life paintings, street scenes, carnival scenes...) illustrate the painter's style: vivid colours and freestyle drawings.

The second, the **Galerie-musée Alexis et Gustav-Adolf Mossa (LR X)** ⊘, houses the works of father, Alexis (1844-1929), and son, Gustav-Adolf (1883-1971). Alexis's works illustrate landscapes (watercolour) and carnival scenes; Gustav-Adolf's, whose artistic career lasted from 1903 to 1917, painted strange and fantastic scenes which rapidly evolved into a symbolism, with morbid undertones.

★ OLD NICE *3 hours*

The castle, place Garibaldi and the hanging gardens, where the River Paillon has been covered over, define the limits of the old town, which forms a network of twisting, narrow lanes and steps on the lower slopes below the castle. The tall houses, bright with flowers or washing, exclude the glare of the sun and keep the streets cool. The many small shops, particularly near boulevard Jean-Jaurès, the bars and the restaurants serving local dishes attract an endless flow of people to the district.

The western section, near the former government office (Palais du Gouvernement) and the town hall, was laid out in the 17C on the grid pattern.

Socca

The day started early in those days in the Nice bar where my uncle and I enjoyed our socca. The ingredients include chick-pea flour, olive oil and salt beaten into a smooth mixture, in a large copper pan. It is baked in a wood fire oven, a cooking time based on exact calculation or long experience and a speedy hand in cutting the cake into pieces when it is served. *Socca* will not wait; it must be eaten piping hot – seasoned with pepper.

The recipe has never changed. This is the same socca which used to be delivered all over the town. It was put in a box with a zinc lid and the trays in the delivery vans were kept warm with charcoal heaters. Nothing was more satisfying to labourers, office workers, women shopping or anyone else overcome by the desire for a little something in the morning. It is the same socca which the dockers, who had knocked back a laced coffee at 5 o'clock, used to consume in the bars of Nice at half past six. It was their breakfast, *merenda*.

Louis Nucera
Chemin de la Lanterne (1981)
Éd. Grasset

Park the car at the end of quai des États-Unis to walk up to the castle. Take the lift (ascenseur) ⊘ – the entrance is to the left of the 400 steps, which also lead to the castle.

Follow the arrows slightly downhill to visit the naval museum.

NICE

B Ancien Palais du Gouvernement	**M⁵** Galerie de malacologie	**S** Chapelle de la Miséricorde
E Monument de Catherine Ségurane	**M⁹** Musée d'Art moderne	**X** Galerie-Musée Alexis
F Chapelle du Saint Sépulcre	et d'Art contemporain	et Gustave-Adolf Mossa
K Maison Lascaris	**R** Chapelle de l'Annonciation	**Y** Galerie-Musée Raoul Dufy

Tour Bellanda (LR) - This enormous circular bastion, for all its appearance, only dates from the 19C, when it was built as an identical replacement for one of the towers of the citadel which had been destroyed by Louis XIV's troops in 1706. The composer Berlioz *(Roméo et Juliette, La Damnation de Faust)* lived here during the time he spent in Nice, which he wrote of with great enthusiasm: "Here I am in Nice, breathing the warm, balmy air... Here life and happiness come running swiftly to greet me, music folds me into her arms, and the future smiles on me... Here I am in Nice, strolling through orange groves..."

Musée naval ⊙ - The naval museum is at the top of the Tour Bellanda. At the entrance are two 17C Portuguese bronze cannons. Inside are models of ships, arms and navigational instruments. The walls are decorated with views of old Nice and there is a model of the port at different periods in its history. A section is devoted to competitive sailing and pleasure boating.

Château (LR) - This is in fact the name given to the 92m - 300ft high hill, arranged as a shaded walk, on which Nice's fortress once stood. Catinat blew up the powder magazine in 1691 and the fortress itself was destroyed in 1706 by the Duke of Berwick, marshal of France (1670-1734), the illegitimate son of James II who served in the French army.
From the wide platform on the summit there is an almost circular **view**★★ *(viewing table)*. Below the terrace is an artificial waterfall fed by water from the Vésubie. On the eastern side the **foundations of an 11C cathedral** (apse and apsidal chapels) have been uncovered. Below these ruins a Roman level and a Greek level have been excavated.
Walk round the ruins. From the northwest corner of castle hill *(follow the arrows to "Cimetière, Vieille Ville")* there is a path affording **bird's eye views** of the roofs of old Nice and the Baie des Anges. Steps lead down from near a chapel on the left.

St-Martin-St-Augustin (LQ) ⊙ - In this, the oldest parish in Nice, Luther, who was an Augustinian monk, celebrated mass in 1510, and Garibaldi was baptised. The church has a fine Baroque **interior**★ with a *Pietà*, the central panel of an altarpiece by Louis Bréa, on the left in the choir.

Outside, opposite the entrance, is a **monument** erected in 1933 to Catherine Ségurane *(See NICE: NIKAIA to NISSA LA BELLA)* (**LQ E**).

Place Garibaldi (**LQ**) – The square was laid out at the end of the 18C in the Piedmont style, the buildings coloured yellow ochre. It marks the northern limit of the old town and the beginning of the new. A statue of Garibaldi stands squarely among the fountains and greenery. The **chapel of Saint Sépulcre** (**LQ F**) on the south side of the square belongs to the Blue Penitents Brotherhood; it was built in the 18C and has a blue Baroque interior.

Rue Pairolière, a shopping street, goes past the St-François belltower, part of a Franciscan convent which moved to Cimiez in the 16C.

Place St-François (**LQ 69**) – A fish market is held here in the mornings round the fountain. To the right is the classical façade of the former town hall now the Labour Exchange (Bourse du Travail).

Fixed to a house on the corner of rue Droite and rue de la Loge is a cannon ball which dates from the siege of Nice by the Turks, allies of François I (1543).

Palais Lascaris (**LQ K**) ⊘ – The palace was built in the Genoese style, influenced by local tradition, from 1648 by J-B Lascaris, a descendant of the Counts of Ventimiglia whose family was allied with the Lascaris, emperors of Nicaea in Asia Minor in the 13C. The façade is decorated with balustraded balconies supported on consoles of carved marble and columns with flowered capitals; scrollwork ornaments the doorway.

On the ground floor a pharmacy from Besançon (1738) has been reconstructed to display a fine collection of flasks and tripods.

A grandiose balustraded **staircase★**, decorated with 17C paintings hanging in rockwork niches and 18C statues of Mars and Venus, leads to the second floor. The salon is hung with Flemish tapestries; the *trompe-l'œil* ceiling is the work of Italian artists from Genoa: the *Fall of Phaeton*, similar to one in Cagnes. In the next room hang two Flemish tapestries from sketches by Rubens. The state bedchamber is separated from the antichamber by a stucco screen supported by atlantes and caryatids.

On the other side of the staircase are the private apartments displaying 18C ceilings, painted medallions framed in stucco work and Louis XV woodwork inlaid with silver beneath landscaped piers.

Ste-Réparate (**KR**) – The **cathedral** was built in 1650 by the Nice architect, J-A Guiberto, and dedicated to the patron of Nice, who was martyred in Asia Minor at the age of 15.

Colours enhance the well-proportioned façade in which the Baroque style is very evident between the ground level and the first cornice in the elegant arcading of the doorway and the decorative niches and medallions. The belltower is 18C and the church is roofed by a magnificent dome of glazed tiles.

The **interior★** is a riot of Baroque plasterwork and marble. The high altar and choir balustrade are of marble adorned with heraldic bearings; the frieze and cornice are particularly graphic; 17C panelling in the sacristy.

★ **St-Jacques** (**LR**) – Built as a chapel in the 17C, this church is reminiscent of the Gesù church in Rome.

Twin fluted columns support a barrel vault opening into side chapels containing loggias for the noble families. The general effect is highly ornate: there are 164 painted and 48 carved cherubs. The ceiling is painted with scenes from the life of St James and there are several paintings presented by various brotherhoods; a 16C *Pietà* stands on the right.

The **sacristy**, formerly the chapter-house, contains 14 huge walnut cupboards (1696), some of which display the church treasure; pyxes, monstrances and reliquaries.

Turn left into rue Droite, right into rue Vieille and left into rue de la Poissonnerie.

Chapelle de l'Annonciation (**KR R**) – Originally dedicated to St Giaume (St James the Apostle), the chapel is known locally as the **Chapelle Ste-Rita**, an Italian saint still venerated in Nice as the armfuls of flowers and pyramids of candles at her altar *(left on entering)* and in the sacristy show.

Midday cannon

Each day at noon a short cannon shot is heard to remind people that it is lunchtime. This custom was introduced by a visiting Englishman, Sir Thomas Coventry, who grew tired of irregular meal times. He offered to buy and maintain a cannon for the town so that each day a shot could be fired at noon from the castle hill. The tradition has been maintained, although the cannon has now been replaced by an explosive device.

The interior is a profusion of local Baroque **decoration**★: altars and rails inlaid with marble, sumptuous altarpieces (in the Lady Chapel, which is adorned with a 16C marble statue of the Virgin), painted and coffered vaults, fine panelling. The entrance door is handsomely carved outside.

Cours Saleya (KR 82) – Once the elegant promenade of old Nice, it is now lined with shops and restaurants. The famous **flower market** is held here in this picturesque quarter.

Go along the right-hand side of cours Saleya.

Galerie de malacologie (KR M⁵) – The gallery, an annexe to the natural history museum, houses a collection of molluscs from all over the world: rare specimens of unusual shape and colour. Fish, molluscs and vegetation from the Mediterranean and the Red Sea are displayed in aquariums.

★ **Chapelle de la Miséricorde (KR S)** ⊘ – The chapel, which belongs to the Black Penitents, is a masterpiece of Nice Baroque (1740) and was designed by the 17C Italian architect, Guarino Guarini. A bowed façade, garlands and oval windows accentuate the rounded motif of the exterior design.

The architect's virtuosity is clearly demonstrated in the chapel's interior: the complex interplay of vaulting in the bays and in the harmonious combination of gold and imitation marble.

In the sacristy there are two early Nice **altarpieces**★ of Our Lady of Pity. Jean Mirailhet's work is in the Gothic tradition but the panel painted some 80 years later by Louis Bréa betrays the influence of the Italian Renaissance and shows the Virgin against a Nice landscape.

To the north is the elegant 18C façade of the old **Palais du Gouvernement (KR B)**, decorated with alternate Corinthian and Doric columns and crowned by a balustrade. The clock tower on the left is 18C.

★★ CIMIEZ (HV) *3 hours 30min*

Cimiez hill is the sophisticated part of Nice with many large houses. At the top of boulevard de Cimiez is a statue of Queen Victoria who used to stay in Cimiez. *Starting from place Jean-Moulin, behind the Acropolis, drive west along boulevard Carabacel and follow the route marked on the plan.*

★★ **Musée Marc-Chagall (GX)** ⊘ – The result of Chagall's donation to France, this museum built in 1972 by A Hermant houses the most important permanent collection of the painter's works. It is built partly in glass and hidden among the trees on a hill in Cimiez. The setting was designed especially bearing Chagall's "Biblical Message" in mind. The canvases are shown to their best advantage owing to the recessed walls and the large windows opening onto the bright Mediterranean light.

Welcoming the visitor into a world of lyrical and almost sacred fantasy is a multi-coloured tapestry (1971) showing Chagall's personal feeling for the Holy Scriptures brought from his past – born (1887) of a poor Jewish family in Vitebsk in Russia. He died at St-Paul in 1985.

This poetical lyricism is visible in all **17 canvases** which make up the "Biblical Message", an endeavour of 13 uninterrupted years (1954-1967). In a large gallery are displayed 12 paintings

Jacob and the Angel by Marc Chagall

Musée Chagall, Nice – © ADAGP, Paris 1996

evoking the Creation of Man, the Garden of Eden, the Story of Noah, Abraham, Jacob and Moses; among Chagall's world of rich translucent colours lies a magic spell of poetic enchantment which yet does not detract from the seriousness of the subject matter. In a nearby gallery are five paintings illustrating the Song of Songs: dreamlike figures drift among glowing colours above the rooftops of sleepy villages.

There are also several sculptures by the artist; from the library door look outside and admire the large **mosaic** (1970), which is reflected in the pool: it represents the Prophet Elijah, taken up to Heaven in a chariot of fire, surrounded by the signs of the Zodiac.

The circular gallery (used for concerts and conferences) is immersed in a bluish light emanating from the three large windows depicting the Creation of the World. The other rooms are either taken up by temporary exhibitions or devoted to the development of the "Biblical Message". There is a series of 39 gouaches painted by the artist in 1931 after his return from Palestine. Some of the themes were taken up again and appear in his larger canvases, 105 etchings and copperplate engravings for the Bible edited by Tériade in 1956; 200 sketches (oils, pastels, gouaches, drawings) showing the artist's preliminary study and a series of lithographs.

★★ **Musée Matisse** (Villa des Arènes) (HV M²)⊙ – This museum is housed in a splendid patrician villa, a typical example of the development of town architecture in Nice. In 1670, on the site of a hut *(cabanoun)* buried in the ancient remains of Cimiez, a folly was built, with numerous symmetrical windows and façades decorated with coloured pebble-dash and *trompe-l'œil* paintings and extended by balustraded terraces. The site of the villa, facing the sea, and the characteristic Genoese architecture are explained by the ease of trade and the links between the rich families of Nice and Liguria. Its owner, the consul of Nice, named it "Palais de Gubernatis". In the 19C successive additions were made by the new owners to adapt it to a large town house. In 1950, when it was *in extremis*, the town of Nice saved it from being divided up and rechristened it Villa des Arènes. Since its redevelopment in 1993, it has housed the collections and administrative offices of the Musée Matisse on its two levels.

A large composition of cut-out gouaches, *Flowers and Fruit*, which is the master's last work (1953), greets visitors at the entrance.

About 30 **canvases** show the progression of the artist from the timid attempts of his early works in 1890, *Still Life: Books*, to his blossoming in 1946, *Rococo Armchair*. He went from a dark realistic style to the discovery of the bright Mediterranean light, passing through the influence of Cézanne with *Still Life: A Harmonium* and Signac, *Young Woman with an Umbrella*, and culminating from 1916, *Portrait of Laurette*, onwards with an explosion of pure and brilliant colour: *Odalisque with Red Case* 1926, *Window in Tahiti* 1935, *Nude in An Armchair* 1937, *Reader at the Yellow Table* 1944, *Still Life: Pomegranates* 1947 as well as the "pure blue" of *Blue Nude* IV (1952).

Drawings from his many different periods are also on display. Among the 235 works, which make the museum's collection the most significant one of the artist's work, are 30 sketches for the mural *The Dance* (1933). There are also many examples of book illustrations.

Matisse's activity as a sculptor is also well represented by 54 of the total of 62 **bronze sculptures** he produced during his lifetime. Note in particular the *Serf* (c1900) and *The Serpentine* (1909). The development of more abstract form shows in the series of *Jeannette (1910-13)*, *The Nudes*, *Henriette* (1925-29) and culminates in the monumental work *Nudes from Behind*. Two rooms contain sketches and models for the chapel at Vence *(See VENCE)*, which Matisse worked on from 1948 to 1951. There are also the silkscreen prints: *The Sea, The Sky* (1947) and a huge Beauvais **tapestry**: *Polynesia*.

Dispersed about the museum are his personal effects, his furniture and his private art collection, all of which are often depicted in his paintings. The museum is also equipped with an auditorium and an information centre on Matisse.

Musée archéologique (HV M')⊙ – Finds excavated at Cimiez (the ancient site of Cemenelum) and around Nice, as well as donations make up the archeological museum's collections.

The ground floor is divided into two sections. The right side exhibits ceramics and bronzes from the great Mediterranean civilizations (Greece, Etruria, Roman Africa); some of the items, such as the superb **mask of Silenus★**, were found in shipwrecks.

The left side concentrates on the Ligurian and Roman civilizations from the region which became, in 14 BC, the Alpes-Maritimes: Bronze Age (statue of a warrior from Mont Bégo), Iron Age (items excavated from perched strongholds – *oppida*), milestones (1C) from the Via Julia Augusta.

Roman civilization is represented by examples of daily life (pottery, glassware, statues, jewellery...), and public life (inscriptions), a display of imperial coins in an interactive glass case, as well as models and maps of Cimiez, statues of the Imperial family (Antonia, Augustus's niece), and Roman cults.

The ground floor presents the funerary customs found at Cimiez: incineration in the 1C and 2C *(stelae)* and inhumation beginning in the 3C *(sarcophagi)*. The tour ends with examples of the paleo-Christian civilization (4C and 5C) with pottery, coins, inscriptions...

★ **Gallo Roman Archeological Site** (Site archéologique gallo-romain) (HV) ⊘ – *Plan of site below*. **Cemenelum**, the seat of the Roman Procurator of the Alpes-Maritimes province, is estimated to have had a population of 20 000 at the end of 2C BC.

Roman Baths – Steps lead down into the *decumanus maximus* (the main east-west street of a Roman town) with its central drain and shops. On the left are the **North Baths**, probably reserved for the Procurator and other worthies. The summer bath (1) consists of a marble basin surrounded by a peristyle with Corinthian capitals.

On the eastern side are the latrines (2). The northern building contains the cold bath (**frigidarium**) – it was vaulted and its dimensions (10m - 33ft high by 9m - 30ft wide) give an idea of the huge scale of the northern baths – the warm room (3) and the hot rooms (4), built above the **hypocaust** (underground stove), and the public rooms, partially excavated.

On the other side of the main street (Decumanus I), are the less elaborate but fully equipped East Baths for the general public, which can be viewed from a walkway.

To the south of these baths is a parallel street (Decumanus II) lined with houses and shops; some of the paving stones remain.

The western end of this street opens into the *cardo maximus* (main street running north-south) which returns to the Matisse Museum. On the left-hand side are the **West Baths** for women only. The fabric is quite well preserved, although it was used as a cathedral in the 5C; the choir (5), in the *frigidarium*, contains traces of an altar and a semicircular stone seat.

The neighbouring room to the north was used as the **baptistery**.

Amphitheatre – The elliptical arena which is only 67m x 56m - 220ft x 184ft, could hold 4 000 spectators.

Traces remain of the gangways and of the sockets on the external façade, which held the posts carrying a huge adjustable awning *(velum)* used to shelter the spectators from the sun and rain. The amphitheatre was designed for spear contests and gladiatorial bouts but not for animal fights. Traditional festivals take place here all year round *(fêtes des Mai, fêtes des Cougourdons*, folk festivals...) and there are performances in the summer months *(see Calendar of Events)*.

Place du Monastère (HV 46) – A twisted column of white marble, rising in the square in front of the church, bears a **Calvary** dating from 1477. On one side is the crucified seraph who appeared to St Francis and imprinted the stigmata of the Passion on his body; on the other, St Clare and St Francis of Assisi stand on either side of the Virgin.

Nearby in the Cimiez **cemetery** are buried the painters Raoul Dufy and Henri Matisse who were leading exponents of Fauvism. The latter's tomb lies in an olive grove to the north of the surrounding wall.

★ **Monastery** (HV Q) – The Franciscans, who in the 16C took over the buildings of a former Benedictine monastery founded in the 9C, restored and several times enlarged the abbey church.

Notre-Dame-de-l'Assomption – The church possesses three **masterpieces**★★ of the early Nice School.

To the right of the entrance a **Pietà** (1475) by Louis Bréa; although a youthful work, it is one of his most perfect. The arms of the cross and the stiff body of Christ emphasise the horizontal composition; the gold background reveals glimpses of a landscape. Weeping cherubs cluster round the Cross while the lonely figure of Mary holds her son on her knees. One of the two side panels represents St Martin sharing his scarlet cloak; the slight inflection of the figures gives a rare elegance to the composition.

Quite different but as beautiful is the **Crucifixion** by the same artist which is on the left in the choir. It is a later work (1512); the gold background has been replaced by an elaborate landscape showing perspective. The predella is masterly, the lances reinforcing Jesus' arrest, in contrast to the oblique treatment of Christ bearing the Cross. In the second chapel to the left lies a recumbent figure of Christ in wood (18C). The **Deposition**, in the third chapel, which is attributed to Louis Bréa completes the Cruxifixion and adheres to Renaissance principles: the figures obliquely aligned on the body of Christ are counterbalanced by the vertical lines of the landscape. A huge half Renaissance-half Baroque altarpiece carved in wood and decorated with gold leaf screens off the monks' choir.

Conventual buildings – *Not open to the public.* These are grouped about two cloisters: the small cloister (16C) on groined vaulting and the great cloister where concerts are given during the summer *(details from the tourist office)*, and which opens on to the Cimiez gardens through a fine gate.
Church service daily at 6.30pm. Entrance via the small cloister.

Musée franciscain ⊙ – The **museum** recalls the work of the Franciscans in Nice from the 13C to the present day. The social and spiritual message of the Franciscans is proclaimed through documents and works of art (frescoes, engravings, sculptures) in a restored section of the old monastery. There is also a fine illuminated antiphonary (17C), the novices' chapel and a restored 17C cell.

Monastery Gardens – On the south side of the monastery there are attractive terraced gardens with flower beds and lemon trees which look down on the Paillon valley from a **viewpoint** over Nice, the castle and the sea, Mont Boron and the observatory to the east. A copse of cypress and holm oak marks the site of the former Ligurian oppidum.

WEST OF TOWN

★★ **Musée des Beaux-Arts (Jules Chéret)** (DZ) ⊙ – The Fine Arts museum has been housed since 1928 in a residence built in 1878 in the Renaissance style of 17C Genoese palaces for the Russian princess Kotschoubey. The museum displays a rich collection of art of all types, built up through donations and legacies around a nucleus of works sent to Nice by Napoleon III in 1860 for the creation of the first museum of fine arts.

Ground floor – On the side of the façade there are three galleries. In the first vaulted gallery, which is devoted to the Italian Primitives, note *Death of Cleopatra* by Francesco Cozza and *David Conqueror of Goliath* by Francesco Guarino. The second gallery displays 18C works such as *Portrait of an Old Man* by Fragonard, *Ollioules Gorges* by Hubert Robert and *Allegory of Human Life* by Donato Creti. The third gallery is given over to the important artistic dynasty, the **Van Loos**, whose most illustrious member, Carle, was born in Nice in 1705. Works of his on display include *Theseus, Conqueror of the Bull at Marathon*. Jean-Baptiste Van Loo executed the famous portraits of Louis XV and Marie Leszczynska. The great gallery which opens off to the right of the entrance is decorated with large official paintings from the Third Republic, such as *Thamar* by Cabanel and some marvellous portraits of women. The patio which follows is home to *Bronze Age* by Rodin and *Triumph of Flora* by Carpeaux.
At the end of the gallery the small room on the right displays miniature 17C and 18C works.

First floor – The main staircase leads to the hall on the first floor which was used originally by musicians because of its acoustics. It is now adorned with the works of **Jules Chéret**, who died in Nice in 1932.
The first floor is mainly devoted to the art of the second half of the 19C and the start of the 20C. The first of four large galleries, all used for temporary exhibitions, concentrates on the academic tradition (Boulanger, Trachel...) and the work of orientalists such as *Rest during the Flight into Egypt* by Merson and the celebrated *Harem Servant* by Trouillebert. Among the sculptures on display is the original plaster cast of *The Kiss* by Rodin.
In the gallery, as well as a Carrière intimist, a fine series of works by the pre-Impressionist Félix Ziem evokes the romantic countryside.
The second gallery behind the façade displays paintings showing the evolution of the French countryside from the classicism of Cordouan to Impressionism represented by Boudin *(Villefranche Anchorage)*, Monet, Sisley *(avenue of Poplars near Moret)* and Bonnard *(Window open on the Seine at Vernonnet)*. The third gallery is hung with pastels by Jules Chéret, the inventor of modern posters. The last room is reserved for collections by lesser-known 19C artists, grouped by subject: nudes, genre paintings, landscapes.
On the right, at the end of the gallery, two rooms display works linked to Maria Bashkirtseff, Bastien-Lepage, her spiritual mentor and to her rival Louise Breslau. The Van Dongen gallery houses the Fauvist artist's major works: *Pious Dream* and the celebrated *Dance of the Archangel*. In the display cases are ceramics by Picasso.

La Madone des sleepings – The young Russian princess Maria Bashkirtseff, nick named Moussia, spend about ten winters in Nice where she carried on a correspondence with Maupassant and was noted for her eccentricity. She was dubbed the *madone des sleepings* (the sleeping-car madonna) by certain writers. A stone slab commemorates her stay at 63 promenade des Anglais.

★ **Musée d'Art naïf Jakovsky** ⊘ – *Avenue du Val-Marie. Leave the town centre by promenade des Anglais* (**DZ**).

The Anatole Jakovsky Bequest comprises 600 canvases *(about half are on show)* illustrating the amateur talents of many countries.

The Croatian artists *(mostly on 1st floor)* include Generalic, Rabuzin, Kovacic and Petrovic. Among the French are Bauchant, Vivin, Vieillard, Restivo and Crociani *(Festival by Night in Nice)* and more dreamlike paintings by Vercruyce and Lefranc *(Clock)*. There are also works by Italians, Swiss, Belgians and Americans, from both the north and the south (particularly Brazil).

There is a section reserved for a series of portraits of Jakovsky and a room devoted to works by unknown artists from the 17C to the 19C.

Musée des trains miniatures ⊘ – *Avenue Impératrice-Eugénie. From promenade des Anglais, go west towards Fabron, then follow the signs (right) to the museum.*

This museum, on a hill from which there is a broad view of Nice, contains a remarkable collection of railway models; there are nearly 10 000 exhibits, the oldest of which date from the end of the 19C. Extensive circuits, with detailed reconstructions, provide varied backgrounds for about 50 miniature trains which represent the evolution of the railways. There are also aircraft models and many old lead figures.

★ **Parc Phœnix** ⊘ – *From promenade des Anglais, head towards the Nice-Côte-d'Azur airport and turn right by the giant greenhouse in Parc Phoenix into the road signed "Parc Phoenix" which leads into the new Arenas complex. There is an underground car park.*

This vast botanical garden (over 7ha – 17 acres), inaugurated in 1991, is organised by theme and contains over 2 000 species of plant from all over the world, grouped with their corresponding animal life. Visitors wander at will in this popular park around five large zones, each reflecting a particular period or climate. The "île des temps révolus" (island of the wheels of time), in the middle of a big lake, takes visitors back into the past with a display of living plant fossils: cycads, ginkgo biloba, tree ferns etc. The crater of scents and colours next to it displays a selection of colours harmonised with the perfumes of each plant.

Throughout the park, discreetly positioned loudspeakers emit the calls and songs of the animals and birdlife which correspond with the particular zone of plant life the visitor is in.

Studios de la Victorine – the story of cinema in Nice

With the dawning of cinema, Nice provided the film-makers with the ideal ingredients for their future success: almost permanent light and sunshine, the sea and the presence of magnificent hotels as natural backdrops.

Louis Feuillade, who made *Fantômas*, was one of the first to spot the potential of the area; the roofs of the Hôtel Négresco passed into cinematic posterity in the Fantômas – Judex chase.

The "azure cinema" really took off in 1920, however, when a large unoccupied property to the town west of the centre, La Victorine, was acquired by the fabulously rich Hollywood producer Rex Ingram, who had launched Rudolf Valentino and Roman Navarro. He produced an epic historical film, *Mare Nostrum*, to promote his new studios.

From that time, La Victorine studios saw both French and European film-makers prosper for the following ten years. Then changes in public tastes brought another decade of inactivity.

The Armistice of 1940 caused French cinema to seek refuge in Nice (Abel Gance, J Prévert, M Carné).

The filming of *Visiteurs du Soir* in 1943 revived the production of large-scale films.

In 1944 came *Les Enfants du Paradis*, co-produced by M Carné and J Prévert with Arletty and J-L Barrault, which was the greatest production at La Victorine. The reconstruction of the "Boulevard du Crime" in the middle of the war required more than 30 tonnes of scaffolding and nearly 3 500m² of fencing for the sets, as well as 2 000 extras who were recruited in Nice.

The worsening of the general situation and lack of money temporarily brought a halt to this creativity.

The 15 post-war years were good ones; they were followed by a lull.

Nowadays, after several abortive projects, a revival of filming seems to be underway.

– In the second zone, an aviary houses a colourful collection of parrots and other tropical birds. The wadi-oasis reconstitutes part of an oasis in the Sahara.

– The **giant greenhouse**★, the "green diamond", is an enormous tropical greenhouse covering 7 000 m² – 75 300ft² beneath a 25m – 82ft high roof in which seven climates of differing temperatures and hygrometry are housed: an orchid garden; a greenhouse containing plants from the southern hemisphere; an underground vivarium-insectarium; a lovely garden of ferns from various places; and in the centre of it all, a large tropical garden containing palm trees and Madagascan traveller's trees as well as trees cultivated for food (banana, breadfruit, coffee, papaya etc). Carry on from the giant greenhouse to see the carnivorous plants and the butterfly house.

Nearby, the information centre or **infothèque** provides visitors with telematic data bases to consult for general and detailed information on tropical plants.

Outside, to the right, a garden of tropical plants and a beautiful rose garden flourish side by side.

The "great Aztec pyramid" is an original way of displaying what goes on below ground level, as regards both plants and the lives of animals which live underground.

A large circular fountain and various musical fountains add the finishing touches to the visitor's voyage of discovery.

Faculté de droit (DZ U) ⊘ – On the first floor landing of the **law faculty** a large-scale **mosaic**★ by Chagall covers the whole of one wall: *Ulysses returns to Penelope in Ithaca*.

ALONG THE PROMENADE DU PAILLON

Muséum d'histoire naturelle (HJY M⁴) ⊘ – The natural history museum, which is linked to a laboratory, houses a curious collection of 7 000 casts of fungi, and an exhibition of minerals. There is also a stratigraphy section which explains the formation of the earth's crust: fossils, geological phenomena.

★ **Palais des Arts, du Tourisme et des Congrès (Acropolis)** (HJY) ⊘ – The building (55 000m² – 592 000 sg ft), which extends (338m – 369yds) between avenue Gallieni and boulevard Risso, is like a majestic vessel anchored to the five robust vaults which span the River Paillon. It was designed by a group of local architects and the names of its various parts were taken from Greek antiquity.

It comprises five floors articulated by the agora, a vast reception hall lit by immense windows and covered by a retracting metal roof; the vast auditorium (2 500 seats), which is on the south side and called Apollo, has exceptionally good acoustics; the north side comprises the conference centre and Athena auditorium (750 seats), the Mediterranean Room, lecture and meeting rooms, radio and television studios etc.

Contemporary works of art, which harmonise perfectly with the architecture, are displayed both inside and outside the building, along both sides and on the esplanade Kennedy in front.

These sculptures, paintings and tapestries are signed by Volti *(Nikaia)*, Vasarely, Arman *(Music Power)*, César *(Thumb)*, Paul Belmondo, Moretti *(Louis Armstrong)*, Cyril de la Patellière *(Homage to the Mediterranean)* etc.

★★ **Musée d'Art moderne et d'Art contemporain** (LQ M⁹) ⊘ – Designed by Yves Bayard and Henri Vidal, the museum of modern and contemporary art is made up of four square towers with roof-top terraces and linked by glass passageways. On the parvis, between the museum and the theatre, stands a monumental stabile by Alexander Calder.

The collections, exhibited in rotation on the two upper floors (first floor is devoted to temporary ex-

Musée d'Art moderne, Nice, ©ADAGP 1994

Nissa Bella by Raysse, Musée d'Art moderne in Nice

hibits), presents French and American avant-garde art movements from the 1960s to the present. Both these countries were developing parallel art movements which evolved from similar experimenting; in France these ideas were often nurtured by artists living on the Riviera. In the 1960s the American **Pop Art** movement and the French **Nouveau Réalisme** *(see Klein below)* attempted to express the reality of daily life in a modern society of consumerism and popular culture. Where Pop artists Andy Warhol, Roy Lichtenstein, Tom Wesselmann, James Rosenquist, George Segal, Robert Rauschenberg etc appropriated objects belonging to mass culture, the New Realists, more derisive, sought inspiration from those same objects as symbols of modern life, by collecting or breaking them (Arman), compressing them (César), capturing them under glass (Spoerri), or packaging them (Christo)...

A section of the museum is devoted to the French painter **Yves Klein** (1928-62), whose monumental work, *Wall of Fire*, is located on the roof-top terrace. Putting aside his association with the French movement (he was the founder of Nouveau Réalisme, a term which means new realism and was coined in 1960 by the art critic Pierre Restany), Klein attempted by monochrome paintings, where gold and especially IKB (International Klein Blue) were used, to capture and express space, energy or the universal essence of things.

Fluxus, an off-shoot of the neo-Dadaist movement, closely linked to music (John Cage), and similar in ideology to the Happenings, was formed by a group of artists centred in Germany in the early 1960s. These artists were opposed to the rift between art and daily life. Their theory was propounded, when Beuys was prompted to question, while holding some lard, why something so essential to daily life could not be used in art? The Nice artists Ben, Serge III, Robert Filliou and Brecht explored this theory in more depth.

During this same decade abstraction in the United States was progressing in several directions: questioning the colour matter with artists Morris Louis and Larry Poons or reflecting on the support itself with artists Frank Stella and Kenneth Noland. This influenced two movements in France, the **Support-Surface** (Viallat, Pagès, Dezeuze, Dolla, Alocco, Cane, Arnal...) and their Nice counterparts who were assembled under the Groupe 70 (Charvolen, Chacallis, Isnard, Maccaferri, Miguel); these two movements sought to reduce painting to its materialistic reality playing with the frame or support and sought ways to apply colour to the surface. They followed Simon Hantaï's (*b* 1922 of Hungarian origin) experimenting with canvas, out of its stretcher, which is cut, suspended, folded... the American **Minimalists** (Sol Le Witt, Richard Serra) reduced to the minimum the artist's intervention by going back to elementary forms, at times using repeated identical units and industrial materials; this idea was not foreign to the French BMPT; a group of artists (Buren, Mosset, Parmentier, Toroni) who in 1966-67 were experimenting with the idea that the work be reduced to its most simple materiality – support, colour, texture.

The 1980s saw the return of figurative art, already announced by such artists as the Dutchman Karel Appel (b 1921; a member of COBRA, a European movement 1948-51). Different methods were used: traditional references for Gérard Garouste (mythological scenes) and Jean-Claude Blais, while rock culture and comics inspired the artists of Figuration Libre (Robert Combas, Hervé Di Rosa, Blanchard...), who sought simply to create without being preoccupied by realism. The museum also holds works by artists belonging to the Nice School, who were closely in tune with the movements flourishing in USA at that time but for the past 30 years have followed their own vision, such as Bernar Venet, Sacha Sosno, Gilli, Jean-Claude Fahri, Robert Malaval, Chubac...

ADDITIONAL SIGHTS

★ **Cathédrale orthodoxe russe St-Nicolas** (EXY) ⊘ – With its six gilded onion domes and its façade of ochre brick, the **Russian Orthodox cathedral** lends an exotic touch to the Nice skyline and symbolises the importance of the Russian colony on the Riviera. It is the largest Russian religious building outside Russia itself. The frequent visits to Nice of the Russian nobility, who were regularly joined by the Imperial Court, gave rise to the erection of an immense Orthodox place of worship. The Villa Bermond was donated by the dowager Empress in 1900 for the construction of the new cathedral. The Russian architect Préobrajensky drew the plans and oversaw the work. The choice of materials was enhanced by the generosity of Tsar Nicolas II: the bricks came from England, the glazed tiles on the domes and the six crosses surmounting them from Italy, the domes are covered with fine gold leaf and the mosaic icons on the façades were handmade by Russian artists. The inauguration took place in December 1912 in the presence of the Imperial Russian family. Other icons and devotional articles were given refuge in the cathedral after 1917.

The interior, in the form of a Greek cross, is richly decorated with frescoes, panelling and icons. At the entrance to the choir is a sumptuous **iconostasis**★ bringing together the finest examples of Russian religious art, taken from the church of Jaroslav and the church of St Basil the Blessed in Moscow. On the right of the choir is an icon of **Our Lady of Kazan**, painted on wood and decorated with chased silver and precious stones. At the end of the park on the left a **Byzantine chapel** is dedicated to Tsarevich Nicolas, the son of Tsar Alexander II, who died of an illness here in 1866. His funeral was an imposing ceremony in Nice at the Russian church in rue Longchamp.

Ste-Jeanne-d'Arc (**FV**) ⊘ – This is a modern church designed by Jacques Droz in concrete with three segmented cupolas and an ellipsoidal porch as main doorway. The belfry wreathed with flames rises to a height of 65m – 215ft. Inside, the soaring vaulting is striking. The stations of the cross are frescoes by Klementief (1934).

Prieuré du Vieux Logis (**EV M⁸**) ⊘ – The museum consists of a priory reconstructed in a 16C farm and richly supplied with works of art, 14C to 17C furniture and items from everyday life (outstanding kitchen). There are numerous statues including a 15C *Pietà* from Franche-Comté.

St-Barthélemy (**EV**) – The church's Renaissance façade, restored in the 19C, is complemented by a modern belltower in the Italian Quattrocento style. Within *(right aisle)* is a triptych by François Bréa: *Virgin in Majesty*.

St-François-de-Paule (**KR**) – The church is a fine example of Nice Baroque. The sanctuary (1750) is surmounted by a belfry roofed with coloured tiles; over the Dominican door on the left is a carving of the Virgin and Child.
The interior has the theatrical and worldly appearance so dear to Baroque art. The choir is surrounded by "stage boxes" behind grills reaching to the upper floor. *The Communion of St Benedict* on the right of the entrance is attributed to Carle Van Loo. The statue of St Dominic (1949) between the two chapels on the left is carved in olive wood.

Port (**JZ**) – For 2 000 years ships simply tied up in the lee of the castle rock. A deep water port was excavated in 1750 under Charles-Emmanuel III, Duke of Savoy, in the marshy ground at Lympia. In 1870 and 1904 it was extended and made deeper; two breakwaters were built to create an outer harbour where the car ferries from Corsica now dock until a new terminal is built. The harbour is busy with craft of all kinds.

Musée de Terra Amata (**JZ M⁶**) ⊘ – A model of a sand dune on a fossil beach, which has been uncovered 26m – 85ft above the present sea-level on the western slopes of Mont Boron, is reproduced on the ground floor of the museum, built on the site of the excavation. An open hearth and a human footprint with a calcified surface were found in the hardened limestone.
Bones, stone tools and traces of fire mark one of the earliest human settlements known in Europe. Articles, drawings, maps and a full-scale reconstruction of a shelter made of branches illustrate the life of the Acheulean hunters some 400 000 years ago (early paleolithic).

BOAT TRIPS ⊘

In the season the *Gallus* boats run cruises ⊘ along the Riviera.

EXCURSIONS

★★ Les Deux Monts

Round trip of 11km – 6 miles – about 45min – local map see Corniches de la RIVIERA.

*Leave Nice from place Max-Barel (**JY**) on N 7, Moyenne Corniche, going east. After 2.5km – 1.5 miles turn sharp right into a forest road. 1km – half a mile further on turn sharp left into a path leading to the fort on Mont Alban.*

★★ **Mont Alban** – Alt 222m – 728ft. A footpath circles the height from which there is a splendid **view**★★ of the coastline: to the east lie Cap Ferrat, Cap d'Ail, the Bordighera headland and the limestone heights of Tête de Chien; to the west lie the Baie des Anges and the Garoupe plateau. The fort, a massive 16C construction with bastions and watchtowers, can be explored on foot.
Return to the fork and bear left to Mont Boron.

★ **Mont Boron** – Alt 178m – 584ft. From the mountains there are **views**★ extending over the Villefranche anchorage and along the coast to Cap d'Antibes. On the horizon can be seen the mountains around Grasse and, further to the left, the Esterel.
Return to Nice along the Corniche Inférieure (N 98).

★★ Plateau St-Michel

Round tour of 19km – 12 miles – about 1 hour – local map see Corniches de la RIVIERA.

Leave Nice going east along avenue des Diables-Bleus and the Grande Corniche (D 2564).

Look back to enjoy views of Nice and the Baie des Anges and later Cap d'Antibes and the Paillon basin. Ahead lie the fort of La Drète in the foreground and Mont Agel further back.

Observatoire du Mont Gros Ⓥ – *The private road to the Nice observatory leads off to the right of the Grande Corniche.*

This famous international centre for astronomical research was founded in 1881 by the scientific patron Bischoffheim. Charles Garnier was responsible for construction of the buildings, while Gustave Eiffel built the metallic frame of the great dome (26m – 85ft in diameter). This houses an astronomical telescope called the "great equatorial". It is 18m – 59ft long with an optical diameter of 76cm – 30in and was for a long time the largest instrument of its type in the world. Note the neo-Classical pediment at the entrance to the dome, typical of its period.

Beyond the 4-Chemins Pass, Cap Ferrat peninsula and Villefranche-sur-Mer anchorage come into view.

Bear right into D 34 and after 500m – 547yds leave the car in the car park.

★★ **Plateau St-Michel Viewpoint** – A viewing table points out all the main features of the coast from Cap d'Ail to the Esterel.

Continue along D 34 and then bear left into the Moyenne Corniche (N 7). After a long tunnel there is a marvellous **view★** of Beaulieu, Cap Ferrat, Villefranche-sur-Mer, Nice and Cap d'Antibes. The road winds round above Villefranche anchorage. After the Col de Villefranche, Nice with its castle hill, the harbour and the Baie des Anges comes into view; on the horizon the outline of the Esterel and the limestone hills of Grasse.

Return to Nice via place Max-Barel.

Michelin Maps (scale 1: 200 000), which are revised regularly, indicate:

– golf courses, sports stadiums, racecourses, swimming-pools, beaches, airfields

– scenic routes, public and long-distance footpaths, viewpoints

– forest parks, interesting sights...

The perfect complement to the Michelin Green Guides
for planning holidays and leisure time
Keep current Michelin Maps in the car at all times

NICE Hinterland★★

Michelin map 84 folds 9, 10, 18, to 20 or 115 folds 6 to 9, 16 to 19, 26 to 28 or 245 folds 25, 26, 38, 39

The Corniches de la Riviera, the breathtaking scenic roads between Nice and Menton, may be the most famous features on this stretch of coast but the Nice hinterland, which is equally mountainous and served by switchback roads, is also worth exploring to discover the hill villages, the wild gorges, the wooded slopes and the glacial cirques.

The **Pre-Alps of Nice**, a chain of mountains oriented north-south, extend from the Var to the Roya and rise to between 600m and 1 800m – 1 969ft and 5 905ft. The land is drained by many river valleys: the two Paillons, the Vésubie, the Bévéra and their numerous tributaries. To the north the mountain chain abuts the crystalline massif of Le Mercantour where the peaks rise to 3 000m – 9 842ft.

★ ☐ TOUR OF MONT CHAUVE

Round tour of 53km – 33 miles – about 2 hours 30min – local map overleaf

From Nice take avenue du Ray north; turn sharp right into avenue de Gairaut, D 14, towards Aspremont and after passing under the motorway (2km – 1.2 miles) bear right following D 14 and then turn left following the signs.

Cascade de Gairaut – In two great steps the waters of the Vésubie Canal, which supplies Nice, tumble down into a basin. From the chapel terrace there is a beautiful view of the town.

Return to D 14.

Soon there are fine views on the left of Nice and Mont Boron and of Cap d'Antibes. As the road climbs to Aspremont, the **view** extends to include the Baous, the Var valley and the mountains.

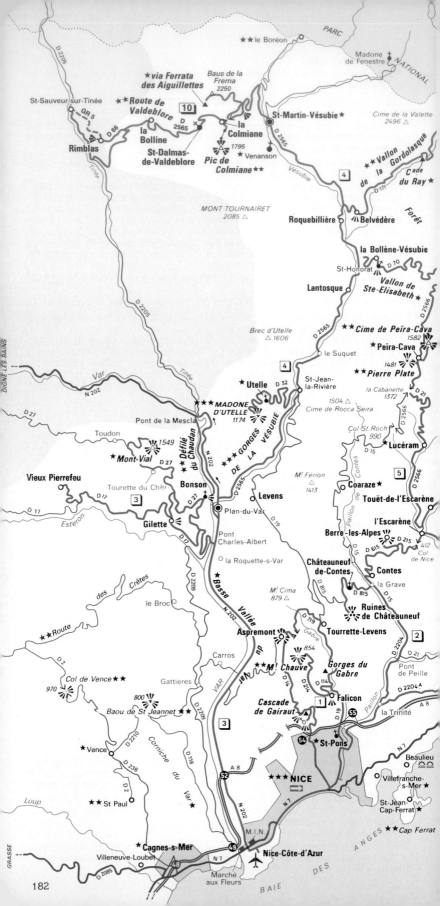

PARC

★★ le Boréon

Madone
de Fenestre

NATIONAL

St-Sauveur-sur-Tinée

★ via Ferrata
des Aiguillettes

Baus de la
Frema
2250

10

la Bolline

la
Colmiane

St-Martin-Vésubie ★

Cime de la Valette
2496 △

D 2205

GR 5

D 66

Rimblas

Route de Valdeblore ★★

D
2565

St-Dalmas-
de-Valdeblore

1795

Venanson

★★ Vallon de
la Gordolasque

4

C.ᵈᵉ
du Ray ★

Pic de
Colmiane ★★

Tinée

D 2205

MONT TOURNAIRET
2085 △

Vésubie

Roquebillière

Belvédère

Forêt

la Bollène-Vésubie

St-Honorat

D 70

Lantosque

Vallon de
Ste-Elisabeth ★

Var

DIGNE-LES-BAINS

N 202

Tinée

Brec d'Utelle
△ 1606

D 2565

le Suquet

★★ Cime de Peïra-Cava
1582

★ Peïra-Cava

1481

★★ Pierre Plate

4

★ Utelle

D 32

St-Jean-
la-Rivière

la Cabanette
1372

D 27

D 2205

★★ MADONE
D'UTELLE
1174

1504 △
Cime de Rocca Seira

D 2566

D 21

Toudon

Pont de la Mescla

GORGES

DE

LA

VÉSUBIE

Col St-Roch
990

Lucéram ★

1549

D 27

★ Mont-Vial

Défilé du Chaudan

M.ᵗ Férion
△
1413

D 15

Contes

5

D 2566

Vieux Pierrefeu

Tourette du Ch.ᵃᵘ

Bonson

D 2565

Levens

★ Coaraze ★

Touët-de-l'Escarène

Esteron

D 17

3

Gilette

D 17

N 202

D 27

Plan-du-Var

D 19

l'Escarène

Berre-les-Alpes

D 215

412
Col
de Nice

Pont
Charles-Albert

o la Roquette-s-Var

Basse

Châteauneuf-
de-Contes

D 615

D 15

Ruines
de Châteauneuf

la Grave

D 815

2

★★ Route

des

Crêtes

le Broc

Vallée

M.ᵗ Cima
879 △

Gorges du
Gabre

Contes

D 815

Pont
de Peille

D 2204

D 21

D 2

Col de Vence ★★

970

Gattières

Carros

N 202

Aspremont

854

Tourrette-Levens

D 719

D 2204

★★ M.ᵗ Chauve

Gabre

D 114

800

Baou de St Jeannet ★★

D 2209

VAR

D 14

D 214

Cascade
de Gairaut

Falicon

D 19

1

la Trinité

D 2204

3

★ Vence

D 2210

Corniche

du

Var

D 118

52

A 8

55

54

★ St-Pons

N 7

Beaulieu

D 236

D 2

Loup

★★ St Paul

★★★ NICE

49

Villefranche-
s-Mer ★

St-Jean-
Cap-Ferrat ★

A 8

M.I.N.

Cap Ferrat ★★

Cagnes-s-Mer

Nice-Côte-d'Azur

ANGES

DES

GRASSE

48

Villeneuve-Loubet

N 7

D 2085

Marché
aux Fleurs

BAIE

182

MⁱCLAPIER 3045 △

★ Cascade de
l'Estrech

Lac Vert

★★ Tende

CUNEO

Roya N 204

8

D 145

MⁱSACCAREL
2200 △

Vⁿ de Fontanalbe

Casterino

Casterine

Val de la

Mⁱ du Grᵈ
Capelet △
2935

Baisse de Valmasque

△ 2872
Mⁱ Bégo

9

Lac des Mesches

la Brigue

D 43

Levense

★ Vallée des
Merveilles

Vallon

de

la

Minière

D 91

St-Dalmas-
de-Tende

D 45

N.-D. des-
Fontaines ★★

2685 △
CIME DU DIABLE

Refuge des Merveilles

DU

Granile

Haute

Vallée

de

la

Roya

MERCANTOUR

Gorges de Bergue ★

N 204

Fontan

l'Authion ★★
1889

pⁿᵗᵉ des
3 Communes ★★
2082

D 68

Mⁱ
aux Morts

D 68

Cabanes Vieilles

★★ Gorges
de Saorge ▲

Saorge ★★

8

1607
Col de Turini

Vallée

Turini

D 2566

Moulinet

Mⁱ Mangiabo
△ 1801

△ 2204

Roya

la Giandola

Breil-s-Roya ●

de

879

Col de Brouis ★

5

N.-D. de
la Menour

la

7

Bévéra

Col du Pérus
654

Piène-Haute ★

N 204

I T A L I A

Gorges du
Piaon ★★

Mⁱ Agaisen
△ 745

Nervia

Col
e Braus
1002

St Roch ☆

Sospel ★

Bévéra

Braus

N 204

Mont Barbonnet △
847

642 △
Col St-Jean

D 2566

Mérlançon

Col de Castillon
707

S 20

Clue de Braus

6

Castillon

▲ Viaduc du Caramel

Roya

Forêt
de Menton

Vallée
du Carei

Monti

GENOVA

es du Paillon

D 21

Peille ★

Ste-Agnès ★

Castellar

A 10

S 1

la Grave

2

Gorbio ★

D 23

Mont Agel
1110 △

Roquebrune-

D 22

59

A 8

D 2566

MENTON ★★

Ventimiglia

Peillon ★

D 53

St-Martin-de-Peille

Cap-Martin ★

N.-D.
e Laghet

57

N 1

Cap Martin ★★

56

la Turbie

MONTE-CARLO ★★★

Èze ★★

MONACO ★★★

Cap-d'Ail

M E R   M É D I T E R R A N É E

ARRIÈRE-PAYS NIÇOIS

0   5 km

183

Aspremont – The village, built to a concentric plan, perches prettily on its hill site. The **church** ⊙ has a Gothic nave, decorated with frescoes and supported on solid cubic capitals; on the left there is a painted wooden Virgin and Child. Above and behind the church once stood the castle, now destroyed. From the terrace which overlooks the town is a **panorama**★ comprising several hill villages, Vence, Cap d'Antibes, the hills behind Nice, Mont Chauve and Mont Cima.

On leaving the village, take the D 719 over a little pass, the Col d'Aspremont, between Mont Chauve and Mont Cima to the rich basin of Tourrette-Levens.

Tourrette-Levens – The village clings to a knife-edged rock. The 18C **church** ⊙ has a fine carved wooden altarpiece, also 18C, of the Virgin between St Sylvester and St Antony (behind the high altar). A short walk through the village to the castle (partially restored) reveals **views** of the neighbouring mountains – Chauve and Ferion – and the Gabre and Rio Sec valleys.

Return to D 19 turning left down into the Gabre valley.

Gorges du Gabre – The ravine walls are limestone.

Bear right into D 114 towards Falicon.

Falicon – Typical Nice village huddled on a rocky outcrop among the olive groves. The Bellevue inn *(panoramic view from the terrace)* displays souvenirs of Jules Romains (1885-1972) who wrote about Falicon in one of his novels.

Other illustrious guests were attracted to the village by its delightful setting. Queen Victoria came from Cimiez and drank tea here; the restaurant has commemorated this visit with a sign: *Au thé de la Reine.*

The **church** ⊙ founded by the Benedictines of St-Pons, has a square belfry and a façade in *trompe-l'œil.* In the nave is a beautiful 17C Nativity framed in gold.

Climb up the stairway to the left of the church and turn right into a path leading to a terrace for a **view**★ of Nice, the sea, the hills and Mont Agel.

Return to D 114; turn left.

At the chapel of St-Sébastien turn right into D 214, a narrow and dangerous road, to Mont Chauve.

Leave the car at the end of the road.

Mont Chauve d'Aspremont – *30min on foot return.* Alt 854m – 2 802ft. "Chauve" means bald, and the mountain lives up to its name. A disused fort stands on the naked summit offering a magnificent **panorama**★★: the snow-clad Alps and the Nice hills and the coast from Menton to Cap Ferrat. On a very fine day Corsica is visible.

Return to D 114 turning left; 2km – 1.2 miles further on turn sharp right into D 19. Go under the motorway; 1km – half a mile later there is a righthand turning up to St-Pons.

★ **St-Pons** – The Benedictine abbey of St Pontius was founded in Charlemagne's reign and played an important part in local affairs for 1 000 years. The **church** ⊙, which was rebuilt early in the 18C, stands on a headland above the Paillon valley, its graceful silhouette and Genoese campanile visible on all sides. The elegant curves and counter-curves of the tall Baroque façade are echoed in the peristyle. The building forms an ellipse, preceded by a vestibule, prolonged by a semicircular choir and ringed by side chapels opening out between powerful columns. Rich plasterwork decoration.

★ ② THE TWO PAILLONS

Round tour of 90km – 56 miles – allow one day – local map above

The Paillon de l'Escarène, the main river, rises to the northeast of the Col St-Roch, while the Paillon de Contes springs from the upper slopes of Rocca Seira to the northwest of the pass; they join at Pont de Peille and reach the coast in Nice. The suggested route goes up one valley and down the other with detours to La Turbie and Peille.

Leave Nice by boulevard J-B-Verany and route de Turin, D 2204 going north. In La Trinité bear right to Laghet.

The road goes up the verdant Laghet valley. The Roman road from La Turbie to Cimiez was on the opposite bank.

Notre-Dame de Laghet – The sanctuary was founded in 1656 and is a pilgrimage centre; its influence is felt on both sides of the border with Italy. Innumerable votive offerings, touching and amusing in their naïvety, cover the church and cloisters. The best of them are displayed in the little **museum** ⊙ in place du Sanctuaire. The interior décor is heavy Baroque. The statue of Our Lady of Laghet on the high altar is carved in wood.

The road winds steeply up through the olive groves to the Grande Corniche; turn left.

★ **La Turbie** – *See La TURBIE.*
Leave La Turbie on D 53 with its views of the sea and the Paillon basin. On the left of the road is the chapel of St-Martin.

St-Martin-de-Peille – The church stands in a lonely but beautiful setting of olive-clad mountains. It is a modern structure of very simple design, with plastic windows; the base of the altar is made from the trunk of a giant olive tree. Wide bays on either side of the altar look out onto the mountains.
The road winds round the lower slopes of Mont Agel before descending to Peille. Near the last tunnel there is a fine **view** of the village of Peille.

★ **Peille** – *See PEILLE.*
Join Paillon valley at La Grave. After 2.5km – 1.5 miles turn left into D 121 which climbs to the eagle's nest of Peillon.

★★ **Peillon** – *See PEILLON.*
Return to D 21 and turn right.
The village of Peille comes into view on the slopes of Mont Castellet *(right).*

★ **Gorges du Paillon** – Beautiful green wooded ravine.

L'Escarène – Built at the junction of the road to the resort of Peïra-Cava and the beginning of the hairpin bends to the Col de Braus, this large town stretches along the bottom of the Paillon valley. It was an important staging post on the old road from Nice to Turin, called the Salt Road **(Route du Sel)**. The old bridge with its single arch and place de la Gabelle remain from that period.
From the Armée des Alpes bridge over the Paillon, there is a good view of the old village.

★ **St-Pierre** – This 17C church, flanked by two chapels of the Black and White Penitents, is the work of the Niçois architect, Guibert, who designed Nice cathedral. It has a very ornate Baroque façade, and the sizeable interior is of the same period. The font on the right is hollowed out of an ancient Gallo-Roman altar topped by a gilded 17C statuette. The organ (1791) is by the Grinda brothers.

On the road to the Col de Turini, the imposing mausoleum to the Ist Division France Libre, inaugurated in 1964 by General de Gaulle, commemorates the sacrifices and battles of the Liberation at the end of the Second World War.
Take D 2204 south to the Col de Nice and turn right into D 215.
Glimpses of Berre-les-Alpes can be had on the drive up.

Berre-les-Alpes – The village has a charming **setting** at 675m – 2 215ft. From the cemetery there is a **panorama★** of the Pre-Alps of Nice and the sea.
Return downhill on the same road bearing right into D 615.
The drive from Berre-les-Alpes to Contes is enchanting. The road winds its way through a typical inland Nice landscape of chestnut and olive groves interspersed with cypress and pine trees and clumps of mimosa on the terraced land.

Contes, Châteauneuf-de-Contes, Old Châteauneuf – *See CONTES.*

Other itineraries – *Local map above*

★ ③ **Lower valley of the Var**
Nice to Pont de la Mescla. *See Basse Vallée du VAR.*

How to recognise a good olive oil

The essential characteristic of virgin olive oil is its extraction by a mechanical process from the first cold pressing without being refined. Six further operations are necessary before the oil is ready to be marketed: grading *(calibrage)* and washing in cold water *(lavage)*, crushing *(broyage)* in a traditional mill, after which the resulting paste is pressed on fibre mats *(scourtins)*. The oil thus obtained is purified by centrifuge (by natural settling and decanting if the traditional process is followed throughout). Regulations define several categories of oil which must be mentioned on the label:
- Extra-virgin oil *(huile vierge extra)* which is easily digested, has most flavour and very low acidity (less than 1%),
- Virgin oil *(huile vierge)* which also has a very good flavour but can have double the acidity of extra-virgin oil
- Olive oil *(huile d'olive)* which has an acceptable taste for local cooking but fairly high acidity (about 3%)
- Refined oil *(huile d'olive lampante)* which is mixed with virgin oil as its acidity (nearly 4%) makes it unsuitable for consumption.

★★ ④ Vésubie valley
Plan-du-Var to the Madone d'Utelle and St-Jean-la-Rivière to St-Martin-Vésubie. *See Vallée de la VÉSUBIE.*

★★ ⑤ Turini forest
L'Authion, the Vallon Ste-Élisabeth and the Col de Braus road, all leaving from the Col de Turini. *See Forêt de TURINI.*

★ ⑥ Col de Castillon
Menton to Sospel. *See MENTON: Excursions.*

★ ⑦ Col de Brouis road
Sospel to La Giandola. *See SOSPEL: Excursions.*

★★ ⑧ Upper valley of the Roya
Breil-sur-Roya to Tende. *See Haute Vallée de la ROYA.*

★★ ⑨ Valley of Les Merveilles
Starting from St-Dalmas-de-Tende. *See Vallée des MERVEILLES.*

★★ ⑩ Route de Valdeblore
Starting from St-Martin-Vésubie. *See Route de VALDEBLORE.*

NOTRE-DAME-DES-FONTAINES★★

Michelin map 84 fold 10 or
115 fold 9 or 245 fold 26
Local map see NICE HINTERLAND

Set alone in the Mont Noir valley, not far from the fascinating Mont Bégo, and overlooking one of the region's many mountain streams, the **chapel** of Notre-Dame-des-Fontaines is a pilgrimage centre on the site of an old sanctuary dedicated to water. It was built at two different periods: the chancel is 12C and the nave 14C; the latter was raised in the 18C in order to add seven clerestory windows. Although the exterior is plain and simple the inside is a marvellous surprise – the walls are covered with **frescoes**.

Jesus questioned by Pilate by J Canavesio

★★★ FRESCOES ⊙

The chancel panels (badly damaged) were discovered in *c*1950 under a coat of wash. They were painted in *c*1451 by **Jean Baleison**, master of the Gothic style in this region of the Alps. These frescoes, peopled with delicate dancing figures, depict the Four Evangelists (on the vault), the Resurrection of Christ and the Virgin's Assumption (on the walls).
The nave, however, was decorated by the Renaissance Primitive **Giovanni Canavesio** (1420 – early 16C), whose exuberant artistic style, always Gothic-inspired, asserts itself with a more lively brush and a better sense of perspective.

1. Jesus entering Jerusalem
2. The Last Supper
3. Jesus washing the feet of the Apostles
4. Jesus betrayed by Judas
5. The agony in the Garden of Gethsemane
6. The Arrest of Jesus
7. Jesus before the high priest Annas
8. Jesus before Caiaphas
9. The scourging of Jesus
10. Peter denying Christ
11. Jesus before Pontius Pilate
12. Jesus mocked by Roman soldiers
13. Jesus before Herod
14. Jesus humiliated before Herod
15. The Crown of Thorns
16. Ecce Homo
17. Judas' repentance
18. Pilate washing his hands
19. Jesus carrying the Cross
20. Jesus nailed on the Cross
21. Jesus' Death on the Cross
22. The Descent from the Cross
23. The Entombment
24. The Resurrection of Christ
25. The Descent into Hell

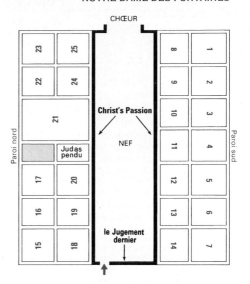

According to the theme and nature of the frescoes, it would seem that Canavesio painted those on the triumphal arch (scenes of the life of the Virgin and Jesus' Childhood) at the same time as Baleison painted those in the chancel.

The frescoes behind the façade and on the sides are dated 12 October 1492 (Latin inscription). They illustrate the Last Judgement and the Passion *(see plan above)*. The compositions, often somewhat elaborate, seem by specific details to want to reveal different levels of interpretation as well as the theories expounded at that time. For example Simon Peter is depicted brandishing a dagger during the Last Supper (2) and a sword during the Arrest of Christ (6); in the Garden of Gethsemane (5) he sleeps lying down and not seated and is found warming his feet during the Denial (10); in the Washing of the Feet, his feet float on top of the water before Jesus washes them. These irregularities may, perhaps, reveal the first hints of the Pre-Reformation, criticising the Papacy as avid of political and temporal (the dagger) power, attached to physical comfort and unconcerned with purity (symbolised by water). Yet in this same scene (3, Washing of the Feet) Judas is the only one to remove his sandals, as if desirous to have his sins washed away; moreover, he is shown barefoot when overcome with remorse (17). His depiction hanged and disembowelled – the same scene uniting both versions of his death – with double internal organs (two hearts, two livers, two intestines), may perhaps symbolise his dual destiny of traitor, essential to the message discussed in the Scriptures, and the Repentant Sinner.

The painted chapels of the Nice hinterland – Scattered in the valleys of the Roya, the Paillon and the Basse-Tinée, many medieval chapels contain superb frescoes designed to teach the Scriptures:

- Coaraze, St-Sébastien;
- Lucéram, N-D de Bon Cœur and St-Grat;
- Peillon, Pénitent chapel;
- Saorge, N-D del Poggio (private chapel);
- St-Dalmas-Valdeblore church;
- Venanson, St-Sébastien;

As well as these remarkable Gothic paintings, there are several modern successors worthy of note: Matisse in Vence, Cocteau in Villefranche and Tobiasse in Le Cannet. The frescoes of the chapels and parish churches of the Tinée valley north of the Alpes-Maritimes are described in the Green guide "Southern Alps".

PEILLE*

Population 1 836
Michelin map 84 fold 19 or 115 north of fold 27 or 245 fold 38
Local map see NICE HINTERLAND

The village, which has maintained its medieval appearance, stands near the ruins of a castle, once the property of the Counts of Provence: three mountains tower over the wild **site** above the Faquin ravine: Pic de Baudon, Mont Agel and Cime de Rastel.

Park the car on the north side of the village by the church, which is approached up a steep slope behind the hospice.

Church ⊙ – The church, dating from the 12C and 13C and with an elegant Romanesque belfry, is formed from two adjoining chapels; the one on the right having rounded vaulting, the one on the left crossed pointed arching. As you enter, an altar against the wall on the left is adorned with a fine altarpiece (16C), divided into 15 panels, by Honoré Bertone. The central panel depicting a Virgin of the Rosary has been removed and replaced by a statue. A picture on the right shows Peille as it was in the Middle Ages. A 14C mural represents St Anne and the Virgin and Child.

★ **The town** – *Car park beside D 53, place de la Tour.*
Go down some steps which lead from D 53 to rue de la Sauterie, a cobbled alley punctuated by steps and covered passageways and sloping down towards place A-Laugier. Rue Centrale on the right leads to a domed 13C building, which used to be the chapel of St-Sébastian. It has been restored and now houses the town hall. Turn left and left again into rue St-Sébastien; on the left of the crossroads stands the former salt tax office (Hôtel de la Gabelle).
The street emerges into place A-Laugier which borders what was once the consuls' residence. At the far end of the square, beyond the Gothic fountain, two arches beneath a house rest on a central Romanesque pillar: pass beneath the right arch and turn right into rue Lascaris, then left into avenue Mary-Garden which goes up to the war memorial.

★ **Viewpoint** – From the memorial there is a view to the north of the gardens of Peille, the Faquin ravine, the church and Pic de Baudon in the distance; to the south the Cime de Rastel and a glimpse of Nice and the Baie des Anges down the Paillon valley.

PEILLON**

Population 1 139
Michelin map 84 fold 19 or 115 fold 27 or 245 fold 38
Local map see NICE HINTERLAND

Set back on a narrow spur overlooking the Paillon valley, Peillon is one of the most spectacular villages on the Riviera. The strict architectural uniformity of the village was imposed by the site and the need for defence.

Pignata-Mont/RAPHO

Christ's Passion by J Canavesio, Peillon

Chapelle des Pénitents Blancs ⊙ – This chapel's most interesting feature is the **frescoes**★ by Giovanni Canavesio: at the far end the Crucifixion with St Antony and St Petronella; on the walls and ceiling scenes from the Passion, in particular the Flagellation and Judas' Kiss, vividly portrayed.
The similarity of style with the chapel of Notre-Dame-des-Fontaines *(see above)* is evident. On the altar stands a *Pietà* in coloured wood.

★ **Village** – Untouched since the Middle Ages, the village has few streets but instead many steep steps and covered alleys between the flower-bedecked houses which crowd upon one another. The 18C church with its octagonal lantern crowns the village; inside are 17C and 18C canvases and an 18C wooden statue of Christ.

PORT-GRIMAUD★

Michelin map 84 fold 17, 114 fold 37 or 245 folds 48 and 49
Local map see Massif des MAURES

Access: follow the signs for Port-Grimaud (Nord) – and not Port-Grimaud (Sud) – to the visitors' car park. Only residents can drive into the town.

Port-Grimaud, which was designed by the architect **François Spoerry**, has a unique charm but is as controversial as Marina Baie des Anges *(See VILLENEUVE-LOUBET)* of which it is in some sense the antithesis. It looks like a Mediterranean fishing village on the north shore of St-Tropez bay *(See illustration in Practical Information)*; in fact it is a modern complex of luxury housing with a fully-equipped marina and a fine beach; it provides facilities for a wide range of leisure activities.

It is pleasant to stroll through this lively village, past the coloured houses covered with Roman tiles linked by canals, narrow alleys, tiny shaded squares and neat little bridges. Public transport is available in passenger barges *("coches d'eau")* which ply the lagoon.

St-François-d'Assise ⊘ – This ecumenical church dedicated to St Francis of Assisi was conceived as part of the overall plan and is resolutely modern although inspired by the Provençal Romanesque style. The interior is plain; no ceiling conceals the wooden roof beams. The stained glass is by Vasarély. The **tower** provides a **view**★ of Port-Grimaud itself, of St-Tropez bay and of the Maures massif.

RAMATUELLE★

Population 1 945
Michelin map 84 fold 17, 114 fold 37 or 245 fold 49 – Local map under Massif des MAURES

The village, which is set among vineyards halfway up a slope, has all the features of an old Provençal town: narrow winding streets with arches and vaults; old houses, now restored, huddled against the old town wall near the church.

In spite of its isolated position, the village fell under the occupation of the Saracens who had otherwise made their lair in La Garde-Freinet. The old prisons are a rare example of their architecture. In 1592, having opted to side with the Catholic League, Ramatuelle was destroyed after a siege. Many door lintels, including that on the doorway of the church, recall the date the village was rebuilt: 1620. The cemetery contains, to the right of the entrance, the ivy-covered tomb of the actor **Gérard Philipe**, born in Cannes (1922-59), and since 1990 that of the writer Anne Philipe, his wife.

Church – The Romanesque church with its flat east end opens through a serpentine door (1620). Inside are two 17C Baroque altarpieces of magnificent gilded wood.

Monument to the Resistance – Facing the cemetery is a monument to the members of the Special Services who died in the Second World War; the submarines which maintained contact with the members of the Resistance used to wait offshore by the Escudelier rock.

EXCURSION

★★ **St-Tropez Peninsula**

See ST-TROPEZ Peninsula.

Ramatuelle from the air

Corniches de la RIVIERA★★★

Michelin map 84 folds 19 and 20 or 115 folds 26, 27 and 28 or 245 folds 38 and 39

The mountains plunge sharply down into the sea between Nice and Menton; the beaches are directly overlooked by the heights along which run the three famous highways known as the Grande Corniche, the Moyenne Corniche and the Corniche Inférieure. The first, which climbs to 450m – 1 476ft, affords the most spectacular views; the second, beautiful vistas along the shore; and the third, access to all the coastal resorts. In 1986 the region was devastated by fire; it will be several years yet before it regains its usual appearance.

The time given for making the tours described below does not allow for visiting Nice or Menton.

★★★ GRANDE CORNICHE

① Menton to Nice

31km – 19 miles – about 3 hours – local map below

The Grande Corniche, built by Napoleon along the route of the ancient Via Julia Augusta is the highest of the three roads, passing through La Turbie from which it looks down from 450m – 1 400ft onto the Principality of Monaco. It provides breathtaking views and access to the hill village of Roquebrune.

★★ **Menton** – *See MENTON. 3 hours.*

From Menton take avenue Carnot and avenue de la Madone (N 7) going west. Either bear left into D 52 to Cap Martin or continue uphill (N 7) bearing right into D 2564 to Roquebrune.

★ **Roquebrune-Cap-Martin** – *See ROQUEBRUNE-CAP-MARTIN.*

From Roquebrune take D 2564 westwards.

★★ **Le Vistaëro** – From nearly 300m – 1 000ft above the sea where the Vistaëro hotel stands, there is a marvellous **view**★★ extending out over Bordighera point, Cap Mortola, Menton, Cap Martin, Roquebrune and, immediately below, Monte-Carlo Beach. To the right lie Monaco and Beausoleil, with the Tête de Chien rising above them. Further inland, in a pass, can be seen La Turbie and the Alpine Trophy.

★ **La Turbie** – *See La TURBIE.*

The Grande Corniche discloses distant **views** of Cap Ferrat and then of Èze village as the road reaches its highest point at 550m – 1 804ft. In Pical a stone cross on the left commemorates Pope Pius VII's return from exile in 1814.

Col d'Èze – Alt 512m – 1 680ft. Extended **view** to the north over the mountains and valleys of the upper Vésubie and Var. Owing to its strategic position, Mont Bastide on the left has been a Celto-Ligurian oppidum and a Roman camp.

Astrorama ⊙ – *On leaving the Col d'Eze towards Nice, turn right into the road going up signed "Parc départemental de la Grande Corniche-Astrorama".*
After a lot of hairpin bends, the road finally reaches a shelf which is home to an old gun battery belonging to the system of defence of Séré de Rivières, positioned between the forts of Drete and Revère, called the Batterie des Feuillerins. This now houses an astronomical study and observation centre designed especially for members of the public with no previous knowledge of the subject: the **Astrorama**.
The staff present will go into detail about the different theoretical and practical aspects of the discovery and observation of space. The site is relatively shielded from the interference of the intense artificial light that there is all along the densely populated coast, and so various sophisticated viewing devices are put at the public's disposal, under the guidance of a member of staff.
It is possible to drive up the road as far as the car park at Fort de la Revère *(No access to the fort)*. From the base of the fort there is a superb **panorama**★★ over the whole Var coast as far as Italy and, in winter, on very clear mornings it is possible to see the outline of Corsica to the southeast.

Belvédère d'Èze – 1 200m – 1 312yds beyond the pass, opposite a small café named the "Belvédère" in a right bend, there is a wide panoramic **view**★★ in which one can distinguish the Tête de Chien, Èze and the sea below, the Cap Ferrat Peninsula, Mont Boron, the Cap d'Antibes, the Lérins islands, the Esterel chain with the summit of Cap Roux, and the French and Italian Alps.

Col des Quatre Chemins – A short way beyond the pass (alt 327m – 1 037ft) one can see the Alps through an opening made by the Paillon valley.
Soon afterwards, the road descends steeply offering a wide **view**★ of the Pre-Alps, and then of Nice and castle hill, the harbour, the Baie des Anges, Cap d'Antibes and the Esterel.

Enter Nice from the east by avenue des Diables-Bleus.

★★★ **Nice** – *See NICE. 1 day.*

★★ MOYENNE CORNICHE

2 Nice to Menton

31km – 19 miles – about 2 hours – local map below

The Moyenne Corniche is a broad modern road, well sited along the mountainside; it tunnels through the larger mountain chains and takes large sweeping curves into the delightful Mediterranean countryside; it offers good views of the coast and the coastal resorts and provides the only access by road to the amazing village of Èze.

As a parapet along a great part of the road obscures the view of the sea and the coast, lay-bys have been provided at all the best viewpoints.

★★★ **Nice** – *See NICE. 1 day.*

From Nice from place Max-Barel take N 7 east.

Initially the view comprises the town, the hill with the old château, the harbour and the Baie des Anges; the Esterel chain and the limestone mountains of Grasse stand out on the horizon to the southwest.

Col de Villefranche – Alt 149m – 489ft. From a bend in the road soon after the pass Villefranche-sur-Mer anchorage and Cap Ferrat come into view.
Just before entering a 180m – 200yd long tunnel, there is a very good **view**★★ of Beaulieu, Cap Ferrat, Villefranche-sur-Mer, Nice and Cap d'Antibes. After the tunnel the old village of Èze comes into view, perched high on its rock against the backdrop of the Tête de Chien (alt 556m – 1 880ft), the mountain promontory dominating Cap d'Ail and Monaco.

★★ **Plateau St-Michel** – *2km – 1 mile from N 7. After the tunnel turn right into the narrow D 34 which climbs back over the tunnel for 2km – 1 mile to a terrace car park.*
Walk up to the viewing table on the edge of the plateau (371m – 1 217ft). The **panorama**★★ extends from the tip of Cap d'Ail to the Esterel.

★★ **Èze** – *See Èze.*

Beyond Èze the Moyenne Corniche circles the rock escarpments of the Tête de Chien and brings into sight new panoramic views overlooking Cap Martin and the long Bordighera headland in Italy. Below, in the foreground, lies the Principality of Monaco.
At the entrance to Monaco bear left into N 7 which skirts the Principality and offers remarkable **views**★ of the Principality, Cap Martin, the Italian coast and the coastal ranges.

★ **Beausoleil** – This resort forms part of the Monte-Carlo conurbation although it is on French territory. Its houses, reached by stepped streets, project from the slopes of Mont des Mules like balconies over the sea.

★ **Mont des Mules** – *Bear left into D 53 – 1km – half a mile plus 30min on foot return along a marked path.* From the top there is a fine **panorama**★ *(viewing table).*
Return to N 7 which passes below the Vistaëro before joining the Corniche Inférieure at Cabbé.

★★ **Cap Martin** – *See ROQUEBRUNE-CAP-MARTIN.*

★★ **Menton** – *See MENTON. 3 hours.*

★★ CORNICHE INFÉRIEURE

3 Nice to Menton

33km – 21 miles – about 6 hours – local map below

The Corniche Inférieure was conceived and built as long ago as the 18C by a Prince of Monaco. The road, running at the foot of the mountain slopes and following the contours of the coast, serves all the Riviera resorts.

★★★ **Nice** – *See NICE. 1 day.*

From Nice take boulevard Carnot, N 98, southeast.

The road skirts the base of Mont Boron with **views**★ of the Baie des Anges, Cap Ferrat, Villefranche-sur-Mer anchorage, Èze and the Tête de Chien in succession.

★ **Villefranche-sur-Mer** – *See VILLEFRANCHE-SUR-MER.*

Start from Pont St-Jean for a tour of the Cap Ferrat peninsula.

★★ **Cap Ferrat** – *Round tour of 10km – 6 miles – about 2 hours 30min. See CAP FERRAT.*

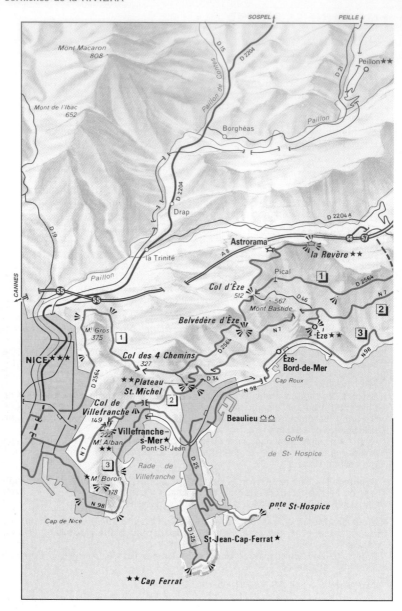

⌂⌂ **Beaulieu** - *See BEAULIEU.*
As the road skirts Cap Roux, there is a view across the water to Cap d'Ail.

Èze-Bord-de-Mer - The resort lies beneath the cliffs below Èze.
As the road hugs the rocky coast, Cap d'Ail is in full view.

Cap d'Ail - Sheltered by pine, palm and cypress trees, the elegant properties of Cap d'Ail cover the lower slopes of the Tête de Chien down to the sea.

★ **Coastal path of Cap d'Ail** - *1 hour on foot return. To the east side of the station go down the steps into a tunnel which comes out on a road. Turn left and at Restaurant La Pinède take another flight of steps on the right down to the sea.* A coastal footpath running eastwards skirts the rocks at the foot of Cap d'Ail, which are pounded furiously by the sea in high winds. To the west lie Beaulieu and Cap Ferrat; gradually Monaco Rock comes into view. The footpath ends on Marquet beach. One can take the road into Monaco or return by the footpath.

★★★ **Monaco** - *See MONACO.*
The road joins the Moyenne Corniche at Cabbé.

★★ **Cap Martin** - *See ROQUEBRUNE-CAP-MARTIN.*

★★ **Menton** - *See MENTON.*

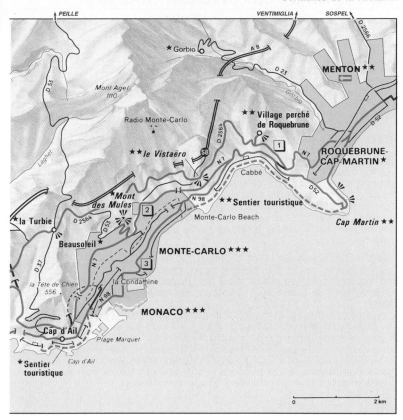

*The Michelin Maps for this region are shown
in the diagram below the table of contents
The text refers to the maps which, owing to their scale or coverage,
are the clearest and most appropriate in each case*

ROQUEBILLIÈRE

Population 1 539
Michelin map 84 fold 16 or 115 fold 16 or 245 fold 25
Local map see NICE HINTERLAND

This important town has been rebuilt six times since the 6C following rock falls and floods. The last landslide in 1926 left some of the austere old houses, but it was necessary to rebuild on the west bank of the Vésubie where the 15C church already stood.

St-Michel-du-Gast ⊙ – *In the new town.* The church is one of many examples in Provence of the Romanesque and Gothic styles combined. Sadly, the Romanesque spire is disfigured by a clock. Three Gothic naves are supported on squat Romanesque columns. An **altarpiece** of the Nice School is dedicated to St Antony; the predella represents scenes from his legend. The Maltese Cross carved on the volcanic stone of the font shows that the church was originally owned by the Knights of St John. Fine collection of 17C and 18C priestly vestments in the sacristy.

EXCURSION

★★ Vallon de la Gordolasque *19km – 12 miles – about 1 hour*

From Roquebillière-Vieux, take D 2565 north; turn right into a narrow road up to Belvédère. See Vallée de la VÉSUBIE: From St-Jean-la-Rivière.

ROQUEBRUNE-CAP-MARTIN*

Population 12 358
Michelin map 84 fold 10 or 20 or 115 fold 28 or 245 fold 39
Local maps see MENTON: Excursions and Corniches de la RIVIERA

This pretty resort which covers the whole of Cap Martin and extends along the coast between Menton and Monte-Carlo, is watched over by the old hill village of Roquebrune and its castle keep.

The Roquebrune enclave is the only example in France today of a Carolingian castle, forerunner of the castles built 200 years later, when the feudal system was dominant.

HISTORICAL NOTES

The castle was built at the end of the 10C by Conrad I, Count of Ventimiglia, to stop the Saracens from establishing themselves once again in the area. For several centuries it belonged to the Grimaldis *(See MONACO)*, who remodelled part of it and introduced artillery in its defences. Originally, the castle was a fortress enclosing the keep and the village within its battlements, which were pierced by six fortified gateways. In the 15C, the keep became known as the castle and the rest of the fortress became the village, which up to the present has preserved its medieval character.

Traditional processions – For the past 500 years a procession, representing the principal scenes of the Passion in six tableaux, is held on the afternoon of 5 August. Unchanged, since it was first performed by those who made a vow in 1467 during an epidemic of the plague, the ceremony goes on for about two hours.

At 9pm on Good Friday, a **Procession of the Entombment of Christ** is held. This procession was instituted by the Brotherhood of the White Penitents, which is now disbanded. A train of some 60 people – representing Roman centurions and legionaries, disciples carrying the statue of Christ and holy women – walk through the streets of the village, which are decorated with lighted motifs recalling the symbols of the Passion and illuminated with hundreds of little lights formed by snail and sea shells filled with olive oil, in which there is a small cotton wick.

** HILL VILLAGE *1 hour*

The town's remarkable situation and the medieval keep are not Roquebrune's sole attractions. To savour its charm, one should stroll through its covered streets, all apparently either steep slopes or stairways, which have preserved their ancient aspect despite the art galleries and craft and souvenir shops which have edged their way between the local tradesmen.

Park in place de la République.

The square was once the barbican – the keep's advanced defence.

* **Rue Moncollet** – Make for place des Deux-Frères and then turn left into rue Grimaldi. Bear left again into the unusual and picturesque rue Moncollet with its long and narrow, covered and stepped passageways. Medieval houses with barred windows, where those invited to join the seigneurial court once lived, give on to the road in front, while at the back they lie against or are cut into the living rock. Rue Moncollet, bending slightly to the right, leads into rue du Château on the left.

* **Donjon** ⊙ – After crossing the "flowered enclosure", you enter the ancient keep of the oldest feudal castle in France. It overlooks by some 26m – 80ft the façades of the houses opposite in rue Moncollet. The walls, which are from 2 to 4m – 6 to 12ft thick, have every sort of defence: cannon embrasures, machicolations, battlements and loopholes, etc.

A flight of 20 steps leads up to the first floor and the Hall of Feudal Ceremonies. Note particularly: the cell recessed into the wall; in the centre, a cube-shaped water tank; and the 15C mullioned window, replacing the oblique slots 20cm – 8in across which once provided light. Below this hall is the storeroom, carved out of the rock. On the second floor is the small guardroom, on the right a comfortable prison and further on the archers' dormitory. On the third floor are the baronial apartments complete with furnishings; dining room, primitive kitchen with bread oven, and a bedroom containing old weapons.

The fourth floor includes the upper artillery platform affording a circular **panorama**** over the picturesque roofs of the village, the sea, Cap Martin, the Principality of Monaco, and Mont Agel (military air base).

Go down by the parapet walk and the so-called English Tower which has been badly restored. You can also visit the light artillery platform and the look-out post.

Olivier millénaire – *Cross place William-Ingram and turn right into rue du Château.*
Opposite a souvenir shop, before reaching the post office, turn left into rue de la Fontaine and the Menton road, which 200m – 219yds beyond the end of the village passes a **1 000-year-old olive tree**, said to be one of the oldest trees in the world.
Return to rue du Château (left) which leads to the church.

Ste-Marguerite ⊙ – The fairly plain Baroque façade masks the original 12C church, which has undergone many alterations over the years. Against the polychrome plasterwork of the interior hang two paintings by a local painter, Marc-Antoine Otto (17C): a *Crucifixion* (2nd altar) and a *Pietà* (above the door).
Turn right into rue Grimaldi which leads, via place des Deux-Frères, to place de la République.

★★ CAP MARTIN

Cap Martin with its magnificent estates is the rich suburb of Menton. It is served by roads which cut through olive groves and clumps of cypresses, perfumed by pinewoods and banks of mimosa.
A massive tower of feudal appearance rises at the centre; it was the old beacon, now converted to a relay station for telecommunications. At its foot lie the ruins of the basilica of St-Martin, part of a priory built by the Lérins island monks in the 11C and destroyed by pirates about 1400.
Local legend gives the following account. One night the Prior, wishing to test the vigilance of the inhabitants who were obliged to protect the monks, sounded the alarm. The people came running, cursed to find it was a false alarm and returned to bed swearing not to be duped again. Some time later the pirates launched an attack; the monks sounded the alarm but nobody came to their rescue; they were massacred and the monastery burned down.

East coast – From the road along the eastern shore there is a marvellous **view**★★ of Menton in its mountain setting and of the Italian coast as far as Bordighera. There are several beaches dominated by the old village: two at Cabbé facing southwest and one at Carnolès on the east side next to Menton.

"Cabanon" de Le Corbusier ⊙ – This cabin, tucked in below promenade Le Corbusier which runs along the coast from Cabbé to Cap Martin, has a deceptively plain exterior. It is, in fact, a unique construction, the dimensions of which were calculated by Le Corbusier using the **Modulor** scale, a measuring tool on a human scale invented by the architect for use in his projects. The Cabanon consists of a corridor decorated with a fresco painted by the architect and a room (10m^2 100ft^2). Each piece of furniture has several functions, even the windows, some of which are jointed, allow the passage of light and also ventilation from the sides. This building, where the architect lived on several occasions, and near where he ended his days, is still an object of curiosity for the layman and a point of reference for schools of architecture. "I have a château on the Riviera which measures 3.66m by 3.66m – 12ft by 12ft (...) It is wonderfully comfortable and pleasant" confided Le Corbusier.
Le Corbusier's tomb, which he designed himself and where he has lain with his wife since 1965, can be seen in Roquebrune graveyard.

★★ Coastal path

A coastal footpath runs from Cap Martin to Monte-Carlo Beach: 4 hours on foot return (preferably in the afternoon). Park in avenue Winston-Churchill car park at the seaward end of Cap Martin. A sign "Promenade Le Corbusier" near a restaurant indicates the beginning of the footpath.
The footpath leads westwards round the headland over the rocks. After several minutes a series of steps and inclines skirts the grounds of private properties through wild and abundant vegetation. Gradually the view takes in Monaco in its natural amphitheatre, Cap Ferrat, the Tête de Chien, La Turbie and Mont Agel behind Monaco, and the old village of Roquebrune with its castle.
A flight of steps on the right crossing the railway line provides a shortcut back to Carnolès Beach via the town hall (Mairie).

The coastal footpath continues beside the railway line to Cap Martin-Roquebrune Station above a sheer drop into the sea. Skirting the Cabbé beaches and the Bon Voyage rocks, the path goes on towards Monte-Carlo (rear view to Cap Martin), leaving La Vieille point to seaward, and ending in a flight of steps near the Monte-Carlo Beach Hotel.
There are frequent trains to Carnolès from Monaco or Cap Martin-Roquebrune. There is also a bus which leaves from the St-Roman district of Monte-Carlo.

Roquebrune-Cap-Martin

EXCURSION

★ **Gorbio** *9km – 5.5 miles – about 45min.*

From Roquebrune-Cap-Martin take D 23 north to Gorbio, a narrow winding road where passing is often difficult.
The Gorbio valley, with its flowers, its olives and pines and its luxurious houses, contrasts with the stark appearance of the village, perched on its wild and rocky **site★**. Near the entrance to the narrow cobbled lanes stands the old Malaussène fountain. The elm tree in the square was planted in 1713. For the feast of Corpus Christi, the villagers organise a very attractive parade, known as the **procession des limaces**, in which everyone carries a snail shell filled with olive oil and lit by a little wick. Rue Garibaldi leads round the church to a fine **viewpoint** looking across to Bordighera point.

ROQUEBRUNE-SUR-ARGENS

Population 10 389
Michelin map 84 south of fold 7, 114 fold 24 or 245 fold 36

The small town of Roquebrune, perched on a rocky peak at the foot of the Rocher de Roquebrune, was most likely founded in the early 11C, after the land had been reconquered from the Saracens *(See La GARDE-FREINET)*. Originally a stronghold, the castrum, located near the church, expanded and was surrounded with a curtain wall (destroyed in 1592 during the Wars of Religion). Traces of the wall are visible, particularly in boulevard de la Liberté (below the church); houses have been built on the rampart's foundations, encompassing the clock tower. At the foot of this tower is the old fountain (known as the Fontaine Vieille), and opposite is the picturesque rue des Portiques, lined with houses, some of which go back to the 16C. Inside the fortifications, the narrow, winding streets and two old doorways recall Roquebrune's medieval past.

St-Pierre St-Paul – The church was built in the 16C in the Gothic style and has an unusual façade, which was added in the 18C.
Inside, on the left, two chapels – remnants of the 11C building modified in the 14C – have thick quadripartite vaulting with rectangular-shaped diagonal and transverse arches. The first of these two chapels contains a wooden altarpiece (1557) of John the Baptist in high relief flanked by St Claudius and St Bridget of Sweden; while the second chapel holds an altarpiece of the same period depicting the Last Judgement. In the nave, on the right on entering, is a 16C altarpiece composed of six carved panels depicting the Passion around a large crucifix. There are two other 16C painted panels in the gallery; large canvases added in the 19C hang in the chancel and side chapels.

Musée de préhistoire et d'histoire locales ⊙ – *Rue de l'Hospice, the continuation of rue des Portiques.*
Located in the old St-Jacques Chapel, the museum houses, for the most part, prehistoric and Roman finds; most of them were excavated in the Bouverie caves (located not far from Roquebrune) which were inhabited without interruption from 30 000 to 8 000BC; this settlement has been identified as Bouverian (*c*15 000 to 10 000BC), a culture unique to south-eastern France, which corresponds to the Magdalenian culture elsewhere.
Also displayed are fine objects from the Neolithic era, and remarkable Roman remains, in a reconstruction of a tomb under **tegulae**. In the sacristy there is a collection of ex-votos and historic documents.
A film *(30min)* on flint-cutting and its industry completes the exhibit.

St-Pierre – *From Roquebrune take D7 southeast.*
The chapel has preserved a Carolingian apse but was rebuilt in the Romanesque style in the 11C, after the Saracen invasion. A recessed tomb has been placed on the façade. The east end is surrounded by an ancient cemetery, the tombs of which were carved into the rock.

★ ROCHER DE ROQUEBRUNE

Round tour of 14km – 8.5 miles – about 1 hour excluding the climb.

Partially covered with cork-oaks, tree ferns and conifers, the proud silhouette of Roquebrune rock forms a small, solitary massif between the Maures and Esterel. Composed of red sandstone subsequently compacted then once again eroded, the rock forms a jagged silhouette which dominates the lower Argens valley in a spectacular fashion.

From Roquebrune-sur-Argens take the small road to the south opposite the graveyard.

Notre-Dame-de-Pitié – The chapel stands on rising ground amid pine and eucalyptus trees at the foot of a majestic red cliff, one of the first heights of the Maures massif. Beyond the screen on the high altar stands a 17C retable framing a *Pietà* similar to a work by Annibale Carracci (in the Louvre in Paris). From the chapel precincts there is a **view**★ of the Argens plain, Fréjus, St-Raphaël and the Esterel heights.

Return to Roquebrune and turn left into D 7. After 500m – 547yds bear left; 1km – half a mile further on turn left again into a forest road. After 2km – 1.5 miles leave the car where a path branches off to the right.

★ **Roquebrune Summit** – *2 hours on foot return of hard walking; keep to the path.* From the summit (alt 372m – 1 073ft), there is an extended **view**★ of the Maures, the lower Argens plain, Fréjus bay, the Esterel and the Alps on the horizon. At the rock's summit stand three crosses of different shapes, which are the work of the sculptor Vernet. They were placed there in memory of three famous Crucifixions painted by Giotto, Grünewald and El Greco, using the summit of the rock to symbolise Golgotha.

Drive down the south face of Roquebrune rock and turn right into D 25. After 1km – half a mile (view of the River Argens) *turn right along the north face.*

The road runs parallel to the motorway. Drive through the hamlet of La Roquette.

Notre-Dame-de-la-Roquette – *30min on foot return. Leave the car in the car park beside the road and take the path on the right.* The ruined chapel, an ancient place of pilgrimage and meeting place for rambles is located in an attractive **setting**★ of lotus, chestnut and holly trees beside a great rock chaos of red sandstone.
From the terrace (alt 143m – 470ft) the **view** includes the lower Argens valley and the Provençal tableland.

Return to the road; turn right to reach D 7 and Roquebrune-sur-Argens.

Michelin Maps (scale 1: 200 000), which are revised regularly, provide much useful information:

- *latest motorway developments and changes*
- *vital data (width, alignment, camber, surface) of motorways or tracks*
- *the location of emergency telephones*

Keep current Michelin Maps in the car at all times

ROUTE DES GRANDES ALPES★★★

Michelin Maps 70, 74, 77, 81, 89, 115 or 244, 245
Local map below
Michelin Green Guides Northern Alps, Southern Alps, French Riviera

The Route des Grandes Alpes is the most renowned of the great routes in the French Alps. It links Lake Geneva with the Riviera along a road which follows the line of the peaks and often runs next to the frontier. In high summer it is only that the road is open through out its length.

The Alps were formed in the Tertiary era, when the two great geological plates, the Italo-African and the Eurasian, collided, forcing up the area between them: this resulted in the great arc of mountain ranges between Nice and Vienna. The Grandes Alpes include the central Massifs and the axial zone (also called the intra-Alpine zone or Alpine axis). The former were part of a very ancient Hercynian chain worn down by erosion, covered with sediment in the Secondary era and forced back up to high altitudes in the Tertiary era; this is a region of great rounded

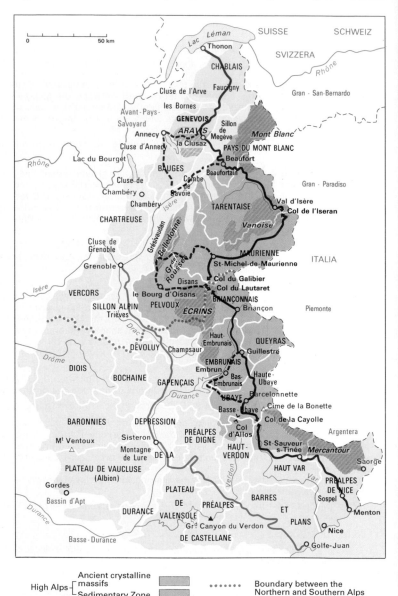

High Alps	Ancient crystalline massifs
	Sedimentary Zone
Pre-Alps	
Sub-Alpine Furrow	
Principal massifs	

•••••• Boundary between the Northern and Southern Alps

District boundary

━ ━ ━ Route des grandes Alpes

──── Route Napoléon

2 day itinerary

It is possible to go from Thonon to Menton in 2 days, with a night in Briançon; this is, however, a tiring trip which entails some sacrifices. It involves leaving out most of the excursions which make the trip worthwhile such as Chamonix with the Aiguille du Midi and the Vallée Blanche, the Gave with the panoramic viewpoint at Chazelet, St-Véran... and allows for only carefully-timed stops.

5 day itinerary

- Thonon – Beaufort: *144km – 90 miles – allow 5 hours 30min (tours included)*
- Beaufort – Val-d'Isère: *71km – 44 miles – allow 3 hours (tours included)*
- Val d'Isère – Briançon: *180km – 111 miles – allow 7 hours 30 min (tours included).*
- Briançon – Barcelonnette: *133km – 83 miles – allow 6 hours 30 min (tours included).*
- Barcelonnette – Menton: *206km – 128 miles – allow 7 hours (tours included).*

or needle-shaped summits, with clear skies, sunny countryside and larch forests; it is sparsely populated. The axial zone is the axis of the upthrust of the range: its sedimentary rocks, often crystallised by the pressure of their own weight and by their heat, gave birth to large sunny valleys, with a mild climate. During the Quaternary era the contours of the High Alps were powerfully shaped by the erosion of great rivers and by four successive glaciations.

At the foot ot the High Alps water drains from their valleys via the Isère and the Drac into a large valley, which makes communications easier: this is the Alpine Sillon (trench). The Durance valley plays a comparable rôle in the southern Alps. The Pre-Alps, a great range of foothills, open out to the south; they are striking because of the ruggedness of their limestone surfaces which are tubular or folded.

★★ ST-SAUVEUR-SUR-TINÉE TO MENTON

100km – 62 miles, allow a day without visits to the villages.

St-Sauveur-sur-Tinée – *See Michelin Green Guide Southern Alps*

From St-Sauveur-sur-Tinée take D 2205 south; after 4 km – 2,5 miles turn left into D 2565.

The road climbs beside the Valdeblore stream to the junction of the Tinée and the Vésubie valleys.

After 7km – 4 miles turn left into a small road which climbs to Rimplas.

Rimplas – Stunning **site**★ on a rocky ridge. There is an extensive view from below the fort.

Continue on D 2565; turn left into the Bramafan valley to St-Dalmas.

La Bolline – The administrative centre for the large commune de Valde-blore, this is a pleasant summer resort in the midst of a vast chestnut grove at the confluence of the Valdeblore and Bramafan streams.

St-Dalmas-de-Valdeblore – *See Route de VALDEBLORE.*

East of Col de St Martin, the road descends to La Colmiane.

La Colmiane – The chalets and hotels of this winter sports resort are scattered in a lovely larch forest.
It is possible to reach the **Pic de Colmiane**★★ by chairlift from Col St-Martin: there is a remarkable **panorama**★★ from the summit.
On coming out of the tunnel there is an attractive view down to St-Martin-Vésubie and *(north)* of the mountain amphitheatre of Le Boréon.

★ St-Martin-Vésubie – *See St-MARTIN-VÉSUBIE.*

From this popular hiking centre, there are walks in the Boréon valley and that of Madone de Fenestre.

Roquebilière – *See ROQUEBILLIERE.*

4km – 2,5 miles after the village of Roquebillière-Vieux, turn left into D 70 towards La Bollène-Vésubie.

The road climbs the small valley of Ste-Élisabeth, tributary of the Vésubie, by means of numerous hairpin bends.

La Bollène-Vésubie – In the heart of a fine chestnut forest, the houses of this summer resort are grouped around the church on top of the hill.

1km – 0.5 mile further on, from the terrace of the chapel St-Honorat, there is a fine view over the Vésubie valley to Lantosque and over the site of La Bollène.

The road then enters the wild gorges of Ste-Élisabeth. As it approaches the Col de Turini, the road seems to be caught between the summit of Calmette (1 787m – 5 863ft) and the Tête de Scoubayoun (1 680m – 5 512ft).

Straddling the valleys of the Vésubie and the Bévéra, the **Turini forest**★★ marks the southern limit of the **Parc national de Mercantour**.

The **Massif de l'Authion**★★, north of the Col de Turini, forms a formidable natural fortress which controls access between the Vésubie and the Roya and thus used to control communications between the Provençal coast and Piedmont. This strategic position

Moving to summer pasture at the Turini Pass

made it the scene of numerous battles in 1793, 1940 and above all in 1944-45. It was one of the last sectors of France to be liberated in April 1945 *(see INTRODUCTION: Provence landings)*.

On the Col, a stone tablet recalls the bitterness of these battles.

Several roads lead from the Col: a winding road goes round the **Pointe des 3 Communes** (2 082 m – 6 831ft) towards the resort of Peïra Cava and the Paillon valley and another goes down beside the Bévéra towards Sospel.

On leaving the Turini forest, the route leads through **Moulinet**, a charming village tucked into a fertile basin, then passes the **chapelle de N-D-de la Menour** the Renaissance façade of which can be seen on the left at the end of an imposing staircase. There is a fine view of the entrance to the gorges from the square in front of the church.

The Bévéra valley forces its way through the **Gorges du Piaon**★★ where the road runs on a ledge over the river. After a pretty waterfall on the left, the valley widens, olive trees reappear and the road reaches Sospel in a wide basin.

★ **Sospel** – *See SOSPEL*

From this hiking centre there is access to the Haute-Vallée de la Roya via the Col de Brouis, to the Paillon valley and to Nice via the Col de Braus and to the Careï valley and Menton via the Col de Castillon.

Take D 2566A from Sospel towards Castillon and Menton.

The road follows the route of the old tramway linking Sospel to Menton, climbing by the Merlanson, a tributary of the Bévéra. On the opposite side, a south-facing slope, the road to Nice over the Col de Braus snakes through olive groves, dominated by the imposing glacis of Barbonnet fort.

Just before the tunnel (D 2566A) the ruins of the old village of Castillon, which was destroyed by an earthquake at the end of the last century, can be seen on a ridge to the right. At the exit from the tunnel a road on the left climbs to the present village of Castillon, brought back to life by craftsmen. The road then begins to go down a series of hairpin bends towards the bottom of the woodel Careï valley where the vestiges of the old tramway line are visible. The succession of bends offers fine views of the sparkling sea below. On the slopes adjoining Italy, the little village of Castellar seems to be pinned to the hills.

After passing through the charming hamlet of Monti dominated by its church and driving under the imposing viaduct of the A8 motorway, the road reaches the suburbs of Menton.

★★ **Menton** – *See MENTON.*

ROUTE NAPOLÉON

Michelin maps 115, 84, 81, and 77 or 245 and 244

The Route Napoléon – Napoleon's Road – follows the Emperor's route on his return from Elba, from the point where he landed in Golfe-Juan to his arrival in Grenoble. The new road was opened in 1932. The commemorative plaques and monuments bear the flying eagle symbol inspired by Napoleon's remark: "The eagle will fly from steeple to steeple until he reaches the towers of Notre-Dame".

FLIGHT OF THE EAGLE

After landing at Golfe-Juan on 1 March 1815, Napoleon and his little troop, preceded by an advance guard, made a brief overnight stop at Cannes. Wishing to avoid the Rhône area, which he knew to be hostile, Napoleon made for Grasse to get to the valley of the Durance by way of the Alps. Beyond Grasse the little column had a difficult time along mule tracks. It halted at St-Vallier, Escragnolles and Séranon, from which, after a night's rest, it reached Castellane on 3 March; by the afternoon it arrived in Barrême. The next day (4 March) the party lunched at Digne. Napoleon halted that evening at the Château de Malijai, impatiently awaiting news from Sisteron, where the fort commanded the narrow passage of the Durance.

Napoleon landing at Golfe-Juan on his return from Elba on 1 March 1815

Sisteron was not guarded. Napoleon lunched there (5 March) and left the town in an atmosphere of growing support for his cause. Once more on a coach road he arrived that night at Gap and there received an enthusiastic welcome. Next day (6 March) he slept at Corps. On 7 March he reached La Mure, only to find troops from Grenoble facing him at Laffrey. This was the site of the famous episode – commemorated today by a monument to Napoleon – which turned events in his favour. That same evening he entered Grenoble to shouts of: "Long live the Emperor".

The route as far as the Col de Valferrière is described below. The continuation north of the route is described in the Michelin Green Guides Alpes du Sud and Alpes du Nord (in French).

The ascent of the Alps by Napoleon

"He disembarked at Golfe-Juan, several hours before nightfall, and established a bivouac. As the moon rose, between one and two o'clock in the morning, the bivouac was struck and they went on to Grasse. There the Emperor expected to find a road over the Alps, which he had ordered to be built under the Empire, but it had never been constructed. He was therefore obliged to attempt difficult passes in deep snow, which meant he had to leave his coach and two cannons in Grasse with the town guard.

... The Emperor moved like lightning. He felt that victory depended on his strength of will and that France would rally to him if he reached Grenoble. There were a hundred leagues to go and we made it in five days, from 2 to 7 March, but on such roads and in such weather..."

Las Cases *(Mémorial)*

GOLFE-JUAN TO THE COL DE VALFERRIÈRE

57km – 35 miles – half a day

⌂⌂ **Golfe-Juan** – *See GOLFE-JUAN.*
From Golfe-Juan take N 7.
The road winds round the west face of Super-Cannes hill, facing the Lérins islands and the Esterel massif. The view is best at sunset.

⌂⌂⌂ **Cannes** – *See CANNES.*
From Cannes take N 85, ④ on the plan.
The road rises above the town and the sea past the hill village of Mougins.

Mouans-Sartoux – This charming village is formed from the union of the *communes* of Sartoux, a medieval village destroyed by the Saracens, and Mouans, once a stronghold protecting the road to Grasse.
In 1588, Suzanne de Villeneuve, the widow of a Huguenot, was defending her village against the troops of the Duke of Savoy. Despite an agreement reached by the two parties, the Duke razed the castle, so Suzanne pursued him as far as Cagnes, where he was forced to pay a heavy fine to recompense the inhabitants.
The château, which is situated in the middle of a pleasant park, has foundations dating back to the 16C despite its late 19C external appearance. It now houses a centre of contemporary art, the **Espace de l'Art Concret** ⊙, which displays an interesting collection of works, supplemented by various temporary exhibitions on particular themes.
On leaving Mouans-Sartoux, the road reveals Grasse spread out across the mountain slope ahead.

★★ **Grasse** – *See GRASSE.*
From Grasse take N 85, ④ on the plan, going northwest.
The road skirts "Napoleon's plateau" where he halted on 2 March outside the town. The route through the Provence plateau and then the Pre-Alps of Grasse, Provence's limestone mountains, crosses three passes in succession: Col du Pilon (782m – 2 566ft), Pas de la Faye (981m – 3 218ft) and Col de Valferrière (1 169m – 3 805ft); the view south is magnificent.

Col du Pilon – From the southern slope there is a **view**★★ of La Napoule bay with the Lérins islands, Grasse, the Lac de St-Cassien, the Esterel and the Maures.

St-Vallier-de-Thiey – *See ST-VALLIER-DE-THIEY.*
As the road climbs to the Pas de la Faye there are very fine **views**★, particularly from the double bend.

★★ **Pas de la Faye** – Similar **view**★★ to that seen from the Col du Pilon. Those travelling south over the pass suddenly see the Mediterranean and the Riviera coastline spread out before them.
The road runs through arid country dominated by the Audibergue and Bleine mountains to the north and the Lachens mountain to the east, with countless **views** to the south. 1km – 0.5 mile before Escragnolles, by a filling station, a road to the Belvédère de Baou Mourine branches off to the left.

★ **Belvédère de Baou Mourine** – *1km – 0,5 mile plus 30min on foot return. Path marked with red arrows.* Terrace **viewpoint**★ over the Siagne valley, La Napoule bay, the Esterel and Maures massifs.
After Escragnolles, where Napoleon made a brief halt, fine views to the south.
For an alternative route to Cannes via Grasse described in reverse order see GRASSE: Excursions.

Haute Vallée de la ROYA★★

Michelin map 84 folds 10 and 20 or 115 folds 8, 9 and 18 or 245 fold 26
Local map see NICE HINTERLAND

When Savoy and the County of Nice were attached to France in 1860, the Italian minister, Cavour, obtained permission from Napoleon III to keep part of the French side of the Maritime Alps – the upper valley of the Roya – so that the sovereign of the new kingdom of Italy could retain his hunting grounds in the neighbourhood of Le Mercantour.
The peace treaty with Italy, confirmed by a plebiscite on 12 October 1947, put an end to this anomaly. The upper valley of the Roya, together with the neighbouring valleys of the Vésubie and the Tinée, were incorporated into France, thus bringing the frontier back to the watershed.
A tributary valley leads to a prehistoric site in the Vallée des Merveilles *(see Vallée des MERVEILLES).*

BREIL-SUR-ROYA TO TENDE

39km – 24 miles – about 3 hours – local map see NICE HINTERLAND

Breil-sur-Roya – *See BREIL-SUR-ROYA.*
From Breil-sur-Roya take N 204 north.
On the left the road to the Col de Brouis *(See SOSPEL)* branches off.

La Giandola – Attractive mountain hamlet with a Renaissance church tower. Beyond La Giandola the road climbs the Roya valley which becomes ever more enclosed.

★★ **Gorges de Saorge** – The road follows the river's every curve in narrow *corniche* style beneath overhanging rocks. The Nice-Cuneo railway also passes through these gorges by way of tunnels and other feats of engineering.
At the end of the gorges, there is a view between two rock cliffs of the extraordinary **setting**★★ of Saorge built in curved tiers, on a hillside clad in olive trees.

★★ **Saorge** – *See SAORGE.*

★ **Gorges de Bergue** – Beyond Fontan, the road ascends gorges cut through red schists where the rock appears deeply coloured and foliated.
The valley widens out into the St-Dalmas-de-Tende-basin.

St-Dalmas-de-Tende – Attractive resort surrounded by chestnut forests. It is a good excursion centre, particularly for the Vallée des Merveilles.

La Brigue – *2.5km – 1.5 miles east of St-Dalmas-de-Tende along the charming Levense valley. See La BRIGUE.*

★★ **Notre-Dame-des-Fontaines** – *4km – 2.5 miles east of La Brigue on D 43 and D 143. For description of chapel, see NOTRE-DAME-DES-FONTAINES.*
Return to St-Dalmas-de-Tende and after 1km – 0,5 mile take D 91 to the Lac des Meshes then turn left in the direction of Granile.

Granile – The road twists for 5km – 3 miles through chestnut woods and Scotch pine before finishing in a cul-de-sac at Granile. This charming village, seemingly isolated on the side of a mountain, has an original look with its mountain houses decorated with wooden balconies and roofs covered with stone slabs. There is an impressive view of the Gorges de la Roya and *(east)* of the ridge of peaks on the frontier.
To the south of the village, a footpath leads either to N204 at the bottom of the valley or to the village of Bergue (or Berghe) further to the south.
Return to St-Dalmas-de-Tende and continue up the valley.
The apple trees in the meadows contrast with the rock-strewn olive groves in the regions round Sospel and Breil. At a bend, Tende comes into view.

★ **Tende** – *See TENDE.*

ST-MARTIN-VÉSUBIE★

Population 1 041
Michelin map 84 fold 19 or 115 fold 6 or 245 fold 25
Local map see NICE HINTERLAND

St-Martin-Vésubie, stretched out along a spiny rock between the Boréon and Madone-de-Fenestre streams, and encircled by tall summits, has become an important summer **mountaineering centre** ⊙ and, because it is so cool, a highly popular resort.

VILLAGE

Start under the plane trees in the beautiful square half way along Allées de Verdun.

Rue du Docteur-Cagnoli – A narrow street, bordered by Gothic houses with handsome porches and lintels, runs north-south through the town with a gutter down the middle.

Chapelle des Pénitents Blancs (B) – A carved façade, a bulb-shaped belltower and, below the altar, a recumbent figure of Christ with cherubs at the four corners holding the instruments of the Passion.

Maison des Gubernatis (D) – No 25 at the bottom of the street, the house built over an arcade, belonged to the Count of Gubernatis.

Place de la Frairie – Turn left into rue du Plan which ends in place de la Frairie marked by a fountain. From the terrace overlooking the Madone de Fenestre Torrent, there is a **view** of the rushing river and of the neighbouring mountains (Cime de la Palu and Cime du Piagu).

Church – The beautiful decoration dates from the 17C. To the right of the choir is a richly dressed statue of Our Lady of Fenestre – the Madone de Fenestre *(see Excursions below)*, a 12C seated figure of polychrome wood. On the last Saturday in June it is carried in procession to her mountain sanctuary where it stays until mid-September.

In the second chapel in the left-hand aisle are two panels from an altarpiece attributed to Louis Bréa: St Peter and St Martin on the left, St John and St Petronella on the right. In the third chapel, a beautiful altar to the Rosary in carved and gilded wood: Virgin and Child surrounded by scenes from the life of Christ (17C).

From the terrace a restricted **view** of the Boréon valley and Venanson village below the round wooded Tête du Siruol.

ST-MARTIN-VÉSUBIE

Docteur Fulconis
  (Allées du) 3
Église (R. de l') 4
Kellerman (Av.) 5
Plan (R. du) 7
Raiberti (Av. Eug.) 8
Saravelle (Av.) 9

B Chapelle des Pénitents Blancs
D Maison des Gubernatis

EXCURSIONS

★★ Le Boréon *8km – 5 miles*

From St-Martin-Vésubie take D 2565 north up the west bank of Le Boréon

The resort stands on a superb site (1 500m – 4 201ft) on the southern edge of the Parc National du Mercantour *(see Introduction)* by the **cascade du Boréon**★ where the river drops 40m – 130ft down a narrow gorge; above the waterfall a small lake adds its calm beauty to the green landscape of pasture and woodland.

Le Boréon is the starting place for walks in the forest, up to the high peaks and mountain lakes. One can drive by car to the Vacherie du Boréon *(2.5km – 1.5 miles to the east)* beneath the distinctive silhouette of La Cougourde.

There is also a road running west along the southern edge of the park for 4km – 2.5 miles up the Salèse valley.

★ Venanson *4.5km – 3 miles*

Leave St-Martin-Vésubie via the bridge over the Boréon and take D 31 south.

From the village square which stands on a rock spike 1 164m – 3 819ft high, there is a good **view**★ of St-Martin, the Vésubie valley and its mountain setting.

St-Sébastien ⊙ – The interior of the chapel is decorated with **frescoes**★ by Baleison. At the far end beneath a Crucifixion, St Sebastian pierced by arrows; on the side walls and the ceiling, scenes from the saint's life inspired by the Golden Legend. Another panel takes prayer as its theme. The thoughts of the two figures are revealed by the direction of the lines from their faces; the one

Le Boréon waterfall, St Martin-Vésubie

Parc national du Mercantour

on the left sees only the wounds of Christ whom he adores while the one on the right concentrates on his house and his wealth which appear behind him.

Parish church – On the left of the entrance is a triptych of the Virgin and Child, flanked by St John and St Petronella. At the high altar is a Baroque altarpiece (1645) of the Coronation of the Virgin featuring the donor. On the right is an altarpiece of the Rosary.

★ **Vallon de la Madone de Fenestre** *12km – 7.5 miles east – about 30min*

From St-Martin take avenue de Saravalle (northeast on the plan). Turn right into D 94.

The road climbs rapidly up the Madone valley between the Cime du Piagu and the Cime de la Palu, crossing and re-crossing the river. A fine forest of pines and larches rises out of heavy undergrowth before giving way to high mountain pasture.

Madone de Fenestre – The road ends in a rugged rock **cirque**★★ much appreciated by mountaineers. Cayre de la Madone, huge and pointed, rises nearby; the slopes of the Cime du Gélas (3 143m – 10 312ft), covered with frozen snow, dominate the northern horizon on the Italian border.

There are pilgrimages to the **chapel** ⊙ on the last Saturday in June, 26 July, 15 August and 8 September. During the summer it houses the statue of Our Lady of Fenestre which returns to St-Martin-Vésubie in solemn procession in the middle of September.

A mountaineering pioneer on the Riviera

The Chevalier Victor de Cessole (1859-1940), a member of an old Nice family, came to climbing late and in an unusual manner; as his doctor had recommended exercise in the fresh air, he enrolled when over 30 in the new Club Alpin Français. His first contact with the high mountains at La Madone de Fenestre awakened a passion for walking in the Alps.

He became a compulsive mountaineer, climbing successively the highest peaks in the Alpes Maritimes (Mont Clapier, Mont Gelas) and setting several records in the Massif de l'Argentera. His recommended walks, described in illustrated brochures, are forerunners of the guide books of today. His activities earned him the presidency of the Club Alpin Français, which he held for 40 years, and enabled him to inaugurate and organise the chain of mountain refuges. In 1901 he opened the Nice refuge above Madone de Fenestre. He initiated the first skiing competitions and is considered to be the founder, in spirit at least, of Beuil, the oldest resort in the area. His interest in nature led him to establish the first measures for the protection of wildlife in the region – the banning of the picking of *Saxifraga florulenta*, now the emblem of the Parc du Mercantour. His large collection of books and papers, acquired during his research, and his interest in the local heritage are now contained in the de Cessole library, bequeathed to the Musée Masséna in Nice.

ST-PAUL★★

Population 2 903
Michelin map 84 fold 9 or 18 or 115 fold 25 or 245 fold 37

The tapering outline of St-Paul stands out from afar above the rolling hills and rich valleys of the Vence countryside in a charming **setting**★. It is typical of the fortified towns which once guarded the Var frontier. Set on a spur, behind ramparts which are still more or less intact (it continued its defensive military activities until 1870), it has retained much of its medieval appearance, while attracting one of the highest numbers of visitors of any village in France.

After a period of prosperity in the Middle Ages, the village declined in the last century to the benefit of Vence and Cagnes. It was "discovered" in the 1920s by painters such as Signac, Modigliani, Bonnard and Soutine who used to meet in a café which has since become the sumptuous Auberge de la Colombe d'Or, its walls covered with paintings as in a gallery. Other artists followed: painters, sculptors, men of letters and entertainers, making St-Paul famous.

SIGHTS

Park the car in one of the car parks provided at the entrance to the village, before passing through the north gate; the protruding muzzle belongs to a cannon captured at the battle of Cérisoles (1544). A square machicolated tower houses the tourist information centre *(Syndicat d'Initiative)* together with a permanent exhibition of modern paintings.

Fountain in rue Grande, St Paul-de-Vence

Rue Grande – Rue Grande is the main street (closed to traffic) running the full length of the village. Many of the arcaded 16C and 17C houses bearing coats of arms are now artists' studios, antique shops and art and craft galleries. The urn-shaped **fountain** with its vaulted washing place in the square is of particular interest.

Climb up the stepped street above the fountain. Take the first right and then the first left to the church.

Church – Gothic building constructed from the 12C to the 13C; the vaulting was rebuilt in the 17C and the belltower in the 18C. The nave and two aisles are divided by massive pillars and contain several works of art. At the end of the north aisle hangs a painting attributed to Tintoretto of St Catherine of Alexandria in a magnificent red cloak, sword in hand.

The choir stalls are 17C carved walnut.

The south transept chapel is particularly noteworthy for the richness of its stucco decoration; before the altar a low relief depicting the martyrdom of St Clement; above the altar a 17C Italian canvas of St Charles Borromeo; on the left, an Assumption from the Murillo school.

The next chapel is adorned with a Madonna of the Rosary (1588) with Catherine de' Medici in the crowd. The Stations of the Cross are modern although painted in tempera, a 16C technique.

The **treasury**, in the side aisle, is rich in 12C to 15C pieces – statuettes, ciborium, processional cross, reliquaries and, in particular, a 13C enamel Virgin and Child; all testify to the skill of Provençal craftsmen. There is also a parchment signed by King Henri III.

Donjon – The **keep** opposite the church is now the town hall.

Return to rue Grande and continue down to the south gate.

★ **Ramparts** – From the bastion of the south gate, overlooking the cemetery, there is a superb **view** of the Alps, the sea (Cap d'Antibes) and the Esterel.

The ramparts remain much as they were when built (1537-47) by François I in answer to the challenge of the Citadel of Nice. Follow them round anti-clockwise using the parapet walk where possible; it commands good views both of the orange trees and flower fields in the valley and of the hills and mountains inland.

Musée d'histoire locale ⊘ – *Place de la Castre.*

This museum offers an interesting summary of the village's history. Eight illustrated scenes with life-size figures depict the stages in its evolution, which often mirror those of the history of Provence itself.

The tour begins with a scene illustrating the arrival of the Count of Provence, Raimond Bérenger V, in St-Paul in 1224. Subsequent scenes include the visit of Queen Jeanne, then that of François I during the "Truce of Nice" *(see Villefranche)*. A visit by Vauban was instrumental in integrating the village into the system of defence of the border. Finally, there are local scenes of the war between the French republicans and the Austro-Sardinian alliance.

An exhibition of photographs of famous people who have stayed in St-Paul adds a contemporary note to this historical display.

★★ **Fondation Maeght** ⊘ – This modern art museum is located northwest of St-Paul in a pinewood on a hill, the Colline des Gardettes.

Using white concrete and rose-coloured bricks the architect José Luis Sert has created an architectural complex in the true Mediterranean style.

Incorporated in the enclosure wall is a mosaic by Tal-Coat; in the park the visitor is greeted by a Calder stabile, as well as mobiles, sculpture, a bronze by Zadkine, Arp's *Giant Pip* and a fountain by Pol Bury. In another garden is the Labyrinth with sculpture and ceramics by Miró and in the Chapel of St Bernard are stained-glass windows by Ubac and Braque; the Stations of the Cross are by Ubac. A Braque mosaic forms the background to a pond while another by Chagall decorates the external wall of the bookshop.

The museum is made up of two buildings divided by a court peopled with sculptures by Giacometti. The collection of modern art is exhibited in rotation in specially designed rooms: canvases, sculpture, ceramics and drawings by Braque, Chagall, Léger, Kandinsky, Miró, Giacometti, Bonnard, Bazaine, Hartung, Tapiès, Alechinsky etc, as well as works by several artists of the younger generation (Adami, Garache, Messagier, Viallat etc).

The Foundation organises annual exhibitions. In summer, during the temporary exhibitions, the permanent collection is not displayed.

ST-RAPHAËL★

Population 26 616
Michelin map 84 fold 8, 114 fold 25, 115 fold 33 or 245 fold 36
Local map see Massif de l'ESTEREL

St-Raphaël, a fashionable summer and winter resort situated on Fréjus bay, has a well-sheltered beach at the foot of the Esterel. The anchorage is deep enough for warships; the old harbour is used by fishing boats and trading vessels; a double marina, including **Santa Lucia**, southeast of the town can accommodate up to 1 800 pleasure craft.

HISTORICAL NOTES

Origins – St Raphaël, like Fréjus, is a daughter of Rome. A Gallo-Roman holiday resort stood on the site now occupied by the large Casino. It was built in terraces, decorated with mosaics, and included thermal baths and a vivarium (fish reserve). At that period rich Romans came here to take the sea air.

In the Middle Ages the villas were plundered by the Saracen pirates. After their expulsion (end of the 10C), the Count of Provence left these deserted lands to the Abbeys of Lérins and St-Victor in Marseille. The monks built a village round the church. In the 12C its defence was entrusted to the Templars. In the 18C the fishermen and peasants who lived in St-Raphaël occupied what are now the old quarters; marsh fever so weakened the inhabitants that they became known in the region as "pale faces".

After Corsica was united with France in 1768, the port of St-Raphaël became the terminus for a short-lived sea link with the island, also known as Ile de Beauté.

Bonaparte in St-Raphaël – On 9 October 1799 the small village was suddenly brought into the limelight, when Bonaparte, returning from Egypt, landed there after a voyage of 48 days (a pyramid standing in avenue Commandant-Guilbaud commemorates this event).

In 1814 St-Raphaël received Napoleon once again, this time as a defeated man leaving for Elba, his new and minute kingdom.

Two men who developed the resort: Alphonse Karr and Félix Martin – Alphonse Karr (1808-1890) was an extravagant personality who used his talents as journalist and pamphleteer to oppose Napoleon III from Nice where he was in exile. His horticultural interests led him to settle in St-Raphaël in 1864 in a villa named "Maison Close" (**XY**). Writing to one of his Parisian friends, he said: "Leave Paris and plant your stick in my garden: next morning, when you wake, you will see that it has grown roses." Writers and artists responded to his invitation: Alexandre Dumas, Maupassant, Berlioz, Gounod.

Félix Martin, local mayor and civil engineer, followed Karr's lead and transformed the village into a smart resort, encouraging building and linking St Raphaël with Hyères (then an expanding resort) by means of a small railway along the coast. Martin engaged the architect Pierre Audlé, who left his mark on the design of the resort.

Illustrious guests marked their stay in St Raphaël with works of art: Gounod composed *Roméo et Juliette* there in 1869, Scott Fitzgerald wrote *Tender is the Night* in St Raphaël and Félix Ziem painted some of his pictures there.

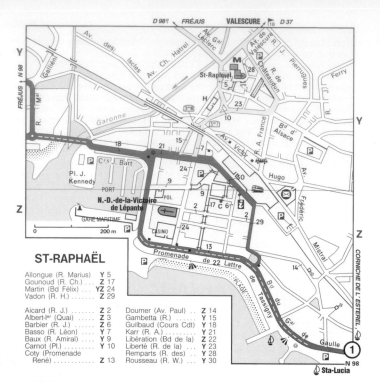

RESORT

The original town centre consists of an important and quite rare collection of seaside architecture from the beginning of the Third Republic.

Seafront – There is great activity on the waterfront by the old harbour stimulated by the cafés and shops which line the broad pavement of cours Jean-Bart and quai Albert-Ier.

From beneath the palms and plane trees of promenade René-Coty and avenue du Général-de-Gaulle, there is a fine **view** of the sea and the twin rocks known as the Land Lion and the Sea Lion. The road follows the coast eastwards to the marina with its terraces, shops and restaurants.

Villas – During the redevelopment of the residential area between promenade René-Coty and rue Alphonse-Karr many of the exotically decorated villa façades were lost. Among those remaining in promenade René-Coty is the Villa Roquerousse (1900) with its exuberant décor; there are also several characteristic façades still in boulevard Félix-Martin: the charming oriental Villa Sémiramis, Villa "Paquerettes" decorated in ceramics; a little further on the shadow of Gounod still haunts "l'Oustelet dou Capelan" ("the priest's house" in Provençal). Both Plateau Notre-Dame and St Sébastien hill are full of remarkable villas and the Palladian inspiration of their designers is evident in the arrangement of the gardens and the flights of stairs.

N-D-de-la-Victoire de Lépante (XY) – This original church, in neo-Byzantine style, was built in 1883 by Pierre Audlé, the architect of many of the villas in St-Raphaël. The church was named by its creator who came from Greece.

Quartier de Valescure – This district, on the right bank of the Garonne, was once much patronised by foreign visitors. The director of the Paris Opera in 1880, Carvalho, laid out, with advice fom Charles Garnier, a park decorated with ornaments which came from the remains of the Palais des Tuileries in Paris. At the crossroads of rue Allongue and rue Maréchal-Leclerc there is a fountain, a remnant of the extravagances of the period, which also came from the Tuileries.

OLD TOWN

North of the railway station, the old town, once surrounded by ramparts, extends beyond the Hôtel de Ville. There are still ramparts to be seen in rue Allongue and in the gardens of the Musée Archéologique; the rue des Remparts follows their original course.

Musée archéologique (Y M) ⊘ – This archeology museum profits from the fact that St-Raphaël was situated at a crossroads for major land (Via Aurelia) and sea routes (between Massalia and the western Mediterranean) and is thus endowed with a rich heritage of archeological remains dating from Antiquity. The rooms on the ground floor display a remarkable collection of **amphorae**★, dating from the 5C BC to the 5C AD. There is also an interesting reconstruction of the loading of a Roman galley. In the garden, there is a milestone dating from 3 BC which was found on Cap Roux. A gallery of technology contains a display on the evolution of scuba diving equipment and of underwater photography, as well as on the process of preserving wood underwater.

On the second floor, two rooms are given over to the finds from the excavation of prehistoric sites in the Esterel which date from the Paleolithic to the Bronze Age.

St-Pierre-des-Templiers (Y) ⊙ – This church, built in the 12C in the Romanesque-Provençal style, served as a fortress and a refuge for the Populationulation in case of attack by pirates. The watchtower, which tops one of the apsidal chapels, brings to mind the military constructions of the Templars.

In one of the side chapels a red sandstone monolith, once a pagan altar, now supports the altar table. The gilded wooden bust of St Peter is carried by the fishermen in procession to the Sea Lion in August.

Near the church are fragments of a Roman aqueduct which brought water to St-Raphaël.

ST-TROPEZ★★

Population 5 754
Michelin map 84 fold 17, 114 fold 37 or 245 fold 49
Local map see Massif des MAURES

On the southern shore of one of the most beautiful bays of the Riviera, facing Ste-Maxime and separated on the east from the elegant bay of Cannébiers by a promontory topped by a citadel, the little port of St-Tropez has become one of the best-known resorts of Europe, a crossroads where journalists and photographers, writers, artists and celebrities all meet.

HISTORICAL NOTES

The legend of St Tropez – Tropez (Torpes), a Christian centurion beheaded in his native Pisa by order of the Emperor Nero, was placed in a boat with his head beside him and cast adrift with a cock and a dog who were meant to devour his remains, which however they left intact. The boat is supposed to have come ashore where St-Tropez now stands.

Republic of St-Tropez (15C-17C) – In 1470 the Grand Seneschal of Provence accepted the offer of a Genoese gentleman, Raffaele de Garezzio, to settle himself and 60 Genoese families at St-Tropez, which had been destroyed by war at the end of the 14C. De Garezzio undertook to rebuild and defend the town on condition that it was freed of all taxes. The town revived rapidly.

St-Tropez became a sort of small republic administered by the heads of the families and, later, by two consuls and 12 councillors who were elected.

Judge Suffren (18C) – Pierre André de Suffren was born in 1729 in St-Cannat in Provence. He first served in the Order of Malta, where he earned his title of judge *(bailli)*, and then in the French Navy. His career advanced slowly; at 55 he was still only a captain. Appointed in 1781 to command five ships being sent as a reinforcement to the Indies, Suffren sailed from Brest with his fellow Provençal, Count de Grasse *(See Le BAR-SUR-LOUP)*, with whom he parted company at the Azores.

Then began an amazing campaign, which went on for two years from the Cape Verde Islands to the Cape of Good Hope, from La Réunion to Ceylon, from Sumatra to Madras. When the *Treaty of Versailles* was signed in 1783, Suffren, by then an Admiral, had to return. He died in 1788 at the age of 59 from an unfortunate blood-letting. A statue has been raised in his honour on the quay in St Tropez.

The "Bravades" – Two *bravades*, or "acts of defiance", take place each year. The first of these acts, a simple religious procession in honour of St Tropez, has maintained its local importance since the end of the 15C. On 16 and 17 May the gilded wooden statue of St Tropez is carried through the town escorted by the town captain, elected by the municipal council, and the corps of *bravadeurs*. Strangers flock to see this picturesque spectacle.

The second act has a page of local history as its origin. On 15 June 1637, 22 Spanish galleys, attempting to take the town by surprise and to make off with four of the king's ships anchored in the port, were forced to flee in the face of the energetic defence offered by the St-Tropez militia.

PRACTICAL INFORMATION

Parking and information
At the entrance to the port, park in the large car park well-placed for the centre of town.
Access to the town by car is difficult and sometimes actually prohibited.
For tours around St-Tropez inquire at the Maison du Golfe de St-Tropez et du Pays des Maures, Carrefour de la Foux. ☎ 04 94 43 42 10

Food, drink and atmosphere
Of the bars along the old port, the most select is *le Sénéquier* where, in its crimson chairs, towards the end of the morning there is always the chance of rubbing shoulders with a star who has come for breakfast.
Lovers of soul, rock and large engines go to the *Café de Paris*, the bikers' meeting place.
The La Ponche district has a choice of Provençal restaurants and a friendly piano-bar, *l'Atelier*. The typically Provençal place des Lices has its regulars who come to sip their apéritif on the terrace of the *Brasserie de la Renaissance* or the *Café des Arts*, and watch hotly contested boules matches.

Discothèques
The most popular with its cosmopolitan customers is *Papagayo*; *Les Caves du Roy* (dresss carefully) at the Hôtel Byblos, as well as *Le Bal*, at the Résidence New-Port are also obligatory ports of call for celebrities.

Markets and shopping
Every Tuesday and, especially, Saturday, in season, there is a lively market in the place des Lices, with a good selection of local crafts.
Shops in the rue Clemenceau, rue Gambetta and rue Allard offer a great variety of good quality articles: pottery, glass and the famous *"tropézienne"* sandals inspired by the ancients and made on the spot. Not to be missed while walking around the shops is a taste of the delicious *"tarte tropézienne"*.

Renown – At the turn of the century St-Tropez was a charming little village unknown to tourists and poorly served by a narrow-gauge branch line. In the harbour tartans (single-masted sailing vessels) laden with sand and wine were moored beside the fishing boats. It was then that Maupassant discovered it. It was however the painters who came in Signac's train who made it more widely known *(see below)*. Between the wars Colette, who used to spend the winter here, contributed to its notoriety. Other famous residents included politicians, the couturier Paul Poiret and later Jean Cocteau.
From the 1950s St-Tropez became the fashion with the literary set from St-Germain-des-Prés in Paris and then with the cinema people, together with their fans, and so became internationally famous.

St-Tropez

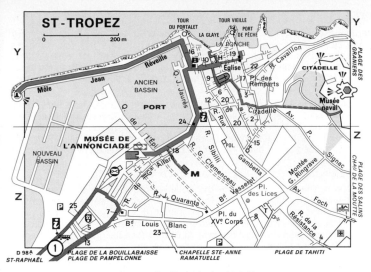

In season the old town is closed to traffic

Aire-du-Chemin (R.)	Y 2	Guichard (R. du Cdt)	Y 9	Péri (Quai Gabriel)	Z 18
Aumale (Bd d')	Y 3	Hôtel-de-Ville (Pl. de l')	Y 10	Ponche (R. de la)	Y 19
Belle-Isnarde (R. de la)	Z 4	Laugier (R. V.)	Y 12	Portail-Neuf (R. du)	YZ 20
Blanqui (Pl. Auguste)	Z 5	Leclerc (Av. Maréchal)	Z 13	Remparts (R. des)	Y 22
Clocher (R. du)	Y 6	Miséricorde (R. de la)	Z 15	Roussel (Av. Paul)	Z 23
Croix-de-Fer (Pl. de la)	Z 7	Mistral (Quai-Frédéric)	Y 16	Suffren (Quai)	Y 24
Grangeon (Av.)	Z 8	Ormeau (Pl. de l')	Y 17	11-Novembre (Av. du)	Z 25

B Château de Suffren **M** Maison des papillons

SIGHTS

★★ **L'Annonciade, Musée de St Tropez (Z)** ⊙ – The chapel of Our Lady of Annonciade, built in 1510 and deconsecrated during the Revolution, was divided into two levels in the early 19C and set up as a museum in 1937.

Georges Grammont (patron of the arts) donated some ten sculptures and about 50 paintings covering 1890-1940. The collection confirms the important role St-Tropez played in the Post-Impressionist movement.

In 1892 **Paul Signac** (1863-1935) landed at St-Tropez. Enthralled by the site, he stopped to paint and ended up living there. Around him gathered other painters – Matisse, Bonnard, Marquet, Camoin, Dunoyer de Segonzac – some residing longer than others. Fascinated by the exceptional light in the region, these artists sought different methods of expressing colour, contributing to, or instigating the great movements of the late 19C and 20C, such as Pointillism *(see Introduction)*, Fauvism, The Nabis and Expressionism.

Tour – Displayed amidst the Pointillists, Signac is represented by his oils and watercolours (exhibited in rotation). He is surrounded by his followers H-E Cross *(St-Clair Beach)*, Théo van Rysselberghe, Maximilien Luce and several artists, like Derain (London scenes) and Picabia, who were momentarily part of the movement before taking a different direction.

The Fauves, delighting in pure colour, are represented by Matisse *(The Gypsy)*, Braque *(Estaque Landscape)*, Manguin, Vlaminck, Kees Van Dongen and Dufy. The Nabis group reacted against Impressionism, painting in primary colours on an essentially flat surface. They are represented by Bonnard, Vuillard *(The Women Under a Lamp)*, Félix Vallotton *(Misia at Her Desk)*...

The Expressionists, who used painting as a means to express the intensity of their emotions, via exaggerated facial expressions for example, are represented by Rouault, Chabaud *(Hôtel-Hôtel)*, Utrillo and his mother Suzanne Valadon. *The Rower*, a Cubist work by Roger de La Fresnaye, landscapes and harbour scenes (Camoin, Bonnard, Marquet) complete this prestigious collection where the various artistic movements all tend to use the human figure as their central theme, regardless of how different their theories may be.

The sculpture, complementing the collection and of the same period, is by Maillol *(Nymph)* and Despiau; note also the sandstone vases by E Decœur.

★★ **Harbour (Port – YZ)** – The harbour teems with life. The fishing boats, commercial vessels and excursion craft share the mooring with a crowd of yachts – from the most humble to the most luxurious. On the waterfront and in the neighbouring streets the old pink and yellow houses have been converted into cafés and pastry shops, cabarets and restaurants, luxury boutiques, galleries and antique shops. In season a picturesque and cosmopolitan crowd strolls beneath the bronze figure of Suffren.

Môle Jean-Réveille (Y) – The attractive **panorama**★ from the top of the jetty includes all of St-Tropez – Portalet tower, the harbour, the town and its commanding citadel; the head of the bay, Grimaud and its castle ruins; Beauvallon; Ste-Maxime; Cap des Sardinaux; Issambres point; Dramont headland; Cap Roux summit and, in the distance, the Esterel and in fine weather, the Alps.

La Ponche Quarter – Turn right at the seaward end of quai Jean-Jaurès into place de l'Hôtel-de-Ville; on the left stands the massive **Château de Suffren** (Y B). Turn left beyond the Hôtel-de-Ville to reach the bay of La Glayel; rue de la Ponche leads through the old gateway to a beach overlooked by the Vieille Tour (old tower) where the fishing boats ride at anchor: two typical corners which have attracted painters.

Retrace your steps, turning left into rue du Commandant-Guichard.

Church (Y) – The 19C edifice is in the Italian-Baroque style; the belltower is crowned with wrought-iron work. The interior contains some finely carved woodwork and to the left of the high altar, a bust of St Tropez, and, laid around it like a tribute of votive offerings, several old blunderbusses which exploded without hurting anyone during a *bravade*. At Christmas a beautiful 19C Provençal crib with dressed figures is brought into the church.

Maison des papillons (Musée Dany Lartigue) (Z M) ⊙ – *9 rue Étienne Berny.*
This charming Provençal house, tucked into an alleyway out of the way of the crowded port, is the former home of the mother of the painter D Lartigue, wife of the photographer J H Lartigue. It houses a collection of nearly 5 000 butterflies, comprising all the diurnal species in France, captured by the artist, as well as a donation of 20 000 exotic specimens. The staircase wall is hung with J H Lartigue's photos and family souvenirs of the composer A Messager, the painter's grandfather. Artistic arrangements show the capacities for mimicry of the insects in their natural surroundings. A pleasant patio with a fountain leads out from this room and contains two paintings illustrating Tropézienne festivals. Upstairs rare and exotic species (such as the famous black Apollon of Mercantour and numerous Zerynthis and Parnassus) are grouped in display cases.

In rue du Clocher turn right towards place de l'Ormeau and right again towards rue de la Citadelle.

★ **Citadelle** (Y) – The citadel stands on a hillock at the east end of the town. A fine hexagonal **keep** with three round towers was built in the 16C. In the 17C a fortified wall was added.
From the ramparts there is a good **panorama**★ of St-Tropez, the bay, Ste-Maxime and the Maures.

Musée naval ⊙ – This maritime museum in the citadel keep is an annexe of the Musée de la Marine in the Palais de Chaillot in Paris. In the courtyard are two handsome 16C Spanish bronze cannons. Within the keep are displayed models of ships (including a reconstruction of a Greek galley), engravings and seascapes

---

La Nioulargue, a sailing festival

This great event at the end of the season in St-Tropez brings together real lovers of the sea and the most aristocratic traditional sailing boats (swans, ketches and schooners built during the 1920s for film stars or famous owners). Since its first meeting in 1981, more than 250 competitors (most of whom have previously taken part in the America's Cup) rush here every year at the beginning of October to take part in this race which has become the great European meeting for old boats.

The course starts at the Tour du Portalet, goes round the shallows marked by the Nioulargue (sea nest, in Provençal) buoy and returns to the port. A spectator who has managed to find himself a good viewing point will be rewarded with the unforgettable sight of these large sailing boats in action. The skilful dances performed by ketches (recognisable by the small mast at the stern) and schooners (with the small mast in the bows) call for miraculous feats in anticipating manœuvres and great strength to move the enormous sails (the stress at the foot of the main mast can be as much as 500 tonnes!).

The best way to follow the race – This can be achieved by boarding the launches run by MMG who operate a shuttle service in the gulf (boarding opposite the restaurant l'Escale in the old port). A more peaceful view of the scene is possible from the buttresses of the citadelle, with a good pair of binoculars.
Lastly, share the hire of a small boat so as to appreciate the skills of the skippers at close quarters.

illustrating the history and local activities of St-Tropez with an explanation of the 1944 Allied Landing. Full-scale cross-section of a torpedo from the local naval shipyard. The exhibition room illustrates a different theme each year.

There is a magnificent **view**★★ from the keep terrace of the town, St-Tropez bay, the Maures and the Esterel; on a clear day the Alps are visible.

Ste-Anne – *0.7km – about half a mile. From St-Tropez take avenue Paul-Roussel and route de Ste-Anne.*

Standing on a volcanic rock spike in the shelter of huge trees, this attractive Provençal chapel is a place of pilgrimage for seafarers and *"bravadeurs" (see above)* with a **view**★ of the sea in all directions, particularly of St-Tropez and the bay.

BOAT TRIPS ⊘

Motorboats run services across and around St-Tropez bay. There are also daily services from St-Tropez to Port-Grimaud, Ste-Maxime, Les Issambres, St-Raphaël, Port-Cros and the Iles de Lérins.

EXCURSIONS

⌂ **Beaches** – The nearest is Bouillabaisse beach *(1km – half a mile by D 98ᴬ, ①️ on the plan)*. To the east of the town is **Graniers beach** *(access from rue Cavaillon)*. Further east round the headland is **Les Salins beach** *(4.5km – 2.8 miles on avenue Foch)*.

For a description of Pampelonne Bay see ST-TROPEZ PENINSULA.

Château de la Moutte ⊘ – *4km – 2.5 miles. From St-Tropez take avenue Foch going towards Les Salins.* This small Provençal castle with its bastide stands in a park shaded by age-old trees. In 1860 it was bought by Émile Ollivier, ex-Minister to Napoleon III, statesman and member of the French Academy. After the Franco-Prussian War in 1870 he retired to this house and wrote a number of works, particularly on politics. He died in 1913 and was buried in a sober granite tomb at the end of Les Salins beach.

The interior decoration of his house has not changed for over a century: numerous souvenirs of Ollivier and the period of the Second Empire.

ST-TROPEZ Peninsula★★

Michelin map 84 fold 17, 114 fold 37 or 245 fold 49

Although in the high season tourism takes over the town of St Tropez, the surrounding country presents a traditional landscape of rectangular vineyards alternating with rows of cypress trees and immaculate farms (*mas*) in the shade of murmuring umbrella pines. The coastline consists of the rocky headlands – Cap Camarat, Cap Taillat and Cap Lardier – and the long ribbon of fine sand in Pampelonne Bay, which has been preserved from the usual concrete invasion by the active intervention of the Coastal Conservatory.

⌂ PAMPELONNE BEACHES

South of St-Tropez, Pampelonne Bay stretches form Cap du Pinet to Cap Camarat and forms part of the commune of Ramatuelle. The main beaches are plage de Tahiti *(accessible from the centre of St-Tropez by rue de la Belle-Isnarde)* and the large sandy plage de Pampelonne *(5km – 3 miles long)*, part of which is privately managed *(admission fee)* and part of which is open to the public. In season, there are several lifeguard posts on the beach *(Main access by car from D 93 via the many side turnings, some of which are unsurfaced; the official signs give directions to the car parks (paying) near the beach; it is best to choose a car park in the shade payable by the day)*.

PRACTICAL INFORMATION

The first part of the walk is along beaches on sandy ground, at least as far as Bonne Terrasse Point at the southern end of Pampelonne Bay.
The next section of the path can be reached from the car park at Bonne Terrasse or at l'Escalet *(turn off D 93)*.
Avoid the hottest hours of the days as heat haze reduces visibility. Pampelonne Beach is well supplied with oper-air cafés but it is advisable to take a good supply of drinks if walking further afield.
Time required to walk from St-Tropez harbour to
- Cannebiers Bay – about 30min
- Salins beach – 2 hours 30min
- Tahiti beach (north end of Pampelonne Bay) – 3 hours 30min to 4 hours.

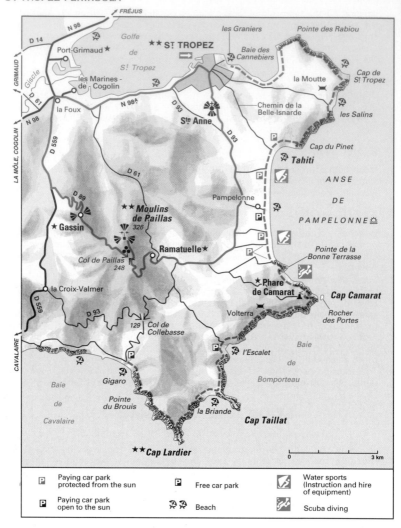

Ⓟ☂	Paying car park protected from the sun	Ⓟ	Free car park
Ⓟ☀	Paying car park open to the sun	🏖🏖	Beach

🏄	Water sports (Instruction and hire of equipment)
🤿	Scuba diving

★★ HEADLANDS BY COASTAL PATH

This path, signposted in yellow, links St-Tropez with Cavalaire Beach via Cap Camarat and Cap Lardier *(about 35km – 22 miles)* but this is not a walk which can be completed in a single day as the time required is more than 11 hours. *See below for a description of the section from St-Tropez to Cap Lardier. For a description of the path from Cavalaire to Cap Lardier see CAVALAIRE.*

St-Tropez to Tahiti beach – *About 3 hours*

The path leaves from Graniers beach at the western edge of the harbour. It follows the contours of the coast and provides superb views of the foothills of the Maures and the overhanging red rocks of the Esterel. Via Rabiou Point and the Cap de St-Tropez, the path reaches Les Salins beach, the first stopping Point where refreshment is available in the open-air cafés *(guingettes)* during the summer season. The path then rounds Cap Pinet and comes out on Tahiti beach at the north end of Pampelonne Bay.

Tahiti beach to Cap Camarat – *About 2 hours 15min*

The path follows a track parallel with the long sandy stretch of Pampelonne beach *(5km – 3 miles)* to Bonne-Terrasse Point. On reaching Bonne-Terrasse Bay, the path climbs the first rocks through thicker vegetation. Near the Rocher des Portes there is a footpath *(right)* towards Camarat lighthouse which is visible through a forest of arbutus and tree ferns.

Cap Camarat to Cap Taillat – *About 2 hours. No refreshments available except in l'Escalet.*

After going around the Rocher des Portes, the path leads to the beach at l'Escalet passing a succession of creeks which are easily accessible and isolated by great rock slabs ideal for sunbathing. During this walk there is the surprising and unexpected sight of the imposing **Château de Volterra** *(closed to the public)* overlooking the bay. The path then reaches Cap Taillat.

★PHARE DE CAMARAT

From Ramatuelle take D93 east; turn right into the road (sign "Route du Phare") which runs along the promontory beyond Les Tournels campsite; park outside the lighthouse enclosure which is a pedestrian area.

Tour ⊘ – This magnificent **lighthouse**, commissioned in 1831, was electrified after the Second World War. It is one of the tallest in France (129.8m – 426 ft above sea-level) and has a range of 60km – 37 miles. Since 1977 it has been completely automatic. From the summit there are superb **views**★★ over Pampelonne Bay, the whole of the peninsula and St-Tropez bay.

★MOULINS DE PAILLAS AND GASSIN *Round tour 28km – 18 miles*

This tour into the countryside around St-Tropez offers extensive views over the coast and the Maures hinterland and includes villages which have retained their original character.

★★ **St-Tropez** – *See ST-TROPEZ.*

Chapelle Ste-Anne – *See St-TROPEZ.*
Take D 93.
The road passes through the vineyards above Pampelonne Bay.
Turn right into D61 towards Ramatuelle.

★ **Ramatuelle** – *See RAMATUELLE.*
Turn right into D89 towards col de Paillas.

★★ **Moulins de Paillas** – Beyond three ruined olive mills, there is a radio beacon on a circular platform. *Follow the signed path.*
On walking round the enclosure, there are glimpses through the trees of a fine **panoramic view**★★ – *(seawards from north to south)* over Cap Roux and the rough peaks of the Esterel, the coast of the Maures Massif, Ste-Maxime, St-Tropez Bay, the long stretch of Pampelonne beach, Cap Camarat lighthouse rising white above the pinewoods, and, out to sea, the Iles du Levant and de Port-Cros; *(inland)* Gassin *(below)*, the Pradels range *(southwest)* and the Sauvette chain *(north-west)*, Cogolin and Grimaud in the valley *(north-northwest)*.
Return to the junction and turn right to Gassin.

Gassin – Alt 201m – 659ft. In contrast to modern resorts this village has proudly retained its Provençal character, with its network of alleyways sometimes linked by flights of steps.

La Briande beach, Ramatuelle

The terrasse des Barri, planted with lotus trees and redolent of the Mediterranean, provides a **view★** over St-Tropez Bay, Cavalaire Bay and the Iles d'Hyères; when the mistral blows, the Alps are visible *(east)*.

Around the town, there are several vineyards producing local AOC Côtes de Provence wines. The festival of St-Laurent, the patron saint of the village, is celebrated with a taste of garlic mayonnaise *(aïoli)*.

Take D559 to return to St-Tropez.

The Customs Officers footpath, which follows the whole of the Var coastline close to she shore, dates from the 1st Empire (early 19C). The path, which was commissioned by Fouché when he was Minister, was originally intended to facilitate the patrols of armed customs officers, who had powers as wide-ranging as the police. They were ordered to suppress the smuggling of salt and, subsequently, of tobacco and arms. Since 1976 the path has been restored and all private properties adjoining the shore are obliged to allow a passage (at least 3m-10ft wide) across their land. Walls and solid fences erected before that date are, however, exempt. Nearly 200km – 124 miles of Varois coastline are affected by this measure.

ST-VALLIER-DE-THIEY

Population 1 536
Michelin map 114 folds 12 and 13, 115 fold 24 or 245 folds 36 and 37

This medieval village, once a Roman stronghold, is situated in the middle of a fertile plateau and is a popular summer holiday destination for the inhabitants of Grasse. The Romanesque church, which dates from the early 12C and was restored in the 17C, has a lovely 13C nave with pointed barrel vaulting and houses two Baroque altarpieces. The belltower is decorated with arcading, a remnant from the original construction, and surmounted by an elegant 19C campanile. The old seigneurial château beside the church now houses the town hall. The line of the neighbouring houses marks the position of the old fortified wall, of which only a fine gateway with loopholes remains.

In the square, a column bearing a statue of Napoleon with bared head commemorates the Emperor's passage on 2 March 1814.

★ **Souterroscope de la Baume Obscure** ⊘ – *From St-Vallier-de-Thiey drive south towards St-Cézaire; turn right into the road to the cemetery (sign "Grotte Baume Obscure"). Continue beyond the cemetery (unsurfaced track) for 2km – 2 188yds to a large car park opposite a shelter built over the ticket office. Audioguide tour 1 hour. Shoes with non-slip soles advised. Narrow passages.*

This cave is in fact more an underground network of galleries, which were not brought to light until 1958 because of the long, narrow tunnels leading to them, which tended to put off early explorers.

The detailed exploration of the selection of galleries currently open to the public was finally completed in 1980, as was the adaptation of the site for visiting by the public.

Baume Obscure, St Vallier-de-Thiey

Experts have explored 1 200m - 1 312yds of the underground network; the tour of the cave actually covers 500m - 547yds and takes visitors down 50m - 164ft to the "Galerie du pas de course". There is a constant temperature of 14ºC - 57ºF.

At the end of a long corridor, once filled in with clay, visitors will discover a series of nine galleries which contain features such as vast domes, natural dams *(gours - see Introduction)* forming cascades and a profusion of thread-like stalactites, resembling thin, straight spaghetti hanging down, an absolute forest of needle-shaped concretions scattered all over the roofs. In the gallery with the *gours*, note the unusual colour of the water brought out by the lighting, and the ground which is formed from an enormous petrified flow of calcite at the base of a stalagmite. This whole network of caves is also widely reputed for the variety of strange formations it contains.

★ PLATEAU DE CAUSSOLS

St-Vallier-de-Thiey to Gourdon

30km - 19 miles - allow 2 hours, excluding the tour of the observatory

On leaving the village, take N 85 towards the Pas de la Faye, then D 5 to the right, which twists and turns along the side of the mountain, giving lovely views over the St-Vallier basin. After going through a pass, the Col de Ferrier, the road overlooks the wooded valley of Nans. Leave the main road which goes round the Audiberghe mountain, taking D 12 which leads off to the right (sign "Caussols").

The **Plateau de Caussols**, at an average altitude of 1 000m - 3 281ft, is itself enclosed by higher land. It is one of the rare examples of karst relief in France. The north of the plateau features a landscape of cultivated land and meadows, thanks to its fertile soil; the south, on the other hand, reflects a less orderly setting, with *dolines*, swallowholes and chasms forming a landscape typical of limestone relief eroded by rainwater. Walkers should take care when near these pits and chasms, especially in rainy weather. There is a particularly spectacular example of this kind of feature to be seen by taking the small road to the right, when leaving the centre of the somewhat dispersed village of **Caussols** to the east. This little road crosses the plateau diagonally to reach **Les Claps★** (Provençal for "rocks"). These are in fact a remarkable rock chaos. The mineral nature of this feature is all the more striking for the absence of any plantlife nearby. Some stone huts *(bories)* indicate that man was once resident here. Turning round to face the plateau opposite gives a view of the domes of the CERGA observatory.

Return to D 12 and follow it for 2km - just over a mile towards Gourdon.

Observatoire du CERGA ⊘ *- 2km - just over a mile after Caussols on the D 12, a road leads off to the left signposted "St-Maurice – Observatoire du CERGA". After passing the houses, carry on past the sign marked "Route privée" which indicates the entrance to the CERGA property.*

The road winds its way round a series of hairpin bends, giving lovely views of Caussols in its dip.

The **Plateau de Calern**, at an altitude of 1 300m - 4265ft, is home to the various installations and equipment of the CERGA (geodynamic and astronomical research and study centre) observatory. The site is unique from a geological point of view. The observatory, inaugurated in 1974, is intended to develop modern instrumentation for astronomy and monitor the movements of the earth. It is part of the Observatoire de la Côte d'Azur, which includes the observatory at Nice.

The tour of the observatory brings visitors into contact with the teams who work with interferometers (for measuring diameters of stars), the Schmidt telescope (for observing the sky), laser telemeters (for measuring the distance from the Earth to the moon and to the satellites) and astrolabes (for calculating the position of the stars).

Return to D 12 and follow it towards Gourdon.

The road carries straight to the eastern edge of the plateau and then begins its descent into Gourdon. There is a lovely **view★** of the Loup valley from the first big bend.

★ **Gourdon** *- See GOURDON.*

Use the **Index** *to find more information about a subject mentioned in the guide*
  - people, towns, places of interest, isolated sites,
    historical events or natural features...

Population 7 364
Michelin map 84 folds 17 and 18, 114 fold 37 or 245 fold 49
Local map see Massif des MAURES

The fashionable resort of Ste-Maxime lies along the north shore of the gulf of St-Tropez. It faces due south in a pretty setting protected from the *mistral* by wooded hills. As well as the fishing harbour there is a well-appointed marina and a beautiful beach of fine sand. In summer the town centre is a pedestrian precinct.

Church – Modern ceramic tympanum above doorway. Inside, fine Baroque (17C), green and ochre marble altar from the Chartreuse de la Verne; 15C choir stalls.

Tour carrée des Dames – *Opposite the church, facing the port.*
A square defensive tower, built in the 16C by the Lérins monks and later used as law courts, has been transformed into a **museum of local traditions** ⓥ. Ste-Maxime and its surrounding area are presented with exhibits on nature (sea), history and traditions (arts and crafts, Provençal dress).

Place Victor-Hugo – Beneath magnificent plane trees, the square leads into tree-lined avenue Charles-de-Gaulle west along the shore. Near the tourist information centre in promenade Simon-Lorière stands the first marker on the route taken by the Allied forces in 1944 from Ste-Maxime to Langres in the north of France.

EXCURSION

Parc de St-Donat – *10km – just over 6 miles north – about 1 hour. From Ste-Maxime take boulevard G-Clemenceau, D 25 north.*
A leisure park has been laid out in the woods between Col de Gratteloup and the chapel of St-Donat. The main attraction is the museum of mechanical musical instruments.

Musée du phonographe et de la musique mécanique ⓥ – The building, which recalls a turn-of-the century barrel organ, houses an astonishing collection of 350 musical instruments and sound recording machines; among the rare and bizarre exhibits are a melophone (1780, forerunner of the accordion), musical boxes from all periods, barrel organs and pianolas, phonographs from 1878 (Edison) to the present day, a 1903 dictaphone, a Pathegraphe for the study of foreign languages (first audio-visual machine) and even a singing bird (Bontemps, 1860).

Michelin on the Net: www.michelin-travel.com

Our route planning service covers all of Europe – twenty-one countries and one million kilometres of highways and byways – enabling you to plot many different itineraries from wherever you are. The itinerary options allow you to choose a preferred route – for example, quickest, shortest, or Michelin recommended.
The network is updated three times weekly, integrating ongoing road works, detours, new motorways, and snowbound mountain passes.
The description of the itinerary includes the distances and travelling times between towns, selected hotels and restaurants.

SANARY-SUR-MER ☆

Population 14 730
Michelin map 84 fold 14, 114 fold 44 or 245 fold 46
Local map see Excursions below
Town plan in the current Michelin Red Guide France

The name Sanary derives from St Nazaire who is venerated in the local church. The charming resort, all pink and white, is popular at every season.

Sanary boasts a smart little harbour, bordered by palms. The bay is fairly well protected from the *mistral* by wooded hills, dominated to the north by the Gros Cerveau, and has fine beaches.

"Capital of German literature" before the Second World War – The little port of Sanary, known to German painters in the 1920s, became a refuge for many intellectuals who fled from Hitler's regime in the 1930s. A German refugee journalist christened Sanary "capital of German literature". Among those who stayed there were Thomas Mann and his brother Heinrich, who stayed at Villa "La Tranquille", the writer Feuchtwanger, as well as Alma Mahler and Franz Werfel. Zwieg visited on his way to the United States.

After the armistice in 1940, many were able to seek refuge in the USA thanks to the intervention of President Roosevelt. Some of the less well-known were interned at Camp des Milles near Aix-en-Provence. In the port, above the bowling area, a plaque commemorates the names of the refugees and a leaflet detailing the principal villas which were used is on sale at the bookshop.

Notre-Dame-de-Pitié – *Access via boulevard Courbet.*

The chapel was built in 1560 on a hillock, west of the town, and is decorated with votive offerings, mostly naïve paintings. From the stepped approach bordered by oratories there is **view★** of Sanary Bay with the Toulon hills in the background, and the coast as far as the Embiez Archipelago behind which rise the heights of Cap Sicié.

EXCURSIONS

★★ ① The Gros Cerveau

13km - 8 miles - about 1 hour 15min - local map below

From Sanary take avenue de l'Europe-Unie D 11 east, ② on the town plan.

Flowers, vines and fruit trees are cultivated on the fertile land.

At the entrance to Ollioules turn left into D 20.

At the start of the drive through terraced gardens and vineyards, the view extends both over the hillock on which the fort of Six-Fours stands and over the inner anchorage of Toulon at the foot of Mont Faron. Gradually the panorama extends southeast over Toulon and the Cap Sicié peninsula from an impressive *corniche* road. Further on the **view★** is magnificent: to the right, the Grès de Ste-Anne – enormous rocks riddled with caves, the Beausset plain, the Ste-Baume massif, the Évenos hills and the Ollioules gorge; on the left, a view of the coast.

8km - 5 miles after Ollioules (sign) make a U-turn to a platform.

A short walk will reveal a marvellous **view★★** of the coast from the Giens peninsula to Ile Verte off La Ciotat.

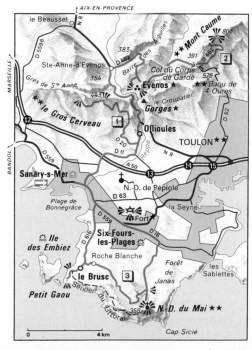

★★ ② Mont Caume

23km – 14.3 miles northeast – about 2 hours

Leave Sanary on avenue de l'Europe-Unie going east and follow D 11 to Ollioules

Ollioules – Old arcaded houses and a Provençal Romanesque church stand at the foot of the 13C castle. A cut-flower market (exporting throughout Europe) is held here.

"Théâtre National de la Danse et de l'image" de Châteauvallon – This centre was designed by Komatis and Gérard Paquet from 1965, and was developed around a 17C walled town, with a large open-air amphitheatre as well as an indoor theatre. Theatre and jazz festivals take place here all year round.

Beyond Ollioules turn left into N 8 which immediately enters the gorge.

★ **Gorges d'Ollioules** – The arid and sinuous gorge was created by the Reppe which tumbles into the sea in Sanary bay. As the road emerges at the northern end there is a view on the left of the Grès de Ste-Anne, a curious mass of sandstone rocks, hollowed and pitted by erosion.

In Ste-Anne-d'Évenos, turn right into D 462.

The road climbs a ravine dominated by the abrupt Barre des Aiguilles on the left.

Turn right towards Évenos and park the car near a cross set in a rock.

★ **Évenos** – *15min on foot return.* The village is a jumble of half-ruined and abandoned houses, built of basaltic stone, clinging to the steep rock slopes. The 13C church has a belltower with two bays. Over all brood the ruins of a 16C castle; the keep, also of basaltic stone, stands on the edge of a volcano from which the lava slag is still visible. From the platform there is a **view** of Destel gorge, Croupatier hill, Ollioules gorge and the Gros Cerveau in the foreground, and of Cap Sicié and the Ste-Baume massif on the horizon.

Continue east along D 62 turning left at the Col du Corps de Garde into D 662.

Mont Caume rises to 801m – 2 628ft. The steep approach road offers fine viewpoints; from the top *(climb the mound)* there is a magnificent **panorama**★★ of the coast, from Cap Bénat to La Ciotat bay and inland to the Ste-Baume massif.

★ ③ Cap Sicié Peninsula

Round tour of 25km – 15.5 miles – about 2 hours (excluding Ile des Embiez)

From Sanary take avenue d'Estienne-d'Orves.

The road skirts Bonnegrâce beach and Pointe Nègre: views of Sanary bay and Bandol.

Le Brusc – Fishing village and resort; ferries to Ile des Embiez leave from the port.

⌂ **Ile des Embiez** – *See Ile des EMBIEZ.*

Petit Gaou – The rocky promontory, once an island, pounded by the sea, resembles a Breton seascape. There is an extensive **view** of the coast and the neighbouring islands.

Return to Le Brusc and take D 16 towards Six-Fours; in Roche-Blanche bear right.

The road runs parallel to the coast about 1km – half a mile inland but gives glimpses of La Ciotat, Bandol and Sanary. At the crossroads there is a **view**★★ of the Toulon anchorage, Cap Cépet, the Giens peninsula and the Iles d'Hyères.

Turn right and park next to the radio station.

★★ **Notre-Dame-du-Mai** ⊙ – *Walk round the radio station to the chapel.*
The chapel is a place of pilgrimage (14 September) dedicated to Our Lady of the May Tree, also known as Our Lady of Good Protection, and contains many votive offerings. From the top of Cap Sicié there is a dizzy drop to the sea and a splendid **panorama**★★ of the coast from the Iles d'Hyères to the *calanques* east of Marseille.

Return to the crossroads continuing straight ahead.

The narrow road cuts through **Janas Forest**, a fine plantation of conifers, before rejoining D 16; turn left.

⌂ **Six-Fours-les-Plages** – *See SIX-FOURS-LES-PLAGES.*

Return to Sanary on D 559.

SAORGE★★

Population 323
Michelin map 84 fold 20 or 115 fold 18 or 245 fold 26
Local map see NICE HINTERLAND

In a rugged **setting**★★ the stone-covered houses and the proud belfries of the church and chapels cling to the steep slopes of a natural amphitheatre where the Roya valley temporarily broadens out. Saorge was originally a Ligurian settlement and then a Roman colony. In the Middle Ages the town was reputed to be impregnable but it has yielded twice: in 1794, to the French under Masséna, and in April 1945.

★ **Old town** – *Park the car at the north entrance.*
The stepped and twisting streets, sometimes arched, make an interesting walk past 15C houses with decorative doorways and carved lintels. On the far side of the square, go straight, then right and right again to reach a terrace offering a beautiful **view**★ into the bottom of the Gorges de la Roya.

St-Sauveur – Built in the 16C and revaulted in the 18C, the church comprises three naves supported on columns with gilded Corinthian capitals and is decorated with altarpieces. The **organ**, which was built in 1847 by the Lingiardi of Pavia, was transhipped by sea from Genoa to Nice and thence to Saorge on muleback. In the south nave is an 18C canvas depicting Elijah with the Virgin and Child; a fine Renaissance tabernacle; a 15C font beneath a painting by a local artist (1532); a Virgin in gilded wood beneath a canopy (1708). To the left is a 16C primitive over the altar of the Annunciation.

Leave from the southern end of the village, bearing right at the road fork.

Madonna del Poggio – *Private property.* The early Romanesque building boasts a soaring **belfry** with six rows of Lombard bands and a fine chevet. The three naves are supported by columns crowned by capitals decorated with a stylised leaf design. This is the oldest religious building in the Roya valley. The return to the village offers a fine **view** of Saorge and the terraced olive groves.

Take a sharp right at the road fork towards the monastery.

Couvent des Franciscains ⊙ – Overlooking the village from the south, the 17C buildings of the Franciscan convent, to which the monks returned in 1969 after a long absence, are prettily set among olive trees. The church, which is in the Baroque style, has a porch surmounted by a balustrade; the belltower is capped by a bulbous roof of coloured tiles. Small **cloisters** are decorated with unrefined but nonetheless pretty paintings on pious themes.
From the terrace, a splendid **view**★★ of Saorge, the Roya and the gorge.

A. Philippon/EXPLORER

Saorge

SEILLANS★

Population 1 793
Michelin map 84 fold 7, 114 fold 11 or 245 fold 36

The village was often visited by Gounod and Alphonse Karr, and the painter Max Ernst chose to live there at the end of his life. The pink and cream houses cascade down the steep slope of the Canjuers plateau. Pleasant cobbled lanes lead up to the church and the old castle with its ramparts and fountain. The main local activity is the production of honey and herbs.

Church ⊘ – The rebuilding in 1477 incorporated a few sections dating from the 11C. The interior is decorated (right) with two beautiful triptychs: a 15C Coronation of the Virgin painted on wood and a marble stoup (1491). From the church there is a fine view over Fayence in the plain to the Tanneron massif.

Notre-Dame-de-l'Ormeau ⊘ – *1km – half a mile southeast on the Fayence road.* The Romanesque chapel, which is dedicated to Our Lady of the Elm Tree, is flanked by a belltower of dressed stone but marred by the later addition of an open porch.
The interior contains a remarkable 16C **altarpiece**★★. In the centre, a crowd of people is climbing the Tree of Jesse; the Adoration of the Shepherds (left) and the Adoration of the Magi (right) are both strikingly expressive. The predella, beneath a wooden peristyle, illustrates (left to right) the life of St Anne, the birth and marriage of the Virgin and the Annunciation.
To the left of the altarpiece is a fine low relief sculpture of the Assumption (17C): to the right, in a recess, an early statue of Our Lady of the Elm Tree.
To the left of the entrance there is a Roman tombstone with an inscription. The walls are adorned with numerous votive offerings dating from around 1800.

Help us in our constant task of keeping up-to-date. Send your comments and suggestions to:

*Michelin Tyre PLC – Tourism Department
38 Clarendon Road – WATFORD Herts WD1 1SX
Tel: (01923) 415000
Web site: www.michelin-travel.com.*

SIX-FOURS-LES-PLAGES ⚓

Population 28 957
Michelin map 84 fold 14, 114 folds 44 and 45 or 245 fold 46
Local map see SANARY-SUR-MER: Excursions

This widespread *commune* encompasses no fewer than 125 hamlets and districts; there are several beaches – the nearest and largest (2km – 1.5 miles of sand) is Bonnegrâce near Sanary.
The name comes from the Latin *sex furni*, a fortified post which was the first sign of settlement left by the Phocaeans from Massilia. During the Middles Ages the village was grouped around the summit of a hill and protected by three rows of ramparts. The Collégiale St-Pierre remains from this highly fortified site.

OLD SIX-FOURS

Access via avenue du Maréchal-Juin; turn left into a narrow road.

The steep climb offers alternating views of Sanary bay and the Toulon anchorage.

★ **Fort de Six-Fours** – Alt 210m – 689ft. From the platform at the entrance to the fort a **panorama**★ extends from east to west over Toulon anchorage, St-Mandrier peninsula, Cap Sicié, Sanary bay, Le Brusc and the Ile des Embiez.

Collégiale St-Pierre ⊘ – At the foot of the fortress stands the church of the now abandoned village of Old Six-Fours. It has two naves at right angles; in the 17C a Gothic-style nave was built. The Romanesque nave contains a polyptych attributed to Louis Bréa. In the Gothic chapels are a late 16C Flemish Descent from the Cross and a Virgin attributed to Pierre Puget.

Coast path – *Start from Bonnegrâce beach (on the edge of Sanary)*. The path runs along the beaches through low thorny vegetation. It leads to the little fishing port of Le Brusc with its busy small boats *(pointus)*. This stretch of the path also crosses the rocky promontory of Petit Gaou *(for description see SANARY-SUR-MER: Cap Sicié)*. There is a fine **view**★ over the southern part of Cap Sicié peninsula.

Experienced walkers may like to attempt the next part of the coast path to N-D-de-Mai, where it is possible to be met by car *(car park at the relais TDF)*.

EXCURSIONS

★★ **Chapelle Notre-Dame-du-Mai** – *For description see SANARY: Cap Sicié Peninsula*.

Cap Sicié – *See SANARY*.

Mediterranean Caviar

Edible sea urchins, known as sea chestnuts, have been appreciated since ancient times for their fine "eggs"; they are therefore intensively harvested, leading to great scarcity on the shores of the Mediterranean. This echinoderm lives on algae, tiny animals and bacteria caught by its spines. It attaches itself to the sea by means of the suckered feet around its mouth. It moves very slowly (about 1 cm – less than 1/2 inch a minute) by moving its spines. At certain times of the year bacterial infection can cause it to lose its spines.

The edible part of the sea urchin consists of the sexual organs, divided into five branches, which are orange in the female and off-white in the male. Fishing for sea urchins is prohibited between May and August (when there is no 'r' in the month); during this period the creatures are empty. Professional fishermen, who use diving equipment, carry a gauge to check that the sea urchins are more than 5cm 2 in in diameter and catch them in large nets which contain up to 20 dozen creatures.

Information campaigns designed to bring about more active conservation of sea urchins are led by the Institut Océanographique Paul-Ricard at Les Emblez and other institutes.

N-D-de-Pépiole – *3km – 2 miles – about 1 hour*
From Six Fours drive north. After a short distance turn left at the roundabout into a narrow road (sign "Monuments historiques"). Park on the terrace, 100m – 110yds from the chapel.

This chapel of yellow, rose and grey stone, surmounted by two charming campaniles, stands in a most attractive **setting**★ of pines, cypress trees, olive trees, vines and broom, against the mountainous backdrop of Toulon.

The chapel **N-D-de-Pépiole** ⊙ (5C-6C) is one of the oldest early Christian buildings in France; for centuries it was hidden under heavy layers of plaster which helped to preserve it. It originally consisted of three separate chapels; in the 12C great lateral arcades of blue stone were added to create a unique place of worship. The chapel on the left contains a 17C statue of Notre-Dame-de-Pépiole.

SOSPEL★

Population 2 592
Michelin map 84 fold 20 or 115 west of fold 18 or 245 folds 25, 26
Local map see NICE HINTERLAND

The old houses of Sospel, a cool mountain resort, line both banks of the Bévéra, making a very picturesque scene. The village lies in a cultivated basin (olive groves) surrounded by high mountains and is a good excursion centre owing to its position at the confluence of the rivers Merlanson and Bévéra, where the road from Menton to the upper Vésubie meets the road from Nice to Turin via the Col de Tende.

Sospel was the capital of the stewardship under the County of Ventimiglia in the 13C, then bishopric during the Great Schism and one of the places travellers had to pass through on the Salt Road *(Route du Sel)* linking the capital of the Kingdom of Sardinia, Turin, to the coast.

★ OLD VILLAGE

South bank – The church and arcaded houses in place St-Michel make a charming sight. The oldest house (palais Ricci) to the right of the church bears a plaque recording Pope Pius VII's stay in 1809, when Napoleon had him brought to France away from the Papal States.

Old bridge, Sospel

St-Michel – At the time of the Great Schism the church was a cathedral. The Romanesque belltower with Lombard bands flanks an imposing Baroque façade. The interior décor is pure Baroque: altar with baldaquin, huge altarpieces, *trompe-l'œil* frescoes, gilding: a denticulated cornice runs the length of the nave walls.

In the north apsidal chapel the Virgin of Mercy does not seem to belong to the Nice School but the **Immaculate Virgin★** is one of François Bréa's best works: a retable of the Virgin against a charming landscape thronged with angels.

To the right of the parvis, large stairways lead to the ruins of a Carmelite convent, now almost hidden by vegetation. Carry on to reach the remains of some fortifications, including a huge 15C corner tower and, further on, a semicircular arched gateway in the curtain wall. Go through this gateway and follow a stairway to the rue St-Pierre, which runs on from the cathedral parvis. The road, which is lined initially by arcades, leads to the little square behind the *mairie* (town hall) in which there is a pretty wall fountain.

In rue St-Pierre are several emblazoned door lintels (nos 3, 20 and 29). Most of these carved stones are surmounted by a grill covering the semicircular archway and providing natural air-conditioning by encouraging the movement of air. There is an interesting façade *(no 30)* endowed with two Renaissance windows. The ground floor, in Gothic style, has a diagonal rib window and door.

Les fontaines – The important commercial role of the town in the past is recalled by numerous sculpted fountains scattered round the village. In place de la Cabraïa, the most imposing fountain has two levels and was used as a drinking trough. This place is in fact named after the flocks of goats which used to be seen here. There are other fountains in place St-Nicolas (the oldest), at the end of rue de la République and in place St-Pierre, behind the town hall.

★ **Old bridge** – The toll tower on the 11C bridge was destroyed during the Second World War. It has been rebuilt and now houses the *syndicat d'initiative* (tourist information) and, in season, an information centre about the Parc National du Mercantour.

North bank – Cross the old bridge, paved with cobblestones, to visit place St-Nicolas with its old houses and pretty paving. Beneath the arcades of the erstwhile community centre, decorated with a paschal lamb in bas-relief, there is a lovely 15C fountain. Rue de la République to the right, once housed numerous small businesses and enormous cellars used as warehouses by passing merchants before they settled their toll at the bridge. The houses along this road feature beautifully carved stone lintels (nos 14, 15, 23 and 51). In a recess *(right, after no 51)* there is an elegant Provençal fountain. The picturesque and narrow rue des Tisserands leads to Ste-Croix (17C chapel).

★ **Fort St-Roch** ⊙ – *1km – just over half a mile south of the village, on D 2204 to Nice. After the cemetery, take an old army road to the right (signed).*
This military construction was designed to block the Bévéra valley and cover the Col de Brouis and the exit of the railway tunnel coming from Breil. Completed in 1932, it amounts essentially to an underground town, 50m – 164ft deep, which was able to survive for up to three months without contact with the outside world. The fort was part of the Alpine Maginot line of fortifications built in the region during the 1930s. The tour covers over 2km – a mile of underground galleries, including the kitchens, an electricity generating station, an operations block, ventilation chambers, the firing stations – up a 45° slope served by a funicular which was used for ammunition, a small cinema and the artillery rooms (81mm mortar and 75mm gun), as well as the periscopes which enabled the inhabitants of the fort to view their surroundings. This interesting visit is completed by a museum containing a retrospective on the Alpine Army between 1939 and 1945.

Botanic path – *1 hour 30 mins return on foot.* This delightful footpath, signed and marked with boards detailing the plants to be seen, is below D93 to the right towards the Olivetta frontier post. Go down the slope from the road towards the railway, then turn left under the bridge. A signpost near a ruin marks the start of the botanic footpath. The path goes through a wood of young oak trees, alders growing in a damp area, and then scrubland which was once cultivated in terraces, and a holm oak wood.

EXCURSIONS

Mont Agaisen

7km – 4,3miles by car and then 2 hours on foot return. From Sospel take the road which runs alongside the Post Office and then climbs up the north bank of the Bévéra. After 1,5km – just under a mile, turn right and follow a road uphill towards Serres des Bérins
The road winds its way up the hillside between orchards, giving pretty glimpses of the valley. On entering the Bérins district, take the surfaced road on the right, heading south. After a short stretch through some woods, the old army road reaches the first small forts of the fortified complex of Mont-Agaisen *(not open to the public).*
It is possible to leave the car at any one of the many lay-bys along the climb. Follow the path that leads to the summit (alt 745m – 2 444ft) on foot. Here and there you will come across a casemate or a firing turret. Heading due south will bring you to the edge of the summit, near a large metal cross. There is a good view of the village, the Bévéra valley and Mont Barbonnet, recognisable by its fortified glacis. There are many other viewpoints on the summit, towards the Col de Brouis, for example, or north towards the sunken valley towered over by the bare peak of Mont Mangiabo (alt 1 801m – 5 909ft).
More experienced walkers may like to try a variation of this excursion, namely leaving from the village and doing the whole of it on foot. In this case, you should leave from the Groupe Scolaire overlooking the village and follow the path which leads off to the right, signed "GR 52 – Mont Agaisen"*(about 3 hour walk).* The track merges with that of the GR 52; follow the red and white flashes along this for about 1km – half a mile. At the junction with a surfaced road, turn left into this and follow it uphill for another half a mile or so until you reach the first ruins of military buildings and rejoin the car itinerary described above.

★ Piène-Haute via the Col de Vescavo
9km – 5.6 miles – allow half a day.

From Sospel take D 2204 east. After 2km – just over a mile turn right into a road signed "Piène-Olivetta".
After 4km – 2.5 miles D 93 reaches the Col de Vescavo (alt 478m – 1 568ft) which overlooks the bank on the Italian side of the Bévéra. The road then wends its sinuous way down through pine trees and then olive groves to the border checkpoint before the Italian village of Olivetta. Follow D 193 to the left as it continues to climb to the charming little village of Piène-Haute. In solitary splendour on an outcrop 613m – 2 011ft in altitude. The best place to park is on the esplanade at the entrance to the village. Before setting off downhill on foot, admire the **view**★ of the tightly packed old houses, overlooked by the ruins of the castle. Tiny streets colourful with flowers lead to the pretty little square in

front of the *mairie* (town hall). The church, on a rise, has a beautiful carved belltower and houses an unusual red marble altarpiece. Above the village, by the castle ruins, there are splendid views of the valley of the Roya and the hamlet of Piène-Basse on the border.

It is possible to extend the excursion from here to the Col de Brouis *(half a day)* or as far as the summit of the Arpette (alt 1 610m – 5 282ft) via the hamlet of Libre and following the line of the crest along the border, overlooking the village.

★ Col de Brouis Road

21km – 13 miles – about 1 hour – local map see NICE Hinterland.

The road is an extension of the Col de Braus Road *(see Forêt de TURINI)* towards Turin (the old "salt road") and links the Bévéra valley to the Roya valley.

From Sospel take D 2204 east.

There is a view to the rear over Sospel guarded by the Fort du Barbonnet.

Col du Pérus – Alt 654m – 2 146ft. The road runs above the Bassera ravine.

★ **Col de Brouis** – Alt 879m – 2 884ft. This pass takes its name from the particular type of heather-like shrub found growing in profusion in this area, known locally as *brouis*. The monument above the car park on the right commemorates the last French attack of April 1945 against the German forces, who had been driven back into the valleys. A broad **view**★ opens up of the peaks on the far bank of the Roya. The road descends 2 steep slope before winding down to La Giandola.

La Giandola – *See Haute Vallée de la ROYA.*

Salt Road

By virtue of its essential role in the preservation of meat and the tanning of hides, salt has always been of strategic interest. Provençal salt-works have supplied Piedmont since the Middle Ages. The salt was unloaded from sailing barges in Nice and transported by mule to Turin. Among the routes used at the time, the one favoured by the princes of Savoy crossed the cols de Braus, de Brouis and de Tende and passed through Sospel and Saorge. This strategic highway became known as the Salt Road *(route du sel)*. The returning caravans carried rice from Piedmont, hemp and cloth. The heavy traffic (more than 5 000 tonnes of salt a year), which by the end of the 18C used nearly 15 000 mules, obliged the authorities to improve the road and make it suitable for carts and carriages; they also drew up plans for a tunnel under col de Tende but it was not finished until 1883.

The road, which is now embellished with works of modern art, is still the main highway between the Riviera and the cities of Piedmont.

Massif du TANNERON

Michelin map 84 folds 8 and 9 or 115 north of folds 33 and 34, or 245 folds 36 and 37

The Tanneron is a northern extension of the Esterel from which it is separated by a shallow depression through which N 7 and the Provençal motorway run.

However, its round contours and the nature of its rocks (gneiss) suggest that it is more closely related to the Maures.

A bouquet of mimosa – The Tanneron is well known for its winter display of brilliant yellow mimosa contrasting with the clear winter sky. The snow-falls and hard frosts in 1985 and 1986 have unfortunately caused considerable damage to this plant.

Once the massif was covered with sea pines and chestnut trees, but the forest has been much reduced under the triple assault of man (cultivation rights have existed since the

N. Thibaut/EXPLORER

Mimosa in bloom

Middle Ages), the cochineal (a parasitic insect which kills the pine trees) and fire. Mimosa was imported into the Mediterranean from Australia in 1839 and is first mentioned near Cannes in 1864. Since then it has invaded the bare slopes of the Tanneron and early this century brought financial success to the region.

Mimosa belongs to the acacia family of plants (not to be confused with the common acacia which is a "false acacia"). There are many different types – some taking the form of shrubs and others growing into trees up to 12m – 40ft high – which flower at different times between November and March; the "four seasons" variety flowers throughout the year. The commonest mimosa grows wild in huge swathes. Flowering can be induced or improved by forcing techniques. Fronds are cut prematurely and shut up in a dark room for two or three days at a temperature of 22-25°C with very high humidity. Mimosa can also be cut when the flowers are still in bud; a special powder mixed with hot water will cause the flowers to open. Tonnes of cut flowers from the Tanneron are sold in France and abroad each year.

ROUND TOUR STARTING FROM CANNES

56km – 35 miles – about half a day

⚏⚏⚏ **Cannes** – *See CANNES.*

From Cannes take N 7, ③ on the plan. For a description of the route as far as the Logis-de-Paris crossroads see Massif de l'ESTEREL ④.

Then turn right into D 237 which offers **glimpses** of La Napoule bay and Mont Vinaigre. Beyond Les Adrets de l'Esterel the view extends to the Pre-Alps of Grasse. The road crosses over the Provençal motorway on the edge of the Montauroux woods before skirting the Lac de St-Cassien.

Lac de St-Cassien – *Before the Pré-Claou bridge turn right into D 38.*

The road rises through a pinewood with pleasant **glimpses** of the lake, the dam and the mountain peaks on the horizon. Near the hamlet of Les Marjoris the road winds over mimosa-clad slopes down to the River Verrerie.

Before reaching Tanneron village, turn right into a steep narrow road.

★ **Notre-Dame de Peygros** – Alt 412m – 1 352ft. From the terrace of the Romanesque chapel, there is a fine **panorama**★ of the Lac de St-Cassien, the Siagne valley and Grasse; Mont Agel on the coast and the Alps on the Italian border stand out to the east; the Esterel and the Maures massifs dominate the southern horizon.

Pass through Tanneron to the Val-Cros crossroads.

The descent reveals fine **views** of Auribeau, of Grasse and the broad Siagne valley.

★ **Auribeau-sur-Siagne** – *7km – 4.3 miles – from Val-Cros crossroads (alt 296m – 971ft).* A narrow twisting road sunk between banks of mimosa leads up to the charming village, which dates from the 12C, on a hill beside the Siagne. It was rebuilt in 1490 by colonists from Genoa. Go through the 16C Porte Soubran, the upper gate, and stroll through the stepped and, at times, narrow streets. The old houses (restored) huddle around the **church** ⊘, which contains a 15C silver-gilt and enamelled reliquary and a 16C chalice.

From the church square the **view** encompasses the wooded hills of the Siagne valley, Grasse and its ring of mountains, the Pic de Courmettes and the Valbonne plateau.

Starting from the church's west façade, take the stepped streets (degrés de l'Église and degrés Soubran) leading to Porte Soutran, the lower gate, which is set in a bend of a street. It is fortified and has a rounded arch.

Return to the Val-Cros crossroads and go straight across towards Mandelieu-la-Napoule, D 92.

★★ **Road to Mandelieu** – The slopes of the massif are covered by scrub. The drive through the mimosa down a steep hill to Mandelieu-la-Napoule is marvellous, with many **views**★★ of the Esterel, the town and its aerodrome, La Napoule bay, Cannes and the Iles de Lérins, the Siagne valley, Grasse and the Pre-Alps. On the horizon loom the Alps.

Mandelieu-la-Napoule – Capital of mimosa country on the banks of the Siagne.

Return to Cannes by D 92 and N 98 along the seafront.

The length of time given in this guide
- *for **touring** allows time to enjoy the views and the scenery*
- *for **sightseeing** is the average time required for a visit*

TENDE★

Population 2 089
Michelin map 84 fold 10, 115 fold 8 or 245 fold 26
Local map see NICE HINTERLAND

Tende (alt 816m – 2 677ft) has a breathtaking **setting★**, in an Alpine landscape on the banks of the Roya beneath the steep rock face of the Riba de Bernou. The tall austere houses beneath their shingled roofs seem to be stacked on top of one another. A jagged tooth of wall sticking 20m – 65ft into the air is all that remains of the former splendour of the Lascaris family, whose castle was pulled down by the French during the war of the League of Augsburg in 1692. A curious terraced cemetery near the walls adds a bizarre touch. Tende commands access to the road over the pass into Italy and, together with St-Dalmas, is the starting point for organised excursions to the Vallée des Merveilles.

M. Braun

Old town, Tende

★ **Old town** – Most of the houses, some dating from the 15C, are built of the local stone, green and purple schist. The maze of narrow streets boasts several carved lintels bearing escutcheons, huge overhanging eaves and balconies on all floors. Note the Renaissance belltowers on the chapels of the Black and White Penitents. From above the town on the site of the old castle, the **view★** looks down onto the village, its shingled-roofed houses and belltowers.

Musée des Merveilles ⊙ – *avenue du 16 Septembre 1947, opposite the Customs*. A visit to this museum, with its modern façade consisting of 12 parallelepiped columns and a square green stone from the Roya depicting rock art motifs, is recommended as the ideal complement to a walk around the sites of Mont Bégo. The history of the Vallée des Merveilles and its inhabitants is illustrated in the museum following three themes: relief models and animations show the regional geology; archeology forms a major exhibit with dioramas reconstructing daily life in the Bronze Age, many casts of the carvings, the original stela known as "**chef de tribu**" (moved because of erosion damage) and objects discovered during excavations; modern popular and pastoral traditions are brought to life in an exhibition of objects and dioramas which show a continuity with prehistoric life. The museum also houses a university training centre and facilities for research into rock art of the period.

Notre-Dame-de-l'Assomption – This collegiate church was built in the early 15C of green schist, except for the Lombard tower capped with a pretty little dome. The Renaissance-style **doorway** is flanked by two Doric columns resting on two lions, inspired by Romanesque art; the entablature is decorated with statues of Christ and the Apostles. The tympanum illustrates the Assumption. The inside is divided equally into three aisles by thick, green-schist (from the Roya) columns. The Lords of Lascaris are buried here. The sacristy ceiling is decorated with 17C frescoes and stuccowork.

Michelin Maps (scale 1: 200 000), which are revised regularly, show at a glance:

    – main roads linking the main towns and sights
    – regional roads
    – side roads for a leisurely drive

Keep current Michelin Maps in the car at all times

Abbaye du THORONET★★

Le Thoronet, the oldest of the three Cistercian abbeys in Provence *(see Michelin Green Guide PROVENCE: Sénanque and Silvacane)* is surrounded by wooded hills in an isolated spot, in keeping with the rigid rules of the Cistercian Order.

From foundation to the present – In 1136 monks from the abbey of Mazan (Haut-Vivarais) settled in the valley of the River Florège near Tourtour, but later they moved to Le Thoronet near Lorgues and finally established themselves on land presented to them by Raymond Bérenger, Count of Barcelona and Marquis of Provence. The abbey soon became prosperous from the many donations it received, particularly from the lords of Castellane. The church, the cloisters and the monastic buildings were constructed between 1160 and 1190.

A few years later the abbey's most famous abbot was appointed – **Folquet de Marseille**. His family came from Genoa but he left the commercial life to devote himself to poetry. He became a famous troubadour, quoted by Dante, and then in 1196 decided to become a Cistercian monk. In 1201 he was appointed Abbot of Le Thoronet and then Bishop of Toulouse in 1205.

Like many other Cistercian abbeys in the 14C, Le Thoronet went into decline. First internal dissension and later the Wars of Religion caused the monks to leave the abbey. In 1787 it was attached to the See of Digne. During the Revolution it was sold and again abandoned. In 1854 it was bought by the State and saved from ruin by the intervention of Prosper Mérimée.

The restoration and consolidation work which has been carried out since then has been made even more necessary by the bauxite extraction site nearby and the subsidence caused by the weather.

TOUR ⊘ *1 hour*

The quality of the buildings that remain (church and cloisters), and their simple but rigorous style, mean that the abbey of Le Thoronet can be considered one of the jewels of Cistercian architecture.

★ **Church** – This was built in the style of the Provençal Romanesque School.

Exterior – The building is squat, austere and rigorously geometric. It is extraordinarily similar in plan to the abbey church at Sénanque. The stonework is remarkable; the blocks have been accurately cut and assembled without mortar. The square belltower of stone is an exception to the architectural rules of the Order, which allowed only simple wooden structures. It was permitted here because of the violent winds and the risk of fire.

In the west front there are four small windows and an oculus but no central door; instead there are two doors opening into the aisles, both surmounted by a small window which is slightly off-centre. The door on the left was for the lay brothers. In the south wall, on the opposite side to the cloisters, is a round-arched niche (1), one of the rare external funerary repositories in Provence.

Interior – The nave is covered with barrel vaulting, slightly pointed, supported on tranverse arches. It consists of three bays, prolonged by a fourth of the same height at right angles to the transept: only the raised arches indicate the presence of two arms of the transept which are vaulted like the nave. As at Sénanque, the eastern wall of each transept opens into two semicircular chapels which, on the outside, are rectangular in shape.

The chancel ends in an oven-vaulted apse, as at Sénanque, and is lit through three windows. It is preceded by a shallow bay, featuring a triumphal arch which is surmounted by an oculus. The aisles are lower than the nave and covered with rampant pointed vaulting supported on transverse arches.

There is hardly any sculpture or carved decoration in the church to detract from its majestic proportions and purity of line. There is, however, a gentle curve on the imposts on the pillars and the half-columns which support the transverse arches and rise to only 2.90m – 9.5ft above the ground according to Cistercian use.

★ **Cloisters** – The cloisters on the north side of the church are austere and solidly built in the form of a trapezium. The south gallery is at about the same level as the church, but the west (exhibition of manuscripts and illuminated texts) and the north and east (which once supported another storey beneath a pitched roof) are lower because of the uneven ground; in all, seven steps were needed to compensate for the change of level. The galleries have transverse arches and barrel vaulting. The solid, round-headed arches which open onto the cloisters' garth (now a garden) are each divided in two by a stout column; the tympanum is pierced by an oculus. Opposite the refectory door, projecting into the garth, is the **lavabo** (2) where the monks washed their hands before meals. The hexagonal structure has been restored; the water container is provided with holes and spouts through which the water ran into the basin below.

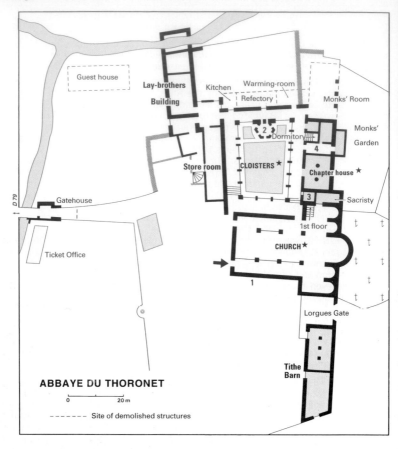

ABBAYE DU THORONET

0   20 m

------ Site of demolished structures

Conventual buildings – These stand on the north side of the church round the cloisters. The door of the library (**armarium** – **3**), which is on the ground floor, is surmounted by a triangular lintel.

The **chapter house**★ dates from the early Gothic period; the ogival vaulting, in which the ribs fan out like palm trees, is supported on two columns with roughly sculpted capitals, ornamented with leaves, pine cones, palm fronds and a hand gripping a staff. These are the only carvings in the abbey. The stone benches have been partially reconstructed. Next to the chapter house is the **parlour** (**4**) which also serves as a passage between the cloisters and the outer garden. The **dormitory** over the chapter house is reached by a vaulted stairway; it is roofed with pointed vaulting supported on transverse arches; the 18 windows with double embrasures have been reglazed. At the southern end, jutting out above the cloisters, is the Abbot's chamber. The doors in the north gallery opened into the monks' room, the warming room, the refectory and the kitchen, which have all disappeared.

The **store room**, on the west side of the cloisters, has pointed vaulting and contains 18C vats for wine and olive oil as well as the remains of a press.

The lay-brother building *(lais)*, at the northwest corner of the store room, was separate housing for the lay-brothers, who carried out manual labour for the monks and who lived a less constrained monastic life. It has been partially restored and comprises a refectory on the ground floor and a dormitory above.

Outbuildings – Beside the stream, the foundations of the **guest house** have been excavated. The **tithe barn** on the south side of the church was later converted into an oil mill and contains some mill stones and a mortar.

Michelin Green Guides are revised regularly
Use the most recent edition to ensure a successful journey

TOULON★★

Population of conurbation 437 553
Michelin map 84 fold 15, 114 fold 45 or 245 fold 46
Local map see Excursions below
Plan of conurbation in the current Michelin Red Guide France

France's second naval port lies behind its **anchorage★★**, one of the most secure and most beautiful harbours of the Mediterranean, surrounded by tall hills crowned by forts. The suburbs lie along the shore and form terraces on the sunny slopes of the surrounding hills.

HISTORICAL NOTES

Toulon purple – In Roman times Toulon was celebrated for the manufacture of the imperial purple. The dye was obtained by steeping the colour glands of the pointed conches (genus *Murex*) which proliferate along the coast in salt solution previously brought to boiling point for ten days in lead vats. The purple obtained was used to dye silk and woollen materials. This sumptuous colour was initially reserved for emperors but later its use spread, though the imperial treasury maintained a monopoly over its manufacture. The foundations of the old Toulon dye-works were uncovered during reconstruction work in the arsenal.

The age of the galleys (17C and 18C) – One of the attractions for travellers of the 17C and 18C was to visit the galleys moored in the old port (Vieille Darse). Each ship had only one bank of oars – 25 or 26 oars per side, each about 16m – 52ft long and manned by four men; the sails were triangular; artillery had begun to be used. Thousands of galley slaves were needed. Criminals and poachers not being numerous enough, political and religious prisoners were added; Turks were bought and there were even some volunteers! All these men were bare-foot, wore a red cloak and a red or green bonnet; faces and heads were clean shaven but the Turks were allowed to retain a tuft of hair and the volunteers their moustaches. On board, the galley slaves rowed with one foot bound to the deck and one wrist chained to the oar, eating and sleeping without leaving their places. The slave-master stimulated their efforts with cuts from a rawhide whip. The slaves were allowed to go ashore but were chained together in pairs. Players of musical instruments were much in demand at weddings,

Toulon Arsenal entrance

J. L. Gallo/MICHELIN

when they played for dancing. In 1748 the galleys were abolished and replaced by naval prisons. In 1854 these disappeared in their turn and the system of transportation overseas followed.

Bonaparte's first feat of arms – On 27 August 1793, Royalists handed Toulon over to an Anglo-Spanish fleet. A Republican army was sent to Toulon; the artillery was under the command of an obscure junior captain called Bonaparte. Between La Seyne and Tamaris where the Fort Carré or Fort Napoléon stands today the British had built a fortification so strong that it was called "little Gibraltar".
A battery was installed facing the British fort, but was subjected to such terrible fire that the gunners faltered. The young Corsican made a sign inscribed "battery of fearless men". He soon had enough volunteers. Bonaparte set the example; he laid the guns and manned the sponge-rod. It was in this engagement that Sergeant Junot distinguished himself. As he was writing down an order being dictated by Bonaparte, a shell burst nearby covering them both with flying earth: "Good!" said Junot, brushing himself down, "now I shall not need any sand to dry the ink". "Little Gibraltar" fell on 17 December. The foreign fleet withdrew after burning the French

PRACTICAL INFORMATION

Information Centres

Monthly programme of events available from the Tourist Office – place Raimu ; ☎ 04 94 363 80. Public road transport and the RMTT provide sea links from quai Cronstadt to La Seyne, Les Sablettes and St Mandrier.

Markets

The atmosphere at the market (open 6am to 1pm) in Cours Lafayette is lively and typical of the *marchés de Provence* celebrated, in song, memorably fragrant, and vividly colourful; do go early, because later in the day it is very crowded.

Market in cours Lafayette, Toulon

Food and drink – some specialities

The café terraces in quai Cronstadt provide a good view of the life of the old port – *Bar du Soleil*, *La Gourmandise* and *Le France.* The natives of Toulon *(moccots)* particularly enjoy l'*escabèche de sardine, la cade* (a flat cake made from chickpeas, similar to *socca* in Nice), *la pompe à l'huile* (a hard cake, oiled and flavoured with orange water) and the famous sweet doughnut *(chichifrei)* which can be bought from the stalls in the Lafayette market. Several restaurants specialise in fish dishes (place du Théâtre and rue Jean-Jaurès).

In **Mourillon** many restaurants have terraces which are ideal places to sit and try the seafood specialities (corniche Henri-Fabre, port St-Louis).

Shopping

The best streets are rue Jean-Jaurès, rue Hoche, place Victor-Hugo and rue d'Alger.
- Christmas crib figures *(santons)* from a craftsman in Pradet – La Santonnerie, rue Alphonse-Daudet;
- Olive oil from the mills on the outskirts of Toulon – Moulin de St-Côme in La Cadière d'Azur; Domaine de Souviou in Beausset; Moulin de Callas in Callas.

Shows and entertainment

Toulon really comes to life when the Mayol stadium is filled with the supporters of the local football team (Racing Club de Toulon – RCT). Large shows and some sporting events are hosted by the multi-purpose hall Zénith-Oméga, boulevard Cdt Nicolas.

In July *Jazz is Toulon* presents a series of free concerts in the square and a gigantic anchovy and olive sandwich *(anchoïade monstre)* is given to the musicians.

ships, the arsenal, and the provision depots, as well as taking part of the population with them. While Napoleon was being made a brigadier-general, Toulon came within a hair's breadth of being destroyed; 12 000 workers were requisitioned to raze "the infamous city", but at the last moment the Convention cancelled the order.

Second World War - In November 1942, in response to the Allied Landings in North Africa, Hitler decided to invade the French free zone. The decision was therefore taken to scupper the French fleet *(see below)*.
On 19 August 1944, four days after the Allied Landing on the Maures beaches, French troops attacked the Toulon defences, a plan of which had been smuggled out in 1942 by sailors in the Resistance. The city was liberated on 26 August. On 13 September the French fleet, which had taken part in the liberation, sailed into the anchorage, where the scuttled ships still lay on the bottom.

Post-war - Up to 1939 Toulon had been too dependent on the naval dockyard and very isolated by its geographic position. After the war an effort was made to diversify: the Arsenal broadened the scope of its production, commercial trade in the port was developed and new industries were set up. The construction of holiday homes in the region sustained the building trade in the period after the post-war reconstruction boom. Improvements in the road network made the town more easily accessible. Tourism, the founding of a university and of the **Centre culturel de Châteauvallon** all underpin hopes for the city's successful future.

★ OLD TOWN *2 hours 30min*

The ancient heart of Toulon, with its characteristic confusion of streets, is bounded to the east by Cours Lafayette, to the west by rue Anatole-France and to the north by rue Landrin, a perimeter which follows the line of the fortifications in the reign of Henri IV. A programme of renovation is planned for the whole town centre, which includes a red-light district (an inevitable part of nightlife in Mediterranean ports) known as "Chicago".

The following itinerary, as well as including a visit on foot to the museums and monuments of the old town, is intended to draw attention to certain alleyways with their unusual façades.

★ **Pedestrian tour of the old town** - Place Raimu, opposite the tourist office, contains the bronze replica of the legendary card game from the film *César* (in which an empty chair represents an invitation). To the north is l'îlot des Riaux, where the Toulon penal colony is recalled in place du Globe with its stylised fountain and fine banana trees. Rue de la Glacière, with many private vaulted passageways leading off it, leads towards place Vezzani *(left)* where a huge stone prow embedded in a wall commemorates shipbuilding. Turn back to the right towards rue Baudin and then into rue des Boucheries which retains its medieval character. In place à l'Huile, named after the oil market which used to take place here and which has been replaced by a shellfish market, the renovated façade of Maison aux Têtes bears witness to the wealth of the Toulon bourgeoisie. In rue Seillan *(right)* there is a balcony with consoles *(no 5)*. To the left of the tourist office is a fine *trompe-l'œil* façade.

For a tour of the monuments and museums of the old town, start in place d'Armes and follow the green route on the plan.

Place d'Armes (EX) - The basic layout of this square, bordered to the south by the Corderie building, was drawn up by Colbert. Originally designed (1683) for troop reviews like the Champs de Mars in Paris, it became a favourite meetingplace for the local bourgeoisie and outward bound naval officers. Concerts take place on Sundays in the bandstand in the centre of the square. The north side is full of popular cafés and restaurants and also houses the offices of leading local newspapers, such as the *Petit Marseillais*.
East of the square is the birthplace *(6 rue Anatole-France)* of the most renowned of local inhabitants, Jules Muraire, know as Raimu (b 1883).

Return to the entrance to the Corderie.

Corderie - *Military property, not open to the public.* This building (320m - 1 050ft long), designed by Vauban to house the naval rope factory, now houses the Naval administrative offices. The fine **door**★ (1689) came from the former Jesuit college and was added to the façade in 1976. Magnificent allegories of Law *(Loi)* and Might *(Force)* frame the top floor.

★ **Musée de la Marine** (EY) ⊙ - The entrance to the naval museum is through an impressive 18C doorway; four marble columns support a pediment, flanked by statues of Mars (left) and Bellona (right). On entering, the visitor might be plunging straight into the Quai de l'Artillerie and the old arsenal - the subject of this large, likelife fresco was taken from a painting (18C) by Joseph Vernet. Note the sky painted in gold leaf. On the ground floor there are large-scale models of a frigate, *La Sultane*, and of an 18C vessel, the *Duquesne*. The room is

Atlantes by Puget on the old town hall, Toulon

decorated with statues of great 17C admirals carved in wood by Puget's pupils and an impressive figurehead of Neptune. Fine paintings by Vernet's pupils, drawings and other exhibits recall Toulon's seafaring history and its prison. Note in the stairwell another figurehead, Bellona in gilded and painted wood (1807). On the first floor there is an interesting collection of model ships and submarines from the 19C to the present.

Quai Cronstadt (EFY) – Attracted by the shops and cafés, an animated crowd throngs the waterfront. The tall modern buildings with their many-coloured windows form a screen between the old port and the old town. The only reminders of the past are the famous **atlantes**★ **(F)** by Pierre Puget, which support the main balcony of the old town hall.

Painted walls of Toulon

The high points of life in Toulon are illustrated by enormous wall frescoes in the town
Place Victor Hugo – The card game from *César*
Rue du Noyer *(corner of place Raimu)* – The glory of the merchant navy
Avenue Franklin-Roosevelt – Félix Mayol
Corner of rue Micholet – Typical activities in 19C Toulon, on three levels

---

St-François-de-Paule (FY) ⊘ – This small church was built in 1744 by the Recollects; its double-arched façade and Genoan belltower identify it with the Nice Baroque style. It has a nave and two aisles separated by coupled columns and galleries with balustrades; the chancel opens into a dome. In the south aisle is a statue of Our Lady of Peace carved in wood by one of Puget's pupils.

Rue Méridienne and place à l'Huile *(see above)* lead to place de la Poissonnerie which for several centuries accommodated the covered Fish Market (Halles aux Poissons), one of the livelier spots in Toulon. The last market building was demolished in 1898.

Ste-Marie (FY) – The cathedral was constructed in the 11C and restored in the 12C. In the 17C it was enlarged and the classical façade was erected; the belltower dates from 1740. The fairly dark interior is a mixture of Romanesque and Gothic, since the 17C architects retained the plan of the earlier building. There are several interesting works of art: in the north aisle, an Annunciation by Pierre Puget; in the south aisle, a canvas by J-B Van Loo, the *Triumph of the Eucharist*, and one by Pierre Puget, *The Vision of St Felix of Cantalice*. The elaborately carved pulpit dates from 1824; the Baroque altar in marble and plasterwork was designed by a pupil of Puget.

Cours Lafayette (FY) – The vegetable and flower market held here every morning is a noisy, bustling, highly coloured occasion.

Musée du Vieux Toulon (FY M²) ⊘ – This museum, located in the headquarters of the old bishopric, is currently undergoing restoration. The two galleries open at the time of going to press display maps, engravings and paintings recalling great moments in the history of the city of Toulon since the Middle Ages. The display cases contain ceramics, statuettes, costumes and exhibits of Provençal traditions. In the second gallery, there is a lovely relief map of the city, made in 1880.

Take rue Garibaldi to Porte d'Italie.

Porte d'Italie (GY) – This bastioned gate, built in 1790 on the site of ancient fortifications, is the only remnant of the defences which surrounded Toulon. Honoré de Balzac used it as a backdrop when Vidocq made use of a funeral cortège to help him escape from the town.

Return to Cours Lafayette and walk along the righthand side.

Fontaine des Trois-Dauphins (FX K) – The character of place Puget is embellished by this curious fountain which was sculpted in 1780 by two local artists; its distinction is due to the plants which have grown in its basins. The three intertwined dolphins are covered in moss and calcium deposits, on which grow ferns, a fig tree, a medlar and an oleander. Place Puget is pleasantly shaded and the cafés surrounding it are ideal places for sitting and enjoying the coolness.

Northwest of Place Puget is **Place des Trois-Dauphins** containing a bust of Raimu.

Rue d'Alger (FY) – This pedestrian precinct is the main commercial street which leads into the old port.

Félix Mayol

The Mayol Centre and Stadium perpetuate the memory of the comedian who was the first of a long line of performers from Toulon. Félix Mayol (1872-1941) was 20 when he started the fashion for the quiff of hair which characterised his silhouette as well as for the bunch of lily of the valley which he always wore in his button hole. In 1910, when he was the comedian at a café-concert in Paris, he bought the hall where he was appearing and rechristened it *Concert Mayol*. From his home town he hired comedians whose fame had not yet spread beyond the Toulon district – including Raimu, Sardou, Tramel and the singer Turcy – who were ironically named *des comiques à l'huile* by the Parisians at their first performances. During his career Mayol produced more than 500 works and light comedies.

ADDITIONAL SIGHTS

St-Louis (EY) – This church is a fine example of neo-Classical architecture, built in the late 18C in the form of a Greek temple. It comprises three naves separated by a double Doric colonnade supporting a coffered vault. Ten Corinthian columns in the choir support a windowed cupola decorated with a foliage frieze. The pulpit is elaborately carved.

Place de la Liberté (EFX) – This square is the heart of the modern town. The monumental fountain, Fontaine de la Fédération, erected for the centenary of the Republic, is the work of André Allar. The superb Grand Hôtel (1870) in the background, with its charming old-fashioned façade, is the last remaining example of the buildings of the Edwardian era.

On either side of the square, boulevard Strasbourg and avenue du Général-Leclerc (built on the site of the ancient fortifications) form the main axis of the town, separating the old town to the south from the new town to the north. The Opéra Municipal (1862), formerly the largest auditorium outside Paris, was the centre of attraction in the evenings until just before the Second World War. The many local cafés and cabarets helped to give this district a festive atmosphere.

Museums (EX M³) – A Renaissance style building houses two interesting municipal collections.

Muséum ⊙ – Two galleries in the right side of the building on the ground floor house the zoological collection (birds, mammals, primates, etc; note the two large sperm whales' jaws.

Musée d'Art ⊙ – In the left side of the building. The Flemish, Dutch, Italian and French Schools (16C-18C) are all represented in the museum's collections, which also include works by 19C artists, including a large number of Provençal painters, such as the Toulon landscapist, Vincent Courdouan.

The museum also possesses a very eclectic collection of contemporary painting and sculpture, exhibited in rotation.

Jardin Alexandre Ier (DEX) – This garden is home to some attractive trees, including magnolias, palms and cedars. The bust of Puget is by Injalbert and the 1914-18 War Memorial is by Honoré Sausse.

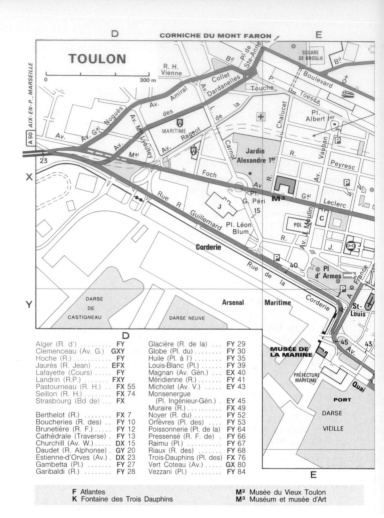

★ THE PORT (DEY) ⊙

Construction of the old port (Vieille Darse or Darse Henri-IV) began in 1589 on the orders of the Duke of Épernon, Governor of Provence. Expenses were borne by the town of Toulon which imposed a 25% tax on olive oil. The two breakwaters, closing the harbour on the south side, except for a 30m – 100ft wide passage across which a chain was slung, were completed in 1610.

At that time there was no royal fleet; when the king required ships, he leased them from lords and captains who had them built, armed and equipped. It was Richelieu who created a military arsenal to build and repair warships. Under Louis XIV the port proved too small and Vauban had the new port (Darse Neuve) excavated between 1680 and 1700. This became the naval port while the old port was turned over entirely to merchant shipping. In the 19C the navy needed yet more space, and in 1836 an annexe, which is still in use, was built at Mourillon. In 1852 Prince Louis-Napoléon established the harbour at Castigneau but 10 years later the port was again declared too small and Napoleon III created the Missiessy Harbour.

While retaining its position as a naval port, Toulon is increasing its commercial role. Merchant shipping is directed to the new facilities in Brégaillon bay on the west side of the inner anchorage, while the east side is used by the passenger ferries plying to the Iles d'Hyères, Corsica and Sardinia and by pleasure boats and cruise liners throughout the year.

Arsenal maritime – The naval arsenal covers some 240ha – 593 acres overall and employs in the region of 6 300 civilians. Its main activity is the maintenance of the French Mediterranean fleet: frigates, aircraft carriers, sloops, submarines and minesweepers. Some of the dry docks date from the 17C.

Bagne de Toulon – The only remains of this terrible penal colony, described in detail by Victor Hugo in *Les Misérables*, is a wall in the Arsenal. The withdrawal of the galleys in 1748 turned the galley slaves into convicts *(see TOULON: Age*

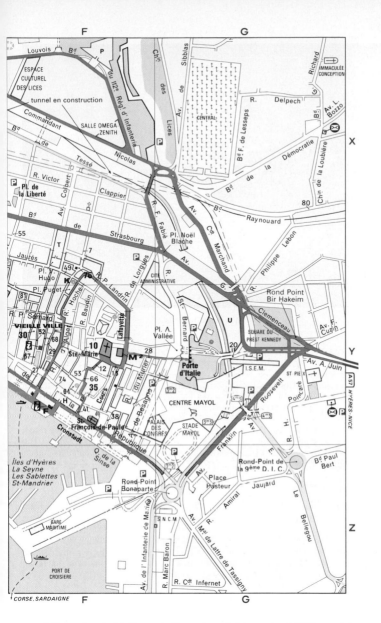

of the galleys). At its peak the colony held nearly 4 000 convicts, employed in shipbuilding and harbour maintenance. They formed a marginal but very structured society, with a common feature – the chain weighing 7kg – 15lbs to which they were permanently attached. The woollen Phrygian caps which they wore indicated their status – a red cap for those convicted for a limited period, a green cap for those sentenced for life and a brown cap for a deserter. Many a novelist was inspired by the inhuman conditions. In 1854 the government introduced transportation to penal settlements in the French colonies, such as Guyana and New Caledonia. The penal colony in Toulon was finally closed on 1 January 1874 when the last 300 inmates were shipped to Cayenne on board the frigate *La Guerrière*.

BOAT TRIPS

★ Tour by boat of the Petite Rade and the Grande Rade ⊘

The tour of the inner and outer harbours leaves from quai Cronstadt in the old port. The Toulon Roads are home to the Force d'Action Navale which includes two aircraft carriers, *Foch* and *Clemenceau*, the largest vessels in the French navy. They alternate between time in port and time on duty patrolling the

Toulon naval harbour

Mediterranean. The military port is lined with naval vessels – minesweepers, anti-submarine or missile-launcher frigates and, sometimes, the slim dark outline of a nuclear submarine.

The tour then passes the naval graveyard, where ships at the end of their useful life wait to be broken up, and approaches La Seyne port with its lifting bridge and the large area once occupied by the shipyards.

The Tamaris coast road leads to Balaguier Bay, where there are two forts – Balaguier and l'Ayguillette. The structures on piles in the centre of the bay mark the position of mussel beds. The tour returns via Lazaret Bay, along the St-Mandrier Peninsula and the long sea wall, which protects the eastern end of the outer harbour.

Scuppering of the French fleet

When German troops entered Toulon on 27 November 1942, 75 ships prevented by the Vichy government from leaving harbour, decided to scupper themselves rather than fall into the hands of the enemy. Among those which did escape were several submarines, including the *Casablanca* which then maintained liaison between the Free French Forces and Corsica. The scuttled ships remained on the bottom until the end of the war. It took 10 years to clear the harbour; 400 000 tonnes of metal were removed.

Ferries; boats to the Iles d'Hyères ⊘

There are several daily services to and from **La Seyne-sur-Mer**, **Les Sablettes** and **St-Mandrier-sur-Mer** *(see below EXCURSIONS).*

This is also the embarkation point for boats to the Iles d'Hyères *(see Iles d'HYERES).*

EXCURSIONS

The roads used in these excursions, although serving military installations, are classified as part of the civilian network. Traffic is permitted up to the entrance of these installations without formality but the military authorities categorically forbid anyone to enter certain places indicated by notices and signposts, particularly at the immediate approaches to the Forts of Croix-Faron, Lieutenant-Girardon and Cap Brun.

★★ ① La Corniche du Mont Faron

30min tour by car – local map see below – plan of conurbation in Michelin Red Guide FRANCE

The Corniche du Mont Faron provides the best view of the whole of Toulon harbour. The best time is late afternoon, when the light is ideal.

To reach the Corniche du Mont Faron take pont de Ste-Anne (DX), avenue de la Victoire and boulevard Ste-Anne (left).

The drive along the magnificent Corniche Marius-Escartefigue and the slopes of Mont Faron provides views of Toulon and its surroundings – the old town clustered round the port and the suburbs backed by the surrounding mountains. The view★ of the anchorage is very fine – the Petite Rade between Le Mourillon and La Seyne backed by the cliffs of Cap Sicié; the Grande Rade, partially enclosed (south) by the St-Mandrier Peninsula and its low narrow isthmus and (east) by Cap Carqueiranne, Giens Bay and the Giens Peninsula.

★★★ ② Mont Faron

Round tour of 18km – 11 miles – about 1 hour 30min – local map below

From Toulon take avenue St-Roch (DX 72), rue Dr-Fontan, avenue Général-Gouraud and avenue des Moulins and then turn right into the road to Fort Rouge.

Mont Faron (alt 584m – 1 916ft) is the small limestone massif, bordered by deep valleys, which immediately overlooks Toulon. It is a pleasant drive in summer over pine-clad slopes providing good views★ of Toulon, the inner and outer anchorages, the St-Mandrier and Cap Sicié peninsulas and Bandol.

Téléphérique du Mont Faron ⊙ – *Take boulevard Ste-Anne (DX) and follow the signs ("Téléphérique du Mont Faron") to the cable-car station in avenue Perrichi. At busy periods it is possible to park below the station on the left.*
The cable-car ride (6min) offers fine views★ over the town, the harbour and the limestone cliffs which surround Toulon. To the left the remains of many small forts can be seen. The view from the terrace of the upper station is for customers only. A pleasant view can also be had by walking about 10m – 33ft to the left along the access road to Mont Faron.

★ **Musée-mémorial du Débarquement en Provence** ⊙ – Installed in the Beaumont tower, left of the road, is the memorial to commemorate the liberation of the southeast of France by the Allies in August 1944. The first section is devoted to the memory of the English, American, Canadian and French who took part. In the second part there is a diorama (12min) of the liberation of Toulon and Marseille and a cinema (documentaries – 15min – filmed during the landing). From the terrace (accessible during a tour of the museum) there is a magnificent circular view★★★ (three viewing tables) of Toulon, the anchorages, the Mediterranean, and the islands and mountains all around Toulon.

Zoo ⊙ – Animals include lions, tigers, jaguars and monkeys.
The road crosses a wooded plateau, which ends abruptly at the foot of a steep slope, and then climbs up to the Fort Croix-Faron from where there is a beautiful view★ of the coast from the Giens peninsula to Bandol. Walk 100m – 110yds north of the fort to enjoy a view of the Provençal Alps.
Return to Toulon by the cable-car or the Faron road turning right into boulevard Faron.

★ ③ Baou de 4 Oures

11km – 6.8 miles northwest – 1 hour – local map below

From Toulon take avenue St-Roch (DX 72), rue Dr-Fontan, avenue Général-Gouraud and then turn left into avenue des Routes; in place Macé turn right into D 62 (avenue Clovis). After 4km – 2.5 miles turn left into D 262.
3km – 2 miles further on is a platform from which there is a magnificent view★★ of Toulon, the anchorages and the coast.
The narrow road to the top (4km – 2.5 miles) crosses a firing range (open to traffic).
At the top there is a fine panorama★★ of the coast from Cap Bénat to La Ciotat and inland from Ste-Baume to the Maures.

★★ ④ Tour of the Anchorage

17km – 10.5 miles south – about 1 hour 30min – local map below

From Toulon take A 50 motorway and D 559.
The road skirts the Brégaillon merchant shipping port.
Turn left towards La Seyne-sur-Mer.

La Seyne-sur-Mer – La Seyne, built beside the bay which bears its name, looks eastwards towards the inner anchorage. It has a harbour for fishing boats and pleasure craft but is basically an industrial town which depended for its livelihood upon the naval shipyards. These were founded in 1856, when they built ships for the merchant navy, as well as producing some of the most outstanding vessels of the war fleets. The site is being modified; it will be rebuilt round the sea while conserving the environment. The old overhead crane at the entrance to the dockyards is still in place.

The road skirts the small bay between forts Aiguillette and Balaguier, which were built in the 17C opposite the Tour Royale *(see ⑥ below)* to seal off the harbour entrance. Close inshore are mussel beds and some old ships at anchor. There is a good view inland across the inner anchorage beyond Toulon to Mont Faron and Le Coudon.

Fort Balaguier – The fort was recaptured from the English in 1793 by the young Napoleon. Set up in the fort's rooms, with walls 4m – 13ft thick, is a **naval museum** ⊙. It contains an interesting collection of model ships and memorabilia of the Napoleonic era. On the walls hang seascapes and paintings of the Toulon region.

The 17C chapel contains objects relevant to the Toulon galleys and naval prisons: registers, chains and works of art made by the prisoners.

From the terrace overlooking the fort's garden and its aviary, there is a remarkable **view★** of the coastline from Toulon to the Ile du Levant.

Toulon anchorage from Mont Faron

Tamaris – In the shady resort on the hillside, George Sand wrote several of her novels. Fine view of St-Mandrier peninsula.

Villa Tamaris-Pacha ⊙ – The history of this magnificent residence, still unfinished, is worthy of the *Arabian Nights*. Towards the middle of the 19C a Frenchman, Michel Pacha, became by a series of happy coincidences the concessionnaire of the lighthouses, quays and warehouses of Constantinople. He was thus the creator of the modern port of Istanbul and of reconnaissance of the coasts under the Ottoman administration. As the Var coast closely resembled the Golden Horn and the Bosphorus he chose to build his wife a palace inspired by Florentine villas in Tamaris. After three years of hard work, when his wife was stabbed by a mentally ill person in 1893, Michel Pacha stopped all work on the villa and the palace stayed uninhabited for a century. Now redeveloped, the villa houses a cultural institution and has exhibitions.

Beside the bay, a luxurious house, the work of Michel Pacha, displays the ornately carved Mauresque style. It houses a Lyonnais university centre.

All along Le Lazaret bay are small cabins perched on stilts above the mussel beds.

Les Sablettes – Long wide beach of fine sand open to the sea. The houses were rebuilt after the last war in the neo-Provençal style, designed by the architect F Pouillon.

The unusual military career of the St-Mandrier peninsula

The hill of La Croix aux Signaux, a secret German naval base, was from September 1943 to August 1944 an assembly base for midget submarines which left via an access tunnel which ended up on Cavalas beach. In 1929, however, the Marine Nationale Française had buried there (14m – 46ft deep) two enormous gun turrets each holding two 340 guns, 17m – 56ft long, covering a sector from Le Lavandou to La Ciotat! Shelling preparatory to the landing in Provence in 1944 brought an end to development of this base.

It was from the rifle range at St-Mandrier that the first French liquid-powered rocket was launched in March 1945, inaugurating the European space race.

P. Ricou

Take the road along the narrow sandy isthmus, which links the peninsula to the land mass. Fine view of Toulon surrounded by mountains.

★ **Presqu'île de St-Mandrier** – The road round the peninsula offers a **view**★ of the whole anchorage and of Toulon and its setting before skirting the bight of St-Georges, which harbours an aeronaval base and training centre for marine engineers as well as the fishing and leisure port of **St-Mandrier-sur-Mer**. A right-hand turning at the entrance to the town climbs steeply to a small cemetery with a **panoramic view**★★ of Toulon, Cap Sicié and the Iles d'Hyères.

★ ⑤ Le Coudon

Round tour of 36km – 22 miles – about 1 hour 30min – local map below

*From Toulon take pont de Ste-Anne (**DX**) and avenue de la Victoire; turn left into boulevard Ste-Anne and right into boulevard Escartefigue.*

★★ **Corniche du Mont Faron** – *See TOULON: Corniche du Mont Faron above.*

At the end of boulevard Escartefigue turn left into avenue de la Canaillette, which leads to D 46. Turn right and right again into D 446, a steep and narrow road.

★ **Le Coudon** – Alt 702m – 2 303ft. At the start of the climb you can see Mont Coudon in its entirety and also La Crau and the surrounding plain. The road, which narrows after going through pinewoods and then olive groves, finally comes out onto a wasteland scattered with evergreen oaks; the **view**★ widens continuously until at the entrance to Fort Lieutenant-Girardon the entire coast from the Giens peninsula to the former island of Gaou near Le Brusc is visible.

Return to D 46 and turn right. After 2.5km – 1.5 miles – D 846 crosses a dam to Le Revest-les-Eaux.

Le Revest-les-Eaux – This is a delightful old village with a 17C church at the foot of Mont Caume overlooked by a Saracen tower. Its 17C château is now an inn.
Return to Toulon through the Las valley (D 846) between the mountains of Faron and Croupatier.

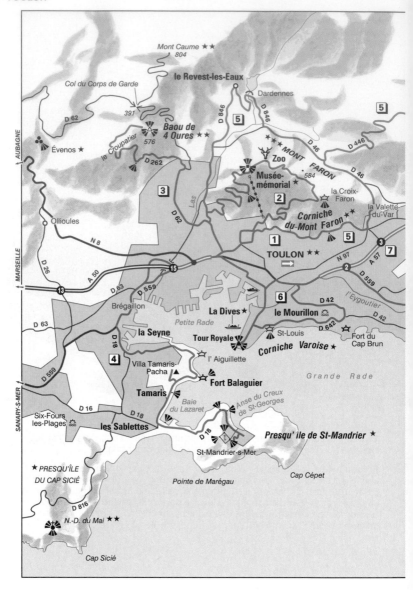

★ ⑥ **Corniche Varoise**
Round tour 11km – 6.8 miles – about 45min – local map above

From Toulon town centre take avenue de l'Infanterie-de-Marine (southeast on the town plan) going straight on into avenue des Tirailleurs-Sénégalais.

★ **Navire-Musée (BDC) "La Dives"** ⊘ – *Car park beside Tour Royale. Guided tour about 45 min.* The ship *La Dives* was used by the French Navy from 1961 to 1986 for landing tanks (BDC = Bâtiment de Débarquement de Chars); it was similar to the American LST landing craft which became famous on the French coast in 1944. The visit begins with a video film about this type of craft, and continues along gangways, through the kitchens, the infirmary and the crew's quarters to the bridge. Original equipment, displayed as it would have been when in service, gives an impression of what life was like on board. With a crew of 70, the ship could carry either 200 people, 4 landing barges or 4 000 tonnes of cargo. The tour ends in a hangar containing a fine collection of military vehicles from the Second World War – a GMC amphibious Dodge, several armoured vehicles and a Sherman M4 which took part in the liberation of St-Tropez.

Tour Royale ⊘ – Known also as the Grosse or Mitre tower, this was built by Louis XII in the early 16C for defensive purpose (its walls are 7m – 23ft thick at the base). It then served as a prison. From the watchpath there is a lovely

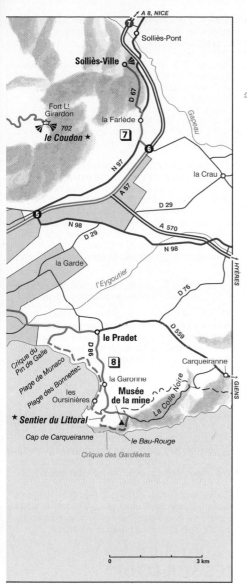

panorama★ of Toulon, with Mont Faron looming behind it, the anchorages and the coast from the Gien peninsula to Cap Sicié.

Return to boulevard Dr-Cunéo and turn right.

⌂ **Le Mourillon** – Drive past the 17C Fort St-Louis; the Littoral Frédéric-Mistral passes through a residential district with fine beaches and a view of the outer anchorage. The coast here thrusts forward into two promontories: Cap Brun and Cap Carqueiranne. The Giens peninsula is outlined on the eastern horizon.

Continue along D 642, known as the "Corniche Varoise".

On the right, overlooking the sea, is the **Fort du Cap Brun** which was built in the mid-19C *(access to the fort and its grounds is strictly forbidden)*. In 1880 it was transferred to the Navy and used at first as barracks. After the Second World War it became a School of Navigation. Now it is the official residence of the Maritime Prefect.

Return to Toulon by D 42.

7 Solliès-Ville

15km – 9.3 miles northeast – 1 hour 30min – local map opposite

From Toulon take A 97 motorway. At the La Farlède junction take the direction to La Farlède and then D 67 to Solliès Ville. The old town of Solliès-Ville clings to the side of a hill overlooking the rich Gapeau plain; below lies Solliès-Pont, a busy market town in a region famous for its cherry orchards and its fig trees. Solliès-Ville markets more than three-quarters of the French production of figs.

Church ⊙ – This building with two naves combines Romanesque traits with Gothic arches. The monolith at the high altar is thought to be a 15C ciborium. The walnut organ case dates from 1499. There is a 17C altarpiece (left) and another from the 16C near the pulpit. The crucifix on the pillar is 13C. The Lords of Solliès are buried in the crypt.

Maison Jean Aicard ⊙ – The house of the poet, novelist and dramatist, Jean Aicard (1848-1921), has been converted into a small museum. He became a member of the Académie Française in 1909.

Esplanade de la Montjoie – From the ruined castle of the Forbins, Lords of Solliès, there is a beautiful **view**★ of the Gapeau valley and the Maures massif.

★ 8 Le Pradet

10km – 6 miles to the east in the direction of Giens – about one day including a tour of the mine – local map above

*From Toulon take avenue du Mal-Juin (**GY 37**) and D 559 to Le Pradet.*
This charming resort which sits below the Massif de la Colle Noire has a good selection of easily accessible small beaches. There is a footpath designed especially for botanical discoveries in Courbebaisse wood.

Musée de la mine de Cap Garonne ⓥ – *In Le Pradet take D 86 southwards towards the Garonne et des Oursinières beach. After the beach, take the road which climbs to the left, signposted "la mine", and continues to Carqueiranne.*

Copper ore was mined here for centuries. The first traces of workings go back to the 16C, but it was only with the concession granted in 1862 that commercial mining began. It went on until 1917, when the reduction in copper content of the ore meant that mining was no longer profitable.

The tour visits the redeveloped part of the mine galleries and shows by means of several reconstructions and animations the evolution over time of working methods and the way of life of the miners at Cap Garonne as well as events during its lifetime such as loading ore for transport to England.

At the end of the tour, in a **great hall**★, there are tables equipped with magnifying glasses with which the many and various colours of copper ore extracted at Cap Garonne can be examined. Particularly notable are the magical blue needles of crystals of **cyanotrichite**, the principal ore of the mine. Two categories of copper ore can be recognised: the oxides (cuprite, malachite, azurite...) which are now mined in Africa and the Far East and the **sulphurated ore**, more widespread, represented above all by the iron-based chalcopyrites. There are also fine green stalagtites which are characteristic of the oxidation of this ore.

A botanical footpath is being developed around the mine area and gives fine views of the Massif de la Colle Noire.

Beaches – The La Garonne bay is punctuated by several attractive creeks. The best way to explore them is to take the coast path which can be followed between each beach accessible by road.

★ **Coast footpath** – *Allow at least 3 hours because of the winding path which is steep in places. Access to the beaches is often by steep steps cut out of the rock.* The route signposted in yellow runs from the car park at the lovely **Crique du Pin de Galle** to Bau Rouge *(It is possible to continue from Bau Rouge to Carqueiranne).*

The steep slope above Pin de Galle beach offers magnificent views over Toulon harbour. The numerous cabins in the pinewood add to the bucolic charm of the setting. The shady path joins the road through the park before descending steeply to **Monaco beach**. At the end of this beach, one part of which is used by nudists, the path begins beyond a low wall and climbs a cliff covered by superb *maquis* (scrub). After a headland, a little further on, there is a lovely view of the indentations along the coast. A well-marked path goes down to **Les Bonnettes beach** at the foot of a remarkable rocky inlet. In season there is a lifeguards'post and an open-air café here. It was from this beach that Murat sailed for Corsica.

The path then links La Garonne beach with that of Les Oursinières. Beyond Oursinières port a footpath to the right leaves the road to Le Pradet. It leads past panoramic viewpoints on the cliffs to Bau Rouge with fine views over the coast eastwards towards Carqueiranne and of the Les Gardéens creek.

TOURRETTES-SUR-LOUP★

Population 3 449
Michelin map 84 fold 9 or 18 or 115 fold 25 (west of Vence) or 245 fold 37

This is violet country; the flowers are cultivated under the olive trees. The unusual fortified village, its outer houses forming a rampart, stands on a rock plateau above a sheer drop; Route des Quenières, the continuation of Route St-Jean, provides the best **view**★. The weavers, potters, sculptors, engravers and painters who have come to live in Tourrettes have made it an arts and crafts centre.

Church – In the 15C nave (south) is a triptych by the Bréa School: St Antony flanked by St Pancras and St Claude. In the chancel (south) a handsome altarpiece in carved wood depicts scenes from the life of the Virgin. There are other altarpieces in the transepts as well as reliquaries and busts from the 15C, 16C and 17C. Behind the high altar stands a Gallo-Roman altar originally dedicated to Mercury.

★ **Old Village** – To see this apparently untouched medieval village, pass under the belfry gate in the south corner of the main square and follow the Grande-rue in a semicircle through the village, re-entering the square through another gate.

St-Jean – This chapel was decorated in 1959 with naïve **frescoes** by Ralph Souplaut. On the far wall are John the Baptist and St John the Divine on either side of the cross, symbolising the link between the Old and New Testaments.

TOURTOUR*

Population 472
Michelin maps 84 fold 6, 114 fold 21 and 245 fold 34

This village, set in a cool and wooded region, flanked on each side by an old castle, occupies a dominant position (alt 625m – 2 050ft) on a ridge backing on to the last foothills of the Pre-Alps, facing the Varois plain.

Here in the 12C Cistercian monks founded the Abbaye de Florielle, before moving to Thoronet. Remains of this abbey can still be seen near the Chapelle de Florielle (southeast).

*VILLAGE

The village has retained its medieval character with the remains of fortifications, attractively restored houses and narrow, sloping streets, linked by vaulted passages, which converge on the central square.

The two large olive trees growing in this square replaced the elms planted at the time of the visit of Anne of Austria in 1638. A vaulted passageway leads from the square beside the Clock Tower (tour de l'Horloge) to an old mill, which now houses the fossil museum.

Musée des fossiles ⊙ – This museum contains an interesting exhibition of local fossils – dinosaur eggs, large ammonites and fossil impressions.

Beside the museum building (left) are the ruins of a 12C castle.

Further on (1km – 0,6 miles) is a two-storeyed medieval tower, Tour Grimaldi. Beside the approach road on the way up is a charming wash-house.

Go down below the old castle to the oil mill.

Moulin à huile ⊙ – This communal oil mill has been in service since the 17C and has three presses. During the autumn, when production takes place, 5 000l – 1 100 gallons of oil are produced here, showing the continuing importance of the industry in this region. During the summer, the mill houses exhibitions of paintings. The town hall occupies the former Château des Raphelis, a solid 16C building with pepperpot towers.

Église St-Denis – This 11C church, standing on its own at the southeastern edge of the ridge, was extensively modified in the last century.

* **Viewpoint** – From the grassy esplanade in front of the church there is a wide **panorama**★ (viewing table) over the Argens and Nartuby valleys, extending (east) to the Maures and (west) to Ste-Baume, Mont Ste-Victoire and the Luberon. A few miles further on (east) is the residential village of St-Pierre-de-Tourtour, in a lovely forest setting, designed in its entirety by Beaumont who was responsible for Les Issambres.

EXCURSIONS

* **Belvédère de Villecroze** – From Tourtour take D 51 towards Villecroze.
The little road winds through woods which soon give way to strangely shaped rocks and caves. About 1km – 0,6 miles before Villecroze, a belvedere can be seen beside the road. The circular **panorama**★ from the viewing table takes in Tourtour, the Plans de Provence, Villecroze, Salernes, Gros Bessillon and (further east) the Maures and Ste-Baume.

Villecroze – See VILLECROZE.

Monastère orthodoxe St-Michel ⊙ – 10km – 6 miles by D 77. This monastery was created by an Orthodox community under the authority of the Patriarch of Antioch. The only part open to the public is the wooden chapel, a miniature replica of Souzdal cathedral in Russia.

Circuit du Haut-Var – Round tour from Aups – 53km – 33 miles. For a description of this tour starting from Aups see AUPS.
It is also possible to make this tour in the opposite direction starting from Villecroze.

La TURBIE*

Population 2 609
Michelin map 84 folds 10 or 19 or 115 fold 27 or 245 fold 38
Local maps see NICE HINTERLAND and Corniches de la RIVIERA

The village of La Turbie was built on the Grande Corniche at an altitude of 480m – 1 575ft, in a pass at the base of the massive Tête de Chien promontory overlooking Monaco, and on either side of the Roman Via Julia Augusta which ran from Genoa to Cimiez. In addition to the Alpine Trophy, a masterpiece of Roman art for which the village is famous, La Turbie boasts splendid panoramas of the coast and Monaco. At night, the lights of Monte-Carlo and Monaco are a magnificent spectacle.

LA TURBIE

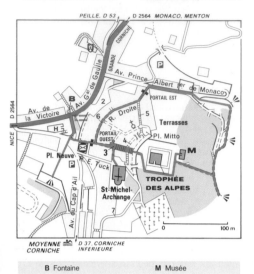

B Fontaine   **M** Musée

HISTORICAL NOTES

When Caesar died, the greater part of the Alps was occupied by several unconquered tribes who posed a constant threat to communications between Rome and her possessions in Gaul and Spain.

Augustus decided to put an end to this situation and extend Roman rule into the Alps. Several campaigns were mounted between 25 and 14 BC; Augustus probably took part in some of them in person and was assisted by Drusus and Tiberius. New provinces were established linking Italy, Gaul and Germania; one of them was the "Maritime Alps" with Cimiez as its capital. In 6 BC the Senate and the Roman people decreed that these important victories should be commemorated by the erection of a trophy. The position chosen was on the Via Julia Augusta, which had been built during the campaigns, at the foot of Mont Agel, where the Mediterranean coast is visible in both directions for several miles. There is only one other Roman trophy still standing (at Adam-Klissi in Romania, 150km – 93 miles from Bucharest). During the years of peace under the Romans a settlement grew up round the monument; its Latin name, *Tropea Augusti*, gradually evolved into La Turbie.

SIGHTS

Start from avenue Général-de-Gaulle and follow the route marked on the town plan.

Fountain (B) – It was built in the 19C at the end of the Roman aqueduct which was brought back into service at the same time.

Place Neuve – From the southwest corner of the square there is a fine **view**★ of the coast as far as the Maures massif.

Rue Comte-de-Cessole (3) – This street, part of the former Via Julia Augusta, built by the Romans, now goes through the West Gate, climbing between medieval houses to the Trophy. A house on the right bears a plaque with the verses Dante dedicated to La Turbie. Another plaque shows that the town appeared in the Antonine Itinerary (a reference list of the staging posts on the main roads of the Roman Empire with the distances between them). Fine view of the Trophy at the top of the street.

St-Michel-Archange – The church, set back from the street, is a fine example of the Nice Baroque style. Built in the 18C on an ellipsoidal plan, it has a shallow concave façade – two storeys beneath a triangular pediment – and a belltower surmounted by a cupola of coloured tiles.

★ **Interior** – *Walk round clockwise*. The decoration of the nave and chapels is Baroque; the cradle vaulting, supported on tall pillars, is adorned with frescoes and mouldings.

There are two paintings by J-B- Van Loo: *St Charles Borromeo* and *Mary Magdalene;* a copy of Raphaël's *St Michael* which is in the Louvre. The chapel on the left of the choir contains a *Pietà* from the Bréa School and a *St Mark Writing his Gospel* attributed to Veronese. The 17C communion table is in onyx and agate. The high altar in multicoloured marble comes from the abbey of St-Pons in Nice and was used for the cult of Reason during the Revolution; above it is an 18C Christ in painted wood. Also 18C are the two triptychs in the choir; the one on the right shows Christ together with the Church, represented as a queen in a white robe, and the Synagogue, turning away so as not to see the truth.

In the first chapel on the right is a canvas attributed to Ribera and a 15C *Virgin and Child*. In the second chapel a painting of *Mary* by the Murillo School and a *Flagellation* in Rembrandt's style; also *St Catherine of Siena* by a pupil of Raphaël.

* **Trophée des Alpes** ⊘ – The **Alpine Trophy**, (50m high × 38m wide 164ft × 125ft) comprised: a square podium bearing a lengthy inscription to Augustus and a list of the 44 conquered peoples; a large circular Doric colonnade with niches containing statues of the leaders who took part in the campaigns; a stepped cone serving as a base for a huge statue of Augustus, flanked by two captives. Stairways gave access to all levels.

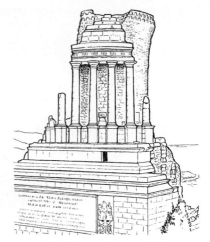

Most of the monument is built of the beautiful local white stone. After the Romans had left, it was damaged and despoiled; in the Middle Ages it was converted into a defensive structure (the blind arcading at the top dates from this period) and so was preserved from further deterioration; it survived Louis XIV's order for it to be blown

Trophée des Alpes, La Turbie

up; later it served as a source of building stone, particularly for the construction of the church of St-Michel-Archange. At the beginning of the modern era all that was left was a ruined tower emerging from a cone of rubble.

Skilful and patient restoration has been carried out through the generous help of Edward Tuck, an American, and directed by Jules Formigé. The trophy has been rebuilt up to about 35m – 115ft high but a large part of it has been left untouched. The inscription has been restored – Pliny had quoted it – and replaced in its original position; it is the longest left to us from Roman times. Its elevated position means that the Trophy is visible from a long way off.

Museum (M) – Plans, drawings and photographs tell the story of the Trophy and its restoration (model reconstruction). The display includes milestones, inscriptions, fragments of the Trophy, pieces of sculpture and documents on the other Roman monuments in Europe.

Terraces – From the raised terraces there is a splendid **panorama**★★★ of the coast from the Italian border, via Cap Martin, the Principality of Monaco 450m – 1 350ft below, Èze and Cap Ferrat to the Esterel; inland is the Laghet valley with Mont Agel behind.

Return along avenue Prince-Albert-I-de-Monaco turning left into rue Droite which passes through the east gate; it follows part of the ancient Via Julia Augusta towards Italy then turns left and becomes rue Incalat.

Forêt de TURINI★★

Michelin map 84 folds 19 and 20 or 115 folds 17 and 18 or 245 fold 25

For people living on the coast between Nice and Menton the forest of Turini evokes another world of cool green shade. The huge forest, only 25km – 15.5 miles from the Mediterranean coast, is unusual, for its trees are commonly found in more northerly latitudes. The lower slopes are covered with maritime sea pines and young oaks but higher up there are maple, beech, chestnut, spruce and superb pine trees, some of which reach 35m – 115ft on the northern slopes. Between 1 500 and 2 000m – 5 000 and 6 500ft the larch predominates. The forest covers a total of 3 500ha – 1 350sq miles between the Vésubie and Bévéra valleys.

Several roads meet at the **Col de Turini**, which is a good starting point for touring this beautiful district.

★★ L'AUTHION

Round tour from Col de Turini

18km – 11 miles – 45min – local map see NICE Hinterland

The roads are usually blocked by snow in winter and sometimes late into spring. A nature trail explains the flora and fauna of the forest.

From the Col de Turini the Authion road (D 68) passes through pine and larch woods. As the road climbs, the mountain scenery becomes more magnificent. 4km – 2.5 miles from the pass stands a war memorial to those who died in 1793 and 1945.

Monte-Carlo Rally

Monument aux Morts – The Authion massif has twice been the backdrop for military action. In 1793 the Convention's troops fought here against the Austrians and Sardinians, and in 1945 there was a bitter struggle before the Germans were driven out. Panoramic **view**★ from the memorial.

Continue along D 68 bearing right at the fork to Cabanes Vieilles, an old military camp which was damaged in the fighting in 1945. The road runs through Alpine pastures and offers marvellous **views**★ of the Roya valley.

Turn right by another monument into a track which leads (500m – 547yds) to a platform where it is possible to turn the car round.

★★ **Pointe des 3-Communes** – At this altitude (2 082m – 6 830ft) there is a marvellous **panorama**★★ of the peaks in the Mercantour national park and of the Pre-Alps of Nice.

Return to D 68; at the war memorial take the road back to Col de Turini.

★ VALLEY OF STE-ÉLISABETH

Col de Turini to the Vésubie

15km – 10 miles – 1 hour – local map see NICE HINTERLAND

The road (D 70) winds northwest cutting its way between the mountain peaks (Cime de la Calmette and the Tête du Scoubayoun) overlooking the small Vésubie tributary which flows down the valley of Ste-Élisabeth.

Gorges de Ste-Élisabeth – This rugged gorge cuts a savage gash between the deep, concertina-like folds in the rock strata.

Soon after the tunnel, at a bend in the road, stop by the chapel of St-Honorat.

★ **St-Honorat Viewpoint** – The view extends from the terrace by the chapel over the hill village of Bollène – the **site** of the village can be seen particularly clearly from this angle; up the Vésubie from Lantosque to Roquebillière; north to the Mercantour peaks.

La Bollène-Vésubie – This pleasant village stands on a hill in a chestnut wood at the foot of a mountain peak, the Cime des Vallières. The streets are laid out concentrically, climbing between the 18C houses to the church.

The road winds its serpentine course down into the valley of the Vésubie, giving breathtaking views at it goes.

★★ COL DE BRAUS ROAD

Col de Turini from Peïra-Cava to the valley of the Bévéra

76km – 47 miles – 1 day – local map see NICE Hinterland

The drive to Peïra-Cava passes through the thickest part of the forest of Turini. There are fine **views** west into the valley of the Vésubie and of the surrounding mountains.

★★ **Cime de Peïra-Cava** – *1.5km – 1 mile – plus 30min on foot return. On entering the village of Peïra-Cava turn left up a steep hill by the post office; bear right at the fork and park in the car park.*
It is an easy climb to the top (follow the lift) for a panoramic **view**★★ of the Vésubie valley and mountains on one side and of the Bévéra valley, Le Mercantour and the high peaks on the Franco-Italian frontier on the other. South beyond the Pre-Alps of Nice lies the sea and, in fine weather, Corsica.

★ **Peïra-Cava** – Alt 1 450m – 4 757ft. The village is a winter sports centre and a summer resort. It stands on a narrow ridge between the Vésubie and Bévéra valleys with an almost aerial view of the district.

Beyond the village a sharp right turn leads to a car park: a walk of 50m – 55yds leads to some steps on the left.

★★ **Pierre Plate** – This peak provides a **panoramic view**★★ similar to the view from the Cime de Peïra-Cava *(viewing table).*
Return downhill to D 2566 and continue south through the forest. In La Cabanette turn left into D 21 to Lucéram. The road descends through a succession of steep bends with magnificent **views**★ on all sides. On the edge of the forest a lefthand turn takes a picturesque route over the Col de l'Orme to the Col de Braus; D 21 continues to Lucéram.

★ **Lucéram** – *See LUCÉRAM.*

South of Lucéram D 2566 descends the Paillon valley to l'Escarène.

L'Escarène – *See NICE Hinterland* ②.
From L'Escarène D 2204 climbs northeast up the Braus valley to Sospel through a series of astonishing bends scaling the Pre-Alps of Nice. The road over the Col de Braus, which links the Paillon and Bévéra valleys, is a section of the old Piedmont Road from Nice to Turin.

Touët-de-l'Escarène – Charming little village with a Baroque church.
The olive groves give way to a poorer landscape of Spanish broom.

Braus Rift – The rift *(clue)* which opens up beyond Touët village is short but impressive. From St-Laurent (hamlet) one can reach the Braus waterfall *(15min return)* leaving the car by the restaurant.
In the next 3km – 2 miles D 2204 winds through 16 bends. As the road climbs the **view**★ extends from the white dome of the Nice observatory on the top of Mont Gros to the Cap d'Antibes and the Esterel massif outlined against the sea.

Col de Braus – Alt 1 002m – 3 287ft. It is interesting to look back down over the series of hairpin bends which carry the road up to the pass.
Beyond the pass the road descends through 18 bends offering extensive **views**★★ of the mountains of the Bévéra Valley, particularly l'Authion and the Cime du Diable ("devil's peak").
The road runs round Mont Barbonnet crowned with the fortifications of Fort Suchet. At the Col St-Jean, between the dwellings on the left, an old army road leads off to the entrance porch of **Fort Suchet** ⊘, built 1883-86 and then modernised in the 1930s. Note in particular the two striking 155mm turrets on top.
After the Col St-Jean, the road draws near the Merlanson valley, and then reaches Sospel. On a level with the casemates of Fort St-Roch, there is a good view of the village.

★ **Sospel** – *See SOSPEL.*
Olive groves reappear in the wide depression at Sospel. D 2566 climbs northwest through the forest up the **Bévéra valley**★. The river has created a very deep, narrow and winding channel lined by rocky and wooded heights. There is a beautiful **waterfall** on the right.

★★ **Gorges du Piaon** – The *corniche* road runs beneath an overhang of rock high above the bed of the stream, which is strewn with huge boulders.

Notre-Dame-de-la-Menour – An oratory marks the beginning of a path (right) which provides a good view of the valley and the gorge. A great flight of steps leads up to the chapel which has a two-storey Renaissance façade.

Moulinet – Charming village in a fresh green hollow.
The road returns through the forest to the Col de Turini.

Respect the life of the countryside
Drive carefully on country roads
Protect wildlife, plants and trees

UTELLE★

Population 456
Michelin map 84 fold 19 or 115 fold 16 or 245 fold 25
Local map see NICE HINTERLAND

At 800m – 2 625ft the village projects like a balcony over the Vésubie valley facing the forest of Turini and the Gordolasque mountains to the north. In the past it was the most important town between the Tinée and the Vésubie. The isolated village has retained its original character: fountain in the square, old houses with sundials, ruined fortifications.

St-Véran – Built in the 14C on the basilica plan and altered in the 17C, the church has an elegant Gothic porch with carved panels illustrating the legend of St Veranus in 12 tableaux.

The architecture of the interior – groin and barrel vaulting supported on archaistic Romanesque columns and capitals – contrasts surprisingly with the generous Classical, even Baroque, decoration. At the high altar a **carved wooden altarpiece**★ representing scenes from the Passion is dominated by a statue of St Veranus. There is an altarpiece of the Annunciation (Nice School) above the first altar in the north aisle and a 13C recumbent Christ below the altar in the south aisle. Fine 17C woodwork (choir, pulpit) and 16C carved font. The sacristy contains some handsome vestments in silk and Genoan velvet.

Chapelle des Pénitents Blancs ⊙ – The chapel, which is near the church, contains a carved wooden altarpiece of the Descent from the Cross by Rubens and six large 18C paintings.

★★★ **Madone d'Utelle Panorama** – *6km – 3.8 miles southwest – See Vallée de la VÉSUBIE.*

Plateau de VALBONNE

Michelin map 84 fold 9 or 115 south of folds 24 and 25 or 245 fold 37

The Plateau de Valbonne slopes gently from the Grasse Pre-Alps to the coast with an average altitude of 200m – 650ft. It comprises some 2 000ha – 4 940 acres of pines and holm oaks and is drained by the Brague and its tributaries, the Bouillide and the Bruguet.

Valbonne – This hospitable spot (*vallis bona* in Latin) has been occupied since Antiquity. In 1199 the Chalais Order founded an abbey, which came under the control of Lérins before becoming the parish **church**. The building, in the form of a Latin cross with a square chevet, has been badly restored on several occasions but has retained the austere character typical of Chalais buildings.

The village is a curious example of ribbon development, with its houses with ramparts and chequerboard districts, having been rebuilt in the 16C by the Lérins monks. The abbey (under restoration) houses an interesting **Musée des arts et traditions populaires** ⊙. The **main square** with its 15C-17C arcades and old elm trees makes an attractive sight. Every year around St Blaise's Day (3 February) the Feast of the "Servan" grape (which ripens late) is celebrated.

Sophia-Antipolis (Parc international d'activités) – *Southeast of Valbonne.* A wooded plateau (2 300ha – 5 683 acres) has been designated an **International Science Park**. About two-thirds of the area has been carefully landscaped to provide a pleasant, natural setting for the third or so that is occupied by offices, housing and leisure facilities. The project which has been completed so far has set up four main categories of business: information technology, electronics and telecommunications; health and biotechnology; teaching and research; science and the environment. These businesses have been integrated with the housing, cultural and sports facilities so as to protect the environment, creating a sort of "international city of knowledge, science and technology".

The park is ideally placed near Nice International Airport and the A 8 motorway; the buildings are decidedly modern. 900 French and foreign enterprises have settled in; among them are the Air France worldwide reservations centre, certain departments of the Centre National de la Recherche Scientifique, the École de Mines, France Télécom and foreign companies specialising in high technology. Further development is planned, particularly to the north of the park, which will double the surface area of the development and the number of businesses it can contain.

This centre of activity is the last stage of the **Route des Hautes-Technologies** which links a number of centres involved in developing the latest technology between Aix-en-Provence and Valbonne.

The key on the inside Front Cover explains
the abbreviations and symbols used in this guide

Route de VALDEBLORE★★

Michelin map 84 folds 18 and 19 or 115 folds 5 and 6 or 245 folds 24 and 25

The road linking the valleys of the Tinée and the upper Vésubie passes through the Valdeblore district, a region of green pastures and wooded slopes high in the mountains.

A memory of one of the lords of Valdeblore, a sort of Bluebeard character, survives in the place names of the region. The sufferings of the monster's wives, who were incarcerated and left to die of hunger, have given rise to Valdeblore (*Val de pleurs* = vale of tears) and Bramafan (*crie la faim* = cry of hunger).

ST-MARTIN-VÉSUBIE TO VALLÉE DE LA TINÉE
29km - 18 miles - about 2 hours 15min

★ **St-Martin-Vésubie** – *See ST-MARTIN-VÉSUBIE.*
From St-Martin Vésubie take D 2565, which climbs north up the valley and overlooks the villages of St-Martin and Venanson. Just before the tunnel, there is a fine **view**★ back down to the Vésubie and St-Martin, up the Madone valley and north to the Boréon.

La Colmiane – A ski resort in the Col St-Martin (alt 1 500m – 4 921ft) composed of chalets and hotels dispersed among the larches and pines.

At the Col St-Martin turn left into a narrow road which leads to the chairlift.

Via Ferrata des Aiguillettes, La Colmiane

★★ **Pic de Colmiane** – *Chairlift to the summit* ⊙. From the top there is an immense **panorama**★★: south over Mont Tournairet, the Vésuble valley and Turini forest; east over the Mercantour chain; north and west over the Baus de la Frema to Mont Mounier with Valdeblore in the foreground.

★ **Via ferrata des Aiguillettes** – *At the col turn right opposite the minigolf (sign "Via ferrata"). There is plenty of space to park on the way up the slope. The Via ferrata begins at the end of the car park, after the information sign.*
Equipment can be hired at the sports shop "Igloo Sport" at the col. A guide to the facilities is available from the tourist office in Valdeblore.
This new development, directly accessible by car, offers ideal facilities for learning rock-climbing and overcoming vertigo. There are three routes graded blue, red and black according to their difficulty. The first course takes at least 1 hour 30min. Those looking for big thrills will particularly enjoy crossing the footbridge (35m – 115ft long; 50m – 164ft above ground level) which links the two rocky peaks of the Aiguillettes.
Beyond the pass the road enters a green gulley, the highest part of the Valdeblore.

St-Dalmas-de-Valdeblore – The Romanesque **church** ⊙ is striking with its pyramidal Alpine-style belltower, its stout buttresses and Lombard bands on the chevet. The church is built on the basilica plan over a pre-Romanesque groin-vaulted crypt. The interior was vaulted in the 17C to hide the original roof. Above the high altar there is a polyptych by Guillaume Planeta of St Dalmas, St Roch and the Evangelists, on the predella the Adoration of the Shepherds and the Wise Men. In the north aisle is an altarpiece of St Francis attributed to André de Cella. Behind an altarpiece of the Rosary (17C) in the south apsidal chapel are the partial remains of some very old frescoes: the history of John the Baptist and Christ in Majesty on the vault.

The road looks down on the Bramafan valley and passes through La Roche at the foot of a grey rock spur.

La Bolline – The town, which is the administrative centre of the Valdeblore district, makes a pleasant summer resort surrounded by chestnut woods which contrast with the Bois Noir (black forest) on the opposite slope.

West of La Bolline turn right into D 66.

Rimplas – The curious **site**★ of the village on a rib of rock (1 000m – 3 281ft high) is very striking. From the chapel, dedicated to Mary Magdalene, at the edge of the ridge below the fort, there is an extensive **view**★ of the Tinée valley, Bramafan valley and the Valdeblore villages.

For an easy route back to St-Sauveur-sur-Tinée, take the path (GR 5) down to the northwest of the village.

To reach the confluence of the Valdeblore and the Tinée return to D 2565, turn right; after 7km – 4 miles turn right into D 2205.

Reintroduction of the "bone breaker" *(casseur d'os)*

The bearded vulture, a magnificent bird with a huge wingspan (2.8m – 9.6ft) is an example of a European endangered species. Its numbers were greatly reduced in the 19C in the Alps, although it survives in the Pyrenees and Corsica. The bearded vulture, which is the largest Alpine bird, has a curious way of life; alternating between soaring flight and perilous aerobatics, it flies over the steep, sloping pastures looking for the carcasses of chamois and sheep from which it takes the large bones (up to 3kg – 6.6lbs). It then drops the bones from a great height on to rocks in order to break them. It used to be looked on as the natural assistant of the shepherd.

The reintroduction of bearded vultures as chicks into the Parc du Mercantour (at Roubion) in 1993 was rewarded with success. It takes eight years for the birds to reach maturity after which they can live for 40 years.

In 1996 five birds were released in the southern Alps and 60 throughout the Alps in an extensive international reintroduction programme, the only one of its kind.

VALLAURIS

Population 24 326 with Golfe-Juan
Michelin map 84 fold 9 or 115 fold 39 or 245 fold 37
For plan of conurbation see CANNES

Vallauris lies close to the sea among rounded hills covered with orange trees and mimosa. The centre is laid out on a grid plan; the town was razed to the ground in 1390 and rebuilt and repopulated in the 16C by immigrants from neighbouring regions. The town's traditional craft of pottery was in decline when Picasso infused it with new life. Vallauris is now an important French centre for ceramics: its Biennial International Festival of Ceramic Art (July to mid-October) has a worldwide reputation. The local commercial scene also includes cut flowers and aromatic plants.

SIGHTS

Château (V D) – Originally a priory attached to Lérins, it was rebuilt in the 16C and is a rare example of Renaissance architecture in Provence. It is a rectangular two-storey building with a round pepperpot tower at each corner. It houses two museums.

★ **Musée national "La Guerre et la Paix"** ⊘ – Only the Romanesque chapel of the priory survived. Deconsecrated, it was decorated in 1952 by Picasso with a huge composition: *War and Peace.* This work evokes the horrors of war; black invaders trampling the symbols of civilization underfoot attack a knight in shining armour who is just (his spear forms the arm of a balance) and peaceful (his shield bears the device of a dove). The figures on the opposite wall are indulging in fruitful work and the innocent joys of peace. The end panel symbolises fraternity between races.

Provençal dragon flask (1952)
ceramic by Pablo Picasso

Musée municipal ⊘ – The ceramics which won awards at the Biennial Festival are displayed in the vaulted rooms.

A fine Renaissance staircase leads to two rooms on the second floor containing ceramics by Picasso (plates, dishes, humorously decorated vases).

Six rooms are devoted to the **Magnelli bequest**: works in oil, collage and gouache together with a large mural. Alberto Magnelli (1888-1971) was born in Florence but spent the greater part of his life in France. The rooms are arranged from left to right to trace the evolution of the artist's style; from large washes of pure colour he turned to abstracts, which he abandoned in the 1920s before returning to them in 1931. Finally, there are some lovely collections of Art Deco, Art Nouveau and 1950s ceramics.

Place Paul-Isnard (V 56) – At the centre of the town, where the market is held in front of the church, stands a bronze statue presented by Picasso to the town of which he became an honorary citizen.

Avenue Georges-Clemenceau (V 25) – Here and in the neighbouring streets (rue Sicard, rue du Plan) are the pottery shops and **workshops** ⊘, their displays of ceramics spilling out onto the pavement. High-quality work vies for attention with second-rate wares. The Madoura studio sells reproductions of Picasso's ceramics as well as its own work.

Musée de la Poterie (V M) ⊘ – *Rue Sicard.* Located in a pottery workshop, which still functions, the pottery museum shows how clay was worked in the first half of the 20C. Displays illustrate the techniques used for extracting the clay from the earth, its preparation, shaping, glazing and baking in the wood-fired kiln. Old pottery is also on view.

A visit to the present workshop helps one to appreciate the evolution of the potter's techniques.

EXCURSION

* **Musée de l'Automobiliste** – *4km – 2.5 miles – about 1 hour 30min. From Vallauris take D 135 north. Cross the motorway and immediately turn left into chemin de Font-de-Currault which leads to the car museum's car park. See MOUGINS: Excursions.*

Basse Vallée du VAR

Michelin map 84 folds 18 and 19 or 115 folds 15, 16 and 26 or 245 folds 24, 25, 37 and 38 – Local map see NICE HINTERLAND

Traditionally there have always been two main highways leading from eastern Provence and the County of Nice into the Alps of Haute-Provence; one is the Var, and the other what is known as the Route Napoléon. The lower reaches of the Var are broad, allowing the passage of heavy traffic in the valley. It is only above the confluence with the Vésubie that the river becomes narrower.

Despite growing industrialisation and urbanisation, the lower valley of the Var has many charms.

NICE TO PONT DE LA MESCLA

66km – 41 miles – 2 hours 30min excluding Nice

*** **Nice** – *See NICE. 1 hour.*

Leave Nice by promenade des Anglais, which becomes promenade Corniglion-Molinier, a pleasant drive along the Baie des Anges.

Turn right into the access road to the airport.

Nice-Côte d'Azur Airport – This is the second largest airport in France in terms of traffic. To meet the growing demand, the airport, which is on the east side of the Var estuary, has been extended out into the sea to provide an additional runway (1983) and terminal number 2 (1987). Freight handling has been improved by the installation of brand-new equipment for this purpose (1991).

Return to N 98, then turn right towards Plan du Var.

N 202 runs north past the Nice flower market and the vast facilities of the Sports Park, then underneath the Provençal Motorway, which swings away east towards Italy negotiating the heights of Nice through a series of engineering feats.

The road hugs the east bank of the Var. In a landscape composed of flower beds and vegetable plots, of vineyards and olive groves, the hill villages of Vence and the Nice hinterland stand out one by one: on the west bank Gattières, Carros and Le Broc; on the east bank Aspremont and Castagniers at the foot of Mont Chauve, followed by St-Martin-du-Var and La Roquette-sur-Var.

The **view**★ includes the snow-capped Alps on the horizon. At St-Martin-du-Var the river is joined by one of its western tributaries, the Esteron.

Cross the river over the Pont Charles-Albert and take D 17 to Gilette.

The site of the village of Bonson on an impressive rock spur high above the river on the west bank comes into view, followed afterwards by Gilette, in its unusual site nestling in a cleft.

Gilette – From place de la Mairie follow the arrows up to the castle ruins for an impressive **view**★ of the *corniche* roads, the Var valley, its confluence with the Esteron and the Pre-Alps of Nice. There is a pleasant walk, bordered by acacias and plane trees, below the castle with fine views of the hill villages – Bonson and Tourette-du-Château - and of the Alps to the north.

From Gilette take D 17 north up the Esteron valley; 2km – 1 mile beyond Vescous turn right into a narrow road which climbs to Vieux-Pierrefeu.

Vieux-Pierrefeu – Alt 618m – 2 028ft. This village, high above the Esteron valley, was a Roman signalling post (Petra Igniaria), a link in the chain which ran from Hadrian's Wall on the border between England and Scotland to Rome and was used to transmit optical messages.
The church just down the road in **Pierrefeu** has been converted into a picture gallery, the **Musée "Hors du temps"** ⊘, on the origins of the world; the unique collection of paintings on the Genesis theme contains the work of 40 contemporary artists including Brayer, Carzou, Folon, Erni, Vicari, Villemont and Moretti. The drive provides views of the Var valley and of Bonson and La Roquette, perched on its rock.

Bonson - It is built on a remarkable **site**★ on a rock spur high above the Var valley. From the church terrace there is an exceptional **view**★★ of the Vésubie emerging from its gorge to join the waters of the Var at the southern end of a narrow gorge, the Défilé de Chaudan *(see below)*. This famous wooded area suffered a terrible fire in 1994 which destroyed everything up to the edge of the village.
The **church** contains three beautiful primitive paintings from the Nice School. On the back wall there is a **retable of St Antony**; the figure of St Gertrude, who was invoked against the plague, is identified by the great rats climbing her shoulders; the painting shows some similarity with the work of Durandi. In the south aisle is a **retable of John the Baptist**, attributed to Antoine Bréa (the centre panel has been spoiled by overpainting). At the high altar, in a Renaissance frame, is a **retable of St Benedict**★, including the figure of St Agatha holding her mutilated breasts.

★ **Mont Vial** – *20 km – 12 miles from Bonson. Take D 27 west towards Toulon.* The picturesque road twists and turns along the flank of the hill with attractive glimpses of Gilette. After Tourette-du-Château take the road going sharply down to the right which winds to Le Vial ridge before reaching the summit (1 549m – 5 082ft) *(U-turns possible)*. An impressive **panorama**★★ will reward the effort of climbing up. In fine weather the view extends over the course of the Var from Puget-Théniers to the mouth of the river.

Return to Bonson by the same route.

Leave Bonson by D 27 going south.

The road loops down to the Pont Charles-Albert, giving beautiful **views**★ of the Var valley.

Cross the bridge and turn left into N 202.

North of Plan-du-Var cross the River Vésubie where it joins the Var. The road to the right climbs up the Gorges de la Vésubie.

★★ **Défilé du Chaudan** – The defile, which is named after the little village of Chaudan at its southern end, has been created by the Var, which has worn a deep, narrow and winding channel through the rocks. The road follows the course of the river in and out of every bend and through four tunnels.
At the northern end, at Pont de la Mescla, the River Tinée flows into the Var.

---

*The Michelin Green Guide **Rome** (French and English editions) proposes many walks in the Eternal City visiting:*
- *the best-known sights*
- *the districts steeped in 3 000 years of history*
- *the art treasures in the museums and galleries*

VENCE*

Population 15 330
Michelin map 84 fold 9 or 18 or 115 fold 25 or 245 fold 37

Vence is a delightful winter and summer resort, 10km – 6miles from the sea between Nice and Antibes, in a countryside where mimosa, roses, carnations and violets are cultivated and where olive and orange trees grow. It is a picturesque old market town, favoured by artists and art galleries, standing on a rock promontory bordered by two ravines and sheltered from the cold north winds by the last foothills of the Alps. The wines from the surrounding stony hillsides (La Gaude, St-Jeannet) are highly regarded.

HISTORICAL NOTES

An episcopal town – Vence, founded by the Ligurians, was an important Roman town. With the coming of Christianity, it took on a new influence, that of an episcopal seat. Among the bishops from 374 to 1790 were St Veranus (5C) and St Lambert (12C), Alessandro Farnese, an Italian prince who became Pope Paul II (16C), Antoine Godeau *(see below)* and Surian, a great preacher.
During the Wars of Religion Vence was besieged by the Huguenot Lesdiguières in 1592, but held out; the victory is commemorated each year at Easter.

The Lords of Vence (13C) – The bishops of Vence were in continual conflict with the barons of Villeneuve, lords of the town. This family drew its fame from **Romée de Villeneuve**, an able Catalan who in the 13C reorganised the affairs of the Count of Provence, Bérenger V. The count had four marriageable daughters and an empty treasury.
Romée induced Blanche of Castille to ask for the eldest, Marguerite, for the future St Louis. Eleanor married Henry II and became Queen of England and another became Empress of Austria. The last daughter, Beatrix, heiress of Provence, married Charles of Anjou, brother of St Louis in 1246, and became Queen of the Two Sicilies.

Bishop Godeau (17C) – The memory of Antoine Godeau has remained vivid throughout the region. His beginnings did not seem likely to lead him to a bishopric: he was the oracle of the House of Rambouillet. Small, skinny, swarthy – in short uncommonly ugly – he was, nevertheless, in great demand among some cultured society ladies *(les précieuses)* because of his wit, his fluency and his rich and ready poetical vein: they called him Julie's dwarf (Julie d'Angennes was the daughter of the Marquise de Rambouillet) and also, tongue-in-cheek, the "Jewel of the Graces". His reputation was unprecedented. Richelieu made him the first member of the French Academy. At the age of 30, Godeau, no doubt tired of verse-making, took holy orders and, the following year, was made Bishop of Grasse and Vence. The towns would not accept a joint bishop and so for several years he remained between the two dioceses, finally opting for Vence. The former wit and ladies' confidant took his new role seriously; he repaired his cathedral, which was falling in ruins, introduced various industries – perfumery, tanning and pottery – and brought some measure of prosperity to his poor and primitive diocese. He died in 1672 at the age of 67.

SIGHTS

★ **Chapelle du Rosaire or Chapelle Matisse (A)** ⊙ – "Despite its imperfections I think it is my masterpiece... the result of a lifetime devoted to the search for truth." This was Henri Matisse's opinion of the chapel which he had designed and decorated between 1947 and 1951. The fame of this artist and the daring of his design, a contemporary echo of the genius of the medieval masters, aroused enormous interest in the building.
From the outside it looks like an ordinary Provençal house with a roof of coloured tiles surmounted by a huge wrought-iron cross with gilt tips.
Inside, the community nave and the parish nave meet at the altar, which is set at an angle.
Everything is white – floor, ceiling, tiled walls – except for the small high stained-glass windows which make a floral pattern in lemon, bottle green and ultra-marine. The decoration, the furnishings, the vestments are strikingly plain and simple. The mural compositions, the Stations of the Cross and St Dominic have been reduced to a play of black lines on a white background. Although not in sequence the Stations of the Cross provide a visual progression towards the Calvary at the climax of the composition. The gallery containing studies made by Matisse for his finished designs is worth a visit.

Place du Frêne (B) – Start from place du Grand-Jardin but before entering the old town look at place du Frêne and the enormous ash tree, which gives the square its name and which, according to legend, was planted in memory of the visit to Vence in 1538 of François I and Pope Paul III.

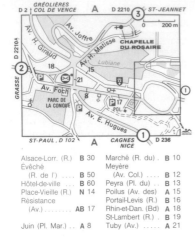

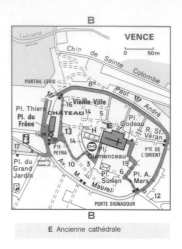

E Ancienne cathédrale

Château de Villeneuve – Fondation Émile Hugues (B) ⊘ – The old castle of the Barons of Villeneuve, built in the 17C, incorporates the 13C watchtower. The foundation was set up to forge a link between local heritage and artistic creativity inspired by the region. Note the lovely interior decoration on each floor. Thematic exhibitions show to full advantage works by the great masters of the 20C, such as Matisse, Dubuffet, Dufy and Chagall, inspired by the time they spent in Vence. Alternating with these are exhibitions of modern and contemporary works.

Old town (Vieille Ville) (B) – The old town was enclosed in elliptical walls, parts of which can still be seen, and which were pierced by five gateways.

Go round the 15C square tower, adjoining the château *(see above)* to reach and pass through the Peyra gateway (1441). This part of town is alive with artists, craftsmen and boutiques.

★ **Place du Peyra** (B 13) – The square is picturesque with a striking square tower and splashing fountain in the form of an urn (1822). It was the forum of the Roman town.

From the south side of the square take rue du Marché and turn left to reach place Clemenceau.

Cathedral (B E) ⊘ – The Roman temple of Mars built on this site was replaced in the 5C by a Merovingian church which was incorporated in later structures. The present unusual church, the old cathedral, was begun in the Romanesque style but was later altered and enlarged several times. Some Roman inscriptions have been included in the Baroque façade; those on either side of the door are dedicated to the emperors, Elagabalus and Gordian.

The interior consists of a nave and four aisles. The tomb of St Lambert and his epitaph are to be found in the second chapel on the right; a 5C Roman sarcophagus, said to be the tomb of St Veranus, is in the third chapel on the right. The north aisle contains a handsome carved doorway with Flamboyant Gothic rose windows; on the same side is a 16C retable of angels. Some fine pieces of Carolingian carving have been incorporated in certain of the pillars. The baptistery contains a mosaic by Chagall of *Moses in the Bulrushes*. The most unusual feature is the **organ loft**; the singing desk and the **choir stalls**★ are admirable: the risers, elbow rests and misericords are the work of Jacques Bellot, a sculptor from Grasse (15C) whose lively imagination sometimes borders on the irreverent.

Ramparts – Leave the church through the east door which opens into place Godeau, overlooked by the square tower with its parapet and surrounded by old houses. At the centre stands a Roman column erected to the god Mars. Take rue St-Lambert and then rue de l'Hôtel-de-Ville to reach the 13C Signadour gateway and turn left.

The next gate on the left is the Orient (east) gateway, opened in the 18C; the date 1592 carved on a stone (top left) refers to the siege of the Protestant Duke François de Lesdiguières during the Wars of Religion. Boulevard Paul-André follows the line of the ramparts; several narrow stepped streets open into it; there are fine **views** of the high peaks *(baous)* and of the foothills of the Alps. Re-enter the old town through the Gothic Lévis gateway (13C) and walk up rue du Portail Lévis between handsome old houses to place du Peyra.

EXCURSIONS

Château Notre-Dame-des-Fleurs ⊘ – *3km – 2 miles northwest along D 2210ᴬ.*

The castle was built in the 19C on the site of an 11C Benedictine abbey, Notre-Dame-des-Crottons (Our Lady of the Caves), which housed the bishops of Vence from 1638-1728. Its name was changed to Notre-Dame-des-Fleurs (Our Lady of the Flowers) by its owner, a Grasse perfumer.
A gallery of contemporary art displays the works of many artists in the rooms and gardens.
From the terrace, decorated with aromatic plants, the **view**★ extends from Cap Ferrat to the Esterel. The pre-10C Romanesque chapel was restored in 1988; its chancel is adorned with a stained-glass window by Bernard Dhonneur.
Nearby, the bishop's private chapel contains a 6C Virgin.

★★ Routes des Crêtes
Round trip of 59km – 37 miles – half a day.

Leave Vence by ③ on the plan, D 2210, going northeast to St-Jeannet.
The road skirts three peaks – Baou des Blancs, Baou des Noirs and Baou de St-Jeannet – and provides a long leisurely view of the **site**★ of St-Jeannet.

Gattières – The hilltop village looks out over vineyards and olive groves to the Var valley and the neighbouring villages. The charming Romanesque-Gothic **church** contains a naïve painted sculpture of St Nicolas and the three children he revived *(right of chancel)* and a beautiful modern Christ in the choir.
Leave Gattières by D 2209 going west and north.

The *corniche* road skirts the edge of the Grasse Pre-Alps overlooking the Var and provides an attractive glimpse of Gattières to the south.

Carros – The old village occupies a remarkable **position**★ huddled round the castle (13C-16C). Just below the village a rock, which bears traces of an old mill, has been made into a terrace: **panorama**★★ *(viewing table).*
The road from Carros to Le Broc provides magnificent **views**★ of numerous hill villages, of the Var, flowing in its several channels round the banks of flat white pebbles which lie in its broad bed, and of its confluence with the Esteron.

Le Broc – This hill village has a fountain (1812) in the square, which is surrounded by arcades. The 16C **church** ⊘ was decorated by the modern painter Guillonet. From the village there is a fine view of the Var valley.
The road overlooks the confluence of the Esteron and the Var before turning west into the Bouyon ravine.

Bouyon – Every part of the village offers a **view**★ of Mont Cheiron, the Var and Esteron valleys and the Alps of the Franco-Italian border.
South of Bouyon the road (D 8) skirts the northern flank of Mont Chiers passing through Bézaudun-les-Alpes to Coursegoules.

Coursegoules – Perched on a rocky spit at the foot of the south face of Mont Cheiron, the tall houses rise above the ravine of the nascent River Cagne. The **church** ⊘ contains a **retable** by Louis Bréa of John the Baptist between St Petronilla and St Gothard; the detail on the latter figure is remarkable.
Take D 2 southeast to Vence.

The road runs through barren countryside beside the River Cagne which turns into a waterfall when it rains. There is always something interesting to look at along this stretch.

★★ Col de Vence – Alt 970m – 3 182ft. Just south of the pass a fine **panorama**★★

opens up: the high peaks east of the Var as far as Mont Agel; along the coast from Cap Ferrat, past the Baie des Anges, Cap d'Antibes and the Lérins islands to the Esterel. To the north the white slopes of Mont Cheiron stand out dramatically against the sky.
The road descends through the barren limestone *garrigue* on the southern edge of the Pre-Alps of Grasse.

★ Haute Vallée du Loup
47km – 29 miles – about 1 hour 30min.

Leave Vence by D 2 going northwest. From Vence to Coursegoules the route is described in reverse order under Route des Crêtes above.

From Coursegoules return to D 2 going west.

The road descends a green valley and suddenly emerges into the **upper Loup valley**★, a beautiful stretch of country with superb views both before and after Gréolières.

Gréolières – This is a hill village at the southern foot of Mont Cheiron; to the north are the extensive ruins of Haut-Gréolières; to the south are the remains of an important stronghold.

The **church**, which has only one aisle, has a Romanesque façade and a squat belltower. On the left (on entering) stands a 15C silver-gilt processional cross and a fragment of a 16C retable of John the Baptist; opposite stands a 14C wooden statue of the Virgin and Child; the finest work (high on the right) is the **retable of St Stephen**★ by an unknown artist with Christ and his Apostles on the predella (15C).

West of Gréolières the road climbs above the village and then snakes westward along the side of the gorge passing in and out of brief tunnels and beneath huge rock spurs of fantastic shape and size. More than 400m – 1 312ft below flows the River Loup.

★ **Gréolières Rift** – The rift *(clue)* was formed by a tributary of the Loup; its bare slopes are pitted with giant holes and spiked with curious dolomitic rocks.
The road emerges from the rift on to a broad alluvial plateau, Plan-du-Peyron.
In Plan-du-Peyron turn right into D 802.

As the road climbs the south face of Mont Cheiron, there are interesting **views** to the west and north.

Gréolières-les-Neiges – Alt 1 450m – 4 757ft. The resort, which is on the north face of Mont Cheiron, is the most southerly of the Alpine ski stations; it is well equipped and easily accessible and attracts a large number of local skiers.

Chartreuse de la VERNE

Michelin map 84 fold 16, 17,
114 fold 35 or 245 fold 48
Local map see Massif des MAURES

The **charterhouse** ⊘ was founded in 1170 on an isolated **site**★ on a wooded slope in the Maures, off the beaten track near a spring. It was rebuilt several times and survived until the Revolution, when the monks abandoned it. Since 1983 it has been occupied by the religious Order of Bethlehem.

The buildings are of brown Maures schist but are distinguished by the use of serpentine (bluish-green polished stone) for the door frames, arcades, vaulting and other decoration.

Porch – The huge doorway is built of serpentine stone; two ringed columns flank the door which is surmounted by a triangular pediment supported on two pilasters; a statue of the Virgin and Child stands in a recess.

Guest house – A path on the right of the porch leads to the guest house. Beyond the reception room is a large courtyard with a fountain at the centre, bordered by the buildings where the guests were received. On the left is the bakery. Opposite is a Classical façade with a Regency panelled door. A porch on the left of this door opens into a passage which leads to the scullery and the 12C **kitchen** with rib vaulting.
Leave the building by the same route.

Conventual buildings – A wooden stair in the courtyard this side of the porch leads to the kitchen and the remains of the **little cloisters**: six barrel-vaulted

E. Baret

La Verne Charterhouse gate

serpentine bays. The monks' refectory is used for exhibitions. The ruins of the Romanesque chapel open off the little cloisters (handsome Renaissance door on the site of the chancel). The **great cloisters** have depressed vaulting and serpentine decoration; they are bordered by the monks' cells – four rooms and an adjoining garden. One of the cells has been restored.

Viewpoint – A Romanesque postern at the far end of the great cloisters leads to the remains of a windmill; from here there is a fine **view** of the chestnut and holm-oak forests on the Maures massif, of the Verne valley and in fine weather of the mountains of Haute-Provence.

Vallée de la VÉSUBIE★★

Michelin map 84 folds 9 and 19 or 115 folds 6, 16 and 17 or 245 fold 25
Local map see NICE HINTERLAND

The Vésubie, an eastern tributary of the Var, is formed by two torrents – the Madone de Fenestre and the Boréon – which rise near the Italian border. Drawing its source amidst mountains of 2 500m – 8 000ft, the Vesubie is fed by the snows of the last high Alpine ranges. The valley, one of the most beautiful above Nice, has a variety of characteristics: the upper valley has Alpine green pastures, pine forests, cascades and peaks while the middle valley, between Lantosque and St-Jean-la-Rivière, shows signs of Mediterranean climate – the slopes are less steep and are partially cultivated in terraces or planted with vines and olive trees. In its lower reaches below St-Jean-la-Rivière, the torrent has created a gorge with vertical walls through which it passes to join the Var as it emerges from the Défilé du Chaudan.

PLAN-DU-VAR TO THE MADONE D'UTELLE

25km – 15 miles – about 1 hour

D 2565 follows the bed of the narrow, winding **Gorges de la Vésubie★★★**: the steep rock walls are layered in many colours.
In St-Jean-la-Rivière turn left into the road (D 32) which climbs towards Utelle, giving **views** of the Vésubie gorge.

★ **Utelle** – *See UTELLE.*

★★★ **Madone d'Utelle Panorama** – The sanctuary of the Madonna of Utelle, founded in 850 by Spanish sailors, who had survived a storm, was rebuilt in 1806. It is a place of pilgrimage: 15 August and 8 September.
A short distance from the chapel there is a viewing table (l 174m – 3 852ft) covered by a dome. Splendid **panorama** over a wide expanse of the Maritime Alps.

ST-JEAN-LA-RIVIÈRE TO ST-MARTIN-VÉSUBIE

85km – 53 miles – about 4 hours

Beyond St-Jean-la-Rivière, the valley squeezes between bluffs of rock, widening slightly at Le Suquet to skirt the eastern foothills of the Brec d'Utelle.

Lantosque – It is sited on a limestone ridge which crosses the valley.

Roquebillière – *See ROQUEBILLIÈRE.*

On leaving Roquebillière-Vieux turn right into a narrow road to Belvédère.

It is a picturesque road up the **Gordolasque valley★★** between the Cime du Diable (devil's peak) and the Cime de la Valette.

Belvédère – The **site★** of this charming village overlooks both the Gordolasque and the Vésubie. From the terrace behind the *mairie* (town hall) there is a fine **view★** of Roquebillière-Vieux immediately below backed by Tournairet mountain, of the Vésubie downstream to Mont Férion and Turini forest.
The road (D 171) continues up the valley past massive rocks and tumbling waterfalls.

★ **Cascade du Ray** – The river divides into two gushing waterfalls.

The road follows the valley due north divided from the eastern parallel valley, Vallée des Merveilles, by the Cime du Diable.

Further north are the indented rocks of the Grand Capelet.

★ **Cascade de l'Estrech** – The road ends near the beautiful Estrech waterfall *(1km – half a mile of mountain track)* which flows down from a **cirque★★** of snow-capped mountains dominated by the Cime du Gélas and Mont Clapier, both of which reach 3 000m – 4 828ft.

Return to D 2565.

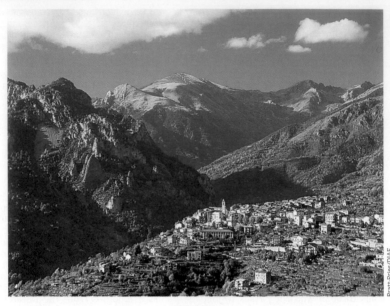

Belvédère

Berthemont-les-Bains – *4km – 2.5 miles from D 2565*. This spa is in a shady setting. The sulphurous, radioactive waters at 30°C were used as long ago as in Roman times. Diseases treated include respiratory, illnesses, rheumatism and diseases of the joints.

As the road climbs, the valley changes to a landscape of chestnuts, pines and green pastures which has earned the region round St-Martin-Vésubie the title of "Suisse niçoise" (Nice's Switzerland). Venanson overlooks the valley from the west bank.

★ **St-Martin-Vésubie** – *See ST-MARTIN-VÉSUBIE.*

Return of the wolf

The presence of wolves *(canis lupus)* in the Parc du Mercantour, detected by tracks found in 1989, was verified during the winter of 1992. Observations made in spring 1995 confirmed the presence of a pack of eight wolves, and also probably an isolated couple.

Arriving in one of the successive migrations from the Abruzzi (Central Italy) where the wolf population is estimated at more than 500, the wolf is constantly searching for new territories where its capacity for adaptation is astounding. The pack is the basic family unit, consisting of the parents and their offspring from the last two years, about six to eight members. The return of the wolf is a sign of ecological health in the area. The Parc du Mercantour conducts a campaign of awareness and education with shepherds who are directly involved in the new problems of living with wolves. Measures have been taken: penning of flocks at night and the introduction of a sheepdog (the Pyrenean Patou) with a great deterrent effect on the wolves' attacks. The creation of a Maison du Loup in the Parc has helped inform the public.

MICHELIN GREEN GUIDES

    Architecture
    Fine Art
    Ancient monuments
    History
    Geography
    Picturesque scenery
    Scenic routes
    Touring programmes
    Places to stay
    Plans of towns and buildings
    A collection of regional guides for France

VILLECROZE

Population 1 029
Michelin map 84 fold 6 (northeast of Salernes),
114 fold 21 or 245 fold 34

The village has grown up round a group of caves, partially converted into dwellings. It lies in the wooded foothills of the Provençal tableland.

Old village – The flavour of the Middle Ages lingers in the clock tower, rue des Arcades and Romanesque church with its wall belfry.

Parc municipal – *Entrance via route d'Aups, then a right-hand turning leading to a car park.* A beautiful waterfall cascades 40m – 130ft down the cliff face and forms a stream in an oasis of greenery beside a lovely rose garden. A marked path leads to the caves *(grottes)*.

Caves ⊘ – In the 16C the caves were partially converted into dwellings by the Lords of Villecroze; some mullioned windows set into the rock remain. The tour includes several little chambers with attractive concretions.

Viewpoint – 1km – half a mile from the village on the Tourtour road, there is a look-out point *(viewing table)*. The **panorama**★ extends from the Provençal tableland over Tourtour, Villecroze and Salernes to the Bessillon peaks, the Maures and Ste-Baume.

VILLEFRANCHE-SUR-MER★

Population 8 080
Michelin map 84 fold 10 or 19 or 115 fold 27 or 245 fold 38
Local map see Corniches de la RIVIERA

Villefranche, a fishing port and holiday resort, is built on the wooded slopes encircling one of the most beautiful **anchorages**★★ in the Mediterranean. The deep bay of 25 to 60m – 13 to 33 fathoms, where cruise liners and warships can lie at anchor, lies between the Cap Ferrat peninsula and the Mont Boron heights.
Villefranche has preserved its 17C character in its ports, citadel and old streets.

The origins of Villefranche – The town owes its name to the Count of Provence, Charles II of Anjou, nephew of St Louis, who founded it at the start of the 14C and gave it commercial freedom. Between its cession to Savoy in the late 17C and the excavation of the Lympia harbour in Nice in the mid-18C, Villefranche was the major port of the Savoyard and then the Sardinian states.

The Congress of Nice – In 1538, the Congress of Nice was convened by Pope Paul III, former Bishop of Vence, to bring peace between François I and Charles V. During the Congress, Charles V stayed in Villefranche, François I in Villeneuve-Loubet and the Pope, acting as intermediary, in Nice.
The Queen of France, sister of Charles V, went to see her brother, whose ship was moored at Villefranche. Charles, giving his hand to the Queen and followed by the Duke of Savoy and lords and ladies of his suite, advanced majestically along the wooden gangway between the jetty and the ship. With a cracking noise the gangway collapsed, and the Emperor, the Queen and the Duke could only splash about helplessly in the water until, soaked and dishevelled, they were pulled ashore by onlookers.
The peace of Nice lasted only five years.

From naval base to zoological station – The Russian presence in Villefranche increased at the end of the 18C and has been remarkably consistent ever since. The strategic potential of the harbour did not escape the notice of the Russian naval authorities of the period. Each conflict between the Russian Empire and Turkey brought about the temporary anchorage of Russian naval units at Villefranche. It was, however, just after the Crimean War, in 1856, that Villefranche harbour became even more useful to the Russian military fleet which was deprived of access to the Mediterranean via the Bosphorus. In 1857 an agreement was made with the King of Sardinia for the transfer of storehouses and of the harbour at Villefranche to Russia which would use it as a depot for fuel and provisions as well as a home base for the Imperial nobility on holiday on the coast. Uniting with the Comté de Nice maintained these arrangements but interest in the site developed at the end of the century.
In 1893 a team of Russian scientists and academics from Kiev replaced the soldiers to carry out oceanographic research, taking advantage of the upcurrent in the harbour. These studies, in spite of political ups and downs between the two nations, continued until the 1930s, when the premises were reclaimed by the Université de Paris who established a marine zoology station of international repute there.

SIGHTS

★ **Old town** – A row of brightly painted houses lines the waterfront of the charming fishing harbour.
Rue du Poilu (**22**) is the main street in a network of narrow streets, some of which are stepped or vaulted, such as the strange **rue Obscure** (**19**) where the population took refuge during bombardments.

St-Michel – This Italian Baroque church contains 18C altarpieces. In the north transept is a crucifix carved with impressive realism from the trunk of a fig tree by an unknown convict in the 17C, and a 16C polychrome wood statue of St Roch and his dog stands against a pillar (left). The typically French organ, dated 1790 and recently restored, was built by the well-known Grinda brothers of Nice.

★ **Chapelle St-Pierre** ⊙ – This chapel was decorated throughout in 1957 by **Jean Cocteau**. The staring eyes on either side of the door – the flames of the Apocalypse – were painted later to look like ceramics.
The frescoes are typical of Cocteau's style of drawing, in precise but ample lines. His theme, the life of St Peter, is illustrated by simple realistic scenes; there are also some secular scenes celebrating the young women of Villefranche and gypsies. They are linked together by geometric decoration.

Harbour (Darse) – Once a military port where galleys were built and manned, this is now an anchorage for yachts and pleasure boats.

Citadelle – The citadel was constructed in 1560 by the Duke of Savoy to guard the port. It was much admired by Vauban and spared by Louis XIV together with Fort du Mont Alban, when the defences of the County of Nice were destroyed.
The building was restored in 1981 and comprises the town hall, the former chapel of St Elmo used for temporary exhibitions, an auditorium and an open-air theatre. The casemates of the citadel house a **collection of submarine archeology** ⊙. The exhibits come from the wreck of a Genoese ship wrecked in the Villefranche anchorage in the 16C and excavated in the 1980s.
They are also home to the **Collection Roux** ⊙, a collection of ceramic figurines displayed in little tableaux evoking everyday life in the Middle Ages and during the Renaissance. These scenes are based on treaties and other documents dating from these periods.

★ **Musée Volti** ⊙ – The main courtyard of the citadel and the surrounding vaulted casemates provide an admirable setting for a collection of sculptures by Antoniucci Volti, a citizen of Villefranche of Italian origin.
His work is strictly representational; he concentrates exclusively on the human body, not without humour, as in the group in beaten copper exhibited in the courtyard. He excels in countless representations of the female figure: supremely elegant *(Parisiennes)*, gracefully reclining *(Nikaïa)*, seated with dignity *(Cachan Maternity)*, crouching or curled up *(Lotus)*.
Some of his most recent works verge on the monumental *(Queen, Minerva...)*. The sculptures are accompanied by several very fine drawings in red chalk.

Villefranche-sur-Mer bay

VILLEFRANCHE-SUR-MER

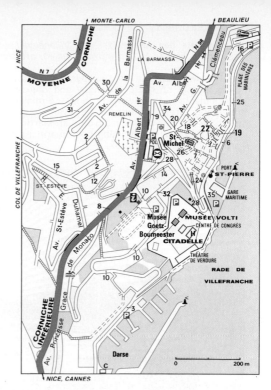

Musée Goetz-Boumeester (M) ⊙ – The main collection was given to the town of Villefranche by the painter-engraver Henri Goetz, born in 1909, and his wife Christine Boumeester (1904-71); there are about 100 works, representing 50 years of pictorial research ranging from the figurative to the abstract. There are also some souvenir works signed by Picasso, Miró, Hartung, Picabia etc.

The annual Michelin Red Guide France
offers comprehensive up-to-date information in a compact format
An ideal companion on holidays, business trips or weekends away
It is well worth buying the current edition

VILLENEUVE-LOUBET

Population 11 539
Michelin map 84 fold 9 or 115 fold 25 or 245 fold 37
Town plan see CAGNES-SUR-MER

The district of Villeneuve-Loubet on the banks of the River Loup is bordered on the coast by a vast beach. The old village is dominated by a medieval **castle**, the property of the Villeneuve family, which was restored in the 19C and is well preserved.

The tall pentagonal keep was begun in the 9C. François I stayed in the castle during his negotiations with Charles V, leading to the *Treaty of Nice* which was signed in the castle in 1538.
The village preserves the traditional form of the Provençal sport *pelota*, which is played without a glove.

★ **Musée de l'art culinaire (Y M²)** ⊙ – The culinary museum occupies the house where **Auguste Escoffier** (1846-1935) was born and contains souvenirs of his career as head chef at the Savoy and the Carlton in London (he was the creator of Peach Melba). There are many documents on the art of cooking; also, amazing show-pieces made of icing sugar or almond paste. The room which has been arranged as a Provençal kitchen leads to an upstairs room displaying a collection of 5 000 menus; some date from 1820.

Musée militaire (Y M³) ⊙ – The military museum is devoted to the great conflicts waged this century: both the First and the Second World Wars (respectively 1914-18 and 1939-45), First Indochina War (1946-54), Algerian War (1954-62), French military intervention in Chad and Zaïre (1969-84) and the Lebanon (1982-87), and the Gulf War (1991). The display includes uniforms, weapons, decorations, flags, posters, photographs etc.

Marina Baie des Anges (z) – *In Villeneuve-Loubet-Plage. Take D 2 south and turn right into N 7 (towards Antibes); after crossing the motorway, turn left.*

The shallow S-bends of the four pyramidal blocks of luxury seafront flats are the brainchild of André Minangoy and one of the most amazing property developments on the Riviera. Each floor diminishes in surface area towards the top storey providing terraces at every level. Their distinctive silhouettes dominate the Baie des Anges from Cap Martin to Cap d'Antibes. The beach is complemented by a swimming pool, marina, cafés, shops and restaurants to form an impressive complex.

Marina Baie des Anges, Villeneuve-Loubet

Long before it became the mecca of the sun-worshipping 20C tourist, the Riviera was popular among foreigners as a winter resort.

Lord Brougham, the Lord Chancellor of England, was accustomed to winter in Nice but in 1834 he was forced by an outbreak of cholera in Provence to stay in Cannes ; he liked it so well that he built a house, where he stayed every winter until his death in 1868.

Other famous Englishmen, who made a home on the Riviera, were the writers, Somerset Maugham in Cap Ferrat, Graham Greene in Antibes and the film actor/writer, Sir Dirk Bogarde, who was President of the Cannes Film Festival in 1984, when he lived near Grasse.

Another foreign colony was the Russian nobility, who until the Revolution in 1917, were regularly joined by the Imperial Court. Their legacy is a number of beautiful Russian Orthodox churches in Cannes, Nice and Menton.

The benefit of the dry climate attracted many patients suffering from tuberculosis, including Katharine Mansfield, a New Zealand writer, who settled in Menton.

The Americans began to make a mark in the 1920s – Douglas Fairbanks and Mary Pickford from the film world, Ernest Hemingway and Scott Fitzgerald, the writers, and other young Americans with money. They introduced jazz, the music of Cole Porter and sunbathing. There was more jazz at the end of the Second World War stimulated by the US Naval base ; the Juan-les-Pins Jazz Festival dates from this period.

In the 1930s many German artists in exile settled in Sanary-sur-Mer. Other communities of artists have been established in Vallauris, where Picasso revived the traditional craft of pottery and which now hosts a bi-annual International Festival of Ceramic Art (July to mid-October), and in St-Paul-de-Vence, where James Baldwin, the American author lived for many years.

Monaco, where fortunes have been lost and won on the gaming tables, still attracts a significant number of wealthy tax exiles.

Practical
information

Planning your tour

Passport – Nationals of countries within the European Union entering France need only a national identity card (or in the case of the British, a passport or a Visitor's Passport). Nationals of other countries must be in possession of a valid national **passport**. In case of loss or theft report to the embassy or consulate and the local police.

Visa – An **entry visa** is required for Canadian and US citizens (for a stay of more than 3 months) and for Australian and New Zealand citizens. Apply to the French Consulate (visa issued same day; delay if request submitted by mail).
US citizens should obtain the booklet *Safe Trip Abroad* ($1), which provides useful information on visa requirements, customs regulations, medical care etc for international travellers. Published by the Government Printing Office, it can be ordered by phone – ☎ (202) 512-1800 – or consulted on-line at www. access.gpo.gov.

Customs – Apply to the Customs Office (UK) for a leaflet on customs regulations and the full range of "duty free" allowances; available from HM Customs and Excise, Dorset House, Stamford Street, London SE1 9PS, ☎ 0171 928 3344. The US Customs Service offers a publication *Know before you go for* US citizens: for the office nearest you, consult the phone book, Federal Government, us Treasury (www.customs.ustreas.gov.).
There are no customs formalities for holidaymakers bringing their caravans into France for a stay of less than 6 months. No customs document is necessary for pleasure boats and outboard motors for a stay of less than 6 months but the registration certificate should be kept on board.

French Government Tourist Offices – For information, brochures, maps and other assistance travellers should contact the official tourist office in their own country.

Australia Sydney – BNP Building, 12 Castlereagh Street, Sydney, New South Wales 2000 ☎ (61) 2-231-5244, Fax (61) 2-221-86-82.

Canada Toronto – 30 St Patrick's Street, Suite 700, Toronto, ONT M5T 3A3 ☎ (416) 593-4723
Montreal – 1981 Ave McGill College, Suite 490, Montreal, PQ H3A 2W9 ☎ (514) 288-4264, Fax (514) 845-4868.

Ireland Dublin – c/o 38 Lower Abbey Street, Dublin 1 ☎ (1) 703 4046, Fax (1) 874 7324.

United Kingdom London – 178 Piccadilly, London WIV OAL ☎ (0891) 244 123, Fax (0171) 493 6594.

United States
France On Call Hotline: 900-990-0040 (US$0.50/min) for information on hotels, restaurants and transportation.
East Coast: New York – 444 Madison Avenue, NY, 10022 ☎ (212) 838-7800, Fax (212) 838-7855.
Middle West: Chicago – 676 North Michigan Avenue, Suite 3360, Chicago, IL60611-2819 ☎ (312) 751-7800, Fax (312) 337-6339.
West Coast: Los Angeles – 9454 Wilshire Boulevard, Suite 715, Beverly Hills, CA 90212-2967 ☎ (310) 271-2693, Fax (310) 276-2835.

Regional and Departmental Tourist Offices – These bodies publish information brochures on their own regions –
- **Comité Régional du Tourisme de Provence-Alpes-Côte d'Azur** – Espace Colbert, 14 rue Sainte-Barbe 13001 Marseille ☎ 04 91 39 38 00.
- **Comité régional du tourisme Riviera-Côte d'Azur** – 55 promenade des Anglais, BP 602, 06011 Nice Cedex 1 ☎ 04 93 37 78 78.
- **Comité départemental du tourisme du Var** – 1 boulevard Foch, BP 99, 83003 Draguignan cedex ☎ 04 94 68 58 33 and 5 avenue Vauban, BP 5147, 83000 Toulon ☎ 04 94 09 00 69.
- **Office de tourisme et des congrès de la Principauté de Monaco** – 2A boulevard des Moulins, 98000 Monaco ☎ 04 93 50 60 88.
- **Fédération départementale des offices de tourisme et syndicats d'initiative des Alpes-Maritimes** – 2 rue Deloye, 06000 Nice.
- **Parc naturel national du Mercantour** – 23 rue d'Italie, 06000 Nice ☎ 04 93 87 86 10.
- **Parc naturel national de Port-Cros** – Castel Ste Claire, rue Ste Claire, 83400 Hyères ☎ 04 94 65 32 98.
- **Fédération Nationale des Comités Départementaux de Tourisme**, 2 rue Linois, 75015 Paris ☎ 01 45 75 62 16.

Tourist Information Centres – The **Michelin Red Guide France** gives the addresses and telephone numbers of the Tourist Information Centres *(Syndicats d'Initiative)* to be found in most large towns and many tourist resorts. They can supply large-scale town plans, timetables and information on local entertainment facilities, sports and sightseeing.

Tourism for the Disabled – Some of the sights described in this guide are accessible to disabled people *(see Admission Times and Charges)*.

The **Michelin Red Guide France** and the **Michelin Camping Caravaning France** indicate hotels and camping sites with facilities suitable for physically disabled people.

The Comité National Français de Liaison pour la Réadaptation des Handicapés, 236 bis rue de Tolbiac, 75013 Paris ☎ 01 53 80 66 66, provides information on travel and holidays.

Information on access to museums is available from Direction des Musées de France, service Accueil des Publics Spécifiques, 6 rue des Pyramides, 75041 Paris Cedex 01 ☎ 01 40 15 35 88.

Useful organisations in the UK include RADAR (Royal Association for Disability and Rehabilitation, 12 City Forum, 250 City Road, London EC1V 8AF, ☎ (0171) 250-3222, Fax (0171) 2580-0212) and Access Project (39 Bradley Gardens, West Ealing, London W13 8HE), who provide specialised practical information about on such matters as health insurance for disabled travellers.

Web-surfers can find information for slow walkers, mature travellers and those with special needs at www.access-able.com.

If you are a member of a sports club and would like to practice your sport in France, or meet others who do, ask the CNRH for information on clubs in the *Fédération Française du Sport Adapté* (FFSA – Paris ☎ 01 48 72 80 72).

Minitel – **Michelin Travel Assistance** (AMI), one of the French Telecom videotex services, is a computerised route-finding system offering integrated information on roads, tourist sights, hotels and restaurants. The service costs 1.27F/min and is always available; the access code is **3615 MICHELIN**.

Minitel terminals are installed in hotel chains and certain petrol stations throughout the country (over six million terminals).

Cyberspace

www.info.france-usa.org
The French Embassy's Web site provides basic Information (geography, demographics, history), a news digest and business-related information. It offers special pages for children, and pages devoted to culture, language study and travel, and you can reach other selected French sites (regions, cities, ministries) with a hypertext link.

www.fr-holidaystore.co.uk
The new French Travel Centre in London has gone on-line with this service, providing information on all of the regions of France, including updated special travel offers and details on available accommodation.

www.ottowa.ambafrance.org
The Cultural Service of the French Embassy in Ottawa has a bright and varied site with many links to other sites for French literature, news updates, E-texts in both French and English.

Climate – The **tourist season** on the French Riviera lasts virtually all year round. The **winter** months are characterised by a mild, sunny climate and are ideal for those who seek to avoid the peak influx of tourists.

Spring and **autumn** can sometimes bring heavy rainfall and a searching wind *(mistral)* for a few days but neither eclipses the magnificent display of plant-life in full bloom at these times.

Summer is of course the best season for bathing and working up a suntan, not to mention participating in the energetic nightlife. Traffic on the coast is, however, always very congested during this period; it can also be difficult to find accommodation so it is advisable to book in advance.

Weather forecasts
Recorded report
- for Alpes-Maritimes – 04 36 65 02 06
- for the Var 04 36 65 02 83

Forecast of conditions at sea
- for Alpes-Maritimes – 04 36 65 08 06
- for Var – 04 36 68 08 83
- 5-day forecasts – 04 36 68 08 08.

Road conditions
- Interservice Route – 02 48 94 33 33
- by Minitel 3615 METEO, 3615 CIEL and 3617 METPLUS

Snowfall in winter sports stations (24 hour) – 04 42 66 64 28

5-day forecast
- for the mountains – 04 36 68 04 04
- snow and avalanche forecast – 04 36 68 10 20

General weather information – 05 45 55 91 09

5-day forecast – 04 36 85 01 01

Travelling

By air

The various national and other independent airlines operate services to Paris (Charles de Gaulle and Orly) and to the major provincial airports (Bordeaux, Lille, Lyons, Marseille, Montpellier, Nantes, Nice, Strasbourg, Toulouse). There are also package tour flights with a rail or coach link-up as well as fly-drive schemes. Information, brochures and time tables are available from the airlines and from travel agents.

The domestic network operates frequent services covering the whole country
- Marseille from Paris-Orly (Air Inter, TAT, AOM and Air Liberté)
- Toulon-Hyères (☎ 04 94 22 81 60) from Paris and Lille (Air Inter)
- Toulon from Brest (Air Provence) and Ajaccio and Bastia (Kyrnair)
- Fréjus-St-Raphaël (☎ 04 94 51 04 07) from Paris during the summer only
- Nice-Côte d'Azur (TAT) – information on Minitel 3615 TAT
- Nice and Marseille from Paris-Orly (AOM 2 rue Halévy 06000 Nice ☎ 04 92 14 67 77)
- Cannes-Mandelieu (☎ 04 93 90 40 40) during the summer only.

There are transfer buses to town terminals and to rail stations. Roissy-Rail, Orly-Rail operate fast rail links to the centre of Paris.

By sea

There are numerous **cross-Channel services** (passenger and car ferries, hovercraft) from the United Kingdom and Ireland and also the rail Shuttle through the Channel Tunnel. For details apply to travel agencies or to –

P & O European Ferries, Channel House, Channel View Road, Dover CT17 9TJ ☎ 01304 203 388.

Stena Sealink, Charter House, Park Street, Ashford, Kent TN24 8EX ☎ 01233 647 047.

Hoverspeed, International Hoverport, Marine Parade, Dover, Kent CT17 9TG ☎ 01304 240 241.

Sally Line, 81 Piccadilly, London WIV 9HF ☎ 0171 409 2240.

Brittany Ferries, Millbay Docks, Plymouth PLI 3EW ☎ 01752 221 321.

Irish Ferries, 24 Merrion Row, Dublin 2 ☎ (353) 1-661 0511.

Le Shuttle-Eurotunnel ☎ (01303) 271 100.

There are regular Mediterranean sealinks
- from **Nice** all year to **Corsica** and in summer to **Italy** – ☎ 04 93 09 50 85 (Port Authority) and ☎ 04 93 13 66 66 (Corsica)
- from **Toulon** all year to **Corsica** and in summer to **Sardinia**; Mediterranean cruise ships also put in to Toulon – ☎ 04 94 22 80 82 (Port Authority).

By rail

British Rail offers a range of services to the Channel ports and French Railways (SNCF) operates an extensive network of lines including many high speed passenger trains and motorail services throughout France. There is a daily service via the Channel Tunnel on Eurostar *(3 hours)* between **London** (Waterloo International Station) and **Paris** (Gare du Nord).

French Railways and Air France also offer special packages combining air and rail travel.

Rail passes (France Vacances Pass) offer unlimited travel; group travel tickets offer savings for parties. Eurorail Pass, Flexipass and Saver Pass are options available in the US for travel in Europe and must be purchased in the US – ☎ (212) 308-3103 (information) and 1-800-223-636 (reservations).

Information and reservations in the UK from French Railways, 179 Piccadilly, London WIV OBA ☎ (1891) 515 477 and from travel agencies.

The Thomas Cook European Rail timetable gives all the train schedules throughout France and useful information on train travel.

Tickets bought in France must be validated *(composter)* by using the orange automatic date-stamping machines at the platform entrance.

Baggage trolleys (10F coin required – refundable) are available at main line stations.

By coach

Regular coach services are operated from London to Paris and to large provincial towns:

Euroways/Eurolines, 52 Grosvenor Gardens, Victoria, **London** SWI OA4 ☎ 0171 730 8235.

28 avenue du Général de Gaulle, 93547 Bagnolet (Paris Region) ☎ 01 49 72 51 51.

Motoring in France

Documents

Nationals of EU countries require a valid national **driving licence**; nationals of non-EU countries require an **international driving** licence (obtainable in the US from the American Automobile Club; US$10 for members, US$22 for non-members).
For the vehicle it is necessary to have the **registration papers** (log-book) and a **nationality plate** of the approved size.

Insurance

Insurance cover is compulsory and although an International Insurance Certificate (Green Card) is no longer a legal requirement in France it is the most effective proof of insurance cover and is internationally recognised by the police and other authorities. Certain UK motoring organisations (AA, RAC) run accident insurance and breakdown service schemes for members. Europ-Assistance (252 High Street, Croydon CR0 1NF) has special policies for motorists. The brochure *Offices to serve you abroad* is published by the American Automobile Club; its affiliated organisation in France is Association Française des Automobile-Clubs, 9 rue Anatole-de-la-Forge, 75017 Paris ☎ 01 42 27 82 00.

Highway code

The minimum driving age is 18 years old. Traffic drives on the right.
It is compulsory for the front-seat passengers to wear **seat belts**; all back seat passengers should wear seat belts where they are fitted. Children under the age of ten should travel on the back seat.
Full or dipped headlights must be switched on in poor visibility and at night; use sidelights only when the vehicle is stationary.
In the case of a **breakdown** a red warning triangle or hazard warning lights are obligatory.
Drivers should watch out for unfamiliar road signs and take great care on the road.
In built-up areas **priority** must be ceded to vehicles joining the road from the right but traffic on roundabouts and on main roads outside built-up areas has priority. Vehicles must stop when the lights turn red at road junctions and may filter to the right only where indicated by a flashing amber arrow.
The regulations on **drinking and driving** and **speeding** are strictly enforced – usually by an on-the-spot fine and/or confiscation of the vehicle.

Speed limits – Although liable to modification these are as follows:
- toll motorways 130kph – 80mph (110kph – 68mph when raining);
- dual carriage roads and motorways without tolls 110kph – 68mph (100kph – 62mph when raining);
- other roads 90kph – 56mph (80kph – 50mph when raining) and in towns 50kph – 31mph;
- outside lane on motorways during daylight, on level ground and with good visibility – minimum speed limit of 80kph – 50mph.

Parking regulations

In town there are restricted and paying **parking zones** (blue and grey zones); tickets must be obtained from the ticket machines (*horodateurs* – small change necessary) and displayed (inside windscreen on driver's side); failure to display may result in a heavy fine or the vehicle being towed away.
In some towns blue parking zones *(zone bleu)* are indicated by a blue line on the pavement or a blue sign with a P and a small square underneath; in the latter case a time disc must be displayed which allows a stay of 1 hour 30min (2 hour 30min at lunchtime) free of charge; time discs *(disque de stationnement)* are on sale in supermarkets and petrol stations.

Route planning

For 24-hour road traffic information: dial 56 96 33 33 or consult Minitel 3615 Code Route (1.29F/min) or Michelin on the Internet: www.michelin-travel.com.
The road network is excellent and includes over 6 400 km – 4 000 miles of motorways, mostly toll-roads *(autoroutes à péage)*. The roads are very busy during the holiday period (particularly weekends in July and August) and to avoid traffic congestion it is advisable to follow the recommended secondary routes *(Dison Futé itinéraires bis)*.

Tolls

In France most motorways are subject to a toll *(péage)* payable by cash or by credit card (Visa, Mastercard); Calais to Marseille costs about 350F per car.

Car Rental

There are car rental agencies at airports, air terminals, railway stations and in all large towns throughout France. Fly-drive schemes are operated by the major airlines. European cars usually have manual transmission but automatic cars are available on demand (advance reservation recommended). An **international driving licence** is required for non-EU nationals.

Car hire is relatively expensive in France; Americans in particular should consider booking before leaving the USA or using a Fly-Drive scheme.

Central reservation in France

Avis	01 46 10 60 60
Budget	01 46 86 65 65
Eurodollar	01 49 58 44 44
Europcar	01 30 43 82 82
Hertz	01 47 88 51 51

Petrol – In France there are four different types of petrol (gas US) –

super leaded	*super*
super unleaded 98	*sans plomb 98*
unleaded 95	*sans plomb 95*
diesel	*diesel/gazole*

Accommodation

Places to stay

The map at the beginning of the guide indicates the recommended places for overnight stops.

The **Michelin Red Guide France** lists a selection of hotels and restaurants in all price categories.

Loisirs Accueil is an officially-backed booking service which has offices in most French *départements* and publishes an annual guide. For information: contact 17 rue de l'Ingénieur Keller, 75015 Paris ☎ 01 40 59 44 12 or Minitel 3615 SLA.

The **Accueil de France** Tourist Offices which are open all year make hotel bookings for a small fee for personal callers only. The head office is in Paris (127 avenue des Champs Élysées – ☎ 01 47 23 61 72 for information only) and there are offices in many large towns and resorts.

The *Relais et Châteaux Hotel Guide* and the *Logis et Auberges de France* brochure are available from the French Government Tourist Office.

Rural accommodation

For a list of relevant addresses apply to **Maison des Gîtes de France**

– 59 rue St-Lazare, 75009 Paris ☎ 01 49 70 75 75

– 78 Piccadilly, London W1V OAL ☎ 0171 493 3480

– Minitel 3615 GITES DE FRANCE.

Gîtes de France – 55 promenade des Anglais, 06000 Nice ☎ 04 93 44 39 39.

The Fédération Française des Stations Vertes de Vacances, Hôtel du Département de la Côte d'Or, BP 1601, 21035 Dijon Cedex ☎ 03 80 49 97 80, publishes two guides (no charge), *Guide des stations vertes de vacances*

Brignoles

E. Baret

and *Guide des villages de neige*, which list accommodation, leisure facilities and natural attractions in rural locations.

A useful guide which provides information on mountain accommodation for those who like walking is *Gîtes-Refuges* by Annick and Serge Moutaret, published by La Cadole, 78140 Vélizy); also available on Minitel 3615 CADOLE. For **families** there is *Partir en famille – Kid des vacances* by Josette Sicsic, published by ETC, which lists accommodation with facilities and leisure activities suitable for parents with young children.

Bed and Breakfast

Gîtes de France (see above) publishes a booklet on bed and breakfast accommodation *(chambre d'hôte)*. Information also available from Bed & Breakfast (France), **International Reservations Centre**, 94-96 Bell St., Henley-on-Thames, Oxon RG9 1XS ☎ 01491 578 803, Fax 01491 410 806. E-mail address: bookings@bedbreak. demon.co.uk.

Youth Hostels

There are two main youth hostel *(auberge de la jeunesse)* associations in France.
- Ligue Française pour les Auberges de la Jeunesse, 38 boulevard Raspail, 75007 Paris ☎ 01 45 48 69 84, Fax 01 45 44 57 47
- Fédération Unie des Auberges de Jeunesse, 27 rue Pajol, 75012 Paris ☎ 01 44 89 87 27, Fax 01 44 89 87 10, Minitel 3615 code FUAJ (1.01F/min). Internet: www.Fuaj.org.

Holders of an International Youth Hostel Federation card should apply for a list from the International Federation or from one of the French organisations (see above). For information on budget accommodation members of American Youth Hostels should call 202 783 6161.

Camping

France has some 11 000 officially graded sites with varying standards of facilities. The **Michelin Guide Camping Caravaning France** lists a selection of camping sites. An International Camping Carnet for caravans is useful but not compulsory; it may be obtained from the motoring organisations or the Camping and Caravanning Club, Greenfield House, Westwood Way, Coventry CV4 8JH ☎ 01203 694 995.

Electricity

The electric current is 220 volts. Circular two pin plugs are the rule – an electrical adaptor may be necessary. US appliances (hairdryers, shavers) will not work without one. Adapters are on sale in electronics stores and also at international airports.

Services

Medical treatment

First aid, medical advice and chemists' night service rota are available from chemists *(pharmacie* – green cross sign). Prescription drugs should be clearly labelled and tourists are advised to carry a copy of prescriptions.

It is advisable to take out comprehensive insurance cover as medical treatment in French hospitals or clinics must be paid for by the recipient. Nationals of non-EU countries should check with their insurance companies about policy limitations. Reimbursement can then be negotiated with the insurance company according to the terms of the policy held.

American Express offers a service, *Global Assist*, for any medical, legal or personal emergency.

British citizens should apply to the Department of Health and Social Security **for Form E 111**, which entitles the holder to urgent treatment for accident or unexpected illness in EU countries. A refund of part of the costs of treatment can be obtained on application in person or by post to the local Social Security Offices (Caisse Primaire d'Assurance Maladie).

Currency

See illustrations overleaf. There are no restrictions on the amount of currency visitors can take into France. To facilitate the export of currency in foreign bank notes in excess of the given allocation, visitors carrying a lot of cash should complete a currency declaration form on arrival.

The unit of currency in France is the French franc (F), subdivided into 100 centimes; Monaco has its own currency, also valid in the Alpes-Maritimes *département* of France. French coins are issued in the following values
- 5, 10, 20, 50 centimes (all gold in colour except the 50 centime coin which is silver)
- 1, 2, 5, 10, 20 francs (all silver except the 10 and 20 franc coins which are silver with a gold band).

French notes are issued in the following values
- 50, 100, 200 and 500 francs; the 20 franc note is being withdrawn.

Banks

Banks are usually open from 9am to 12 noon and 2pm to 4pm and are closed on Mondays or Saturdays (except if market day); some branches open for limited transactions on Saturdays. Banks close early on the day before a bank holiday. A passport is necessary as identification when cashing cheques in banks. Commission charges vary and hotels usually charge more than banks for cashing cheques for non-residents.

Most banks have **cash dispensers** (ATM) which accept international credit cards and are easily recognised by the CB logo. American Express cards can be used only in dispensers operated by the Crédit Lyonnais Bank or by American Express.

Credit cards – American Express, Visa (Carte Bleue), Mastercard/Eurocard and Diners Club are widely accepted in shops, hotels and restaurants and petrol stations. In the case of a lost or stolen credit card, ring the following 24-hour numbers

American Express	01 47 77 72 00
Visa	01 42 77 11 90
Mastercard/Eurocard	01 45 67 84 84
Diners Club	01 47 62 75 50

Such loss or theft must also be reported to the local police who will issue a certificate to show to the credit card company.

Post

Post Offices open Mondays to Fridays, 8am to 7pm, Saturdays, 8am to 12 noon. Smaller branch post offices generally close at lunch-time between 12 noon and 2pm and at 4pm. Postage via air mail to
- UK letter (20g) 3F
- US letter (20g) 4.40F
- US postcard 4.10F.
- Australia and New Zealand letter (20g) 5.20F.

Stamps are also available from newsagents and tobacconists.

Stamp collectors should ask for *timbres de collection* in any post office.

Poste Restante mail should be addressed as follows: Name, Poste Restante, Poste Centrale, postal code of the *département* followed by town name, France. The Michelin Red Guide France gives local postal codes.

Embassies and Consulates

Australia	Embassy	4 rue Jean-Rey, 75015 Paris ☎ 01 40 50 33 00, Fax 01 40 59 33 10
Canada	Embassy	35 avenue Montaigne, 75008 Paris ☎ 01 44 43 29 00, Fax 01 44 43 29 99
Ireland	Embassy	4 rue Rude, 75016 Paris ☎ 01 45 00 20 87, Fax 01 45 00 84 17
New Zealand	Embassy	7ter rue Léonard-de-Vinci, 75016 Paris ☎ 01 45 00 24 11, Fax 01 45 01 26 39
UK	Embassy	35 rue du Faubourg St-Honoré, 75008 Paris ☎ 01 42 66 91 42, Fax 01 42 66 95 90
	Consulate	16 rue d'Anjou, 75008 Paris ☎ 01 42 66 06 68 (visas)
		9 avenue Hoche, 75008 Paris ☎ 01 42 66 38 10
		24 avenue Prado, 13006 Marseille ☎ 04 91 15 72 10, Fax 04 91 37 47 06
USA	Embassy	2 avenue Gabriel, 75008 Paris ☎ 01 42 96 12 02, Fax 01 42 66 97 83
	Consulate	2 rue St-Florentin, 75001 Paris ☎ 01 42 96 14 88
		12 boulevard Paul-Peytral, 13006 Marseille ☎ 04 91 54 92 00
		31 rue du Maréchal-Joffre, 06000 Nice, ☎ 04 93 88 89 55.

Conversion tables

Weights and measures

1 kilogram (kg)	2.2 pounds (lb)	2.2 pounds
1 metric ton (tn)	1.1 tons	1.1 tons

to convert kilograms to pounds, multiply by 2.2

1 litre (l)	2.1 pints (pt)	1.8 pints
1 litre	0.3 gallon (gal)	0.2 gallon

to convert litres to gallons, multiply by 0.26 (US) or 0.22 (UK)

1 hectare (ha)	2.5 acres	2.5 acres
1 square kilometre (km²)	0.4 square miles (sq mi)	0.4 square miles

to convert hectares to acres, multiply by 2.4

1 centimetre (cm)	0.4 inches (in)	0.4 inches
1 metre (m)	3.3 feet (ft) - 39.4 inches - 1.1 yards (yd)	
1 kilometre (km)	0.6 miles (ml)	0.6 miles

to convert metres to feet, multiply by 3.28, kilometres to miles, multiply by 0.6

Clothing

Women	EU	US	UK		EU	US	UK	Men
	35	4	2½		40	7½	7	
	36	5	3½		41	8½	8	
	37	6	4½		42	9½	9	
Shoes	38	7	5½		43	10½	10	**Shoes**
	39	8	6½		44	11½	11	
	40	9	7½		45	12½	12	
	41	10	8½		46	13½	13	
	36	4	8		46	36	36	
	38	6	10		48	38	38	
Dresses &	40	8	12		50	40	40	**Suits**
Suits	42	12	14		52	42	42	
	44	14	16		54	44	44	
	46	16	18		56	46	48	
	36	08	30		37	14½	14,5	
	38	10	32		38	15	15	
Blouses &	40	12	14		39	15½	15½	**Shirts**
sweaters	42	14	36		40	15¾	15¾	
	44	16	38		41	16	16	
	46	18	40		42	16½	16½	

Sizes often vary depending on the designer. These equivalents are given for guidance only.

Speed

kph	10	30	50	70	80	90	100	110	120	130
mph	6	19	31	43	50	56	62	68	75	81

Temperature

Celsius (°C)	0°	5°	10°	15°	20°	25°	30°	40°	60°	80°	100°
Fahrenheit (°F)	32°	41°	50°	59°	68°	77°	86°	104°	140°	176°	212°

To convert Celsius into Fahrenheit, multiply °C by 9, divide by 5, and add 32.
To convert Fahrenheit into Celsius, subtract 32 from °F, multiply by 5, and divide by 9.

Notes and coins

500 Francs featuring
scientists
Pierre and Marie Curie
(1858-1906), (1867-1934)

200 Francs featuring
engineer Gustave Eiffel
(1832-1923)

100 Francs featuring
painter Paul Cézanne
(1839-1906)

50 Francs featuring
pilot and writer
Antoine de Saint-Exupéry
(1900-1944)

20 Francs

10 Francs

5 Francs

2 Francs

1 Franc

50 Centimes

20 Centimes

10 Centimes

5 Centimes

Telephoning

Public telephones

Most public telephones in France use pre-paid phone cards *(télécarte)*. Some booths accept credit cards (Visa, Mastercard/Eurocard; minimum monthly charge 20F). Phone cards *(télécarte)*, for 50 or 120 units, which are available from post offices, branches of *France Télécom*, authorised cigarette sales point *(bureaux de tabac)* and newsagents, can be used for inland and international calls. Calls can be received at phone boxes where the blue bell sign is shown.

Internal calls

Telephone numbers in France have 10 digits, of which the first two indicate the region as follows -

01	Paris and the Paris region
02	northwest France
03	northeast France
04	southeast France and Corsica
05	southwest France.

The ringing tone is a series of long tones; the engaged (busy) tone is a series of short beeps.

International calls

To call Paris from abroad, dial the country code 33 + 1 + 8-digit number. For the provinces the country code 33 + 9-digit number (omit the initial zero).

When calling abroad from France dial 00, wait until the continuous tone recurs, then dial the country code and dialling code and the number of the correspondent. For international enquiries dial 00 33 12 + country code; there may be a wait of up to an hour.

To use a personal card dial BT – 00-0044   Mercury – 00-00944
AT & T – 00-0011   MCI – 00-0019.

Telephone rates from a public telephone at any time (approximate)
  – France to the UK – 3F/min
  – France to the USA and Canada – 4F

Periods when reduced rates are in force

to the UK	– Mondays to Fridays, 9.30pm to 8am
	– Saturdays from 2pm
	– Sundays and public holidays, all day.
to the USA and Canada	– lowest rates from 2am to noon all week
to Australia	– Mondays to Saturdays, 9.30pm to 8am
	– Sundays, all day.

International dialling codes

61	Australia	64	New Zealand
1	Canada	44	United Kingdom
353	Ireland	1	United States of America

Freephone/toll free numbers

In France numbers beginning 0 800 are free of charge.

Emergency numbers -

17 Police – 18 Fire *(pompiers)* – 15 Ambulance *(SAMU)*

Cellular phones – In France these have numbers which begin with 06. Two-watt (lighter, shorter reach) and eight-watt models are on the market, using the Itinéris (France Télécom) or SFR network. Cell phone rentals (delivery or airport pickup provided):

Ellinas Phone Rental	☏ 01 47 20 70 00
Euro Exaphone	☏ 01 44 09 77 78
Rent a cell Express	☏ 01 53 93 78 00

Shopping

Opening hours

The big stores and larger shops are open Mondays to Saturdays from 9am to 6.30 or 7.30pm. Smaller, individual shops may close during the lunch hour. Food shops – grocers, wine merchants and bakeries – are open from 7am to 6.30 or 7.30pm; some open on Sunday mornings. Many food shops close between 12 noon and 2pm and on Mondays. Hypermarkets usually open until 9pm or 11pm.

People travelling to the USA cannot import plant products or food, especially fruit and cheeses. Visitors returning home may import, tax-free, goods to the following total values

Americans	US$400 maximum
Canadians	CND$300 maximum
British	£136 maximum
Australians	AUS$400 maximum
New Zealanders	NZ$700 maximum.

Specialities

A catalogue of all the desirable products of France would make a very long list. The map in the Introduction – *Specialités et Vignobles* – shows the main centres for craftwork and local produce.

Some specialist producers are listed in the Practical Information sections in the chapters on the large towns.

For further information on markets, local produce and crafts see below.

Wildlife – Parc National du Mercantour

Mercantour national park, the last of the French National State Parks, was created in 1979 and covers an area of 68 500ha – 169 267 acres in the Alpes-Maritimes and Alpes-de-Haute-Provence *départements* (encompassing 22 and 6 *communes* from each respectively).

The park, which was once the French part of Italian royal hunting grounds and extended over both sides of the Alps prior to 1861, has been twinned since 1987 with the Italian Argentera nature park with which it has a common border of 33km - 20.5 miles. These two organisations share the management of introducing and monitoring animal species in the whole of this protected region. In this way, ibexes which have wintered in the Argentera arrive to spend the summer months in the Mercantour, while wild sheep (moufflons) do the opposite.

The Mercantour is a high, mountainous park, with terraces from 500m to 3 143m – 1 640ft to 10 312ft in altitude, offering breathtaking views of natural amphitheatres, glacial valleys and deep gorges.

It contains a rich variety of flora; over 2 000 species have been counted there, including **Saxifraga florulenta** which was for a time the park's emblem. All levels of vegetation are present, from olive trees to rhododendrons and the gentians which make such a splendid display of colour in the spring.

Fauna includes some 6 300 chamois, nearly 300 ibex and 1 250 moufflons which are well adapted to the Mediterranean climate. The wooded slopes at medium altitude are home to various deer and smaller mammals such as hares, ermines and marmots. Feathered members of this community include black grouse, ptarmigans and splendid examples of birds of prey such as the short-toed eagle *(circaëtus)* and the golden eagle. The reintro-

Marmot

278

PARC NATIONAL DU MERCANTOUR

P **Maison du Parc**

🛈 **Tourist information centre**

M **Museum or exhibition**

🛡 **Main shelters or overnight accommodation**

🚶 **Footpath**

duction of the bearded vulture was achieved successfully in the summer of 1993. There are now five birds in the park. For the first time in France since 1942, wolves have returned of their own accord to live in the park. They come from Italy where this protected species is now spreading.

The 600km – 373 miles of footpaths laid out within the park's boundaries enable tourists to discover the park on foot. These include the GR5 and the GR52A④, or the Mercantour panoramic footpath which crosses the Merveilles valley, as well as footpaths at l'Authion, Le Boréon and Madone de Fenestre.

This guide describes the regions of the Vésubie and Merveilles valleys, the Authion massif and Turini forest.

Mountain bikes are not allowed in the central area of the park.

Recreation

OFFSHORE

Boat trips

There are regular ferries to the Iles de Bendor, des Embiez, d'Hyères and de Lérins, and also boat trips from the following resorts

Port of embarkation	Destination
BANDOL	Les Embiez – Toulon via Cap Sicié Gare maritime ☎ 04 94 32 51 41 Cassis and the Calanque d'En-Vau via la Ciotat – Whole day to the Château d'If and Le Frioul – Underwater exploration with l'Aquascope (Cie Atlantide)
SANARY	Iles des Embiez – Toulon Anchorage and Cap Sicié – Calanques de Cassis
Le LAVANDOU	Ile du Levant
CAVALAIRE	Iles d'Hyères
St TROPEZ	Iles d'Hyères (Cie MMG ☎ 04 94 96 51 00) – Ste Maxime (shuttle) – St-Raphaël (in summer)
Ste MAXIME	St-Tropez (shuttle) – Iles d'Hyères
CANNES	Iles de Lérins – excursion to St-Tropez and Monaco on a catamaran (Cie Chanteclair ☎ 04 93 39 11 82)
JUAN LES PINS	Underwater viewing cruise off Cap d'Antibes (departure from Ponton Courbet)
NICE	Iles de Lérins – La Riviera (Cie Gallus ☎ 04 93 26 54 60)
MENTON	St-Jean-Cap-Ferrat (and Villefranche Bay) – Monaco (with and without stopping) (Cie Hippocampe ☎ 04 93 35 51 72)

Sailing

Most of the seaside resorts on the French Riviera, from Lecques to Menton, have well-equipped marinas, so that this coast is the best in France for sailing.

Although nearly every port has moorings with good facilities, the enthusiasm for sailing is such that enormous marinas have been constructed with extensive services to satisfy even the most exacting yachtsman. Ports providing over 1 000 berths are Bandol, Toulon, Hyères (Port-St-Pierre), La Londe (Port Miramar), Le Lavandou, St-Raphaël (Ste-Lucia), Cannes (Pierre Canto and the Vieux Port), St Laurent-du-Var and Antibes (Port-Vauban), which is the largest to date.

The marinas which are open to visiting crafts are marked on the Places to Stay Map at the beginning of the guide.

There are sailing clubs which provide lessons in most resorts; during the summer it is possible to hire craft with or without crew.

Port-Grimaud

On the ocean wave

Sailing boat

Speedboat

Traditional fishing boat

Motor yacht

Catamaran

Cabin cruiser

Motor launch

Luxury cruiser

The services available in each port are listed in the *Guide du plaisancier* en Méditerranée, published by Ed France Yachting Service.

Further information available from each port authority and from the Fédération Française de Voile, 55 avenue Kléber, 75084 Paris Cedex 16 ☎ 01 43 89 39 89.

Scuba diving

There are many clubs providing scuba diving lessons accompanied by instructors. The main centres are Bendor (Centre Padl is one of the largest in Europe), Le Pradet (Garonne Beach), Giens (la Tour Fondue), Sanary, Cavalaire, Ramatuelle (l'Escalet), St-Tropez, Ste-Maxime, St-Raphaël, La Napoule, Cannes and Villefranche.

A brochure listing all the local clubs is available from La Maison du tourisme du Golfe de St-Tropez in Gassin (☎ 04 94 43 42 10).

Excursions to explore the Mediterranean flora and fauna are provided by the Centre du Rayol-Canadel and the Parc National de Port-Cros.

The Fédération Française d'Études et de Sports sous-marins (24 quai de Rive-Neuve, 13007 Marseille ☎ 04 91 33 99 31) is an umbrella organisation, comprising 100 local clubs, which publishes a comprehensive yearbook covering all sub-aqua activity in France.

Information also available from Comité régional Côte d'Azur des sports sous-marins, Cap Blanc, Port de Bormes, 83230 Bormes-les-Mimosas ☎ 04 94 71 63 43.

Finest underwater landscapes – The coves of the Maures and the Esterel on the Var coast and the clear water round the Iles d'Hyères are invitations to discover the charm of the Mediterranean *(la Grande Bleu)* and of the silent underwater world. The volume of marine traffic over the centuries has turned the seabed into a museum of shipwrecks – about 100 ships and upwards of 20 aircraft have sunk along this coast. Most of them are lying in more than 20m – 65ft of water, accessible only to experienced divers who are members of specialist clubs. Other wrecks, lying in shallower water, can easily be visited by amateurs. Information about underwater centres near such wrecks is available from the Fédération des sports sous-marins in Marseille.

The wrecks of the Provençal coast and their history are described in *Naufrages en Provence* by J-P Joncheray.

Underwater fishing

The abundance of creeks along the coast should satisfy all demands. The sport is strictly regulated; the essential regional regulations are given below.

Underwater fishing is forbidden in certain areas of the coastline from early November to the beginning of March. It is essential to check with the local maritime authority – Toulon, 244 avenue de l'Infanterie de Marine ☎ 04 94 46 92 00 and Nice, 22 quai Lunel ☎ 04 92 00 41 50.

Some areas are out of bounds to fishing all the year round – south coast of St-Mandrier Peninsula, part of Porquerolles Island, Port-Cros Island and its neighbouring islets.

There are underwater nature reserves, marked by buoys, near Golfe-Juan, Beaulieu and Roquebrune-Cap-Martin. Villefranche Anchorage is a protected area. Underwater fishers must comply with general fishing regulations and bear in mind that in the Mediterranean Sea

- it is illegal to catch or fish for grouper and oysters (for mother-of-pearl)
- it is illegal to fish for sea urchins from 1 May to 30 September
- it is illegal to pursue or catch marine mammals (dolphins, porpoises), even without intending to kill them
- the minimum size of catch is 12cm – 4.72in (except for sardines, anchovies), 18cm – 7.09ins for crayfish.

Whatever the circumstances, it is illegal to be in possession of both diving equipment and an underwater gun.

Underwater safety – Enthusiasm for exploring the superb underwater landscape of the Riviera should not blind the occasional diver to the need to observe certain regulations

- never dive alone, nor after eating a heavy meal, nor after drinking alcohol or fizzy drinks, nor when tired
- avoid shipping lanes and areas used by wind-surfers
- when signalling for help, make it known that it is a diving accident so that the rescuers can prepare a decompression chamber, which is the only effective aid in diving accidents, even minor ones.

Sea fishing

In Sanary, in the Cogolin Marina and in Ste-Maxime there are organisations through which visitors may hire out boats and professional fishermen for sea fishing or join a sea fishing party (usually in summer from 6am to 10am).

Underwater exploration

Other seaside activities

The long stretches of Var coast, consisting of beaches where the *mistral* blows, have become some of the most popular locations in the Mediterranean for those who enjoy riding the waves on a **sail-board** (wind-surfing) or **a funboard**; the shorter board used for the latter makes acrobatics possible. Almanarre Beach on the west side of the Giens Peninsula has become a mecca for funboarders and played host to the World Championships. More technical skill is required on other beaches such as Six-Fours-les-Plages and the two sides of Cap Nègre.

For a different view of their favourite beaches, holidaymakers can fearlessly indulge in the joys of **parascending** – flying over the water below a parachute which is towed by a motorboat. The aim is to stay in the air for as along as possible and as high as possible. Instruction in this sport is available on nearly all the organised beaches, where there is enough wind.

Jet-skiing is practised on certain stretches of coast, which have been carefully chosen and are not accessible from the land. The sport provides a superb experience of moving alone at speed. It is, however, strictly regulated

– machines must be 150m – 164yds apart;
– machines may operate only during the day;
– machines may operate between 300m – 328yds outside the channels and up to 1 nautical mile
– in future pilots must hold a proficiency (Mer) certificate. Most of the large resorts offer jet-ski hire by the hour or the half day. It is also possible to hire sea canoes in Salins d'Hyères and certain resorts on the Var coast.

Motor vessels are forbidden within 300m – 328yds of the shore (except in the access channels) and must not exceed 5 knots in certain restricted areas (Iles d'Hyères, Iles de Lérins et Villefranche Anchorage). Elsewhere the top speed is 10 knots.

Coastal walks

Before the recent building boom the famous Customs Path ran all along the Riviera coast; some particularly picturesque sections still survive and have been developed by the Coast Conservancy *(Conservatoire du Littoral)*.

There are several signed country footpaths along the Var coast, of which about 10, from Bandol to St-Aygulph, are described in a Topo-Guide published by the Fédération Française de la Randonnée Pédestre.

INLAND

Rambling

A network of waymarked paths covers the region described in this guide.

GR (Grande Randonnée) paths, which are fully open only from the end of June to early October, are for experienced ramblers who are competent in mountain conditions

- **GR 5**, the oldest and most majestic, which terminates in Nice after crossing Europe; the last section from Nice to St-Dalmas-Valdeblore passes through Aspremont, Levens, the Vésubie gorge and Madone d'Utelle.
- **GR 52**, from St-Dalmas-Valdeblore to Menton via le Boréon, la Vallée des Merveilles, Turini Forest, Sospel and Val Rameh Tropical Garden
- **GR52A**, among the peaks in the eastern part of the Parc national du Mercantour beyond the Col de Tende

  Other paths, open all year, for walkers of all levels of competence
- **GR 4**, from Grasse via Gréolières and Entrevaux to the Verdon Gorge
- **GR 51**, nicknamed "the Mediterranean balcony", from Castellar (east of Menton) to Col de la Cadière (Estérel) providing panoramic views of the coast from the first ridge
- **GR 510**, entirely in the Alpes-Maritimes region, from Breil-sur-Roya via Sospel, Villars-sur-Var, Puget-Rostand, Roquestéron, St-Auban and Escragnolles to St-Cézaire-sur-Siagne, discovering another valley dotted with hill villages at each stage of the 10 days' ramble
- **GR 9**, from Signes through the Massif des Maures to St-Pons-les-Mûres
- **GR 99**, from Toulon through the Brignolais country to the Verdon Gorge
- **GR 90**, the shortest, from Le Lavandou through the Massif des Maures to Notre-Dame-des-Anges, where it meets the GR 9.

Various bodies organise rambles adapted to the competence of those taking part.

Week-long rambles in the Vallée des Merveilles are organised by Destination Merveilles, Le Grand Provence, 38 rue Clément Roussal, 06100 Nice ☎ 04 93 16 08 72.

Topo-guides for the Grandes and Petites Randonnées are published by the Fédération Française de la Randonnée Pédestre – Comité National des Sentiers de Grande Randonnée, and are obtainable from the Centre d'Information, 64 rue de Gergovie, 75014 Paris ☎ 01 45 45 31 02 and from the Comité départemental des Alpes-Maritimes de randonnée pédestre ☎ 04 93 66 39 48 (Monsieur Santerre).

Lac Vert, Fontanalbe

A. Philippon/EXPLORER

Over the frontier

The old royal hunting ground of the Sardinian monarchy extended until the Second World War over the two slopes of the Mercantour and the Marguareis. Since then the Italian section has been administered as a nature reserve with an active policy for the conservation of species and habitats. Two large natural parks have been created – **Parco dell'Argentera**, the largest, and **Alta Valle Pesio**, further east. Together with the Parc du Mercantour they have conducted a campaign for the reintroduction of endangered species – bearded vulture and ibex. In the Parco dell'Argentera there are many "royal" botanical paths which are easily accessible to ramblers from the French side of the border by the frontier passes – Col de la Lombarde and Col de Tende. From the latter pass two paths *(each about 3 hours)* follow the peaks towards Rocca dell'Abisso (2 755m – 9 039ft – west) and Cima di Pepino (2 335m – 7 661ft – east).

The **Alta Valle Pesio** park, in the Marguareis, is the wildest and least easy to reach from France. Ramblers should branch into the northeast route from Limone-Piemonte or go up the valley from Savone.

The Vermenagna valley which extends from Col de Tende to the Cuneo plain is still within the range of the Provençal culture; Provençal spectacles *(Roumiage de Provenço)* are held in Grana valley in July. Among the specialities of the district is a famous cheese, Castelmagno, and hand-made cutlery, such as the Vernantino pocket knife.

Parco naturale regionale dell'Argentera – Corso Dante Livio Bianco 5 – 12010 Valdieri (CN) ☎ 39 171 97 397

Parco naturale regionale Alta Valle Pesio e Tanaro – Via Sta Anne 34 – 12013 Chiusa Pesia (CN) ☎ 39 171 73 40 21

Tourist Office in Limone-Piemonte – Via Roma (CN) ☎ 39 171 92 101.

Riding

Ligue Provence – Côte d'Azur de tourisme équestre – 19 boulevard Victor Hugo, 06130 Grasse ☎ 04 93 42 62 98

Comité départemental d'équitation de randonnée des Alpes-Maritimes – Mas de la Jumenterie, route de St-Cézaire, 06460 St-Valleir-de-Thiey ☎ 04 93 42 63 98 (Mr Desprey)

Comité départemental du tourisme équestre du Var – Centre de tourisme équestre de l'Estérel, les 3 Fers, Domaine du Grenouillet, Agay 83700 St Raphaël ☎ 04 94 82 75 28

Association varoise de développement du tourisme de randonnée (AVDTR) – 1 boulevard Foch, 83000 Draguignan ☎ 04 94 68 97 66, which publishes the brochure *Guide annuaire de cavalier varois*

Exploring the border on horseback – This is an unusual way of exploring the Massif du Mercantour. There is a waymarked route on the **Franco Italian Natural Spaces Equestrian Itinerary** *(Itinéraire Équestre des Espaces Naturels Franco-Italiens – Itinerario Equestre degli Soazi Naturali Franco-Italiani)* from St-Martin-Vésubie through the Italian parks – Argentera and Alta Valle Pesio – to Certosa di Pesio; there are 10 staging posts with facilities for riders and their mounts.

Practical information is available from the Parc du Mercantour and the Parco dell'Argentera Information Offices *(see Rambling)*.

The Parc du Mercantour publishes a brochure containing various bridle routes and staging posts in the Argentera and Mercantour highlands.

Winter sports

It is only a short distance (less than 2 hours by car) from the coast to a range of winter sports stations

La Colmiane-Valdeblore

Boréon-St-Martin-Vésubie

Peïra-Cava

L'Audibergue

La Gordolasque-Belvédère

Turini-Camp d'Argent

Gréolières-les-Neiges

There are off-piste runs near la Haute-Roya – La Brigue (alt 900m – 2 953ft) and Tende-Val Casterino (alt 1 500m – 4 921ft).

The proximity of the Italian ski resort, Limone-Piemonte, which can be reached by rail, means that many types of snow sport are available.

Mountaineering

There is a large variety of climbing in the highlands from the Pre-Alps of Nice via the steep faces of the *baous* in the Var valley and the Rock in Roquebrune-sur-Argens to the rock faces of the Verdon Gorge.

Guided excursions in rock-climbing, mountaineering, rambling, downhill skiing and overland skiing are organised by
– the Club Alpin Français, 25 rue Victor-Clappier, 83000 Toulon
– the Club Alpin Français, 14 avenue Mirabeau, 06000 Nice ☎ 04 93 62 59 99

- the Association des guides et accompagnateurs des Alpes Méridionales
  Roquebillière ☎ 04 93 03 44 30
  St-Martin-Vésubie ☎ 04 93 03 26 60
  Tende ☎ 04 93 04 69 22 or 04 93 04 68 72.
- Bureau des Guides de la Côte d'Azur
  3 rue de la Suisse, 06000 Nice ☎ 04 93 3964 77
  06450 St-Martin-Vésubie ☎ 04 93 03 26 60
- Compagnie des guides du Mercantour
  place du Marché, 06450 St-Martin-Vésubie
  Tende ☎ 04 93 04 77 85

Hunting

For details on hunting, contact
- St-Hubert Club de France, 10 rue de Lisbonne, 75008 Paris ☎ 01 45 22 38 90
- local offices of the Fédération départementale de chasse.

Caving and potholing

The Var has many sites of original configuration; the Siou Blanc plateau is a catalogue of variants of chasms and potholes which the amateur can explore. Among these is the deepest pothole in the region (350m – 1 148ft). The Grotte de Mouret, near Draguignan, is useful for practice.
In the Alpes-Maritimes, both the Pays Grassois and the Caussols Plateau offer many opportunities for seasoned cavers. The legendary Massif du Marguareis (northeast of Tende), the site of the exploits of the potholer Michel Siffre in the 1960s, is still a paradise for the experienced caver. This immense chalky plateau is peppered with sinkholes, with vertiginous rock faces overhanging the Italian slopes, and contains deep chasms (more than 900m – 2 953ft).
Information available from
- **Comité départemental de spéléologie du Var**, l'Hélianthe, rue Émile-Olivier, 83000 Toulon ☎ 04 94 31 29 43
- **Comité départemental de spéléologie des Alpes-Maritimes**, boulevard Paul-Montal, bâtiment 5, l'Alsace, 06200 Nice ☎ 04 93 62 09 54
- Spéléologie divisions of the Club Alpin Français in Nice or Toulon.

Water sports

Canoeing – Some of the rivers in the Alpes-Maritimes can be explored by canoe throughout the year but the best time is in spring. In any season beware of sudden floods caused by heavy rain upstream.
The most attractive stretches of river are to be found just inside the boundaries of the Mercantour or near St-Martin-Vésubie. Excursions shooting rapids through gorges accompanied by experts are organised by the Toulon division of the Club Alpin Français. Those offering the best services are awarded the title **Point-Canoë-Nature** by the Fédération Française de canoë-kayak; list available from the federation and on Minitel 3615 Canoë 24.
Fédération Française de canoë-kayak, 87 quai de la Marne, 94340 Jonville-le-Pont ☎ 02 48 89 39 89.

Canyoning – The most attractive stretches of water provided by the Alpes-Maritimes for this activity, which combines rock-climbing, potholing and swimming in running water, are to be found within the Parc du Mercantour and in St-Martin-Vésubie. There are also two exceptional sites in the valley of the Haute-Roya near Saorge – La Maglia (through caves) and la Bendola (2 days in the water). Canyoning is strictly forbidden in the central part of the Parc du Mercantour.
Between St-Martin-Vésubie and its confluence with the Var, the River Vésubie offers a variety of canyons – Duranus, the agreeable site at l'Imberguet, la Bollène and Gourgas, which is technically demanding.
The Estéron, an eastern tributary of the Var, provides classic stretches in exceptional settings between Roquestéron and St-Auban.
The network of rivers in the Var provides many opportunities for canyoning, with 11 authorised sites of varying difficulty suitable to all levels of competence. The Destel Gorge, between Caramy and Carcès, the lower stretches of the Jabron (downstream of Trigance) and the Pennafort Gorge are suitable for beginners. Seillans-la-Cascade, the Nartuby and the Destéou in the Maures demand greater skill.
At all times of the year there is a risk of sudden increases in the volume of water following a storm upstream and the sudden release of retained water.
Canyoning trips with guides are organised by the Toulon branch of the Club Alpin Français.
Information is also available from the Comité départemental de spéléologie du Var (☎ 04 94 87 42 72).

Lakes – The largest lake in the Estérel, **Lac de St-Cassien** (430ha – 1 062 acres), not only supplies electricity and water to the eastern Var and provides water for the fire-fighting aircraft but also has a nature reserve at the west end with a reed-bed where more than 150 species of over-wintering migrating seabirds have been recorded. There are facilities for wind-surfing and pedalo – tuition from the base and equipment for hire from the open-air cafés along the sometimes steep banks; motorised vessels are forbidden.

Centre régional d'entraînement et de formation à l'Aviron – Lac de St Cassien 83440 Montaurous ☎ 04 94 76 43 08

The **Lac de Carcès** (100ha – 247 acres) is a reservoir formed by a dam and fed by the River Argens. There is a pleasant wooded road along the eastern bank; the opposite bank, more rural, is much used by fishermen. Canoeing in kayaks is permitted.

Coarse angling – Local and national fishing regulations apply to fishing in lakes (Carcès and St Cassien) and in rivers (Gapeau, Réal Martin, Argens, Roya, Bévéra etc). It is also advisable to join the Association de Pêche et de Pisciculture in the area in question by paying the annual fees appropriate to the form of fishing practised and then by buying a daily permit from an authorised vendor.

Trout fishing is permitted from the 2nd Saturday in March to the 3rd Sunday in September; pike fishing is allowed only between 31 January and 15 April. Fishing for common grayling in the Siagne is banned through the year.

Up-to-date information available from
- **Fédération départemental du Var** ☎ 04 94 69 05 66
- **Fédération départemental des Alpes-Maritimes** ☎ 04 93 72 06 04
- **Conseil Supérieur de la Pêche**, 134 avenue Malakoff, 75016 Paris ☎ 01 45 01 20 20, which provides a leaflet *Pêche en France*.

Cycling and mountain biking

The diversity of terrain inland and the network of cycle tracks along the coast and in the Massifs of the Estérel and the Maures are very popular with mountain bike enthusiasts. Many organisations, hotels and clubs in the region hire out this kind of bicycle and provide details of local cycle tracks. Lists of suppliers are also available from local tourist offices.

Main railway stations – Antibes, Bandol, Cagnes-sur-Mer, Cannes, Hyères, Juan-les-Pins, St-Raphaël – hire out various types of bicycle, which can be returned to a different station.

The regulations concerning admission to the Parc du Mercantour apply also to cyclists; details available from the Maisons du Parc and the headquarters (23 rue d'Italie, Nice).

The Comité départemental du Tourisme du Var distributes a leaflet describing more than 20 signed routes for cyclists; among the principal ones are
- Roof of the Var *(Toit du Var)* (70km – 43 miles)
- Bauxite Road *(route de la bauxite)* (80km – 50 miles)
- North face of the Maures *(l'Ubac des Maures)* (80km – 50 miles)
- Maures chestnut woods *(châtaigneraies des Maures)* (90km – 56 miles)

One of the most famous mountain biking events in Europe is the Roc d'Azur at Ramatuelle with a height difference of nearly 200m – 656ft (50km – 31 miles long) *(see Calendar of Events)*.

Comité départemental de cyclotourisme des Alpes-Maritimes, 22 bis rue Trachel, 06000 Nice ☎ 04 93 82 16 39 (Mr Rény Bernage)

Comité départemental de cyclotourisme du Var, Les Ibis, bâtiment A, avenue de Bellegou, 83000 Toulon ☎ 04 94 46 00 25 (Mr J-Marc Pappon)

Fédération Française de Cyclotourisme, 8 rue Jean-Marie-Jégo, 75013 Paris ☎ 01 45 80 30 21.

Aerial sports

Hang-gliding, parachuting and ultra-light craft – There are about 20 suitable sites for parachuting, hang-gliding *(vol libre)* and ultra-light craft *(planeur ultra léger motorisé)*. For a list of centres consult
- Minitel 3615 FFLV
- **Comité départemental de vol libre varois**, Domaine de la Limatte, 83870 Signes ☎ 04 94 90 86 13
- **Fédération Française de vol libre**, 4 rue de Suisse, 06000 Nice ☎ 04 93 88 62 89
- **Fédération Française de Planeur Ultra Léger Motorisé**, 96 bis rue Marc-Sangnier, 94700 Maison-Alfort ☎ 05 49 81 74 43.

Gliding – The main gliding centre, which is run by l'Association aéronautique Provence-Côte d'Azur, is near Fayence where the aerological conditions are exceptional. It has become the leading gliding centre in Europe and has contributed to the rapid development of glider aerobatics. Each year champions from all over the world demonstrate their skill at the *Open de France de Planeur*.

- **Association aéronautique Provence-Côte d'Azur**, 83440 Fayence ☎ 04 94 76 00 68.

Air trips – It is possible to fly over part of the Riviera such as the Bay of St-Tropez, the Estérel, the Iles de Lérins, Monaco and the Verdon Gorge.

For details of timetables and fares contact the following companies, all based at the international airport of Cannes-Mandelieu, 06150 Cannes-la-Bocca
- **Compagnie Air Nice** ☎ 04 93 90 40 26, Cannes-Mandelieu Airport, 06150 Cannes la Bocca
- **Toulon-Hyères Airport** ☎ 04 94 22 81 60.

Short trips over the Riviera by **helicopter** are available from
- **Héli-air-Monaco**, Monaco-Fontvieille heliport ☎ 00 377 92 05 00 50.

Unusual Sites and Themed Itineraries

UNUSUAL VIEWS OF THE COTE D'AZUR

Riviera Caves – The limestone region of the Pays Grassois (especially the Caussols Plateau) boasts many interesting geological features dating from different periods – the caves *(grottes)* at St-Cézaire *(see GRASSE)*, the potholes within gigantic limestone crevices such as the Grotte des Audides *(see CABRIS)* or the original caves consisting of a succession of natural dams *(gours)* such as the Grotte de Baume Obscure *(see St-VALLIER-de-THIEY)*. The **Grottes de Villecroze** near Draguignan *(see VILLECROZE)* are formed of tufa.

Other caves, which are accessible with adequate equipment and some technical knowledge, belong in the caving category *(see above)*. People with no caving experience can receive an impression of the activity in the first section (about 12m – 39ft) of the **Embut de Caussols** (*embut* is the Provençal word for swallowhole).

Military Fortifications of the Alpes-Maritimes – The strategic significance of the frontier zone in the southeast, identified by Vauban, was exploited from 1880 onwards by the system of defence begun by Sérés de Rivières. The project was completed and improved from 1929 by its integration into the Maginot line which defended the eastern frontier from Dunkirk to Menton. The whole construction gives an interesting view of military architecture in the 19C and 20C. Some of the buildings have been disarmed, restored by associations and are accessible to visitors
- Fort de Ste-Agnès *(see MENTON)*
- Fort du Barbonnet *(see FORET DE TURINI)*
- Fort Suchet (19C), the only one which can be visited *(see FORET DE TURINI)*
- Fort St-Roch *(see SOSPEL)*.

Other less interesting forts make pleasant destinations for walks with fine views. *Visitors should bear in mind that, although the buildings of the Maginot line appear to be in good condition, they may conceal indoor wells or dangerous passages. Some properties are private property as they have been acquired by private individuals.* In the highly strategic sector of l'Authion, near the Col de Turini *(see FORET DE TURINI)*, several structures designed by Sérés de Rivières have survived and can be reached by the loop road which encircles the Massif
- Fort des Mille Fourches
- La Forca
- Redoute des 3 Communes (1897), the first building constructed of reinforced concrete.

From Mont Chauve d'Aspremont *(see NICE Hinterland)* there is a brilliant view of the whole coast in ideal high-pressure conditions. On the summit (854m – 2 802ft) is a Sérés de Rivières fort with a monumental south façade typical of the period; it is occupied by the Service des Télécommunications. Mont Chauve de Tourette is visible further north capped by a fort of similar period.

The section near Col de Tende, which was Italian from 1860 to 1947, is an impressive example of the Italian system of defence. The remarkable central fort is set on top of the col and approached by the narrow road which branches off by the entrance to the road tunnel; each of its façades has a different architectural style. The interior *(access difficult)* resembles a small town, self-sufficient in supplies.

On the track of Macaron – The old track bed of one of the dismantled sections of the pine-cone train *(train des pignes)*, which linked Toulon to St-Raphaël from early in the 20C to 1950, is open to walkers. Although the track and stations have mostly disappeared owing to the effects of time and events, such as the allied landings at the end of the Second World War, works of art and some stations (Carqueiranne) have survived. The tunnels are often used by walkers as short cuts, providing unusual and surprising glimpses of the Maures Coast.

FOREST PARKS

All along the Alpes-Maritimes coast there are islands of greenery *(parcs forestiers départementaux)* provided for walkers of all ages
- **Parc de la Grande-Corniche** à Èze (access from Col d'Èze on the Grande Corniche)
- **Parc de Vaugrenier** (access by N 7 between Antibes and Baie des Anges Marina)
- **Parc de la Vallée de la Brague** (at the northern end of Biot village)
- **Parc du San Peyre** (from La Napoule towards A 8 motorway and a left turn into Route du Cimetière), a former look-out post (alt 131m – 430ft) which offers a superb panorama of Cannes Bay
- **Parc de la pointe de l'Aiguille** (car park on N 98 at the edge of Théoule).

THEMED ITINERARIES

Route Historique des Hauts-Lieux de Provence – a circuit from St-Maximin-la-Ste-Baume via Draguignan and Les Arcs to Fréjus returning along the coast to Toulon, organised by an association at the Office de Tourisme 83460 Les Arcs sur Argens ☎ 04 94 73 37 30.

Route des Côtes de Provence – *See CRAFTS and FOOD AND DRINK.*

FOR CHILDREN AND THEIR ESCORTS

For a change from the beach, on cloudy days or when the *mistral* is blowing, there are many attractions all along the Riviera – leisure pools, animal parks and miniature collections. For the opening times of the main attractions see the Admission Times and Charges *(below)*.

Leisure pools

- Parc nautique Niagara, route du Canadel, 83310 La Môle ☎ 04 94 49 58 87
- Aquasplash, RN7, 06600 Antibes ☎ 04 93 33 49 49
- Aquatica, RN98, 83600 Fréjus ☎ 04 53 58 58
- Aqualand, 559 chemin départemental, 83270 St-Cyr-sur-Mer ☎ 04 94 32 09 09

Animal collections

- Sanary-Bandol – Zoo
- Toulon – Zoo du Mont-Faron
- La Londe-les-Maures – Jardin d'Oiseaux tropicaux (see HYÈRES)
- Gonfaron – Village des Tortues (see Massif des MAURES)
- Fréjus – La Jungle des Papillons, La Petite Ferme, le Golf Adventureland and Marineland
- St-Jean-Cap-Ferrat – Chimpanzee shows at the Zoo
- Monaco – Jardin d'Acclimatation

Miniature parks

- Brignoles – Parc Mini-France
- Nice – Parc des Miniatures (boulevard Impératrice Eugénie)

Specialist fairs in the Var

2 February	Grimaud	Candlemas fair
14 April	Six-Fours-les-Plages	Plant fair
Ascension Day	Grimaud	Wool fair
8 June	Les Issambres	St Médard fair
24 June	Le Beausset	Leatherwork fair
1st Sunday in July	Trigance	Craft fair
2-10 July	Draguignan	Olive fair
24 July	La Verdière	Dog fair
26 July	St-Tropez	St Anne's fair
mid-August	Seillans	Decorated earthenware fair
17-18 August	Barjols	Leatherwork fair
28 August	La Garde-Freinet	Pottery market
1st weekend in September	Le Val	Sausage fair
2 September	La Garde	Garlic and livestock fair
8-9 September	Cogolin	Provençal fair
19 September	Lorgues	St Ferréol fair
29 September	Many villages	Michaelmas fairs
6 October	Fréjus	Garlic fair
Monday after 11 November	Collobrières	St Martin's fair
3rd Sunday in November	Taradeau	New wine *(vin nouveau)* fair
30 November	Ramatuelle	St Andrew's fair

Santons fairs in the Var

These are exhibitions by craftsmen, who make *santons* for sale; *Santons* are the human and animals figures which make up a Christmas crib.

Carqueiranne	2nd weekend in December
La Celle	last weekend in November
Draguignan	a week before Christmas in Bon-Pasteur chapel
Entrecasteaux	1st fortnight in December
Fréjus	week before Christmas
La Garde	week before Christmas – *foire aux santons de la Farigouleto*
Hyères	mid-July
Ollioules	December at the Vieux-Moulin
Puget-Ville	2nd week of December
Signes	1st fortnight in November
Solliès-Ville	2nd fortnight in December at Moulin d'Oli
La Valette	2nd fortnight in December at Moulin d'Ardouvin

Great sporting events on the Riviera

End January	Monte-Carlo Automobile Rally
2nd or 3rd weekend in April	Sailing competitions in St-Tropez
Ascension weekend	Grand Prix Automobile de Formula 1 in Monaco
Last weekend in May	Truck driving Grand Prix (with trailer-handling displays) at Le Castellet circuit
3rd weekend of September	Bol d'Or (Golden Bowl for motorcycles) at Le Castellet circuit
1st weekend of October	La Nioulargue (sailing regatta) in St-Tropez
Weekend in mid-October	Roc'Azur (motorcross – championnat de VTT) in Ramatuelle

Scenic rail journeys

The single track main railway line between Nice and Cuneo in Italy crosses the old county of Nice passing through Peille, L'Escarène, Sospel, Breil-sur-Roya, Fontan-Saorge, St-Dalmas-de-Tende, Tende, Vievola and finally Limone in Italy. The track was built from 1920 onwards and incorporates some spectacular feats of engineering as it twists and turns through the dramatic mountain landscapes, sometimes even spiralling to change level. The train gives wonderful views which are not always obtainable from the road, particularly between L'Escarène and Sospel and between Breil and Tende along the rugged gorge of the River Roya. The line is 119km – 74 miles long; over a stretch of 85km – 53 miles it rises from sea-level to 1 279m – 4 196ft at the entrance to the tunnel bored through the Col de Tende. The French section of the line suffered extensive damage during the Second World War and the repair work was not completed until 1980. On the Italian side of the border, the line descends less steeply down to Cuneo through the charming Vermegnagna Valley.

The frequent service enables skiers to reach the Massif du Mercantour and spend the day skiing in the Italian winter sports resort of Limone-Piemonte.

There are at least 4 daily return services to and from Nice-Ville station. In Breil-sur-Roya the line joins the main line between Ventimiglia and Cuneo, which has better interconnections with the Italian train network; for timetable information ☎ 04 93 87 50 50.

Provençal railway

The famous pine-cone train *(train des pignes)* is named after the pine cones which were used as fuel to stoke the locomotives. It runs between Nice and Digne-les-Bains (150km – 93 miles) passing through Puget-Théniers, Entrevaux, Annot, St-André-les-Alpes. The single track was constructed from 1890 to 1911 and comprises 60 remarkable feats of engineering – metal bridges, viaducts, tunnels (one of which is 3.5km – 2.3 miles long). It is a relic of a vast regional network which early in the 20C served the whole inland area from Toulon to Draguignan. The journey, 2hr by train, 3hr by omnibus, passes through five valleys, offering fine views of the landscape and hill villages which are often difficult to reach by road.

All year round it is possible to take the train to Lac de Castillon, the Verdon Gorge and the winter sports stations in the Alpes-Maritimes *département*. From Plan-du-Var there is a service to the walking country in the Vésubie Valley. In summer the **Alpazur** service runs from Nice as far as Grenoble and there is a tourist steam train on the Puget-Théniers section. There are wayside halts at which walkers can leave or rejoin the train at the beginning and end of a day's rambling.

The violent storms in autumn 1994 caused serious damage to some sections of the line so it is advisable to check the availability of trains with the Chemins de Fer de Provence (4 rue Alfred Binet, 06000 Nice ☎ 04 93 82 10 17).

Scarassoui Viaduct, Nice-Cuneo railway

Crafts, souvenirs and activities

In the season many village and resorts organise craft courses – painting on porcelain in Le Cannet, weaving and woodwork in the Cannes district and regional cooking in St-Martin-Vésubie.
The names of the appropriate bodies are available from the Comités départementaux de tourisme in Toulon and in Nice.

PROVENCAL MARKETS

Typical markets, perfumed with thyme, tarragon and garlic, as well as the sound of cicadas and the fragrance of lavender, are part of the traditional vision of the South of France.
As a general rule during the summer season, stalls selling fruit and vegetables and craftwork can be found under the plane trees of even the smallest villages.
The most picturesque and lively markets of the Var and the days on which they take place are listed below.

Aups	Wednesdays, Saturdays
Bargemon	Thursdays
Le Beausset	Fridays (fair)
Bormes-les-Mimosa	Wednesdays
Brignoles	Saturdays
Callas	Tuesdays, Saturdays
Cogolin	Wednesdays, Saturdays (fair)
La Croix-Valmer	Sundays
Draguignan	Wednesdays, Saturdays
Fayence	Tuesdays, Thursdays (fair)
Fréjus	Wednesdays, Saturdays (fair)
La Garde	Tuesdays, Saturdays (fair)
Grimaud	Thursdays (fair)
Hyères	Tuesdays, Thursdays (fair)
Le Lavandou	Thursdays
Lorgues	Tuesdays
Le Luc	Fridays
Ramatuelle	Thursdays, Sundays (fair)
St-Tropez	Tuesdays, Saturdays (fair)
Ste Maxime	Thursdays (fair)
Toulon (Cours Lafayette)	daily
Tourtour	Tuesdays, Saturdays
Trans-en-Provence	Sundays
Villecroze	Thursdays (fair)

A list of traditional craft markets, where the products of the Var region are sold, is published annually by the Chambre des métiers, BP 69 – 83402 Hyères Cedex ☎ 04 94 21 00 57.

Crystallised fruit

WINE TASTING AND REGIONAL PRODUCE

The main areas where craftwork and local produce can be bought by visitors from the producers are shown on the map – Spécialités et Vignobles *(see INTRODUCTION)*.

Further information on specialist products

Sweets – Confiserie des Gorges du Loup, Le Pont du Loup, 06140 Tourrettes-sur-Loup ☎ 04 93 59 32 91

Marrons glacés and preserved chestnuts – Nouvelle Confiserie Azuréenne, boulevard Koenig, Collobrières ☎ 04 94 48 07 20

Glassware – Verrerie de Biot in Biot where it is possible to watch master glassblowers at work

Leather – The *tropézienne* sandal is the same model which has been made since 1927 by the same company in rue Clemenceau in St-Tropez.

Wine cooperative cellars – The **Côte de Provence** wine road winds its way through the vineyards; the wine cellars which are open for tasting are advertised on the roadside signs.

There are three vineyards on Ile de Porquerolles producing an AOC *(Appellation d'Origine contrôlée)* Côte de Provence wine and all offer wine tasting
- Domaine de l'Ile, the oldest
- Domaine Perzinsky
- Domaine Courtade.

Another wine road *(route du vin)* advertises the wine of Bandol.

Information from the Syndicat des Domaine en Appellation Bandol Contrôlée, Les Domaines du Bandol, allées Viven, 83150 Bandol ☎ 04 94 29 45 03.

The *vin de Bellet* is produced on the hillsides behind Nice round St-Romain-de-Bellet; it is on sale in the cellars which are open to the public; further information from the Nice Tourist Office.

Major summer aïoli festivals in the Var
(see INTRODUCTION : Food and Wine)

8-11 July	Châteauvieux
8 August	Mazaugues
9 August	Entrecasteaux (one of the largest)
12 to 15 August	La Motte du Var
12 to 15 August	La Celle
12 to 16 August	Collobrières
14 to 16 August	Ampus
20 to 22 August	Solliès-Ville
26 to 28 August	Fayence

(Admission by reserving and paying the entrance fee at the local Tourist Office).

Spotlight on the Riviera

Because of the abundance and diversity of its sites and the quality of the light, the whole of the Riviera seems to have been predestined to become a backdrop for all the varied scenarios of the film-makers. Here are the main locations which have featured in the history of the cinema.

The steep inlets of the south coast of the Ile de Porquerolles enabled J-P Belmondo to show what he was capable of in *Pierrot le fou*. Several districts of Hyères can be recognised in *Le Passager de la pluie* by René Clément, with Marlène Jobert, as well as in *Vivement Dimanche !* by Truffaut.

Roger Vadim launched both Brigitte Bardot and **St-Tropez** with his imaginative *Et Dieu créa la femme*. The resort is renowned in the world of the cinema and has provided the setting for many location shots – *La Collectionneuse* by Rohmer, *La Cage aux folles* by Édouard Molinaro and, of course, the celebrated series *Gendarme de St-Tropez* by Jean Girault with Louis de Funès, six episodes of which were filmed between 1964 and 1982.

The old port in Cannes still contains the galleon *Neptune* on which *Pirates* by Polanski was set in 1986; admirers of *Mélodie en sous-sol* by Henri Verneuil will be nostalgic at the sight of the Palm Beach casino.

The **Studios de la Victorine** in **Nice** have been closely involved in the birth and development of cinema on the Riviera *(see NICE)*. In 1929 *A propos de Nice* by **Jean Vigo** focussed on the contrast between the holidaymakers on the beach and the working-class districts.

La Nuit Américaine by Truffaut, partly filmed at the Studios de la Victorine, used several natural locations on the coast – Atlantic Hotel in Nice, the Vésubie Valley and the Nice hinterland.

The location shots for *Visiteurs du soir* were filmed in Tourrette-sur-Loup by Marcel Carné in 1942. Villefranche-sur-Mer and its picturesque *rue obscure* were used by Jean Cocteau in *Testament d'Orphée*. The medieval setting of **Sospel** was ideal for cloak-and-dagger scenes in *Masque de fer* (1962) by Henri Decoin with Jean Marais and, more recently, in *Sac de Billes* by Jacques Doillon.

Ever since *Max à Monaco* with Max Linder was made in Monaco in 1913, the principality has been popular with film-makers looking for exotic locations. The jet set clientele of the Monte-Carlo casino has inspired several directors, including Lubitsch who made *Monte-Carlo* with Jeanette MacDonald in 1930.

The impressive drops of the Grande Corniche made a marvellous backdrop for *La Main au collet* (1956), a thriller by Alfred Hitchcock with Cary Grant and Grace Kelly; this film also provides an unintended record of the urban development of the Principality. The comic adventures of *la Coccinelle* throughout the world had to include an episode in Monaco – *La Coccinelle à Monte-Carlo* (1977) by V McEveety. The film *Le Fils préféré* by Nicole Garcia (1994) with G Lanvin makes use of the natural setting of Nice, Menton and Grasse.

Provençal cinema – Local writers – Jean Aicard, Marcel Pagnol etc – and famous southern comedians are among those involved in the cinema who have drawn on local traditions. The location shots for *La Femme du boulanger* (1938) by Pagnol were filmed in Le Castellet.

Together with Pagnol, the film-maker André Hugon, who made the first French talking film, and who was fond of the Mediterranean coast, portrayed typical Provençal characters – *Maurin des Maures* (1932), *L'Illustre Maurin* and *Gaspard de Besse*.

The colourful pre-war setting of **Toulon** has made a contribution to Provençal cinema – *César* (1936) by Marcel Pagnol with the local film actor **Raimu** *(see COGOLIN)*, *L'Étrange Monsieur Victor* (1937) by J Grémillon, also with Raimu, and *Fleur d'amour* (1927) by Maurice Vandal, which portrays the formerly "hot" district of "Chicago". Other works made in the Var – *Les Démons de l'aube* (1945) by Yves Allégret about the Provençal landings and *En haut des marches* (1982) by Paul Vecchiali with Danielle Darrieux, the behind-the-scenes story of historical events in Toulon.

FURTHER READING

A Little Tour in France H James
Art Speak R Atkins
Bonjour Tristesse F Sagan
Collected Short Stories K Mansfield
Earthly Powers A Burgess
Fauvism S Whitfield
Fragrance: The Story of Perfume from Cleopatra to Chanel E T Morris
France Today J Ardagh
J'accuse G Greene
Matisse L Gowing
Perfume from Provence W Fortescue
Primitivism in 20C Art ed W Rubin
Provence and the Côte d'Azur J Bentley
Riviera was Ours P Howarth
Short Stories S Maugham
Tender is the Night F Scott Fitzgerald
The Rock Pool C Connolly

VIRTUAL RIVIERA

Here are a few selected sites for surfers.

www.beyond.fr "Beyond the French Riviera" is a site in English with lots of links, information on places, sports, history, lodging and more; practical and complete.

www.provenceweb.fr "Provence on the Web" includes an on-line magazine with featured villages, upcoming events, recipes, and touring suggestions (thematic tours, bike tours...) for do-it-yourselfers.

www.monaco.mc "Welcome to Monaco" brings the ancient principality up to date – but gives plenty of pages over to dynastic history (no gossip); Grand Prix updates; information for tourists and business travellers.

Calendar of events

Battle of flowers in Nice

J. Sierpinski/SCOPE

Penultimate weekend in May
Grasse . . . . Rose Festival

16-18 May
St-Tropez . . . . Processions *(Bravades)*

Late May to mid-July
Toulon . . . . Music Festival and International Music
Competition (wind instruments)

Mid-June
St-Tropez . . . . Spanish Procession *(Bravades)*

29 June
St-Tropez . . . . Votive Fishermen's Festival

Late June to late September
Peille . . . . Musical Evenings ☎ 04 93 79 90 32
Cagnes-sur-Mer . . . . International Art Festival

Early July to late September (even years)
Vallauris . . . . Biennial International Festival of Ceramic Art
(next in summer 2000)

1st or 2nd Sunday in July
Cap d'Antibes (La Garoupe) . . . . Seamen's Festival

July
Hyères . . . . Festival of Jazz and Lyric Song
Vence . . . . Classical Music Festival: ☎ 04 93 58 78 75

First fortnight in July
Nice (Cimiez: Amphitheatre) . . . . . Jazz in Nice: ☎ 04 93 87 16 28

1st weekend in July
Villefranche-sur-Mer . . . . Feast of St Peter

2nd Sunday in July
Tende . . . . Feast of St Eligius, patron saint of muleteers

Mid-July
Cannes (Le Suquet) . . . . Musical evenings

3rd Sunday in July
Villeneuve-Loubet . . . . Shingle Castle Competition

2nd fortnight in July
Juan-les-Pins-Antibes . . . . World Jazz Festival

July and August
Cannes . . . . American Festival. Sea Theatre: Jazz concerts,
variety shows and theatre
St-Tropez . . . . Music Festival (evenings)

Mid-July to mid-August
Cotignac . . . . La Falaise Theatre Festival

13 August
Vallauris . . . . Pottery Festival

Mid-August
Entrecasteaux . . . . Chamber Music Festival: ☎ 04 94 04 44 83

August
Menton . . . . Chamber Music Festival
(about 13 concerts are held in front of the Church
of St-Michel)

1st fortnight in August
Abbaye du Thoronet . . . . Poetry Festival
Ramatuelle . . . . Theatre Festival ☎ 04 94 79 20 50

1st Sunday in August
Grasse . . . . Jasmine Festival
Fréjus . . . . Grape Festival

5 August
Roquebrune-Cap-Martin . . . . . Passion Procession through the old village streets
(4pm to 6pm)

15 August

Bendor . . . . Fishermen's Festival

September

Cannes . . . . Royal Regattas

1st week-end in September

Peille . . . . Folk Festival *Festin des Baguettes* in honour of a young dowser-shepherd, who during a drought found water with a divining rod made from an olive branch

3rd weekend in September

Monaco . . . . Vintage Car Rally

1 October to 30 November

Gonfaron . . . . Chestnut Festival

1 to 3 October

Ollioules . . . . Olive Festival

16 to 30 October

Collobrières . . . . Chestnut Festival

21 to 23 October

Entrecasteaux . . . . Flower Show

23 October

La Garde-Freinet . . . . Chestnut Festival

19 November

Monaco . . . . Monaco's National Day

Last week in November

Cannes . . . . International Dance Festival

1st Sunday in December

Bandol . . . . Wine Festival

24 December

Lucéram . . . . The Shepherds' Christmas Offering and Provençal mass

Admission Times and Charges

The information given below applies to individual adults. Reduced rates may be available for families, children, students, senior citizens (old-age pensioners) and the unemployed. In some cases there is no admission charge on certain days. Special rates and admission times are generally available for group bookings. As admission times and charges are liable to alteration, the information printed below is for guidance only. Where it has not been possible to obtain up-to-date information, the times and charges from the previous edition of the guide are printed in italics ⊙.

Religious buildings are closed during services. Some churches and most chapels are often closed and admission times and charges are given if the interior is of special interest. Where visitors must be accompanied by the keyholder, a fee may be payable or a donation expected. In some places, guided tours of the whole town or historical districts only are available throughout the tourist season. These are mentioned at the start of the admission times and charges for the towns concerned. In Art and History Towns (Villes d'Art et d'Histoire) and Art Towns (Villes d'Art) 🅰, *they are conducted by lecturers from the Historic Monuments Association (Caisse Nationale des Monuments Historiques et des Sites).*

Where there are facilities for the disabled, the symbol &. *is shown after the place-name.*

Many shops, museums and other monuments may be closed or vary their times of admission on public holidays, listed below. National museums and art galleries are closed on Tuesdays, municipal museums are usually closed on Mondays. School holidays include mid-term breaks (10-14 days) in February and early November.

1 January – New Year's Day
Easter Sunday and Monday (Pâques)
1 May
8 May – Victory in Europe (1945) Day
Whit Sunday and Monday (Pentecôte)
Ascension Day (Ascension)
14 July – Bastille Day national holiday
15 August – Feast of the Assumption of the Virgin Mary (Assomption)
11 November – All Saints' Day (Toussaint)
25 December – Christmas (Noël)

A

ANTIBES 11 place du Général-de-Gaulle – 06200 ☎ 04 92 90 53 00

Musée Archéologique – *Open all year except November, daily except Mondays, 10am to 12 noon and 2pm to 6pm. Closed public holidays. 10F* ☎ *04 92 90 54 35.*

Musée Peynet – Open daily except Mondays, 10am to 12 noon and 2pm to 6pm. Closed public holidays. 20F (children under 15 and St Valentine's Day, no charge). ☎ 04 92 90 54 30.

Musée de la Tour des Arts et Traditions populaires – Open Wednesdays, Thursdays and Saturdays, April to September, 4pm to 7pm; October to March, 3pm to 5pm. 10F. ☎ 04 93 34 50 91.

Musée Picasso – Open daily except Mondays, June to September, 10am to 6pm; October to May, 10am to 12 noon and 2pm to 6pm. Closed public holidays. 30F. ☎ 04 92 90 54 20.

Excursions

Marineland – &. Open all year from 10am. Afternoon shows at 2.30pm and 4.30pm. Evening show at 6pm (according to time of year). Late evening show July and August at 9.45pm. 116F (children 3-12 78F); inclusive tickets covering neighbouring attractions available. ☎ 04 93 33 49 49.

Jungle des papillons – &. Open daily, 10am to sunset. 36F (child 24F). ☎ 04 93 33 49 49.

Parc Aqua-Splash – Open mid-June to early September, daily. 89F (adult). ☎ 04 93 33 49 49.

Cap d'ANTIBES

Sanctuaire de la Garoupe – &. Open daily, 9.30am to 12 noon and 2.30pm to 7pm; in winter 10am to 5pm. ☎ 04 93 67 36 01.

Phare de la Garoupe – Guided tour (30 min) all year, 3pm to 5pm (May to September, 6pm). ☎ 04 93 61 57 63.

Jardin Thuret – Open Mondays to Fridays, 8am to 6pm (5pm in winter). Closed public holidays. No charge. ☎ 04 93 67 88 66.

Musée naval et napoléonien – Open all year except October, daily except Saturday afternoons and Sundays, 9.30am to 12 noon and 2.15pm to 6pm. Closed public holidays. 20F. ☎ 04 93 61 45 32.

LES ARCS
🚊 place du général De Gaulle - 83460 ☎ 04 94 73 37 30

Excursions

Chapelle Ste-Roseline – Open daily except Mondays, June to September, 3pm to 7pm; March to May, 2pm to 6pm; October to February, 2pm to 5pm). No charge. ☎ 04 94 73 37 30.

ASPREMONT

Église – *Closed temporarily.*

AUPS
🚊 place de la Mairie - 83630 ☎ 04 94 70 00 80

Collégiale St-Pancrace – Usually open. To visit the Treasury, apply to the Office de tourisme or Mr le Curé, 2 rue Jules Philibert. ☎ 04 94 70 00 53.

Musée Simon-Ségal – Open 15 June to 15 September, daily, 10.30am to 12 noon and 4pm to 7pm. 13F. ☎ 04 94 70 01 95.

AURIBEAU-SUR-SIAGNE

Église – Open Sundays, 12 noon to 6.30pm. ☎ 04 93 42 25 46.

B

BANDOL

Notre-Dame du Beausset-Vieux – Open daily 2pm to 5.30pm. ☎ 04 94 98 61 53.

BEAULIEU-SUR-MER
🚊 place Georges Clémenceau - 06310 ☎ 04 93 01 02 21

Villa grecque Kérylos – Open July to September, daily, 10am to 7pm (6pm September); mid-February to June and October, daily, 10.30am to 12.30 and 2pm to 6pm; mid-December to mid-February, weekdays, 2pm to 6pm; during Christmas holidays, 10.30am to 12.30pm and 2pm to 6pm. Closed 1 January, 12 November to 20 December and 25 December. 40F. ☎ 04 93 01 01 44.

Île de BENDOR 🚊
allée Vivien à Bandol - 83150 ☎ 04 94 29 41 35

Access – Every 30 min from Bandol (7 min). 25F return. ☎ 04 94 29 44 34.

Exposition universelle des vins et spiritueux – Open April to September, daily except Wednesdays, 10am to 12 noon and 2pm to 6pm. No charge. ☎ 04 94 29 44 34.

BIOT 🚊 place de la Chapelle - 06410 ☎ 04 93 65 05 85

Musée National Fernand-Léger – ♿ Open daily except Tuesdays, 10am to 12.30pm and 2pm to 5.30pm. Closed 1 January, 1 May and 25 December. 30F. ☎ 04 92 91 50 20.

Villa Kerylos, Beaulieu-sur-Mer

BIOT

Bonsaï-arboretum – Open May to September, daily except Tuesdays, 10am to 12 noon and 3pm to 6.30pm; October to April, 10am to 12 noon and 2pm to 5.30pm. 25F. ☎ 04 93 65 63 99.

Verrerie de Biot – Open July and August, Mondays to Saturdays, 9am to 8pm, Sundays and public holidays, 10am to 1pm and 3pm to 7pm; September to June, Mondays to Saturdays, 9am to 6pm, Sundays and public holidays, 10.30am to 1pm and 2.30pm to 6.30pm. Closed 25 December. 20F. ☎ 04 93 65 03 00.

Musée de Biot – Open all year except November, Wednesdays to Sundays, 2.30pm to 6.30pm (2pm to 6pm out of season). Closed public holidays. 10F (no charge Sundays). ☎ 04 93 65 54 54.

BORMES-LES-MIMOSA   🖥 83230 ☎ 04 94 71 15 17

Musée «Arts et Histoire» – *Open July and August, Mondays and Wednesdays to Saturdays, 10am to 12 noon and 4pm to 6pm; Sundays, 10am to 12 noon; also Wednesday, Friday and Sunday evenings, 9pm to 11pm; September to June, Wednesdays, 10am to 12 noon and 3pm to 5pm; Sundays, 10am to 12 noon. 5F.* ☎ *04 94 71 56 60.*

BREIL-SUR-ROYA   🖥 06540 ☎ 04 93 04 99 76

Écomusée du haut-pays – *Open mid-June to mid-September, daily except Tuesdays, 10am to 12 noon and 3.30pm to 6.30pm. 17F.* ☎ *04 93 04 99 76.*

BRIGNOLES   🖥 place des Augustins - 83170 ☎ 04 94 69 01 78

Musée du pays Brignolais – Open daily except Mondays and Tuesdays, April to September, 9am to 12 noon and 2.30pm (3pm Sundays) to 6pm; October to March, 10am to 5pm. Closed public holidays. 20F. ☎ 04 94 69 45 18.

La BRIGUE

Chapelle de l'Assomption – *Closed temporarily.*

Chapelle de l'Annonciation : Musée du Trésor – *Open July and August, daily, 3pm to 6pm.*

Le BROC

Église – Guided tour daily on application to the town hall. ☎ 04 93 29 08 06.

C

CABASSE

Église St-Pons – Apply to the bar-tabac, place de la République, or on Wednesdays to the presbytery. ☎ 04 94 80 22 37.

CABRIS

Grottes des Audides – Autoguide tour July and August, daily, 10am to 12 noon and 12.30pm to 5.30pm; September, October and mid-February to June, daily except Mondays and Tuesdays, 2pm to 5.30pm; November to mid-February, telephone in advance. 25F. ☎ 04 93 42 64 15.

CAGNES-SUR-MER   🖥 6 boulevard Maréchal-Juin - 06800 ☎ 04 93 20 61 64

Église St-Pierre – Open daily, 2pm to 7pm. Closed on wet days. ☎ 04 93 20 67 14.

Chapelle N.-D.-de-Protection – Open all year except November, daily except Tuesdays and Fridays, 2pm to 5pm (6pm in winter). No charge. ☎ 04 93 20 87 29.

Château-Musée – *Open daily except Tuesdays, May to September, 10.30am to 12.30pm and 1.30pm to 6pm (5pm October to April). Closed 1 January, 20 October to 21 November and 25 December. 20F.* ☎ *04 93 20 85 57.*

Musée Renoir – Open daily except Tuesdays, May to September, 10.30am to 12.30 pm and 1.30pm to 6pm (5pm October to April). Closed 20 October to 9 November and 25 December. 20F. ☎ 04 93 20 61 07.

CALLAS

Église – Open Sundays on application to the parish priest of Bargemon.

CANNES   🖥 Palais des Festivals, 1 la Croisette - 06400 ☎ 04 93 39 24 53

Musée de la Castre – Open all year except January, daily except Tuesdays, July to September, 10am to 12 noon and 3pm to 7pm (6pm April to June, 5pm February, March and October to December). 10F. ☎ 04 93 38 55 26.

La Malmaison – Open daily except Tuesdays; times vary according to exhibitions. 10F. ☎ 04 93 38 55 26.

Chapelle Bellini – Open Mondays to Fridays, 2pm to 5pm (6pm June to August). No charge. ☎ 04 93 38 61 80.

Église orthodoxe St-Michel-Archange – Open weekdays by request. ☎ 04 93 43 00 28.

Le CANNET
🛈 avenue du Campon – 06110 ☎ 04 93 45 34 27

Musée Tobiasse – Open all year, daily except Tuesdays and Thursdays, 2pm to 6pm. Closed 1 January and 25 December. No charge. ☎ 04 93 45 34 27.

CAP FERRAT
🛈 59 avenue Denis-Semeria, St-Jean-Cap-Ferrat-06230 ☎ 04 93 76 08 90

Musée Île-de-France – Open daily February to October, 10am to 6pm (7pm July and August); November to 8 February, 2pm to 6pm. Closed 25 December. 46F. ☎ 04 93 01 45 90.

Grand parc d'acclimatation – Open daily, 9.30am to 7pm (5.30pm mid-September to May). 55F (child 40F). ☎ 04 93 76 04 98.

Phare – Closed temporarily for safety reasons. Enquire at the Office de tourisme in St-Jean-Cap-Ferrat.

Le CASTELLET

Circuit du Castellet Paul-Ricard – Track enclosure open 8am to 6pm. No charge except on race days. Closed 25 December to 1 January. ☎ 04 94 98 45 00.

Musée du modélisme – Open daily, July to September, 10am to 7pm; October to June, 10am to 1pm and 2pm to 6pm. Closed 1 January and 25 December. 35F. ☎ 04 94 90 61 90.

CAVALAIRE-SUR-MER
🛈 maison de la mer – 83240 ☎ 04 94 64 08 28

Excursions to the îles d'Hyères – Operate all year. Day and half-day trips comprising a circuit of the three islands, a coastal tour of the three headlands and excursions to the islands. ☎ 04 94 64 08 04 (Vedettes Îles d'Or) and ☎ 04 94 64 48 38 (Bateaux Verts).

La CELLE

Abbaye de La Celle – Open daily except Saturday and Sunday mornings, July to October, 10am to 12 noon and 2pm to 6pm (5pm April to June); November to March, closed Saturdays and Sundays. Closed public holidays. 20F. ☎ 04 94 59 19 05.

CHATEAUNEUF-DE-CONTES

Église – *Closed Sunday afternoons. For a guided tour, apply to Mme Diribarne.* ☎ *04 93 79 23 76.*

CHATEAUNEUF-LES CONTES

Église «Madame de Villevieille» – Open July and August, 8.30am to 6pm, September to June, 10am and 3pm (except Sunday afternoons) by arrangement with Mme Odette Diribarne. b 04 93 79 23 76 or 04 93 79 03 65.

COARAZE
🛈 montée du Portal – 06390 ☎ 04 93 79 37 47

N.-D.-de-la-Pitié – Open by arrangement. Apply to the Syndicat d'initiative or Bar des Arts (closed Mondays), place Ste Catherine.

COGOLIN
🛈 place de la République – 83310 ☎ 04 94 54 63 18

Manufacture des tapis – Exhibition and salesroom only open Mondays to Fridays, 8.30am to 12 noon and 2pm to 6pm (5pm Fridays).

Espace Raimu – Open daily except Sunday mornings, July to September, 10am to 12 noon and 4pm to 7pm; October to June, 10am to 12 noon and 3pm to 6pm. 20F. ☎ 04 94 54 18 00.

COURSEGOULES

Église – *Open mornings, 9am to 12 noon.*

D

DRAGUIGNAN
9 9 avenue Georges-Clemenceau - 83300 ☎ 04 94 68 63 30

Guided tour of the town – Apply to the Office de tourisme.

Tour de l'Horloge – Access only during guided tour of the town organised by the Office de tourisme.

Église St-Michel – Closed Sunday afternoons.

Musée – Open daily except Sundays, 9am to 12 noon and 2pm to 6pm. No charge. ☎ 04 94 47 28 80.

Musée des Arts et Traditions de moyenne Provence – Open daily except Mondays and Sunday mornings, 9am to 12 noon and 2pm to 6pm. Closed 1 January, 1 May and 25 December. 20F. ☎ 04 94 47 05 72.

Cimetière américain et mémorial du Rhône – Open daily, 9am to 5pm. No charge. ☎ 04 94 68 03 62.

Musée du canon et des artilleurs – Open 15 January to 15 December, Mondays to Fridays, 8.15am to 11am and 2.15pm to 5pm. Closed public holidays. No charge. ☎ 04 94 60 23 85 or 04 94 60 23 86.

E

ÎLE des EMBIEZ

Access – By boat from Le Brusc port (10 min), 17 to 23 crossings daily in both directions depending on the season. 31F return.

Centre de plongée des Embiez – For information on diving courses, telephone 04 94 34 12 78.

Aquascope – Operates June to September. For timetable and charges, telephone 04 94 34 01 48.

Institut Océanographique Paul-Ricard – Open July and August, daily, 10am to 12.30pm and 1.30pm to 6.30pm (5.30pm April to June and September and October); November to 30 December, closed Wednesday and Saturday mornings; 2 January to 30 March, closed Wednesday afternoons and Saturday mornings. Closed 1 January and 25 and 26 December. 20F (child 10F). ☎ 04 94 34 02 49.

ENTRECASTEAUX

Château – Open 15 March to 15 February, daily except Wednesdays, 11am to 12.30pm and 2.30pm to 6pm. 30F. ☎ 04 94 04 43 95.

ÈZE
9 place du Général de Gaulle - 06360 ☎ 04 93 41 26 00

Chapelle des Pénitents Blancs – Works of art permanently on display can be seen through the wrought iron grille in the entrance. Guided tour on application to the Office de tourisme.

Jardin exotique – Open daily, July and August, 9am to 8pm; September to June, 9am to 12 noon and 2pm to 5pm (7pm Easter to June). 12F. ☎ 04 93 41 10 30.

Parfumerie Fragonard – ♿ Guided tour (30 min), 16 March to October, 8.30am to 6.30pm; November to 15 March, 8.30am to 12 noon and 2pm to 6pm. No charge.

Excursions

Astrorama – Guided tour (2hrs) from 6.30pm, July and August, daily except Sundays, May to September, Tuesdays and Fridays. 40F; 60F including show. ☎ 04 93 85 85 58.

F

FALICON

Église – Open Thursday afternoons, 3.30pm to 6pm.

FAYENCE
9 place Léon-Roux - 83440 ☎ 04 94 76 20 08

Excursions

N.-D.-des-Cyprès – *Apply to Mr Rebuffel at the wine cellar at the east end of the church.*

FRÉJUS

🛈 325 rue Jean-Jaurès – 83600 ☎ 04 94 51 83 83.

Guided tour of the town  – Apply to the Office de tourisme.

Cathedral close – Cloisters and museum open April to September, daily, 9am to 7pm; October to March, daily except Mondays, 9am to 12 noon and 2pm to 5pm. Closed 1 January, 1 May, 1 and 11 November and 25 December. Portal and baptistery with guided tour only. 25F. ☎ 04 94 51 26 30.

Cathédrale– Closed 12 noon to 4pm.

Arènes – Open daily except Tuesdays, 9am to 12 noon and 2pm to 6.30pm (4.30pm October to March). Closed 1 January and 25 December. No charge.

Petit train du soleil – Operates (40 min) mid-May to September, daily, every hour from 2pm. 25F. ☎ 04 93 09 40 60.

Pagode bouddhique Hong-Hien - Open daily, 9am to 7pm (10am to 6pm out of season). 5F. ☎ 04 94 53 25 29.

Mémorial d'Indochine – *Open daily except Tuesdays, 10am to 5.30pm (museum 5pm). Closed 1 January, 1 May and 25 December. No charge.* ☎ 04 94 44 42 90.

Musée des troupes de marine – Open daily except Tuesdays and Saturdays, mid-June to mid-September, 10am to 12 noon and 3pm to 7pm; mid-September to 24 December and 2 January to mid-June, 2pm to 5pm. No charge. ☎ 04 94 40 81 75.

Fréjus Baptistery, door

Parc zoologique – Open May to September, 9.30am to 6.30pm; October to April, 10am to 5pm. 61F (child 37F). ☎ 04 94 40 70 65.

Chapelle N.-D.-de-Jérusalem – *Open daily except Tuesdays, 2pm to 6pm (5pm October to March).* ☎ 04 94 17 19 19.

Aquatica – Open June to 15 September, 10am to 6pm (evenings also July and August). 98F (child 76F). ☎ 04 94 51 82 51.

G

La GARDE-FREINET

🛈 place de la mairie – 83310 ☎ 04 94 43 67 40

Chapelle St-Éloi – Closed for restoration.

GONFARON

Écomusée du liège – *Open daily except Mondays, April to September, 2pm to 6pm; October to March, 10am to 12 noon and 2pm to 4pm. 25F.* ☎ 04 94 78 25 65.

Village des tortues – Open March to November, daily, 9am to 7pm; closed December to February. 40F. ☎ 04 94 78 26 41.

GOURDON

Château – Guided tour (20 min) daily except Tuesdays, June to September, 11am to 1pm and 2pm to 7pm; October to May, 2pm to 6pm. 25F. ☎ 04 93 09 68 02.

GRASSE

Guided tour of the town – Apply to the Office de tourisme.

Musée d'Art et d'Histoire de Provence – *Open June to September, daily, 10am to 7pm; October and December to May, Wednesdays to Sundays, 10am to 12 noon and 2pm to 5pm. Closed public holidays. 25F.* ☎ *04 93 36 01 61.*

Musée international de la Parfumerie – Open June to September, daily, 10am to 7pm; October and December to May, Wednesdays to Sundays, 10am to 12 noon and 2pm to 5pm. 20F. ☎ 04 93 36 80 20.

Musée de la marine – *Open June to September, daily, 10am to 7pm; October to May, daily except Sundays, 9am to 12 noon and 2pm to 6pm. Closed 1 to 15 November. 20F.* ☎ *04 93 09 10 71.*

Musée Jean-Honoré Fragonard – Same admission times and charges as the musée d'Art et d'Histoire de Provence (see above).

Perfumeries:

Parfumerie Molinard – Open April to September, daily 9am to 6.30pm; October to [March], daily except Sundays, 9am to 12.30pm and 2pm to 6pm. No charge. ☎ 04 93 36 01 62.

Parfumerie Galimard – Open daily, April to October, 9am to 6.30pm; November to March, 9am to 6pm. No charge. ☎ 04 93 09 20 00.

Parfumerie Fragonard – Open daily, April to October, 9am to 6.30pm; November to March, 9am to 12.30pm and 2pm to 6pm. No charge. ☎ 04 93 36 44 65.

GRIMAUD

H

HYÈRES

Ancienne collégiale St-Paul – Open weekdays, 2.30pm to 5pm.

Jardins Olbius-Riquier – Open 8am to 7pm.

Serre tropicale – Open daily, 8am to 8pm (7pm in low season). ☎ 04 94 35 90 65.

Villa de Noailles – Open mid-June to mid-September. Guided tour (2 hr) mid-June to mid-September, Thursdays at 9am. 30F. Apply in advance to the Office de tourisme.

Musée municipal – *Open Mondays, Wednesdays, Thursdays and Fridays, 10am to 12 noon and 3pm to 6pm. Closed public holidays.* ☎ *04 94 35 90 42.*

Parc du château Ste-Claire – Open 8am to 7pm (5pm in winter). No charge.

Îles de HYÈRES

Access – By ferry from **Hyères** to the Îles de Port-Cros (1 hr) and Îles du Levant (1 hr 30 min). Société de Transports Maritimes et Terrestres du Littoral Varois, Port St Pierre. 83400 Hyères. ☎ 04 94 57 44 07.

– By ferry from La Tour Fondue (Giens) to the Île de Porquerolles (20 min). ☎ 04 94 58 21 81.

– By ferry from **Le Lavandou** (35 min) and from **Cavalaire** (54 min). Compagnie de Transports Maritimes «Vedettes Îles d'Or», 15 quai Gabriel-Péri, 83980 Le Lavandou. ☎ 04 94 71 01 02.

Île de Porquerolles

Bureau d'information – In the village harbour. Open 1 June to 30 September. ☎ 04 94 58 33 76.

Fort Ste-Agathe – Open 2 May to September, daily, 10am to 12 noon and 2pm to 5.30pm. 25F.

Phare – Guided tour (30 min) in season, mornings and afternoons (maintenance work permitting). No charge. ☎ 04 94 58 30 78.

Île de Port-Cros

Parc national – Information from Castel Ste Claire 83418 Hyères, ☎ 04 94 12 82 30, or from the Centre d'Information de Port-Cros, first building to the left of the landing stages in the harbour (summer only), ☎ 04 94 05 90 17.

Fort de l'Estissac – Open 2 May to September, 10.30am to 12.30pm and 2pm to 6pm. No charge.

Underwater path – Open to the public, 15 June to 15 September, 10am to 5pm. Accompanied dives in summer in groups of 7 to 8 from La Palud beach.

Unaccompanied dives by following the buoys using plastic-coated booklets (available for hire from the Maison du parc in the harbour) attached to the wrist to identify plant and animal species. Own diving equipment recommended (no aqualung required).

Boat trips with underwater view – Operate mid-April to early September, daily, at 9am, 10.15am, 11.30am and 2.30pm; Wednesdays and weekends the rest of the year; enquire about departure times in advance. 60F (child 30F). ☎ 04 94 05 92 22.

Île du Levant

Access – By ferry from the port of **Hyères** (1 hr). Société de Transports Maritimes et Terrestres du Littoral Varois, Port St Pierre, 83400 Hyères. ☎ 04 94 57 44 07.

By ferry from **Le Lavandou** (35 min) and **Cavalaire** (54 min). Compagnie de Transports Maritimes «Vedettes Îles d'Or», 15 quai Gabriel-Péri, 83980 Le Lavandou. ☎ 04 94 71 01 02.

L

Le LAVANDOU
🛈 quai Gabriel Péri - 83980 ☎ 04 94 71 00 61

Boat trips – Many services operate all year to the Îles d'Hyères; also daily, 9am to 7pm, underwater viewing trips aboard *"Seascope"*, a specially adapted trimaran. Prices from Compagnie de Transports Maritimes «Vedettes Îles d'Or». ☎ 04 94 71 01 02.

Les LECQUES

Musée romain de Tauroentum – Open July to September, daily except Tuesdays, 3pm to 7pm; October to June, Saturdays and Sundays, 2pm to 5pm. Closed 25 December. 15F. ☎ 04 94 26 30 46.

Îles de LÉRINS

Access – *By ferry from Cannes, daily. Ile Ste-Marguerite 45F; Ile St-Honorat 50F; both islands 70F.* ☎ *04 93 39 11 82 (Compagnie Esterel Chanteclair). Cruise (1 hr 30 min) on board Nautilus, a glass bottomed boat, in season only, 70F; excursions to St-Tropez or Monaco 100F;* ☎ *04 93 38 66 33.*

Île Ste-Marguerite

Botanical nature trail – In July and August, guided walk daily except Mondays, at 10.30am, 2.30pm and 4.30pm. No charge. Information from the ONF. ☎ 04 93 43 49 24.

Fort Royal – Musée de la mer – Open all year except January, daily except Tuesdays, July to September, 10.30am to 12.15pm and 2.15pm to 6.30pm (5.30pm October to June). 10F. ☎ 04 93 43 18 17.

Île St-Honorat

Église abbatiale du monastère moderne – *Open all year, daily except Sunday mornings, 8.30am to 11.15am and 2pm to 4.30pm. Closed public holidays. Donation welcome.* ☎ *04 93 48 68 68.*

Ancien monastère fortifié – *Open daily except Sunday mornings, July and August, 10am to 12 noon and 2.30pm to 4.30pm. 10F; September to June, 9am to 4pm. No charge. Closed public holidays.* ☎ *04 93 48 68 68.*

LEVENS
🛈 12, rue du Docteur Faraut - 06670 ☎ 04 93 79 71 00

Mairie – *To see the frescoes, apply to the secretariat, Mondays to Fridays, 9am to 12 noon and 2pm to 6pm.*

La LONDE-les-MAURES

Jardin des oiseaux exotiques – Open daily, June to September, 9.30am to 7.30pm; October to May, 2pm to 6pm. 40F (child 25F). ☎ 04 94 35 02 15.

LORGUES
🛈 - 83510 ☎ 04 94 73 70 06

Chapelle N.-D.-de-Benva – Closed temporarily. Apply to the ASFVL. ☎ 04 94 73 70 53.

Saut du LOUP

Continuous access June to September. Charge not available.

Le LUC   🅱 Château de Vintimille, place de la Convention - 83340 ☎ 94 60 74 51

Musée Historique de centre-Var – Open daily except Sundays, July to mid-September, 3pm to 6pm; June and mid-September to mid-October, 2.30pm to 5.30pm. No charge. ☎ 04 94 60 70 12.

Musée régional du timbre et de la philatélie – Open mid-June to August, daily except Tuesdays, 2.30pm to 6pm; September to mid-June, daily except weekday mornings, 10am to 12 noon and 2.30pm to 5.30pm. Closed 1 January, 1 May and 25 December. 10F. ☎ 04 94 47 96 16.

LUCÉRAM

Église – *For a visit with lighting and commentary, apply to the presbytery the previous day.* ☎ *04 93 79 51 87.*

Chapelle N.-D.-de Bon Cœur – *Apply to the parish priest at the presbytery.* ☎ *04 93 79 51 87.*

Chapelle St-Grat – *Apply to the parish priest at the presbytery.* ☎ *04 93 79 51 87.*

M

MAGAGNOSC

St-Laurent – *Closed 11.30am to 3pm.* ☎ *04 93 42 78 55.*

Statue of St Margaret and the dragon in Lucéram Church Treasury

B. Régent/DIAF

MENTON   🅱 Palais de l'Europe - 06500 ☎ 04 93 57 57 00
🅱 Maison du patrimoine, 5 rue Ciapetta - 06500 ☎ 04 93 10 33 66

Guided tour of the town – Tuesday afternoons from the Church of St Michel. Apply to Maison du patrimoine.

Boat trips – Operate mid-April to mid-October, at 2.30pm and 4pm, Mondays, Wednesdays and Fridays, to Monaco with commentary but without stopping (60F), and Tuesdays, Thursdays and Sundays to St-Jean-Cap-Ferrat with commentary (90F); mid-June to mid-September, Tuesdays and Thursdays, day trip to Monaco (80F); July and August, Saturdays, day trip to Villefranche bay (110F); day trips to St-Tropez (200F) and San Remo in Italy (110F) by Bateaux Gallus. Information from Compagnie Navigation et Tourisme, Vieux port, quai Napoléon III. ☎ 04 93 35 51 72.

Musée Jean-Cocteau – Open daily except Tuesdays, 10am to 12 noon and 2pm to 6pm. Closed public holidays. No charge. ☎ 04 93 35 49 71.

Église St-Michel – Closed 12 noon to 3pm and major public holidays. ☎ 04 93 35 81 63.

Musée des Beaux-Arts (Palais Carnolès) – Open daily except Tuesdays, 10am to 12 noon and 2pm to 6pm. Closed public holidays. No charge. ☎ 04 93 35 49 71.

Hôtel de Ville – Salle des mariages Jean Cocteau open Mondays to Fridays, 8.30am to 12 noon and 1.30pm to 4.45pm. Closed public holidays. 5F. ☎ 04 93 10 50 00.

Musée de préhistoire régionale – Same admission times and charges as the Musée des Beaux-Arts *(see above).*

Église orthodoxe russe – Guided tour fourth Saturday in the month at 2.30pm, organised by the Maison du patrimoine. 30F.

Jardin de Maria Serena – Guided tour (2 hr) Tuesdays at 10am. 30F. ☎ 04 92 10 33 66.

La Serre de la Madone – For information about guided tours, telephone 04 92 10 33 66.

Garavan:

Jardin du Val Rameh – Open May to September, 10am to 12.30pm and 3pm to 6pm; October to April, 10am to 12.30pm and 2pm to 5pm. 20F. ☎ 04 93 35 86 72.

Jardin des Colombières – Closed for restoration. For information, telephone 04 92 10 33 66.

Jardin des Romanciers (villa Fontana Rosa) – Guided tour (2 hr) of the jardin des Romanciers second and fourth Friday and third Saturday in the month at 10am. 30F. ☎ 04 92 10 33 66.

Chapelle de l'Annonciade (Monastère de l'Annonciade) – Open 9am to 12 noon and 2pm to 6pm. **Service** Sunday mornings. ☎ 04 93 35 76 92.

Excursions

Fort de Ste-Agnès – *Open June to September, daily, 3pm to 6.30pm; October to May, weekends, 2.30pm to 5.30pm. 20F.* ☎ *04 93 35 84 58.*

Vallée des MERVEILLES
🛈 avenue du 16 septembre 1947 – 06430 Tende
☎ 04 93 04 73 71

Guided tour of the engravings – July and August, daily:
Secteur de l'Arpette from les Merveilles refuge at 7.30am, 11am and 3pm; 12 July to 16 August, 1pm also. ☎ 04 93 04 68 66.
Secteur de Fontanalbe from Fontanalbe refuge at 8am and from lacs Jumeaux at 11 am and 2pm. ☎ 04 93 04 89 79.
Both sectors, 7 to 28 June and 6 to 27 September, Sundays only, 8am and 1pm. Bureau des guides Val des Merveilles in Tende. 35F (children under 10, no charge). ☎ 04 93 04 67 00.

Excursions by jeep or on horseback – Excursions on horseback (1/2 day and full day) from Tende and Castérino (prices unavailable); excursions from Tende to Fontanalbe and Les Merveilles refuges in a 4-wheel-drive vehicle (including a section on foot). Apply to the Office de tourisme de la Haute-Roya in Tende for list of organisers. ☎ 04 93 04 73 71.

Principality of MONACO
🛈 2a boulevard des Moulins – 98000 ☎ (377) 92 16 61 66

To telephone Monaco from France, dial 00 followed by 377 (code for Monaco) and the 8-digit telephone number.

Jardin exotique – Open daily, mid-May to mid-September, 9am to 7pm; between 5pm and 6pm the rest of the year, according to the month. Closed 19 November and 25 December. 39F (ticket also valid for the grotte de l'Observatoire and musée d'Anthropologie préhistorique). ☎ 93 15 29 80.

Grotte de l'Observatoire – Open 10am to 6pm; otherwise as for the Jardin exotique (see above).

Musée d'Anthropologie préhistorique – Open May to August, daily, 9am to 7pm; September to April, 9am to 6pm (5pm November to January). Closed 19 November and 25 December. 39F (ticket also valid for the Jardin exotique and grotte de l'Observatoire). ☎ 93 15 80 06.

Église St-Martin – Closed Ascension Day and following Sunday.

Collection de voitures anciennes du prince de Monaco – ♿ Open all year except November, daily, 10am to 6pm. 30F (child 15F). ☎ 92 05 28 56.

Musée des timbres et des monnaies – ♿. Open daily, 10am to 5pm (6pm in summer). 20F. ☎ 93 15 41 50.

Musée naval – Open daily, 10am to 6pm. 25F. ☎ 92 05 28 48.

Musée océanographique – ♿ Open July and August, 9am to 8pm; September, October and March to June, 9.30am to 7pm; November to February, 10am to 6pm. Closed Sunday of Monaco Grand Prix. 60F. ☎ 93 15 36 00.

Musée de la chapelle de la Visitation – Open daily except Mondays, 10am to 4pm. 20F. ☎ 93 50 07 00.

Petit train touristique «Azur Express» – *Operates February to October, daily, 10.30am to 12 noon and 2pm to 6pm. Monaco-Ville (10 min) 16F; Monaco-Ville to place du Casino (35 min). 32F.* ☎ *92 05 64 38.*

Spectacle audiovisuel Monte-Carlo Story – ♿ Show (35 min) March to October, daily, every hour from 11am to 5pm (6pm July and August); November, January and February, 2pm to 5pm. 38F (child 20F). ☎ 93 25 32 33.

Historial des Princes de Monaco – ♿ Open March to September, daily, 9.30am to 6.30pm; October to February, 11am to 4pm. Closed 15 November to 25 December and 10 January to 31 January. 26F. ☎ 93 30 39 05.

Palais du Prince – Open June to September, daily, 9.30am to 6.30pm; October, 10am to 5pm. 30F. ☎ 93 25 18 31.

Musée napoléonien et des archives du Palais – Open June to September, daily, 9.30am to 6.30pm; October to 11 November, daily, 10am to 5pm; 17 December to May, daily except Mondays, 10.30am to 12.30pm and 2pm to 5pm. Closed 1 January and 25 December. 20F (40F including entrance to the Palais du Prince). ☎ 93 25 18 31.

Jardin animalier – Disabled symbol. Open June to September, daily, 9am to 12 noon and 2pm to 7pm; October to May, 10am to 12 noon and 2pm to 5pm (6pm March to May). 20F. ☎ 93 25 18 31.

Boat trips with underwater views – *Operate June to mid-September, at 11am, 2.30pm, 4pm and 5.30pm for a trip around Monaco (55 min) aboard "Monte-Carlo", a glass-bottomed catamaran. 70F. Day trips to Îles de Lérins also available. 130F.* ☎ 92 16 15 15.

Hôtel de l'Ermitage, Monte-Carlo

Casino de Monte Carlo – ♿ No admittance to persons under 21. Open all year from 12 noon. European salons 50F; private salons 50F supplement. ☎ 92 16 23 00.

Jardin japonais – Open daily, 9am to an hour before sunset. No charge.

Musée National de Monaco (dolls and automata) – Open from Easter to August, daily, 10am to 6.30pm; September to Easter, 10am to 12.15pm and 2.30pm to 6.30pm. Closed 1 January, 1 May, Ascension Day, 19 November, 25 December and during the Monaco Grand Prix (4 days). 26F. ☎ 93 30 91 26.

MONS
🛈 place St-Sébastien – 83440 ☎ 04 94 76 39 54

Église – Guided tours daily, 2pm to 6pm. Apply to the Office de tourisme.

MOUANS-SARTOUX

Château de Mouans (Espace de l'Art concret) – Open daily except Tuesdays, June to September, 11am to 7pm; October to May, 11am to 6pm. 15F. ☎ 04 93 75 71 50.

MOUGINS

Ermitage N.-D.-de-Vie – Open only for Sunday morning mass.

Musée de l'Automobiliste – Open April to September, 10am to 7pm (6pm in October and December to March). 40F. Closed 24, 25 and 31 December and morning of 1 January. 40F. ☎ 04 93 69 27 80.

Clocher de l'église – Open all year except November, daily except Tuesdays, 1pm to 6pm (8pm July and August). Closed 1 January, 1 May and 25 November. For the key, apply to the Musée de la photographie *(see below)*. No charge. ☎ 04 93 75 85 67.

Musée de la photographie – Open daily except Tuesdays, July and August, 2pm to 11pm; September, October and December to June, 1pm to 6pm. Closed 1 January, 1 May and 25 December. 5F. ☎ 04 93 75 85 67.

Musée municipal – Open all year except November, daily except weekends out of season, 10am to 12 noon and 2pm to 6pm. No charge. ☎ 04 92 92 50 42.

N

ERMITAGE N.-D.-DES-ANGES

Ermitage N.-D.-des Anges – Chapel open all year. Gîte for rent April to October. Apply to the Ermitage. ☎ 04 94 59 00 69.

La NAPOULE

Château-musée – Guided tour (1 hr) July and August, daily except Tuesdays, 3pm, 4pm and 5pm; March to June, September and October, 3pm and 4pm. Closed 1 May. 25F. ☎ 04 93 49 22 93.

NICE   ▣ avenue Thiers - 06000 ☎ 04 93 87 07 07

Guided tour of the town 🅰 – Apply to the CAIDEM ☎ 04 93 62 18 12.

Tour of old Nice – Guided tour Tuesdays and Sundays at 3pm, from palais Lascaris, 15 rue Droite. Apply to the CAIDEM ☎ 04 93 62 18 12.

Musée Raoul Dufy – ♿ Dufy's works are currently exhibited at the Musée Chéret. Open daily except Sunday mornings and Mondays, 10am to 12 noon and 2pm to 6pm. Closed 1 January, 1 May and 24, 25 and 31 December. 15F. ☎ 04 93 62 31 24.

Musée Alexis et Gustav-Adolf Mossa – Open daily except Sunday mornings and Mondays, 10am to 12 noon and 2pm to 6pm. Closed public holidays. 15F. ☎ 04 93 62 37 11.

Ascenseur du château – Operates daily, January, February, March, October and November, 10am to 6pm; April, May and September, 9am to 7pm; June, July and August, until 8pm. 3.50F single, 5F return. ☎ 04 93 85 62 33.

Musée naval – *Open daily except Tuesdays, 10am to 12 noon and 2pm to 5pm (7pm June to September). Closed mid-November to mid-December. 15F.* ☎ *04 93 80 47 61.*

Église St-Martin et St-Augustin – Open Tuesdays to Saturdays and Sunday mornings. When closed, apply to the archpriest *(archiprêtre)* at the cathedral.

Palais Lascaris – Open all year except November, daily except Mondays, 10am to 12 noon and 2pm to 6pm. Closed public holidays. 25F. ☎ 04 93 62 05 54.

Chapelle de la Miséricorde – Open only for lecture tours organised by the CAIDEM, Tuesdays and Sundays at 3pm, starting from the palais Lascaris. 45F.

Promenade en train touristique – Operate all year except 5 January to 25 January and 15 November to 20 December, 10am to 6pm, every 30 min (40 min journey). 30F.

Musée national Message biblique Marc-Chagall – ♿ Open daily except Tuesdays, July to September, 10am to 6pm; October to June, 10am to 5pm. Closed 1 January, 1 May and 25 December. 30F (supplement during exhibitions); 20F Sundays. ☎ 04 93 53 87 20.

Musée Franciscain – Open daily except Sundays, 10am to 12 noon and 3pm to 6pm. Closed 1 January, Easter and Whit Monday, 1 and 8 May, Ascension Day, 14 July, 15 August, 1 and 11 November and 25 December. No charge. ☎ 04 93 81 00 04.

Musée Matisse – Open daily except Tuesdays, April to September, 10am to 6pm; October to March, 10am to 5pm. 25F. ☎ 04 93 81 08 08.

Musée Archéologique – Disabled symbol. Open daily except Mondays, April to September, 10am to 12 noon and 2pm to 6pm; October and December to March, 10am to 1pm and 2pm to 5pm. Closed 1 January, Easter, 1 May and 25 December. 25F (including entrance to archeological site). ☎ 04 93 81 59 57.

Site archéologique gallo-romain – Same admission times and charges as for the musée Archéologique *(see above)*.

Arènes – Open 8am to 6pm (8pm in summer). No charge.

Musée des Beaux-Arts – Open daily except Mondays, 10am to 12 noon and 2pm to 6pm. Closed 1 January, Easter, 1 May and 25 December. 25F. ☎ 04 92 15 28 28.

Musée d'Art naïf Jakovsky – Open daily except Tuesdays, 10am to 12 noon and 2pm to 6pm. Closed 1 January, Easter, 1 May and 25 December. 25F; no charge on first Sunday of the month. ☎ 04 93 71 78 33.

Musée des trains miniatures – Open daily, 9.30am to 7pm (5pm out of season). 30F (child 20F). ☎ 04 93 97 41 40.

Parc Phoenix – Open 15 March to 15 October, 9am to 6pm; 15 October to 15 March, 9am to 5pm (last admission 4.15pm). 40F. ☏ 04 93 18 03 33.

Faculté de droit – Chagall mosaic can be seen during university year, Mondays to Fridays, 9am to 11.30am and 2pm to 5pm. ☏ 04 93 97 70 01.

Acropolis – Palais des Arts, du Tourisme et des Congrès – Guided tour by appointment. ☏ 04 93 92 82 35.

Musée d'Art moderne et d'Art contemporain – Open daily except Tuesdays, 11am to 6pm (10pm Fridays). Closed public holidays. 25F; no charge on first Sunday of the month. ☏ 04 93 62 61 62.

Muséum d'Histoire naturelle – *Open daily except Tuesdays, 9am to 12 noon and 2pm to 6pm. Closed 1 January, Easter, 1 May, 15 August to 15 September and 25 December. 25F.* ☏ *04 93 55 15 24.*

Palais Masséna – Musée d'Art et d'Histoire – Open daily except Mondays, 10am to 12 noon and 2pm to 6pm. Closed 2 weeks in November and public holidays. 25F. ☏ 04 93 88 11 34.

Cathédrale orthodoxe russe – Open May to September, 9am to 12 noon and 2.30pm to 6pm (5pm October to April). Closed on Orthodox holidays. 12F. ☏ 04 93 96 88 02.

Église Ste-Jeanne-d'Arc – Open daily; Sundays, 5pm to 7pm only.

Prieuré Vieux-Logis – *Guided tour (1 hr 30 min) Wednesdays, Thursdays, Saturdays and first Sunday in the month, 3pm to 5pm. Closed 1 January and Christmas. No charge.* ☏ *04 93 84 44 74.*

St Réparate Cathedral, Nice

Musée de Terra Amata – Closed temporarily. ☏ 04 93 55 59 93.

Boat trip – Apply to S. A. Bateaux Gallus, 24 quai Lunel. ☏ 04 93 89 79 09.

Observatoire du Mont-Gros – Guided tour (1 hr 30 min) Saturdays at 3pm. 20F. ☏ 04 93 85 85 58.

NOTRE-DAME-DE-LAGHET

Musée et sanctuaire N.-D.-de-Laghet – Open all year 3pm to 5pm. No charge. ☏ 04 93 41 09 60.

Chapelle N.-D.-DE-PEYGROS

N.-D.-de-Peygros – Apply to the Syndicat d'initiative. ☏ 04 93 60 71 73.

Chapelle N.-D.-des-FONTAINES

Open May to October, daily, 9.30am to 7pm; November to April, apply to the cafés and restaurants in La Brigue where the key can be borrowed in exchange for a passport or identity card. ☏ 04 93 04 76 73 (La Brigue town hall).

P

PEILLE

Église– Closed temporarily.

PEILLON

Chapelle des Pénitents Blancs – Closed temporarily.

PORT-GRIMAUD

Église – Open daily, 9am to 7pm (preferably not during services). **Tower open** daily, 9am to 7pm. 5F.

Le PRADET
🛈 place général de Gaulle - 83220 ☏ 04 94 21 71 69.

Musée de la mine de Cap Garonne – Guided tour (45 min), mid-June to mid-September, daily, 2pm to 5.30pm; mid-September to mid-June, Wednesdays and weekends, 2pm to 5pm. Closed 1 January and 25 December. 35F (child 15F). ☏ 04 94 08 32 46.

R

RAYOL-CANADEL-SUR-MER
🛈 place du Rayol - 83240 ☏ 04 94 05 65 69

Domaine du Rayol – Open daily, July and August, 9.30am to 12.30pm and 4.30pm to 8pm; September to June, 9.30am to 12.30pm and 2.30pm to 6.30pm. Guided tour (2 hr) July and August at 9.30am, 10am, 10.30am, 4.30pm, 5pm and 5.30pm; September to June at 3pm. Closed 21 November to 31 January. 40F. ☏ 04 94 05 32 50.

Underwater path – Guided tour (1 hr 30 min approximately), July and August, daily except Mondays. Book by previous day at latest at the Domaine du Rayol. 70F (child 50F). Price includes loan of diving equipment (wetsuit, mask, flippers and snorkel, no aqualung).

ROQUEBILLIÈRE

Église de St-Michel-du-Gast – Open weekends. Closed December and January. ☏ 04 93 03 45 62.

ROQUEBRUNE-CAP-MARTIN
🛈 20 avenue Paul-Doumer - 06190 ☏ 04 93 35 62 87

Donjon – Open daily (except Fridays in winter), 10am to 12 noon and 2pm to 5.30pm (7pm mid-April to mid-September). Closed 1 May and mid-November to mid-December. 20F. ☏ 04 93 35 07 22.

Église de Ste-Marguerite – Open daily, 3pm to 6pm. ☏ 04 93 35 01 18.

Cabanon de Le Corbusier – Guided tour Tuesdays at 9.30am by appointment with the Office de tourisme.

ROQUEBRUNE-SUR-ARGENS
🛈 1 rue Jean-Aicard - 83520 ☏ 04 94 45 72 70

Musée de Préhistoire et histoire locale – *Open June to September, Tuesdays to Saturdays, 10am to 12 noon and 2pm to 6pm; October to May, Thursdays and Fridays only. Film show on request. 10F. ☏ 04 94 45 75 51.*

S

ST-CÉZAIRE-SUR-SIAGNE

Grottes de St-Cézaire-sur-Siagne – Guided tour (45 min), July and August, 10.30am to 6.30pm; June and September, 10.30am to 12 noon and 2pm to 6pm; October to May, 2.30pm to 5pm. Closed November to 15 February. 27F. ☏ 04 93 60 22 35.

SAINT-DALMAS-VALDEBLORE

Église – To visit in summer, apply to Mr Jean Alloi at "Les Mollières" restaurant. ☏ 04 93 02 82 29.

ST-MARTIN-VÉSUBIE
🛈 place Félix Faure - 06450 ☏ 04 93 03 21 28

Centre d'alpinisme – Guided walks and mountain climbs by two organisations:
– Bureau des guides de la Haute Vésubie. Office open July to September, slide shows in late afternoon). ☏ 04 93 03 26 60 and 04 93 03 44 30 (outside holiday season).
– Guides du Mercantour. Office open July to September. ☏ 04 93 03 31 32.

Madone de Fenestre – Open June to 15 September, 9am to 6pm. ☏ 04 93 03 23 24 (presbytère de St-Martin-Vésubie).

ST-PAUL
🛈 rue Grande - 06570 ☏ 04 93 32 86 95

Musée local d'histoire – Open mid-June to mid-September, daily, 10am to 6pm (5pm mid-September to mid-June). Closed 1 January and 1 to 25 December. 20F. ☏ 04 93 32 41 13.

ST-PAUL

Fondation Maeght – Open July to September, 10am to 7pm; October to June, 10am to 12.30pm and 2.30pm to 6pm. Permanent collection not on display during temporary exhibitions. 40F (supplement for exhibitions). ☎ 04 93 32 81 63.

ST-PONS

Église – Open Sunday mornings until 11am. Advisable to telephone in advance. ☎ 04 92 03 83 42.

ST-RAPHAËL
🆔 rue Waldeck Rousseau - BP 210 - 83700 ☎ 04 94 19 52 52

Musée Archéologique – Open mid-June to mid-September, daily except Tuesdays, 10am to 12 noon and 3pm to 6pm; mid-September to mid-June, daily except Sundays, 10am to 12 noon and 2pm to 5pm. No charge. ☎ 04 94 19 25 75.

Église St-Pierre-des-Templiers – Closed temporarily. Enquire at the Office de tourisme.

ST-TROPEZ
🆔 quai Jean-Jaurès - 83990 ☎ 04 94 97 45 21

L'Annonciade, musée de St-Tropez – Open June to September, daily except Tuesdays, 10am to 12 noon and 3pm to 7pm; October and December to May, 10am to 12 noon and 2pm to 6pm. Closed 1 January, 1 May, Ascension Day and 25 December. 30F. ☎ 04 94 97 04 01.

Maison des papillons – Open April to 1 October, daily except Tuesdays, 10am to 12 noon and 3pm to 7pm; 2 October to March, daily except Sundays, 3pm to 6pm. 20F. ☎ 04 94 97 63 45.

Musée Naval – Open all year except November, daily except Tuesdays, 10am to 6pm (5pm in low season). 25F. ☎ 04 94 97 59 43.

Château de la Moutte – Guided tour (45 min) May to September, by appointment. No charge. Apply in advance in writing or by telephone to Mme Anne Troisier de Diaz, Château de la Moutte, route des Salins, 83990 St-Tropez, ☎ 04 94 97 03 26.

Boat trips in the bay – Operate regularly from St-Tropez
– to Ste-Maxime, April to October (64F return).
– to les Issambres, July and August (68F return).
– to Port-Grimaud, July to mid-September (502F return).
– to baie des Cannebiers, daily at 3.30pm from St-Tropez (50F) and at 3pm from Ste-Maxime (80F).
Information and reservations available at the landing stages and from Compagnie de Transports Maritimes MMG. ☎ 04 94 96 51 00.

Presqu'île de ST-TROPEZ

Phare de Camarat – Open 10am to 12 noon and 2pm to 6pm. ☎ 04 94 79 80 65.

ST-VALLIER-DE-THIEY

Souterroscope de Baume Obscure – Autoguide tour (1 hr) all year except January, Wednesdays to Sundays, 10am to 5pm (7pm weekends and July and August). 50F. ☎ 04 93 42 61 63.

Observatoire du CERGA – Open May to September, Sundays at 3.30pm. 20F. ☎ 04 93 85 85 58.

STE-MAXIME
🆔 promenade Simon Lorière - 83120 ☎ 04 94 96 19 24

Musée des Traditions – *Open daily except Tuesdays, July to September, 10am to 12 noon and 4pm to 7pm; October to March, 3pm to 6pm; April to June, 10am to 12 noon and 3pm to 6.30pm. 15F. ☎ 04 94 96 70 30.*

Musée du phonographe et de la musique mécanique – Open Easter to October, Wednesdays to Sundays, 10am to 12 noon and 3pm to 6pm. 15F. ☎ 04 94 96 50 52.

SANARY-SUR-MER
🆔 Jardins de la Ville - 83110 ☎ 04 94 74 01 04

Zoo Jardin exotique de Sanary-Bandol – Open daily, 8am to 12 noon and 2pm to 6pm. Closed Sunday mornings October to March. 40F (child 25F). ☎ 04 94 29 40 38.

Chapelle de Notre-Dame-du-Mai – Guided tour daily in May, Easter Monday, 15 August and 14 September. No access by car 15 June to 15 September. Apply in advance to Mr Pastourelly. ☎ 04 94 34 54 93.

SAORGE

Couvent des Franciscains – *Open June to September, daily, 2pm to 6pm; October to May, Saturday afternoons only. ☎ 04 93 88 90 87.*

SEILLANS

☎ 83440 ☎ 04 94 76 85 91

Église – When closed, apply to the presbytery. ☎ 06 12 89 10 92.

Notre-Dame de l'Ormeau – Open July and August, Sundays, 10.30am to 6pm. Apply to Annie Riche. ☎ 04 94 76 97 65.

Open Thursdays, 11am to 12 noon by appointment. Apply to the Office de tourisme. ☎ 04 94 76 85 91.

La SEYNE-SUR-MER

🖪 place Ledru-Rollin – 83500 ☎ 04 94 94 73 09

Musée naval du Fort Balaguier – Open daily except Mondays, July and August, 10am to 12 noon and 3pm to 7pm; September to June, 10am to 12 noon and 2pm to 6pm. Closed 1 January, 1 May and 25 December. 10F. ☎ 04 94 94 84 72.

SIX-FOURS-LES-PLAGES

Collégiale St-Pierre – Open in summer, 3pm to 7pm; in winter, 2.30pm to 6pm. ☎ 04 94 34 24 75.

Chapelle de Notre-Dame-de-Pépiole – Guided tour in summer 3.30pm to 6.30pm. ☎ 04 94 63 38 29.

SOLLIÈS-VILLE

Maison Jean-Aicard – Guided tour (15 min) all year except October, daily except Wednesdays, 10am to 12 noon and 3pm to 6pm. Closed Easter and Christmas. No charge. ☎ 04 94 33 72 02.

Église – Guided tour at same opening times as maison Jean-Aicard by museum attendant. Apply preferably in advance to maison Jean-Aicard. ☎ 04 94 33 72 02.

SOSPEL

🖪 Pont-Vieux – 06380 ☎ 04 93 04 15 80

Fort St-Roch – Guided tour (1 hr 30 min), July to September, daily except Mondays, 2pm to 6pm; April to June and October, Saturdays and Sundays, 2pm to 6pm. Closed November to March. 25F.

Fort Suchet (on the col St-Jean) – *Open July and August. Enquire at the Syndicat d'initiative.*

T

TAMARIS-SUR-MER

Villa Tamaris-Pacha – Open daily except Mondays, 2pm to 6.30pm. Closed 1 January and 25 December. No charge. ☎ 04 94 06 84 00.

TENDE

🖪 06430 ☎ 04 93 04 73 71

Musée des Merveilles – ♿ Open daily except Tuesdays, 10.30am to 6.30pm (9pm Saturdays in season; 5pm mid-October to April). Closed 1 January, 12 to 25 March, 13 to 25 November and 25 December. 30F. ☎ 04 93 04 32 50.

Abbaye de THORONET

Open April to September, daily, 9am to 7pm (closed 12 noon to 2pm Sundays); October to March, 10am to 1pm and 2pm to 5pm. Closed 1 January, 1 May, 1 and 11 November and 25 December. Guided tour (1 hr) available. 35F. ☎ 04 94 60 43 90.

TOULON

🖪 place Raimu – 83000 ☎ 04 94 18 53 00

Boat tour of Toulon harbour – Tour of Toulon harbour with commentary (50 min) from landing stage, quai Cronstad, opposite Cuverville statue, mid-April to October, mornings and afternoons; November to mid-April, afternoons only. 42F.

Musée de la Marine – Open daily except Tuesdays, 10am to 12 noon and 1.30 to 6pm (7pm July and August). Closed public holidays except Easter and Whitsun. No closures during July and August. 25F. ☎ 04 94 02 02 01.

Église St-François-de-Paule – Closed Sundays and Mondays.

Musée du Vieux Toulon – Open daily except Sundays, 2pm to 6pm. Closed public holidays. No charge. ☎ 04 94 62 11 07.

Muséum – Open daily, 9.30am to 12 noon and 2pm to 6pm. Closed public holidays. No charge. ☎ 04 94 93 15 54.

Musée d'Art – Open daily except Sundays, 1pm to 6pm. Closed all public holidays. No charge. ☎ 04 94 93 15 54.

Harbour – Warship lying at anchor in the roads can usually be visited mid-June to September, Saturdays, Sundays and some public holidays. Apply to boatmen, quai de Cronstadt.

Navire de débarquement "La Dives" – Guided tour (1 hr) June to September, daily, 10am to 7pm. 25F.

Boat trips to Sablettes and St Mandrier – Regular launch service operating all year from landing stage in Toulon (Ponton SITCAT/RMTT, quai Cronstadt) to La Seyne-sur-Mer, les Sablettes, Tamaris and St-Mandrier-sur-Mer, provided by SITCAT as part of the public transport network of Toulon (same tickets as for buses). Information and ticket sales at the Ponton de Toulon (quai Cronstadt) and Ponton de La Seyne (quai Cronstadt) and from RMTT/ALLOBUS. ☎ 04 94 03 87 03.

Boat trips to the Îles d'Hyères – Tour of Toulon harbour with commentary (50 min), mid-April to October, mornings and afternoons; November to mid-April, afternoons only. 42F.

Cruise to Île de Porquerolles, mid-June to mid-September, daily; cruise around the Îles d'Hyères or inlets of Cassis, May to September, daily.

Departures from quai Cronstadt (opposite Cuverville statue). Information and reservations from SNRTM, 1247 route du Faron, 83200 Toulon; ☎ 04 94 62 41 14.

Téléphérique du Mont Faron – Operates July and August, daily, 9.30am to 7.45pm; September to June, daily except Mondays, 9.30am to 12 noon and 2pm to 5.30pm (according to the month, until 6pm). Closed 1 May and 1 November. 37F return; joint ticket with the Zoo 55F. ☎ 04 94 92 68 25.

Musée-mémorial national du débarquement en Provence – Open in summer, 9.30am to 11.30am and 2.30pm to 5.30pm ([5.30pm] the rest of the year). Closed Mondays in winter. 25F. ☎ 04 94 88 08 09.

Zoo du Mont Faron – Open July to mid-October, 10am to 7pm; mid-October to June, 2pm to 6pm. 40F (child 30F). ☎ 04 94 88 07 89.

Tour Royale – Open daily except Tuesdays, July to 1 August, 9.30am to 12 noon and 3pm to 7pm; the rest of the year, 9.30am to 12 noon and 2pm to 6pm. Closed public holidays except Easter and Whitsun. 29F. ☎ 04 94 02 02 01.

TOURRETTE-LEVENS

Château-Musée d'entomologie – Open daily, 2pm to 7pm (5.30pm November to April). No charge. ☎ 04 93 91 03 20.

Église – Open 3.30pm to 5pm.

Figurehead, Musée de la Marine, Toulon

Lerault/DIAF

TOURTOUR

🖪 place des Ormeaux - 84690 ☎ 04 94 70 54 36

Musée des Fossiles – Open mid-June to mid-September, daily except Tuesdays, 3pm to 7.30pm. No charge. ☎ 04 94 70 57 20.

Moulin à huile – Mill operates December to early February (visitors may assist with the work); February to June, apply to the Town Hall; June to end September, exhibitions. No charge.

Excursions

Monastère orthodoxe St-Michel – Chapel open Sunday mornings. ☎ 04 94 73 75 75.

La TURBIE

Trophée des Alpes – Open April to 20 September, daily, 9.30am to 6pm; 21 September to March, daily except Mondays, 10am to 5pm. Closed 1 January, 1 May, 1 and 11 November and 25 December. 25F. ☎ 04 93 41 20 84.

U

UTELLE

Église St-Véran – *To visit in summer, apply to Mr Fernand Belletini.* ☎ *04 93 03 15 22.*

Chapelle des Pénitents Blancs – *Apply to Mr Fernand Belletini.* ☎ *04 93 03 15 22.*

V

Le VAL

Musée du Santon – Open daily, 9am to 12 noon and 2pm to 5.30pm. Closed 25 December. 10F. ☎ 04 94 37 02 21.

Musée d'Art Sacré – Same admission times and charges as the musée du Santon (see above).

Musée de la Figurine historique – Same admission times and charges as the musée du Santon (see above) but closed Mondays.

VALBONNE

Musée des Arts et Traditions Populaires – Open daily except Mondays, June to September, 3pm to 7pm; October to May, 2pm to 6pm. Closed January. 10F. ☎ 04 93 12 96 54.

VALDEBLORE 🛈 06000 ☎ 04 93 02 88 59

Pic de la Colmiane – Chairlift reserved for skiers 15 December to 15 April, daily. No walkers or tourists. 23F single; season ticket available.

VALLAURIS 🛈 84, avenue de la Liberté – 06220 ☎ 04 93 73 63 12

Musée National «La Guerre et la Paix» – Same admission times and charges as for the musée Magnelli – musée de la Céramique (see below).

Musée Magnelli – musée de la Céramique – Open July and August, daily except Tuesdays, 10am to 12.30pm and 2pm to 6.30pm (6pm September to June). Closed public holidays. 17F. ☎ 04 93 64 16 05.

Ateliers de céramique – Some are open to the public. Apply to the Association Vallaurienne d'Expansion Céramique, 15 rue Sicard. ☎ 04 93 64 66 58.

Musée de la Poterie – Open daily, May to September, 9am (2pm Sundays) to 6pm; October, November and February to April, 11am (2pm Saturdays and Sundays) to 6pm. Demonstrations of turning during opening hours. 10F. ☎ 04 93 64 66 51.

VARAGES

Musée de la faïence – Open July to mid-September, daily, 3pm to 7pm; mid-September to June, by appointment. 10F. ☎ 04 94 77 83 18.

Église – *Open Sundays for mass at 9.30am. On other days, by prior arrangement with the parish priest of Barjols.* ☎ *04 94 77 00 43.*

Atelier de la faïence – Open daily with demonstrations in July and August.

VENANSON

Château St.-Sébastien de Venanson – Apply to "La Bella Vista" restaurant. ☎ 04 93 03 25 11.

VENCE 🛈 place du grand jardin – 06140 ☎ 04 93 58 06 38

Chapelle du Rosaire (chapelle Matisse) – Open Tuesdays and Thursdays, 10am to 11.30am and 2.30pm to 5.30pm. Closed Sundays, Mondays, public holidays and 1 November to 14 December. Otherwise apply 48 hours in advance to Soeur Magdalena, Foyer dominicain Lacordaire, avenue H Matisse, 06140 Vence. ☎ 04 93 58 03 26.

Château de Villeneuve – Open daily except Mondays, 10am to 12.30pm and 2pm to 6pm (summer, 10am to 6pm). 25F. ☎ 04 93 58 15 78.

Ancienne cathédrale – Guided tour of the choir stalls in summer. Apply in advance to the Cité Paroissiale, 3 avenue Marcelin Maurel, Vence. ☎ 04 93 58 42 00. Donation welcome.

Château N.-D.-des Fleurs – Open daily except Sundays, 11am to 7pm. ☎ 04 93 24 52 00.

Chartreuse de la VERNE

Open all year except November, daily except Tuesdays, 11am to 6pm in summer and 11am to 5pm in winter. Closed Easter and Christmas. 30F. ☎ 04 94 43 45 41. As this is a working monastery, appropriate dress should be worn and animals are not allowed.

VIEUX-PIERREFEU

Musée "Hors du temps" du vieux Pierrefeu – Open by prior arrangement. 20F. ☎ 04 93 08 56 44 or 04 92 08 98 63.

VILLECROZE

Grottes – Guided tour (20 min) July to mid-September, daily, 10am to 12 noon and 2.30pm to 7pm; May and June, daily, 2.30pm to 7pm; mid-September to April, Saturdays and Sundays, 2pm to 6pm. Closed 15 October to 10 February. 10F. ☎ 04 94 70 63 06.

VILLEFRANCHE-SUR-MER   🚇 Jardin François Binon – 06230 ☎ 04 93 01 73 68

Guided tour of the town – Apply to the Office de Tourisme.

Chapelle St-Pierre – Open daily except Mondays, July to September, 10am to 12 noon and 4pm to 8.30pm; October to June, 9.30am to 12 noon and 2pm to 6pm (5pm in winter and 7pm in spring). Closed mid-November to mid-December. 12F. ☎ 04 93 76 90 70.

Cocteau frescoes, Chapelle St Pierre, Villefranche-sur-Mer

Submarine archeology collection – Same admission times and charges as the Musée Goetz-Boumeester (see below).

Collection Roux – Same admission times and charges as the Musée Goetz-Boumeester (see below).

Musée Volti – Same admission times as the Musée Goetz-Boumeester (see below). No charge. ☎ 04 93 76 33 33.

Musée Goetz-Boumeester – Open daily except Tuesdays and Sunday mornings, July and August, 10am to 12 noon and 3pm to 7pm (6pm June to September and 5pm October to May). Closed November. No charge. ☎ 04 93 76 33 44.

VILLENEUVE-LOUBET

Musée militaire – *Open July and August, Tuesday to Friday, 9am to 12 noon and 2pm to 5pm; Saturdays and Sundays, 10am to 12 noon. Closed public holidays. 10F.* ☎ *04 93 02 60 39.*

Musée de l'Art culinaire – Open all year except November, daily except Mondays, 2pm to 6pm (7pm in summer). Closed public holidays. 10F. ☎ 04 93 20 80 51.

Index

MANUFACTURE FRANÇAISE DES PNEUMATIQUES MICHELIN

Société en commandite par actions au capital de 2 000 000 000 de francs

Place des Carmes-Déchaux – 63 Clermont-Ferrand (France)

R.C.S. Clermont-Fd B 855 200 507

© Michelin et Cie, Propriétaires-Éditeurs 1997

Dépôt légal juillet 1997 – ISBN 2-06-133503-9– ISSN 0763-1383

Printed in the EU 04-98/3

Photocomposition : MAURY-Imprimeur S.A. – Malesherbes

Impression-Brochage : AUBIN Imprimeur à Ligugé.

Illustration de la couverture par Patricia HAUBERT

Michelin Green